American Poetry 1915 to 1945

Titles in the CRITICAL COSMOS series include

AMERICAN FICTION

American Fiction through 1914
American Fiction, 1914–1945
American Fiction, 1946–1965
American Fiction, 1966 to the Present
American Jewish Literature
American Women Novelists and Short
  Story Writers
Black American Fiction

AMERICAN POETRY, DRAMA,
  AND PROSE

American Drama to 1945
American Drama 1945 to the Present
American Poetry through 1914
American Poetry, 1915–1945
American Poetry, 1946–1965
American Poetry, 1966 to the Present
American Prose and Criticism to 1945
American Prose and Criticism, 1945 to
  the Present
American Women Poets
Black American Poetry

BRITISH LITERATURE THROUGH 1880

British Drama: 18th and 19th Centuries
Eighteenth-Century Fiction and Prose
Eighteenth-Century Poetry
Elizabethan and Jacobean Drama
Elizabethan Poetry
Elizabethan Prose and Fiction
English Romantic Fiction and Prose
English Romantic Poets
Medieval Literature
Seventeenth-Century Poetry
Seventeenth-Century Prose
Victorian Fiction
Victorian Poetry
Victorian Prose

FRENCH LITERATURE

French Drama through 1915
French Fiction through 1915
French Poetry through 1915
French Prose and Criticism through 1789
French Prose and Criticism, 1790 to the
  Present
Modern French Drama
Modern French Fiction
Modern French Poetry
Modern French Prose and Criticism

GERMAN LITERATURE

German Drama through 1915
German Fiction through 1915
German Poetry through 1915
German Prose and Criticism through 1915
Modern German Drama
Modern German Fiction
Modern German Poetry
Modern German Prose and Criticism

MODERN BRITISH AND
  COMMONWEALTH LITERATURE

Anglo-Irish Literature
British Prose, 1880–1914
British World War I Literature
Canadian Fiction
Canadian Poetry and Prose
Commonwealth Poetry and Fiction
Contemporary British Drama, 1946 to the
  Present
Contemporary British Fiction, 1946 to the
  Present
Contemporary British Poetry
Contemporary British Prose
Edwardian and Georgian Fiction,
  1880–1914
Edwardian and Georgian Poetry,
  1880–1914
Modern British Drama, 1900–1945
Modernist Fiction, 1920–1945
Modern Poetry and Prose, 1920–1945

OTHER EUROPEAN AND LATIN
  AMERICAN LITERATURE

African Anglophonic Literature
Dadaism and Surrealism
Italian Drama
Italian Fiction
Italian Poetry
Jewish Literature: The Bible through 1945
Modern Jewish Literature
Modern Latin American Fiction
Modern Scandinavian Literature
Modern Spanish Fiction
Modern Spanish and Latin American
  Poetry
Russian Drama
Russian Fiction
Russian Poetry
Scandinavian Literature through 1915
Spanish Fiction through 1927
Spanish Poetry through 1927

THE CRITICAL COSMOS SERIES

American Poetry 1915 to 1945

Edited and with an introduction
by *HAROLD BLOOM*
Sterling Professor of the Humanities
Yale University

CHELSEA HOUSE PUBLISHERS ◇ 1987
New York ◇ New Haven ◇ Philadelphia

© 1987 by Chelsea House Publishers, a division
of Chelsea House Educational Communications, Inc.
    95 Madison Avenue, New York, NY 10016
    345 Whitney Avenue, New Haven, CT 06511
    5014 West Chester Pike, Edgemont, PA 19028

Introduction © 1987 by Harold Bloom

Printed and bound in the United States of America

∞The paper used in this publication meets the minimum
requirements of the American National Standard for
Permanence of Paper for Printed Library Materials,
Z39.48-1984.

Library of Congress Cataloging-in-Publication Data
America poetry, 1915–1945.
    (The Critical cosmos)
    Bibliography: p.
    Includes index.
    1. American poetry—20th century—History and
criticism.   I. Bloom, Harold.   II. Series.
PS324.A4   1986   811'.52'09   86-17632
ISBN 0-87754-952-4

Contents

Editor's Note

This volume gathers together a selection of what I judge to be the best criticism available on the principal American poets whose work centered in the three decades 1915–1945. The essays are arranged here, as far as is possible, in the order of the dates of the poets' births. I am grateful to Daniel Duffy for his aid in editing this volume.

My introduction covers Robinson, Frost, Stevens, Williams, Pound, Moore, Eliot, and Hart Crane, whom I judge to be the most eminent figures in their era. Conrad Aiken, poet and poetic critic, reviewing a later volume of Edwin Arlington Robinson, celebrates the earlier work instead, *The Man against the Sky* in particular. The relation of the distinguished black poet Paul Laurence Dunbar to the tradition of dialect verse is explored by Myron Simon.

Robert Frost and Wallace Stevens, our greatest poets since Walt Whitman and Emily Dickinson, receive two essays each. Richard Poirier, Frost's foremost critic, analyzes his "life-long commitment to certain theories of sound and poetic form," while Charles Berger intricately examines Frost's concern with origins and echoes. Stevens's majestic, late masterpiece, *An Ordinary Evening in New Haven*, is given an elaborate reading by a certain ordinary critic in New Haven, after which Marie Borroff contributes a marvelous study of this great poet's diction, the always incipient cosmos constituted by his world of words.

Six once famous poets, now in their long decline, are defended genially but reservedly by Hyatt Waggoner. The "Cornhuskers" or "Chicago poets"—Vachel Lindsay, Edgar Lee Masters, and Carl Sandburg—are combined here with three women poets who emphasized their erotic sorrows and who have achieved no particular favor with recent feminist criticism—Sara Teasdale, Elinor Wylie, and Edna St. Vincent Millay (once celebrated as a female Byron).

With Paul Mariani's fierce manifesto for the *Paterson* of William Carlos Williams, we return to a poet of more permanent achievement, though perhaps of a more problematic order than his admirers concede. Ezra Pound, an even more questionable over-reacher, is depicted in his relation to the American literary tradition by Kathryne V. Lindberg.

Brother Antoninus (the poet formerly called William Everson) champions the now neglected Nietzschean dramatic poetry of Robinson Jeffers, certainly one of the most ambitious poets in the American tradition. An immense contrast to the sublime and violent intensities of Jeffers is provided by Marianne Moore, whose subtle and ironic artistry is investigated here first by Bonnie Costello, who finds in Moore a dignity of diction that belies most male notions of what constitutes "feminine language." In another exegesis, John M. Slatin uncovers something of the repressed complexities of Moore's relation to the poetic traditions of our language.

A figure rising in esteem, particularly in an age of feminist criticism, H. D. is seen here by Susan Gubar as the master of a new kind of long poem, an assertion eloquently offered by Gubar but perhaps difficult to define. The more traditional aesthetic virtues of John Crowe Ransom's courtly and elegant poetry are set forth here by Randall Jarrell, his poetic and critical follower a generation later. T. S. Eliot, the major cultural spokesman (or the Matthew Arnold) of his era, is studied here in two very different ways. The first is the exegesis of *Ash Wednesday* by Hugh Kenner, Eliotic critic and Modernist mandarin, while the other is the very different tracing of Eliot's authentic agon with the American and British Romantic poetic tradition, expertly carried through by Gregory S. Jay.

Conrad Aiken, an uneven but greatly gifted poet now greatly neglected, is examined here in two brief overviews by the poets Delmore Schwartz and Dudley Fitts. Schwartz emphasizes Aiken's cosmic vision of the self isolated in the coldness of space, while Fitts chooses to concentrate on Aiken's undoubted technical mastery. Something less than mastery, in the control of poetic language by E. E. Cummings, is exposed perhaps too positively by R. P. Blackmur. John Brooks Wheelwright, a flamboyant and permanent poet, difficult and magnificent, is rendered a moving tribute by the great poet John Ashbery.

With Allen Tate, perhaps a more eminent critic than he was a poet, we receive a persuasive and formidable defense of poetic achievement by Cleanth Brooks, indomitable New Critic and Southern man-of-letters. Tate's friend, Hart Crane, who had the greatest natural poetic gift of any American poet, ever, is described here by the critic Sherman Paul, who expounds the superb "Proem: To Brooklyn Bridge" as the threshold to Crane's vision in *The Bridge*.

This volume concludes with essays upon two of the most vital poets of the Harlem Renaissance—Langston Hughes and Countee Cullen. Hughes is portrayed by Raymond Smith as an ironist who pioneered in the poetic use of black urban folkways, while the more traditional Cullen is seen by Ronald Primeau as a noble but necessarily only partly successful agonist, who attempted the impossible in seeking to bring together the procedures of Romantic poetry and the necessarily recalcitrant material of the dilemmas of his own people.

Introduction

EDWIN ARLINGTON ROBINSON

Emerson himself was a product of New England and a man of strong moral habits. . . . He gave to American romanticism, in spite of its irresponsible doctrine, a religious tone which it has not yet lost and which has often proved disastrous. . . . there is a good deal of this intellectual laziness in Robinson; and as a result of the laziness, there is a certain admixture of Emersonian doctrine, which runs counter to the principles governing most of his work and the best of it.

—YVOR WINTERS

The Torrent and the Night Before (published late in 1896 by Robinson himself) remains one of the best first volumes in our poetry. Three of its shorter poems—"George Crabbe," "Luke Havergal," "The Clerks"—Robinson hardly surpassed, and three more—"Credo," "Walt Whitman" (which Robinson unfortunately abandoned), and "The Children of the Night" (reprinted as title-poem in his next volume)—are memorable works, all in the earlier Emersonian mode that culminates in "Bacchus." The stronger "Luke Havergal" stems from the darker Emersonianism of "Experience" and "Fate," and has a relation to the singular principles of *Merlin*. It prophesies Robinson's finest later lyrics, such as "Eros Turannos" and "For a Dead Lady," and suggests the affinity between Robinson and Frost that is due to their common Emersonian tradition.

In *Captain Craig* (1902) Robinson published "The Sage," a direct hymn of homage to Emerson, whose *The Conduct of Life* had moved him profoundly at a first reading in August 1899. Robinson had read the earlier Emerson well before, but it is fascinating that he came to essays like "Fate" and "Power" only after writing "Luke Havergal" and some similar poems, for his deeper nature then discovered itself anew. He called "Luke Havergal" "a piece of deliberate degeneration," which I take to mean what an early letter calls "sympathy for failure where fate has been abused and self demoralized." Browning, the other great influence upon Robinson, is obsessed with "deliberate degeneration" in this sense; Childe Roland's and Andrea del Sarto's failures are wilful abuses of fate and demoralizations of self. "The Sage" praises Emerson's "fierce wisdom," emphasizes Asia's influence upon him, and hardly touches his dialectical optimism. This Emerson is "previsioned of the madness and the mean," fit seer for "the fiery night" of "Luke Havergal":

1

But there, where western glooms are gathering,
The dark will end the dark, if anything:
God slays Himself with every leaf that flies,
And hell is more than half of paradise.

These are the laws of Compensation, "or that nothing is got for nothing," as Emerson says in "Power." At the depth of Robinson is this Emersonian fatalism, as it is in Frost, and even in Henry James. "The world is mathematical," Emerson says, "and has no casualty in all its vast and flowing curve." Robinson, brooding on the end of "Power," confessed: "He really gets after one," and spoke of Emerson as walloping one "with a big New England shingle," the cudgel of Fate. But Robinson was walloped too well, by which I do not mean what Winters means, since I cannot locate any "intellectual laziness" in Emerson. Unlike Browning and Hardy, Robinson yielded too much to Necessity. . . . Circumstances and temperament share in Robinson's obsession with Nemesis, but poetic misprision is part of the story also, for Robinson's *tessera* in regard to Emerson relies on completing the sage's fatalism. From Emerson's categories of power and circumstance, Robinson fashions a more complete single category, in a personal idealism that is a "philosophy of desperation," as he feared it might be called. The persuasive desperation of "Luke Havergal" and "Eros Turannos" is his best expression of this nameless idealism that is also a fatalism, but "The Children of the Night," for all its obtrusive echoes of Tennyson and even Longfellow, shows more clearly what Robinson found to be a possible stance:

It is the crimson, not the gray,
    That charms the twilight of all time;
It is the promise of the day
    That makes the starry sky sublime;

It is the faith within the fear
    That holds us to the life we curse;—
So let us in ourselves revere
    The Self which is the Universe!

The bitter charm of this is that it qualifies so severely its too-hopeful and borrowed music. Even so early, Robinson has "completed" Emersonian Self-Reliance and made it his own by emphasizing its Stoic as against its Transcendental or Bacchic aspect. When, in "Credo," Robinson feels "the coming glory of the Light!" the light nevertheless emanates from unaware angels who wove "dead leaves to garlands where no roses are." It is not that Robinson believed, with Melville, that the invisible spheres were formed in fright, but he shrewdly suspected that the ultimate world, though existent, was nearly as destitute as this one. He is an Emersonian incapable of transport, an ascetic of the Transcendental spirit, contrary to an inspired saint like Jones Very or to the Emerson of "The Poet," but a contrary, not a negation, to use Blake's distinction. Not less gifted than Frost, he achieves so much less because he gave himself away to Necessity so soon in his poetic life. Frost's Job quotes "Uriel" to suggest that confusion is "the form of forms," the way all things return upon themselves, like rays:

> Though I hold rays deteriorate to nothing,
> First white, then red, then ultra red, then out.

This is cunning and deep in Frost, the conviction that "all things come round," even the mental confusions of God as He morally blunders. What we miss in Robinson is this quality of savagery, the strength that can end "Directive" by saying:

> Here are your waters and your watering place.
> Drink and be whole again beyond confusion.

To be beyond confusion is to be beyond the form of forms that is Fate's, and to be whole beyond Fate suggests an end to circlings, a resolution to all the Emersonian turnings that see unity, and yet behold divisions. Frost will play at [yielding to Necessity], many times, but his wariness saved him from Robinson's self-exhaustions.

There is a fine passage in "Captain Craig" where the talkative captain asks: "Is it better to be blinded by the lights, / Or by the shadows?" This supposes grandly that we are to be blinded in any case, but Robinson was not blinded by his shadows. Yet he was ill-served by American Romanticism, though not for the reasons Winters offers. It demands the exuberance of a Whitman in his fury of poetic incarnation, lest the temptation to join Ananke come too soon and too urgently to be resisted. Robinson was nearly a great poet, and would have prospered more if he had been chosen by a less drastic tradition.

ROBERT FROST

"Directive" is Frost's poem of poems or form of forms, a meditation whose rays perpetually return upon themselves. "All things come round," even our mental confusion as we blunder morally, since the Demiurge is nothing but a moral blunderer. Frost shares the fine Emersonian wildness or freedom, the savage strength of the essay "Power" that suggests a way of being whole beyond Fate, of arriving at an end to circlings, at a resolution to all the Emersonian turnings that see unity, and yet behold divisions: "The world is mathematical, and has no casualty, in all its vast and flowing curve." "Directive" appears to be the poem in which Frost measures the lot, and forgives himself the lot, and perhaps even casts out remorse. In some sense, it was the poem he always wrote and rewrote, in a revisionary process present already in *A Boy's Will* (1913) but not fully worked out until *Steeple Bush* (1947), where "Directive" was published when Frost was seventy-three. "The Demiurge's Laugh" in *A Boy's Will* features a mocking demonic derision at the self-realization that "what I hunted was no true god."

North of Boston (1914) has its most memorable poem in the famous "After Apple-Picking," a gracious hymn to the necessity of yielding up the quest, of clambering down from one's "long two-pointed ladder's sticking through a tree / Toward heaven still." Frost's subtlest of perspectivizings is the true center of the poem:

> I cannot rub the strangeness from my sight
> I got from looking through a pane of glass
> I skimmed this morning from the drinking trough
> And held against the world of hoary grass.
> It melted, and I let it fall and break.

The sheet of ice is a lens upon irreality, but so are Frost's own eyes, or anyone's, in his cosmos. This supposed nature-poet represents his harsh landscapes as a full version of the Gnostic *kenoma*, the cosmological emptiness into which we have been thrown by the mocking Demiurge. This is the world of *Mountain Interval* (1916), where "the broken moon" is preferred to the dimmed sun, where the oven bird sings of "that other fall we name the fall," and where the birches:

> shed crystal shells
> Shattering and avalanching on the snow crust—
> Such heaps of broken glass to sweep away
> You'd think the inner dome of heaven had fallen.

Mountain Interval abounds in images of the shattering of human ties, and of humans, as in the horrifying "Out, Out—." But it would be redundant to conduct an overview of all Frost's volumes in pursuit of an experiential darkness that never is dispelled. A measurer of stone walls, as Frost names himself in the remarkable "A Star in a Stoneboat," is never going to be surprised that life is a sensible emptiness. The demiurgic pattern of "Design," with its "assorted characters of death and blight," is the rule in Frost. There are a few exceptions, but they give Frost parodies rather than poems.

Frost wrote the concluding and conclusive Emersonian irony for all his work in the allegorical "A Cabin in the Clearing," the set-piece of *In the Clearing* (1962), published for his eighty-eighth birthday, less than a year before his death. Mist and Smoke, guardian wraiths and counterparts, eavesdrop on the unrest of a human couple, murmuring in their sleep. These guardians haunt us because we are their kindred spirits, for we do not know where we are, since who we are "is too much to believe." We are "too sudden to be credible," and so the accurate image for us is "an inner haze," full kindred to mist and smoke. For all the genial tone, the spirit of "A Cabin in the Clearing" is negative even for Frost. His final letter, dictated just before his death, states an unanswerable question as though it were not a question: "How can we be just in a world that needs mercy and merciful in a world that needs justice." The Demiurge's laugh lurks behind the sentence, though Frost was then in no frame of spirit to indulge a demiurgic imagination.

Frost would have been well content to give his mentor Emerson the last word, though "content" is necessarily an inadequate word in this dark context. Each time I reread the magnificent essay "Illusions," which concludes and crowns *The Conduct of Life*, I am reminded of the poetry of Robert Frost. The reminder is strongest in two paragraphs near the end that seem to be "Directive" writ large, as though Emerson had been brooding upon his descendant:

> We cannot write the order of the variable winds. How can we penetrate the law of our shifting moods and susceptibility? Yet they differ as all and nothing. Instead of the firmament of yesterday, which our eyes require, it is to-day an eggshell which coops us in; we cannot even see what or where our stars of destiny are. From day to day, the capital facts of human life are hidden from our eyes. Suddenly the mist rolls up, and reveals them, and we think how much good time is gone, that might have been saved, had any hint of these things been shown. A sudden rise in the road shows us the system of mountains, and all the summits, which have been just as near us all the year, but quite out of mind. But these alternations are not without their order, and we are parties to our various fortune. If life seem a succession of dreams, yet poetic justice is done in dreams also. The visions of good men are good; it is the undisciplined will that is whipped with bad thoughts and bad fortunes. When we break the laws, we lose our hold on the central reality. Like sick men in hospitals, we change only from bed to bed, from one folly to another; and it cannot signify much what becomes of such castaways,—wailing, stupid, comatose creatures,—lifted from bed to bed, from the nothing of life to the nothing of death.
>
> In this kingdom of illusions we grope eagerly for stays and foundations. There is none but a strict and faithful dealing at home, and a severe barring out of all duplicity or illusion there. Whatever games are played with us, we must play no games with ourselves, but deal in our privacy with the last honesty and truth. I look upon the simple and childish virtues of veracity and honesty as the root of all that is sublime in character. Speak as you think, be what you are, pay your debts of all kinds. I prefer to be owned as sound and solvent, and my word as good as my bond, and to be what cannot be skipped, or dissipated, or undermined, to all the *éclat* in the universe. This reality is the foundation of friendship, religion, poetry, and art. At the top or at the bottom of all illusions,

I set the cheat which still leads us to work and live for appearances, in spite of our conviction, in all sane hours, that it is what we really are that avails with friends, with strangers, and with fate or fortune.

WALLACE STEVENS

"Leave the many and hold the few," Emerson advises in his late poem "Terminus," thus sanctioning the democratic poet, like Whitman, in the pragmatic address to an actual elite. Stevens needed little sanctioning as to audience, but he was rather anxious about his own constant emphasis upon the self as solitary "scholar," and his recourse was to plead "poverty." He cannot have been unaware that both "scholar" and "poverty" in his rather precise senses were Emersonian usages. A great coverer of traces, Stevens may be judged nevertheless to have turned more to a tradition than to a man. American Romanticism found its last giant in Stevens, who defines the tradition quite as strongly as it informs him.

"The prologues are over. . . . It is time to choose," and the Stevens I think we must choose writes the poems not of an empty spirit in vacant space, but of a spirit so full of itself that there is room for nothing else. This description hardly appears to flatter Stevens, yet I render it in his praise. Another of his still neglected poems, for which my own love is intense, is entitled simply "Poem with Rhythms":

> The hand between the candle and the wall
> Grows large on the wall.
>
> The mind between this light or that and space,
> (This man in a room with an image of the world,
> That woman waiting for the man she loves,)
> Grows large against space:
>
> *There the man sees the image clearly at last.*
> *There the woman receives her lover into her heart*
> *And weeps on his breast, though he never comes.*
>
> It must be that the hand
> Has a will to grow larger on the wall,
> To grow larger and heavier and stronger than
> The wall; and that the mind
> Turns to its own figurations and declares,
> *"This image, this love, I compose myself*
> *Of these. In these, I come forth outwardly.*
> *In these, I wear a vital cleanliness,*
> *Not as in air, bright-blue-resembling air,*
> *But as in the powerful mirror of my wish and will."*

The principal difference between Stevens and Whitman appears to be that Stevens admits his mind is alone with its own figurations, while Whit-man keeps inaccurately but movingly insisting he wants "contact" with other selves. His "contact" is an Emersonian term, and we know, as Whit-man's readers, that he actually cannot bear "contact," any more than Emer-son, Dickinson, Frost, or Stevens can tolerate it. "Poem with Rhythms," like so much of Stevens, has a hidden origin in Whitman's "The Sleepers," particularly in a great passage apparently describing a woman's disap-pointment in love:

> I am she who adorn'd herself and folded her hair
>   expectantly,
> My truant lover has come, and it is dark.
>
> Double yourself and receive me darkness,
> Receive me and my lover too, he will not let me go without
>   him.
> I roll myself upon you as upon a bed, I resign myself to the
>   dusk.
>
> He whom I call answers me and takes the place of my lover,
> He rises with me silently from the bed.
>
> Darkness, you are gentler than my lover, his flesh was
>   sweaty and panting,
> I feel the hot moisture yet that he left me.
>
> My hands are spread forth, I pass them in all directions.
> I would sound up the shadowy shore to which you are
>   journeying.
>
> Be careful, darkness! already, what was it touch'd me?
> I thought my lover had gone, else darkness and he are one,
> I hear the heart-beat, I follow, I fade away.

This juxtaposition of major Whitman to relatively minor Stevens is not altogether fair, but then I don't think I hurt Stevens by granting that Whit-man, upon his heights, is likely to make his descendant seem only a dwarf of disintegration. Whitman-as-Woman invokes the darkness of birth, and blends himself into the mingled Sublimity of death and the Native Strain. Stevens-as-Interior-Paramour invokes only his mind's own figurations, but he sees himself cleansed in the vitalizing mirror of will as he could never hope to see himself in the mere outwardness of air. Whitman oddly but beautifully persuades us of a dramatic poignance that his actual solipsism does not earn, while Stevens rather less beautifully knows only the non-dramatic truth of his own fine desperation.

What then is Stevens giving us? What do we celebrate with and in him when he leads us to celebrate? His vigorous affirmation, "The Well Dressed Man with a Beard," centers on "a speech / Of the self that must sustain itself on speech." Is eloquence enough? I turn again to the fountain of our will, Emerson, who had the courage to insist that eloquence was enough, because he identified eloquence with "something unlimited and boundless," in the manner of Cicero. Here is Stevens mounting through eloquence to his individual sense of "something unlimited and boundless," a "something" not beyond our apprehension:

> Last night at the end of night his starry head,
> Like the head of fate, looked out in darkness, part
> Thereof and part desire and part the sense
> Of what men are. The collective being knew
> There were others like him safely under roof:
>
> The captain squalid on his pillow, the great
> Cardinal, saying the prayers of earliest day;
> The stone, the categorical effigy;
> And the mother, the music, the name; the scholar,
> Whose green mind bulges with complicated hues:
>
> True transfigurers fetched out of the human mountain,
> True genii for the diminished, spheres,
> Gigantic embryos of populations,
> Blue friends in shadows, rich conspirators,
> Confiders and comforters and lofty kin.
>
> To say more than human things with human voice,
> That cannot be; to say human things with more
> Than human voice, that, also, cannot be;
> To speak humanly from the height or from the depth
> Of human things, that is acutest speech.

A critic who has learned, ruefully, to accept the reductive view that the imagination is only decaying sense, must ask himself: Why is he so moved by this transfiguration of language into acutest speech? He may remember, in this connection, the prose statement by Stevens that moves him most:

> Why should a poem not change in sense when there is a fluctuation of the whole of appearance? Or why should it not change when we realize that the indifferent experience of life is the unique experience, the item of ecstasy which we have been isolating and reserving for another time and place, loftier and more secluded.

The doctrinal voice of Walter Pater, another unacknowledged ancestor, is heard in this passage, as perhaps it must be heard in any modern Epicureanism. Stevens, I suggest, is the Lucretius of our modern poetry, and like Lucretius seeks his truth in mere appearances, seeks his spirit in things of the weather. Both poets are beyond illusions, yet both invest their knowing of the way things are with a certain grim ecstasy. But an American Lucretius, coming after the double alienation of European Romanticism and domestic Transcendentalism, will have lost all sense of the communal in his ecstasy. Stevens fulfilled the unique enterprise of a specifically American poetry by exposing the essential solipsism of our Native Strain. No American feels free when he is not alone, and every American's passion for Yes affirms a hidden belief that his soul's substance is no part of the creation. We are mortal gods, the central strain in our poetry keeps saying, and our aboriginal selves are forbidden to find companionship in one another. Our ecstasy comes only from self-recognition, yet cannot be complete if we reduce wholly to "the evilly compounded, vital I . . . made . . . fresh in a world of white." We need "The Poems of Our Climate" because we are, happily, imperfect solipsists, unhappy in a happily imperfect and still external world—which is to say, we need Stevens:

> There would still remain the never-resting mind,
> So that one would want to escape, come back
> To what had been so long composed.
> The imperfect is our paradise.
> Note that, in this bitterness, delight,
> Since the imperfect is so hot in us,
> Lies in flawed words and stubborn sounds.

WILLIAM CARLOS WILLIAMS

Poetic influence, an intensely problematical process, normally brings together a strong poet's earliest and final phases. Williams's true precursor, necessarily composite and in some sense imaginary, was a figure that fused Keats with Walt Whitman. Such a figure has in it the potential for a serious splitting of the poetic ego in its defense against the poetic past. The "negative capability" of Keats sorts oddly with Whitman's rather positive capability for conveying the powerful press of himself. "Memory is a kind / of accomplishment," Williams wrote in "The Descent," a crucial poem in his *The Desert Music* (1954). The descent to dying beckons to a return of the dead precursors in one's own colors, even as Keats and Whitman beckoned Williams to ascend into his own poetry. But the poem "The Descent" Williams shrewdly quarried from book 2 of his own major long poem, *Paterson*, a quarrying that suggests his pride in his own continuities.

Those continuities are massive throughout Williams's best work, which can be cataloged (against the numerous Williams idolators) as a limited yet still remarkably diverse canon: *Paterson* (book 1), *Kora in Hell, Spring and All,* "The Widow's Lament in Springtime," "To Waken an Old Lady," "The Trees," "The Yachts," "A Coronal," "These," "The Poor," "A Marriage Ritual," "Raleigh Was Right," "Burning the Christmas Greens," "A Unison," and the grand return of Keats-as-Williams in *Asphodel, That Greeny Flower.*

The best lyrics and book 1 of *Paterson* are of a higher order, though they also betray darker anxieties of influence than even Williams's defiances dared to confront. They display also another kind of agon, the anxiety as to contemporary rivals, not so much Pound and Eliot as Wallace Stevens and Hart Crane, heirs to Keats and to Whitman, even as Williams was. No two readers are likely to agree upon just which shorter poems by Williams are his strongest, but the one that impresses and moves me most is "A Unison," where the title seems to comprehend most of the dictionary meanings of "unison": an identity of pitch in music; the same words spoken simultaneously by two or more speakers; musical parts combined in octaves; a concord, agreement, harmony. Thomas R. Whitaker, one of Williams's best and most sympathetic critics but no idolator, gives the best introduction to "A Unison":

> It is like an improvisation from *Kora in Hell*—but one with the quiet maturity of vision and movement that some three decades have brought. . . . As the implicit analogies and contrasts accumulate, we discover (long before the speaker tells us) that we are attending a "unison and a dance." This "death's festival"—*memento mori* and celebration of the *"Undying"*—evades neither the mystery of transience nor that of organic continuance, though neither can be "parsed" by the analytical mind. . . . In this composed testament of acceptance, Williams's saxifrage ("through metaphor to reconcile / the people and the stones") quietly does its work. . . . Not since Wordsworth has this natural piety been rendered so freshly and poignantly.

I would not wish to quarrel with Whitaker's judgment, yet there is very little Wordsworth and (inevitably) much Whitman and considerable Keats in "A Unison." Indeed, the poem opens with what must be called an echo from Whitman, in what I assume was a controlled allusion:

> The grass is very green, my friend,
> And tousled, like the head of—
> your grandson, yes?

We hear one of the uncanniest passages in Whitman, from "Song of Myself" 6:

> This grass is very dark to be from the white heads of old
>   mothers,
> Darker than the colorless beards of old men,
> Dark to come from under the faint red roofs of mouths.

Whitman's great fantasia answers a child's question: *"What is the grass?"* As an Epicurean materialist, Whitman believed that the *what* was unknowable, but his remarkable troping on the grass takes a grand turn after his Homeric line: "And now it seems to me the beautiful uncut hair of graves."

Williams simply borrows the trope, and even his "very green" merely follows Whitman's hint that a "very green" becomes a "very dark" color, in the shadow of mortality. "A Unison" insists upon

> —what cannot be escaped: the
> mountain riding the afternoon as
> it does, the grass matted green,
> green underfoot and the air—
> rotten wood. *Hear! Hear them!*
> *the Undying.* The hill slopes away,
> then rises in the middleground,
> you remember, with a grove of gnarled
> maples centering the bare pasture,
> sacred, surely—for what reason?

Williams does not know whether he can or cannot say the reason, but the allusion is to Keats's characteristic, Saturnian shrine in *Hyperion*. For Williams it is "a shrine cinctured there by / the trees," the girdling effect suggested by the natural sculpture of Keats's shrine. Where Keats as the quester in *The Fall of Hyperion* pledges "all the mortals of the world, / And all the dead whose names are in our lips," and where Whitman insists, "The smallest sprout shows there is really no death," Williams neither salutes the living and the dead nor folds the two into a single figuration. Rather, he *hears* and urges us to: "*Hear the unison of their voices.*" How are we to interpret such an imaginative gesture? Are we hearing more, or enough more, than the unison of the voices of John Keats and Walt Whitman? Devoted Williamsites doubtless would reject the question, but it always retains its force nevertheless. It is not less true of *The Waste Land* than it is of Williams. Eliot revises Whitman's "When Lilacs Last in the Dooryard Bloom'd" by fusing it with Tennyson (among others, but prime among those others). Image of voice or the trope of poetic identity then becomes a central problem.

Whitman once contrasted himself to Keats by rejecting "negative capability" and insisting instead that the great poet gave us the "powerful press of himself." Admirable as *Paterson* is (particularly its first book), does even it resolve the antithesis in Williams between his "objectivism" or negative capability, and his own, agonistic, powerful press of himself? Paul Mariani ends his vast, idealizing biography by asserting that Williams established "an American poetic based on a new measure and a primary regard for the living, protean shape of the language as it was actually used." J. Hillis Miller, even more generously, tells us that Williams gave us a concept of poetry transcending both Homer and Wordsworth, both Aristotle and Coleridge:

> The word is given reality by the fact it names, but the independence of the fact from the word frees the word to be a fact in its

own right and at the same time "dynamizes" it with meaning. The word can then carry the facts named in a new form into the realm of imagination.

Mariani and Miller are quite sober compared to more apocalyptic Williamsites. Not even Whitman gave us "a new measure," and not Shakespeare himself freed a single word "to be a fact in its own right." William Carlos Williams was, at his best, a strong American poet, far better than his hordes of imitators. Like Ezra Pound's, Williams's remains a fairly problematical achievement in the traditions of American poetry. Some generations hence, it will become clear whether his critics have canonized him permanently or subverted him by taking him too much at his own intentions. For now he abides, a live influence, and perhaps with even more fame to come.

EZRA POUND

I have brought the great ball of crystal; who can lift it?
—Canto 116

I do not know many readers who have an equal affection for the *Cantos* and for, say, Wallace Stevens's *An Ordinary Evening in New Haven* or his *The Auroras of Autumn*. Doubtless, such differences in poetic taste belong to the accidents of sensibility, or to irreconcilable attitudes concerning the relation of poetry to belief. They may indeed belong to more profound distinctions; in judgments as to value that transcend literary preferences. I do not desire to address myself to such matters here. Nor will I consider Pound's politics. The *Cantos* contain material that is not humanly acceptable to me, and if that material is acceptable to others, then they themselves are thereby less acceptable, at least to me.

My subject here, in necessarily curtailed terms, is Pound's relation to poetic tradition in his own language, and to Whitman in particular. Pound's critics have taken him at his word in this regard, but no poet whatsoever can be trusted in his or her own story of poetic origins, even as no man or woman can be relied on to speak with dispassionate accuracy of his or her parents. Perhaps Pound triumphed in his agon with poetic tradition, which is the invariable assertion of all of his critical partisans. But the triumph, if it occurred, was a very qualified one. My own experience as a reader of the *Cantos*, across many years, is that the long poem or sequence is marred throughout by Pound's relative failure to transume or transcend his precursors. Their ancestral voices abound, and indeed become more rather than less evident as the sequence continues. Nor is this invariably a controlled allusiveness. Collage, which is handled as metaphor by Marianne Moore and by the Eliot of *The Waste Land*, is a much more literal process in Pound, is more scheme than trope, as it were. The allusive triumph over tradition in Moore's "Marriage" or *The Waste Land* is fairly problematical, yet nowhere near so dubious as it is in the *Cantos*. Confronted by a past poetic wealth in figuration, Pound tends to resort to baroque elaborations of the anterior metaphors. What he almost never manages is to achieve an ellipsis of further troping by his own inventiveness at metaphor. He cannot make the voices of Whitman and Browning seem belated, while his own voice manifests what Stevens called an "ever early candor."

I am aware that I am in apparent defiance of the proud Poundian dictum: *Make It New*. Whitman made it new in one way, and Browning in another, but Pound's strength was elsewhere. Anglo-American Poetic "Modernism" was Ezra Pound's revolution, but it seems now only another continuity in the long history of Romanticism. Literary history may or may not someday regard Pound as it now regards Abraham Cowley, John Cleveland, and Edmund Waller, luminaries of one era who faded into the common light of another age. But, as a manneristic poet, master of a period style, Pound has his deep affinities to Cowley, Cleveland, and above all Waller. He has affinities also though to Dante Gabriel Rossetti, a permanent poet who suffered from belatedness in a mode strikingly akin to that of Pound. Poundian critics tend to regard Rossetti as a kind of embarassing prelude to their hero, but I certainly intend only a tribute to Pound in comparing him to Rossetti. It is, after all, far better to be called the Dante Gabriel Rossetti than the Edmund Waller of your era.

Pound, brash and natural child of Whitman and Browning, found his idealized forerunners in Arnaut Daniel and Cavalcanti, Villon and Landor. Oedipal ambivalence, which marks Pound's stance towards Whitman, never surfaces in his observations on Cavalcanti and Villon, safely remote not only in time and language, but more crucially isolated from the realities of Pound's equivocal relation to his country and compatriots.

I find Whitman quite unrecognizable in nearly every reference Pound makes to him. Our greatest poet and our most elusive, because most figurative, Whitman consistently is literalized by Pound, as though the Whitmanian self could be accepted as a machine rather than as a metaphor.

Many Poundians have quoted as evidence of their hero's esteem of Whitman a bad little poem of 1913:

A PACT

I make a pact with you, Walt Whitman—
I have detested you long enough.
I come to you as a grown child
Who has had a pig-headed father;
I am old enough now to make friends.
It was you that broke the new wood,
Now is a time for carving.
We have one sap and one root—
Let there be commerce between us.

"Truce," the original word in the first line, is more accurate than "pact," because truly there was a failure in commerce between Whitman and Pound. Whether Pound remembered that Whitman's father was a carpenter, and that Whitman himself had worked, with his father, at the trade, is beyond surmise. The root, as Pound perhaps knew, was Emerson. It is no accident that Whitman and Emerson return to Pound together in *The Pisan Cantos*, with Whitman central in the eighty-second and Emerson in the eighty-third of the *Cantos*. Emerson, I think, returns in his own trope of self-identification, the Transparent Eyeball, yet in Pound's voice, since Emerson was at most Pound's American grandfather. But Whitman returns in Whitman's own voice, and even in his own image of voice, the "tally," because the obstinate old father's voice remains strong enough to insist upon itself:

> "Fvy! in Tdaenmarck efen dh' beasantz gnow him,"
>   meaning Whitman, exotic, still suspect
>   four miles from Camden
>   "O troubled reflection
>   "O Throat, O throbbing heart"
>   How drawn, O GEA TERRA,
>   what draws as thou drawest
>   till one sink into thee by an arm's width
>   embracing thee. Drawest,
>   truly thou drawest.
>   Wisdom lies next thee,
>   simply, past metaphor.
> Where I lie let the thyme rise . . .
> ·   ·   ·   ·   ·   ·   ·   ·   ·   ·   ·   ·
>   fluid ΧΘΟΝΟΣ, strong as the undertow
>   of the wave receding
>   but that a man should live in that further terror, and live
>
>   the loneliness of death came upon me
>   (at 3 P.M., for an instant)   δακρύων
>   ἐντεῦθεν
>   three solemn half notes
>   their white downy chests black-rimmed
>   on the middle wire
>   periplum

Pound begins by recalling his German teacher at the University of Pennsylvania, forty years before, one Richard Henry Riethmuller, author of *Walt Whitman and the Germans* (1966), an identification I owe to Roy Harvey Pearce. Riethmuller (Pound got the spelling wrong) had contrasted Whitman's fame in the professor's native Denmark to the bard's supposed obscurity in the America of 1905, a contrast that leads Pound to a recall of

Whitman's "Out of the Cradle Endlessly Rocking." Whitman's poem is an elegy for the poetic self so powerful that any other poet ought to be wary of invoking so great a hymn of poetic incarnation and disincarnation. Whitman's "O troubled reflection in the sea! / O throat! O throbbing heart!" is revised by Pound into "O troubled reflection / O throat, O throbbing heart," with "in the sea" omitted. These are the last two lines of the penultimate stanza of the song of the bird lamenting his lost mate:

> *O darkness! O in vain!*
> *O I am very sick and sorrowful.*
>
> *O brown halo in the sky near the moon, drooping upon the sea!*
> *O throat! O throbbing heart!*
> *And I singing uselessly, uselessly all the night.*

Canto 82 rather movingly has shown the incarcerated poet studying the nostalgias of his early literary life, while meditating upon the unrighteousness of all wars. A vision of the earth now comes to him, in response to his partly repressed recall of Whitman's vision of the sea. Marrying the earth is Pound's counterpart to Whitman's marrying the sea, both in "Out of the Cradle Endlessly Rocking" and in "When Lilacs Last in the Dooryard Bloom'd," and both brides are at once death and the mother. "Where I lie let the thyme rise," perhaps repeating William Blake's similar grand pun on "thyme" and "time," is a profound acceptance of the reality principle, with no more idealizations of a timeless order. Whitman returns from the dead even more strongly in the closing lines of Canto 82, where Pound lies down in a fluid time "strong as the undertow / of the wave receding," which invokes another great elegiac triumph of Whitman's, "As I Ebb'd with the Ocean of Life." The two song-birds of "Out of the Cradle," with Whitman their brother making a third, utter "three solemn half notes" even as the loneliness of death came, for an instant, upon Whitman's son, Pound. Most powerful, to me, is Pound's recall of Whitman's great image of voice, the tally, from "Lilacs," "Song of Myself," and other contexts in the poet of night, death, the mother, and the sea. In Whitman, the tally counts up the poet's songs as so many wounds, so many auto-erotic gratifications that yet, somehow, do not exclude otherness. Pound, marrying the earth, realizes his terrible solitude: "man, earth: two halves of the tally / but I will come out of this knowing no one / neither they me."

Kenner is able to read this as commerce between Whitman and Pound, and insists that "the resources in the Canto are Pound's, as are those of Canto 1." But Homer, ultimate ancestor in Canto 1, was safely distant. Whitman is very close in Canto 82, and the resources are clearly his. Pound does better at converting Emerson to his own purposes, a canto later, than he is able to do with Whitman here. Would the following judgment seem valid to a fully informed and dispassionate reader?

> Pound's faults are superficial, he does convey an image of his time,
> he has written histoire morale, as Montaigne wrote the history of

his epoch. You can learn more of 20th century America from Pound than from any of the writers who either refrained from perceiving, or limited their record to what they had been taught to consider suitable literary expression. The only way to enjoy Pound thoroughly is to concentrate on his fundamental meaning.

This is Pound on Whitman from the *ABC of Reading* (1934), with Pound substituted for Whitman, and the twentieth for the nineteenth century. Pound was half right about Whitman; Whitman does teach us his country in his century, but his form and his content are not so split as Pound says, and his fundamental meaning resides in nuance, beautifully shaped in figurative language. Pound's faults are not superficial, and absolutely nothing about our country in this century can be learned from him. He conveys an image only of himself, and the only way to enjoy him is not to seek a fundamental meaning that is not there, but to take his drafts and fragments one by one, shattered crystals, but crystalline nevertheless. He had brought the great ball of crystal, of poetic tradition, but it proved too heavy for him to lift.

MARIANNE MOORE

For Plato the only reality that mattered is exemplified best for us in the principles of mathematics. The aim of our lives should be to draw ourselves away as much as possible from the unsubstantial, fluctuating facts of the world about us and establish some communion with the objects which are apprehended by thought and not sense. This was the source of Plato's asceticism. To the extent that Miss Moore finds only allusion tolerable she shares that asceticism. While she shares it she does so only as it may be necessary for her to do so in order to establish a particular reality or, better, a reality of her own particulars.

—WALLACE STEVENS

Allusion was Marianne Moore's method, a method that was her self. One of the most American of all poets, she was fecund in her progeny; Elizabeth Bishop, May Swenson, and Richard Wilbur being the most gifted among them. Her own American precursors were not Emily Dickinson and Walt Whitman—still our two greatest poets—but the much slighter Stephen Crane, who is echoed in her earliest poems, and in an oblique way Edgar Poe, whom she parodied. I suspect that her nearest poetic father, in English, was Thomas Hardy, who seems to have taught her lessons in the mastery of incongruity, and whose secularized version of Biblical irony is not far from her own. If we compare her with her major poetic contemporaries— Frost, Stevens, Eliot, Pound, Williams, Aiken, Ransom, Cummings, H. D., Hart Crane—she is clearly the most original American poet of her era, though not quite of the eminence of Frost, Stevens, or Crane. A curious kind of devotional poet, with some authentic affinities to George Herbert, she reminds us implicitly but constantly that any distinction between sacred and secular poetry is only a shibboleth of cultural politics. Some day she will remind us also of what current cultural politics obscure: that any distinction between poetry written by women and poetry by men is a mere polemic, unless it follows upon an initial distinction between good and bad poetry. Moore, like Bishop and Swenson, is an extraordinary poet-as-poet. The issue of how gender enters into her vision should arise only after the aesthetic achievement is judged as such.

Moore, as all her readers know, to their lasting delight, is the visionary of natural creatures: the jerboa, frigate pelican, buffalo, monkeys, fish, snakes, mongooses, the octopus (actually a trope for a mountain), snail, peacock, whale, pangolin, wood-weasel, elephants, race horses, chameleon, jellyfish, arctic ox (or goat), giraffe, blue bug (another trope, this time for a pony), all of La Fontaine's bestiary, not to mention sea and land unicorns, basilisks, and all the weird fabulous roster that perhaps only Borges also, among crucial modern writers, celebrates so consistently. There is something of Blake and of the Christopher Smart of *Jubilate Agno* in Moore, though the affinity does not result from influence, but rather is the consequence of election. Moore's famous eye, like that of Bishop after her, is not so much a visual gift as it is visionary, for the beasts in her poems are charged with a spiritual intensity that doubtless they possess, but which I myself cannot see without the aid of Blake, Smart, and Moore.

I remember always in reading Moore again that her favorite poem was the Book of Job. Just as I cannot read Ecclesiastes without thinking of Dr. Johnson, I cannot read certain passages in Job without recalling Marianne Moore:

> But ask now the beasts, and they shall teach
> thee; and the fowls of the air, and they shall
> tell thee:
> Or speak to the earth, and it shall teach thee:
> and the fishes of the sea shall declare unto thee.
> Who knoweth not in all these that the hand of
> the Lord hath wrought this?
> In whose hand is the soul of every living
> thing . . .

This, from chapter 12, is the prelude to the great chant of Yahweh, the Voice out of the whirlwind that sounds forth in the frightening magnificence of chapters 38 through 41, where the grand procession of beasts comprehends lions, ravens, wild goats, the wild ass, the unicorn, peacocks, the ostrich, the sublime battle-horse who "saith among the trumpets, Ha, ha," the hawk, the eagle, and at last behemoth and leviathan. Gorgeously celebrating his own creation, Yahweh through the poet of Job engendered another strong poet in Marianne Moore. Of the Book of Job, she remarked that its agony was veracious and its fidelity of a force "that contrives glory for ashes."

"Glory for ashes" might be called Moore's ethical motto, the basis for the drive of her poetic will towards a reality of her own particulars. Her poetry, as befitted the translator of La Fontaine and the heir of George Herbert, would be in some danger of dwindling into moral essays, an impossible form for our time, were it not for her wild allusiveness, her zest for quotations, and her essentially anarchic stance, the American and Emersonian insistence upon seeing everything in her own way, with "conscientious inconsistency." When her wildness or freedom subsided, she produced an occasional poetic disaster like the patriotic war poems, "In Distrust of Merits," and " 'Keeping Their World Large.' " But her greatest poems are at just the opposite edge of consciousness: "A Grave," "Novices," "Marriage," "An Octopus," "He 'Digesteth Harde Yron,' " "Elephants," the deceptively light "Tom Fool at Jamaica."

Those seven poems by themselves have an idiosyncratic splendor that restores my faith, as a critic, in what the language of the poets truly is: diction, or choice of words, playing endlessly upon the dialectic of denotation and connotation, a dialectic that simply vanishes in all Structuralist and post-Structuralist ruminations upon the supposed priority of "language" over meaning. "The arbitrariness of the signifier" loses its charm when one asks a Gallic psycholinguistifier whether denotation or connotation belongs to the signifier, as opposed to the signified, and one beholds blank incredulity as one's only answer. Moore's best poems give the adequate reply: the play of the signifier is answered always by the play of the signified, because the play of diction, or the poet's will over language, is itself constituted by the endless interchanges of denotation and connotation. Moore, with her rage to order allusion, echo, and quotation in ghostlier demarcations, keener sounds, helps us to realize that the belated Modernism of the Gallic proclamation of the death of the author was no less premature than it was, always already, belated.

T. S. ELIOT

Thomas Stearns Eliot is a central figure in the Western literary culture of this century. His undoubted achievement as a lyric and elegiac poet in itself would suffice to establish him in the main Romantic tradition of British and American poetry that moves from Wordsworth and Whitman on to Geoffrey Hill and John Ashbery, poets of our moment. There is an obvious irony in such a judgment. Eliot's professed sense of *the* tradition, *his* tradition, was rather different, tracing as it did the true line of poetry in English from its origins in medieval Provence and Italy through its later developments in France (I borrow that remark from Northrop Frye). Eliot's polemical stance as a literary critic can be distinguished from his rhetorical stance as a poet, and both postures of the spirit are fortunately quite distinct from his cultural position, self-proclaimed as Anglo-Catholic, Royalist and Classical.

An obsessive reader of poetry growing up in the 1930s and 1940s entered a critical world dominated by the opinions and example of Eliot. To speak out of even narrower personal experience, anyone adopting the profession of teaching literature in the early 1950s entered a discipline virtually enslaved not only by Eliot's insights but by the entire span of his preferences and prejudices. If one's cultural position was Jewish, Liberal, and Romantic, one was likely to start out with a certain lack of affection for Eliot's predominance, however much (against the will) the subtle force of the poetry was felt. If a young critic particularly loved Shelley, Milton, Emerson, Pater, and if that same critic did not believe that Blake was a naive and eccentric genius, then regard for Eliot seemed unnecessary. Whatever he actually represented, a neochristian and neoclassic Academy had exalted him, by merit raised, to what was pragmatically rather a bad eminence. In *that* critical climate, Hopkins was considered the only valid Victorian poet, greatly superior to Browning and Tennyson, while Whitman seemed an American nightmare and Wallace Stevens, if he passed at all, had to be salvaged as a Late Augustan. Thirty years on, these views have a kind of antique charm, but in 1954 they were at least annoying, and if one cared enough, they had some capacity for infuriating.

I resume these matters not to stir up waning rancors, but to explain why, for some critics of my own generation, Eliot only recently has ceased to represent the spiritual enemy. His disdain for Freud, his flair for demonstrating the authenticity of his Christianity by exhibiting a judicious anti-Semitism, his refined contempt for human sexuality—somehow these did not seem to be the inevitable foundations for contemporary culture. Granted that he refrained from the rhetorical excesses of his ally Ezra Pound; there is nothing in him resembling the Poundian apothegm: "All the jew part of the Bible is black evil." Still, an Academy that found its ideology in Eliot was not a place where one could teach comfortably, or where one could have remained, had the Age of Eliot not begun to wane. The ascendency of Eliot, as a fact of cultural politics, is something many among us could not wish to see return.

Eliot asserted for his poetry a seventeenth-century ancestry, out of Jacobean dramatists and Metaphysical lyricists. Its actual forerunners are Whitman and Tennyson, and Eliot's strength is felt now when we read "When Lilacs Last in the Dooryard Bloom'd" and "Maud: A Monodrama," and find ourselves believing that they are influenced by *The Waste Land*. It is a neglected truth of American poetic history that Eliot and Stevens are more Whitmanian than Hart Crane, whose allegiance to Whitman was overt. Though Eliot and Stevens consciously did not feel or know it, their poetry is obsessed with Whitman's poetry. By this I mean Whitman's tropes and Whitman's curious transitions between topics, and not at all the example of Whitman, far more crucial for Crane and many others.

It is the pattern of Eliot's figurations that is most High Romantic, a pattern that I suspect he learned from Tennyson and Whitman, who derived it from Keats and Shelley, who in turn had been instructed by Wordsworth's crisis lyrics and odes, which go back yet further to Spenserian and Miltonic models. Consider Eliot's *Ash-Wednesday*, his conversion-sequence of 1930. The poem's six movements are not a Dantesque *Vita Nuova*, despite Eliot's desires, but a rather strict re-enactment of the Wordsworthian drama of experiential loss and compensatory imaginative gain:

(I) This is an ironic movement that says "I rejoice" but means "I despair," which is the limited irony that Freud terms a "reaction formation," or an emotion masking ambivalently as its opposite. Despite the deliberate allusions to Cavalcanti and Dante, Ezekiel and the Mass, that throng the poem, the presumably unintended echoes of Wordsworth's Intimations of Immortality Ode carry the reader closer to the center of the poet's partially repressed anxieties and to his poetic anxieties in particular. "The infirm glory" and the "one veritable transitory power" are stigmata of the visionary gleam in its flight from the poet, and if what is lost here is more-than-natural, we remember that the loss in Wordsworth also transcends nature. Though Eliot employs the language of mysticism and Wordsworth the language of nature, the crisis for each is poetic rather than mystical or natural. Eliot's renunciation of voice, however ironical, leads directly to what for many readers has been the most memorable and poignant realization in the sequence: "Consequently I rejoice, having to construct something / Upon which to rejoice." No more illuminating epigraph could be assigned to Wordsworth's Intimations Ode, or to "Tintern Abbey" or "Resolution and Independence." The absence lamented in the first part of *Ash-Wednesday* is a once-present poetic strength, whatever else it represented experientially. In the Shakespearean rejection of the desire for "this man's gift and that man's scope," we need not doubt that the men are precursor poets, nor ought we to forget that not hoping to turn again is also an ironic farewell to troping, and so to one's own quest for poetic voice.

(II) The question that haunts the transition between the first two sections, pragmatically considered, is, "Am I, Eliot, still a poet?" "Shall these bones live?" is a synecdochal question, whole for part, since the immortality involved is the figurative survival of one's poetry: "As I am forgotten / And would be forgotten, so I would forget." Turning around against himself, this poet, in the mode of Browning's Childe Roland, asks only to be numbered among the scattered precursors, to fail as they have failed: "We have our inheritance."

(III) After such self-wounding, the poet seeks a kind of Pauline *kenosis*, akin to Christ's emptying himself of his own Divinity, which here can only mean the undoing of one's poetic gift. As inspiration fades away willfully, the gift wonderfully declares itself nevertheless, in that enchanted lyricism Eliot never ceased to share with the elegiac Whitman and the Virgilian Tennyson: "Lilac and brown hair; / Distraction, music of the flute, stops and steps of the mind over the third stair." The figurative movement is metonymic, as in the displacement of poetic power from the speaker to the curiously Pre-Raphaelite "broadbacked figure drest in blue and green," who is anything but a possible representation of Eliot's own poetic self.

(IV) This is the daemonic vision proper, allowing a sequence that denies sublimity, to reattain a Romantic Sublime. In the transition between sections 3 and 4, Eliot appears to surmount the temptations of solipsism, so as to ask and answer the question, "Am I capable of loving another?" The unnamed other or "silent sister" is akin to shadowy images of desire in Tennyson and Whitman, narcissistic emblems certainly, but pointing beyond the self's passion for the self. Hugh Kenner, indubitably Eliot's best and most Eliotic critic, suggestively compares *Ash-Wednesday* to Tennyson's "The Holy Grail," and particularly to the fearful death-march of Percivale's quest in that most ornate portion of *The Idylls of the King*. Kenner of course awards the palm to Eliot over what he dismisses as a crude "Victorian ceremony of iterations" as compared to Eliot's "austere gestures of withdrawal and submission." A quarter of a century after he made them, Kenner's judgments seem eminently reversible, since Tennyson's gestures are, in this case, palpably more austere than his inheritor's. Tennyson has, after all, nothing quite so gaudy as "Redeem / The unread vision in the higher dream / While jewelled unicorns draw by the gilded hearse."

(V) Percivale's desert and the wasteland of Browning's Childe Roland join the Biblical wildernesses in this extraordinary *askesis*, a self-curtailing rhapsody that truncates Romantic tradition as much as it does Eliot's individual talent. One could assert that this section affirms all the possibilities of sublimation, from Plato through Nietzsche to Freud, except that the inside/outside metaphor of dualism confines itself here only to "The Word without a word, the Word within." Eliot, like all his Romantic ancestors from Wordsworth to Pater, seeks a crossing to a subtle identification with an innocent earliness, while fearing to introject instead the belatedness of a world without imagination, the death-in-life of the poet who has outlasted his gift.

(VI) This is one of Eliot's triumphs, as an earliness is recovered under the sign of contrition. The "unbroken wings" still flying seaward are a beautiful metalepsis of the wings of section I, which were "merely vans to beat the air." A characteristic pattern of the Romantic crisis lyric is extended as the precursors return from the dead, but in Eliot's own colors, the "lost lilac" of Whitman and the "lost sea voices" of Tennyson joining Eliot's "lost heart" in the labor of rejoicing, having indeed constructed something upon which to rejoice.

That Eliot, in retrospect, will seem the Matthew Arnold rather than the Abraham Cowley of his age, is the sympathetic judgment of A. Walton Litz. For motives admitted already, one might prefer to see Eliot as the Cowley, and some celebrated passages in *Four Quartets* are worthy of comparison with long-ago-admired Pindarics of that forgotten wit, but Arnold's burden as involuntary belated Romantic is indeed close to Eliot's. A direct comparison of Eliot's elegiac achievement to Whitman's or Tennyson's seems to me both more problematical and more inevitable. "Gerontion" contrasts unfavorably to "Tithonus" or "Ulysses," while *The Waste Land*, despite its critical high priests, lacks the coherence, maturity, and experiential authenticity of "When Lilacs Last in the Dooryard Bloom'd." And yet it must be admitted that Eliot is what the closing lines of *The Waste Land* assert him to be: a shorer of fragments against his (and our) ruins. The phantasmagoric intensity of his best poems and passages can be matched only in the greatest visionaries and poets of Western literature. It is another paradox that the Anglo-Catholic, Royalist, Classical spokesperson should excel in the mode of fictive hallucination and lyric derangement, in the fashioning of nightmare images perfectly expressive of his age.

Eliot's influence as a poet is by no means spent, yet it seems likely that Robert Penn Warren's later poetry, the most distinguished now being written among us, will be the final stand of Eliot's extraordinary effort to establish an anti-Romantic counter-Sublime sense of *the* tradition to replace the continuity of Romantic tradition. That the continuity now has absorbed him is hardly a defeat; absorption is not rejection, and Eliot's poetry is securely in the canon. Eliot's strength, manifested in the many poets indebted to him, is probably most authentically commemorated by the poetry of Hart Crane, which engages Eliot's poetry in an agon without which Crane could not have achieved his difficult greatness. One can prefer Crane to Eliot, as I do, and yet be forced to concede that Eliot, more than Whitman, made Crane possible.

HART CRANE

Again the traffic lights that skim thy swift
Unfractioned idiom, immaculate sigh of stars,
Beading thy path—condense eternity:
And we have seen night lifted in thine arms.

Under thy shadow by the piers I waited;
Only in darkness is thy shadow clear.
The City's fiery parcels all undone,
Already snow submerges an iron year . . .

O Sleepless as the river under thee,
Vaulting the sea, the prairies' dreaming sod,
Unto us lowliest sometime sweep, descend
And of the curveship lend a myth to God.
                                  —"Proem" to *The Bridge*

Hart Crane in *White Buildings* is wholly Orphic, in that his concern is his relation, as poet, to his own vision, rather than *with* the content of poetic vision, to utilize a general distinction inaugurated by Northrop Frye, following after Ruskin. The peculiar power of *The Bridge* at its strongest is that Crane succeeds in becoming what Pater and Nietzsche urged the future poet to be: ascetic of the spirit, which is an accurate definition of a purified Gnosis. Directly before these three final quatrains of "To Brooklyn Bridge," Crane had saluted the bridge first as Orphic emblem, both harp and altar, but then as the threshold of the full triad of the Orphic destiny: Dionysus or prophet's pledge, Ananke or prayer of pariah, and Eros, the lover's cry. It is after the range of relations to his own vision has been acknowledged and accepted that a stronger Crane achieves the Gnosis of those three last quatrains. There the poet remains present, but only as a knowing Abyss, contemplating the content of that knowing, which is a fullness or presence he can invoke but scarcely share. He sees "night lifted in thine arms"; he waits, for a shadow to clarify in darkness; he knows, yet what he knows is a vaulting, a sweep, a descent, above all a curveship, a realization of an angle of vision not yet his own.

This peculiarly effective stance has a precursor in Shelley's visionary skepticism, particularly in his final phase of *Adonais* and *The Triumph of Life*. Crane's achievement of this stance is the still-unexplored origin of *The Bridge*, but the textual evolution of "Atlantis," the first section of the visionary epic to be composed, is the probable area that should be considered. Lacking space here, I point instead to the achieved stance of "Voyages" 6 as the earliest full instance of Crane's mature Orphism, after which I will conclude with a reading of "Atlantis" and a brief glance at Crane's testament, "The Broken Tower."

The governing deities of the "Voyages" sequence are Eros and Ananke, or Emil Oppfer and the Caribbean as a Whitmanian fierce old mother moaning for her castaways. But the Orphic Dionysus, rent apart by Titanic forces, dominates the sixth lyric, which like Stevens's "The Paltry Nude Starts on a Spring Voyage" partly derives from Pater's description of Botticelli's Venus in *The Renaissance*. Pater's sado-masochistic maternal love-goddess, with her eyes smiling "unsearchable repose," becomes Crane's overtly destructive muse whose seer is no longer at home in his own vision:

> My eyes pressed black against the prow,
> —Thy derelict and blinded guest
>
> Waiting, afire, what name, unspoke,
> I cannot claim: let thy waves rear
> More savage than the death of kings,
> Some splintered garland for the seer.

The unspoken, unclaimed name is that of Orpheus, in his terrible final phase of "floating singer." Crane's highly deliberate echo of Shakespeare's Richard II at his most self-destructively masochistic is assimilated to the poetic equivalent, which is the splintering of the garland of laurel. Yet the final stanza returns to the central image of poetic incarnation in Crane, "Repose of Rivers" and its "hushed willows":

> The imaged Word, it is, that holds
> Hushed willows anchored in its glow.
> It is the unbetrayable reply
> Whose accent no farewell can know.

This is the achieved and curiously firm balance of a visionary skepticism, or the Orphic stance of *The Bridge*. It can be contrasted to Lawrence, in the "Orphic farewell" of "Medlars and Sorb Apples" in *Birds, Beasts and Flowers*. For Lawrence, Orphic assurance is the solipsism of an "intoxication of perfect loneliness." Crane crosses that intoxication by transuming his own and tradition's trope of the hushed willows as signifying an end to solitary mourning and a renewal of poetic divination. "Voyages" 6 turns its "imaged Word" against Eliot's neo-orthodox Word, or Christ, and Whitman's Word out of the Sea, or death, death that is the Oedipal merging back into the mother. Crane ends upon "know" because knowledge, and not faith, is his religious mode, a Gnosis that is more fully developed in *The Bridge*.

The dozen octaves of the final version of "Atlantis" show Crane in his mastery of the traditional Sublime, and are wholly comparable to the final seventeen stanzas of Shelley's *Adonais*. Crane's absolute music, like Plato's, "is then the knowledge of that which relates to love in harmony and system," but Crane's love is rather more like Shelley's desperate and skeptical outleaping than it is like Diotima's vision. For six stanzas, Crane drives upward, in a hyperbolic arc whose burden is agonistic, struggling to break beyond every achieved Sublime in the language. This agon belongs to the Sublime, and perhaps in America it is the Sublime. But such an agon requires particular contestants, and "Atlantis" finds them in *The Waste Land* and, yet more repressedly, in Whitman's "Crossing Brooklyn Ferry," the great addition to the second, 1856, *Leaves of Grass*, and Thoreau's favorite poem by Whitman.

Much of Crane's struggle with Eliot was revised out of the final "Atlantis," but only as overt textual traces; the deep inwardness of the battle is recoverable. Two modes of phantasmagoria clash:

> Through the bound cable strands, the arching path
> Upward, veering with light, the flight of strings,—
> Taut miles of shuttling moonlight syncopate
> The whispered rush, telepathy of wires.
> Up the index of night, granite and steel—
> Transparent meshes—fleckless the gleaming staves—
> Sibylline voices flicker, waveringly stream
> As though a god were issue of the strings.
>
> · · · · · · · · · · · · · · · · · · ·

A woman drew her long black hair out tight
And fiddled whisper music on those strings
And bats with baby faces in the violet light
Whistled, and beat their wings
And crawled head downward down a blackened wall
And upside down in air were towers
Tolling reminiscent bells, that kept the hours
And voices singing out of empty cisterns and exhausted wells.

The latter hallucination might be called an amalgam of *Dracula* and the Gospels, as rendered in the high style of Tennyson's *Idylls of the King*, and obviously is in no sense a source or cause of Crane's transcendental opening octave. Nevertheless, no clearer contrast could be afforded, for Crane's lines answer Eliot's, in every meaning of "answer." "Music is then the knowledge of that which relates to love in harmony and system," and one knowledge answers another in these competing and marvelous musics of poetry, and of visionary history. Crane's bridge is to Atlantis, in fulfillment of the Platonic quest of Crane's Columbus. Eliot's bridge is to the Inferno, in fulfillment of the neo-Christian condemnation of Romantic, Transcendentalist, Gnostic quest. Crane's Sibylline voices stream upward; his night-illuminated bridge becomes a transparent musical score, until Orpheus is born out of the flight of strings. Eliot's Sibyl wishes to die; her counterpart plays a vampiric score upon her own hair, until instead of Orphic birth upwards we have an impotent triumph of time.

This contrast, and others equally sharp, constitutes the context of Crane's aspiration in "Atlantis." But this aspiration, which is for knowledge, in the particular sense of Gnosis, yields to Eliot, as it must, much of the world of things-as-they-are. The closing images of "The Tunnel," the section of *The Bridge* preceding "Atlantis," combine *The Waste Land*'s accounts of loss with Whitman's darker visions of those losses in "Crossing Brooklyn Ferry":

And this thy harbor, O my City, I have driven under,
Tossed from the coil of ticking towers. . . . Tomorrow,
And to be. . . . Here by the River that is East—
Here at the waters' edge the hands drop memory;
Shadowless in that abyss they unaccounting lie.
How far away the star has pooled the sea—
Or shall the hands be drawn away, to die?
Kiss of our agony Thou gatherest,
                    O Hand of Fire
                              gatherest—

Emerson's was a Gnosis without Gnosticism; Crane's religion, at its darkest, shades from Orphism into Gnosticism, in a negative transcendence even of the Whitman who proclaimed, "It is not upon you alone the dark

patches fall, / The dark threw its patches upon me also." The negative
transcendence of "Atlantis" surmounts the world, history, and even precursors as knowing, in their rival ways, as Eliot and Whitman. Crane con-
denses the upward intensities of his first six octaves by a deliberate recall
of his own Columbus triumphantly but delusively chanting: "I bring you
back Cathay!" But Crane's Columbus invoked the Demiurge under Emily
Dickinson's name for him, "Inquisitor! incognizable Word / Of Eden." This
beautiful pathos of defeat, in "Ave Maria," was consonant with Whitman's
"Prayer of Columbus," where the battered, wrecked old mariner denied
all knowledge: "I know not even my own word past or present." Crane's
American burden, in the second half of "Atlantis," is to start again where
Dickinson and Whitman ended, and where Eliot had sought to show no
fresh start was possible. Knowledge in precisely the Gnostic sense—a
knowing that knows the knower and is, *in itself*, the form of salvation—
becomes Crane's formidable hymn addressed directly to itself, to poem and
to bridge, until they become momentarily "—One Song, one Bridge of
Fire!" But is this persuasively different from the "Hand of Fire" that gathers
the kiss of our agony?

The dialectic of Gnosticism is a triad of negation, evasion, and extravagance. Lurianic Kabbalah renders these as contraction, breaking-of-the-
vessels, and restitution. Fate, freedom, power is the Emersonian or American equivalent. All of these triads translate aesthetically into a dialectic of
limitation, substitution, and representation, as I have shown in several
critical books starting with *A Map of Misreading*. Crane's negation or limitation, his contraction into Fate, is scarcely different from Eliot's, but then
such rival negative theologies as Valentinian Gnosticism and Johannine
Christianity are difficult to distinguish in their accounts of how to express
divinity. Gnostic evasion, like Crane's notorious freedom and range in
troping, is clearly more inventive than authorized Christian modes of substitution, just as Gnostic extravagance, again like Crane's hyperbolical Sublime, easily surpasses orthodox expressions of power.

Crane's elaborate evasiveness is crucial in the seventh stanza of "Atlantis," where the upward movement of the tropology has ended, and a
westward lateral sweep of vision is substituted, with the bridge no longer
confronted and addressed, but seen now as binding the continent:

> We left the haven hanging in the night—
> Sheened harbor lanterns backward fled the keel.
> Pacific here at time's end, bearing corn,—
> Eyes stammer through the pangs of dust and steel.
> And still the circular, indubitable frieze
> Of heaven's meditation, yoking wave
> To kneeling wave, one song devoutly binds—
> The vernal strophe chimes from deathless strings!

The third line implies not merely a circuit of the earth, but an achieved peace at the end of days, a millennial harvest. When the bridge returns in this stanza's last four lines, it has become heaven's own meditation, the known knowing the human knower. And such a knowing leads Crane on to the single most central stanza of his life and work:

> O Thou steeled Cognizance whose leap commits
> The agile precincts of the lark's return;
> Within whose lariat sweep encinctured sing
> In single chrysalis the many twain,—
> Of stars Thou art the stitch and stallion glow
> And like an organ, Thou, with sound of doom—
> Sight, sound and flesh Thou leadest from time's realm
> As love strikes clear direction for the helm.

Contrast the precise Shelleyan equivalent:

> The One remains, the many change and pass;
> Heaven's light forever shines, Earth's shadows fly;
> Life, like a dome of many-colored glass,
> Stains the white radiance of Eternity,
> Until Death tramples it to fragments.—Die,
> If thou wouldst be with that which thou dost seek!
> Follow where all is fled!—Rome's azure sky,
> Flowers, ruins, statues, music, words, are weak
> The glory they transfuse with fitting truth to speak.

Superficially, the two stanzas are much at variance, with Crane's tone apparently triumphal, Shelley's apparently despairing. But the pragmatic or merely natural burden of both stanzas is quite suicidal. The bridge, as "steeled Cognizance," resolves the many into One, but this music of unity is a "sound of doom" for all flesh and its senses living in time's realm. Love's "clear direction," as in Shelley's climactic stanza, is towards death. But Shelley is very much involved in his own relation, as poet, to his own vision. Crane's role, as known to the bridge's knower, forsakes that relation, and a terrifyingly free concentration on the content of poetic vision is the reward. "Of stars Thou art the stitch and stallion glow" Marlowe himself would have envied, but since both terms of the trope, bridge and stars, exclude the human, Crane is impelled onwards to extraordinary achievements in hyperbole. When the bridge is "iridescently upborne / Through the bright drench and fabric of our veins," then the human price of Gnosticism begins to mount also. Crane insists that all this is "to our joy," but that joy is as dialectical as Shelley's despair. And Crane, supremely intelligent, counts the cost, foreknowing all criticism:

> Migrations that must needs void memory,
> Inventions that cobblestone the heart,—
> Unspeakable Thou Bridge to Thee, O Love.

> Thy pardon for this history, whitest Flower,
> O Answerer of all,—Anemone,—
> Now while thy petals spend the suns about us, hold—
> (O Thou whose radiance doth inherit me)
> Atlantis,—hold thy floating singer late!

Would it make a difference if this read: "Cathay,—hold thy floating singer late!" so that the prayer of pariah would belong to Columbus and not to Orpheus? Yes, for the final stanza then would have the Orphic strings leap and converge to a question clearly different:

> —One Song, one Bridge of Fire! Is it Atlantis,
> Now pity steeps the grass and rainbows ring
> The serpent with the eagle in the leaves . . . ?

Crane's revision of the Orphic stance of *White Buildings* here allows him a difference that is a triumph. His serpent and eagle are likelier to be Shelley's than Nietzsche's, for they remain at strife *within* their border of covenant, the ring of rainbows. Atlantis is urged to hold its Orpheus late, as a kind of newly fused Platonic myth of reconcilement to a higher world of forms, a myth of which Gnosticism was a direct heir. "Is it Cathay?," repeating the noble delusion of Columbus, is not a question hinting defeat, but foreboding victory. Yet Orphic victories are dialectical, as Crane well knew. Knowledge indeed is the kernel, for Crane astutely shows awareness of what the greatest poets always know, which is that their figurations intend the will's revenge against time's "it was," but actually achieve the will's limits, in the bewilderments of the Abyss of troping and of tropes.

The coda to Crane's poetry, and his life, is "The Broken Tower," where the transumption of the Orphic quest does allow a final triumph:

> And so it was I entered the broken world
> To trace the visionary company of love, its voice
> An instant in the wind (I know not whither hurled)
> But not for long to hold each desperate choice.

Crane mentions reading other books by Pater, but not the unfinished novel *Gaston de Latour*. Its first few chapters, at least, would have fascinated him, and perhaps he did look into the opening pages, where the young Gaston undergoes a ceremony bridging the spirit and nature:

> Gaston alone, with all his mystic preoccupations, by the privilege
> of youth, seemed to belong to both, and link the visionary com-
> pany about him to the external scene.

The "privilege of youth" was still Crane's when he died, and "The Broken Tower" remains as one of those links. Such a link, finally, is not to be judged as what Freud called "a false connection" or as another irony to be ironically recognized, but rather as a noble synecdoche, self-mutilating perhaps as is a steeled Cognizance, but by its very turning against the self, endlessly reconstituting the American poetic self, the *pneuma* or spark of an American Gnosis.

Edwin Arlington Robinson

Conrad Aiken

Of his story "The Altar of the Dead" Henry James observed that it was on a theme which had been bothering him for years, but of which the artistic legitimacy was suspect; he had to write it, but he knew it to be pitched in a richly sentimental key which, under the hands of another, he might have condemned. His story *The Turn of the Screw*, surely one of the finest ghost stories in any language, he frankly derided as a potboiler, making no reservations for its brilliance. He was, of course, right in both of these opinions: he was a better judge of Henry James than any other critic has been, he knew his parerga when he saw them, he could afford to wave them blandly aside. We should think, perhaps, a little less of him, as we are tempted to do of any artist, if he had taken his parerga too seriously—if he had appeared to see only dimly, or not at all, any distinction between these things, which were carved from stones flawed at the outset, and those others, which no flaw rebukes.

Thus, toward Mr. Edwin Arlington Robinson, whom we are accustomed to think of as the most unfailing artist among our contemporary poets, one looks with the barest shade of suspicion after reading his latest book, *Avon's Harvest*. One has, of course, with the critic's habitual baseless arrogance, no hesitation in placing it—it fits, in Mr. Robinson's list, in so far as it fits at all, very much as *The Turn of the Screw* fits in the completed monument of Henry James. One is not disposed, that is, to take it with too great a seriousness. More precisely, the degree of our seriousness will depend on the degree of Mr. Robinson's seriousness; if we had any reason to suppose that Mr. Robinson regards *Avon's Harvest* as he regards *Merlin* or *Lancelot* or *The Man against the Sky*, then we should accept it with concern.

From *A Reviewer's ABC*, edited by Rufus A. Blanshard. © 1958 by Conrad Aiken. Meridian Books, 1958.

For, clearly, it is not as good as these, and the most cursory inquiry into the reasons for its comparative unimportance will disclose its defects as not merely those of technique but, more gravely, those of material—as in the case of "The Altar of the Dead." We must grant, at this point, that to every artist come moments when he delights in abandoning for an interim the plane of high seriousness, to allow play to lesser and lighter motives: when Keats dons the "Cap and Bells," the critic, smiling, doffs robe and wig. This is both legitimate and desirable. By all means let the poet have his scherzo! We shall be the richer for it, we shall have, as audience, a scrap the more of the poet's singular soliloquy. But it is imperative that the poet, if his scherzo be abruptly introduced, and amid the graver echo of graver music, should accompany it with an appropriate twinkle of eye. Otherwise his audience may do him the dishonor of supposing that he has nothing more to say.

We prefer to believe, then, that Mr. Robinson does not himself intend *Avon's Harvest* as weightily as many of his other things. It is a ghost story, and a fairly good one. That Mr. Robinson should deal with an out-and-out ghost is not surprising, for ghosts have figured in his work from the very outset—ghosts, that is, as the symbols of human fears or loves, ghosts as the plausible and tangible personifications of those varieties of self-tyranny which nowadays we call psychotic. For this sort of ghost there need be no justification, no more than for the ghost of Banquo. If Mr. Robinson had been content with this, if his ghost in *Avon's Harvest* had been simply this— as it might well have been—we should have less cause to quarrel with him. As it is, we are bound to observe that he has *not* been content with this, that he has yielded to the temptation, which an unfailing realist would have resisted, of heightening the effect of the supernatural for its own sake. The knife, with which in a fulminous nightmare the ghost assails Avon, must later be re-introduced by Avon as a knife or ponderable enough reality, which the ghost, in evaporating, left behind. The actuality of the knife's presence there, after the admirable nightmare, might indeed have been explained by another mechanism than that of the supernatural; but no such explanation is hinted at, or, for that matter, can be hinted at, since Avon is himself the narrator. This is a grave defect; but a graver one is that which again calls to mind "The Altar of the Dead" as a fine thing made of flawed material—the psychological weakness with which the theme is conceived. If Mr. Robinson wished to give us, in Avon, a case of incipient insanity, with a pronounced persecutional mania, then he should have given us, for this aspect, a better lighting. Either we should have been made, therefore, before Avon uttered the first word of his story, more dubious of the man's soundness of mind; or else there should have been, in the story itself, more light upon Avon's character as a thing easily shaken and destroyed—ready, in short, for the very insignificant provocation which was to turn out as sufficient to make a ruin of it. But we are assisted in neither of these ways, and in consequence the provocative action cannot help striking us as disproportionately and incredibly slight: we accept it, as necessary to the story, very much as we often accept a ridiculous element in the plot of a photo-play—accept because acceptance conditions pleasure, not because we believe. We waive our incredulity for the moment; but it returns upon us at the end with the greater weight.

One wonders, in this light, whether it would be unjust, after our provisos for the artist's right to the scherzo, to see in *Avon's Harvest*, as one often sees in an artist's less successful work, a clearer indication of Mr. Robinson's faults and virtues than might elsewhere be palpable. The poem is extravagantly characteristic of its author—there is perhaps no other poet, with the exception of Mr. Thomas Hardy, who so persistently and recognizably saturates every poem with his personality. We have again, as so many times before, the story told by the retrospective friend of the protagonist—apologetic, humorous, tartly sympathetic, maintaining from beginning to end a note about midway between the elegiac and the ironic. This is the angle of approach which has been made familiar to us in how many of the short ballad-like narratives of Mr. Robinson, of which the characteristics were almost as definite and mature in the first volume as in the last: "John Evereldown," "Richard Cory," "Luke Havergal," "Reuben Bright," in that volume, and after them a crowd of others; and then, with the same approach again, but in long form, "Captain Craig," and "Ben Jonson Entertains a Man from Stratford," and "Isaac and Archibald." What we see here, in short, is an instinctive and strong preference for that approach which will most enable the poet to adopt, toward his personae, an informal and colloquial tone, a tone which easily permits, even invites, that happy postulation of intimacy which at the very outset carries to the reader a conviction that the particular persona under dissection is a person seen and known. The note, we should keep in mind, is the ballad note—best when it is swiftest and most concise. If, as we observed above, the elegiac also figures, it is as a contrapuntal device (by "device" one does not mean to suggest, however, a thing deliberated upon), with a clear enough melodic line of its own. To narrative speed much else is ruthlessly sacrificed. Should we admit also, in our effort to place this very individual note, an element suggestive of the rapid lyrical summary, cryptically explanatory, a little subdued and brooding, as under a giant shadow—of the choruses in the tragedies of Aeschylus and Sophocles? In one respect Mr. Robinson's briefer narratives appear closer to these than to the English ballad—the action is so consistently a thing known rather than a thing seen. The action is indeed, in the vast majority of cases, an off-stage affair, the precise shape and speed of which we are permitted only to know in dark hints and sinister gleams.

The dark hint and sinister gleam have by many critics been considered the chief characteristics of this poet's style; and it is useful to keep them in mind as we consider, in a workshop light, his technique and mode of thought. Technique, for our purpose, we cannot regard as a mere matter of iambics and caesuras; it is perhaps merely a more inquisitive term for "style," by which, again, I suppose we mean the explicit manifestation of an individual mode of thought. At all events, technique and mode of thought are inseparable, are two aspects of one thing, and it is impossible to discuss any artist's technique without being insensibly and inevitably led into a discussion of his mode of thought. Thus it is permissible, in the matter of the dark hint and the sinister gleam, to isolate them either as tricks of technique or as characteristics of a particular way of thinking: and it does not greatly matter which way we choose.

If we examine Mr. Robinson's early work, in *The Children of the Night* or *The Town down the River*, in search of the prototype of the "hint" and "gleam" which he has made—or found—so characteristic of himself, we discover them as already conspicuous enough. But it is interesting to observe that at this stage of his growth as an artist this characteristic revealed itself as a technical neatness more precisely than as a neatness of thought, and might thus have been considered as giving warning of a slow increase in subservience of thought to form. The "subtlety"—inevitable term in discussing the gleaming terseness of this style—was not infrequently to be suspected of speciousness. In "Atherton's Gambit," and other poems, we cannot help feeling that the gleam is rather one of manner than of matter: what we suspect is that a poet of immense technical dexterity, dexterity of a dry, laconic kind, is altering and directing his theme, even inviting it, to suit his convictions in regard to style. Shall we presume to term this padding? Padding of a sort it certainly is; but Mr. Robinson's padding was peculiar to himself, and it is remarkable that precisely out of this peculiar method of padding was to grow a most characteristic excellence of his mature manner. For this padding (the word is far too severe) took shape at the outset as the employment, when rhyme-pattern or stanza dictated, of the "vague phrase," the phrase which gave, to the idea conveyed, an odd and somewhat pleasing abstractness. Here began Mr. Robinson's preference, at such moments, for the Latin as against the English word, since the Latin, with its roots in a remoter tongue, and its original tactilism therefore less apparent, permits a larger and looser comprehensiveness; and for such English words as have, for us, the dimmest of contacts with sensory reality. However, it must be remarked that, for the most part, in the first three volumes, the terse "comprehensiveness" thus repeatedly indulged in was often more apparent than real: one suspects that behind the veil of dimness, thus again and again flourished before us by the engaging magician, there is comparatively little for analysis to fasten upon. The round and unctuous neatness of the poems in these volumes has about it just that superfluity which inevitably suggests the hollow. This is not to imply that there are not exceptions, and brilliant ones—"Isaac and Archibald" is a wholly satisfying piece of portraiture, and "Captain Craig" has surely its fine moments. But for the development of this characteristic into something definitely good one must turn to the volume called *The Man against the Sky* and to the others that followed it. Here we see the employment of the "vague phrase" made, indeed, the keynote of the style—the "vague phrase," no longer specious, but genuinely suggestive, and accurately indicative of a background left dim not because the author is only dimly aware of it, but because dimness serves to make it seem the more gigantic. That, if true of the background, a strange, bare, stark world, flowerless, odorless, and colorless, perpetually under a threat of storm, is no less true of the protagonists. These, if their world is colorless, are themselves bodiless: we see them again and again as nothing on earth but haunted souls, stripped, as it were, of everything but one most characteristic gesture. If they are shadowy they seem larger for it, since what shadow they have is of the right shape to "lead" the eye; if their habiliments of flesh, gesture and facial expression are few, we see them the more clearly for it and remember them the better. This is the style at its best, but if we move on once more to the last volume, *The Three Taverns*, and *Avon's Harvest*, even perhaps to some things in *Lancelot* (though here there are other inimical factors to be considered), we shall see a deterioration of this style, and in a way which, had we been intelligent, we might have expected. For here the "vague phrase" has become a habitual gesture, otiose precisely in proportion as it has become habitual. The "vague phrase" has lost its fine precision of vagueness, the background has lost its reality in a dimness which is the dimness, too often, of the author's conception, and the one gesture of the protagonist is apt to be inconsiderable and unconvincing. We savor here a barren technical neatness. The conjuror more than ever cultivates a fine air of mystery; but nothing answers the too-determined wand.

In connection with this characteristic vague phrase, with its freight of hint and gleam, it is useful to notice, as an additional source of light, Mr. Robinson's vocabulary. We cannot move in it for long without feeling that it indicates either a comparative poverty of "sensibility" or something closely akin to it; either a lack of sensibility, in the tactile sense, or a fear of surrendering to it. We have already noted, in another guise, the lack of color; we must note also the lack of sense of texture, sense of shape. As concerns his meter these lacks manifest themselves in a tendency to monotony of rhythm, to a "tumbling" sort of verse frequently out of key with the thought. It is an iron world that Mr. Robinson provides for us: if roses are offered they are singularly the abstractions of roses, not at all the sort of thing for the senses to grow drunk on. He gives us not things, but the ideas of things. We must be careful not to impute to him a total lack of sensory responsiveness, for, as we shall see in *The Man against the Sky* and *Merlin*, this element in his style reaches its proportional maximum and betrays a latent Mr. Robinson, a romanticist, who, if he uses color sparingly, uses it with exquisite effect.

In general, however, Mr. Robinson's eye is rather that of the dramatist than of the poet—it is perceptive not so much of the beautiful as of significant actions; and the beautiful, when it figures here at all, figures merely as something appropriate to the action. In this regard he is more akin to Browning than any other modern poet has been, if we except Mr. Thomas Hardy. Like Browning, he is a comparative failure when he is an out-and-out playwright; but he is at his most characteristic best when he has, for his poetic framework, a "situation" to present, a situation out of which, from moment to moment, the specifically poetic may flower. This flowering, we are inclined to think, is more conspicuous and more fragrant in *The Man against the Sky* and *Merlin* than elsewhere, most fragrant of all in *Merlin*. Differences there are to be noted—"Ben Jonson Entertains a Man from Stratford" represents the perfection of Mr. Robinson's sense of scene and portraiture, sees and renders the actual, the human, with extraordinary richness. In *Merlin*, however, where Mr. Robinson's romantic alter ego, so long frustrated, at last speaks out, we cannot for long doubt that he reaches his zenith as a poet. The sense of scene and portraiture are as acute here, certainly, but the fine actuality with which they are rendered is, as in the best poetry, synonymous with the beautiful; and the poem, though long, is admirably, and beyond any other American narrative poem, sustained. The "vague phrase" here swims with color, or yields to the precise; the irony (Mr. Robinson's habitual mode of "heightening," so characteristically by means of ornate understatement) is in tone elusively lyrical. Merlin and Vivien move before us exquisitely known and seen, as none of the people whom Tennyson took from Malory ever did. It is one of the finest love stories in English verse.

It is not easy to explain why Mr. Robinson should thus so superlatively succeed once, and not again. Shall we say that, if intellectually and ironically acute, he nevertheless lacks "energy"? There is no Chaucerian or Shakespearean breadth here; it is the closer and narrower view in which Mr. Robinson excels, and it may well be this, and the lack of energy (aspects of one thing?) which have in the main led him to a modern modification of the ballad form, in which simplification and the "hint and gleam" may take the place of the richly extensive. These are not the virtues on which to build in long form: they are stumbling-blocks in a long narrative poem, since if they are allowed free rein they must render it fragmentary and episodic. These stumbling-blocks Mr. Robinson amazingly surmounted in *Merlin*, thanks largely, as we have said, to the fact that here at last a long-suppressed lyric romanticist found his opportunity for unintermittent beauty. But in *Lancelot*, fine as much of it is, failure may be noted almost exactly in proportion as Mr. Robinson's theme has compelled him to "broaden" his narrative stream. Of the soliloquy he can be a master, and even, as in *Merlin*, of the duet; but when the stage fills and the necessity is for a franker, larger, more robustious and changeable complex of action, as in *Lancelot*, poetic energy fails him, he resorts to the factitious, and is often merely melodramatic or strained. We grant the nobility of theme, the austerity of treatment, and, of the latter half especially, the beauty. But the poem as a unit is not a success.

When we have considered *Merlin* and *The Man against the Sky*, it becomes unjust to consider again *The Three Taverns* or *Avon's Harvest*. We feel a technical and temperamental slackening in these, a cyclic return to the comparatively illusory "depth" of the earlier work. They are parerga which we must hope do not indicate an end.

Paul Laurence Dunbar and Dialect Poetry

Myron Simon

Reading Dunbar, one is forcibly reminded that black poetry in America has issued from two quite different sources. One stream, beginning with Phillis Wheatley and Jupiter Hammon, and continuing with George Moses Horton, Frances Watkins Harper, James Whitfield, Albery Whitman, and Joseph Seaman Cotter, carefully observed the margins of the Anglo-American literary tradition and accordingly committed itself to formal modes of expression entirely remote from the vernacular of the black community, which was still chiefly Southern and rural during Dunbar's lifetime. The other stream, beginning with the anonymous authors of spirituals, blues, protest and work songs, was compelled by the residual experience of the black community and faithful to its vernacular until, in the last decades of the nineteenth century, transcription of the black oral tradition was initiated by white Southern writers like Irwin Russell, Joel Chandler Harris, and Thomas Nelson Page and by black writers like Daniel Davis, James Campbell, James Corrothers, and Dunbar. These writers were interested in Southern rural black speech largely as a vehicle for amiable humor and pathos, and thus employed the vernacular selectively for literary effect. Although Harper, Whitman, and Cotter occasionally wrote in the vernacular, up to the time of Dunbar the two streams had remained quite pure. Indeed, Dunbar kept them so perfectly separate in his work that he became the prototype of the black poet with two different voices: the one cultivated and non-racial or only faintly racial; the other solecistic and black.

Dunbar manifestly preferred his literary to his vernacular voice, but his mastery of both was widely praised. And he was, consequently, the first black poet to become celebrated—albeit sometimes by different audi-

From *A Singer in the Dawn: Reinterpretations of Paul Laurence Dunbar*, edited by Jay Martin. © 1975 by Jay Martin. Dodd, Mead, 1975.

ences—for his work in both standard literary English and in the "plantation" dialect. Dunbar explicitly separated the two modes only in *Majors and
Minors* and *Lyrics of the Hearthside*, the second of his four "Lyrics" volumes,
where "The Paradox" and "Sympathy" stand apart from "Little Brown
Baby" which appears in a concluding section called "Humor and Dialect."
In the other volumes, the two modes sit familiarly together on the same
or facing pages, "An Ante-Bellum Sermon" close against the "Ode to Ethio-
pia." Thus, one of the reasons for Dunbar's great importance in the history
of black poetry is that in his books the two channels through which black
poetry emerged in America—the literary and the oral traditions—begin to
come together: they inhabit the same mind, are bound between the same
covers.

As Dunbar knew, there was abundant precedent in Anglo-American
literary tradition for the introduction of the vernacular into poetic composition. In terms of theory, the classical doctrine of decorum had long
sanctioned the use of ordinary or rough expression when the character
represented was understood to be humble or rude or comic. In terms of
practice, Dunbar could draw reassurance from the work of "standard" poets
like Burns or Lowell, whose use of the Scots or New England vernaculars
had been acclaimed. Burns had artfully combined the literary and vernacular styles in poems like "The Cotter's Saturday Night"; and Lowell's use
of rural New England speech in *The Biglow Papers* had only enhanced his
reputation as the author of "The Vision of Sir Launfal." Evidently committed to this tradition, Dunbar wrote alternately in the literary and vernacular modes from the outset of his poetic career to its very end. Two-
thirds of Dunbar's poetry is in standard literary English, and the literary
mode is more dominant in *Lyrics of Lowly Life* than in any of the succeeding
volumes. But, overall, the balance between the two modes is rather evenly
maintained throughout the four volumes which comprise the *Complete
Poems*. Too much has perhaps been made of Dunbar's uneasiness over the
popularity of his vernacular—i.e., dialect—poems. There is no reason to
believe that, given the achievements in the vernacular by major poets of
the previous century in England and America, he thought his dialect poems
greatly inferior to his more dignified and elegant performances. It is more
likely that he was progressively disheartened by the capacity of the poems
he had written in dialect to obscure the larger part of his poetry. What he
seems to have wished was a celebrity for his genteel verses equal to that
which the public had bestowed upon the dialect poems.

However, what worked for Lowell did not work as well for Dunbar,
since the circumstances of the two poets could scarcely have been more
different. Lowell, deeply rooted in his region and the issue of its highest
culture, moved easily between Harvard rationalism and Yankee village
shrewdness. The "reality" underlying Hosea Biglow's dialect speech is not
disjunct from the values and the sense of life which inform the self-assured
wit of "A Fable for Critics." Because Hosea Biglow is as much a part of

New England culture as the Brahmin editor of the *Atlantic Monthly*, there is no impediment to Lowell's employment of two quite different poetic voices. That is, Lowell occupied his region, his country, and his role as a poet unselfconsciously, without any sense that in writing "The Vision of Sir Launfal" he was shirking obligations to his contemporaries; and he could write his *Biglow Papers* playfully, without feeling that he was demeaning his literary gifts.

But Dunbar—born in a region different from the one in which his parents had been reared, the son of self-taught former slaves and largely self-taught himself—was unselfconsciously at home neither in the South nor the Midwest, neither in standard literary English nor the rural black vernacular. As [Benjamin] Brawley tells us, Dunbar was early drawn to Shelley, Keats, Tennyson, Poe, and Longfellow; and he gave most of his poetic career to writing their kinds of poetry. In consequence of his unwavering loyalty to traditional diction and prosody, most of Dunbar's genteel poems have the slightly labored, uneasy look of set pieces and imitations. Pastoral lyrics like "Retort" and "Farewell to Arcady," Longfellowesque fables like "The Seedling," a classical romance like "Ione," and dutiful exercises like "Columbian Ode," "Dirge," and "Madrigal" in their uniform facility suggest only how often Dunbar's study lamp burned late. As for the dialect poems, he wrote them—he told James Weldon Johnson self-reproachfully—to "gain a hearing," i.e., to capitalize upon his facility in a form of writing which had become enormously popular during the preceding generation. Dunbar's assessment of personal motive may have been too harsh: dialect poems like "When Malindy Sings" and "The Party" almost certainly were written out of more than ambition and self-interest. His best dialect poems work not through disingenuous manipulation of the reader's emotions, but by generating their own emotion out of Dunbar's unmistakable empathy for a rural black world that seemed stable and out of his nostalgia for its close, well-defined human relationships. But, in any event, the operative conventions of "local color" writing had been effectively codified by the time Dunbar made his earliest attempts at it. The formulas by which the post–Civil War reading public was to secure more realistic representations of the full variety of American life found their principal apologist in William Dean Howells and their chief Southern practitioners in J. A. Macon, Irwin Russell, Joel Chandler Harris, and Thomas Nelson Page. Their sense of the content of plantation culture was undoubtedly assimilated by Dunbar. And both from them and James Whitcomb Riley he derived much of his sense of how rural life and speech were to be imitated in literature. Thus equipped, Dunbar found it difficult to get beyond the deceptive surface of black rural life to those ineluctable qualities for which no black poet had yet found an adequate language.

As the example of Lowell indicates, a poet may employ two widely discrepant voices concurrently without loss if, in the profoundest manner of possession, both speech styles are his own. Or, as in the case of Burns, a poet may employ two voices when one is clearly a more "natural" and powerfully wielded instrument than the other. But Dunbar's two voices, whatever their immediate popularity, evidently left him feeling dissatisfied and unfulfilled. Neither language was finally his own; neither was adequate to the task of apprehending and articulating the very reality that his black sensibility was distinctly fitted to engage. In his conversations with Johnson in 1901, Dunbar not only spoke self-reproachfully of his commitment to dialect poetry but implied that the poems he wished to write would not be in literary English. Johnson "surmised" that it was Dunbar's ambition to write poems in "straight English that would relate to the Negro." However, at the end—five years later—he could only report disconsolately to Johnson, "I've kept on doing the same things, and doing them no better. I have never gotten to the things I really wanted to do."

Little more than a decade after Dunbar's death, the emergence of the New Negro movement—with its assertions of racial pride—provoked a sharp reaction against the Plantation Tradition in black writing. Johnson led the attack on precisely those forms and attitudes in dialect poetry of which Dunbar was the acknowledged master. If the direct influence of Dunbar persisted, it was through his verses in literary English—especially the high Romantic strain, which Countee Cullen admired and successfully emulated. But less obviously and more importantly, Dunbar's central dilemma survived in a line of black poets who oscillated—early in their careers—between the two voices that he had never managed either to make his own or to reject. Although Johnson's reservations about the validity of poetry in the plantation or minstrel dialect date from the turn of the century, his first book of poems, *Fifty Years and Other Poems* (1917), is clearly in the line of Dunbar. It has a section of dialect poems that are directly indebted to Dunbar, the most famous of them being "Sence You Went Away"; the poems in the other section, like "O Black and Unknown Bards" and "Fifty Years," are conspicuously accomplished, fastidious performances in literary English. In Langston Hughes's first book, *The Weary Blues* (1926), the same bivocalism is evident. Although the literary voice, under Imagist influence, has been purged of the late Romantic mannerisms so pronounced in Dunbar (see, for example, the sections "Water-Front Streets" and "Shadows in the Sun"), it is yet plainly disjunct from Hughes's vernacular voice, his slightly unsure first attempts to characterize the speech of the urban working-class black in such poems as "Blues Fantasy" and "Mother to Son." By the same token, Sterling Brown's *Southern Road* (1932) is about evenly divided between literary and dialect expression. Such carefully measured statements of near despair—in the style of Housman—as "Salutamus," "Challenge," "Rain," and "Nous n'irons plus au bois . . ." contrast oddly with Brown's dialect presentation of similar Housmanian ironies in poems like "Old Man Buzzard" and "Mister Samuel and Sam." Moreover, this radical division in the languages of black poetry was carried forward into at least the 1940s, as may be seen in Gwendolyn Brooks's *A Street in Bronzeville* (1945) and

Owen Dodson's *Powerful Long Ladder* (1946). Although most of the poems in both volumes are in literary English and the occasional uses of dialect continue the endeavor of Hughes and Brown to abandon phonetic caricature for a more subtle or muted representation of black speech, there is still the effect of speech styles colliding incongruously in Brooks's "The Date" ("If she don't hurry up and let me out of here") and "Firstly Inclined to Take What It Is Told" ("Thee sacrosanct, Thee sweet, Thee crystalline, / With the full jewel wile of mighty light") and in Dodson's "Poem for Pearl's Dancers" ("My lips taste blood, / And in they souls they's blood. / My tongue can't joy no future in this blood") and "Pearl Primus" ("Is it Cassandra as she saw the dark wolf / And caught him fast and dug her prophetic fingernails / To below the hair into the flesh / Feeling a dark blood world of hate?"). In the tension between these styles, bespeaking ultimately an alienation from both, one may perceive the crux in respect to which these very different poets are all close to Dunbar.

Although we may dissent from his reasons, Howells was surely right in pronouncing Dunbar's dialect poems more valuable than his poems in literary English. He judged some of the latter to be "very good, and even more than very good, but not distinctively his contribution to the body of American poetry":

> What I mean is that several people might have written them; but I do not know any one else at present who could quite have written the dialect pieces. These are divinations and reports of what passes in the hearts and minds of a lowly people whose poetry had hitherto been inarticulately expressed in music, but now finds, for the first time in our tongue, literary interpretation of a very artistic completeness.

If we turn it around, Howells's argument suggests why Dunbar's critics, during the Harlem Renaissance and after, have usually felt more dissatisfied with his dialect poems than with those in literary English. The black experience surrounded him, still virtually untouched, awaiting "literary interpretation of a very artistic completeness"; and Dunbar's best chance to engage it lay—as Howells perceived—in the black vernacular, the "tongue" he was better fitted than any white writer to make into the authentic voice of that experience. However, Howells credited him with having achieved precisely what he failed to provide: a true and complete account of what was most distinctive in that part of the American or human experience which he really knew at first hand. Dunbar's failures in literary English, as Sterling Brown has observed, were no worse than those of "the school of American Tennysonians to which he belonged." But his failures in dialect were not so easily extenuated, even by a sympathetic critic; for he omitted much and idealized what he did not omit. Whatever the reason, "the fact of omission remains." Since Dunbar's dialect poems have now come through more than a half-century of growing indifference and censure, it may be useful to examine some of the assumptions underlying those responses.

The reasons for this disaffection from poems once so popular are not always persuasive. Some of the reasons have little direct bearing upon the specific qualities of Dunbar's dialect poems. To begin with, dialect writing as a genre was falling into disrepute by the time of Dunbar's death. It had been so heavily associated with rural America, with all that had begun to seem most ephemeral in American life and literature, that the new artistic predilections for urban and industrial life appeared to render it obsolete. Accordingly, when Langston Hughes commenced his experiments with the language of uneducated working-class blacks who lived not in Kentucky but in Washington, Chicago, and New York, few perceived that he had selected the *dialect* of the newly emergent black urban proletariat as his model; such unprecedented literary speech sounded too natural to be termed "dialect." Rather, it was generally understood that Hughes had abandoned dialect, with its sterotypical portrayal of the Negro. Thus, Dunbar's dialect poetry shared in the general devaluation of local color writing that accompanied the introduction of subtler and tougher minded modes of realistic writing at the beginning of the new century. Moreover, the New Negro movement—with its revisionist stress upon authentic knowledge of the black community—broadened doubts about the adequacy of Dunbar's understanding of rural black life in Kentucky that had been suggested a generation earlier in Joseph Seaman Cotter's ironic "Answer to Dunbar's 'After a Visit.'" Brawley is quick to point out that "Born in Dayton, in the Middle West," Dunbar "had only limited opportunity to study the Negro." Brawley's concession that Dunbar nevertheless "gave a better interpretation than any writer who had preceded him" is nicely ambiguous praise; for, despite the fact that Brawley was speaking thirty years after Dunbar's death, he restricts Dunbar's superiority to the writers who preceded him. There is, of course, a basis in common sense for such doubts; but, clearly, a poet's firsthand knowledge of his subject must be taken as a sufficient and not as a necessary condition of his art. Finally, many criticisms of the dialect poems have questioned the accuracy of Dunbar's representations of black speech in Kentucky or elsewhere in the Southern Midlands. And this has seemed a serious charge because it is generally, if erroneously, believed that the merit of a literary dialect depends upon its correspondence with actual speech. Brawley, eager to defend Dunbar's skill in the employment of dialect, if not his understanding of black life, claims that when—during his boyhood—Dunbar listened to his mother's stories of old Kentucky he was "unconsciously impressed by his mother's inimitable phrasing." "And where," he asks in reference to the artistic progress evident in *Majors and Minors*, "did the young man who had never been South gets this exquisite finish for his Negro dialect? Where but in the stories heard at his mother's knee even from his earliest years?" But critics before and after Brawley have more typically found Dunbar's dialect too remote from the actual speech he sought to represent, too literary in the fashion of Russell and Riley.

Dunbar's most penetrating comment on the use of dialect in literature appears in a letter to Helen Douglass:

> As to your remarks about my dialect, I have nothing to say save that I am sorry to find among intelligent people those who are unable to differentiate dialect as a philological branch from Negro minstrelsy.

That is, linguistics and "minstrelsy" (here meaning poetry, not blackface comedy) provide functionally distinct reports of a dialect because, as George Philip Krapp has observed, they engage actual speech differently:

> The relations of literary dialects to "real" dialects are not easily explicable, mainly because "real" dialects themselves are elusive and hard to define. Literary dialects, on the other hand, depend for their success upon being positive and readily recognizable.

Although the linguist undertakes to provide a full report of his elusive quarry, Krapp denies that the writer of dialect is under any obligation to conform to what the linguist takes the reality of a given variety of English to be. The linguist "at least attempts to exhaust all the details of dialect speech which can come under his observation, thus arriving at a finality of some kind"; the writer, on the other hand, "utilizes only as much of his material as he thinks he needs for his special literary purposes":

> The literary artist attempts by occasional suggestion to produce the illusion of a distinct and "real" dialect speech, but the scientist endeavors to attain a different conception of reality with an analytic method and an exhaustive examination of the material open to him for observation.

Thus, in the case of Dunbar or any other dialect writer, whether literary dialect has been managed well or ill depends not upon its literal accuracy, its closeness to the actual speech which it has selectively approximated, but rather upon how well it works as a creative means of constituting the writer's experience.

Sumner Ives has noted that, despite the popularity of dialect in American literature, there has been very little investigation of the ways in which authors have represented dialects that goes beyond the pioneer chapter on "Literary Dialects" in Krapp's *The English Language in America*. Ives himself advanced the study of literary dialects by the intelligence with which he promptly applied the new evidence and insights of the *Linguistic Atlas of the United States* to the task of illuminating the subtle relationships between actual dialects and their literary representations in the work of such writers as Lowell, Twain, and Joel Chandler Harris. But there has been no comparable study of black dialect writing, so that critics who have commented either affirmatively or negatively on Dunbar's use of dialect appear similarly unaware of the distinctions between Southern plantation speech and Southern mountain speech, on the one hand, and—yet more basically—between

Southern speech and Southern Midland speech, on the other. Since these dialects are not easily differentiated and since, in any event, we have no reliable records of the black speech in these dialect areas during Dunbar's lifetime, it is impossible to say with certainty which dialect he was imitating. We know only that he derived from his mother some indication of black speech in Kentucky; that he had direct knowledge of the speech of black communities in Ohio, Kentucky, Maryland, and the District of Columbia; that he was well acquainted with the conventions in dialect writing practiced by his contemporaries; and that he distinguished the poet's description of a dialect from the linguist's.

There is a sense in which Brawley could rightly imply that by the time of the publication of *Majors and Minors* early in 1896 Dunbar had nearly outgrown the influence of white dialect poets like Russell, Riley, and Will Carleton. That is, he was by then no longer content to imitate them. But one must not too hastily conclude from this judgment that, as Dunbar matured, he abandoned their fundamental assumptions about how dialect was to be rendered. Krapp's principal conclusion about American dialect writers in the nineteenth century is that they were far more attentive to those characteristics of speech that were social—and, hence, cut across geographical lines—than they were to those characteristics that were purely regional. He amasses substantial evidence to show that American dialect writers conceived vernacular speech in terms of class rather than place, and notes the rudimentary ways in which a class dialect "distinguishes between popular and cultivated or standard speech":

> The impression of popular speech is easily produced by a sprinkling of such forms as *aint* for *isn't*, *done* for *did*, *them* for *those*, and similar grammatical improprieties. This impression is often assisted by what may be termed "eye dialect," in which the convention violated is one of the eye, not of the ear. Thus a dialect writer often spells a word like *front* as *frunt*, or *face* as *fase*, or *picture* as *pictsher*, not because he intends to indicate here a genuine difference of pronunciation, but the spelling is merely a friendly nudge to the reader, a knowing look which establishes a sympathetic sense of superiority between the author and reader as contrasted with the humble speaker of dialect.

The first principle that guided the selections of dialect writers from actual speech was their desire to create the impression of uneducated speakers. It was largely in other ways that they sought to register regional and racial differences. Whatever the presumed locale of the speaker, his rusticity or lower-class status was made dominant by the reiteration of nonstandard forms that characterized uncultivated speech throughout the nation. And, as Sumner Ives puts is, the greater the density of nonstandard forms, "the greater the rusticity or the lower the class." Whether purporting to represent the speech of New England, the Southwest, the South, the Midlands or the Negro, most dialect writing was based upon uneducated lower-class usage with a highly selective admixture of local dialect words. Consequently, the special qualities of local color in dialect literature derived far less from the language than from the subject matter itself, i.e., from setting, characterization, and incident.

Krapp remarks of the transcription of black dialect provided by Joel Chandler Harris that, "If there is such a thing as classic Negro literary dialect, it is to be found in the speech of Uncle Remus," However, after careful linguistic examination of a typical passage, he concludes that the "general effect produced by the Uncle Remus stories is strongly dialectal" but that "relatively little in them is found to be dialectally peculiar":

> That the speech of Uncle Remus as Joel Chandler Harris heard it differed markedly even from Southern low colloquial is possible, but if so, his literary transcription of the dialect of Uncle Remus gives remarkably few clues which will enable one to realize this difference. The speech of Uncle Remus and the speech of rustic whites as Harris records it are so much alike that if one did not know which character was speaking, one might often be unable to tell whether the words were those of a white man or of a Negro.

He maintains, "Whether these literary transcriptions are true to the 'real' Negro dialect is one of those questions impossible to answer in the lack of any accepted definition of the essential elements of Negro English." But what seems to him more worthy of note—as a correction of received opinion—is that between the *literary* transcriptions of Negro and white rural speech there was little material difference in the writings of Harris and his contemporaries. In his later study of Harris, Sumner Ives was able to refine Krapp's conclusions with respect both to the relation of literary to actual dialect and the relation of the Negro literary dialect to the white:

> Actually the field records of the Linguistic Atlas, aside from a very few Gullah records, show hardly any usages in Negro speech which cannot also be found in rustic white speech. And there are many similarities in usage as Harris wrote the dialects. However, the peculiarity of his Negro speech, in addition to the features already listed, consists in the greater density of nonstandard forms, and in the fact that the nonstandard items include, in greater number, features which are associated with Southern plantation speech rather than with Southern mountain speech. Since the same features can actually be found in the speech of both Negro and rustic white, Harris could more justly be accused of exaggerating the actual difference than of failing to indicate it.

The last point is an especially telling one, for it is precisely in this regard that we can see how closely Dunbar's dialect conformed to the conventions of literary dialect which Krapp and Ives have been the first to explicate.

Like Harris, Dunbar employed both Negro and white dialect. Indeed, no less than a fifth of the dialect poems in the *Complete Poems* are in white dialect, i.e., in a dialect that Dunbar plainly distinguished from the poems in Negro dialect. Two of them, "Appreciation" and "Circumstances Alter Cases," are attempts to represent ethnic dialects, German and Irish respectively, although the former is not made entirely clear. The other white dialect poems are "The Old Apple-Tree," "The Lawyers' Ways," "The Rivals," "Deacon Jones' Grievance," "After a Visit," "The Spellin'-Bee," "Keep A'Pluggin' Away," "An Easy-Goin' Feller," "The Ol' Tunes," "A Confidence," "Speakin' o' Christmas," "Lonesome," "Growin' Gray," "My Sort o' Man," "Possum Trot," "Breaking the Charm," "What's the Use," "Bein' Back Home," "Till the Wind Gets Right," "When a Feller's Itchin' to Be Spanked," "A Summer Pastoral," and "James Whitcomb Riley." These are the poems that have invited comparison with the work of Riley, and properly so; for they are unmistakably intended as representations of white rural speech. Unfortunately and unfairly, Dunbar's critics have sometimes assumed that all the poems in dialect were intended to represent Negro speech; and the poems listed above have, accordingly, seemed glaring examples of Dunbar's ignorance of or indifference to authentic black speech. But in his portrayal of rural dialect Dunbar consistently differentiated black speech from white. And he did so through reliance upon conventions that had been standardized by Harris and other white dialect writers of the period.

The most obvious of Dunbar's dialect practices is his introduction of many more solecisms into Negro speech than are present in his representation of white speech. Lapses of agreement like "him dat," "we is," "we chooses," and "you does" simply do not appear in his white dialect poems. Nor do such nonstandard usages as "ax" for "ask" or "gin" for "give." And the effect of illiterate usage is greatly magnified by Dunbar's heavier reliance upon "eye dialect" in his Negro dialect poems, where "as" becomes "ez," "says" becomes "sez," "if" becomes "ef," "or" becomes "er," "take" and "make" become "tek" and "mek," "like" becomes "lak," and "sort" becomes "sawt." Some of these specimens of "eye dialect"—e.g., "tek" and "lak"—appear only in his Negro dialect. Another principle of Dunbar's Negro dialect that sets it apart from his white dialect is the replacement of medial "r" with an apostrophe, as in "ca'iage" for "carriage," "diff'ent" for "different," "f'om" for "from," "ha'd" for "hard," "hea't" for "heart," and "co'se" for "course." Moreover, the white dialectal representation of "for" as "fur" becomes "fu" in Negro dialect. Similarly, terminal "r" or "er" or "ure" is consistently represented as "ah," as when "our" becomes "ouah," "where" becomes "whah," "master" becomes "mastah," and "censure" becomes "censuah." Following both rules, Dunbar represents "mourner" as "mou'nah." The use of "d" for voiced "th" is another clear indication that Dunbar wishes to be understood as rendering Negro rather than white rural speech. Accordingly, he represents "though" as "dough," "they" as "dey," "than" as "dan," "then" as "den," "the" as "de," "that" as "dat," "this" as "dis," "there" as "dere" or "dah," "them" as "dem," and "without" as " 'dout." His use of final "f" for voiceless "th" is a similar convention, as in "souf" for "south," "mouf" for "mouth," "wif" for "with," and "bofe" for "both." The substitution of "b" for medial and final "v" is also distinctive in Dunbar's portrayal of Negro dialect, as in "heaben" for "heaven," "ebenin' " for "evening," "nebbah" for "never," and "dribe" for "drive." "Just," commonly represented as "jest" in white dialect, becomes "jes' " or "des" in Dunbar's Negro dialect poems; similarly, white "when" becomes Negro "w'en." Finally, there is more loss of initial unstressed syllables—e.g., " 'case" for "because"—in the Negro dialect. Through such well-established conventions of dialect writing, Dunbar sought to impart the flavor of both Negro and white rural life in the Southern Midlands during the heyday of the "local color" movement.

But Dunbar's relation to the local color writers extends beyond the conception of literary dialect which he derived from them. He acquiesced as well in their nationalism, on the one hand, and their pastoralism, on the other. Claude Simpson finds a major stimulus to local color writing in the conciliatory spirit that emerged after the Civil War:

> The concept of the Union had been established . . . But the difference between legal unity and cultural diversity was as great as ever, and many persons seem to have felt a pressing need for a depth of understanding that slogans and propaganda had made impossible during the era of conflict.

That is, local color writers were, of course, the interpreters of regional and ethnic constituencies: interpreters, however, of one constituency to the others and, collectively, interpreters of all to the nation at large. Even while amiably asserting special modes of thought and behavior, they stressed sympathies and concerns uncontained by regional or national boundaries. Thus, Mrs. Stowe avowed that her object was "to interpret to the world the New England life and character." Significantly, she was drawn not to the contemporary circumstances of her region but to "that particular time of its history which may be called the seminal period." For in the aftermath of the Civil War, the great transformation from agrarian and mercantile capitalism to industrial capitalism had radically altered the American scene and engendered a vast nostalgia for antebellum, i.e., preindustrial, times. This nostalgia for a vanishing pastoral world provided the other major stimulus to local color writing. Leo Marx has delineated the versions of pastoral to which this sense of loss gave rise, and his distinction between sentimental and complex pastoralism may be usefully applied to the local colorists. Unlike such complex pastoralists as Emerson, Hawthorne, and Twain who struggled to comprehend the garden in relation to the machine, the local color writers sentimentally withdrew from history into an idealized rural past.

According to Brawley, "Dunbar's conception of his art was based on his theory of life. He felt that he was first of all a man, then an American, and incidentally a Negro." There is no reason to doubt Brawley's judgment; his biography appeared so many years after Dunbar's death that any merely pious effort to brighten Dunbar's reputation might more reasonably have produced a different emphasis. Brawley's point helps us to understand the convictions that disposed Dunbar to render black vernacular as he did. I take Brawley's statement to mean that Dunbar understood poetry, in the context of Romantic expressive theory, to arise from the thought and feelings of the poet as a kind of representative man; that is, he understood poetry to be the product of impulses both deeper and more universal than questions of nationality and race. Thus, as an urban intellectual nostalgic for a lost world of innocence and peace, his impulse to pastoral expression was the controlling principle of his dialect poems. It has often been too easily concluded that Dunbar really knew very little about rural Negro speech or that he was insufficiently committed to the black community. But there is no reason to believe that Dunbar was less familiar with authentic Negro speech or less loyal to his cultural origins than James Weldon Johnson, who succeeded in revolutionizing poetic use of the rural black vernacular. It is, rather, a case of his having been committed to a theory of lyric expression which predisposed him to minimize the differences between Negro and white swains. Dunbar undoubtedly wished to interpret the Negro to the nation; but, given his conception of the poet, he placed the burden of that interpretation upon the Negro's essential humanity and not upon his blackness. If the Negro who delivers "An Ante-Bellum Sermon" is only superficially distinguished from the white populist who speaks in "My Sort o' Man," that was precisely Dunbar's vision of their identity; for they share a common humanity and the same democratic faith. As practiced by Dunbar and the other local colorists, dialect writing typically revealed many more common than individuating features. To give Dunbar his due as a dialect poet, it is necessary to view his work not normatively but within a particular historical moment and literary tradition. So positioned, Dunbar will surely survive in our literature as a major local color poet and, even more certainly, as the best of the black local color poets.

It was Dunbar's fate to achieve recognition as a dialect writer at the very time when a revolutionary change in the character of poetic language was occurring which would obliterate the distinction between the two voices he had cultivated and make his conception of dialect speech obsolete. For almost a century before Dunbar, American writers had experimented with the literary possibilities of dialect speech. And by the 1880s Twain had demonstrated that the vernacular could be fashioned into a richly expressive literary language. But the efforts of poets to achieve the sound of a resonantly human voice, what Robert Frost called the "sound of sense," through a comparable use of vernacular diction and rhythms lagged behind accomplishments in the short story and the novel or were not so readily accepted. Whitman was virtually ignored by his countrymen in the 1890s, and the subtle employments of the vernacular by Robinson and Frost were not favorably acknowledged until the second decade of the new century. So it is hardly surprising that Dunbar failed to comprehend that a new, more dramatic mode of poetic speech was already supplanting both literary dialect, on the one hand, and elegant literary English, on the other.

It fell to James Weldon Johnson to come upon Whitman in 1900, and he was "engulfed and submerged" by *Leaves of Grass*. At a time when most of the poems he was writing were in dialect "after the style of Dunbar," he was "set floundering again" by his discovery of Whitman and "got a sudden realization of the artificiality of conventionalized Negro dialect poetry . . . of its limitation as an instrument of expression." He made some tentative experiments with Whitman's free verse forms, and early in 1901 confided his reservations about dialect poetry to Dunbar:

> I could not tell him what the things were that I wanted to do, because I myself didn't know. The thing that I was sure of and kept repeating to him was that he had carried traditional dialect poetry as far as and as high as it could go; that he had brought it to the fullest measure of charm, tenderness, and beauty it could hold.

When he showed Dunbar his new work in the style of Whitman, Dunbar expressed both dislike and puzzlement; and his response to Johnson's readings from *Leaves of Grass* was the same. In order to respond differently, Dunbar would have had to reconceive his sense of the nature and function of poetry. For not content with the restriction of poetry to those experiences and ideas most amenable to direct expression in the traditional forms of narration, description, and analysis, Whitman meant to penetrate the inner reality of things and reveal their actual character without falling into the abstractness of direct expression. In his effort to suggest inner states and relationships remote from conventional literature and ordinary experience, he abandoned direct presentation and invented a persona capable of articulating the full range and complexity of human experience. Desirous of writing a poem that engaged experience in a way that was both inclusive and democratic, Whitman abandoned meter and rhyme in favor of more fluid and capacious kinds of parallelism; and he abandoned the distinction between vernacular and cultivated speech styles in favor of a new, programmatically indiscriminate language of his own which blended such vernacular expressions as "so long" (i.e., "good-bye") with literary words like "circumambient," together with assorted foreign words. It was some years later before Johnson was able to provide a clear statement of his reasons for repudiating Dunbar's dialect practice and a program outlining a new conception of the use of vernacular in black poetry. But his reading of

Whitman seems to have confirmed him in his belief that the "minstrel" dialect employed by local colorists like Dunbar had touched only the clichéd surface of black experience and that a new language was essential to the task of exploring its full range and complexity.

The key to Johnson's reform of the language of black poetry—which had shifted so uneasily and inadequately between literary English and literary dialect—was apparently found in his subsequent reading of John Millington Synge's folk dramas. Or, at least, Synge's example offered a closer parallel than Whitman's to the situation of the black writer. In the first place, Synge moved between two cultures: between a sophisticated Anglo-European culture and Irish folk culture. And after committing himself heavily to the former, he turned away from it to the Irish folk culture and found there in abundance the materials for his great literary achievements. Johnson, like Synge, made a belated discovery of the richness of his folk culture and recognized an experiential range and complexity in its oral narratives, spirituals, and blues that belied the restriction of black experience to humor and pathos in the work of the plantation dialect writers. In the second, like the black writer, the Irishman had originally possessed two languages; but with the emergence of the Anglo-Irish vernacular early in the nineteenth century, the languages coalesced, Irish vocabulary, syntax, and speech rhythms blending into a rather old-fashioned standard English. By the end of the century Lady Gregory and Synge had begun to demonstrate the extraordinary literary uses to which this vernacular lent itself:

> in countries where the imagination of the people, and the language they use, is rich and living, it is possible for a writer to be rich and copious in his words, and at the same time to give the reality, which is the root of all poetry, in a comprehensive and natural form.

Given a rich and living popular culture of his own, the poet requires a language adequate to it and to the fictive uses he means to make of it, which he draws from the folk culture itself but imaginatively fuses with standard literary English in order to produce an expressive instrument of maximal subtlety and force. Synge based his dramatic speech upon the actual vernacular of the Irish folk; he did not, however, make a point-by-point transcription of it. Rather, he combined it with the conventions of literary English to produce a new literary language with a capacity for expressiveness that neither cultivated nor folk speech possessed when taken singly. He did not attempt to reproduce the Anglo-Irish vernacular phonetically—in the manner of Finley Peter Dunne's "Mr. Dooley" sketches—by substituting apostrophes for terminal "g" and "d" or by employing such nonstandard spellings as "dacent" for "decent" and "niver" for "never." Instead, he accurately reflected its idiom (i.e., its vocabulary) and its syntax (i.e., its word order, phrasal structure, and intonation patterns).

By 1922 Johnson had publicly rejected traditional dialect poetry because its popularity was based upon an absurdly limited conception of Negro life. He called for an expanded portrayal of that life, and named Synge as the model whom black poets should emulate. But in doing so he was careful to point out that he was not repudiating dialect itself, only its conventional use. Because Johnson was not always entirely clear in his pronouncements on this subject, some critics have described Johnson as an opponent of dialect and have said that his later work—like *God's Trombones*—was written in "straight English" or "non-dialect English." Synge's use of the Anglo-Irish vernacular suggested to him a way of liberating rural black vernacular from certain restrictive literary mannerisms and making it into a far more natural voice for black poets. Thus, Johnson was calling not for an end to the use of dialect but a profound alteration in the nature of its composition and the manner of its use. As an alternative to Dunbar's dialect voice, he proposed building on the actual voice of the black vernacular, which he likened to a trombone, "the instrument possessing above all others the power to express the wide and varied range of emotions encompassed by the human voice—and with greater amplitude." Johnson contemplated the emergence of new black folk poets whose use of black speech was, first, valid for themselves and for their "own group" and, only second, for the larger reading public. In such poets as Don L. Lee, Nikki Giovanni, and the later Gwendolyn Brooks, his expectations appear to have been fulfilled. As for Dunbar, Johnson wrote with characteristic generosity, "I have frequently speculated upon what Dunbar might have done with Negro dialect if it had come to him fresh and plastic."

Robert Frost: Choices

Richard Poirier

Frost could never blame the "age" for anything, or even blame what he did himself at a certain age for what might have happened to him subsequently. This was the virtue of his pride. Moral and literary accomplishment are of a piece in his poetry because of his near-mystical acceptance of responsibility for himself and for whatever happened to him. His biographer [Lawrance Thompson] misses this entirely. In his harsh, distorted, and personally resentful view of Frost's manipulative, calculating use of other people, Thompson sees only the determinations of a man who wanted fully to control his career and his public image. Unquestionably, that was one of the things he was doing. He was also revealing something wonderful about human life, or, if you wish, about his sense of what it was. He was communicating his conviction that, mysteriously, nothing happens to us in life except what we choose to have happen. A conscious "use" of other people, a conscious exploitation of them in order to be lazy, in order to get work done, or to get good reviews—this was at least making yourself, and others, aware of what you were doing. What is conspicuous about Frost's letters when he is asking for a favor is their uncommon forthrightness. There is in them the relish of self-exposure. He tries to make visible the choices he is making for his life, choices which were there anyway, invisibly at work on himself and on others. What he calls "the trial by existence" in the magnificent Dantesque poem of that title in *A Boy's Will* is "the obscuration upon earth" of souls that have chosen to leave heaven and to accept whatever human life might have in store for them. Even after a soul is saved, even after the "bravest that are slain" on earth find themselves in heaven, they discover another opportunity for bravery and choice, an

---

From *Robert Frost: The Work of Knowing*. © 1977 by Oxford University Press.

opportunity all the more daring because the choice will not, once taken, even be remembered:

> 'Tis of the essence of life here,
>   Though we choose greatly, still to lack
> The lasting memory at all clear,
>   That life has for us on the wrack
> Nothing but what we somehow chose;
>   Thus are we wholly stripped of pride
> In the pain that has but one close,
>   Bearing it crushed and mystified.

There are two kinds of choice here. We "greatly choose" some things and we "somehow chose" all the things that happen to us. The pride we may take in conscious choices is stripped away not by any obvious predominance of the unconscious ones but rather by our being ignorant of how much more inclusive they are. That is, the individual is denied the *privilege* of knowing that in fact no one else has made his life as it is. Frost was always seeking for the restitution of that lost and diminished sense of responsibility even while he was at the same time exalted by the mystery of not being able to fully grasp it. This divided consciousness helps explain the perplexing ways in which a poet who attaches so much value to form, with all the choice that involves, attaches equal value to freedom in the movement of the poem toward a form. The perplexity is not lessened by the fact that within the freedom there are the elements which he also "somehow chose." Thus he will write, in "The Figure a Poem Makes" that a poem "has an outcome that though unforseen was predestined from the first image of the original mood—and indeed from the very mood." For him, life and poems work in much the same way. In both, there is a wondrous emergence into consciousness of those selections, impressions— and choices—that were not available to consciousness when first made.

> The impressions most useful to my purpose seem always those I was unaware of and so made no note of at the time when taken, and the conclusion is come to that like giants we are always hurling experience ahead of us to pave the future with against the day when we may want to strike a line of purpose across it for somewhere. The line will have the more charm for not being mechanically straight. We enjoy the straight crookedness of a good walking stick. Modern instruments of precision are being used to make things crooked as if by eye and hand in the old days.
>   ("The Figure a Poem Makes")

It is not stretching the point to say that this intimation of the peculiar and mysterious workings of choice is what made him so resolute and even ruthless when choice became incumbent or conscious. It was as if the free movement in his life demanded of him that he then do what had to be done either with his career, with a poem, or with a book. Despite differences, he is in this more like Lawrence than like any other writer of the century. And yet it seems apparent that form, for Lawrence as much as for Frost, the more formalistic of the two, by being necessarily to some degree conscious was also, to some degree, imposed, and that what Frost says about "modern instruments of precision" might sometimes apply to his own work on a poem. His claims, again in "The Figure a Poem Makes," to the "wildness of logic" are apt to strike some readers as disingenuous. The "logic" of even some of the best poems, as illustrated by "Spring Pools," does not, as the reader experiences it, appear to be "more felt than seen ahead like prophecy." Some of that, yes—but also a good deal of premeditation and preplotting. Frost is best appreciated if we let him *try* to do the best he can within the drama of form and freedom, and it is in that light that we can understand the design he gave to *A Boy's Will* using some of the poems he then had available. It is a matter of his using "experience," in this case poems, that he had paved "the future with against the day when [he would want] to strike a line of purpose across it somewhere."

A *Boy's Will* is an appropriate place for a poem about choices of lives, like "The Trial by Existence." The design of the book—what is put in, what is left out, the groupings of the poems, the headnotes—expresses a "choice" about the portrait of man and poet that Frost wanted to present. Or rather what can be inferred from these "choices" of inclusion and exclusion are three portraits whose details sometimes coincide, sometimes blur, sometimes block one another out. One, the cosiest, most availably public, and closest to the glosses, is of a young man who develops a fulfilling relationship to the world after passing through a period of alienation and trial. Another is of a young man trying to shape the complex tension within himself between sexuality and creative powers, between the calls of love and of poetry. This is a more submerged portrait than the first, and its features will remain both more indelible and more obscure all the way through Frost's work. And then there is a darker version of this second portrait, a kind of *pentimento*, a possible portrait later painted over by an author who "repented" and wanted to block out certain features. He kept this portrait hidden, as it were, by the omission of a poem that could have fitted into this volume (bringing with it a darkening of all that would surround it) with at least as much effectiveness as it did into a later group that includes "Never Again Would Birds' Song Be the Same" and "The Most of It" in *A Witness Tree* of 1942. I am referring to "The Subverted Flower," the first draft of which had been written so early, if we are to believe what Frost himself told Thompson, that it could have been published in *A Boy's Will*.

Taken together these three overlapping portraits, while they do not account for all the poems in the volume—two of the best, "Mowing" and "The Tuft of Flowers," discussed [elsewhere]—do include most of them and the overall "plot" of the book. In discussing the alternate and inter-woven portraits I want above all to insist that none of the features come inadvertently into prominence. Frost knew exactly what he was doing; he was never innocent of what his poems imply. His original omissions and discriminations are the result of his loyalty to the complex and mystifying way in which languages appropriate to sexuality, poetic practice, and nature are, in his consciousness of them, not to be separated one from the other. The elements of intentional disguise in any one of the tracings of the poetic self should not, that is, make anyone think that the other disguises, found beneath the obvious ones, were therefore unconscious. Frost was at once too doggedly responsible for whatever he did about himself and too mis-trustful of himself and of his imagination ever to have said more than he knew.

Thompson's discussions of how the book was put together are at the outset too vague to be useful and too simple to be true. "Alone one night, he sorted through the sheaf of manuscripts he had brought with him and could not resist the impulse to see if he had enough to make up a small volume . . . [which] would represent his achievement up to the age of thirty-eight." "Impulse"? For one thing, he had far more than "enough" to make a book, and a better book than the one he put together. For another, what he did pick out for *A Boy's Will* did not begin to represent the variety, much less the size, of his accomplishment up to the age of thirty-eight. Evidence of this is in Thompson's own research into the dates of compo-sition. No dramatic narratives are included in the book, for example, though at least three that were to appear the next year, 1914, in *North of Boston* had been written as early as 1905 and 1906—"The Death of the Hired Man," "The Black Cottage," and "The Housekeeper." In addition, he had on hand over a dozen poems, all written before 1913, and including some of his best. "Bond and Free" was written in the period 1896–1900, and twelve more were written (or at least begun) in Derry between 1900 and 1911, including "An Old Man's Winter Night," "The Telephone," "Pea Brush," "An Encounter," "Range-Finding," "Loneliness," "The Line Gang," "The Flower Boat," and "The Subverted Flower." In addition, some of the great sonnets were written during 1906–7: "The Oven Bird," "Putting in the Seed," and the fifteen-line sonnet variant "Hyla Brook." All these were held until the third book, *Mountain Interval*, in 1916.

Of course Frost may not have "brought with him" (the precise mean-ing, if any, of Thompson's phrase is never made clear) some of the poems destined for later printing. In that unlikely case, there would be a still stronger indication of some prior decision not to put into his first book works that would presumably fit better into some design of a poetic prog-ress which was to be revealed in subsequent volumes. But there is no evidence that he did not have all of his manuscript poetry with him. Ob-viously he had to have the poems destined for *North of Boston* since this was printed before he left England. In fact, as soon as *A Boy's Will* was out, he began to play tricks with the whole revered critical notion of chronology and "development," using one of the poems he had had around since 1905–6. His specifically intended victim was also his most renowned admirer, Ezra Pound. Knowing that, when the facts became public, Pound, and the usual cant about newness, would be made to look silly, he gave him "The Death of the Hired Man" as a "new poem." After publication in *Poetry* of his review of *A Boy's Will*, which Frost and his wife found condescending, Pound promised Harriet Monroe, the editor, that he would have something new from Frost "as soon as he has done it." "He has done a 'Death of the Farmhand' since the book [*A Boy's Will*]," he wrote his father on June 3, 1913, and adds with yet another example of his wholly engaging generosity of feeling, that this poem "is to my mind better than anything in it. I shall have that in *The Smart Set* or in *Poetry* before long." One thing is sure— that many of the poems held back were incomparably superior to at least three that he chose to publish but would eventually delete from later printings of his poems: "Spoils of the Dead," "In Equal Sacrifice," and "Asking for Roses." The last of these is a fair sample of all three. It is mildly interesting because it offers an early example of Frost's obsession with human dwellings that are impoverished and apparently deserted, and because it is a kind of *Lied* with echoes of Burns and Tom Moore. As the young lovers pass the house, they notice a garden of "old-fashioned roses":

> "I wonder," I say, "who the owner of those is."
> "Oh, no one you know," she answers me airy,
> "But one we must ask if we want any roses."

It is astonishing to learn, if Frost's own testimony is to be believed, that at the time he was willing to see in print this embarrassing poem about a man, a woman, and flowers, he held back "The Subverted Flower" which makes use of the same three items. The complex dramatic interaction between flowers (which are a symptom in the poems of seasonal fertility), sexuality, and poetry is one of the important but uninsistent lines of coherence in the volume. Frost's own awareness of it and of its implications is best indicated by his omission of a poem whose inclusion would have suggested very dark, psychological shadings in the sexual areas which, by the implications of Frost's language in his poetry and in his prose, provide some of the metaphors for artistic creativity. It would also have indicated that he was to some degree victimized by unrequited love and that his career was not as simple an unfolding of self as he wants to suggest.

From the outset "The Subverted Flower" establishes the powerful authority, the psychotic necessity, of its macabre imagery and the relentlessness of its movement. It is the sexual nightmare of an adolescent blankly registering the descent, through sexual repressions, of himself and the girl he desires into different forms of bestiality. The four-beat lines are rhymed in a staggered way that allows sudden accelerations past one fixation, like a nightmare image being recollected, on to the next, where we are suspended as in a trance until a disyllabic rhyme chooses to complete the frame. Except for a few of Meredith's sonnets in "Modern Love" there is little in any poetry before Frost that can approach the direct and graphic sexual terror of this poem, the first lines of which follow:

> She drew back; he was calm:
> "It is this that had the power."
> And he lashed his open palm
> With the tender-headed flower.
> He smiled for her to smile,
> But she was either blind
> Or willfully unkind.
> He eyed her for a while
> For a woman and a puzzle.
> He flicked and flung the flower,
> And another sort of smile
> Caught up like finger tips
> The corners of his lips
> And cracked his ragged muzzle.

The poem could refer to an incident of so-called indecent exposure in Frost's courtship of Elinor White, but the details make it likely that it is an account of a nightmare in which such an incident was symbolically enacted. This would be a good reason for his wanting to withhold it, and the probability that the poem has *something* to do with Elinor White is advanced by Thompson as the sole reason for Frost's delaying publication until 1942, after her death. The subject, Frost was later to say in his *Paris Review* interview, was "frigidity in women."

There are, however, complicated literary as well as personal reasons for his not having printed the poem in *A Boy's Will*, reasons that became apparent when we see that, except for its style, the poem would not have been out of place, and, oddly enough, would have easily fitted in thematically. The problem would have been that the poem excites a kind of autobiographical speculation that would have materially altered the "portrait of an artist" that Frost wanted to project. To begin with, the strangeness of the poem is considerably lessened once it is placed among those in *A Boy's Will* wherein flowers are a token of either a precarious movement toward sexual, seasonal, and artistic fulfillment or the failure of these. Or perhaps one should say that its strangeness informs and significantly alters these other poems. The volume as a whole begins with landscapes that are barren, even funereal, and in which the young man walks forth conspicuously alone. Following on the barren landscapes of the first three poems, "Into My Own," "Ghost House," and "My November Guest," whose name is Sorrow, we come upon the just-married couple of "Love and a Question." The bride and groom are visited by a tramp in need of shelter. The bridegroom turns him away from the door, and yet is peculiarly equivocal as he "looked at a weary road" while his bride sits behind him at the fire: "But whether or not a man was asked / To mar the love of two / By harboring woe in the bridal house, / The bridegroom wished he knew." Then in the next, or fifth poem, "A Late Walk," there is a faint signal of a new vitality. A "flower" is just barely rescued from the desolation which has dominated the scene up to that point. The young man is still , though married, walking alone amidst "withered weeds," bare trees, except for "a leaf that lingered brown." But his walk ends in a gesture of unification with what little is still alive in the landscape and with the life that awaits him at home:"I end not far from my going forth, / By picking the faded blue / Of the last remaining aster flower / To carry again to you."

From this point on, the isolated "I" who has only begun to express the intimacy of his feeling for "her" is replaced with "we" and "our." But the world continues nevertheless to be found cold and threatening. The next poem is "Stars" with its landscape of snow in which the lovers might be lost "to white rest and a place of rest / Invisible at dawn"—an accent of Emily Dickinson unusual for Frost. In the poem that follows, "Storm Fear," the young man still lies alone in his wakefulness, but he is apparently with his wife and fears not for himself so much as for her and the children. Following on these it is proposed in "Wind and Window Flower" that she is a "flower" and that he is a winter wind "concerned with ice and snow, / Dead weeds and unmated birds / And little of love could know."

Even before this we have become aware that the threat to love has been gradually internalized by the young poet and that the landscape is an imaginary one of those moods, depressions, and melancholies which threaten their love with devastation and aridity. Only with the next four poems—"To the Thawing Wind" ("Give the buried flower a dream"), "A Prayer in Spring" ("Oh, give us pleasure in the flowers today"), "Flower Gathering," and "Rose Pogonias"—does the young poet escape from "dead weeds and unmated birds." Along with them the poet has himself been seen as a force for frigidity working in conjunction with the most malevolent aspects which he selects or imagines in the natural environment.

Though thematically "The Subverted Flower" could obviously belong to this grouping, it would have materially changed the implication of these poems insofar as they are about the nature of Frost's sexual-poetic imagination. By including it, Frost would have transferred responsibility from the young man to "her," or Elinor. As a result, he would have obscured the fact that the poems in this volume are essentially concerned with the connections between his poetic prowess and his power to find love within a landscape of the mind as well as in relation to another person. The poems trace out the effort to free his imagination so that it might work toward some harmony with natural cycles both of the seasons and of sexuality. With inclusion of "The Subverted Flower," the interest in the volume would have become more psychological than literary; it would have placed greater emphasis on the hazards of sexuality to the confusion of a Wordsworthian subject which more classically includes sexuality: the "Growth of a Poet's Mind." "The Subverted Flower" is not, as are the others, about *his* potentially frigid mind or imagination but about hers. His delicacy about Elinor White Frost was real enough, no doubt, but equally real was the desire to make himself responsible for anything that might have affected his poetry. It was Frost's enormous desire for control, form, design that forbade his including a poem which might imply, even by blaming another, that he was not the master of his literary fates.

The exclusion of this poem helps explain a number of things implied by his also having left out the other poems I have mentioned. First of all, the selection for *A Boy's Will* was not governed in any thoroughgoing way by the novelistic and self-revelatory scheme he himself claimed to have set up: "The psychologist in me," he was to say later on, "ached to call it 'The Record of A Phase of Post Adolescence.' " Second, the nature of the volume, and the determination of the order of poems, suggest other reasons for leaving out "The Subverted Flower," reasons having to do with Frost's imagination of a poetic career and with his fierce determination to control the public shaping of his life. He would rather have let at least some people think that part of the structure of *A Boy's Will* was dictated by "the seasons," which is superficially true, than allow most people freely to discover that the seasons are finally only a metaphor for the possible and always threatened perversion or subversion of the poetic imagination by the disasters of love. He would rather have pretended that the volume is about "A Phase of Post Adolescence" than have us ask if the connection in his work between sexuality and the progress of poetry is not far more complicated than he chooses to admit. Which is a way of saying that while he knew everything that was going on in his poetry he was not always anxious that we should know as much as he does.

Many of the early poems, offering some of the psychological and structural sources of all of Frost's poetry, are about this relation of love to poetic making, to making in all other senses of the word. A brief biographical digression might be useful here, a recapitulation of Frost's stormy and passionate courtship of Elinor White, with whom he seems to have fallen in love at first meeting. He was seventeen, she nearly two years older, and they sat next to one another in Lawrence High School (Massachusetts). From the outset her ability as a poet (she stopped writing poems before she married him and in later life tried to disguise and disown those that had appeared in the *School Bulletin*), her knowledge of literature, her marks in school (they were co-valedictorians, but her average was finally higher), her ability as a painter, her suitors at St Lawrence University at Canton, New York, all excited his competitive admiration and jealousy. Her attendance at college meant their separation, with Frost going to Dartmouth for a short time, then to teach in the Methuen schools until March 1893, then to act as helper and guardian to Elinor's mother and two of her sisters in

Salem, New Hampshire. Before she left for school and on her vacations in Lawrence he courted her with the help of Shelley's poetry, especially "Epipsychidion," with its inducements to ignore the institution of marriage. And of course he wooed her with poems of his own.

Indeed, his first volume, strictly speaking, was not *A Boy's Will* of 1913, when he was thirty-nine, but *Twilight* in 1894 when he was twenty, the one surviving copy of which is in the Barrett Collection at the University of Virginia. Only two copies were printed, one for Frost and one for Elinor. It included, in addition to "My Butterfly" which was later to appear in *A Boy's Will*, four other poems full of literary echoes ranging from Sidney to Keats, Tennyson to Rossetti, as in the opening lines of the title poem:

> Why am I first in thy so sad regard,
> O twilight gazing from I know not where?
> I fear myself as one more than I guessed!

He carried Elinor's copy on an unannounced trip to her college boarding house in Canton. Surprised, bewildered, prevented by the rules from inviting him in or from going out herself, she accepted her copy in what seemed a casual but was perhaps a merely preoccupied way. She told him to return home at once. He did so, but only to pack a bag and leave for a suicide journey that took him to Virginia and through the Dismal Swamp at night, "into my own," so to speak. The danger was very real. "I was," he later said, "trying to throw my life away." Through this and subsequent travails, torments, threats, and melodramatic scenes, he convinced her to marry him before she could finish school and before he had any secure means of support.

Such briefly are the biographical elements probably at play in some of the early poems. But the biographical material does not tell us as much about the man as the poetry does. By that I mean that the poetry does not necessarily come from the experiences of his life; rather, the kind of poetry he wrote, and the kind of experiences to which he was susceptible, both emerge from the same configuration in him, prior to his poems or to his experiences. Sex and an obsession with sound, sexual love and poetic imagination, success in love and success in art—these conspire with one another. A poem is an action, not merely a "made" but a "making" thing, and "the figure a poem makes," one remembers, "is the same as for love." It is as if in talking about the direction laid down by a poem he instinctively uses a language of ongoing sexual action:

> No one can really hold that the ecstasy should be static and stand still in one place. It begins in delight, it inclines to the impulse, it assumes direction with the first line laid down, it runs a course of lucky events, and ends in a clarification of life—not necessarily a great clarification such as sects and cults are founded on, but in a momentary stay against confusion. . . . It finds its own name as

it goes and discovers the best waiting for it in some final phrase
at once wise and sad—the happy-sad blend of the drinking song.
("The Figure a Poem Makes")

Three early poems, "Waiting," "In a Vale," and "A Dream Pang,"
coming nearly in the middle of *A Boy's Will,* illustrate the connections,
implicit in the structuring of the whole volume, between sexual love and
poetic making, between the "sounds" of love and a poet's love of sound.
None of the three is in any sense considerable. Frost's investment in them
is relatively slight; they are shy of the complications which, when they
emerge in later poems, are more consciously and subtly managed. And yet
the poems are the stranger for *not* showing very much acknowledgment
of their strangeness. It is as if initially the imagination of the sexual self
and of the poetic self were so naturally, so instinctively identified as not
to call for comment.

The three poems are published in sequence in *A Boy's Will,* always an
important and calculated factor in Frost. They are all what can be called
dream poems, and each suggests a different aspect of the dreamlike relationship between poetic and sexual prowess. In the first, "Waiting," the
figure of the poet is "specter-like," as he wanders through a "stubble field"
of tall haycocks, a bit like the "stubble-plains" in the last stanza of Keats's
ode "To Autumn"; the "things" about which he has waking dreams are
mostly the surroundings and their noises. From the outset his condition
seems peculiarly vulnerable to sights and sounds, and it is not till the final
lines that one can attribute this to the fact that what means most to him
in his dream is not anything present to his senses but rather "the memory
of one absent most," the girl he loves:

Waiting
Afield at Dusk

What things for dream there are when specter-like,
Moving among tall haycocks lightly piled,
I enter alone upon the stubble field,
From which the laborers' voices late have died,
And in the antiphony of afterglow
And rising full moon, sit me down
Upon the full moon's side of the first haycock
And lose myself amid so many alike.

I dream upon the opposing lights of the hour,
Preventing shadow until the moon prevail;
I dream upon the nighthawks peopling heaven,
Each circling each with vague unearthly cry,
Or plunging headlong with fierce twang afar;
And on the bat's mute antics, who would seem
Dimly to have made out my secret place,
Only to lose it when he pirouettes,

And seek it endlessly with purblind haste;
On the last swallow's sweep; and on the rasp
In the abyss of odor and rustle at my back,
That, silenced by my advent, finds once more,
After an interval, his instrument,
And tries once—twice—and thrice if I be there;
And on the worn book of old-golden song
I brought not here to read, it seems, but hold
And freshen in this air of withering sweetness;
But on the memory of one absent, most,
For whom these lines when they shall greet her eye.

Before the mention of his beloved, in the next to last line, the poem is filled with evocations of natural sounds in the "stubble field" where "the laborers' voices late have died"; there is also the "vague unearthly cry" of the nighthawks who plunge "headlong with fierce twang afar"; there are the "bat's mute antics," the "rasp" of a creature who, "silenced by my advent, finds once more, / After an interval, his instrument." But what is apt to seem most provocative—given its place at the end of the poem and its uniqueness among all the references of natural sound—is an allusion to poetic sound, to the "worn book of old-golden song." It, too, is a carrier of sound, very likely of sound that helped (even more than did the sounds of nature) during his courtship of the one now "absent." But however much our literary-critical dispositions might prompt us to separate this item of sound from others, as being more centrally important, it is necessary to note that the young poet-specter tends merely to put the poetic within the sequence of other items. It is joined to them casually with another of the many "ands" that make up the listing. Apparently he does not intend to even read the book in order to bring her closer to mind. More than that, though the book is "worn" and though the poetry is itself "old," his reasons for holding onto it are that it may "freshen in this air," this Keatsian air "of withering sweetness."

The "old-golden song" is to be freshened, strangely enough, by something that is more apt to dry it, to "wither" it. We are readied by this paradox for the introduction, as in "Pan with Us," of the theme of "new" song, new sounds, something poetic for the future—in short, the very poem we are reading which is destined for her: "for whom these lines when they shall greet her eye." With the vitality of "shall greet her eye" the poet is no longer "specter-like." He has gotten past a number of by-ways: of possible dreams on other sounds, of the invitation to do no more than dream, of losing himself to these sounds—a danger only less intense than that in the later "Stopping by Woods on a Snowy Evening." Past all this, the young lover is able to envision a future in love inseparable from a future in poetry. He has been able to do this because, all the while, as the poem moves along, he has been "making it"; he has been writing "these lines."

One indication of the peculiar nature of Frost's reputation as a poet, when compared to an Eliot or a Yeats, is that few have bothered with poems so clearly not of his best like "Waiting" or the two others grouped with it. His admirers are defensively anxious to show only the favorite things, when some of the lesser ones are often even more revealing of his preoccupations with the plights and pleasures in the life of the poetic self. "In a Vale" is, even more than "Waiting," fin de siècle in conception and language. With its "vale," "maidens," "fen," and with words like "wist," "list," "dwelt," there is little going on that predicts the later Frost except the penultimate and best stanza. And yet it is still a most ingratiating poem—like an early picture of someone we have gotten to know only in later years—and it tells us perhaps even more than do more posed sittings:

> When I was young, we dwelt in a vale
>   By a misty fen that rang all night,
> And thus it was the maidens pale
> I knew so well, whose garments trail
>   Across the reeds to a window light.
>
> The fen had every kind of bloom,
>   And for every kind there was a face,
> And a voice that has sounded in my room
> Across the sill from the outer gloom.
>   Each came singly unto her place,
>
> But all came every night with the mist;
>   And often they brought so much to say
> Of things of moment to which, they wist,
> One so lonely was fain to list,
>   That the stars were almost faded away
>
> Before the last went, heavy with dew,
>   Back to the place from which she came—
> Where the bird was before it flew,
> Where the flower was before it grew,
>   Where bird and flower were one and the same.
>
> And thus it is I know so well
>   Why the flower has odor, the bird has song.
> You have only to ask me, and I can tell.
> No, not vainly there did I dwell,
>   Nor vainly listen all the night long.

The time scheme of these poems is importantly suggestive of poetic gestations, of a way past and present provide the nutrients for a poetic future. In "Waiting" we are in the present, witnessing the impressions made upon a young poet who holds the past in his hand—Palgrave's *Golden Treasury*—while composing in his head the "lines" which will in future "greet" his beloved. "In a Vale" is a dream wholly of the past, but it, too, looks ahead to a future wherein the past will have been redeemed by the writing of the poems inspired by it: "You have only to ask me, and I can tell. / No, not vainly there did I dwell, / Nor vainly listen all the night long." The listening, again, is to voices or sounds that he has managed to supersede: "a misty fen that rang all night"; the voices that have "sounded in my room" and that "brought so much to say." The dream is a rather wet one ("the last went, heavy with dew") and it is from these nocturnal experiences that he learns what, in the later daytime of publication, he "can tell." With Lucretius, he can tell that "the bird and flower were one and the same." However, he can also tell a more American and Emersonian story: of a world again, which reveals itself in forms (odor and song) which have in part been placed there by the human imagination, including human dreams.

An absent lover imagined in"Waiting" as a future reader, ghostly lovers or maidens whose sayings "In a Vale" will in some future time allow him to "tell" readers about birds and flowers—these figurations are brought together in the last of the three poems, "A Dream Pang." There the poet is discovered in bed with his lover beside him, her very presence proving that his song has been answered by the something more fulfilling than the echoing sounds of nature. This early poem is thereby a prelude to later ones like "Come In" or "A Leaf-Treader," where Frost is in danger of succumbing to the call of nature, of losing himself, of having his sound in words absorbed into the sounds made by the natural elements. In this poem he is not learning to "tell" or expecting the "lines" he is writing to be read; here he is already a poet whose song, in his dream, has been endangered by her denials and by his proud withdrawals:

> I had withdrawn in forest, and my song
> Was swallowed up in leaves that blew alway;
> And to the forest edge you came one day
> (This was my dream) and looked and pondered long,
> But did not enter, though the wish was strong:
> You shook your pensive head as who would say,
> "I dare not—too far in his footsteps stray—
> He must seek me would he undo the wrong."
>
> Not far, but near, I stood and saw it all,
> Behind low boughs the trees let down outside;
> And the sweet pang it cost me not to call
> And tell you that I saw does still abide.
> But 'tis not true that thus I dwelt aloof,
> For the wood wakes, and you are here for proof.

Now, as she lies beside him ("this was my dream . . . you are here for proof") the poem can come to articulation; before, while they were alienated from one another "my song / Was swallowed up in leaves."

Without her, he and his song are lost to the vagaries of nature and its noises; with her, nature, or the "wood," comes to a more orderly life outside their place: "the wood wakes, and you are here." The implications take us to a variety of poems in which Frost can feel momentarily and terrifyingly included, as he says in "Desert Places," in the loneliness of nature "unawares." Cut off from the communion of human sex and human love, he is answered either by random, accidental, teasing responses, like that of the little bird in "The Wood-Pile," or by evidences of brutish indifference such as greet the speaker of "The Most of It":

> He would cry out on life, that what it wants
> Is not its own love back in copy speech,
> But counter-love, original response.
> And nothing ever came of what he cried
> Unless it was the embodiment that crashed
> In the cliff's talus on the other side.

The failure of love, of love-making, the failure to elicit "counter-love" means, as in "The Subverted Flower," that the young poet cannot finally be joined to that human communication with nature which Emerson promised might be found there. Here as elsewhere Frost's Emersonism is grounded in certain basic actualities, especially the sexual relations of men and women, which Emerson himself tended to pass over with little more than citation. Within this sequence of three poems, "A Dream Pang" looks ahead to the implications of a more considerable sequence of three poems, already mentioned, that includes "The Most of It," "Never Again Would Birds' Song Be the Same," and "The Subverted Flower." The implication, briefly noted also in "The Vantage Point," is that a man alone ("he thought he kept the universe alone") cannot see or hear anything in nature that confirms his existence as human. If he is alone, he cannot "make" the world; he cannot reveal himself to it or in it; he becomes lost to it; it remains alien. He cannot make human sound. In "The Subverted Flower" he can at first hope that the impasse " 'has come to us / And not to me alone.' " But even this proposition falls on deaf ears, or essentially deaf ears. It is something "she thought she heard him say; / Though with every word he spoke / His lips were sucked and blown / And the effort made him choke / Like a tiger at a bone."

In the early, as in the later sequence, Frost is concerned in various ways with the possibilities of the sounds of the man-poet-lover in situations where there are competing sounds and where, if he cannot "make it" with his beloved, he cannot "make it" either in competitions with sounds in nature or in other poetry. He cannot "make it" with words so shaped as to reveal his participation in poetry, and—equally important—that such participation is "natural." He is not content to have *"his* song" swallowed up in leaves either of a tree, merely, or of a book, merely. His poetry, his song, must include both.

In the light of this ambition we can best understand Frost's life-long commitment to certain theories of sound and poetic form. The commitment is implicit in all of the poems and in the structural organization of *A Boy's Will*. It was to find theoretical expression somewhat later, in letters written at the time of the publication of the book, and later still in essays and talks. In a letter to the black poet-critic-anthologist William Stanley Braithwaite, on March 22, 1915, for example, Frost said:

> It would seem absurd to say it (and you mustn't quote me as saying it) but I suppose the fact is that my conscious interest in people was at first no more than an almost technical interest in their speech—in what I used to call their sentence sounds—the sound of sense. Whatever these sounds are or aren't (they are certainly not of the vowels and consonants of words nor even of the words themselves but something the words are chiefly a kind of notation for indicating and for fastening to the page) whatever they are, I say, I began to hang on them very young. I was under twenty when I deliberately put it to myself one night after good conversation that there are moments when we actually touch in talk what the best writing can only come near. . . . We must go into the vernacular for tones that haven't been brought to book. We must write with the ear on the speaking voice. We must imagine the speaking voice.

"Sentence sounds" does not refer to the meaning the words give to a sentence but to the meaning the sound of the sentence can give to the words, which is why Frost is so difficult to translate into any other language. It is a matter of stress patterns. Thus, the line, "By June our brook's run out of song and speed" is arranged so that the potential of the word "song"—as a possible allusion to "poetry"—is markedly diminished by putting it immediately after the quickly paced vernacular phase "run out of." The word "song" would be far more potent, but altogether too archly so, if it traded places with the word "speed": "By June our brook's run out of speed and song." Some of these distinctions are clarified in a letter written over a year before, February 22, 1914, to his friend John Bartlett, a newspaper man who was one of his favorite students at Pinkerton Academy:

> I give you a new definition of a sentence:
> A sentence is a sound in itself on which other sounds called words may be strung.
> You may string words together without a sentence sound to string them on just as you may tie clothes together by sleeves and stretch them without a clothes line between two trees, but—it is bad for the clothes. . . . The sentence sounds are very definite entities.(This is no literary mysticism I am preaching.) They are as

definite as words. It is not impossible that they could be collected in a book though I don't at present see on what system they would be catalogued.

They are apprehended by the ear. They are gathered by the ear from the vernacular and brought into books. Many of them are familiar to us in books. I think no writer invents them. The most original writer only catches them fresh from talk, where they grow spontaneously.

A man is all a writer if *all* his words are strung on definite recognizable sentence sounds. The voice of the imagination, the speaking voice must know certainly how to behave [,] how to posture in every sentence he offers.

When Frost refers to the "vocal imagination" (in the essay "The Constant Symbol") he makes it synonymous with what he calls "images of the voice speaking." Frost listens for these images as much in nature as in human dialogue. But there is an important difference in what he wants and expects to hear from these two different places: only in human dialogue can such images emerge as "sentence sounds" rather than as mere echoes, or vagrant, only potentially significant noises, like "The sweep / Of easy wind and downy flake," or what Thoreau calls "brute sounds." Furthermore, Frost's capacity even to find "images of the voice speaking" in nature depends upon human love; it can be crippled or thwarted by the lack of it. The matter might be put in a three-part formula: (1) the "artist as a young man," if doomed to "keep the universe alone," can only call forth from it alien and terrifying sounds, and is in danger of becoming either a mere passive receiver of these sounds or himself a brute; (2) the "artist as a young man" in a reciprocal relationship of love with another human can, as a result, also find "images of the voice speaking" in some rudimentary form in nature, though it is important to know that what he finds is only an image, nothing wholly equivalent to the human voice speaking: "The Need of Being Versed in Country Things" is that one is thereby allowed "Not to believe the phoebes wept." This brings up the third and most important point: (3) that the clearest, but not only, differentiation of human sound from sounds in nature is poetry itself, the making of a poem, the capacity literally to be "versed" in the things of this world. Any falling—of leaves, of snow, of man, of the garland of roses which Adam is holding when he first sees Eve in her fallen state—can be redeemed by loving, and the sign of this redemption is, for Frost, the sound of the voice working within the sounds of poetry. It could even be said that the proper poetic image of the Fall and of the human will continually to surmount it is—given accentual-syllabism's unique role in the handling of English rhythm—the mounting from unstressed to stressed syllables in the iambic pentameter line. Thus, the oven bird can "frame" the question of "what to make of a diminished thing" in "all but words." The words are at the call of the poet; the "making" is in his power. It consists precisely in his showing how the verse form works with and against mere "saying":

He sáys | thė eaŕ | lẏ pét | ȧl fáll | iṡ pást,

Whėn peár | aṅd chér | rẏ bloóm | weṅt dówn | iṅ shów | eṙs.

The glory of these lines is in the achieved strain between trochaic words like "early" and "petal," "cherry" and "showers," and the iambic pattern which breaks their fall. The meter is a perfect exemplification of what the poem is about, of the creative tension between a persistent rising and a natural falling—a poise of creativity in the face of threatened diminishments.

Echoing Eden: Frost and Origins

Charles Berger

Of the major modern poets, Frost seems the least driven to create myths or fictions of origin, the least prone to mystify beginnings. He will have nothing to do with the sacred investiture of the past, whether historical or autobiographical. He resembles Stevens in the belief that the sense "of cold and earliness is a daily sense, / Not the predicate of bright origin" (*An Ordinary Evening in New Haven*), but does not share Stevens's obsession with finding first ideas apart from authoritarian first principles. Though Frost is most profoundly an exploratory poet, whose work indeed is knowing, as Richard Poirier's title tells us, he would not hymn the search for the ground of such knowing as Stevens does. "To re-create, to use / The cold and earliness and bright origin / Is to search." Frost privileges neither the constructed locus of origin nor the search for it with Stevens's high eloquence. At the same time, one cannot read through Frost's poetry and fail to notice how many of his poems engage, however playfully or sceptically, those issues we group under the figurative heading of "origins," even to the point of his invoking Eden and the Fall to describe ongoing moments in consciousness. In his poems of brooks, pools, and gardens, in his speculations on the wellsprings of sound and song, Frost shows an uncanny ability to approach the formerly sacred source, to broach the beginning of things, without yielding to their hieratic lure. Frost plays upon the prestige of these themes, but ends by including or accommodating them within, not outside, the range of lyric discursiveness. His poetic intelligence thrives on the recognition that all beginnings are fictions.

A good example of how Frost can play with the subject of beginnings comes in a little-discussed poem called "The Valley's Singing Day":

73

The sound of the closing outside door was all.
You made no sound in the grass with your footfall,
As far as you went from the door, which was not far;
But you had awakened under the morning star
The first songbird that awakened all the rest.
He could have slept but a moment more at best.
Already determined dawn began to lay
In place across a cloud the slender ray
For prying beneath and forcing the lids of sight,
And loosing the pent-up music of overnight.
But dawn was not to begin their "pearly-pearly"
(By which they mean the rain is pearls so early,
Before it changes to diamonds in the sun),
Neither was song that day to be self-begun.
You had begun it, and if there needed proof—
I was asleep still under the dripping roof,
My window curtain hung over the sill to wet;
But I should awake to confirm your story yet;
I should be willing to say and help you say
That once you had opened the valley's singing day.

This remarkably subtle poem avoids claiming too much for the action
it describes, while at the same time showing how easy—how natural—it
would be to magnify such an incident. The teasing enjambment of the
fourth line makes us first take "awakened" as intransitive (helped in this
by the poetical "under the morning star"), accustomed as we are to the
heightened rhetoric of beginnings. As we read on, we discover that the
action can be explained a little less hyperbolically; something has been jarred
from sleep, simply awakened by a nearly inaudible sound. But the initial
suggestion roused in us will not entirely disappear and the identification
of the bird as "the first" perhaps keeps us within an enlarged sphere of
possibility.

But the poem scales down to anecdote, to "story," as if to imply that
all accounts of beginnings or awakenings contain their share of arbitrariness
or accident. The comedy of disproportion here arises from the gap between
effort and effect: so little goes into achieving what might be regarded, in
another poem, as so much. Placing oneself at the dawn, inserting oneself
at the opening of day so that song would not be "self-begun" but originated
by an outside, prevenient presence, this sounds like the plot of a revised
hymn to sunrise—but of a different poem, as well. These "larger" themes
are echoed playfully throughout this singing day's valley. But it would not
be play, as Frost says elsewhere, were it not for mortal stakes.

The dialectical complement of Frost's wary attraction to original sites
and sounds may be discovered in his many poems about *echo*. Its obvious
associations with pastoralism matter less for the interpreter of Frost than

the use of echo as a figure for repetition and reflection (to bring in the visual analogue). Frost's poetry complicates the hierarchical opposition between the fullness of original sound and the faintness of echo. If he does not go all the way toward regarding repetition as mastery or originality, he certainly avoids seeing it as diminution. A central distinction made by John Hollander in *The Figure of Echo* between echo and allusion helps to explain Frost's attitude toward verbal repetition:

> We might, indeed, propose a kind of rhetorical hierarchy for the relationship of allusive modes. Actual quotation, the literal presence of a body of text, is represented or replaced by allusion, which may be fragmentary or periphrastic. In the case of outright allusion . . . the text alluded to is not totally absent, but is part of the portable library shared by the author and his ideal audience. Intention to allude recognizably is essential to the concept. . . . But then there is echo, which represents or substitutes for allusion as allusion does for quotation. . . . In contrast with literally allusion, echo is a metaphor of, and for, alluding, and does not depend on conscious intention.

By these criteria, Frost would certainly have to be considered a poet of echo rather than allusion. Echo is less referential and intentional than allusion, while at the same time being more figurative. Rather than calling attention to a particular passage, it makes the reader aware of temporality in its pure state. Echo acknowledges indebtedness by figuratively indicating the temporality of the poet's discourse, but works to free that dependence from association with the notion of poetic property, thereby easing the burden of belatedness. Frost's concept of "sentence sounds," preexisting patterns of sound belonging to the genius of the language, amounts to just such a theory of echoing:

> They are apprehended by the ear. They are gathered by the ear from the vernacular and brought into books. Many of them are already familiar to us in books. I think no writer invents them. The most original writer only catches them fresh from talk, where they grow spontaneously.

No critic writing today would have any difficulty exposing the idealizations of this passage, its accordance of priority to speech over writing, or its natural analogues for the process of composition: sounds, which "grow spontaneously" in nature, are gathered (as are crops) or caught (as are animals). Frost himself leaves it an open question as to whether we apprehend sentence sounds from talk or from books. But priority is not really the issue here. What matters for Frost is that the poet capture what Marie Borroff, in her study of Frost's language, terms "native" dialect, the strength of the vernacular. Such a concept seems to fuse origin and echo, insofar as the quest for the vernacular always implies a figurative return to "authentic" language, language at the source, "first" words. But this return also involves a repetition, since the vernacular keeps such language alive and in circulation. It might be said that for Frost the ideal of the native stands in for the stricter sense of the origin that one encounters in other poets. A poem such as "Hyla brook"—"our brook," as Frost calls it—with its refusal to pursue the stream underground in a quest for the deep source, typifies this attitude. The resonances of native speech represent an accommodated purity, for Frost is not the poet of the still center. Poirier distinguishes Frost from some of the romantics in that he does not regard human consciousness as a burden. I would also add that, as opposed to some of his nearer contemporaries, he does not regard the inherently figurative nature of language to be a burden either, and so does not seek radical cures for the imprecisions of language.

In what follows, I will be considering a series of poems on the subject of origins and echoes. These poems should give a strong sense of the different guises under which this central concern appears in Frost. I hesitate to call it an obsession, since that word does not square with the subtlety of Frost's artistry. Although the sequence I have chosen ends with "Directive"—a poem that ends a number of other essays on Frost—I do not intend that poem to be regarded as a culmination, or summa, of Frost's thinking on the subject. Frost's *oeuvre* is the most decentered of any major, modern poet and for the critic to construct a central poem would be to violate the sceptical integrity of his work. All these poems echo each other, in their strategies of covering and recovering the origin.

I

"The Aim Was Song" begins, "Before man came"—but nothing in Frost's rhetoric suggests that he wishes to capture the accents of this prehistoric, prelinguistic moment. Frost does not mystify the subject of "Before man"; indeed, it remains for him a subject, capable of being declaimed upon along with other subjects. Frost does not try to use language to express the epoch *before* language. Poetic primitivism is not his way:

> Before man came to blow it right
>   The wind once blew itself untaught,
> And did its loudest day and night
>   In any rough place where it caught.
>
> Man came to tell it what was wrong:
>   It hadn't found the place to blow;
> It blew too hard—the aim was song.
>   And listen—how it ought to go!
>
> He took a little in his mouth,
>   And held it long enough for north

To be converted into south,
　And then by measure blew it forth.

By measure. It was word and note,
　The wind the wind had meant to be—
A little through the lips and throat.
　The aim was song—the wind could see.

Scattered throughout the poem are teasingly moral terms, such as "right," "wrong," and "ought." The wind itself must be taught. And yet these moral terms have an aesthetic basis to them: "measure" is not so much a moral as an aesthetic category. Learning to measure and order the instrument means learning to play it right, learning to find the smooth as opposed to the rough places. Civilization is a form of measure. Morality might sneak in here in the sense that there is a guiding principle to the search for measure. That is, Frost may be implying that moral systems grow out of a deep-seated, instinctual urge for measure and order, a need on our part to convert things to human scale.

The process of turning undifferentiated wind into the measures of "word and note" involves an act of conversion—"North . . . converted into south"—a turning of the wind against itself, so to speak. Wind is drawn in and then returned as the exhalation of song. Insofar as song is composed partly of natural wind, it is mimetic, a point Frost makes through the mirroring of the word in the line, "The wind the wind had meant to be." But nature is also changed by song's superaddition of meaning, even if such a gesture works to restore a sense of natural mimesis by ascribing a similar meaning to nature itself. In his half-jocular way, Frost stands the Wordsworthian model of nature as pedagogue on its head, by having man become the instructor. The lesson learned, "the wind could see."

The conversion of natural wind into song marks a triumph of human scale and meaning. Sound is converted into song through a twisting or a wrenching, a turning of strength inside out. In making of the wind a human song, we thereby create a sense of order: the measures of song precede the measures of law. If the aim is song, then to be wrong is to misaim, to hit the wrong note, the wrong target, to be guilty of *hamartia*.

"Sitting by a Bush in Broad Sunlight" has drawn surprisingly little comment from the critics, as if its underlying complexities were only too readily translated by confident artistry. The poem's tetrameter couplets invoke Emerson's oracular meter, but the trumpeting is muted here, the line more flexible. The poem's overt subject is entropy, the decline from fire to mere warmth, with the specter of winter not far removed:

When I spread out my hand here today,
I catch no more than a ray
To feel of between thumb and fingers;
No lasting effect of it lingers.

There was one time and only the one
When dust really took in the sun;
And from that one intake of fire
All creatures still warmly suspire.

And if men have watched a long time
And never seen sun-smitten slime
Again come to life and crawl off,
We must not be too ready to scoff.

God once declared He was true.
And then took the veil and withdrew,
And remember how final a hush
Then descended of old on the bush.

God once spoke to people by name.
The sun once imparted its flame.
One impulse persists as our breath;
The other persists as our faith.

Though the poem is startlingly literal in its declaration that "There was one time and only the one," Frost displays little sense of loss, little elegiac lament. To state the terms of decline so boldly is perhaps to expose the impossibility of the original moment—that "one time"—from which we appear to have fallen. Sentences such as "God once spoke to people by name," or "The sun once imparted its flame," are possible only because of "once," the signifier of irrecoverable priority. "Once" marks the precincts of *illo tempore*, the sacred space of story time, of origin conceived as a story. Throughout the poem, Frost threatens to convert these absolute statements into terms of wit, thereby bringing the sacred into the social realm. The act of spreading out "here today" takes priority over the loss of elemental fire. Frost is able both to describe his inability to catch fire, to "take" in the sun, and his inability to mourn the loss of such elemental power.

"Sitting by a Bush in Broad Sunlight" is balanced between scoffing tones and tones of awe, between the coyness of "God . . . took the veil and withdrew," and the imagining of a moment when "dust really took in the sun," a moment when it was possible to catch fire from the source of fire. Frost also plays with two creation stories here, one divine, one natural: the spark of genesis comes from God's Word, it comes from the sun's flames. I have deliberately omitted "or" from the last clause, for the two accounts need not be competing ones. Frost has united the images of speech and fire as we find them in the story of the burning bush. God's speech issues in fire: prophetic or pentecostal speech. Frost's poem has no real room for speculation on this kind of speech, nor does Frost do so elsewhere in his poetry, but he gives us a glimpse of such a conjunction in this poem. Frost assumes that we are separated from such fiery speech, just as we are separated from the truth, once declared but now withdrawn, and he does not mourn the loss of such verbal immediacy. The poem's opening line presents an image of the hand as an emblem of artistic technique and Frost chooses it over the burning tongue of prophetic discourse. Along these same lines, he reveals himself to be a watcher, not a seer: "And if men have watched a long time / And never seen."

The act of sitting by a bush in broad sunlight is, of course, a pale echo of Moses' stance before the burning bush; Frost's speaker is more like Mordechai before the palace gates. Frostian wit, the power of his epigrammatic style, tempers both the pain of loss and quizzes the reality of the supposed lost object. The last stanza of the poem makes it clear that Frost is interested primarily in what he calls our persistence: this is his strong word for echoing, repetition, continuation. The last lines rhyme "faith" and "breath"—though they are the most pronounced off-rhymes in the poem—but the possibility of chiastic structuring makes it impossible to assign these terms with certainty to either sun or God. Does our breath derive from God's speech or the sun's flame? Fire has been allied with suspiration throughout the poem, so it might be natural to assume that the sun's imparted gift still persists as our breath. God's speech, then, is our faith. But these terms could just as easily be reversed. Is breath stronger than faith? And, if so, is it stronger because it comes from nature and not God?

II

The conjunction of green and gold in "Nothing Gold Can Stay" merges myths of the garden and the golden age, while also introducing, through "gold," an artifical note into the account. *Firstness*, Frost seems to say, has an unnatural cast to it.

> Nature's first green is gold,
> Her hardest hue to hold.
> Her early leaf's a flower;
> But only so an hour.
> Then leaf subsides to leaf.
> So Eden sank to grief,
> So dawn goes down to day.
> Nothing gold can stay.

The ability to distinguish a green that differs from itself, a green that is gold, argues an artificial perspective—the Yeatsian "artifice of eternity"—that can only momentarily be held, whether in Nature or the poet's mind. Such a distinction is doomed to slip away or be elided, a process the poem enacts through the grammatical elision of "Her early leaf's a flower." At the same time, the natural process of growth and expansion is implicated in the loss of earliness to a grosser lateness. What one scale of measurement registers as growth, another sees as loss, diminution, entropic dwindling.

The sense of a Fall, made explicit throughout in words such as "sank" and "goes down," is also reinforced by the dominant falling rhythm of the trochaic line. When the word "grief" enters the poem, it has the force of "misery" in Stevens's "The Snow Man," a word which reveals the human reverberations of this apparently impersonal process.

But the loss is not absolute, for the poem proffers a counter-cycle of repetitive restitution. Dawn goes down today but will rise again tomorrow. The hour will again come round. The final line becomes the poem's title and undoes finality by beginning the poem over again. The last line goes down in order to come up again, like the sun. Echoing the title, it takes on the force of a refrain, a daily dirge rather than an epitaph. The first idea, as Stevens says in *Notes toward a Supreme Fiction,* comes and goes, comes and goes, all day. Golden vision yields to the day's green going. Art itself is synecdochal, an hour to a day, but an hour that is guaranteed, even as it cannot be prolonged.

"These pools," the emblematic focus of meditation in "Spring Pools," are curiously double in nature: conceived as wellsprings or sources, they nevertheless reflect as well as generate. And in this reflection they do not lose or diminish that which they reflect. If we regard reflections as the visual equivalent of echo, then what is reflected (echoed) is given back nearly in its entirety, or its totality, as Frost puts it: "These pools that, though in forests, still reflect / The total sky almost without defect." So the spring pools, as first idea, as picture of nature in the cleanliness of the first idea, is already a reflection. Derrida might be invoked here, in a comment upon the impossibility of simple unity even at the point or place of origin: "There are no simple origins, for what is reflected is split *in itself* and not only as an addition to itself of its image; the reflection, the image, the double, splits what it doubles." If we privilege the pools as "clear" or "invisible" ink, linked to inner sight, over the darkening scrawl of the summer trees, then we need to remember that the pools are not a transparency but a reflection.

The sense of doubling, or narcissistic reflection culminates in the image of "flowery waters and watery flowers." The doubling of self through reflection is set against the doubling or extension of self through biological propagation, as in the generative power of the trees to produce leaves. It is not a question of poetry being more like one paradigm than the other, more narcissistic than generative; rather, poetry is both at the same time. The poem tricks us into thinking that one phase yields to the other, as early spring to summer, in a mimesis of natural process. Keats said that if poetry comes not as easily as leaves to the tree, it had better not come at all, but poetry also comes as easily as Narcissus to his image. In many poems, Frost is only too willing to align poetry with so-called "natural" generation, but here he reminds us that poetry is also a cold pastoral, fixed on itself, a power not to be used for something else.

The same idea of a cold paradise can be found in "A Winter Eden," another cold pastoral in which the ideal moment proves curiously sexless. The poem combines much of the thinking found in "Nothing Gold Can Stay" and "Spring Pools," but it is a more animated, playful poem. By the calendar of its emblematic setting, "A Winter Eden" takes place earlier than "Spring Pools"; snow remains unmelted, the hibernating trees do not start from their winter sleep:

> A winter garden in an alder swamp,
> Where conies now come out to sun and romp,
> As near a paradise as it can be
> And not melt snow or start a dormant tree.
>
> It lifts existence on a plane of snow
> One level higher than the earth below,
> One level nearer heaven overhead,
> And last year's berries shining scarlet red.
>
> It lifts a gaunt luxuriating beast
> Where he can stretch and hold his highest feast
> On some wild apple-tree's young tender bark,
> What well may prove the year's high girdle mark.

In the great line "So near to paradise all pairing ends," Frost, with the grave whimsy he manages so well, imagines a point at which the marriage-duty ends and, along with it, the duty to be a poet of marriage:

> So near to paradise all pairing ends:
> Here loveless birds now flock as winter friends,
> Content with bud-inspecting. They presume
> To say which buds are leaf and which are bloom.

Whereas "Spring Pools" emphasized a chilly narcissism, "A Winter Eden" plays up the sportiveness of its scene. In both poems the moment itself is valued, as opposed to anything it might induce, even though the "hour of winter day" is shadowed throughout by knowledge of its brevity. The poem's couplets—its "double knock," to use the phrasing of the last stanza—keep this sense of closure before us at all points, culminating in the dirge-like "This Eden day is done at two o'clock." Though such a day is short, we find no sense here that "Eden sank to grief." Not the fruit, but the bark of the "wild apple tree" is eaten; perhaps the absence of marriage sets a limit to disobedience. Frost contrives a language of innocence in "A Winter Eden," in which words such as "romp" and "sport" seem to find their proper place, salvaged from the bin of anachronism by inclusion in a deliberately anachronistic scene, as any return to Eden must be.

III

"The Most of It" presents us with yet another version of the American Adam, our native solitary, willfully establishing himself in a wilderness

Eden and echoing Adam's lament over lack of suitable companionship. Poirier is right to point out the absurdity of imagining a dramatic situation here, but surely Frost has nevertheless drawn a recognizable character, however allegorical. And this character, as is often the case in lyric, is a narrower consciousness than its author, distorted through exaggeration. The outrageous presumption of the opening line—"He thought he kept the universe alone"—dwindles into the foibles of an Adamic literalist, one who would go about "recreating" the original story, who would literally place himself in Adam's position in order perhaps to experience the inauguration of a new "counter-love, original response":

> He thought he kept the universe alone;
> For all the voice in answer he could wake
> Was but the mocking echo of his own
> From some tree-hidden cliff across the lake.
> Some morning from the boulder-broken beach
> He would cry out on life, that what it wants
> Is not its own love back in copy speech,
> But counter-love, original response.

Voice calls to voice here, but the solitary receives a debased echo, an echo described as "mocking." This is not a tautological description; other forms of echo abound and the poetic tradition, not to mention Frost's poetry, is filled with them. This echo validates nothing. It issues from a source that remains hidden, a "tree-hidden cliff"; within the cliff, perhaps there is a cave, a hidden mouth. This mocking voice bounces off the cliff-side, not from out of the oracular voice of caves.

The satire here, among numerous possibilities, is that this American Adam should seek an "original response," while remaining himself such a literalist of the original story. A copy himself, he hopes to break the mold. His delusion is to think that by copying Adam he will raise the copy of Eve, another Eve. But though he disclaims any narcissistic motive (and is mocked by Echo), I think that readers can decipher the self-aggrandizing mode of one who thinks he keeps the universe alone. For this character is only self-sponsored; he enters on no colloquy, such as the original Adam. Yet he is also too weak to glory in his solipsism, for perhaps at bottom he realizes that it is indeed derivative. Raising echoes, he himself is an echo. Without the strength either to imagine a fit companion or actually summon the embodiment of his desire, his cry trails off into pathos. The humor in "The Most of It" comes from a weak poet figure placing himself in a situation where impossible strength is required, the strength either to persist in one's own delusion and crown it with the honorific "imagination," or to seduce another into sharing one's solitude. Both solipsism and relationship are equally beyond this crier's powers. Unlike the married solitaries in Frost's earlier narrative poems, he generates no dialogue.

The joke played on him from line ten onwards begins with the qualifier "unless" casting doubt over all that follows. There is no doubt as to the event, but only its connection to the solitary's mating call. Is this a response? Does the solitary recognize it as such? If it is a response, then it belongs to that species of oracular answer in which the supplicant gets what he literally asks for, as if to teach him the necessary deviousness of erotic fulfillment.

> And nothing ever came of what he cried
> Unless it was the embodiment that crashed
> In the cliff's talus on the other side,
> And then in the far-distant water splashed,
> But after a time allowed for it to swim,
> Instead of proving human when it neared
> And someone else additional to him,
> As a great buck it powerfully appeared,
> Pushing the crumpled water up ahead,
> And landed pouring like a waterfall,
> And stumbled through the rocks with horny tread,
> And forced the underbrush—and that was all.

The Adamic parody is heightened by the way in which the buck's coming is described. Frost likens it to a heavenly descent appropriate to a messenger from the other side: first the creature crashes, then makes its way from the far-distant shore. And when it finally appears, streaming with power, its emblematic significance is hard to avoid, though Frost Americanizes it as a buck, no royal stag, a rough beast standing for nothing other than its own powerful presence—and that was all. By the end of the poem, the solitary is measured against Adam, the namer, and Orpheus, the tamer, of beasts, but neither name nor music issues from his muted lips. Whatever stature he does achieve comes from this muteness at the close, as he and the reader stand witness to a rugged appearance of original power.

Whereas the opening line of "The Most of It" records a delusion—and a weak delusion at that—the beginning of "Never Again Would Birds' Song Be the Same" presents a central figure (less distinguishable from the poet) capable of recognizing a fable strong and apt enough to inspire belief. Once again, as in "The Most of It," Frost undoes specificity of place; the visionary marker "there," as well as the inclusive "in all the garden round," tells us that we are in the region of no place in particular, the region of Utopia:

> He would declare and could himself believe
> That the birds there in all the garden round
> From having heard the daylong voice of Eve
> Had added to their own an oversound,
> Her tone of meaning but without the words.
> Admittedly an eloquence so soft

Could only have had an influence on birds
When call or laughter carried it aloft.
Be that as may be, she was in their song.
Moreover her voice upon their voices crossed
Had now persisted in the woods so long
That probably it never would be lost.
Never again would bird's song be the same.
And to do that to birds was why she came.

Access to Edenic origin in this poem is not hedged about by fear of dread; the spot is not ringed by a *cordon sanitaire.* Access to the spot proceeds through the corridors of belief. The declaring and believing poet gets there on his own, gets there "himself." One reason for this relaxation of the rigors of original pursuit is that the origin, the garden, lies all around us, if we can only hear it in the overtone of the birds, those mocking generations. These are the self-same birds who heard, not the sad voice of Ruth, but the laughing voice of Eve. After all these birds seem to pattern themselves on Eve's daylong voice; they are not nighttime warblers, darkling singers. The "daylong voice of Eve" goes back to the the sense of day in "Nothing Gold Can Stay," only here the point is precisely that the golden voice of Eve, voice of the golden age, does indeed stay, or persist, in the birds' song about us. The sense of happy mimicry pervading the poem is picked up in the line "Admittedly an eloquence so soft," where Frost's own lines mimic the soft eloquence of Eve—her tone of meaning, but this time with the words. As we repeat the repeating birds, we experience Eve's influence. Here we approach the idea of an originality available through repetition, repetition seen not as curse but as a form of renewal. In line with this emphasis, Frost has little anxiety about the mixing of human and natural orders, little desire to scrutinize the boundaries of contamination. He merely asserts: "she was in their song." There is no effort to separate realms as in Stevens's "The Idea of Order at Key West." Instead, Frost accepts the crossing of voices: "her voice upon their voices crossed." Suspended in the line's final position, "crossed" raises the specter of conflict, as in a crossing of swords, but Frost raises it only to dispel it. He is interested in a creative crossing, a blending, a warp and woof of voice, creating a seamless verbal tapestry.

The nearly hidden ambiguity of "crossed" gets more openly expressed in the way "Never Again" carries elegiac hints only to undo them. The title (especially its first two words) taken alone, seems to indicate loss; the change it augurs appears to be a change for the worse. But the point of the poem is that what we thought was lost has actually persisted—or "probably" has, to use Frost's own qualifier, if only we know how to read that persistence, how to discover its strands of filiation back to the first story. "Persistence" is a virtue Frost also celebrated at the close of "Sitting by a Bush in Broad Sunlight." One of the subtlest ways Frost finds to undo this elegiac impulse comes again by using enjambment to create an undertone. "Moreover her voice upon their voices crossed / Had now persisted in the woods so long," makes us pause at "so long," only to realize as we read on further that the words mean exactly what they say: the phrase does not mean good-by in this context.

"Never Again" tells us that our route back to the garden runs through Eve, not Adam. We follow her verbal trace. Interestingly Frost associates Eve not only with song, which would square with the Miltonic account, but also with eloquence, a faculty more often associated with Adam. According to this song, eloquence is song, song eloquence; we are not in the realm of the oven bird, who learns in singing not to sing. If Adam appears at all in this poem, it may be in the guise of the "He" who inaugurates the fable. This would be Frost's true version of the American Adam—not someone who forges his own discourse as if made new, but a singer who is also a listener, a repeater of the sounds of originality.

The poignance of this poem might also have something to do with the fact that it was written soon after Elinor Frost's death. As Frost wrote in a letter: "she has been the unspoken half of everything I ever wrote." This might explain the terms of Eve's influence as described here [in this] poem. So "Never Again Would Birds' Song Be the Same" can also be read as a kind of elegy to Elinor which turns out in the end not to be an elegy at all, because her sound still persists in the sound of birds: "probably it never would be lost."

IV

From the beginning of "Directive" the movement back toward an earlier time is viewed as a return to simplicity, in the root sense of oneness, that which is not compounded or confused, to draw on the poem's last word. To go back behind—or beyond—confusion is to return to the unity of wholeness. This movement, from the beginning, is seen as a fashioned action—"a time made simple"—and a violent one as well. The simple thing, here at the beginning, is seen not so much as totality, but as a synecdoche, a microcosm. Wholeness is not achieved without the violence of prior fragmentation. And the word "simple" of course carries its negative connotations as well, so that the loss of detail could lead to a damning as well as a saving simplicity, could lead to forgetfulness as much as remembrance. Simplicity here is achieved through the loss of what Frost terms "detail," a word that can be taken in a number of contexts, either as richness or as superfluity. How much of a loss *is* the loss of detail.

And this action of burning, dissolving, breaking off—is it a healing violence, a counter-violence aimed against the wounds of the past? Even before Frost reaches the series of famous paradoxes—"a house that is no more a house . . . "—the poem is riddled with dark sayings about the nature of this regenerative return to the simple past, filled with the poet's sense of the double nature of what he is doing even as he asserts the triumph of the *simplex*, the single thing that can save us.

Despite its emphasis on wholeness and simplicity, "Directive" also has a kind of division built into it in the form of the split between the narrating guide and his audience. "Let us go then, you and I," goes the poem's implicit beginning; and the poem's action needs an auditor, an interpreter, an other, present at the site, to complete its meaning. One of the poem's many open questions is whether or not narrator and auditor merge at the close in the shared gesture of drinking the waters of the source. The offer is certainly made, but whether or not it is accepted depends upon the reaction of the reader-initiate. Equally unclear is whether the narrator drinks. Is he a guide whose mission is to lead others to a sacred spot he himself is barred from knowing? Or has he already tasted the waters? Poetic tradition certainly offers examples of guides, such as Virgil, or the Ancient Mariner, who can save others but not themselves. One way of saving others is to warn them against the sins of the guide, and in this sense it is worth thinking about the narrator's implication in the scene of ruin he brings us to face. For this site in the woods may also be thought of as a scene of the crime. Indeed, if the allusion to St. Mark's cryptic passage points to the necessity of interpreting parables, then surely one of the poem's prime riddles is what connection can this speaker have to this landscape. To leave the house as merely a generalized example of human decay would seem to solve the riddle too quickly. Why does this speaker take us here? Why is he the only survivor of this house? Where is everyone else? Without joining the biographical debate over Frost's character, I find it perplexing that commentators have not called attention to the ruin of Frost's own "house" in treating the site of "Directive." The grim line "This was no playhouse but a house in earnest" seems to lose all resonance otherwise. Here we have "Home Burial" carried to the extreme: the home, "now slowly closing like a dent in dough," is being buried before our eyes.

Indeed, Frost inscribes himself upon the landscape through a favorite trick: ringing changes on his own name. The spirit of this place is "an enormous Glacier"—'Frost' writ large:

> You must not mind a certain coolness from him
> Still said to haunt this side of Panther Mountain.

As Stevens put it, "Cold is our element," and for Frost there is a kind of mystic attunement, a baptismal bond, between his own name and the waters he calls "Cold as a spring as yet so near its source." To introduce another metaphor, the difficult return to the site resembles the salmon's swim upstream, back to its spawning grounds and its death. Return to the origin can thus itself become the sign of death, death conceived not as alienation but as recognition. Here, the return merges with the great theme of the *nostos*.

As Allen Grossman has pointed out in an essay on Hart Crane and the question of origins, there are two great archetypes of the *nostos* motif:

One is the return to the remembered place (like Odysseus' return to Ithaka); the other is the return to the unremembered place of origins (like Socrates' return to the Idea, or Shelley's "Die, / If thou woulds't be with that which thou dost seek!" The return to the remembered place through the good use of time leads to an enhancement of the mortal self, involving an internalization by the voyager of his own past and then its revalidation in the external world (recovery of Ithaka and remarriage with Penelope). The return to the unremembered place is by contrast sacrificial, requiring and justifying the destruction of time and the self at home in it.

Part of the difficulty posed by "Directive" is the way it seems equally poised between the remembered and the unremembered place. The poem is clearly a journey homeward, but to home as remembered place, or to the home that never was? In this sense the real paradox would run: "There is a house that never was a house." The medicinal or healing drink offered at the end of the poem does not appear to cure the wounds of time within time, for the fragmented debris of the past can never be made whole again. The dishes remain shattered, the grail broken, the house slowly closing. These wounds receive the purgatorial waters of tears, not the purifying waters of origin: "Weep for what little things could make them glad. / Then for the house that is no more a house." Nor does it appear that a return is possible to the mortal world. It is more a question of returning to the Idea that underlies the temporal house, the idea of the pure stream of the origin, "A brook that was the water of the house." Before one calls this the waters of life, it should be noted that the house fed by this brook is now a ghost house. Indeed, the kind of cold Frost associates with the brook has its correlative in poets such as Stevens and Bishop, where it is a kind of deathly cold, an inhuman cold, a cold inhospitable to human life. There is the cold of "The Snow Man.": "One must have a mind of winter . . . And have been cold a long time." And there is the frigid water of Bishop's "At the Fishouses": "Cold dark deep and absolutely clear, / èlement bearable to no mortal." For Bishop, one reason the water is "bearable to no mortal" has to do with the fact that it is *absolutely* clear. She means that adverb with dead seriousness. This absoluteness also underscores the danger of the cold in "The Snow Man" and, I would argue, in "Directive" as well, where absolution is achieved only by contact with the absolute, that which Frost describes as "Too lofty and original to rage." But such absolution signifies death as well as life. Within the Christian matrix of paradoxes, we can accept the idea of dying to the world only to live in a transcendent sphere, but does "Directive" sustain such faith? Though the poem is filled with parodic Christian symbolism, best detailed by Marie Borroff, it remains, as Borroff herself writes: "not Christian . . . the revelation the poem brings is moral rather than supernatural." Yet this is a hard morality indeed, hard on others, hard on the self.

The question of the poem's allusions to New Testament doctrine culminates, of course, in the reference to the passage in Mark on the role of parable:

> And he said unto them, Unto you it is given to know the mystery of the kingdom of God: but unto them that are without, all these things are done in parables:
>   That seeing they may see, and not perceive; and hearing they may hear, and not understand; lest at any time they should be converted, and their sins should be forgiven them.

Frank Kermode's *The Genesis of Secrecy* takes this passage from Mark as adumbrating the essential condition of interpretive communities:

> In this tradition insiders can hope to achieve correct interpretation, though their hope may be frequently, perhaps always, disappointed; whereas those outside cannot. There is seeing and hearing, which are what naive listeners and readers do; and there is perceiving and understanding, which are in principle reserved to an elect.

It is perhaps this seemingly smug courting of the fit audience, though few, that leads Poirier to complain that the poem's ironies are "consequential" only to those "who have enclosed themselves within the circuit of Frost's own work." There are few other instances of such direct allusion in Frost's poetry, so we have little precedent for how to read such open quotation in his work. "Out, Out—"represents another example and I think interpetation of that poem has suffered for critics taking the allusion with too little sense of its dialectical complexities. The passage from Mark is notoriously "dark" itself and would thus be a strange example to choose in the hope of stabilizing one's meaning. The phrasing of "as Saint Mark says they mustn't," with its prissy tone of smug election, serves to mock rather than enforce any easy distinction between elect and outcast, insider and outsider. And when Frost talks about the "wrong ones," nothing in the poem would lend itself to taking "wrong" as a moral category. After all, the notion of right and wrong is considerably complicated by the fact that the narrator admits to having stolen the goblet.

Poirier asks the crucial question of whether it is *good* to get beyond confusion and surely the answer to this question—if answer is the appropriate response—determines whether one accepts the offered potion. To be "whole" is to return to the unremembered place of origins; it stands in opposition to the remembered place, the slowly closing "hole" of the natural landscape. Such wholeness seems a kind of self-healing, though it cannot reconstitute the ruinous fragments of history or of the self's actions in history. Surveying it own past, the self may stand confused, but this is at least a sign of moral sentience.

The final line of "Directive" will always seem to tear free from context, for what does its action describe if not an escape from the confinement of context and all its confusions? To be untouched by confusion must mean that one is untouched by life and indeed there seems no possibility of return after drinking the potion. Or, if return is possible, it may only be at the cost of becoming confused again. We remain whole only so long as we remain in this spot. Frost brings us to a point where origin and end merge and the story ceases. So does representation: Frost can only call the spring "cold." He has deliberately elided the Keatsian phantasia of the Nightingale Ode, whose magic potion is the wellspring of a gorgeous chain of romance associations, culled from the region of the "warm South," a region not native to Keats and certainly not to Frost. The draught of Keatsian vintage inspires a chain of figurations, whereas Frost's chills language. Keats's flight takes him far away, Frost's to earthward.

For Frost, the enemy of imagination seems to be "confusion," the loss of self in a proliferation of motives, deeds, and events that carry one far from both the remembered place (the home) and the unremembered place of origin. But return to that place of fabricated wholeness can also destroy the imagination. Confronted with the evidence of his actions, the ruins of his historical house, the poet might indeed have given himself up to that "rage" (etymologically, "madness") which it is the presumed power of the spring to cure. As it is, the poem shows Frost succumbing neither to madness nor to radical cure: the cup is suspended, the spring as yet but "so near" its source. This saving distance from the source is also a form of salvation: the necessary scepticism that keeps one from drowning in one's own fiction.

Stevens's *An Ordinary Evening in New Haven*

Harold Bloom

The poet who writes *An Ordinary Evening in New Haven* is about to turn seventy, but as a poet he is never less desiccated or leafless. Nothing else by Stevens is more exuberant or extravagant than this second longest and most indirect of all his poems. Yet even the indirection is Whitmanian and exhibits a passion for yes that could not be broken.

Stevens sanctioned the shorter, eleven-section original version of *An Ordinary Evening* by including it in his carefully chosen British *Select Poems*. I will take as text here the definitive, thirty-one-section poem, which scrambles the continuity of the final three sections with poetically happy results, and I will introduce comparisons with the original sequence when I approach the poem's conclusion. But I will note which sections were part of the original as I go, for structural reasons which should become apparent.

I am going to assert more for *An Ordinary Evening* than criticism as yet allows it, and so I will begin by giving something of the contrary case. By this, I do not intend the merely ignorant hostility of many negative critics of the poem, but rather its very best expositor, Helen Vendler, for whom the poem is strong only where she judges it to be a portrayal of desiccation, of an old man's most deliberately minimal visions. The critic, though I judge her to be mistaken here, is formidably eloquent:

> In this, the harshest of all his experiments, Stevens deprives his poetry of all that the flesh, the sun, the earth, and the moon can offer, and, himself a skeleton, examines the bare possibilities of a skeletal life. . . . It is, humanly speaking, the saddest of all Stevens' poems. One wants it to have succeeded totally, to have proved

From *Wallace Stevens: The Poems of Our Climate.* © 1976 by Cornell University. Cornell University Press, 1976.

that Stevens could find in life's most minimal offering, something which would suffice. . . . *An Ordinary Evening* is, in short, almost unremittingly minimal, and over and over again threatens to die of its own starvation.

I myself, as I read *An Ordinary Evening*, encounter a very different poem from the one just described. There is much harshness, yes, but a great deal also that is rather more genial than is usual in Stevens. There is some deprivation, and yet the flesh, the sun, the earth, and the moon are all there, and so are a surprising vigor and joy. The poem I read is threatened not by its own starvation but by its own copiousness, its abundance of invention that varies the one theme, which is the problematic Stevensian image that he unhelpfully always called "reality." Critics can diverge absolutely on this poem because the text is almost impossible to read, that is the text keeps seeking "reality" while continually putting into question its own apotheosis of "reality." Stevens said of the poem: "Here my interest is to try to get as close to the ordinary, the commonplace and the ugly as it is possible for a poet to get. It is not a question of grim reality but of plain reality." We can observe that this intention is wholly Whitmanian, and on that basis we might doubt Vendler's judgment that the celebrated title is polemic. "Ordinary" here seems to mean "true" or at least "not false," but true in the root sense of "ordinary," *ar* or "fitted together." New Haven is simply any city that is not home, a city that unsettles the self just enough so that it is startled into meditation, but close enough to home so that the meditation keeps contact always with the commonplace.

Kermode usefully points to the prose first section of *Three Academic Pieces* for a sentence that illuminates Stevens's intentions: "What our eyes behold may well be the text of life but one's meditations on the text and the disclosures of these meditations are no less a part of the structure of reality." But that leaves us with the word "reality" in Stevens, a word I wish Stevens had renounced, since it takes away more meaning than it tends to give. He was addicted to it in prose; he used some form of it well over a hundred times in his poetry, and it appears in thirteen different sections of *An Ordinary Evening*. The best attempt to reduce it to order is made by Frank Doggett in his useful book *Stevens' Poetry of Thought:*

> *Reality,* in Stevens' use of the word, may be the world supposed to be antecedent in itself or the world created in the specific occurrence of thought, including the thinker himself and his mind forming the thought. Often the term offers the assumption that if the self is the central point of a circle of infinite radius, then reality is the not-self, including all except the abstract subjective center. Sometimes *reality* is used in the context of the nominalist position— then the word denotes that which is actual and stands as a phenomenal identity, the existent as opposed to the merely fancied. Stevens usually means by *reality* an undetermined base on which

a mind constructs its personal sense of the world. Occasionally he will use the word *real* as a term of approval, as a substitute for the word *true*, and, therefore, no more than an expression of confidence.

All of these meanings of "reality" occur in *An Ordinary Evening*. The commonest is the Emersonian one in which reality is the not-self, or as Emerson said, Nature or the Not-Me, including one's own body, other selves, the external world, and the anteriority of art. That leaves only one's own mind or imagination to set against a reality that comprehends all otherness, in a dialectical struggle without a victory.

An Ordinary Evening begins, "The eye's plain version is a thing apart" and ends with the premise that reality, rather than being a solid, "may be a shade that traverses / A dust, a force that traverses a shade." The eye's plain version *is* the First Idea as an imagined thing, abstracted, "a thing apart," and like reality this plain version is force, shade, dust, and so a palpable crossing into an impalpable. "Crossing" is of the essence, because "traverses" means "crosses." Force or a trope of Power crosses shade or the residuum of the Freedom of meaning, and shade crosses dust or a trope of Fate. Reality or the eye's plain version thus turns out to be only a crossing between turnings, a continual troping in, through, and with the eye. Haunting *An Ordinary Evening*, as Vendler demonstrates, are three ancestral versions of the eye: Keats's bright star, Milton's universal blank, and Emerson's transparent eyeball. All these return us ultimately to the *res* or thing that is close to the root of reality, that root being *rei*, meaning "possession." "Plain" for Stevens also goes to the root, to flat, clear vision of what is spread out before us, as in the 1952 poem "The Plain Sense of Things":

> After the leaves have fallen, we return
> To a plain sense of things. It is as if
> We had come to an end of the imagination,
> Inanimate in an inert savoir.
>
> It is difficult even to choose the adjective
> For this blank cold, this sadness without cause.
> The great structure has become a minor house.
> No turban walks across the lessened floors.
>
> The greenhouse never so badly needed paint.
> The chimney is fifty years old and slants to one side.
> A fantastic effort has failed, a repetition
> In a repetitiousness of men and flies.
>
> Yet the absence of the imagination had
> Itself to be imagined. The great pond,
> The plain sense of it, without reflection, leaves,
> Mud, water like dirty glass, expressing silence

> Of a sort, silence of a rat come out to see,
> The great pond and its waste of the lilies, all this
> Had to be imagined as an inevitable knowledge,
> Required, as a necessity requires.

A total leaflessness returns us to a plain sense of things, yet at first this plainness is not ordinary. That is, it does not help fit things together. The "blank cold" seems to defy imagination, and yet is shown to be itself an imagining, though not yet a reimagining. That "a fantastic effort has failed" hardly can be an indictment of nature, but refers back to *Blue Guitar*, 11, where repetition is a nightmare: "The fields entrap the children, brick / Is a weed and all the flies are caught."

The difference is in the vision of Ananke, if not quite of a Beautiful Necessity, since Stevens considers his reduction to a First Idea as an inevitable knowledge: "Yet the absence of the imagination had / Itself to be imagined." What "The Plain Sense of Things" omits is a reimagining; for Stevens in his early seventies, to live with the First Idea alone was no longer wholly dehumanizing.

An Ordinary Evening opens with a five-canto meditation upon just such a plain sense of things, culminating in canto 5 with an Emersonian vision of the fall of the self. Cantos 2 through 5 are all organized as commentaries upon canto 1, which suggest the curious, genetic principle of structure in the longer, thirty-one-canto version of *An Ordinary Evening*. All of the twenty cantos added to the later version are in support of, or in apposition to, the eleven cantos of the shorter version. Since the shorter version itself followed the characteristic image patterns of the post-Wordsworthian crisis-poem, the two can be mapped together, with some revealing emphasis. Here are the poem's divisions, in the longer version, with the first canto in each group occupying also its position in the original sequence, except at the end:

1. 1–5
2. 6–8
3. 9–10
4. 11
5. 12–15
6. 16–21
7. 22–27
8. 28
9. 30
10. 31
11. 29

In the original eleven-canto poem, cantos 5–7 are a unit, and 7–11 are another. Indeed, the same division prevails in the longer version, which thus falls into the familiar patterns of the post-Romantic crisis-poem:

Clinamen	1–5
Tessera	6–8
Kenosis	9–10
Daemonization	11
Askesis	12–27
Apophrades	28–31

It will be observed that, in the poem's amplification, its movement of metaphoric sublimation, the *askesis* of the original cantos 5–7, was elaborated into cantos 12–27; or sixteen out of thirty-one cantos, more than half the poem. This accounts for that curious impression of "total leaflessness," as Stevens endlessly elaborates, usually by apposition, a brilliant series of images that substitute for his poem's central trope, "the eye's plain version" that begins it, in a swerve initially away from Emerson. The epigraph to *An Ordinary Evening* might well have been from the first paragraph of Emerson's "Circles," an essay that could have been called "Freedom" or "Wildness":

> The eye is the first circle; the horizon which it forms is the second; and throughout nature this primary figure is repeated without end. . . . Our life is an apprenticeship to the truth that around every circle another can be drawn; that there is no end in nature, but every end is a beginning; that there is always another dawn risen on mid-noon, and under every deep a lower deep opens.

Emerson genially undoes, in that closing trope, the Miltonic, tragic moral of Satan's self-realization on Mt. Niphates. An American Satan merely discovers, "There are no fixtures in nature. The universe is fluid and volatile." Emerson's nature is, as we will see, Stevens's "reality," and the fitting together on an ordinary evening in an ordinary city of the different degrees of reality will expose a volatile interplay of ocular circles. So, at the start, the thing apart or abstracted is again the First Idea as an imagined thing, the perceptual language of experience. "Experience" is as central and as precise a term here as it is in Emerson. The root of "experience," *per*, means "risk," and Stevens like Emerson had used "experience" as a mode opposed to the higher activity of perception. "Poem Written at Morning," in *Parts of a World*, insists, "The truth must be / That you do not see, you experience, you feel," and "Description without Place" had set description as a revelation by seeing against "the experience of sun / And moon." The late poem "Recitation after Dinner" was to venture a final definition of experience:

> Is it experience, say, the final form
> To which all other forms, at last, return,
> The frame of a repeated effect, is it that?

An Ordinary Evening labors to bring experience and seeing together, but inevitably they keep parting, and Stevens will opt for the priority and necessity of seeing even what you cannot hope to feel, whether ever or ever again. But he knows his own preferences from the start, and these are the "an and yet, and yet, and yet" that parodistically start off his poem, genially mocking his own incessant self-qualifications. Where "experience" risks the beginnings of thought as an activity of testing, "description" attempts an image-thinking that cannot be bounded by the otherness of "reality." Freud had remarked that it was an error to apply the standards of "reality" to repressed psychical structures, and we can note that everything Stevens sees in *An Ordinary Evening* inhabits the same universe as such structures. This means that "the never-ending meditation" is not "experience" but rather the process of Stevens's writing, which asks the question that reduces to the First Idea and its thinker, the giant; the question being how to begin perceiving the inconceivable idea of the sun. The second giant that kills the first is once again the reimagining of any single First Idea, and the similitude suggested by that idea invokes a familiar compound ghost in Stevens's poetry:

> Much like a new resemblance of the sun,
> Down-pouring, up-springing and inevitable,
> A larger poem for a larger audience,
>
> As if the crude collops came together as one,
> A mythological form, a festival sphere,
> A great bosom, beard and being, alive with age.

It was Whitman's ambitious dream, in particular, to write "a larger poem for a larger audience," and the "festival sphere" or eye as first circle is Whitman-as-Jehovah, the paternal affirming, farewell-saying figure throughout Stevens. Yet this is not Whitman or any man, because the collops or crude rolls of flesh are being fitted together as myth, and Stevens's own ambivalence is conveyed by the adjective "festival," though the Transcendental image of spheral man or human globe is scarcely qualified by Stevensian anxiety. Nor are anxieties emphasized in the cantos of commentary that follow the originary text of this canto. In canto 2, Stevens internalizes New Haven as a visionary city, impalpable as we are impalpable, because we live in the mind. New Haven too is half sun, half mind, as much poem, or trope as it is anything else, if only imagined but imagined well. So dialectical is this canto that the reader can judge no longer whether New Haven is an image of total presence or of total absence, and a curiously complex irony is developed as Stevens exploits a synesthesia of the spirit: "impalpable town," "impalpable bells," "transparencies of sound," "transparent dwellings" "impalpable habitations," "seem to move," "obscure," "uncertain," "indefinite, confused illuminations and sonorities," "cannot tell apart." Presumably, these all are part of "the hum of thoughts evaded in the mind," part of a dilemma that is "so much ourselves." The dilemma is neither philosophic nor psychological, though it can be mistaken for both. Most simply, it is a need for poetry that cannot be satisfied by poetry whether written or to-be-written. This is Stevensian "poverty" or "misery," too rich in desire to be gratified by fulfillment, too imaginative in need to be redressed by imagination. No attitude toward poetry could be more American or more Emersonian, more hopeful or more frustrating. "The misery of man is to be balked of the sight of essence and stuffed with conjectures," said Emerson cheerfully, as he proceeded to deplore "the coldness and poverty of our view of heaven," while dialectically humming, "Dependence is the only poverty." Stevens puts his earlier version of this best in "Poetry Is a Destructive Force": "That's what misery is, / Nothing to have at heart. / It is to have or nothing." His definitive meditation upon "misery" and "poverty" is "In a Bad Time," written the year after *The Auroras of Autumn*, and a year before *An Ordinary Evening*, and constituting a powerful commentary upon both major long poems:

> How mad would he have to be to say, "He beheld
> An order and thereafter he belonged
> To it"? He beheld the order of the northern sky.
>
> But the beggar gazes on calamity
> And thereafter he belongs to it, to bread
> Hard found, and water tasting of misery.
>
> For him cold's glacial beauty is his fate.
> Without understanding, he belongs to it
> And the night, and midnight, and after, where it is.
>
> What has he? What he has he has. But what?
> It is not a question of captious repartee.
> What has he that becomes his heart's strong core?
>
> He has his poverty and nothing more.
> His poverty becomes his heart's strong core—
> A forgetfulness of summer at the pole.
>
> Sordid Melpomene, why strut bare boards,
> Without scenery or lights in the theatre's bricks,
> Dressed high in heliotrope's inconstant hue,
>
> The muse of misery? Speak loftier lines.
> Cry out, "I am the purple muse." Make sure
> The audience beholds you, not your gown.

The order of the northern sky initially was Sublime terror and then was transformed into innocence in *The Auroras of Autumn*, an innocence close to a poverty that "becomes his heart's strong core." Theatre, for Stevens always a negative image, belongs here to a sordid muse of tragedy, akin to Coleridge's wind in "Dejection: An Ode," which is addressed as an actor rather too close to perfection in all tragic sounds. Stevens ends "In a Bad Time" by advising Melpomene to be more like Hoon, which means that she too must find herself more truly and more strange. This attitude informs the difficult canto 3 of *An Ordinary Evening*, which returns "desire" to its root meaning of "longing for by shining forth," *sweid*, and so can locate it "deep in the eye, / Behind all actual seeing." This is desire transcending the world of Keats's Grecian Urn, for this emptiness and denial are only potentially a porcelain, being still in the state of the bats or lumps of clay out of which the artifact is to be formed.

A crucial image of voice, the savage cry of a savage assuagement, rises in canto 4, as another commentary upon the plainness of plain things or the achieved abstraction of a First Idea. Like so many fierce cries in Stevens, this goes back to Whitman's ocean crying for its castaways and suggests something of the cost of poetic incarnation. Canto 4 begins as ironic comedy, with Stevens himself as the "man who has fought / Against illusion and was." "Illusion" here is the pathetic fallacy, and "was" is time's "it was" against which Nietzsche urged the will's revenge. The cry, as a "mating of surprised accords," undoes the pain of the seasonal cycle, rendering the reduction of cold into a similitude of "a sheen of heat romanticized." Again, we have an argument against illusion conveyed in the *illusio* of irony, as the supposedly plain version of the eye turns out to be a wholly visionary or Transcendental circle. This irony emerges overtly in canto 5, to conclude the poem's first movement. Reality or the Not-Me is itself found to be "inescapable romance, inescapable choice / Of dreams." Stevens resumes the self-mockery of *Auroras*, 5, when he brings his chant of the inauthentic to its pitch by declaiming, "Everything as unreal as real can be, / In the inexquisite eye," a long fall from having been the nomad exquisite of *Harmonium*. A precisely Emersonian fall of the self is then recorded, albeit with considerable gusto:

> Why, then, inquire
> Who has divided the world, what entrepreneur?
> No man. The self, the chrysalis of all men
>
> Became divided in the leisure of blue day
> And more, in branchings after day. One part
> Held fast tenaciously in common earth
>
> And from central earth to central sky
> And in moonlit extensions of them in the mind
> Searched out such majesty as it could find.

There is no better description in Stevens's poetry of his characteristic dualism and of his precise variety of self-consciousness. The poetry of earth is only one part of him; the Transcendental searcher is after all the more dominant part. What has the eye's plain version to do with this questing after majesty, with these moonlit extensions? I read Stevens as answering such a question himself, by the disjunction between cantos 1–5 and 6–8. Canto 6, the second section of the poem's original, short version, presents a fable of naked Alpha, the ever-early candor, and the hierophant Omega, the late plural. When we pass from "searched out such majesty as it could find" to "Reality is the beginning not the end," we negotiate, with Stevens, a Crossing of Election, another testing of his poethood. Canto 6 shows a fresh triumph in such a crossing:

> Reality is the beginning not the end,
> Naked Alpha, not the hierophant Omega,
> Of dense investiture, with luminous vassals.
>
> It is the infant A standing on infant legs,
> Not twisted, stooping, polymathic Z,
> He that kneels always on the edge of space
>
> In the pallid perceptions of its distances.
> Alpha fears men or else Omega's men
> Or else his prolongations of the human.
>
> These characters are around us in the scene.
> For one it is enough; for one it is not;
> For neither is it profound absentia,
>
> Since both alike appoint themselves the choice
> Custodians of the glory of the scene,
> The immaculate interpreters of life.
>
> But that's the difference: in the end and the way
> To the end. Alpha continues to begin.
> Omega is refreshed at every end.

So inspired is this synecdochal representation that at first we may miss the sense in which Stevens turns against himself here, though the two cantos 7 and 8, added as commentary, clarify the compensating sorrows that pay for this poetic election. Naked Alpha or the infant A is the reduction of the Not-Me, of reality as an otherness. The aged Z occupies the position that the palm at the end of the mind holds in Stevens's death-poem "Of Mere Being," at the edge of space, beyond the last thought, and therefore can be called the final reimagining of all First Ideas. We live with both "characters," beginnings and ends of alphabets, and we depend upon both, and though Stevens seems to insist upon the difference between them there now seems less distinction between abstraction or Alpha and reimagining or Omega than ever before. To continue to begin is to be refreshed at every end, which means that reality as Alpha does the same work for us that the finished fiction of the self does as Omega. A variation occurs in canto 7, where the chapels and schools of New Haven, the visible towers of Yale, play the role of Omega, redressing the poverty or imaginative need of their makers but also of Stevens as spectator, the poet as Alpha or representative of reality. New Haven as vision of Omega or the incredible ends by becoming again the credible day of the eye's plain version.

More interesting is the variation of canto 8, where Stevens descends out of his hotel onto the streets of New Haven, and finds his love of the real leading him to "the syllable / Of recognition, avowal, impassioned cry, / The cry that contains its converse in itself." This cry is a recognition of origins, here "the origin of a mother tongue," and should arouse in the reader a recognition of how prevalent and central in Stevens such a cry is, taking him back to Whitman's fierce old mother, the sea, crying out in the night for her sons, the poets, who have been cast away from her, who have fallen down into the occasions that are the cries of their poems.

A new movement, this time of undoing or emptying out of the poetic self, begins in canto 9 and receives its commentary in canto 10. In 9, the third canto of the original poem, Stevens returns to the hotel as the real to seek "the poem of pure reality, untouched / By trope or deviation," which is necessarily not a poem at all but rather New Haven as seen through the Emersonian transparent eyeball, "the eye made clear of uncertainty, with the sight / Of simple seeing, without reflection." Where the Emersonian epiphany is invoked, we can expect high vision to follow:

> We seek
> Nothing beyond reality. Within it
>
> Everything, the spirit's alchemicana
> Included, the spirit that goes roundabout
> And through included, not merely the visible,
>
> The solid, but the movable, the moment,
> The coming on of feasts and the habits of saints,
> The pattern of the heavens and high, night air.

Some critics have deplored this vision as not being Stevens's own, or at least as not being the authentic speech of his own self. Yet the passage is the purest Stevens, though this is the central Whitmanian strain in Stevens. It is the poet of "Song of Myself" who keeps going "roundabout / And through," and who is likely to see visions in the high, night air. Stevens qualifies, as elsewhere, by stressing the moment-to-moment, glimpsing nature of his vision, and also by stressing that what he seeks is part of "the coming on" and not part of what already is. But, most of all, this is not poetry, not "of the hymns / That fall upon it out of the wind." By going "straight to the transfixing object," Stevens is destroying the only language in which poems can be written. The commentary on this metonymic rejection of poetry comes in canto 10, where the drive "straight . . . to the object / At the exactest point at which it is itself" is severely qualified by the admission "We do not know what is real and what is not." But this is then shown to be a saving ignorance, part of living in change, which is repetition as the fulfillment of expectations, spoken of as "this faithfulness of reality." The rejection of a poetry of language for the poem of pure reality is itself partly undone by Stevens's praise for a mode of being, the joyous acceptance of change, that makes "gay the hallucinations in surfaces." It does not matter if they are hallucinations, particularly since the crossing to the poem's next movement juxtaposes "Make gay the hallucinations in surfaces" with "In the metaphysical streets of the physical town." This is a disjunction that does the work of a Crossing of Solipsism, as Stevens mounts into a very Emersonian version of the American Sublime:

> In the metaphysical streets of the physical town
> We remember the lion of Juda and we save
> The phrase . . . Say of each lion of the spirit
>
> It is a cat of sleek transparency
> That shines with a nocturnal shine alone.
> The great cat must stand potent in the sun.
>
> The phrase grows weak. The fact takes up the strength
> Of the phrase. It contrives the self-same evocations
> And Juda becomes New Haven or else must.
>
> In the metaphysical streets, the profoundest forms
> Go with the walker subtly walking there.
> These he destroys with wafts of wakening,
>
> Free from their majesty and yet in need
> Of majesty, of an invincible clou,
> A minimum of making in the mind,
>
> A verity of the most veracious men,
> The propounding of four seasons and twelve months,
> The brilliancy at the central of the earth.

Except for the poem's final four cantos, this fourth canto of the shorter version is the only one upon which Stevens wrote no commentary in the form of interpolated cantos. No qualification or expansion seemed possible because of the strength of this lyric. The lion, here as elsewhere in Stevens an emblem of the power and menace of poetry, enters as the traditional phrase "the lion of Juda" and is then converted into each or any lion of the spirit, Transcendentalist in its imagery:

> Say of each lion of the spirit
>
> It is a cat of a sleek transparency
> That shines with a nocturnal shine alone.

Though this is metaphysical, high and bright, it is in the physical town that mere being centers itself: "the great cat must stand potent in the sun." The fact takes up the phrase's strength, or rather the phrase alters itself to "the lion of New Haven," so that the lion of the spirit participates also in the being of fact. Stevens, the subtle walker in New Haven's metaphysical streets, is accompanied by the profoundest forms of lions as he goes. Any waft of wakening can destroy these irrealities, and yet Stevens needs them as evidences of the majesty of poetry. The invincible *clou*, the peg or point of greatest interest for Stevens, is still a point of brightest origin in a logocentric universe of discourse. Stevens acquires daemonic or Sublime force as he mounts into the hyperboles he insists are for him the given: a Gnostic, Emersonian uncreated element or "minimum of making in the mind" and an attendant truth founded upon the seasonal cycle and the earth's central splendor. The strength of repression in Stevens here is awesome, yet it is the menace of the lions that is being repressed when the poet too easily says that he is free from their majesty.

It is vital to any interpretation of *An Ordinary Evening* that the reader consider how extraordinary an elaboration Stevens made of cantos 5–7 of the original version, which in the final text become cantos 12, 15, and 22. With the cantos written as commentary upon them, these form now the long movement 12 through 22. This dominant movement is the most protracted and ambitious development, in all of Stevens's poetry, of the revisionary ratio I have called *askesis*. The huge curtailment or limitation of meanings centers upon two Shelleyan metaphors: the fiction of the leaves in cantos 12 and 16, and the image of the evening star in canto 22. The movement is through three phases of an ascetic reduction of the image-making power, from "leaves . . . resembling the presence of thought" on to "the total leaflessness" and then at last to the internalization of the star so that, like desire, "it shines / From the sleepy bosom of the real."

Stevens begins this movement of self-deconstruction with one of his major triumphs or central poems, another revision of the "Ode to the West Wind," the eloquent cry of canto 12:

> The poem is the cry of its occasion,
> Part of the res itself and not about it.
> The poet speaks the poem as it is,
>
> Not as it was: part of the reverberation
> Of a windy night as it is, when the marble statues
> Are like newspapers blown by the wind. He speaks
>
> By sight and insight as they are. There is no
> Tomorrow for him. The wind will have passed by,
> The statues will have gone back to be things about.
>
> The mobile and the immobile flickering
> In the area between is and was are leaves,
> Leaves burnished in autumnal burnished trees
>
> And leaves in whirlings in the gutters, whirlings
> Around and away, resembling the presence of thought,
> Resembling the presences of thoughts, as if,

> In the end, in the whole psychology, the self,
> The town, the weather, in a casual litter,
> Together, said words of the world are the life of the world.

An occasion is an event or happening, but its etymological meaning is a falling down, and its Indo-European root means falling *or* dying. To be the cry of fallen leaves is to be a cry in the etymological sense of crying out or imploring the aid of one's fellow citizens ("cry" is from the Latin *quiritare*, in turn from *quiris* for a Roman citizen). A poem is a cadence, and so etymologically a dying fall, as when in *Credences of Summer*, 8, the poem's "resounding cry / Is like ten thousand tumblers tumbling down." In what had been the next canto of the shorter version, now canto 16, Stevens associates himself as his poem's speaker with the occasion as a falling into or near death: "The venerable mask, / In this perfection, occasionally speaks / And something of death's poverty is heard." Here, in canto 12, the poem as deathly cry is "part of the res itself and not about it," which means that the thing itself is death or the reality principle. Speaking the poem as it is, not as it was, is to speak the poem as part of the reverberation of a night when the wind, more even than in *The Auroras of Autumn,* is blowing one toward destruction, as indeed it did in Shelley's "Ode." "Reverberation" is a peculiarly rich word for and in Stevens, meaning not only a re-echoing or resounding (etymologically a relashing, as of a whip) but also a re-wording or reverbalization, here of Shelley, but also of earlier Stevens. "Man and Bottle" had featured the realization that "the poem lashes more fiercely than the wind," that is, the poem reverberated more in the fierce mode of the maternal sea than even the Shelleyan wind rebounded against Stevens's precursor. Two cantos on, in 14, "reverberation" receives Stevens's own commentary when "the point of reverberation" is identified as "not grim / Reality but reality grimly seen / And spoken in paradisal parlance new." Reverberation that is a grim seeing of the reality principle is now precisely the Stevensian *askesis,* but by no means the final resting point of his vision, even in canto 12 of this poem.

In the present that is more absence than presence, Stevens locates his poem or fiction of the leaves "in the area between is and was." The trope is exactly Shelley's "my dead thoughts . . . like withered leaves," and the occasion is not wholly dissimilar: "What if my leaves are falling like its own!" Nor are the conclusions fundamentally different, though Shelley even in despair is a prophet, and Stevens merely meditates upon loss and gain. Shelley also "said words of the world are the life of the world," though the Shelleyan hope for "a new birth" was not to be Stevens's until the final phase, when it emerges in "A Discovery of Thought" and some related lyrics.

Cantos 13–15 scarcely come near the achievement of 12, but they do illuminate it, as is their function. Stevens himself is the solitary ephebe of 13, defining his enterprise in terms taken from his anti-Eliotic lyric, "The

Creations of Sound." Professor Eucalyptus, the Canon Aspirin of New
Haven, makes his first entrance in 14 as a parody of Stevens, not so much
mocking the quest for reality as repeating it in a coarser tone. But canto 15
raises Eucalyptus to a first glory and implicitly reveals why the Yale Professor of Metaphysics has received the name of so aromatic a tree. The
flowering leaf of the eucalyptus is a well-covered flower until it opens,
hence the tree's name from the Greek for "covered" or "hidden." One of
Stevens's early "Primordia" poems thirty years before had spoken of a

> Compilation of the effects
> Of magenta blooming in the Judas-tree
> And of purple blooming in the eucalyptus—
> Map of yesterday's earth
> And of tomorrow's heaven.

Professor Eucalyptus is himself a mapper of yesterday's earth and tomorrow's heaven:

> The instinct for heaven had its counterpart:
> The instinct for earth, for New Haven, for his room,
> The gay tournamonde as of a single world
>
> In which he is and as and is are one.

Either Stevens remembered "Primordia" across thirty years, or else we
have yet another instance of the uncanny persistence of his work. "Tournamonde" is his own coinage, of which he said, "For me it creates an image
of a world in which things revolve and the word is therefore appropriate
in the collocation of is and as." We can say that "tournamonde" is an
economical equivalent of the Nietzschean motive for metaphor: "The desire
to be different, to be elsewhere." Professor Eucalyptus merges into Stevens
as the meditation attains a majesty of fresh desire, as much a part of this
poem as is any vision of a reality principle:

> The hibernal dark that hung
> In primavera, the shadow of bare rock,
>
> Becomes the rock of autumn, glittering,
> Ponderable source of each imponderable,
> The weight we lift with the finger of a dream,
>
> The heaviness we lighten by light will,
> By the hand of desire, faint, sensitive, the soft
> Touch and trouble of the touch of the actual hand.

This hushed eros, so little credited to Stevens, is wholly characteristic of
him. Though the image here is of a world in which things revolve, Stevens
subtly sublimates the summer of that revolution, as the passage goes from
wintry dark hanging in early spring, or bare rock, to glittering rock of

autumn. Summer would be too imponderable a source, as *Credences of Summer* had shown its poet, who nevertheless remained uniquely grateful for that poem and who echoes it again in canto 17. Too large for the somewhat sublimated desires of this poem, summer by its absence qualifies this final commentary upon the ways in which "words of the world are the life of the world."

Canto 16, originally 7, begins another submovement of Stevens's triple *askesis*, setting the image of "the total leaflessness" against the fiction of the leaves. Though I will dispute an aspect of Helen Vendler's interpretation of canto 16, like her I am moved by its expressive power, astonishing even for Stevens:

> Among time's images, there is not one
> Of this present, the venerable mask above
> The dilapidation of dilapidations.
>
> The oldest-newest day is the newest alone.
> The oldest-newest night does not creak by,
> With lanterns, like a celestial ancientness.
>
> Silently it heaves its youthful sleep from the sea—
> The Oklahoman—the Italian blue
> Beyond the horizon with its masculine,
>
> Their eyes closed, in a young palaver of lips.
> And yet the wind whimpers oldly of old age
> In the western night. The venerable mask,
>
> In this perfection, occasionally speaks
> And something of death's poverty is heard.
> This should be tragedy's most moving face.
>
> It is a bough in the electric light
> And exhalations in the eaves, so little
> To indicate the total leaflessness.

This, to Vendler, is "desiccation itself," and "the venerable mask" is hieratic, hiding, "with its stiff grandeur, the unimaginable ruin which has befallen the lapidary rock." The issue between interpretations here turns upon tone, so frequently uncanny in the later Stevens. I take "venerable mask" as ironic metaphor, since "venerable" and "mask" both have an ironic anteriority in Stevens's poetry. Stevens had played upon the venery in "veneration" in *Le Monocle de Mon Oncle*: "Most venerable heart, the lustiest conceit / Is not too lusty for your broadening"; and he had ended the paternal canto 4 of *The Auroras of Autumn* with the bitter rhetorical question "What company, / In masks, can choir it with the naked wind?" As "the wind whimpers oldly of old age / In the western night," Stevens assumes the mask of the most venerable of hearts, in the double sense of age and of a barren desire, "above / The dilapidation of dilapidations," his decayed body, but more significantly and particularly his sexual power. A "dilapidation" is what has fallen into a state of ruin, but etymologically it means to throw the stones apart, and it is like Stevens to play at so elegant a sexual bitterness. Reality or the Not-Me comprises for him, as it did for Emerson, four sundries: nature, art, other persons, and one's own body. Art here is represented by "time's images," nature by night, day, and the night wind, other persons by the obscure contrast between the Oklahoman and Italian blue skies, evidently standing for feminine and masculine meeting: "Their eyes closed, in a young palaver of lips." Like the decayed body, all this is estrangement for Stevens, an otherness, ironically "this perfection," that he cannot address, because reality seems complete without him. His stance approximates that of Yeats in the first stanza of "Sailing to Byzantium" and recalls also "The Poems of Our Climate," where "the imperfect is our paradise" because the perfect, being finished or done completely, does not allow for the delight that "lies in flawed words and stubborn sounds." The mask of aged desire, speaking as the cry of its occasion, speaks the poem of death's poverty, which fails to be "tragedy's most moving face," because it is still only a mask that we hear speaking.

But what does it mean that Stevens compares his own poem to "a bough in the electric light" or to "exhalations in the eaves"? Are those analogues of what is "altogether drier and more brittle," as Vendler says? A bough in artificial light makes a very different and doubtless more qualified impression than a bough in sunlight, yet it is a bough. Exhalations in the eaves are spookily out of context, yet remain exhalations. *An Ordinary Evening in New Haven* is an index, a forefinger indicating much by little, and here at the close of canto 16 it does show the total leaflessness of Stevens's still poignant desire. Yet this is only the start of the middle movement of the Stevensian *askesis*, and from the deliberate nadir at his poem's midpoint we will watch Stevens slowly, steadily, and as deliberately rise to "an alteration / Of words that was a change of nature."

Cantos 17 through 21, the commentary upon 16, adumbrate the total leaflessness and in every instance mitigate it. In 17, the Arnoldian high seriousness is saluted, with the effect of dismissing comedy and tragedy alike in the name of commonplace reflection, or a mirroring of reality by that "dominant blank" that Stevens had seen, in *The Auroras of Autumn*, as Emerson saw it, but now sees as the true mode, the eye's plain version. This is severely said, but its rhetoric is uneasy, as when Stevens too insistently deprecates his usual repressed combination of Jehovah and Whitman:

> Like blessed beams from out a blessed bush
>
> Or the wasted figurations of the wastes
> Of night, time and the imagination.

The repetitions of "blessed," and "wasted" and "wastes," are an index of Stevensian anxiety.

More persuasive is the fable of the carpenter in 18, where the "clear water in a brilliant bowl, / Pink and white carnations" of "The Poems of Our Climate" are reduced to "a fuchsia in a can." The eye's plain version being a thing apart, not of the mere present, and life and death being at least as much metaphysical as physical, even so "this carpenter," Stevens, lives and dies in perceiving the poems, "a carpenter's iridescences," of his own climate. New Haven, "slapped up like a chest of tools," rises in the poet's mind as an iridescence of purged thought, a sublimation of reality. The sublimating force is personified in the less vital canto 19 as "a figure like Ecclesiast," whose chant presumably would be the traditional "all is vanity."

Another of Stevens's fierce reductions dominates canto 20, with a characteristic reimagining coming on as fiercely in 21. Both of these cantos again are uncannily Emersonian if we think of the Emerson of *The Conduct of Life* rather than of *Nature*. Stevens begins canto 20 by apprehending the cloudiness for him, now, of his past poems and his memories of his own past feelings. New Haven, juxtaposed with such an estrangement, is "a neuter shedding shapes in an absolute," not even an auroral serpent of a change. Yet it remains "a residuum," reminding us of the positive coloration that word has elsewhere in Stevens, the sense it conveys of a reduced substance in us that nevertheless prevails. In canto 19, thinking back to the nineteenth century and to the celebration of great and central men, Stevens had invoked the personage who was the axis of vision for his time, Emerson, as "an image that begot its infantines." Here in 20, Stevens deliberately becomes a bitter version of the transparent eyeball, an infant of solipsism:

> In this chamber the pure sphere escapes the impure,
>
> Because the thinker himself escapes. And yet
> To have evaded clouds and men leaves him
> A naked being with a naked will!
>
> And everything to make. He may evade
> Even his own will and in his nakedness
> Inhabit the hypnosis of that sphere.

But this Emersonian reduction becomes Emerson again, at the opening of canto 21, in what could be the epigraph to *The Conduct of Life:*

> But he may not. He may not evade his will,
> Nor the wills of other men; and he cannot evade
> The will of necessity, the will of wills.

The power of necessity restitutes every ascetic movement of the spirit, though it be a power at last of death's necessity. Cythera, island of Venus, appears as Baudelaire's isle of Cythère, and yet Stevens's "black shepherd's isle" is secondary here in comparison to "another isle," where the senses give without taking, an island of a more sympathetic imagination:

> The opposite of Cynthère, an isolation
> At the centre, the object of the will, this place,
> The things around—the alternate romanza
>
> Out of the surfaces, the windows, the walls,
> The bricks grown brittle in time's poverty,
> The clear. A celestial mode is paramount,
>
> If only in the branches sweeping in the rain:
> The two romanzas, the distant and the near,
> Are a single voice in the boo-ha of the wind.

The "romanza out of the black shepherd's isle" joins with Stevens's "alternate romanza" in the single voice of the wind, yet Stevens's kind of poetry is near, "this place, / The things around." Such a finding cannot alter the interpretation of the wind of section 16; it still "whimpers oldly of old age / In the western night," yet those "branches sweeping in the rain" have more life in them than their status as commentary upon "the total leaflessness" might indicate.

With the reentrance of Professor Eucalyptus in canto 22 (originally 7), Stevens begins the final phase of his threefold *askesis,* this one comprising six cantos, 22–27. As before, Eucalyptus parodies Stevens, and the high pomposity scarcely conceals the intensity of Stevens's own quest: "The search / For reality is as momentous as / The search for god." The inside/ outside jugglings between philosopher and poet betray the obsessiveness of Stevens's lifelong anxieties concerning the rival authorities of philosophy and poetry. More impressive is Stevens's conscious palinode in the matter of the First Idea, "the inhalations of original cold / And of original earliness." The First Idea is no longer seen as a reduction, "the predicate of bright origin," but simply as the eye's plain version, the daily sense of cold and earliness. Returning to Crispin, and to Crispin's precursor in the Poet of *Alastor,* Stevens now dismisses the romance of the solitary quester: "Creation is not renewed by images / Of lone wanderers." Reimagining from the eye's plain version is still praised, though Stevens's example of such re-creating is beautifully equivocal:

> Likewise to say of the evening star,
> The most ancient light in the most ancient sky,
>
> That it is wholly an inner light, that it shines
> From the sleepy bosom of the real, re-creates,
> Searches a possible for its possibleness.

This is primarily the evening star of *Adonais* and of many other Shelleyan texts, but "the sleepy bosom of the real" may be an allusion to Keats's sonnet "Bright Star," where the poet wants to be at once the star "in lone splendour" but also pillowed upon the sleepy bosom of the real, which for him is "my fair love's ripening breast." The evening star is one of time's images, ancient in its anteriority. By saying that it is an inner light and then calling its home the real, Stevens has introjected reality even as he tries to draw the star out of the Not-Me into the me. Re-creating the High Romantic metaphor of the star as the endurance and immortality of poetry involves a troping from metaphor to metalepsis, to the Power or *pathos* of possibleness or *potentia*. The evening star remains, in part, a sublimating metaphor, but rather less so than the fictions of the leaves or of leaflessness.

Canto 23, which begins the commentary upon the evening-star canto, is one of my special favorites. Having written of it elsewhere at length, particularly in *Poetry and Repression*, I will note here only the link between its repressed Whitmanian desire for the "cozening and coaxing sound" of the maternal sea of night and the Shelleyan and Keatsian use of the evening star as an emblem of the persistence of desire. After this strength, canto 24 disappoints in its rhetorical execution, though its importance for Stevens is clear. The "escape from repetition," at the edge between afternoon and evening, hints at the difficult theme of the last of Stevens, after *The Rock*, the topography of a new birth into Transcendental perceptiveness. As New Haven poises at the horizon's dip, Stevens prepares for the visions that will begin for him a year later, in 1950, with "A Discovery of Thought."

There is a sudden onslaught of Stevens's uncanny power again in canto 25, with its obsessive imagery of eyes, looks, watched, stared, as the poet confronts man with the blue guitar, earlier form of his own vocation and identity, and so his Whitmanian *daimon*, akin to the figure who mocks Whitman on the beach in "As I Ebb'd." The demands made upon Stevens by the hidalgo are necessarily too stern, reminding us that "hidalgo" means "son of something" where "something" is substance or property. There may be a memory here of the bitter "Thought Revolved," 4, published with the *Blue Guitar:*

> Behold the moralist hidalgo
> Whose whore is Morning Star.

"Description without Place," 7, spoke of how "the hard hidalgo / Lives in the mountainous character of his speech." The hidalgo of *An Ordinary Evening* is both a moralist and a hard looker, "a hatching that stared and demanded," the egg of the eye never quite hatched. Though "permanent, abstract," the hidalgo is hardly a muse but more nearly a superego, whose scrutiny withers every privileged moment. This withering extends into canto 26, which is a kind of late revision of "Sea Surface Full of Clouds." Stevens would like to indulge in the perspectives of distance and so to see the earth as inamorata. But with the attentive eyes of his own hidalgo-aspect upon him, he regards the earth in a plainer version in canto 27:

> Again, "The sibilance of phrases is his
> Or partly his. His voice is audible,
> As the fore-meaning in music is." Again,

> "This man abolishes by being himself
> That which is not ourselves: the regalia,
> The attributions, the plume and helmet-ho."

As so many times, elsewhere, Stevens is at his most tender, even Whitmanian, when he accepts a self-imposed poverty of vision. The whole of this most extensive of all his sublimations ends in this flamboyant canto, the fable of the Ruler of Reality and his spouse, the Queen of Fact. If reality is the otherness beheld by the eye, then the unreal self is the peculiar kingdom ruled by the Queen of Fact. The scholar's *Segmenta* are Stevens's own notes for an unwritten poem, and they celebrate a major man precisely like the MacCullough of *Notes toward a Supreme Fiction*. Like the MacCullough or like the Whitman of *Sea-Drift*, the Ruler of Reality lies lounging by the sea, doubtless "reading in the sound, / About the thinker of the first idea." Yet the later fable is fuller, because of the presence of the Queen of Fact, or theorist of death, the true muse of Stevens's poetry.

In the transition from "and, with the Queen / Of fact, lies at his ease beside the sea" to the final four cantos, we move with Stevens through the most complex of all his Crossings of Identification, because on the other shore of this disjunction he makes a truly central defense of his own poetry, a defense that turns against his worthiest opponent, himself:

> If it should be true that reality exists,
> In the mind: the tin plate, the loaf of bread on it,
> The long-bladed knife, the little to drink and her
>
> Misericordia, it follows that
> Real and unreal are two in one: New Haven
> Before and after one arrives or, say,
>
> Bergamo on a postcard, Rome after dark,
> Sweden described, Salzburg with shaded eyes
> Or Paris in conversation at a café.
>
> This endlessly elaborating poem
> Displays the theory of poetry,
> As the life of poetry. A more severe,
>
> More harassing master would extemporize
> Subtler, more urgent proof that the theory
> Of poetry is the theory of life,
>
> As it is, in the intricate evasions of as,
> In things seem and unseen, created from nothingness,
> The heavens, the hells, the worlds, the longed-for lands.

This, the eighth of the original eleven cantos, is the most famous and I think the best, surpassing even "The poem is the cry of its occasion." The key word is "misericordia," a dispensation from the ordinance of fast-ing and, in this context, a release from the necessities of reduction and from the anxieties of seeking to determine the divisions between real and unreal. On the premise that reality has been taken up into the mind, that the First Ideas of nature, other persons, art, and one's own body have been reimagined fully, then it follows at last that real and unreal, reduction and expansion, are two in one; both of them are synecdoches for the desire to be elsewhere, the desire to be different, to be anywhere in the world except New Haven, or anywhere out of the world except the poem of *An Ordinary Evening in New Haven*. The rocking cradle that endlessly vexed Yeats's rough beast to nightmare, or that earlier first stirred Whitman to the life of poetry, has become in Stevens his variational appositional stance. Stevens elaborates precisely as the Whitmanian maternal ocean rocks, because he too is calling home his castaway, whose name is reality.

Always precise about language, Stevens does not deprecate his poem by describing it as "endlessly elaborating." To elaborate is to execute with truly painstaking detail, to pay attention so that every part is in place, to work the poem out. Yet Stevens says "elaborating" and not "elaborated," which means not that his is a process-poem but that it demands active reading even as it actively reads. "Theory" etymologically means a "viewing," as at a theatre, and "life" goes back to a root meaning "to adhere or stick," or charmingly enough, "fat." To "display" is to "exhibit" yet goes back through a word meaning "scatter" to a root meaning "plait" or "weave." Endlessly working itself out, *An Ordinary Evening in New Haven* scatters and weaves a vision of poetry as being that which sticks or adheres in poetry, the fat of poetry as it is of life. We have met this viewing throughout the poem's theatre, and we now can name it for what it is, the attempt to see earliest, the Emersonian and American doomed attempt to establish a priority in seeing, as though Europe had seen nothing before us. Stevens knows himself to be a great elaborator of this program, but he cannot extemporize as subtly and as urgently as the greatest of all poetic extemporizers, Whitman.

Whitman's art, far more than Stevens's, is to give the effect of an impromptu, to deceive us into the confidence that we listen to an orator who can function without a prepared text. Stevens cannot harass us as Whitman can; his poem is not as severe as "Song of Myself" or "The Sleepers," because "severe" in its root means "true" and Stevens is too Nietzschean to assert that his poem can give truth. "Life, as it is, in the intricate evasions of as" is the enormous, the truly supreme fiction of Whitman, not of Stevens, who knows that what he believes in cannot be true. Yet Stevens is never more moving than when he affirms the Transcendental nostalgia by negating it. Out of the nothingness of his fictive self, Whitman, no snow man, created "the heavens, the hells, the worlds, the longed-for lands." Stevens is not, cannot be, such a master, but no proclamation of his poverty, and of ours, is more poignant than this great canto that concludes by singing so passionately what Stevens says he cannot sing.

When we reach the final three cantos of *An Ordinary Evening*, we confront the complexity of Stevens's self-revisionism, since cantos 9, 10, 11 of
the shorter version appear in the definitive poem as 30, 31, 29. Since I am
following here the sequence of the later, longer version, I pass now to canto
29, yet it remains important to remember that this had been the original
closure of the poem. Canto 29 is as brilliant a fable as Stevens wrote, yet
it may be a fable impossible to interpret, a text too problematic to read fully
or at least for the reader to persuade himself or others that he has read
severely enough:

> In the land of the lemon trees, yellow and yellow were
> Yellow-blue, yellow-green, pungent with citron-sap,
> Dangling and spangling, the mic-mac of mocking birds.
>
> In the land of the elm trees, wandering mariners
> Looked on big women, whose ruddy-ripe images
> Wreathed round and round the round wreath of autumn.
>
> They rolled their r's, there, in the land of the citrons.
> In the land of big mariners, the words they spoke
> Were mere brown clods, mere catching weeds of talk.
>
> When the mariners came to the land of the lemon trees,
> At last, in that blond atmosphere, bronzed hard,
> They said, "We are back once more in the land of the elm
>   trees,
>
> But folded over, turned round." It was the same,
> Except for the adjectives, an alteration
> Of words that was a change of nature, more
>
> Than the difference that clouds make over a town.
> The countrymen were changed and each constant thing.
> Their dark-colored words had redescribed the citrons.

There are two lands in this fable, or rather there is only one land, since
the real land of the elm trees, New Haven, and the unreal, Goethean
paradise or Stevensian Florida of the citrons are two in one. The mariners
desire to be elsewhere, to be different, to forsake the fulfillments of reality
for an Eden of language or simply to be poets. But they take New Haven
with them, and neither they nor Stevens (since they *are* Stevens) can decide
whether this means that nothing can change or whether it means that there
is nothing except change.

In the *Harmonium* world of "dangling and spangling, the mic-mac of
mocking birds," the yellow of the lemons was both blue and green, pun-
gencies alike of mind and of earth. In New Haven, traditionally the land
of the elm trees (Stevens writes just before the major elm blight of the
1950s), wandering, big mariners (or Odysseus assimilated to Stevens) stare

at autumnal women, women more of the earth and its ripeness than of the mind's desires. Language also is gaudy, in the *Harmonium* world, but the language of New Haven is again too much of the earth our mother. Presumably, it is in search of a language "to roll / On the expressive tongue, the finding fang" that the mariner Stevens comes to the land of citrons. But his representatives, arriving at last in their Eden, proclaim, "We are back once more in the land of the elm trees, / But folded over, turned round." I know of nothing else in Stevens so problematic in tone; is this a lament, a defiance, or simply a kind of statement as to that which is? Vendler, with a most acute ear, reads the third possibility:

> This possibly depressing recognition is certainly anticlimactic, but Stevens expresses it without tone, as though he wished the moment to be neutral. The repetitiveness of experience is no new theme in Stevens, but here he refuses to speak of it either as pleasurable or as diminishing. Instead, it is factual; and he has it both ways.

The recognition, as I read it, is not depressing or toneless, but positive, even a touch truculent and defiant. An adjective is an addition, something thrown on to something else, so that to say, "It was the same, / Except for the adjectives" is more self-contradictory than dialectical. The mariners have been troped in being "folded over, turned round"; they have been recolored, and so the mariner Stevens is not just a permanently dark-colored self. He is not within the difference, but beyond the difference, in the faith that "an alteration / Of words that was a change of nature" may be an authentic alteration in the fiction of the self.

What was the force of the original close of the poem, when it ended that "Their dark-colored words had redescribed the citrons"? Too hopeful an earliness, is surely part of the answer. After so many sublimations, so ever-early a candor would not have been appropriate. With marvelous judgment, Stevens took the original cantos 9 and 10 and placed them after the fable of the mariners as cantos 30 and 31. It is not a total leaflessness that is observed in 30, but what nevertheless presents itself as a barrenness:

> The last leaf that is going to fall has fallen.
> The robins are là-bas, the squirrels, in tree-caves,
> Huddle together in the knowledge of squirrels.
>
> The wind has blown the silence of summer away.
> It buzzes beyond the horizon or in the ground:
> In mud under ponds, where the sky used to be reflected.
>
> The barrenness that appears is an exposing.
> It is not part of what is absent, a halt
> For farewells, a sad hanging on for remembrances.

It is a coming on and a coming forth.
The pines that were fans and fragrances emerge,
Staked solidly in a gusty grappling with rocks.

The glass of the air becomes an element—
It was something imagined that has been washed away.
A clearness has returned. It stands restored.

It is not an empty clearness, a bottomless sight.
It is a visibility of thought,
In which hundreds of eyes, in one mind, see at once.

After so many dominant blanks, so many staring eyes hatching like an egg, so many parodied transparent eyeballs, as well as eyes' plain versions, inexquisite eyes, and assorted reflections, we experience a profound sense of liberation when we are told: "A clearness has returned. It stands restored." Truly, the clarity has its menace; it is the moment poised just before winter. But though those hundreds of eyes may belong to the animal kingdom, to the huddled squirrels sensing the imminence of winter, they suggest also Shakespeare's play upon a bottomless dream, and more directly the American Transcendentalist dream of open vision, of seeing as Whitman hoped to see, with the eyes of a multitude. Something strange begins to come on and come forth in Stevens, that "visibility of thought" which will be the discovery of the final phase, when the course of all the particulars of vision and visionary sound is finally tracked. Summer was imagined well but has been washed away, and what remains is no longer an abstraction or reduction to a First Idea. This is revelation without description, tentative and yet definitive, and rhetorically a troping upon all the earlier undoings and sublimations in the poem. There is no finer example in Stevens of a scheme of transumption or metaleptic reversal, the far-fetching of an antipodal creature, worthy of birth.

Stevens does not end the poem upon this introjection of a fresh earliness that huddles expectantly, waiting for the blasts of winter. He goes back to the central Paterian trope of *Harmonium*, the apprehension of reality as the solipsistic recognition of privileged moments, sudden perfections of sense, flakes of fire, fluttering things having distinctive shapes:

The less legible meanings of sounds, the little reds
Not often realized, the lighter words
In the heavy drum of speech, the inner men

Behind the outer shields, the sheets of music
In the strokes of thunder, dead candles at the window
When day comes, fire-foams in the motions of the sea,

Flickings from finikin to fine finikin
And the general fidget from busts of Constantine
To photographs of the late president, Mr. Blank,

These are the edgings and inchings of final form,
The swarming activities of the formulae
Of statement, directly and indirectly getting at,

Like an evening evoking the spectrum of violet,
A philosopher practicing scales on his piano,
A woman writing a note and tearing it up.

It is not in the premise that reality
Is a solid. It may be a shade that traverses
A dust, a force that traverses a shade.

The first six lines refine *Harmonium*, but the next three genially mock the Hoonian vision. "Flickings from finikin to fine finikin" transumes earlier Stevensian intimations as to the high fastidiousness of poetry and of poetic perception, of which the crucial instance is "Like Decorations," 32:

Poetry is a finikin thing of air
That lives uncertainly and not for long
Yet radiantly beyond much lustier blurs.

The mockery in that early passage is overbalanced by the praise of poetry, and so it is here in the final canto of *An Ordinary Evening*. Even "the general fidget," the nervous decline of representation "from busts of Constantine" to the aptly named Mr. Blank, perhaps a departed insurance executive, is redeemed as one of "the edgings and inchings of final form," of history getting at getting it right. There is no full stop in the canto until evening evokes, the metaphysician plays, and the woman makes up and unmakes her mind, presumably upon an issue of erotic choice. What are all these but variant versions, analogues, of Stevens's own appositional method in *An Ordinary Evening*? They share Stevens's achieved premise, that reality, whether it be nature, art, others, or one's body is a crossing or transition, a disjunctive versing of force, shade, dust. "Dead candles at the window" may be only a poignant emblem of ineffectual inchings toward final form, when the sun comes up, yet they are part of the emblematic reality of poet or scholar, the solitary outward form of his internalization of the evening star. Stevens ends his great poem on "shade," but the final emphasis is upon a force crossing a shade, and so freshly breaking a form, writing another canto on an ordinary evening in New Haven.

Wallace Stevens's World of Words:
An Always Incipient Cosmos

Marie Borroff

The exact repetition in the present of the verbal and other forms of behavior used on ceremonial occasions in the past has always been an important means of inducing or perpetuating reverence for authority. Despite Wallace Stevens's insistent and sometimes rude repudiations of the cultural establishment, including the academies and their old descriptions of the world, the first thing to be noted here is his consistent and thorough exploitation of the inherited resources of high formal language. These of course include elevated diction (sporadically undercut, as we have observed, by eccentric word combinations); they also, less obviously, include a repertoire of grammatical constructions, ways of putting together and connecting phrases, clauses, and sentences whose expressive power consists in our conscious or unconscious identification of them with certain kinds of formal context. Two areas of culture and the literary genres connected with them are of especial importance for Stevens. We find them reflected in a scholarly or discursive and a sacred or hierophantic strain, respectively, in his idiosyncratic version of the high style.

The scholar in Stevens's poetry (more narrowly, the philosopher) expounds and excogitates in a language whose forms and patterns suggest the treatise, the textbook, or the classroom lecture. This discursive voice sounds sporadically in single lines and short line sequences; it is most conspicuously audible in whole poems or sections of poems explicitly dramatized as philosophic essays—for example, "Study of Two Pears" (an "opusculum paedagogum"), "The Glass of Water," "Connoisseur of Chaos," *Description without Place*, and parts of *Notes toward a Supreme Fiction* and *An Ordinary Evening in New Haven*.

From *Language and the Poet: Verbal Artistry in Frost, Stevens and Moore.* © 1979 by the University of Chicago. University of Chicago Press, 1979.

In such passages and poems, terminology and syntax are characterized by the preponderance of nominal over verbal and adjectival elements; abstract nouns of course occur frequently as does the verb *to be* in its role of copula. [Unless otherwise specified, page references are to *The Collected Poems* (New York, 1954).]

> If seeming is description without place,
> The spirit's universe, then a summer's day,
> Even the seeming of a summer's day,
> Is description without place;
>
> (p. 343)

> The freshness of transformation is
>
> The freshness of a world. It is our own,
> It is ourselves, the freshness of ourselves,
> And that necessity and that presentation
>
> Are rubbings of a glass in which we peer.
> (p. 398)

> The poem is the cry of its occasion,
> Part of the res itself and not about it.
> (p. 473)

Another feature of importance in these examples is the reiteration of key words and phrases. The effect is didactic; the pace of exposition seems to be deliberately held back while thought is elaborated and qualified, as if by a careful teacher. With regard to larger grammatical structures, Stevens's poetry of course presents us with a host of examples of the patterns traditionally used in formal discourse and excluded, by and large, from spontaneous utterance—multiple subordinations, compoundings of subordinate and independent clauses, participial or infinitive constructions where everyday speech would prefer a finite verb. But sentence structure in Stevens's discursive language may go to the opposite extreme, with a brevity and simplicity as remote from ordinary speech as the conventional elaborations and complications of formal syntax.

> The pears are not viols,
> Nudes or bottles.
> They resemble nothing else
>
> . . . .
> The shadows of the pears
> Are blobs on the green cloth.
> The pears are not seen
> As the observer wills.
> (pp. 196–97)

Ideas are men. The mass of meaning and
The mass of men are one. Chaos is not

The mass of meaning. It is three or four
Ideas or, say, five men or, possibly, six.
                                                        (p. 255)

Again we note the reiteration of key words and phrases; again there is an effect of didactic emphasis and retardation of pace. A minor feature of similar import is the sequence of numbers or letters conventionally serving to mark off the divisions of a text or the points of an argument—the Roman numerals preceding the stanzas of "Study of Two Pears," the "A" and "B" propositions and "Projections" of "Connoisseur of Chaos" and "So-and-So Reclining on Her Couch," the numbered descriptive "exfoliations" of "Someone Puts a Pineapple Together," part 3.

A second realm from which Stevens draws traditionally formal features of language is the sacred or hierophantic, and, in looking to this source, we must recognize that the formal language of religion cannot be fully distinguished from that of poetry itself. Much of the most important poetry of the earlier periods of English, as of other European literatures, is explicitly Christian. And those later poets who found Christianity inadequate or rejected it entirely have themselves tended to assume the role of nondenominational or secular priest, proselytizing in the very accents of religious authority. Stevens himself is a notable case in point. Though he is capable of lashing out ironically against major articles of the Christian faith, of calling the resurrected Jesus a "three-days' personage" (p. 97) and the crucifixion a "glamorous hanging" (p. 192), his poetry from first to last uses Christian imagery for its own purposes with utmost seriousness, having its "dove, alighting" (p. 357), its "communion" (p. 253), its "Candle a Saint" (p. 223), its "chants" of "final peace" (p. 258), its "pastoral nun" whose final vision identifies poetry with apotheosis (p. 378), even its "sudarium" (p. 188) and "wounds" transfigured into roses (p. 318). Genres and modes of discourse associated with the sacred—invocation, prayer, prophecy, hymn, litany, parable—frequently give form to single lines and short passages and, on a larger scale, to poems and sections of long poems; "To the One of Fictive Music," "The Idea of Order at Key West," "Chocorua to Its Neighbor," *The Owl in the Sarcophagus*, and parts of *Esthetique du Mal, Notes*, and *An Ordinary Evening* are important examples.

Terminology and syntax are here characterized by the predominance of nominal and adjectival over verbal elements, with heavy reliance on qualitative terms of solemnizing or celebratory import, some venerable, some innovative:

                        The brilliant height
And hollow of him by its brilliance calmed,
Its brightness burned the way good solace seethes.

> This was peace after death, the brother of sleep,
> . . . .
> Adorned with cryptic stones and sliding shines,
> An immaculate personage in nothingness.
>
> (p. 434)

We find inversions of word order of the time-honored poetic sort ("Green is the night" [p. 223], "In his poems we find peace" [p. 251], "By one caterpillar is great Africa devoured" [p. 456]); the negative qualifications and logical connections among clauses characteristic of the discursive mode give way to appositives and series of nouns and adjectives (also, strikingly, of finite verbs). These may accumulate with a rhythmic continuity furthered by the use of linking conjunctions that eliminate pauses and with an intensity enhanced by traditionally "rhetorical" repetitions of meanings, words, and sounds:

> There was
> Only the great height of the rock
> And the two of them standing still to rest.
>
> There was the cold wind and the sound
> It made, away from the muck of the land
> That they had left, heroic sound
> Joyous and jubilant and sure.
>
> (p. 126)

> And I walked and talked
> Again, and lived and was again, and breathed again
> And moved again and flashed again, time flashed again.
>
> (p. 238)

When the discursive content itself of Stevens's poetry takes on a solemn aura, as it frequently does, the propounding and sanctifying voices merge. Thus the sixth section to "Description without Place" moves from its expository opening,

> Description is revelation. It is not
> The thing described, nor false facsimile,

to a climax in which definition and distinctions give way to celebratory variations on the symbolic theme of a "text we should be born that we might read,"

> the book of reconciliation,
> Book of a concept only possible

> In description, canon central in itself,
> The thesis of the plentifullest John.
>
> (p. 345)

We see the abstract concept of revelation turning into the Book of Revelation as philosophic statement becomes colored by Christian allusion.

The inherited language of the formal modes of discourse in English is, as we know, associated with elevated diction of the sort tending to give rise to statistically high percentiles of words of Romance and Latinate origin. It is thus to be expected that successive Romance-Latinate percentiles of 20 and over will be found in poems like *Credences of Summer* and others in which the discursive and hierophantic modes predominate. The diction of this and other similar poems is to some degree bound to the subject matters or areas of culture associated with these two modes, as is apparent in the passages quoted above in words like *description, presentation, res, state, concept,* and *thesis,* on the one hand; and *peace, immaculate, revelation, reconciliation,* and *canon,* on the other. But subject matter cannot fully account for the presence in these same passages of other words of Romance and Latinate origin such as *cry, resemble, brilliant, adorned, cryptic, personage, facsimile,* and *central.* These latter must be recognized as symptoms of the pervasive bias in Stevens's language we noted earlier, its persistent exploitation, for all its flamboyant originality, of the inherited features of high formal style. An abundance of such features may even make his most opaque passages *rhetorically* intelligible, directly conveying such qualities as discursive seriousness or visionary exaltation:

> This is the the mirror of the high serious:
> Blue verdured into a damask's lofty symbol,
>
> Gold easings and ouncings and fluctuations of thread
> And beetling of belts and lights of general stones,
> Like blessed beams from out a blessed bush
>
> Or the wasted figurations of the wastes
> Of night, time and the imagination,
> Saved and beholden, in a robe of rays.
>
> (p. 477)

Here the words themselves dazzle not only in the intricacies of their sounds and rhythms and their qualities as diction but in their unaccustomed combinations and applications as well, whether or not we grasp their meanings as metaphorical and symbolic description. The reader of such a passage may well feel that in it rhetoric has shouldered meaning aside to an extent verging on self-indulgent display—a vice of style that is perhaps inevitable, given so tremendous a virtuosity.

Stevens's pervasive formal bias, then, manifests itself on the level of diction not only in learned and allusive language but also in the frequent occurrence of distinctively formal words of Romance and Latinate origin, tied neither to any particular area of meaning nor to any particular genre or set of genres, for which native synonyms belonging to the common level of diction are available. Examples of such "free formal" tags are *desire* versus *want, distant* versus *far, edifice* versus *building, interior* versus *inner/inside, labor* versus *work, possess* versus *own,* regard in the meaning it shares with *look* (*at*), and *respond/response* versus *answer.* Another such symptom is the use of full, in preference to contracted, forms of the verb: "*Let us* make hymns" (p. 151), "I *cannot* bring a world quite round" (p. 165), "*We are* conceived in your conceits" (p. 195), "*It is* how he gives his light. *It is* how he shines" (p. 205), "It *has not* always had / To find" (p. 239), "We *do not* say ourselves like that in poems" (p. 311).

While fully exploiting the inherited repertoire of formal Romance and Latinate diction, Stevens by no means neglects that other traditional means of elevation in English, described in the preceding chapter, which involves the use of simple words mostly of native origin, associated since early modern times with poetry and the Bible. Except in the case of archaisms and archaic forms (e.g., *begat, spake*), our recognition of such associations and our response to the stylistic qualities generated by them are dependent on the contexts in which the words appear—on relationships among the ideas expressed and on the cooperative presence of other words of similar potential. In this respect, poetic-biblical diction differs from diction of the ornate, elevated variety. The word *argentine,* for instance (used memorably by Stevens in the third part of *Notes*), has its distinctively formal quality regardless of context; the word *silver* belongs to the common level of diction but has certain biblical associations (most notably in connection with the thirty pieces of silver paid to Judas) which might or might not be evoked and form part of its expressive value in a literary work.

To follow this allusive process in operation, let us look at what happens to the word *know,* among others, in "The Hand as a Being." The poem is written in the form of a parable or simple allegorical narrative; its story is located at the outset "in the first canto of the final canticle" and is thereby linked in significance to the similarly allegorical (or at least traditionally allegorized) Song of Songs, also known as Canticles. Like the Songs, "The Hand as a Being" has an ostensibly sexual theme. In it, the beneficent seduction of the central figure by a mythic feminine being symbolizes a change within the mind from confusion to order. Having been "too conscious of too many things at once," "our man" becomes "composed," with a play on the meanings "serene" and "put into form." At the end of the poem, diction modulates to the extreme of simplicity and Romance and Latinate elements all but disappear:

> Her hand took his and drew him to her.
> Her hair fell on him and the mi-bird flew
>
> To the ruddier bushes at the garden's end.
> Of her, of her alone, at last he knew
> And lay beside her underneath the tree.
>
> (p. 271)

Of the preceding forty-four words, only *garden* is non-native (Romance).

(I consider *mi-* to be a sound-symbolic coinage, as it is also in "the thinnest *mi* of falsetto" in "Parochial Theme" [p. 191], and not the Latinate name of the third note of the musical scale.) In context, the potential biblical suggestiveness of the words *garden* and *tree* and, retrospectively, of *naked* in the first stanza of the poem, is realized with specific reference to the fall of man, and "the hand appeared" of stanza 5 may be seen as alluding to the story of Belshazzar's feast. The verb *drew* in the passage quoted has archaic-poetic status in the sense of "pulled," and *lay beside* is reminiscent of the archaic expression *lie with*, designating sexual intercourse. The prediction of the materializing hand, unlike that of the Old Testament story, is favorable; enlightenment does not bring perdition but comes as a saving grace. The play on the modern and biblical senses of *know*, bringing together the concepts of intellectual enlightenment and sexual consummation, epitomizes the basic symbolic equation of the poem.

So far, we have considered formality in Stevens as a means of associating his poetry with the inherited forms, and thus imputing to it the inherited values of literary and cultural tradition. But it serves other purposes as well, and these should at least be mentioned briefly. First, the solemnity of tone reinforced by formal language in much of the poetry is consonant with Stevens's often-expressed belief in the importance and dignity of the imaginative enterprise, in the poet's public role of helping people to lead their lives. Second, learned diction and other features of elevated language serve here as elsewhere (the point is so obvious that we tend to overlook it) as a kind of accreditation, investing the user with a believable authority. Entirely apart from the significance of each in its context, the foreign words and wide-ranging references to persons and places which appear throughout Stevens's poetry are impressive in general as "verbal credentials." We respect the desire to repudiate the past in the man who proves himself thoroughly conversant with it. And there is a heightening of dramatic intensity in the longing of such a man to divest himself of his knowledge, his melancholy conviction that mental nakedness is a condition of imaginative vitality.

> It may be that the ignorant man, alone,
> Has any chance to mate his life with life
> That is the sensual, pearly spouse, the life
> That is fluent in even the wintriest bronze.
>
>   (p. 222)

Such lines, paradoxically redolent of erudition, bring to mind the speaker of Yeats's "The Dawn," whose longing to be "ignorant" is tacitly frustrated by the knowledge displayed in the very poem in which the longing is expressed. Third and last, formality in the sense in which I have been using the word is consonant with formality in the different but related sense of dignity or aloofness of manner. The "central man" of Stevens's poetry is not only an erudite scholar and polyglot but also an austere personage who keeps his distance from us and confides nothing, seeming to dismiss as trivial all personal griefs and joys, if not all personal relationships what-soever. A symptom of his loftiness of tone is his preference for the im-personal pronoun *one* over a possible *I* or *you:* "One has a malady here" (p. 63); "Among the dogs and dung, / One would continue to contend with one's ideas" (p. 198).

To recognize the pervasive formality of Stevens's poetic language is not to say that the formality is unremittingly sustained. Colloquial phrase-ology was, in fact, exemplified by one of the passages cited [elsewhere]. But such passages are hard to come by in Stevens, and it is surely significant that statements of major importance in his poetry do not sound like any-thing anyone would actually say. It is instructive to compare him in this respect with Frost, setting such lines as "Home is the place where,when you have to go there, they have to take you in"; "Something has to be left to God"; "We have ideas yet we haven't tried"; and "It's knowing what to do with things that counts" side by side with "The gaiety of language is our seigneur"; "Life consists / Of propositions about life"; "The reason can give nothing at all / Like the response to desire"; and "The sentiment of the fatal is part / Of filial love." (Though I cannot resist citing a delightful counterinstance, from "Parochial Theme": "Piece the world together, boys, but not with your hands.") Colloquial phrases may appear in the immediate neighborhood of important pronouncements ("That's it: the more than rational distortion, / The fiction that results from feeling. Yes, that" [p. 406]), but they serve as intensifiers of tone rather than as content carriers, conveying the urgency and excitement attendant upon insight rather than insight itself:

> That's it. The lover writes, the believer hears,
> The poet mumbles and the painter sees,
> Each one, his fated eccentricity.
>
> (p. 443)

More typically, the colloquial note is sounded when all is not well—to express a failure of inner vitality ("My old boat goes round on a crutch / And doesn't get under way" [p. 120]) or the speaker's sense of a stale past or an inane present ("Panoramas are not what they used to be" [p. 134]; "The solar chariot is junk" [p. 332]; "All sorts of flowers. That's the sen-timentalist" [p. 316]). Beyond this, it serves in a few poems to give a deceptively casual air to symbolic or mythic narration ("Sure enough, the thunder became men" [p. 220]; "So you're home again, Redwood Roamer, and ready / To feast" [pp. 286–87]).

A particularly interesting and significant aspect of Stevens's poetic language, considered in conjunction with its prevailingly formal tenor, is his vocabulary of sound-symbolic words, including frequentatives and it-eratives. This vocabulary bulks large in both number of items and fre-quencies of occurrence; some of the words in it are used a dozen times or more: for example, *flash* (21), *hum* (20), *boom* (13), and the frequentatives *glitter* (31), *dazzle* (14), *flutter* (14), *sparkle* (12), and *tumble* (12). *Flick* and *flicker* (13 total) and *glisten* (16) should also be listed here; the latter, though labeled sound symbolic neither by the *Oxford Dictionary of Etymology* (1966) nor by the *Shorter Oxford English Dictionary* (3d ed., 1973), has obvious affinities of phonetic shape and meaning with *glitter* and the archaic word *glister*. Such words are inherently sensory and specific, with an immediacy that can animate scenic description (the more so in that many of them literally designate some sort of rapid motion or change), or, in startling metaphorical translation, relieve the dryness of abstract discourse:

> Air is air.
> Its vacancy glitters round us everywhere.
> (p. 137)

> The banners of the nation flutter, burst
> On the flag-poles in a red-blue dazzle, whack
> At the halyards.
> (p. 390)

> Then Ozymandias said the spouse, the bride
> Is never naked. A fictive covering
> Weaves always glistening from the heart and mind.
> (p. 396)

> The satisfaction underneath the sense,
> The conception sparkling in still obstinate thought.
> (p. 448)

Substitution of either a simpler or a more elevated word for any of the sound-symbolic words in the passages above (*brightness* or *glory* for *dazzle*, *shinning* or *luminous* for *glistening* or *sparkling*) throws into relief the latter's peculiar expressive force.

Many, if not most, of the sound-symbolic words in Stevens are in fact assigned metaphorical roles. Reviewing the examples amassed in chapter 3 in relation to the topics of laughing and crying, we find that, of the sound-symbolic words listed there, Stevens has *chuckle, guffaw, titter, blubber,* and *sob. Guffaw* and *sob* occur once each in their literal meanings (pp. 15, 317), but *blubber, chuckle,* and *titter,* each used once, refer to sounds made by tom-toms, birds, and locusts, respectively (p. 41; *Opus Posthumous* [*O.P.*], pp. 28, 71), while *sob* denotes the cooing of the turtledove, called "turtle" in biblical fashion (*O.P.*, p. 71), and, with bitter paradoxical force, the sharp intake of breath in "the laughter of evil" (p. 253). The dramatic qualities deriving from the affinities of such words with the spoken language is retained in metaphorical application, while any suggestion of triviality vanishes in strangeness. The shift of reference may be from one physical agency to another, as when frogs boom (p. 17), water makes a blather (p. 22), the blue guitar chatters or buzzes (p. 167), thunder straggles (p. 208), grass dithers (p. 234), roses tinkle (p. 252), fire fidgets (p. 352), wind whimpers (p. 477), and crickets babble (p. 523). A more radical shift is that from the sensory to the abstract, as in "the pitter-patter of archaic freedom" (p. 292), "the hullabaloo of health and have" (p. 292), a "flick" of feeling (p. 407) or "false flick false form" (p. 385), "a strength that tumbles everywhere" (p. 354), and "form gulping after formlessness" (p. 411). Words are said to make "glistening reference to what is real" (p. 309), and in "apparition" there are "delicate clinkings not explained" (p. 340). Perhaps most characteristically of all, such metaphors figure in an interpenetration of substance and thought, as, for example, in "The Bouquet":

> The bouquet stands in a jar, as metaphor,
>
> . . . .
>
>   [as] a growth
> Of the reality of the eye, an artifice,
> Nothing much, a flitter that reflects itself,
>
> . . . .
>
>   The bouquet is part of a dithering:
> Cloud's gold, of a whole appearance that stands and is.
>
>   (pp. 448, 452)

An especially remarkable metaphorical operation is performed on certain sound-symbolic words which, as normally used, designate partly audible or intelligible speech and have some degree of derogatory force, but which in Stevens are applied to fully articulate speech, including the language of poetry itself. In "The Reader," the statement

>   Everything
> Falls back to coldness,
> Even the musky muscadines,
> The melons, the vermilion pears
> Of the leafless garden,

emanates from a disembodied voice described as "mumbling" (p. 147), while in "Examination of the Hero in Time of War" the hero is said to glide

>   to his meeting like a lover
> Mumbling a secret, passionate message.
>   (p. 276)

In "A Primitive like an Orb," the speaker concludes that

>   the lover writes, the believer hears,
> The poet mumbles and the painter sees,
> Each one, his fated eccentricity.
>   (p. 443)

In *An Ordinary Evening in New Haven*, cosmic "actors . . . walk in a twilight muttering lines" (p. 497), and "milky [Stevens-ese for "spiritually nourish-ing"] lines" are muttered by "the philosophers' man" of "Asides on the Oboe" (p. 250). Elsewhere, Stevens refers to hymns that buzz (p. 65), "a crackling of voices" (p. 292), a lecturer who hems and haws a disquisition on "This Beautiful world of Ours" (p. 429), "the tragic prattle of the fates" (*O.P.*, p. 34), and "the poet's hum" (*O.P.*, p. 71).

By all odds, the most significant instance of this sort of metaphorical use is the word *gibberish* in its three occurrences toward the end of the second section, "It Must Change," of *Notes toward a Supreme Fiction:*

> The poem goes from the poet's gibberish to
> The gibberish of the vulgate and back again,

and "It is the gibberish of the vulgate that [the poet] seeks" (pp. 396–97). I shall return to this important passage later. Here the point is that *gibberish,* like other sound-symbolic words similarly translated, dramatizes Stevens's paradoxical insistence that poetic language remain partly inarticulate, partly inhuman, that it incorporate within itself something of "the incommunic-able mass" (p. 328) of external reality. The "necessary angel of earth," speaking to the countrymen who have welcomed him, tells them and us that

> in my sight, you see the earth again,

> Cleared of its stiff and stubborn, man-locked set,
> And, in my hearing, you hear its tragic drone

> Rise liquidly in liquid lingerings,
> Like watery words awash; like meanings said

> By repetitions of half-meanings.
>
>   (p. 497)

The expressive powers of the sound-symbolic word, half meaning, half echo, fit this description with uncanny aptness.

It is now time to [consider] the perceptible diversity of Stevens's poetic language and particularly his use of many different kinds of words. In terms of the variables included in the spectrum of diction, we can now say that, on a scale of levels of formality, his vocabulary runs from common to elevated while on a scale of frequencies of use it runs from common to rare, transcending the established boundaries of the language with a pro-fusion of innovative borrowings and formations of both learned and pop-ular types. Colloquial elements, save for a sprinkling of contracted verb forms, are almost wholly lacking. Sound-symbolic words are an important expressive resource for Stevens, but the colloquial tendencies of these are modified by their use in metaphorical meanings. As one element of a pre-vailingly formal style, diction figures in the production of a variety of effects, from a studied simplicity (with or without biblical allusiveness) to elaboration and exoticism. Odd verbal combinations are a hallmark of his style; among these, we can single out one type as especially worthy of note: that in which Latinate (*L*) and sound-symbolic (*s-s*) words appear side by side. The examples "A syllable [*L*], / Out of these gawky [*s-s*] flitterings [*s-s*], / Intones [*L*] its single emptiness"; "addicts [*L*] / To blotches [*s-s*], angular [*L*] anonymids [*L*], Gulping [*s-s*] for shape"; and "the honky-tonk [*s-s*] out of the somnolent [*L*] grasses," which were cited earlier, may now be supplemented by "the irised [*L*] hunks [*s-s*]" (p. 227); "sprinklings [*s-s*] of bright particulars [*L*] from the sky" (p. 344); "delicate [*L*] clinkings [*s-s*]" (p. 340); "the dazzle [*s-s*] / Of mica [*L*], the dithering [*s-s*] of grass, / The Arachne [*L*] integument [*L*] of dead trees" (p. 234); and "Alive with an enigma's [*L*] flitterings [*s-s*]" (*O.P.*, p. 105). Iterative coinages appear in "A shiddow-shaddow [*s-s*] of lights revolving [*L*]" (p. 279) and "a destroying spiritual [*L*] that digs-a-dog" [*s-s*] (p. 332). Such sequences become the more conspicuous as one's ear is alerted to their peculiar timbre; they are dramatically significant in that they blend abstraction with sense perception, solemnity with familiarity, embodying on the level of diction one kind of "choice [not] / Between, but of" (p. 403).

To understand how diversity of diction in Stevens is dramatically motivated, we need to think of it in terms not of static patterns of contrast but of temporal unfolding. From this point of view, diversity is change, perceived as we read a number of poems or a single long poem—as we pass, say, from "The Idea of Order at Key West" to "The American Sublime" in the *Collected Poems*, or from "Chocorua to its Neighbor" to "So-and-So Reclining on Her Couch" in *The Palm at the End of the Mind*, or from section 4 to section 5 of "The Bouquet," or from section 3 to section 4 of *Esthetique du Mal*. Within such lines as "addicts / To blotches, angular anonymids / Gulping for shape" or "alive with an enigma's flittering," change is kaleidoscopic, the hand of the poet all but deceiving the eye. We may be aware of a pleasant strangeness in the proportion, without knowing exactly wherein that strangeness consists.

What the reader perceives as change, a diversity enacted in successive periods or instants of time, may also be described in terms of the activity of the poet. As everyone knows, the basic concerns and preoccupations of Stevens's poetry remained the same from first to last. His essential theme, the interplay of imagination and reality, may be defined, in terms of the plots dramatized in the poems themselves, as the relationship of a central consciousness to its perceived world. From this relationship real people and the real events and circumstances of the poet's life are almost wholly excluded (an important exception is "To an Old Philosopher in Rome"). Such autobiography as there is remains implicit in the seasonal movement, to summer and then to autumn, of the titles of the successive volumes, and in the long backward perspective of the last poems, as, for example, in the opening of "Long and Sluggish Lines," "It makes so little difference, at so much more / Than seventy, where one looks, one has been there before," and the first section, entitled "Seventy Years Later," of "The Rock." Good and bad fortune consist wholly in the success or failure of the mind in its lifelong attempt to achieve, and simultaneously to find words for, a satisfying apprehension of reality. This activity and the writing of poetry are one and the same; thus Stevens can say that "Poetry is the subject of the poem. / From this the poem issues and / To this returns" (p. 176) and that "Life consists / Of propositions about life" (p. 355). The poems may be seen in their entirety as the record of a "never-ending meditation" (p. 465), so defined, as "makings of [the] self" which are "no less makings of the sun" (p. 532). But vitality is change, "life is motion" (p. 83), no less for the mind than for the world which is the mind's necessary complement. And herein we detect a paradox as dramatically fruitful as it is logically insoluble. Poetic statement is language set into form, sequences of words which are and must remain fixed, so that the mind's attempt to give definitive expression to its sense of an "always incipient cosmos" (*O.P.*, p. 115), is doubly self-defeating. "It must be abstract"; "it must change"; these two equally important dicta regarding the supreme fiction meet each other head-on. The very word *abstract*, it should be noted, is in origin a past participle, designating the result of an action that has already taken place; it properly applies neither to natural nor to mental process. Thus

> There's no such thing as life; or if there is,
>
> It is faster than the weather, faster than
> Any character. It is more than any scene.
>   (p. 192)

(*Character* here may well mean "written letter" as well as *dramatis persona;* cf. "written in character" [p. 257].) The vital formulation loses vitality in the very moment of utterance, as the iridescent scented rushes gathered by Alice from the boat in *Through the Looking-Glass* became instantly dull. We see language in Stevens straining through time to express instantaneity:

> The breadth of an accelerando moves,
> Captives the being, widens—and was there.
>   (p. 440)

So too the giant conjured up in the present tense in "Poem Written at Morning" immediately reverts to the past: "Green were the curls upon that head." The mind must constantly discard its own representations. "Goodby, Mrs. Pappadopoulos, and thanks" (p. 296), or, in the more solemn accents of *The Auroras of Autumn*, "Farewell to an idea."

Just as we see the Stevens of the *Collected Poems* turning from one metaphor, one analogy, one symbolic setting, person, or event to another, so also we see him turning from one expressive means to another, trying out now this kind of language, now that, now this kind of word, now that, in the incessant attempt to express what remains perpetually "beyond the rhetorician's touch" (p. 431). And in this same restlessness of mind, these same rejections not only of the past but also of the present which has already become the past, we can see a motive for his ransacking of the lexicon, his borrowings from foreign languages, his creation of new metaphorical meanings, the coinages and innovative formations that mark his diction. "It is never the thing but the version of the thing" (p. 332); Stevens's poetic language is diverse, versatile, full of *divertissements*, in the root sense of all those words, knowing that "what it has is what is not" and turning from it "as morning throws off stale moonlight and shabby sleep" (p. 382). These turnings or shiftings at the verbal level are analogous to the changes with which the poems are concerned in their subject matter and descriptive detail—the cycles of day and night and the seasons, the rising and falling of waves or, on a geological time scale, of mountains, the endless transformations of the weather. The world of Stevens's poems may well be described, adopting one of his happiest coinages, as a *tournamonde* (p. 476) in large and in little, from the grandiose "shiddow-shaddow of lights revolving" at the climax of "Examination of the Hero in Time of War" to the single leaf "spinning its eccentric measure" toward the end of *Notes*. Cyclical change, despite Stevens's cynical treatment of the theme in *Le Monocle de Mon Oncle*, is for him most characteristically a source of pleasure–not the fateful intersecting gyres of a Yeats or the monotonous "birth, copulation, and death" of an Eliot but "The Pleasures of Merely Circulating," repetition felt as "beginning, not resuming" (p. 391), necessity accepted without tragic posturing as "final . . . and therefore, good,"

the going round
And round and round, the merely going round,
Until merely going round is a final good,
The way wine comes at a table in a wood.

(p. 405)

The last line of this passage, to my mind one of the finest touches in *Notes*, deserves further comment. From the point of view of the reader, it both signifies and accomplishes the giving of pleasure and so accords with the title of the last section of the poem, to which it belongs. Unanticipated by anything that precedes it and no sooner introduced than dropped, it typifies the prodigality of Stevens's inventiveness, an ever-accruing wealth which need never hoard itself but can be spent at once. As an event in the mind of the speaker of the poem, it represents a refreshment of life following the acceptance of finality, an ending giving way to a new beginning. Such freshness and spontaneity are thematic. If the moment of imaginative satisfaction, resulting as it does from an encounter between two changing entities, is fleeting, it is by that same token unpredictable. "One looks at the sea / As one improvises, on the piano" (p. 233). A poem entitled "The Sense of the Sleight-of-Hand Man" opens with a statement of this theme, leading off characteristically with a series of three alternative images:

> One's grand flights, one's Sunday baths,
> One's tootings at the weddings of the soul
> Occur as they occur.
>
> (p. 222)

The speaker now asks rhetorically, introducing yet another image, "Could you have said the bluejay suddenly / Would swoop to earth?" He continues,

> It is a wheel, the rays
> Around the sun. The wheel survives the myths.
> The fire eye in the clouds survives the gods.
> To think of a dove with an eye of grenadine
> And pines that are cornets, so it occurs.

These lines make clear that what are called "occurrences" belong both to the external world (the sun with its rays, the red eye of the dove, the sound of wind in the pine trees) and the world within (the metaphors of wheel, eye, grenadine and cornets). To the day-by-day vagaries of wind, weather, and cloud within the framework of seasonal change, the mind responds in accordance with its own fluctuations of vitality and mood, constantly rising to unforeseen occasions. Reality "occurs" independently of our expectations; we say of it what it "occurs" to us to say.

As in the opening lines of "The Sense of the Sleight-of-Hand Man," the grammatical device of the series—whether of words, phrases, or similarly constructed clauses or sentences—lends itself in Stevens to the expression of alternative and equally valid apprehensions. Such sequences dramatize the rapid "play" of thought upon object or idea, and the mind appears in them as "playful" in that its activity is self-sufficing, intrinsically pleasurable without regard to what it accomplishes.

> The wind is like a dog that runs away.
> But it is like a horse. It is like motion
>
> That lives in space. It is a person at night.
> A member of the family, a tie,
> An ethereal cousin, another milleman.
>
> (p. 352)

Some of the poems, indeed, consist largely or wholly of lists of appellations amounting to so many descriptive "hypotheses" among which no choice need be made—or, rather, all of which must be chosen. In "Jumbo," for example, the figure named in the title is a tempest, plucking the trees like the "iron bars" of a huge stringed instrument, or as a captive elephant might pluck apart the iron bars of his cage. The speaker's question to himself, "Who was the musician . . . wildly free," is answered in the last three stanzas of the poem:

> The companion in nothingness,
> Loud, general, large, fat, soft
> And wild and free, the secondary man,
>
> Cloud-clown, blue painter, sun as horn,
> Hill-scholar, man that never is,
> The bad-bespoken lacker,
>
> Ancestor of Narcissus, prince
> Of the secondary men. There are no rocks
> And stones, only this imager.
>
> (p. 269)

Another grammatical device, the appositive, may similarly express an un-anticipated turn of thought, as in the famous manifesto of *Notes:*

> the sun
> Must bear no name, gold flourisher, but be.
>
> (p. 381)

"Gold flourisher" is of course a name for the sun, but in appositive use it strikes us as a designation that occurs to the speaker at this moment, as he thinks about the necessity of freeing the sun from the designations of the past. The same effect of a mental occurrence or event is similarly produced in "Two Versions of the Same Poem," which opens with the lines

> Once more he turned to that which could not be fixed,
> By the sea, insolid rock, stentor.
>
> (p. 353)

Later, the sea is addressed as "Lascar, and water-carcass never named."

If there is something both "shifty" and "makeshift" about the imagination's endlessly self-destructing output, there is also something tentative. Again and again, the poet-speaker speaks of what he has achieved so far as "Segmenta" (p. 485), "fragments found in the grass" (p. 515), "patches and pitches" (*O.P.*, p. 114), "edgings and inchings of final form" (p. 488). We remember in this connection that Stevens thought of calling *Harmonium*, his first book, *The Grand Poem: Preliminary Minutiae* and of calling the *Collected Poems* in turn *The Whole of Harmonium*. If the full experience of reality resists even momentary expression, how much more unlikely of accomplishment is the grand poem itself, the supreme fiction in which being will come true and the structure of ideas will be one with the structure of things. We hear, in Stevens's poems, of total edifices, compositions of the whole, summaria in excelsis, but these projects remain forever "possible"; we do not see them realized. The most important of the long poems, *Notes toward a Supreme Fiction, The Auroras of Autumn,* and *An Ordinary Evening in New Haven,* lack the architectonic unity, the linear movement toward culmination and resolution or systems of complementary relationships among parts, of "When Lilacs Last in the Dooryard Bloomed," "The Tower," *Four Quartets,* or even *The Waste Land*—though each has its own emotional climate, its dramatic succession of moods and modes, its risings and fallings off of intensity, its thematic repetitions. In a sense, each is a collection of shorter poems, a set of variations rather than a symphonic movement. When Stevens does develop a single fictional concept at length, as in "Examination of the Hero in Time of War," "Chocorua to Its Neighbor," and "The Owl in the Sarcophagus," he is not at his most compelling. Something in him did not love the building of massive monolithic structures.

At the end of "The Owl in the Sarcophagus," Stevens's solemn "mythology of modern death" gives way to a simple and self-deprecatory image:

> It is a child that sings itself to sleep,
> The mind, among the creatures that it makes,
> The people, those by which it lives and dies.
>
> (p. 436)

This conception of the imagination's lifework as child's play is a sign of another happy paradox: the presence, in so austere and abstruse a poet and one who took the poetic vocation so seriously, of so much that does not take itself seriously. Our pleasure in Stevens has its source in the picnics as well as the parades and processions, the clowns as well as the rabbis, the ithy oonts and long-haired plomets as well as the lions and swans, the banjo's twang as well as the reverberations of choirs and bells, the beating of the lard pail as well as the blows of the lyre, the hair ribbons of the child as well as the glittering belts and flashing cloaks of the stars. And then there is the irrepressible gaiety and glitter of the language itself, the embellishments of its verbal music "lol-lolling the endlessness of poetry" (p. 458), its flashes of immediacy amid the most abstract or solemn statements, its "tootings at the weddings of the soul" (p. 222). This strain of unpretentiousness and playfulness finds expression in the *Letters* as well as the poems. "People ought to like poetry," Stevens wrote, "the way a child likes snow" (p. 349); and "Many lines exist because I enjoy their clickety-clack in contrast with the more decorous pom-pom-pom that people expect" (p. 485). From the *Letters*, too, we learn that for a long time Stevens thought of adding other sections to *Notes toward a Supreme Fiction* and "one in particular: *It Must Be Human*" (pp. 863–64).

Toward the end of the second section of *Notes*, "It Must Change," there occurs a statement that I quoted earlier in another connection: "The poem goes from the poet's gibberish to / The gibberish of the vulgate and back again." The description of imaginative activity as a dialectic in process leads to a series of questions:

> Does it move to and fro or is it of both
>
> At once? Is it a luminous flittering
> Or the concentration of a cloudy day?
> Is there a poem that never reaches words
>
> And one that chaffers the time away?
> Is the poem both peculiar and general?

As is usually the case in Stevens when the nature of poetry is in question, all these pairs of alternatives apply, even, or rather especially, when they contradict each other (so too, later in the poem, with the Canon Aspirin's mutually exclusive alternatives, thought as thought and fact as fact, both of which must be chosen [p. 403]). This is made clear by the definitive statement at the end of the passage, where it is said of the poet that

> He tries by a peculiar speech to speak
>
> The peculiar potency of the general,
> To compound the imagination's Latin with
> The lingua franca et jocundissima.

Lingua franca, that is, "a mixed language or jargon," is an apt metaphor for the element of "gaiety" in Stevens's diction—his borrowings from modern foreign languages, his sound-symbolic vocabulary, his playful alterations and coinages. Nor is it surprising that the words used in this passage themselves exemplify the opposite extremes which must be fused into a single voice—*flittering* and *chaffers* belonging to the *lingua franca; luminous, concentration*, and others, to the imagination's Latin.

The power to bring about such compoundings remained undiminished in Stevens's last years, and the late poems collected in "The Rock" and *Opus Posthumous* make manifest his continuing delight in "reality as an activity of the most august imagination" (*O.P.,* p. 110). As a final emblem of delight and renewal, we may take the description of the chapel rising from "Terre Ensevelie" beside the ruins of the church in "St. Armorer's Church from the Outside." The church is replaced by the chapel as the past, for him who chooses to remain on the "outside," is perpetually replaced by the present:

> The chapel rises, his own, his period,
> A civilization formed from the outward blank,
> A sacred syllable rising from sacked speech,
>
> . . . .
> Time's given perfections made to seem like less
> Then the need of each generation to be itself,
> The need to be actual and as it is.
>
> St. Armorer's has nothing of this present,
> This *vif*, this dizzle-dazzle of being new
> And of becoming, for which the chapel spreads out
> Its arches in its vivid element,
>
> In the air of newness of that element,
> In an air of freshness, clearness, greenness, blueness,
> That which is always beginning because it is part
> Of that which is always beginning, over and over.

The chapel underneath St. Armorer's walls,
Stands in a light, its natural light and day,
The origin and keep of its health and his own.
And there he walks and does as he lives and likes.

With its high-style rhetoric, its mixture of common native words with elements of the imagination's Latin and of the *lingua franca* (foreign borrowing, sound-symbolic coinage, and all), its play on the ordinary and archaic poetic meanings of *keep*, it succession of equally valid descriptive formulations, its protracted series of nouns and nominal phrases giving way in the last line to a flurry of finite verbs (couched in the simplest of diction), this passage speaks a language such as we find in no other poet—abstract, changing, pleasure giving, and human.

Sic Transit Gloria: Six Famous Poets: Vachel Lindsay, Edgar Lee Masters, Carl Sandburg, Sara Teasdale, Elinor Wylie, Edna St. Vincent Millay

Hyatt Waggoner

We do not, with sufficient plainness, or sufficient profoundness, address ourselves to life, nor dare we chant our own times and social circumstance. . . . We have yet had no genius in America, with tyrannous eye, which knew the value of our incomparable materials, and saw, in the barbarism and materialism of the times, another carnival of the same gods whose picture he so much admires in Homer; then in the middle age; then in Calvinism. Banks and tariffs, the newspaper and caucus, Methodism and Unitarianism, are flat and dull to dull people, but rest on the same foundations of wonder as the town of Troy, and the temple of Delphos, and are as swiftly passing away.

—EMERSON, "The Poet"

The impulse of the new verse [of the 1920s] seems to abide in the poets, all Westerners, who trumpeted, as if in obedience to Emerson and Whitman, America's common moods.

—STANLEY T. WILLIAMS, *American Literature*, 1933

Literary historians of the "New Poetry" movement of the second and third decades of this century have often started their story with the founding of *Poetry: A Magazine of Verse* by Harriet Monroe in Chicago in 1912, and then gone on from there, keeping their eyes on the early issues of the magazine, struggling to bring some kind of order out of the multifarious and undigestible facts before them. Trying to discern the defining characteristics of the movement, they have found themselves faced with the impossible task of generalizing about poets who had nothing in common but their "newness."

Within a year and a half or so of its first issue of October 1912, *Poetry* had published the work of Ezra Pound and Grace Hazard Conkling; William Vaughn Moody and H. D.; Tagore and John Gould Fletcher; Vachel Lindsay and Robert Frost; Amy Lowell and Carl Sandburg. By 1915 it had added Wallace Stevens and T. S. Eliot to its roster. Having started from the perspective provided by *Poetry*, our poetic historians have asked: What do all these poets have in common?

From *American Poets: From the Puritans to the Present.* © 1968 by Hyatt Waggoner. Houghton Mifflin, 1968.

With the distance afforded by the passage of half a century, it would appear now that the only answer that would not do violence to some of the evidence would be "not much." We can learn more about the characteristics of the poetry that dominated the first half of our century by looking long at the work of Pound, Eliot, Stevens, and Williams than we are likely to by any survey, no matter how prolonged, of the early years of *Poetry* magazine.

Between its founding and about 1920, the magazine championed "free verse" and Imagism. Perhaps it was fortunate, in the long run, that Miss Monroe had only a vague notion of what her two causes entailed; for if she had been clearer in her mind about them, she might not have welcomed to her magazine's pages so many poets who were neither Imagists nor writers of "free" verse. Her own taste was strongly for the simple, direct, and native in poetry, but she let Pound bludgeon her into publishing Eliot, and, at Pound's urging again, gave Frost his first American publication in an important national magazine. She managed to pay her contributors, and she was hospitable to unpublished writers. Her magazine did more for poetry than we would be led to expect if we knew only her autobiography, *A Poet's Life,* or her own slender volume of verse. *The Difference and Other Poems* is the only book of poetry I have ever seen that both opens and closes with a photograph of the author, who looks very distinguished in both poses. In between the handsome portraits there is some very undistinguished verse.

As a native Chicagoan who was proud of her city and hopeful that it might become a center for the arts, Miss Monroe was especially on the lookout for midwestern talent. Vachel Lindsay, Edgar Lee Masters, and Carl Sandburg, all from Illinois, seemed for a while, not only to her but to others like Amy Lowell, who ranked them in her *A Critical Fable* just after Frost and Robinson and just before herself, to justify her regionalist expectations. That the first two of them have almost completely ceased to be read by people under fifty and that the third has come to be known chiefly as a folklorist, ballad-singer, and biographer of Lincoln, is the kind of historical irony that makes critics and editors apprehensive about recognizing new talent.

VACHEL LINDSAY

Vachel Lindsay might really have been what he has been called, a "folk poet," if the conditions for true folk poetry had existed in this country in the first third of the century. Again, if he had had more intelligence and self-restraint, it might not have been merely a wry joke to call him, as Peter Viereck has, "the Dante of the Fundamentalists." If self-criticism had been possible for him, he might have created more than an occasional poem capable of reminding us of Blake and Emerson and Whitman.

In a confused and thoroughly subintellectual way, Lindsay tried to re-express for mid-America in the twentieth century the visionary romantic affirmations of these three. His Disciples of Christ (Campbellite) religious background gave him millennial hopes. He had been touched by Swedenborg, through friends in Springfield. Curiously, several of the influences on him paralleled those that affected Blake and Emerson. As an art student in Chicago Lindsay had made copious notes on Blake and had tried, he tells us, to learn to draw like him. When we glance through the final edition of his *Collected Poems,* with its endpaper drawings of the "Village Improvement Parade," its "mystic" "Map of the Universe," and its insistence that we study certain drawings and poems for their hidden meanings, we see a Blakean influence that Lindsay never adequately acknowledged. Reading the poems, we find frequent verbal echoes as well as thematic parallels in poems on children, the poor, and the immanent divinity. But more often than not, Blake's visions seem ludicrous in Lindsay's version. Mysticism has been vulgarized to mystagoguery when a poet can speak so easily of "mystic Springfield" and say that "Swedenborg should be rewritten in Hollywood."

Emerson and Whitman are the only American poets mentioned in Lindsay's "Litany of Heroes"—

> Then let us seek out shining Emerson,
> Teacher of Whitman, and better priest of man,
> The self-reliant granite American,

but Lindsay's work does not make it entirely clear how much or how well he knew their writings. In the first of his "Three Poems about Mark Twain," he contrasts them both with the "genius of the stream" whom one cannot dodge:

> All praise to Emerson and Whitman, yet
> The best they have to say, their sons forget.

Still, no poet in this century wrote more as though he had not forgotten Emerson's advice in "The Poet" to write about the "poem" of America. With Whitmanic inclusiveness, Lindsay sang the praises of Johnny Appleseed and John L. Sullivan; General William Booth and Lincoln; liberal Governor Altgeld of Illinois and William Jennings Bryan; Jane Addams and Theodore Roosevelt; Pocahontas and the bronco that would not be broken. And once at least, in one of his best poems, he must have been remembering Emerson's very words about the carnival of the gods, Troy, and the "foundations of wonder." "Kalamazoo" opens with the fine lines,

> Once, in the city of Kalamazoo,
> The gods went walking, two and two,

but soon appears to be breaking down into sentimentality and gaucherie:

> For in Kalamazoo in a cottage apart
> Lived the girl with the innocent heart.
> Thenceforth the city of Kalamazoo
> Was the envied, intimate chum of the sun,

only to rise to authentic expression again as the humor and the wonder are played off against each other, almost as though Lindsay were adding a note to Emerson's comment on the Troys of America, saying that one need not be solemn about seeing beauty and romance in the awkward. The girl with "the innocent heart," which was perhaps not so innocent after all, his Helen,

> made great poets of wolf-eyed men—
> The dear queen-bee of Kalamazoo
> With her crystal wings and her honey heart.
> We fought for her favors a year and a day
> (Oh, the bones of the dead, the Oshkosh dead,
> That were scattered along her pathway red!)
> And then, in her harum-scarum way,
> She left with a passing traveller-man—
> With a singing Irishman
> Went to Japan.
>
> . . . .
> Who burned this city of Kalamazoo—
> Love-town Troy-town Kalamazoo?

Lindsay did not often write so well. When the subject was closer to him, he was likely to fall back on flat assertions like those with which "Johnny Appleseed's Hymn to the Sun" opens—

> Christ the dew in the clod,
> Christ the sap in the trees,
> Christ the light in the waterfall,
> Christ the soul of the sun.

In general, the Johnny Appleseed poems are among Lindsay's best, but simply to assert the idea of immanence this way is to leave a good many readers unpersuaded. Jones Very would no doubt have liked the lines, since they say what he had said, often more strikingly. But it is not hard to imagine Pound's reaction.

With an almost complete incapacity for self-criticism, Lindsay was capable of writing not simply flat lines but whole poems we can only call bathetic and absurd. The *Collected Poems* is full of verse that is embarrassing to read—if one sees any merit at all in Lindsay. One example will speak for all. "A Rhyme about an Electrical Advertising Sign" could be called Emersonian in its perceiving the "foundations of wonder" on which the then novel product of technology rests; or Whitmanic in "singing the strong light works of engineers"; it might be noted that it states one of the chief themes in Hart Crane's *The Bridge*. But noting how central it is, thematically, in the native romantic tradition cannot save it as a poem. Lindsay's millennial expectations seem only naive when applied to this subject, so that a cynical rejoinder is likely to be the reader's only response to its vision of spiritual progress without pain. Very soon now, the poem says, the newly invented signs will cease to advertise men's collars and new fashions for "shame-weary girls," and will help us ascend to the divine—perhaps by advertising church services?

> The sings in the street and the signs in the skies
> Shall make a new Zodiac, guiding the wise,
> And Broadway make one with that marvellous stair
> That is climed by the rainbow-clad spirits of prayer.

When *this* happens, one assumes that the ladder of spiritual contemplation will have been made plain and easy for the masses.

When we have read this and a good many other poems equally bad, and when we have noted that "The Congo" is absurd if it is read as its subtitle directs us to read it, as a "study" of the Negro race, and that the syncopated rhythms of both "The Congo" and "General Booth" get tiresome before the poems end—when we have noted all this and more that is damaging to what little reputation Lindsay still has, we are likely to conclude that he ought to be totally forgotten.

But we should be wrong. This poet who pleased patriotic critics like Amy Lowell by being so unmistakably grass-roots American, progressive, liberal, and wholesome—all in contrast with the attitudes of expatriates like Pound and Eliot—actually wrote quite a few fine poems and dozens of memorable ones. The Johnny Appleseed poems are worth reading once at least, and several other celebrations of the land and its people are unsurpassed of their kind—"The Golden Whales of California," "Abraham Lincoln Walks at Midnight," "The Eagle That Is Forgotten," for instance. "The Leaden Eyed" expresses Lindsay's thoroughly democratic sympathies far more effectively than "Why I Voted the Socialist Ticket." There are even moving passages in "Bryan, Bryan, Bryan, Bryan," in which the naive Populism is rendered as the memory of what it was like to be sixteen and in love and a Democrat in 1896 in Springfield. The best of Lindsay is worth saving.

EDGAR LEE MASTERS

That cannot be so definitely said about another poet immensely popular for a few years, whom Amy Lowell ranked higher than Pound or Eliot or Stevens. Edgar Lee Masters has more recently been called a "one book" poet, but it begins to appear that that too is an exaggeration. Reading his work along with that of Vachel Lindsay and the early work of Carl Sandburg, all of whom were enthusiastically welcomed by most of the "best critics" in the country at the time, we get a fresh insight into the excuse the American cultural scene offered for Pound's inveterate rage and Eliot's gesture of disaffiliation. *Spoon River Anthology* became in 1915 that rare phenomenon, a book of poetry that is a "best-seller," and remained so for several years, while Frost and Williams were still having difficulty getting published.

Lindsay's life ended badly, in bitterness, insanity, and finally suicide, but his verse at least was full of exuberance. Masters's work was almost as depressed from the beginning as the man himself became in his later years. The sketches of the inhabitants of Spoon River include some of people who found satisfaction in their lives, to be sure, but neither Masters nor his readers could identify with them enough to remember them. As in Sherwood Anderson's fictional counterpart of *Spoon River*, *Winesburg, Ohio*, published just three years later, repression, frustration, and eventual defeat seem to be the rule in the community, and the elegiac tone is unbroken even in the sections that tell of characters like Lucinda Matlock, who *says* she loved life, but protests too much in saying it.

Symptomatically, Father Malloy is not allowed to speak for himself as the others do who lie in the cemetery on the hill. Buried in "holy ground"— the separate Roman Catholic cemetery—he is said to have "believed in the joy of life." He "did not seem to be ashamed of the flesh" and he "faced life as it is." The speaker in Father Malloy's section thinks of Father Malloy as "Siding with us who would rescue Spoon River / From the coldness and the dreariness of village morality." But the speaker cannot imagine what the priest would *say* if he spoke for himself; the faith that produced his joy and his healthy moral realism remains a total mystery.

In the "Father Malloy" section we come to understand the double focus of the whole poem. Implicitly, two different, and conflicting, general meanings emerge from this work that avowedly offers us only a realistic cross-section view of the village life. Self-consciously, Masters is contributing his bit to the "revolt from the village" and the repudiation of lingering "Puritanism," a revolt that would continue to gain momentum for at least the next ten years, especially in works of fiction. From this point of view, Father Malloy offers the model for the better life. But at the same time, more or less unconsciously, Masters is saying, less explicitly but with more feeling, that the real enemy is not Puritan morality but "the nature of things," which to a thinking person made impossible the faith that sustained Father Malloy and Lucinda Matlock, who speaks as from Heaven. If life without the religious faith of these two is simply depressing, and if faith is impossible even to imagine except in Catholic priests and women who died long ago at ninety-six, then it would seem that the achieved meaning of the book is not that we ought to leave the village and cease being Puritans but that life's woe is irremediable.

In his introduction to Robinson's *King Jasper*, Frost would later praise

Robinson for having treated "immedicable" woes, "griefs" instead of merely "grievances." Masters and Robinson have in common a kind of grayness of tone. But there is an important difference between them: Robinson fully understood how "immedicable" the griefs that concerned him were, while it is not clear from *Spoon River Anthology* whether Masters did or not. It seems rather more likely that he didn't know exactly what he *did* mean, or what he intended, in the poem.

Though he had written a good many verses in formal meters before *Spoon River*, this first—and, as it turned out, last—great success spurred Masters on to rapid production. In the following year he brought out two more books of poems, *Songs and Satires* and *The Great Valley*. Not one poem in either book gives us any clue to the success of *Spoon River*, but a good many of them point to the unmentioned source of that poem's depressed tone. "Terminus," for example, in *Songs and Satires*, makes no secret of what the real source of the depression is:

> There is a void that the agèd world
> Throws over the spent heart.

If the metaphor seems mixed here, the *idea* is clear enough. Later in the poem we get a specific statement of what makes the heart empty and the sky "hollow." If we recall that Christ spoke of himself as a vine, the reason for the void in the heart is sufficiently plain:

> Oh, heart of man and heart of woman,
> Thirsting for blood of the vine,
> Life waits till the heart has lived too much
> And then pours in new wine!

In *The Great Valley* we find a more impressive, because better written, clue to the unacknowledged meaning of *Spoon River*. In the long dramatic poem "The Gospel of Mark," in which Mark speaks to a younger disciple, the negative language and the agonized tone of Mark's final words remind us of many passages in similar poems by Robinson:

> No, it cannot be.
> Man's soul, the chiefest flower of all we know,
> Is not the toy of Malice or of Sport.
> It is not set apart to be betrayed,
> Or gulled to its undoing, left to dash
> Its hopeless head against this rock's exception,
> No water for its thirst, no life to feed it,
> No law to guide it. . . .
>
> . . . .
> Go write what I have told you, come what will
> I'm going to the catacombs to pray.

Masters explained the title of his next book of verse, in 1918, this way, in his dedication to William Marion Reedy: "I call this book 'Toward the Gulf,' a title importing a continuation of the attempts of Spoon River and The Great Valley to mirror the age and the country in which we live." Taking Masters at his word, we turn to one of the sketches in the book:

> Louise was a nymphomaniac.
> She was married twice.
> Both husbands fled from her insatiable embraces.
> At thirty-two she became a woman on a telephone list,
> Subject to be called,
> And for two years ran through a daily orgy of sex,
> When blindness came on her, as it came on her father before
> her,
> And she became a Christian Scientist,
> And led an exemplary life.

It is clear that Louise had a lot of hard luck, except for those two fortunate years when she could combine her vocation and her avocation, but it is not clear just what aspects of the age and the country her story mirrors. Could it be the rising divorce rate, or the rapid growth of the Christian Science Society, during those years?

The title of Masters's book of 1919, *Starved Rock*, could have been explicated with the same statement he made about *Toward the Gulf*, and in his very long *Domesday Book* of 1920 he returned to the formula of *Spoon River*, except that he now used blank verse instead of free verse. After this came many books, including *The New Spoon River* in 1924. Masters died in 1950, fifteen years after his last work, a study of Vachel Lindsay. His life is as sad a story as any he told in his verse. A few of the original *Spoon River* sketches are worth keeping in the anthologies to represent the short-lived attempt at "realism" in poetry, but nothing else by Masters is really worth reading. Lindsay originally was, and Sandburg eventually became, better poets.

CARL SANDBURG

Even if there had never been any New Critics to denigrate it, Sandburg's early work, with the exception of several short poems, would surely have been recognized by this time for what it was, an expression of the times that came as close to being subliterary as the work of any American poet of comparable reputation ever has. It is much more difficult, today, to understand why *this* poetry was once so greatly admired than it is to think ourselves back into the situation in which Whittier's poems were read with pleasure. However much we may approve of Sandburg's humanitarian and socialist views, and his efforts to write poetry in which "democratic" and "realistic" would amount to the same thing, we are likely to find the poetry itself, when we actually *read* it, more remote than Tuckerman's. Much of it reads like the worst of Whitman, if Whitman had had only ideology to guide him.

"I Am the People, the Mob," from the "Other Days (1900–1910)" section of *Chicago Poems* (1916), is typical. It begins, "I am the people—the mob—the crowd—the mass," and ends with these two lines":

> When I, the People, learn to remember, when I, the People,
>   use the lessons of yesterday and no longer forget who
>   robbed me last year, who played me for a fool—then
>   there will be no speaker in all the world say the name:
> "The People," with any fleck of a sneer in his voice or
>   any far-off smile of derision.
> The mob—the crowd—the mass—will arrive then.

If there is anything here to lift this above the level of socialist political oratory, it is difficult to see what it is. The outlook being expressed is no more and no less difficult to take seriously than Lindsay's Populism or Whitman's radical democracy and nationalism, though Sandburg looks for revolution to accomplish what they thought evolution would do. The trouble with these verses is that neither in terms of metrics nor in terms of imaginative use of language nor in any other way do we feel in them the presence of a "shaping spirit" doing anything to vivify the abstractions. If the poem calls forth *any* response from us, it will be a purely political one: Some people hope for, and some dread, revolution. If we do neither, we are likely to feel nothing at all. We turn the pages looking for a better poem.

Better ones are hard to find, but there are a few. "Fog" and "Nocturne in a Deserted Brickyard" are the poems most often anthologized, and they do seem less unimaginative than the rest, but Amy Lowell and a dozen other minor poets of the time wrote as memorably. "Chicago" is probably the poem for which the volume will ultimately be remembered, if it is remembered at all. The poem was praised at the time for being just as raw, violent, and unformed as its subject, for its "realism," in short. "The crude violence of the poem is the violence of the city itself," readers were told. The naturalistic aesthetic common at the time placed a high value on direct imitation. Art should be a replica. "Chicago" is full of the "raw material of poetry in all its rawness" that Marianne Moore would soon call the distinguishing mark of genuine poetry. But if the "toads" were "real" enough, there seems to be no "imaginary garden."

Sandburg's early work is full of things that remind us of other poets at the time, nearly always to Sandburg's disadvantage. "Prufrock," for example, which had appeared in *Poetry* the year before *Chicago Poems* was published, identified fog with a cat. The metaphor gains meaning and force in Eliot's poem from its context, including Prufrock's fear of the "animal" side of his nature and his ambivalent use of other animal images. Sandburg makes the identification the substance of the whole poem in "Fog." Lacking any context, his metaphor seems relatively pointless: Like cats, fogs come silently.

Pound's work supplies another parallel. The primitivism of his "Salutation," which contrasts the "thoroughly smug and thoroughly uncomfortable" with the happy "fishermen picnicking in the sun" in the company of their "untidy families," is suggested by Sandburg's "Happiness," which concludes that happiness is reserved for "a crowd of Hungarians under the trees with their women and children and a keg of beer and an accordion." But Pound's last line lifts "Salutation" far above "Happiness": "And the fish swim in the lake and do not even own clothing." We think of the healthy exuberance of the young Whitman, wishing to turn and live with the animals. Sandburg's poem makes us think only of our abstract objections to an abstract primitivism.

The poems in the next volume, *Cornhuskers,* in 1918, are generally less shapeless. Sandburg feels no need, now that life in small towns and on the farm, and memories of prairie scenes, have taken the place of Chicago as the subject, to make the poems "sprawl like the city." It is partly no doubt for this reason, and partly because memory has now replaced political preachment, that there are more realized poems in the volume. "Loam," "Godwing Moth," "Cool Tombs," and "Grass" all come from *Cornhuskers.* Still, when Sandburg writes on subjects others have treated, his inferiority is generally clear, as a comparison of his "Buffalo Bill" with Cummings's "Buffalo Bill's" illustrates. Sandburg's poem expresses simple nostalgia for the lost world of the child, to whom Buffalo Bill was the embodiment of romance. Cummings's poem does this too but adds a witty adult question about how genuine that romance was, and then, with its suggestion of an equation between Buffalo Bill and Christ, enlarges the question still further. Are all such "romantic" figures the creations simply of wish?

After almost half a century of devoting his energies chiefly to things other than his own poetry, Sandburg published his best volume of verse in 1963. *Honey and Salt* would be a remarkable achievement for any poet, but for a poet in his middle eighties who gained his fame with "Chicago," it is extraordinary. The poems no longer demand to be classified as tough or tender, violent or sentimental. There is in them the mellowness and wisdom of age, which we should like to feel we could expect of very aged poets, but hardly dare to; and there is much more. This volume reminds us of the development of Williams in his last decade, both in sound and in sense. The lines now are much more strongly cadenced, yet still "free." The sound of "the American idiom," as Williams called it, is in fact more evident here than in the earlier, more "realistic," verse. And the sense is as different as the sound from what the early work prepared us to expect. The old reliance on ideology has been replaced by a concern for actual people and their actual experience and actual needs, without any loss in the strength of the vision of the family of man. (A few years before *Honey and Salt,* Sandburg did the captions for that wonderful book of photographs which had *The Family of Man* for its title.) The old tendency to fall back from ideology into pure sentimentalism is gone, too, without any loss of the genuine, controlled and meaningful, tenderness that was the chief distinction of the best early poems. In its place, we find a mature romantic imagination manifesting itself chiefly thorugh sympathetic identification with all forms of life.

This is as different as it could be from the identification of the speaker's *interests* with those of "the mass—the mob" that we find in the early poems, and different also from the sentimental celebrations of corn and Buffalo Bill. Some of these late poems come very close to the spirit of Zen—a possibility always latent in the early poems, but never actualized there. "Foxgloves" will illustrate:

> Your heart was handed over
> to the foxgloves one hot summer afternoon.
> The snowsilk buds nodded and hung drowsy.
>   So the stalks believed
>   As they held those buds above.
>   In deep wells of white
> The dark fox fingers go in these gloves.
>   In a slow fold of summer
> Your heart was handed over in a curve
>   from bud to bloom.

The new tendency to *meet* man and nature, instead of trying to manipulate them "for their own good," in the case of man, or submit to them, in the case of nature, leads to an explicitly religious consciousness in these poems—again, always implicit in Sandburg's early work, but in conflict, there, with both political ideology and his notion of "reality." In *Honey and Salt* we are reminded of Frost's late stress on the incarnational idea: In these poems, God is "no gentleman"; he "gets dirty running the universe." But his immanence does not now lead the poet to the vaguely suggested pantheism of the early poems. God is the Creator, and so transcendent, as well as immanent, a point very much emphasized in the climactic passage of the longest, and last, poem in the book, "Timesweep."

Our chief impression from this volume is likely to be that Sandburg has at last grown up to something like the level of his prototype, Whitman. His early work, in contrast, generally sounded either like the worst of Whitman, the lines we wish Whitman had left out of "Song of Myself" and "Starting From Paumanok," or like an unsuccessful adaptation of the Whitman whose chief preoccupations were love and death. In the more than half a century between the earliest poems in the Chicago volume and these last poems, Sandburg discovered in depth the meaning of the tradition in which he had always tried to work. Perhaps the years devoted to study of Lincoln, and the further years of collecting and singing American folksongs and ballads, helped. At any rate, line after line, and a good many whole poems, now remind us of the Whitman we value: "The personal idiom of a corn shock satisfies me. . . . The light of the sun ran through the line / of the water and struck where the moss on / a stone was green. . . . Sheet white egg faces, strong and sad gorilla / mugs, meet yourselves, meet each other." Whitman would have felt, I like to think, that Sandburg's career justified him in the end. At any rate, he might have noted that there was no theme and no effect in *Honey and Salt* that he had not already suggested somewhere. Which would be a way of praising Sandburg, not of damning him. Whitman's vision has not been easy to recover in our century.

For anyone who still enjoys contemplating the ironies of history and the fickleness of literary fortune, the careers of the three best-liked women poets of the 1920s and early 1930s could be an interesting subject of study. Sara Teasdale, Elinor Wylie, and Edna St. Vincent Millay were thought great by many who were themselves thought great, and are now nearly forgotten, except by a few of those who were young when they were young. When we set them against Emily Dickinson, who was not only almost unknown during her lifetime but rejected by those few who knew her work, the irony deepens. Those of us old enough to have a little Latin are likely to find themselves pondering on *ubi sunt* and *sic transit gloria mundi* themes.

The spectacle of three such similar poets suffering similar fates ought to be instructive, we are likely to feel. But how? There is a good deal that is calculated to induce melancholy, both in their work and in their lives, but very little to be learned, it would seem; not even the lesson that bad poets are sometimes temporarily popular with those who should know better; for they were not "bad" poets, just minor ones with the bad luck to be born in a revolutionary time which they were only partly prepared to understand. The one lesson that emerges from their examples with any clarity, we are likely to feel we do not need, having already learned it from such poets as James Russell Lowell and William Vaughn Moody: that a poet who borrows language and feeling from the Romantics, without being able to think as the Romantics did, is not likely to produce great poetry.

SARA TEASDALE

Between 1907 and 1933 Sara Teasdale published eight books of verse. After her first two slender volumes, devoted mostly to character studies, the rest is all of a piece, with one tone (elegiac), one overarching theme whatever the subject (the inevitability of loss and despair), and several related subjects, chiefly love, beauty (of nature, mostly), death, and the necessity of cultivating courage. The sense of life that dominates her poetry, giving it just one tone no matter what the subject, even when the poem means to affirm a momentary joy or triumph, is explicitly stated in her address "To

an Aeolian Harp," the instrument that Emerson and Melville had written
about:

> The winds have grown articulate in thee,
> And voice again the wail of ancient woe
> That smote upon the winds of long ago;
> The cries of Trojan women as they flee,
> The quivering moan of pale Andromache,
> Now lifted loud with pain and now brought low.
> It is the soul of sorrow that we know,
> As in a shell the soul of all the sea.

Memories of a lost faith dominate all the work, once again, whatever
the subject. In "The Inn of Earth" memory and loss combine to create the
subject, privation. The first of the five stanzas sets the pattern for the rest:

> I came to the crowded Inn of Earth,
>   And called for a cup of wine,
> But the Host went by with averted eye
>   From a thirst as keen as mine.

Privation enforced calls forth willed renunciation. Voicing a simplified
version of Stevens's mighty theme, Teasdale sought refuge in poetry from
her "spirit's gray defeat," her "pulse's flagging beat" and her "hopes that
turned to sand,"

> For with my singing I can make
> A refuge for my spirit's sake,
> A house of shining words to be
> My fragile immortality.

Beauty found in experience would do, would *have* to do, if the poems didn't
come. It would distract one from thinking of "Atoms as old as stars, /
Mutation on mutation, / Millions and millions of cells / Dividing," and other
similarly depressing subjects. " . . . Forever / Seek for Beauty, she only /
Fights with man against Death!" If only one could *really* love "all lovely
things," then one might sing "as children sing / Fitting tunes to everything,
/ Loving life for its own sake."

Again and again Teasdale makes the claim that she actually *does* love
all lovely things and love life for its own sake, but the brittleness of the
affirmation is not only revealed by the rest of her poetry, it is exposed even
in the affirmation itself, though not with the effect of intended irony. The
poet says she has *"tried* to take" (my italics) the "stings" of "all lovely
things" lightly, "with gay unembittered lips."; she has, she says, been
"careless" if her "heart must break." Beauty "stings" of course because it
is not permanent, perhaps not even "real." One thinks of Cummings's
satirical poem on this theme that was so common in the 1920s, particularly
in the work of the women poets—"Poem, or Beauty Hurts Mr. Vinal."

"Spare us from beauty," Teasdale, Wylie, and Millay all cried out over and over, in between statements that only beauty mattered. "Spend all you have for loveliness" might have been written by any of the three: Teasdale wrote it. Do so, she said, even though it hurts almost beyond bearing.

Teasdale writes often, in her later volumes, on another theme that both Frost and Stevens had made their own—not that she seems in any way indebted to them. I mean that "One must have a mind of winter" theme. Since everything, most especially the fleeting quality of beauty and love, makes the poet think of "The clock running down, / Snow banking the door" ("Winter Night Song"); and since she can only picture her life as a tune that "climbs. . . . / High over time, high even over doubt" but then, having climbed so high, "pauses / And faltering blindly down the air, goes out," she spends a good deal of time renouncing every hope and insisting that she has "ceased to fear," as once she feared, "The last complete reunion with the earth." She will find peace when the rooftops are "crowned with snow," once she has become "cold with song."

The words ring hollow today, though they didn't seem to do so to many in her generation. She seems to have had no resources to fall back on except the determination of the agonized consciousness to create a "music of stillness" out of the "dream" of the "lonely mind." But she knew the music was only fictive, and therefore not sufficient. Even when she most earnestly asserts its supremacy, she does not convince, either herself or us. Only in her last volume, *Strange Victory*, when she had stopped trying to convince anyone of anything, when she had stopped hoping she could move beyond tragedy, did she begin to write in a way that does not seem embarrassing. Now she perceived that the "long tragic play" of life is "acted best when not a single tear / Falls" and "when the mind, and not the heart, holds sway." For *her* poetry, this was a discovery worth making. *Strange Victory* is a very slender volume containing just twenty-two short lyrics, but it not only contains Teasdale's best work, it is a book any poet might be glad to have written. Perhaps half the poems in it are free from any pretense or any affectation, which had been her ruling vices. But the strange victory she had gained after her hope was lost, though it was salutary for her art, did not suffice the woman. Having at last learned to write well, she committed suicide in 1933.

ELINOR WYLIE

Expressing very similar attitudes, developing often the same themes, in a style derived, like Teasdale's, from the English Romantics, particularly from Shelley, Elinor Wylie created more poems that are still good to read. The several best of them, especially "Wild Peaches" and "Innocent Landscape," are very good. Wylie's spirit was tougher than Teasdale's had been before *Strange Victory*, and her mind clearer.

But what we are likely to notice first, as we read through her collected poems, is the similarity of the two. Among poets less gifted than the major figures of the age, the number of possible reactions to "the modern temper" was severely limited. Thus Wylie, echoing Teasdale, writes often of the advantages of a cold mind and of the heart's strategies of survival with a minimum of sustenance. In her best-known poem, "Let No Charitable Hope," she writes, "I live by squeezing from a stone / The little nourishment I get." She is preoccupied always with erecting defenses against both "love's violence" and the knowledge of impending doom. Hearing continuously "the end of everything" approaching with a sound "insane, insistent," she seeks out ways to "be fugitive awhile from tears" and finds one of them in listening to a "Viennese Waltz":

> Now falling, falling, feather after feather,
> The music spreads a softness on the ground;
> Now for an instant we are held together
> Hidden within a swinging mist of sound.

So sad have the strains of a gay waltz become to ears attuned to "Doomsday" sounds. "Malicious verity" has touched everything, even Beauty and Love.

Often, reading poems like "Viennese Waltz," we wish for the astringencies of Marianne Moore or the intellectual firmness of Dickinson. This is a reaction especially hard to avoid when the poet attempts affirmations of self-sufficiency after the example of Emerson and Shelley. "Address to My Soul" begins,

> My soul, be not disturbed
> By planetary war;
> Remain securely orbed
> In this contracted star.
> Fear not, pathetic flame;
> Your sustenance is doubt:
> Glassed in translucent dream
> They cannot snuff you out.

"They" floats freely in the sentence, not needing to be attached to anything; readers of the period knew well enough who the enemies of the soul were. The "chaos" and "void" and "dissolving star" mentioned later in the poem were understood before being named as the reasons why the soul must try to "be brave." And the poem's concluding advice to the soul could also be anticipated: "Five-petalled flame, be cold."

Shelley has been drawn upon here to help Wylie make her affirmation ("Life, like a dome of many-colored glass, stains the white radiance of eternity"), and Emerson, with his confidence in the "singular" soul's ability to move through its "predestined arc." (One wonders why the poet never acknowledged her debt to Emerson as she did that to Shelley, calling herself once "a woman by an archangel befriended," with Shelley in the angelic role; and on another occasion spreading "A Red Carpet for Shelley.") But the use made of both older poets is ultimately superficial. Something has been borrowed from the superstructure of their vision, but the foundations have been omitted—both the pantheism suggested by Shelley's "white radiance of eternity," and Emerson's faith in the Soul, and in growth, in process.

Sometimes Wylie's debt to Emerson is more specific than that to Shelley. When it is, her way of contracting his meaning becomes, unfortunately, even clearer. "Beauty," for instance, draws from both "Each and All" and "The Rhodora," but what it omits from Emerson's poems and what it adds to them makes apparent the thinness of Wylie's romanticism. Emerson had said that "Beauty is its own excuse for being," which becomes Wylie's initial injunction, "Say not of Beauty she is good, / Or aught but beautiful." Emerson had warned that the bride would diminish from "fairy" to "gentle wife" when caged in marriage, as a "bird from the woodlands" would cease to sing in captivity. Wylie expressed this by saying that beauty must be left "innocent and wild": "Enshrine her and she dies."

What she has omitted is the Emersonian vision that gives his maxims their meaning. He had concluded "The Rhodora" by saying that "The selfsame Power that brought me there brought you," which is to say, both flower and observer are directly related to, and derive their meaning from, the Over-Soul, and from this relationship get their relationship to each other. In "Each and All," he had discovered the organic unity of being which made futile all efforts to separate truth and beauty for the purpose of analysis. The speaker "yielded" himself "to the perfect whole," secure in the faith that nature was "Full of light and of deity." The beauty of every concrete aspect of being derives from, and is symbolic of, unconditioned Being. Thus it is that beauty needs no practical ("humanistic") justification, that it cannot be analyzed or controlled, that it disappears when separated, and that it can only be intuited in submission to the "perfect Whole." These are some of the meanings underlying and giving shape to Emerson's two poems.

Naturally enough, such Transcendental faith was impossible for Wylie. When she borrowed from Emerson, she could not borrow *this*. But to paraphrase Emerson's conclusions without supplying any substitute for the rejected religious vision on which they ultimately rested was to diminish the Transcendental to the merely sentimental.

Wylie's other borrowings from Emerson are similar. In "The Eagle and the Mole" she sounds very Emersonian, though she is probably also remembering Blake, when she counsels the soul to "Avoid the reeking herd" and "The huddled warmth of crowds," but what the eagle will gain, except possibly blindness, when he "stares into the sun," or what the mole will discover in his "intercourse / With roots of trees and stones, / With rivers at their source," the poem does not say or in any way suggest. Similarly, in "Let No Charitable Hope," the poet who lives, as she puts it, by squeezing her nourishment from a stone, says she looks on time without fear as

> In masks outrageous and austere
> The years go by in single file.

The metaphor is adapted from Emerson's "Days," in which the days march by the speaker "single in an endless file," but there is no relation in *meaning* between Emerson's poem and Wylie's.

It is hardly surprising, therefore, that her best poems are those in which she seems most remote from either Emerson or Shelley. Her sense of man's plight in a meaningless universe was her own, not borrowed and not wished for. From it came the "mind of winter" poems that are generally her best. "Innocent Landscape," for instance, notes that though the "reverential" trees look "like saints,"yet

> Here is no virtue; here is nothing blessèd
> Save this foredoomed suspension of the end;
> Faith is the blossom, but the fruit is cursèd;
> Go hence, for it is useless to pretend.

"Wild Peaches" is her finest poem. In it she manages to make the familiar "mind of winter" theme seem fresh and compelling. For one thing, the personal approach, with its "I" and "we," suits her talent better than the bardic tone of her more openly "philosophic" poems. The poem means more than her other poems partly because it seems not to be *trying* to say so much, merely to be saying "I hate," and "I love"; and partly because its texture is richer than is common in her work.

The poem consists of four sonnets so closely linked that in effect they are stanzas in a single poem. The first three describe a kind of return to an unfallen Eden on "the Eastern Shore" reached by "a river-boat from Baltimore":

> We'll live among wild peach trees, miles from town,
> You'll wear a coonskin cap, and I a gown
> Homespun, dyed butternut's dark gold colour.

There the two will "swim in milk and honey," and find "All seasons sweet, but Autumn best of all"; there the squirrels will fall to the hunter "like fruit" and the "autumn frosts will lie upon the grass / Like bloom on grapes." The spring in that mild climate will begin "before the winter's over" and with it the months that are like "brimming cornucopias" spilling out their gifts of nature's richness.

The poem succeeds as well as it does partly because the picture in the first three stanzas of a friendly and fruitful earth is so concrete. We see and smell and taste lovely things until the senses are cloyed and we are

ready for the last stanza's renunciation, its turn to the bareness and whiteness of a real winter:

> Down to the Puritan marrow of my bones
> There's something in this richess that I hate.
> I love the look, austere, immaculate,
> Of landscapes drawn in pearly monotones.
> There's something in my very blood that owns
> Bare hills, cold silver on a sky of slate,
> A thread of water, churned to milky spate
> Streaming through slanted pastures fenced with stones.

The reason—never stated, fortunately—for the speaker's preference
for the bare winter New England landscape to the friendlier Eastern Shore
of Maryland is that it is more "real." Innocence has been lost for good,
and nature as a whole is *not* friendly, however fertile Maryland soil may
be. The "Puritan" sensibility responds to severity. Looking at the seasons
of man's life, it sees that spring is "briefer than apple-blossom's breath"
and summer is "much too beautiful to stay." Its own seasons are

> Swift autumn, like a bonfire of leaves,
> And sleepy winter, like the sleep of death.

Sara Teasdale had not yet written so well as this, and Elinor Wylie, who
died young in 1928, would not again. Edna St. Vincent Millay, the youngest
of the three, would come close to it only at the very beginning of her career,
but for a while in the 1920s and 1930s she was more famous than either of
the others.

EDNA ST. VINCENT MILLAY

When Elizabeth Atkins published the first book on Millay in 1936, she began
her introduction with a disarmingly modest paragraph in which there are,
nevertheless, certain certainties:

> Continually in England and America one hears the question, "Who
> is our finest living poet?" God help me, I think I know the answer.
> But I am in no mood to divulge it, for I am pacific and vulnerable,
> and it is terrifying to be set upon by a mob of militant believers
> in divers other poets. This book grows out of the safer question,
> "Who is our most popular and representative poet?" At that ques-
> tion the most disputatious roomful calms into agreement in an
> instant. Everyone recognizes that Edna St. Vincent Millary rep-
> resents our time to itself, much as Tennyson represented the pe-
> riod of Victoria to itself, or Byron the period of Romanticism. She
> is the only living poet who is casually quoted in philosophical
> treatises and in moving-picture magazines, in churches and in

night clubs, in the rural schools of Oregon and in the Sorbonne of Paris. It is this character of Edna St. Vincent Millay as our representative-at-large—the incarnation of our *Zeitgeist*—which has set me wondering.

So large a claim, which the author was by no means alone in making, sets *us* to wondering, too. If it is really true that Millay was the incarnation of the *Zeitgeist*, what a melancholy time to have lived in! But then, we reflect, *whose Zeitgeist*, or whose interpretation of the *Zeitgeist*? May we not learn more about the age by reading "Prufrock" or *The Waste Land*, or by thinking hard about all the implications of *The Comedian as the Letter C*? But perhaps it might be objected that Eliot and Stevens, like major artists in any age, were not so much simply reflecting the age as taking its measure prior to deciding what their own role in it should be.

Only two years after she had been celebrated as our "most . . . representative" living poet by Miss Atkins, Millay was wondering rather bitterly why she had not received the Pulitzer Prize for her work since 1923, while Robinson and Frost had received it several times each. Writing another "traditional" poet—that is, not "Modernist," as I have let the Imagists, and Pound, Eliot, and Stevens define the term—Arthur Davison Ficke, she said that in considering those who ought to have been honored but had not, she had thought first of Elinor Wylie, then of Ficke himself, then of Robinson Jeffers, then of herself. She supposed that Wylie had never received it because "she had left her husband and her child to run off to Europe with a married man." Concerning Ficke, she thought of his resignation from his position as curator of Japanese prints at Harvard and of "all the circumstances attending the resignation." Concerning her own failure to get the prize, she was sure she knew the answer. She had been arrested and taken to jail for carrying a placard up and down before the State House in Boston protesting the execution of Sacco and Vanzetti. Robinson and Frost, on the other hand, had apparently led "blameless" lives, she supposed, "both sexual and political," which would be a sufficient explanation of their getting the prize again and again.

Or perhaps, she thought on other occasions, there was another reason for her declining fame, more important, finally, than anything in her private life. After the affair of the Bollingen Prize award to Pound in 1949, which had the effect on Williams of sending him into a temporary breakdown, she read Robert Hillyer's *Saturday Review of Literature* attacks on Eliot and Pound, and on the Committee for awarding the Prize to Pound, and thought the articles "brilliant and truly witty." Perhaps, as Hillyer had proposed, both Eliot and Pound were in effect conspirators, both of them enemies of direct, simple, sensuous, and intelligible poetry, Pound an enemy of the state as well. Perhaps *this* was why her fame had suffered. Writing her publisher, she said she had produced, after reading the Hillyer articles, "a satire in verse against T. S. Eliot."

In her last years she spent much time looking for a demon to blame for her frustration. If she had been able to think about the matter more calmly and self-critically, she might have hit upon another explanation: She had probably never written so well again as she had in the poem which first brought her fame, *Renascence*, which she completed in 1912 when she was twenty and published in 1917. *Renascence* is a romantic poem about an experience of "Cosmic consciousness," to use Bucke's phrase. The tone is excited, girlish, and naively ejaculatory, as why should it not be when a Maine seacoast girl of less than twenty (she held the poem and revised it for several years then sent it out for the Lyric Year contest in 1912) had had such an experience? If the tone were cooler, more "modern," we should suspect the whole business of having been "thought up" to make a poem. Its emotions seem genuine, unforced.

The events narrated in *Renascence* fit the classic accounts of mystical vision. If we are to understand the poem, prior to evaluating it, we must do so in terms supplied by such writers on mysticism as Underhill and Bucke, James and Stace. Point by point, for instance, the speaker's report on the "meaning" of the illumination parallels Whitman's in "Song of Myself"—the same sense of the identity of all being, of the unity of life and death and time and eternity, of the ultimate "rightness" of what *is*, coming after an experience of the death of self. All this and more would make it easier to read this poem in terms of Underhill's schematization of mystical experience than James Miller found it to be with "Song of Myself." To say this is not, obviously, to suggest that there would be any *other* point in comparing the two poems as works of art. It is only to say that insofar as the subject of "Song of Myself" is mystical experience, the subjects of the two poems overlap. Even more clearly, the poem states the central meaning of *satori*, "enlightenment," in Zen.

> In this condition [*satori*] we lose our sense of Self, and know ourselves to be part of the great Oneness of all. Knowing ourselves to be part of Absolute Being, our ego and our problems of ego— sin, pain, poverty, fear—all dissolve.

The importance of this observation is that until we have noted what a poem is *about*, we are not in a position to say anything else about it, including anything about the form it takes.

Although it is written in the idiom of the Romantic poetry of the preceding century, *Renascence* is remarkably free from any suggestions of specific literary indebtedness to nineteenth-century writers. Parallels might be found with religious poets like Henry Vaughan and Thomas Traherne, but if Millay had any specific models in mind, they are certainly not evident in the poem. To be sure, the final twelve lines devoted to explicit interpretation of the experience express ideas that sound like those we have seen in Emerson, Whitman, and Dickinson, but in each case, it is the *idea* rather than the expression of it that reminds us of the older poets, who had, or believed in, or at least knew about, mystical experience. The parallels with certain passages in "Song of Myself" are especially striking.

The sensitive, intense, visionary country girl from Maine never fulfilled the early promise of *Renascence*. Her later attempts to affirm meaning sounded increasingly hollow as the years went by. Vassar and Greenwich Village in the 1920s undid her, perhaps, making her distrust the veracity of her own experience. At any rate, whatever the cause, all her affirmations came to have a quality of shrillness. More and more she sought moments of intense experience, but if she found them, the poetic result does not suggest that they brought any illumination. Her assertions that all was well with her came to seem to rest partly upon the necessities of rhyme and partly upon the felt *need* to cheer herself and others. She insisted that the candle she was burning at both ends gave "a lovely light," but "lovely" or not, the light did nothing to dispel her anguish.

She tried to settle for simple endurance, discovering that "Life must go on," though, as she said, she forgot just why. She was tortured by the spectacle of April coming "like an idiot" who babbled and strewed flowers. More and more often she felt herself "lost in whistling space" and sensed "anonymous death" in the "bubbling bowl" of the sun.

Toward the end of her life, she tried devoting her poetry to good causes to fill the emptiness within her, writing for instance a "Poem and Prayer for an Invading Army" to be read over the radio by Ronald Coleman on the Second World War's D-Day, but afterward she blamed herself for writing "propaganda" instead of poetry. Her love poems had always been rather fevered and brittle. Now, in her last years, tired and ill, she began to wish only for peace. She hoped that others might hope, as she once had.

She was not sure what happened to deprive her of "the sure song" she could no longer sing. Her many admirers wondered too and were no more sure of the answer than she was.

The Eighth Day of Creation:
Rethinking Williams's *Paterson*

Paul Mariani

Even before he finished the last part of *Paterson* as he had originally conceived it—with its four-part structure—Williams was already thinking of
moving his poem into a fifth book. The evidence for such a rethinking of
the quadernity of *Paterson* exists in the manuscripts for book 4, for there
Williams, writing for himself, considered extending the field of the poem
to write about the river in a new dimension: the Passaic as archetype, as
the River of Heaven. That view of his river, however, was in 1950 premature, for Williams still had to follow the Passaic out into the North
Atlantic, where, dying, it would lose its temporal identity in the sea of
eternity, what Williams called the sea of blood. The processive mode of
Paterson 1–4 achieved, however, Williams returned to the untouched key:
the dimension of timelessness, the world of the imagination, the quiet,
apocalyptic moment, what he referred to as the eighth day of creation.

The need for imaginatively apprehending such a dimension had impressed itself on Williams in several ways: two operations in 1946, a heart
attack in early 1948, and the first of a series of crippling strokes which began
in 1951 and continued thereafter with increasing violence until his death
in 1963. The impulse for summing up the life of the man / city Paterson in
the mode of the eighth day of creation—a gesture that finds its analogue
in the image of a Troilus viewing his Cress and his embattled city from the
seventh sphere—is no doubt anterior to these repeated intimations of immortality, but such accidents did reinforce the necessity for a new mode
of saying, and, with it, a new way of seeing. But perhaps "new" verges
on an unnecessary immensity, since it does not place the emphasis precisely
where it belongs. "Life's processes are very simple," Williams wrote in his
late thirties. "One or two moves are made and that is the end. The rest is

From *Twentieth Century Literature* 21, no. 3 (1975). © 1975 by Hofstra University Press.

repetitious." So the apocalyptic mode is not really *new* for Williams in the sense that basically new strategies were developed for the late poems. Williams had tried on the approach to the apocalyptic moment any number of times; so, for example, he destroyed the entire world, imaginatively, at the beginning of *Spring and All* to begin all over again, in order that his few readers might see the world as new. And in *Paterson* 3, the city is once again destroyed in the imagination by the successive inroads of wind, fire, and flood, necessary purgings before Dr. Paterson can discover the scarred beauty, the beautiful black Kora, in the living hell of the modern city. These repeated de-creations are necessary, in terms of Williams's psychopoetics, in order to come at that beauty locked in the imagination. "To refine, to clarify, to intensify that eternal moment in which we alone live there is but a single force," Williams had insisted in *Spring and All*. That single force was the imagination and this was its book. But *Spring and All* was only *one* of its books or, better, perhaps, *all* of Williams's books are one book, and all are celebrations of the erotic/creative power of the imagination.

What *is* new about the late poems is Williams's more relaxed way of saying and with it a more explicit way of seeing the all-pervasive radiating pattern at the core of so much that Williams wrote. In fact, all of *Paterson* and *Asphodel* and much else that Williams wrote, from *The Great American Novel* (which finds its organizing principle in the final image of the machine manufacturing shoddy products from cast-off materials, the whole crazy quilt held together with a stitched-in design) to "Old Doc Rivers" (which constructs a cubist portrait of an old-time doctor from Paterson by juggling patches of secondhand conversations, often unreliable, with old hospital records), to "The Clouds" (which tries to come at Williams's sense of loss for his father by juxtaposing images of clouds with fragmentary scenes culled from his memory), in all of these works and in others Williams presents discrete objects moving "from frame to frame without perspective / touching each other on the canvas" to "make up the picture." In this quotation Williams is describing the technique of the master of the Unicorn Tapestries, but it serves to describe perfectly his own characteristic method of presentation. It was a method he learned not only by listening attentively to Rimbaud, Stein, and Pound, but by having watched such cubist masters as Picasso and Juan Gris and Braque in the years following the Armory Show. "The truth is," Wallace Stevens remarked in an essay called "The Relations between Poetry and Painting" which he read at the Museum of Modern Art in January 1951, "The truth is that there seems to exist a corpus of remarks in respect to paintings, most often the remarks of painters themselves, which are as significant to poets as to painters . . . because they are, after all, sayings about art." Williams would have agreed wholeheartedly.

It is, specifically, this cubist mode, eschewing the fictions of perspective for a strategy of multiple centers mirroring one another, that suggests Williams's radical departure from a logocentric poetics, such as we find in the poems of Hart Crane or T. S. Eliot. So, for example, in the late winter of 1938, Williams uses Dante's *Divina Commedia* and "the fat archpriest" of Hita's *El Libro de Buen Amor* as analogues, modes for two antithetical traditions: the tradition exemplified by T. S. Eliot (Williams's archenemy) and Williams's own tradition. Dante, Williams felt, had laced himself too tightly within the constrictions of two formal "necessities": the philosophical and theological underpinnings that everywhere ground the *Comedy*, and the triadic mode of the *terza rima*. But the Spanish priest, with his looser, episodic structure and his "flat-footed quadruple rhyme scheme," placed no barriers between himself and his imagination. What Williams sensed in the priest's open form was a texture that at least manured "the entire poetic field." There was in his poem a tolerance for the imperfect, "a glowing at the center which extends in all directions equally, resembling in that the grace of Paradise." Whether that phrase describes *The Book of Love* or not, it neatly encapsulates two of Williams's long poems: *Asphodel* and *Paterson 5*. (It also describes the *Pictures from Brueghel* sequence read as parts of a single poem, but since Williams was returning in the very late work to the sharper, more nervous mode of *Spring and All*, was in a sense leaving Paradise by the back door, they belong to another meditation.)

The formal emphais we are searching for might be phrased this way: what marks poems like *Asphodel* and *Paterson* 5 as different from his earlier poetry is that Williams has come out on the other side of the apocalyptic moment. He stands, now, at a remove from the processive nature of the earlier poetry, in a world where linear time—the flow of the river—has given way to the figure of the poet standing above the river or on the shore: in either case, he is removed from the violent flux, from the frustrations of seeing the river only by fits and starts. Now the whole falls into a pattern: in book 5 Paterson is seen by Troilus/Williams from the Cloisters at Fort Tryon Park, the line of the river flowing quietly toward the sea, the city itself visible as a pattern of shades, a world chiming with that of the Unicorn Tapestries, the world of art that has survived. From this heavenly world, the old poet can allow himself more space for rumination, for quiet meditation. It is a world that still contains many of the jagged patterns of Williams's own world of the early fifties: The Rosenberg trial, the cold war, Mexican prostitutes and G.I.'s stationed in Texas, letters from old friends and young poets. But all of these are viewed with a detached philosophical air, as parts of a pattern that are irradiated by the energy of the imagination. For it is Kora who, revealed in the late work, glows at the center of the poetry, extending her light generously and tolerantly "in all directions equally." It is Kora again who, like the Beautiful Thing of *Paterson* 3, illuminates the poem, but it is a Kora apprehended now quite openly as icon, the source of permanent radiance: the fructifying image of the woman, the anima so many artists have celebrated in a gesture that Williams characterizes as a figure dancing satyrically, goat-footed, in measure before the female of the imagination. Now, in old age, Williams too kneels before the woman who remains herself frozen, a force as powerful and as liberating as Curie's radium, supplying light and warmth to all the surrounding details, tolerantly, democratically.

The icon presupposes a kind of paradise, or, conversely, most paradises are peopled at least at strategic points with figures approaching iconography. Dante for one felt this. It is no accident, then, that, as Williams moves into that geographical region of the imagination where the river of heaven flows, he will find other artists who have also celebrated the light. And there, in the place of the imagination expressly revealed, will be the sensuous virgin pursued by the one-horned beast, the unicorn/artist, himself become an icon in this garden of delights. Three points demand our attention, then: (1) the movement toward the garden of the imagination, where it is always spring; (2) the encounter with the beautiful thing, Kora, the sensuous virgin to whom the artist pays homage; (3) the figure of the artist, both the all-pervasive creator who contains within himself the garden and the virgin and also the willing victim, a figure moving through the tapestry, seeking his own murder and rebirth in the imagination.

First, then, the fitful but insistent movement in the late poetry toward paradise, toward what Williams called the river of heaven, the Passaic seen in its eternal phase. While Williams was at Yaddo in July and August of 1950, writing furiously to complete the last book of *Paterson* as he had until then conceived of it—as a four-part structure—Nicolas Calas (another poet and artist-in-residence at the colony and an old acquaintance of Williams) showed him the work he had been doing on Hieronymus Bosch's fifteenth-century triptych, the *Garden of Delights*. Calas had pored over every inch of Bosch's work with microscopic care, using hundreds of photographic close-ups to examine the plenitude of detail that makes up the painting. As Williams read through Calas's commentary—his working papers— which attempted to decipher the painting's total complex of meanings, Williams was "appalled," as he said in the *Autobiography*, at the sheer amount of scholarship that had been brought to bear on this medieval artifact. Calas's study of Bosch's apocalyptic icons stuck with Williams. A year later, in August 1951, while he was still recovering from the stroke he had suffered in March, Williams wrote an appreciation of Calas's achievement in giving the modern world a contemporary Bosch. "It makes the 15th century come alive to us in a way which is vivid with contemporary preoccupations," Williams wrote (Calas). It was *not* the revelation of the *medieval* imagination that Calas had stressed, but the *timeless* imagination. Here was one of the old masters whose way of seeing his fifteenth-century world differed only in accidentals from twentieth-century man's way of looking at his own world. Calas had made Bosch's mind work "as if it were a contemporary mind," and—Williams threw out in an important parenthetical aside—"we know the mind has always worked the same" (Calas). In this view, then, Bosch was brother to the surrealists, whose chief importance, Williams had said elsewhere, was that they too had managed, through the use of free association, to liberate the imagination.

And Bosch was also brother to the cubists. In presenting his subjects without worrying about the illusion of perspective, a later preoccupation inherited from the Renaissance, he, like other old masters, had refused, like Williams, to see time as predominantly linear, or, even worse, progressive. What Williams discovered was that the old masters had had their own way of transcending the idiocy of the single, fixed perspective. Like the cubists with their multiple perspectives, their discrete planes apprehended simultaneously, the old masters had also moved their subjects outside the fixed moment. They were able, therefore, to free themselves to present their figures in all of their particularity both within a specific moment and at the same time as universal types or patterns, moving frequently to the level of icon. This shift in perspective helps to explain the similarity (*and* difference) between the achievement, say, of a volume like *Spring and All* and the later poems: the analogue, except in terms of scope, is between the cubist perspectives of a still life by Juan Gris and the multiple perspectives of the unicorn tapestries centered around the central icons of the virgin and the unicorn.

But what apparently struck the most responsive chord in Williams was that Bosch, in Calas's judgment, had managed to achieve the eighth day of creation, the apocalyptic vision itself, had in fact managed to annihilate time, to be in at the end, to see the pattern of his life as something accomplished, the artist looking in upon his own world and finding himself there. "Men do not die if their meaning is kept alive by their work," Williams wrote in the same essay, with an eye turned on himself, "hence the masters secreted their meaning in their paintings to live" (Calas). Williams was willing to acknowledge the need for the hermetic nature of Bosch's painting, which, elucidated by the teachings of St. Augustine and St. Gregory, pointed toward "the disastrous effects of the teachings of heresy generally over against the solid foundation in virtues of the true church" (Calas). But the *particular* force of the triptych came from the face looming out of the right corner, much larger than any other and the only face in the painting showing any particular character. This nearly disembodied face was, according to Calas (and Williams agreed) the face of the artist himself, looking back "with a half suspected smile . . . directly at the beholder" (Calas). This face, peering out from the mass of hundreds of fantastic and monstrous details, amounted to a "confession" of sorts, the artist revealing his subconscious world with all of its attendant erotic fantasies. Together, the hundreds of human and animal and abstract figures, many of them frankly sexual, provided an explanation or, better, an "evocation" into the inner reality of Bosch himself. In revealing or confessing himself so fully, Bosch had transcended the limitations of the self, giving those who could read him an intimate glimpse into themselves as well. Here was a "picture of how a contemporary mind, with all its shiftings as in the subconscious, in dreams, in the throes of composition, works" (Calas).

In a sense, then, Bosch, like Williams, had read Freud's *Interpretation of Dreams* to good advantage. The left triptych represents the earthly paradise, the only kind, finally, Williams was concerned with. And there Christ, the figure of the Creator, is about to present the virgin, Kora, as Eve, to the bridegroom. In that primal gesture, Bosch seems to suggest, nature has begun to manifest its tensions. Already death has entered the garden; the monstrous, as in the two-legged dog, has infiltrated Bosch's world. Williams's garden of delights in *Asphodel* contains the same kinds of potential tensions but all are presented tolerantly, all, even the damned, sharing the light of the imagination. Bosch's triptych, I suggest, then, chimes with Williams's *Asphodel*, a poem in three parts and a coda. Both are, basically, confessions; both present a series of discrete images held on the same plane by the artist. Linearity is eschewed for a mode of cubist simultaneity, and both poem and painting contain versions of the garden. Moreover, if one "reads" Bosch not from left to right but as one might read one's image in a mirror, in reverse, then one begins with the artist in hell and moves to a new beginning, with the bridegroom beholding the luminous bride, the sensuous virgin, apprehended on the eighth day as in the primal garden.

In originally conceiving of *Paterson* in four parts, Williams had, as he pointed out, added Pan to the embrace of the Trinity, much as he felt Dante had unwittingly done in supplying a "fourth unrhymed factor, unobserved" to the very structure of the *Commedia*. (This factor appears if we note the creative dissonance developed by the unrhymed ending reappearing in any four lines after the initial four.) The world of *Paterson* 1–4 is very much a world in flux, a world in violent, haphazard process, where objects washing in or crashing against the surfaces of the man/city Paterson are caught up into the pattern of the poem even as they create in turn the pattern itself. So such things as the chance appearance of a nurse who was discovered to have a case of *Salmonella montevideo*, written up into a case history in the *Journal of the American Medical Association* for July 29, 1948, or a letter from a young unknown poet from Paterson named Allen Ginsberg, or a hasty note scribbled by Ezra Pound from St. Elizabeth's Hospital in Washington, letters from Marcia Nardi or Fred Miller or Josephine Herbst or Edward Dahlberg or Alva Turner find their way into the action painting of the poem. The lines too are jagged, hesitant, coiling back on themselves, for the most part purposely flat, only in "isolate flecks" rising to the level of a lyricism that seems without artificiality or undue self-consciousness, a language shaped from the mouths of Polish mothers, but heightened.

The first four books of *Paterson* are, really, in a sense, the creation of the first six days, a world caught up very much in the rapid confusion of its own linear, processive time, where the orphic poet like the carnival figure of Sam Patch must keep his difficult balance or be pulled under by the roar of the language at the brink of the descent into chaos every artist encounters in the genesis of creation. What Williams was looking for instead in a fifth book, after resting from his unfolding creation, was to see the river at the heart of his poem as the ourobouros, the serpent with its tail in its mouth, the eternal river, the river of heaven. This meant, of course, that time itself would have to change, and a new time meant a relatively new way of measuring, meant a more secure, a more relaxed way of saying. That was a question, primarily, of form, and the emphasis on the variable foot, which the critics went after all through the fifties and sixties like hounds after an elusive hare, was in large part a strategy of Williams's own devising. But it was an absolutely necessary strategy for him, because just here the real revolution in poetry would have to occur: here with the river, metaphor for the poetic line itself.

The river of heaven became almost an obsession for Williams in the early fifties. First he had considered viewing *Paterson* 4 under that rubric; then he had begun a long poem called *The River of Heaven*, which became instead *Asphodel*. In June 1950, Allen Ginsberg had written Williams (in a letter that finds itself caught in the grid of *Paterson* 4) that he'd been "walking the streets of Paterson and discovering the bars." "I wonder," he asked, "if you have seen River Street most of all, because that is really at the heart of what is to be known." There were a number of bars along River Street, especially in the black section, which he recommended to Williams in the summer of 1952. "What I want of your son," Williams wrote Louis Ginsberg, "is for him to take me to a bar on River street. . . . I don't know what the joint is like or whether we'd be welcome there but if it's something to experience and to see I'd like to see it for I want to make it the central locale for a poem which I have in mind—a sort of extension of *Paterson*." From River Street, one of the oldest streets in Paterson, which follows the course of the Passaic, Williams could view through the painted glass of an old tavern-turned-bar the Passaic River surrounded by a cosmic harmony of sorts: the dance of the satyrs, swinging to jazz, on the eighth day of creation. Things have a way of changing, however, and the river of heaven finds its enactment not in the back room of the Bobaloo, but as it flows through the unicorn tapestries, the unicorn emerging from its waters, having escaped the silent hounds, threaded teeth bared, baying his imminent murder.

"Maybe there'll be a 5th book of Paterson embodying everything I've learned of 'the line' to date," Williams told Robert Lowell in March 1952. And, indeed, much of the new book does incorporate Williams's late development with the line, including the three-ply line of *Asphodel*. But the manuscripts reveal an interesting change in Williams's collage for book 5, which refocuses the emphasis of the entire book and brings us from the river to the icon. Williams had intended to include a long letter to him from Cid Corman dealing with the whole question of modern prosody and, in fact, even in the galleys, he had included that letter. But in its place Williams inserted at the last minute a letter from Edward Dahlberg that he had received in late September 1957 when he was putting the finishing touches on book 5.

What Williams saw in Dahlberg's letter was a modern, living, breathing analogue for Brueghel's *The Adoration of the Kings* in the Danish woman surrounded by the police, and the placement of Dahlberg's letter focuses the attention away from the question of the line (which had in any event been attended to by Sappho and Bessie Smith) and onto the modern representation of the central icon of book 5, the beautiful thing, Kora. It is the icon that includes, really, all of her sisters, from the "young woman / with rounded brow" who listens to the "hunter's horn" and who alone can lure the unicorn-poet, to Williams's own English grandmother (whose presence had marked his initiation into the filthy Passaic forty years before and who rounds off the conclusion of *Paterson*). And it includes as well the virgin in Lorca's *The Love of Don Perlimplin,* Osamu Dazai's saintly sister, "tagged" by her lover in *The Setting Sun,* those Mexican whores turning up their dresses in a short sketch by a young writer named Gilbert Sorrentino who had sent Williams his manuscript for the poet's comments, a young girl Williams remembered who'd gone swimming naked with him and all the boys at Sandy Bottom some sixty years before, and, finally, Sappho singing and Bessie Smith singing and the 3,000 years between them now as nothing.

In his 1928 novel, *A Voyage to Pagany,* Williams removed what is in fact the central chapter because the editors found the book too long to print in its original form. That chapter, "The Venus," describes a scene between a young fräulein and Dev (for Evans Dionysius) Evans. There the American doctor and the German girl sit in a quiet spot south of Rome which still bears evidences of having been in some remote past a pagan grotto, while Evans tries to explain the elusive beauty he is searching for in America. It is clear from Williams's description that Evans is in fact speaking to a modern-day incarnation of Venus herself, specifically Botticelli's sensuous virgin. But this Venus is about to enter a convent because she has not found the figure of the artist who can fully liberate her, although Evans's new-world paganism attracts her. The steady glance of this German Venus continued to haunt Williams, and he found that glance again in the figure of another Venus in a garb very like a nun's: Brueghel's Virgin. A buxom German peasant girl, she holds her baby boy upon her knee, as later, in the *Pictures from Brueghel,* she will pose in icon fashion, detached from the quotidian bustle everywhere apparent, as she does too in Giotto's *Adoration of the Magi,* which Williams celebrated in "The Gift," a poem also from the mid-fifties.

It is she, Kora, around whom all of *Paterson* 5 radiates, and, in the tapestries, she appears again with the tamed unicorn amidst a world of flowers where Williams had always felt at home. In a sense, Marianne Moore's real toad in an imaginary garden finds its correlative here in Williams's icons of the virgin / whore situated among "the sweetsmelling primrose / growing close to the ground," "the slippered flowers / crimson and white, / balanced to hang on slender bracts," forget-me-nots, dandelions, love-in-a-mist, daffodils, and gentians, and daisies. We have seen this woman before: she is the woman in *Asphodel* caring for her flowers in winter, in hell's despite, another German Venus, Floss Williams. Which, then, is the real, Williams's wife seen or his icon of the wife? And his wife seen now, at this moment, or his wife remembered, an icon released by the imagination from time, ageless, this woman containing all women? Rather, it is the anima, the idea of woman, with its tenuous balance between the woman glimpsed and the woman realized, the hag language whored and whored again but transformed by the pet-lover's desire into something virginal and new, the woman and the language translated to the eighth day of creation, assuming a new condition of dynamic permanence. In this garden, the broken, jagged, random things of Williams's world are caught up in a pattern, a dance where the poem, like the tapestries themselves, can be possessed a thousand thousand times and yet remain as fresh and as virginal as on the day they were conceived, like Venus, from the head of their creator.

The woman is of course all-pervasive in Williams's poems. What is different now is the more explicit use of Kora as the symbol, in fact, the central icon in the late poems. Two examples from the earlier sections of *Paterson* will serve to illustrate differences in the handling of his women. In *Paterson* 1, Williams sketches the delineaments of the giants, the female of the place, Garrett Mountain, resting against the male of it, the city of Paterson. "Paterson," the genesis of book 1 begins, "lies in the valley under the Passaic Falls / its spent waters forming the outline of his back." Over "against him, stretches the low mountain. / The Park's her head, carved, above the Falls, by the quiet river." Williams, as Michael Weaver has noted, may even have had Pavel Tchelitchew's *Fata Morgana*, his painting of two reclining earth figures, a man, a woman, in mind. This pattern of the unroused lovers is evoked obliquely later in book 2 when Paterson/Williams, walking on Garrett Mountain, notices a young couple lying partly concealed by some bushes, intent on each other while Sunday strollers float past them on all sides:

> But the white girl, her head
> upon an arm, a butt between her fingers
> lies under the bush
>
> Semi-naked, facing her, a sunshade
> over his eyes,
> he talks with her
>
> the jalopy half hid
> behind them in the trees—
> I bought a new bathing suit, just
>
> pants and a brassier:
> the breasts and
> the pudenda covered—beneath

the sun in frank vulgarity.
Minds beaten thin
by waste—among

the working classes SOME sort
of breakdown
has occurred.

Mural has become cameo, but the image of reclining lovers remains, substantially unchanged. In terms of strategy, however, Williams has purposely not pressed his parallel home. For the attention must be riveted first on the actuality of the encounter: it is midmorning in late May, probably 1942 or 1943. Or for that matter 1933 or 1973. These are probably young second-generation Polish- or Italian-Americans, surprised by eros on this, their day off, intent on seizing the day before returning to the silk mills or locomotive works in the industrial town sprawled out below them. But for this moment, the pattern of young lovers persists as archetype, fleshed out in these particular working-class people who impinge upon Williams's consciousness.

There is another interesting image that Williams found *too* explicit to finally place in book 4, but the various manuscripts for that book mention it several times. In the modern Idyll that begins *Paterson* 4, Williams gives us a strange love triangle that spells frustration from whatever angle of incidence we follow: the love triangle between Corydon, an aging, lame lesbian and would-be poetess, well educated in the classics and in French literature, whose penthouse apartment in the East fifties overlooks the river; her masseuse, a young (twenty-one-year-old) nurse from Ramapo (perhaps a Jackson White) trained at Passaic General Hospital in Paterson (where Williams served for some forty years), and Dr. Paterson himself, that married man and aging lover. Paterson is driven wild by the young virgin's beauty; indeed he cannot even think unless she first removes her clothes. For Williams she is, explicitly, the very incarnation of Goya's famous Maja Desnuda. And if for Dr. Paterson she remains the elusive new-world beauty who cannot give herself to the new-world poet but follows instead the old-world hag (Europe) into a world cold and alien, she is first and foremost a real woman, someone from Williams's own past, an incarnation of the unattainable reclining nude, the odalisque, Olympia, more fleshly cousin of Stevens's Mrs. Pappadoppoulos. Goya's nude seems to have informed Williams's realization of Phyllis in the unpublished sheets of the Idyll, but Williams carefully removed the scaffolding in the published version.

Paterson 5 eschews such oblique stratagems, however. Williams has made that consummate metapoem far more explicit for several reasons, one comes to realize: first, because no critic, not even the most friendly and the most astute, had even begun to adequately sound the real complexities of the poem by 1956, ten years after *Paterson* 1 appeared. (Indeed an adequate critical vocabulary for the kind of thing Williams was doing does not seem to have been available then to the critics and reviewers.) Second, Williams felt the need to praise his own tradition, his own pantheon of artists, to pay tribute to those others who had also helped to celebrate the light. Williams would show that, on the eighth day of creation, all of the disparate, jagged edges of *Paterson* could, as he had said in his introduction, multiply themselves and so reduce themselves to unity, to a dance around the core of the imagination.

In the dreamlike worlds of *Asphodel* and *Paterson* 5, filled as they are with the radiant light of the imagination, all disparate images revolve around the virgin/whore, including the "male of it," the phallic artist who is both earthly Pan and unicorn, that divine lover, who dances contrapuntally against his beloved. Williams, perhaps sensing that the old, crude fight against the clerks of the great tradition had been sufficiently won by that point to let him relax, chooses now to celebrate a whole pantheon of old masters in *Asphodel* and again in *Paterson* 5.

And if the presences of Bosch, Brueghel, and the master of the unicorn tapestries are the central presences in the three late long poems, still, there is room to celebrate a host of other artists who dance in attendance on the woman as well. We can do little more at this point than enumerate some of them: Toulouse-Lautrec, who painted the very human turn-of-the-century Parisian prostitutes among whom he lived; Gauguin, celebrating his sorrowful reclining nude in *The Loss of Virginity*; the anonymous Inca sculptor who created the statuette of a woman at her bath some 3,000 years ago; the 6,000 year-old cave paintings of bison; Cézanne for his patches of blue and blue; Daumier, Picasso, Juan Gris, Gertrude Stein, Kung; Albrecht Dürer for his *Melancholy*; Audubon, Ben Shahn, and Marsden Hartley.

We come, then, finally, to our third point: the figure of the artist himself, the male principle incessantly attracted to and moving toward the female of it: the anima. And here we are confronted with the comic and the grotesque: the figure of Sam Patch or the hydrocephalic dwarf or the Mexican peasant in Eisenstein's film, and, in the late poems, the portrait of the old man, all of these finding their resolution and comic apotheosis in the captive, one-horned unicorn, a figure, like the figure of the satyr erectus, of the artist's phallic imagination. There is, too, Brueghel's self-portrait, as Williams thought, re-created in the first of Williams's own pictures taken from Brueghel, and imitated in a cubist mode. That old man, with his "Bulbous nose" (one thinks of Williams's own early poem celebrating his own nose) and his "eyes red-rimmed / from over-use" with "no time for any / thing but his painting." And, again, there is the head of the old smiling Dane, the Tollund Man, seen in a photograph; it is a portrait of a man, a sacrificial victim, strangled as part of some forgotten spring rite, the features marvelously preserved intact by the tanning effects of the bogs from which he had been exhumed after twenty centuries of strong silence, that 2,000-year-old face frozen into something like a half-smile. That face chimes with Brueghel's face as both chime with the strange, half-smiling face of Bosch peering out from his strange world where order has given way to an apocalyptic nightmare.

But the male remains the lesser figure of the two in Williams. As he told Theodore Roethke in early 1950, "All my life I have hated my face and wanted to smash it." (It was one reason, he told Roethke in the same letter, that he could not even bear to speak of Vivienne Koch's critical study of him which had just appeared. What mattered was not the man himself, but the man's work.) He was willing, however, to let the icon of the unicorn, the one-horned beast, stand. And he let it stand because it represented the necessary male complement to the female of it, the object desired, the beautiful thing: the language in its impossible edenic state. No one but the virgin can tame the unicorn, the legend goes, and Williams had, like other artists before and after him, given himself up to that elusive beauty. Like Hart Crane in another mode, he had given himself up to be murdered, to offer himself not, as Pound had, to the pale presences of the past, virtually all of them male voices, but for the virgin, Kora. And yet, there was a way out, a hole at the bottom of the pit for the artist, in the timeless world of the imagination, the enchanted circle, the jeweled collar encircling the unicorn's neck. In the final tapestry of the series, the unicorn kneels within the fence paling, (pomegranates bespeak fertility and the presence of Kora), at ease among a panoply of flowers forever on the eighth day of creation, a world evoked for Williams out of the imagination, the source from which even the author of Revelation must have created his own eighth day in his time.

What was of central importance to Williams was not the artist, then, whose force is primarily directional and whose presence is in any event everywhere, but the icon that motivates the artist and urges him on: the icon of Kora, the image of the beloved. And this figure appears, of course, everywhere in Williams's writing, assuming many faces, yet always, finally one. Asked in his mid-seventies what it was that kept him writing, Williams answered that it was all for the young woman whose eyes he had caught watching him out there in some audience as he read his poems. It was all for lovely Sappho, then, and all for Venus. Consider for a moment the example of other modern poets: Yeats's Helen of Troy, Stevens's fat, voluptuous mundo, or Pound, finding a shadow of his ideal beauty in the *yeux glauques*, the lacquered eyes of Jenny in those Burne-Jones cartoons, or the eyes of the goddess momentarily penetrating through the very walls of Pound's tent at the U.S. Army Detention Center at Pisa in that summer of 1945. With them Williams places his own icon of the woman rising out of the hell of his own repressions. In the world of art, in that garden where spring is a condition of permanence, where the earthly garden chimes perfectly with the garden of paradise, the eye of the unicorn is still and still intent upon the woman.

Rhizomatic America: Ezra Pound

Kathryne V. Lindberg

*Far too as her splendors shine, system on system shooting like rays,
upward, downward, without center, without circumference—in the mass
and in the particle, Nature hastens to render account of herself to the
mind. Classification begins . . . and so, tyrannized over by its own
unifying instinct, [the mind] goes on tying things together, diminishing
anomalies, discovering roots running under ground whereby contrary and
remote things cohere and flower out from one stem.*
                                    —EMERSON, "The American Scholar"

A PACT

*I make a pact with you, Walt Whitman—
I have detested you long enough.
I come to you as a grown child
Who has had a pig-headed father;
It was you that broke the new wood,
Now is a time for carving.
We have one sap and one root—
Let there be commerce between us.*
                                    —POUND, *Personae*

At times, Pound's desire for a compatible and legitimate tradition led him
to renounce his Americanism and to abjure modernism altogether. Nevertheless, whether under the name of "Make It New" or "The American
Risorgiamento," his historical and/or aesthetic project is articulated in terms
which belie any simple desire to keep THE TRADITION intact. He wanted
to *drill* a certain version of America into modern letters, to *graft* fragments
of modern life onto the trunk of European art, and at the same time, to
carve out an American heritage. I emphasize Pound's recurrent metaphors
of grafting and drilling, of the organic and even the sculptural as against
the architectonic. These figures, endemic to American poetics, at once
ground and unsettle the edifice—or is it the system of poetic roots and
shoots?—Pound hoped to erect or resurrect as an American tradition. One
might note in passing that an American tradition, let alone one that combines the mutually exclusive models of the organic and the monumental,
has always seemed oxymoronic if not downright impossible.

   In "What I Feel about Walt Whitman," a note written in 1909 but left
unpublished until 1955, Pound outlined a strange genealogical reconstruc-

From *Reading Pound Reading: The Nietzschean Indirections of Modernism.* © 1986 by Oxford
University Press.

171

tion in characteristically mixed metaphors and catachreses. Presenting the old saw, that is, "the family tree," perhaps too graphically, he says of Whitman that "the vital part of my message, taken from the sap and fibre of America, is the same as his" [*Selected Prose*]. This American tree, of which Whitman and Pound are parts, though not simply living trunk and branch, is indeed an unnatural one. Growing backward in time, it has not yet taken root. In fact, Pound suggests that both he and Whitman are misplaced and untimely. If Whitman was an imperfect beginning, Pound is the repetition of such a beginning. In this way, Pound marks both a repetition of and a revolution against Whitman, who, for better or worse, found himself in a similar position of at once taking up and overthrowing his European and American heritage(s).

Pound and Whitman are hardly alone in recognizing America's ambiguous cultural imperatives. Indeed, Henry Adams, for whom American culture was inescapably problematic, translated the search for roots into the broader and no less heterogeneous areas of pedagogy, medieval art history, and the new sciences of geology, genetics, and physics. Adams recognized that Americans' need for cultural legitimacy necessarily involved the breaking of discursive categories to say nothing of the laws of literary genre. This can be seen as much in the strange mixed genre of his own autobiographical history texts (*Mont St. Michel and Chartres* and *The Education*) as in his ironic treatment of the presumably pure disciplines out of which he created such heterogeneous and heterodox categories as "Conservative Christian Anarchism." I will have something more to say about Adams later, but first, it is necessary to look more closely at the relations between Pound and Whitman as a crisis of moment for modernism and Americanism in which current literary theory, itself riddled with generic and genealogical anxieties, still has a stake.

Early and late, American writers have sung of themselves as additions to or parasites upon an unbroken legacy of Western Art—marking both its completion and its unaccountable excess. Thus, not without quoting Whitman, Pound claims his American heritage and more: "I am (in common with every educated man) an heir of the ages and I demand my birth-right. Yet if Whitman represented his time in language acceptable to one accustomed to my standard of intellectual-artistic living he should belie his time and nation. Yet I am but one of his 'ages and ages' encrustations' or to be more exact an encrustation of the next age" [*Selected Prose*]. Whitman is honored there, as Pound would always honor him, for faithfulness to his time and language; like Dante in Italy and Chaucer in England, Whitman wrote in his native or vulgar tongue and thereby created the possibility of a new Poetry if not of an American language.

Pound is torn between refining the American, that is, the Whitmanesque, idiom and acquiring greater erudition and a more impressive ancestry. At the same time that he complains of Whitman's inadequacies, Pound approves his nativist project. Yet he does so by translating it into a series of metaphors—the organic and the destructive, the archeological and the archeoclastic, the genetic and the accidental—for that American mythos of history that has always been similarly befuddled. Thus Whitman is the encrustation upon as well as the founder of a still uncertain "American tradition" to which Pound turns in order to overturn. And Pound is part of the new which is an encrustation upon both the last and the next ages, only a moment of transition between two disjunct poetic and genealogical lines.

However "congenial" or genealogically amenable Pound insists he is to the more recognized precursors of the Eliotic Tradition, when he equates Dante and Whitman the earlier poet necessarily suffers a diminution. And, more importantly, the poetic hierarchy undergoes a leveling in which the privileged category of Poetry hardly remains intact. Pound both acknowledges and represses these difficulties in charting an ancestry which is, if geometry and genealogy permitted such aberrations, a series of intersecting parallel lines of poet-hybrids who cut across several languages, artistic genres, and historical periods.

Just so, "textbooks" such as "How to Read" and *The ABC of Reading* privilege those writers who worked radical innovations *within* the very tradition Pound seems to propogate. Even as early as "I Gather the Limbs of Osiris" (1911–12), he proposes to anthologize and canonize the " 'donative' author who seems to draw down into the art something that was not in the art of his predecessors. If he draws from the air about him, he draws latent forces, of things present or unnoticed, or things perhaps taken for granted but never examined" [*Selected Prose*]. Such an author/reader— let alone the modern reader who discovers and (re)positions him—automatically destabilizes the tradition by changing his inheritance and his legacy, that is, the "Art of his predecessors."

Whitman, the acknowledged inventor of "free-verse" and of the "democratic epic," necessarily disrupts poetry's old generic categories. And Pound, while always dissatisfied with Whitman's characteristic lack of refinement, tended to praise his forebear for such violations and to affect such crudities in order to disturb the genteel tradition and inscribe his personal signature of the prodigal modern. Further, he proposes separating Whitman's meaning from his verse, thus performing an operation which rests on the assumption that *Leaves of Grass* is not an organic poem; it does not, unlike his favorite Provençal poems, require full quotation or "direct presentation." According to Pound, this is because Whitman was so open to history and to the non-poetic that *Leaves of Grass* is as much history as it is poetry. If anything, Pound wants Whitman to be less "poetic"—at least along the old lines—and more iconoclastic.

Indeed, it is Whitman the reader of culture and the *scourge* of tradition Pound adopts as his American ancestor, as for instance, in *The ABC of Reading*, when he says: "If you insist, however, in dissecting his language you will probably find out that it is wrong NOT because he broke all of what were considered his day 'the rules' but because he is spasmodically conforming to this, that or the other . . . using a bit of literary language." However uneasy Pound might be about adopting the style of *Leaves of Grass* for his own poetic or pedagogical strategies, he never ceases acknowledging Whitman's *critical* (both crucial and interpretative) function of turning the European poetic tradition toward the broader area of (American) culture. As we will see, the replacement of "tradition," a word that must be associated with Eliot's fabrication of his conservative modernism, by "culture," and finally Pound's neologism, *Kulchur,* graphically as well as semantically marks disruption of the generic and genealogical orders.

Of his own relationship to Whitman, Pound says, "Personally I might be very glad to conceal my relationship to my spiritual father and brag about my more congenial ancestry—Dante, Shakespeare, Theocritus, Villon, but the descent is a bit difficult to establish. And, to be frank, Whitman is to my fatherland what Dante is to Italy and I at my best can only be a strife for a renaissance in America" [*Selected Prose*]. From a certain perspective, Whitman occupies the position of first poet, the flower of that belated and imported "American Renaissance" that originated in Emerson, or even the position of the disseminator of an American, in contrast to the English, poetic language. By these accounts, he is no more than an interloper in Europe, especially the idealized Europe of pre-Renaissance Italy where Pound would situate himself and his American ancestor. Whitman is both the origin of American poetry and its unaccommodated original; perhaps because he was thus, like Americans generally, obsessed with origins yet compelled to be original in the exercise of individuality. At least Pound seems to say as much when he is at pains to decide where Whitman belongs in the greater scheme of things—as well as in the recent history of Poetry.

Faced with a similar dilemma in the figure of that evolutionary glitch, the ganoid fish *Pteraspis,* a still extant paleolithic species passed over by evolution, Henry Adams observed that "to an American in search of a father, it mattered nothing whether the father breathed through lungs, or walked on fins, or on feet." Surely Pound's choice of precursors is not quite that indiscriminate. Whitman's centrality to a nativist poetics is hardly in doubt; nevertheless, he resists incorporation into an organic tradition or literary history as fiercely as Adams's fish resists Darwin's neat taxonomy.

Yet Whitman himself had deliberately reorganized more than one category within the poetic tradition and the larger province he named "American culture," a recurrent phrase, if not a new and privileged Idea, in his criticism as well as his poetry. In terms Pound would use in his poetry as well as his "culture criticism," Whitman had tried to redefine "culture" and his own European cultural inheritance. Not surprisingly, "culture" was a troublesome word for the egalitarian "rough" whose poetry and polemics were deployed against the narrow definitions of poetry and art advanced by "gentlemen of culture." In "Democratic Vistas," for example, Whitman asks how an American culture might be cultivated. One should note that his analysis proceeds by a series of agricultural metaphors resting on a pun:

> The writers of a time hint the mottoes of its gods. The word of the modern, say these voices, is the word Culture.
>
> We find ourselves abruptly in close quarters with the enemy. *This word Culture*, or what it has come to represent, *involves, by contrast, our whole theme*, and has been, indeed, the spur, urging us to engagement.
>
> Certain questions arise. . . . *Shall a man lose himself in countless masses of adjustment, and be so shaped with reference* to this, that, and the other, *that the simply good and healthy and brave parts of him are reduced and clipp'd away, like the bordering of a box in a garden?* You can cultivate corn and roses and orchards—but who can cultivate the mountain peaks, the ocean, and the tumbling gorgeousness of the clouds? Lastly—is the readily given reply that *culture only seeks to help, systematize, and put in attitude, the elements of fertility and power*, a convulsive reply?
>
> *I do not so much object to the name, or word, but I should certainly insist, for the purposes of these States, on a radical change of category*, in the distribution of precedence [italics mine].

Like Whitman, Pound felt uneasy about the limited and privileged term "culture," which he figures as both a continuum and a wearing down of classical unity into indistinct fragments. Here is one of his most quoted definitions of "culture," one which is nonetheless not granted the complexity and inconsistency it clearly presents: "European civilization or, to use an abominated word *'culture'* can best be understood as a *medieval trunk with wash after wash of classicism going over it*. That is not the whole story, but to understand it, you must think of that *series of perceptions, as well as of anything that has existed or subsisted from antiquity*" [*The ABC of Reading*].

Pound has again resorted to catachresis, to mixed metaphors that jumble the classical inheritance with subsequent revivals or "perceptions" of it. In a fiction that does not resolve as smoothly as Eliot's "Tradition and the Individual Talent," culture is here imaged as both the perennial family tree and as a shore or even a painting effaced by waves or washes of color. Like "encrustations of the next age," washes cover over and, at least to all appearances, change what is underneath. In the case of white-wash or of watercolor washes, such simple distinctions as object and covering can become completely obscured. Furthermore, in Pound's model, "classicism," which should by rights precede the "medieval," comes later, as a series of additions to, rather than a revelation of, previous cultures. Thus belated, American literature which began in New England or Brooklyn or, as Pound claims, in Virginia, was in a position to work a renaissance or a rejection of the old cultural forms—or perhaps to have it both ways, as Emerson and, to some extent, Whitman hoped.

In speaking of an American culture, in repeating once again that American gesture of mapping a national history, Pound suggests that America should open art and literature to the non-literary and the inartistic. In "The Jefferson-Adams Letters as a Shrine and a Monument," for instance, he insists that American literature originated or culminated in the fugitive journals and correspondence of John Adams, Jefferson, Franklin, and Van Buren. Pound denies any fall away from classicism and thereby endorses the heterogeneity characteristic of America and modernism, thus: "Our national culture can be perhaps better defined from the Jefferson letters than from any three sources and mainly to its benefice" [*Selected Prose*].

Jefferson and the other founding fathers are praised for repeating the ordered multiplicity Pound had uncovered in Dante. With regard to the Presidential correspondence, he recalls Dante's phrase, " 'in una parte piu e meno altrone.' " He translates the phrase as suggesting that Jefferson and Adams were polymaths who nevertheless maintained a sense of proportion and a scale of values. In describing the "palimpsest" of their "Mediterranean state of mind" as the best "intellectual filing system," Pound admits that the world and works of his favorite Americans contained "things neither perfect nor utterly wrong, but arranged in a cosmos, an order, stratified, having relations with one another." Despite the fact that here and in the "Jefferson/Adams Cantos" Pound tends to focus on those details that refuse incorporation into any sort of organic whole, and on the infinitely interpretative relations among writers and writings rather than on monolithic Ideas, he memorializes the Jefferson/Adams letters in the following terms: "The implication is that they stand for a life not split into bits. Neither of these two men would have thought of literature as something having nothing to do with the nation, the organization of government" [*Selected Prose*]. Pound's category of American culture or the American "cosmos" (the unacknowledged adoption of the Whitmanesque term startles) is large enough to accommodate a great deal more than traditional art and literature, however miniscule Pound's quotations from the text of America eventually become.

Not without contradiction, then, Pound endorses the thrust of Whitman's change in the category "Culture," and thus tacitly approves the democratic and even the anti-poetic elements of *Leaves of Grass*. Rather than smooth Whitman's roughneck image or remake his poem into a part of an epic continuity, Pound employs the earlier American as laborer against the conservative and elitist aesthetic which he nevertheless hoped to export intact back to America, as that "high modernism" he is credited with founding. His motives as well as his metaphors are mixed, and his translation of the European into an American culture is neither direct nor untroubled. Playing more on the architectonic than the organic, and in the name of Whitman as well as the names of more accepted figures, Pound issues a sort of Americanist manifesto: "It seems to me I should like to drive Whitman into the old world, I sledge, he drill—and scourge America with all the old beauty . . . and with a thousand thongs from Homer to Yeats, from Theocritus to Marcel Schwob" [*Selected Prose*].

In his proposed destruction and reconstruction of the old beauty, Pound equates Whitman, Homer, Yeats, and the historian Marcel Schwob in a list he would supplement and reassemble throughout his literary career, adding, as time went on, writers from disparate ages and discourses. This was one strategy by which he would, as he said, "make all ages contemporaneous." But the cost of this ahistoricism or cultural relativism is a destabilizing of the poetic as well as the political hierarchies and privileges he never ceases claiming for Poetry, the acme of culture by his own definition(s).

Pound wanted both the stability of cultural monuments (though hardly Matthew Arnold's "touchstones") and the untameable action of new discoveries and unusual methods. Leo Frobenius's *Kulturmorphologie* and specifically the figure of "paideuma" satisfied Pound's conflicting desires for novelty and respectability. Under various names, "paideuma" runs throughout *Guide to Kulchur* and his other writings on American history. At one point, he says: "The history of culture is the history of ideas going into action" [*Guide to Kulchur*]. Later, in contrasting Frazier's mythography to Frobenius's archeology, Pound suggests that "paideuma" violates chronology in his favorite way; it turns the distant past into a new prospect: "His [Frobenius's] archeology is not retrospective, it is immediate. . . . To escape a word or set of words [culture and tradition] loaded with dead associations Frobenius uses the term Paideuma for the tangle or complex of the inrooted ideas of any period" [*Guide to Kulchur*].

It is not going too far to claim that Pound enlisted the quirky German anthropologist for his on-going Americanist project of troping historical and cultural "retrospection" into nativist "prospect," or even a prospectus. After all, it was Emerson, that original American reviser, who began *Nature* with the familiar admonition: "Our age is retrospective, it builds the sepulchres of the fathers. It writes biographies, histories, and criticism. The foregoing generations beheld God and nature face to face; we through their eyes. Why should not we also enjoy an original relation to the universe." Pound articulated his similar concern about immediacy and originality in terms of original interpretations of the whole of culture. Yet, for all his efforts at erecting original and paradoxically *living* and *inrooted* "monuments" to Jefferson, Adams, Homer, Dante, *et alia*, Pound more than once echoes Emerson in defining his own project: "The reader, who bothers to think, may now notice that in the new paideuma I am not including the retrospect, but only the pro-spect" [*Guide to Kulchur*].

In spite of himself, Pound proposes to undermine, if not to dismantle, those artistic structures which had never been successfully transplanted onto American soil. This is to say that when Pound supplements American poetry with European beauty, he exaggerates the stability and coherence of the "American" as well as that of the "other" order he calls tradition. Yet he neglects to note Whitman's ambivalence toward the European tradition and thus he forgets the admixture of traditionalism and iconoclasm already stamped into "the American." His "feelings about Walt Whitman" are in fact characteristic of the schizophrenic loyalties the American writer has always felt toward the old and new worlds. A longer essay might consider other segments of the broken and often subterranean line that stretches from Emerson to those post-modern writers who still answer "The American Scholar" 's call to an American poetics. But instead, I would like at this point to make a kind of European and post-modern detour, in order to call upon an even more recent commentary on what we have come to call American modernism. I will refer to a programmatic essay by Gilles Deleuze and Felix Guattari, entitled "Rhizome" [in *On the Line*, tr. John Johnston (NY: *Semiotext(e)*, Columbia University, 1983)].

"Rhizome" was undertaken to explain the Frenchmen's micro-political assaults upon such entrenched conventions of Western philosophical and literary discourse as the single author, the unified book, and the segregation of disciplines within the academy. The essay opens, for instance, with Deleuze and Guattari positioning—or, better, "deterritorializing"—themselves in the midst of an ongoing cultural exchange that will not admit of *their* own uniqueness. Their very insistence on shared and unaccountable authorship is an embarrassment to literature, psychology, and philosophy, all disciplines that privilege individual consciousness as primary to systematic and serious discourse. They begin thus, conscious of a belatedness that includes their own past writings:

> We wrote *Anti-Oedipus* together. As each of us was several, that already made quite a few. . . .
> A book has neither subject nor object; it is made up of variously formed materials, of very different dates and speeds. As soon as a book is attributed to a subject this working of materials and the exteriority of their relations is disregarded. A benificent God invented geological movements. In a book, as in everything else, there are lines of articulation or segmentation, strata, territorialities; but also lines of flight, movements of deterritorialization and of destratification.

A similar and even more anxiety-ridden sense of belatedness has characterized American writing from Emerson to the present, and, as we have seen, applies even to Whitman, despite the critics' tendency to accept his immediate and "barbaric yawp" as a return to the primal voice. Marking this self-consciousness, which wants to preserve a genealogical sense of order yet claim a sense of individual identity in its own disruptiveness, is a gesture that Pound whimsically called, in a letter to William Carlos Williams, "the American habit of quotation." Quoting and stealing, the American writer from Emerson to Poe on would "deterritorialize" his past. But this also meant subverting any claim to originality and authority over his own text.

Indeed, Pound [in *Guide to Kulchur*] calls into question his own authority if not his own authorship, as he persists in valuing the unstoppable exchanges of subjects and objects within the culture and its adequate history:

> We do NOT know the past in chronological sequence. It may be convenient to lay it out anesthetized on the table with dates pasted on here and there, but *what we know we know by ripples and spirals eddying out from us* and from our own time.
>
> There is no ownership in most of my statements and *I cannot interrupt every sentence or paragraph to attribute authorship* to each pair of words, especially *as there is seldom an a priori claim even to the phrase or half phrase* [my italics].

I do not wish to exaggerate the similarities between Pound and the two French writers who have no reason to think like the traditionalist/ modernist/fascist writer, whom they instead have every reason to reject. Nevertheless, Pound, and Whitman as well, pushed against the limitations of books and logical discourse in much the same way as Deleuze and Guattari propose to do:

> A tiresome feature of the Western mind is that it relates actions and expressions to external or transcendent ends, instead of appreciating them on the plane of immanence according to their intrinsic value. For example, insofar as a book is made of chapters, it has its culminating and terminal points. What happens, on the contrary, with a book made of plateaus, each communicating with the others through tiny fissures, as in the brain? We shall call a "plateau" every multiplicity connectable with others by shallow underground stems, in such a way as to form and extend a rhizome. We are writing a book as a rhizome.

If such radical deployments of the problems inherent in writing remain—or have again become—surprising to the American critical ear, questions such as "What is an Author?" "What are the ends of philosophy?" and the like, have become thematic commonplaces in recent continental thought. Yet one might claim that they are native to American poetics and certainly to Pound's version of the modern, both of which unsettle categories of the Western literary tradition. Although they make no reference to Pound's modernist interventions, Deleuze and Guattari suggest as much when they say that Western culture, which they trace back to its roots in agriculture, has always privileged trees, if in a most ambivalent fashion: from the Edenic tree of knowledge to the family tree of Indo-European languages. Borrowing a distinction from botany and amplifying its metaphoric resonance, they oppose the *arborescent* or tree-like culture to their own *rhizomatic* or weed-like writing. And, most important here, they find their precedent in America's weedlike multiplication of influences and tangled roots.

To summarize briefly the botanical definitions: trees have fixed roots and structural permanence; rhizomatic plants, which include most tubers, orchids, and such virulent weeds as the "Virginia creeper," lack fixed roots and instead have filamental shoots that grow horizontally just beneath the surface of the ground and sometimes project aeriel roots in all directions. Trees grow vertically; rhizomatic plants grow horizontally. With work, trees can be cut down, but rhizomes left in the ground can hide, hibernating and spreading subterraneously until they eventually give rise to new plants or more weeds, often in surprising locations and configurations. By extension, and to quote Guatarri and Deleuze, "Arborescent systems are hierarchical systems comprised of centers of significance and subjectivization, of autonomous centers. . . . It is curious how the tree has dominated Western reality, and all of Western thought, from botany to biology and anatomy, and also gnosticism, theology, ontology, all of philosophy . . . the root-foundation, *grund*, fundaments."

Rhizomes can, however, masquerade as trees. Sometimes, as is the case with Pound and Adams, the grafting of a family tree of poetry and the other disciplines becomes a subtle parody of the search for origins. Or, as in Whitman, one cannot find the trees for all the individual, heterogeneous and heteroclite leaves of grass and of paper. Curiously enough, Deleuze and Guattari claim that "American literature," notwithstanding its perennial search for origins and originality, is the exemplary rhizomatic text, both for its origins of European and its writings about American culture. If the Frenchmen might be said to give "America's rhizomatic literature" a univocity *we all* know it lacks, they nevertheless expose the tangled themes of the Americanist problematic. I quote one particularly stunning segment:

> America should be considered a place apart. Obviously it is not exempt from domination by trees and the search for roots. This is evident in its literature, in the quest for a national identity, and even for a European ancestry or genealogy. . . . Hence the difference between an American book and a European book, even when an American sets off pursuing trees. A difference in the very conception of the book: 'Leaves of Grass.' Nor are directions the same in America: the east is where the arborescent search and the return to the old world takes place; but the west is rhizomatic, with its Indians without ancestry, its always receding borders, its fluid and shifting frontiers.

Notwithstanding the rather complex and foreign, not to say subversive, character of Deleuze and Guattari's argument, it would seem that much of American writing has been involved with rhizomes, that is, with the wild weed-like growths that undermine the organic or agricultural order so fundamental to Western thought and its literature. Emerson, the putative founder of what is now recognized as a de-centered—if not a rhizomatic—American poetic tradition, has a good deal to say about the American underbrush which refuses to sustain trees or other rooted structures. One of his most striking and heuristic uses of the botanic metaphor takes the form of a self-conscious complaint against the very diffuseness and errancy epitomized by his own essays, journals, and miscellaneous notes. In a journal passage dated 1847, he says, "Alas for America as I must so often say, the ungirt, the profuse, the procumbent, one wide juniper, out which no cedar, no oak will rear up a mast to the clouds! It all runs to leaves, to suckers, to tendrils, to miscellany."

Guattari and Deleuze were probably not thinking of Emerson at all, nor were they embarrassed by Whitman's *Leaves of Grass* in quite the same way as were modern American poets like Pound, Eliot, and Williams. Yet what in "Rhizome" appears as a privileged, cross-discursive miscellany and the projection of a subterranean American counter-tradition (poetic counter-culture?) is related to the ambiguous nationalism of Pound's modernist program. Moreover, as we have seen with regard to Whitman's *sledging* and his *sap* of nativism, Pound's thoughts about American poetics are frequently conveyed in strained botanic metaphors.

Pound certainly set out "pursuing trees," if with the quixotic or at least the unnatural aim of grafting an ancient European genealogy onto the new growth of American literature to which Whitman was both precursor and product. Despite continual efforts to repair the rootlessness of *Leaves of Grass*, Pound's own long poem, and his criticism both in and out of that poem, share much with the text Deleuze and Guattari somewhat cryptically identify as representative of "the American rhizome." Like Whitman's poem, *The Cantos* is heterogeneous, insistently incomplete or provisional; composed of fragments of various historical themes and poetic forms, it too changed over the history of its writing. Indeed, the further back in time and the farther East Pound ventured in search of his "legitimate ancestry," the more fragmentary his poem became; that is, the more history Pound included in his poem, and the more ancestors and antecedents he collated into metaphors and models of his tradition, the more insistent became his questioning of the fundamental concepts and figures comprising any nostalgic quest for origins. Perhaps this contradiction is most pronounced in "The Chinese Cantos," which record four thousand years of Dynastic history in genealogical tables which Pound interrupts with distracting and often idiosyncratic programmatic statements. This textual layering is conveyed by a mixture of organic, economic, and architectural metaphors, comprising at best simulacra of System or tradition.

"The Chinese Cantos," published with the "Jefferson/Adams Cantos" and obsessed with order and systematization, are composed of virtually unreadable fragments translated through French transliterations of often corrupt and incomplete records written by thousands of court historians whose interested selections can hardly be considered the work of objective or accurate historiography; nor can their various styles and themes be gathered into any sort of coherent book, let alone an organic American epic.

Nevertheless, Pound was expressly attempting to use these texts to establish a general economy or cultural paradigm that could in some way mark a continuity between the ancient agrarian civilization of China and such later idealized cultural repetitions as Jeffersonian democracy. Despite the efforts of sympathetic critics to translate Pound's stated intention into an organic poem or an epic held together by such devices as "subject rhymes" and "nodal repetitions," both in theme and form the text remains a kind of natural hybrid (to use an oxymoron), exhibiting the sort of rootlessness and excess Deleuze and Guattari call rhizomatic. Perhaps more than any of the Cantos except for "Rock Drill," the Chinese sequence exceeds even the "wash upon wash of classicism" that Pound both charted and descried. Moving away in both directions from European Classical culture (east and backward in time to China as well as west and forward in time to America), the Cantos are rhizomatic, that is, not rootless but, as Pound said, "the tangled and inrooted ideas of any age."

Two examples from "The Chinese Cantos" will suffice to show that Pound's own self-conscious metaphors undercut the organic or, more precisely, the "arborescent" tradition he set out to recover and, as it turned out, to cut and graft into a different sort of growth. Canto 52 reintroduces and augments the series of ostensibly architectonic metaphors and mythological systems that weave through *The Cantos* like tendrils, surfacing only as new sources and themes are introduced or old ones modified. At this point, Pound signals a turn from sixteenth-century Venetian economics back to the mythic founding of an agriculture in prehistoric China. Preceding the Canto proper, one of the poem's few prose notes announces the theme of the two decads which encompass Chinese history and the Jefferson/Adams period of America. Here, Pound feels compelled to reflect on what impedes or disrupts his own elucidation of this linkage.

After a table of contents more appropriate to a textbook like his own *Guide to Kulchur* than to an epic, he makes his excuses in somewhat misleading advice to the reader:

> Note the final lines in Greek, Canto 71, are from Hymn to Cleanthes, part of Adams' *paideuma*: Glorious, deathless of many names, Zeus eye ruling all things, founder of the inborn qualities of nature, by laws piloting all things.
> [*The Cantos of Ezra Pound* (NY: New Directions, 1975), p. 256]

On the one hand, he insists that the Eleusinian or agricultural Zeus serves as a principle of order and exact repetition; on the other hand, he underscores the problems inherent in translating proper names and ideas from one culture into another and, by extension, the difficulties of substituting one set of organizing or textual metaphors for another. Rather than mutually translatable or originary ideas of order, Pound offers a series of mixed metaphors, which gain complexity as he traces them back through time and across cultures: nature vies with classical poetry, agricultural myths with avant-garde art, for preeminence in an "American *paideuma*," which names the roots and shoots that form textual tangles rather than the permanent roots and organized structures of (family) trees. While it seems to retain a grounding in nature or vegetation myths, Pound's cultural history uses a different organic/botanic model. In his repeated efforts at "clearing the underbrush" and breaking ground aside, Pound seems always to focus on the wayward and weed-like proliferation of words and of translations.

In *The Cantos'* American *paideuma*, historical particularity and clear definitions give way to heterogeneity and lawlessness that might permit his manner of grafting what had seemed independent and incompatible systems, to the point where it is no longer possible to distinguish a main stem from dependent offshoots. In the cultural exchange between revolutionary America and Imperial China, John Adams, like Pound's rather idiosyncratic Zeus, figures centrally in the founding of both governmental and agricultural systems. Adams and Jefferson are praised for erecting monuments, including statues of Washington, and for valuing the active and revolutionary over the static and monumental. By way of reconstructing viable poetic and economic programs for modern America—or creating them for the first time out of fragments of an old "American Dream"—Pound advances a wayward textual economy of multiplying references or, in his phrases, "spermatic thought" and "interpretative metaphors." His text embraces as many contradictions, and includes as many senses of "culture," as Whitman's.

As though to compound the disorder of his various systems, and to deny the fundamental principle of Imagism by which he rejected rhetorical ornament, Pound claims that his use of Chinese *ideograms* and all the other foreign quotations is almost purely supplementary and ornamental. In the "Chinese Cantos" one suspects that Pound's simply erroneous translations and transliterations border on irony, since he seems to know more about the complexities of cultural exchanges and translations than he practices. In the note preceding Canto 52, he seems to warn and yet to reassure the reader, aware at least that he is complicating linguistic and cultural matters: "Foreign words and ideograms both in these two decads and in earlier cantos enforce the text but seldom if ever add anything not stated in the English, though not always in lines immediately contiguous to these underlinings" (52: 256).

Indeed, for most readers, the Chinese glyphs and Pound's other interpolations add little to the English, though they are likely to erupt weed-like into the English text at places where their meaning remains indeterminate. Not only do Pound's foreign usages violate Imagist doctrine, but he also seems willing to court uncontainable metaphoricity, not to say rhetorical ornament, for the sake of inclusiveness and, perhaps, in order to appear "cultured" in a random sort of way. Chinese characters often stand as signs of the exotic, as metonymines for incompatible or irreducable systems, and, more to Pound's purpose, as impressive monuments to genealogical and State order. In this way, Pound complicates recurrent Classical references by interpolating into his text less congenial precursors of his ideal America—even in the very name of the Adams family line, and using Brooks Adams's notion of cultural/economic exchange. Pound is often self-conscious and always deliberate about his unorthodox precedures for fabricating what he will claim is an organic tradition.

The very claim that his text can be easily domesticated, that foreign borrowings contribute emphasis rather than meaning, involves Pound in a play of figures, a questioning of language, that he could not contain. Rather than "underlining" significant connections or tracing subterranean root systems among the various languages, arts, and sciences he wanted to appropriate, his Chinese and other foreign inscriptions radiate tangled lines of force and influence in all directions, jumping from plateau to plateau and following the "lawless laws" of rhizomes.

One of the more suggestive instances of these fertile outcroppings occurs in Canto 53, where Pound's nostalgic record of the agricultural and monetary reforms instituted by the founder of the ancient Shang dynasty is punctuated by that frequently cited modernist imperative, "Make It New." I quote: "In 1760 Tching Tang opened the copper mine / (ante Christum) / made discs with square holes in their middles / and gave them to the people / wherewith they might buy grain. . . . Tching prayed on the mountain and / wrote MAKE IT NEW / on his bath tub. / Day by day make it new / cut the underbrush, pile the logs / keep it growing" (53: 264–65). Pound's free translation of the imperial motto, which had been coined by Confucius roughly a millennium after Tching's reign, performs the same sort of destructive and/or reconstructive (one could nearly say de-con-structive) task for which the latter-day American enlisted Whitman as "drill." Thus, even in this most radical effort to affirm genealogical order, an absolute origin and continuity to culture, Pound uncovers the ubiquitous conflict of tradition and innovation in which history, science, and poetry must begin over again—and differently—every day.

Pound was compelled to reflect on the plethora of masterpieces, discourses, and traditions which lend to his poem a chaos of systems that cannot be reduced to a master System. Often his self-reflections on this palimpsestic structure involve an uneasy mixture of the organic and the architectonic; his reflections become inextricable from the textual machine he had set in motion. Especially in the later Cantos, Pound addresses what we have been calling the American rhizome as against European and Asian arborescence. For instance, in Canto 85, the first poem of "Rock Drill," where he recalls the natural basis of sound economy and right government from the Shang dynasty to the present, Pound refers to the sacred ash of Norse mythology: "From T'ang's time until now / That you lean 'gainst the tree of heaven / and know Ygdrasil" (85: 545).

A few pages later in the same Canto, however, Pound tries to translate the myth of an originary unity, or transplant a rooted tradition, into the hostile climate of America. By this account, his native culture has "No classics, / no American history / no centre, no general root" (85: 549). This particular turn or translation back into the American literary scene ends on of *The Cantos'* many catalogues of those non-literary disciplines (including philology, geology, mathematics, biology, and publishing) from which Pound, rather like Henry Adams, borrowed tags and the proper names of culture heroes, though not System. Moreover, his very complaint places him in a certain pattern of anxiety-reaction to America's de-centeredness and miscellaneousness. As we have seen, Emerson, whose writings epitomize the very tendencies they dismiss, was already in this tenuous and, it would seem, *American* position.

Finally, in the "Draft of Canto 113" Pound's own system building culminates in an unsteady equation of three metonyms (rather improperly used proper names of the key figures from disparate arts) associated with the unrelated though internally coherent disciplines of music, taxonomy, and genetics. He depicts Paradise thus: "Yet to walk with Mozart, Agassiz and Linnaeus / 'neath overhanging air under sunbeat / Here take thy mind's space / And to this garden" (113: 786). In this way, Pound's poem—for which a *baroque gallery* (a bust of Mozart here, a specimen chest in the style of Goethe's study there, and, in the midst of all these monuments, the artist creating new masterworks at an easel or writing desk surrounded by discarded drafts) would be a more fitting metaphor than even that untamed mental landscape or garden of the muses—collects fragments, tags, and whole strata of traditions and discourses.

The poet was not unconcerned about his tendency to miscellany. After all—and *after all*—he says, in the fragment of Canto 116, "I am not a demigod, / I cannot make it cohere. . . . Disney against the metaphysicals. . . . a nice quiet paradise over the shambles" (116: 786). If we take seriously Pound's sometimes tragic and sometimes more strategically ironic comments about the incoherence of his poem and of the culture which willy-nilly gave rise to it, we come to recognize that he poses fundamental challenges not only to Poetry but to virtually all those Western scientific and metaphysical traditions that have become the targets of current post-structuralist readings in the texts of Deleuze, Guattari, and certain wayward tendrils of recent American criticism.

Yet this deconstructive strain, this self-conscious tendency to subvert self-reflection, has always been present at least on the margins of American literature. No writer has been more crucial in this regard than Henry Adams, though one hesitates to name so insistently *marginal* a figure as central to America's critical—let alone its literary—tradition. As he visited the cultural shrines of Europe, Adams insisted that he was a tourist and an uncle, neither an expert nor the father of a new historiography or a new critical method. He discovered neither a continuous line of descent nor a completed circle of cultural achievements; instead, he multiplied genealogical anxieties until his recuperation of European culture became a parody of itself, a swirl of interpretations launched against the desire for *closure*—at least on the model of the hermeneutical circle of the autotelic test. His choice of literary and architectural monuments at least anticipates Pound's, even as it follows Hawthorne's *The Marble Faun* and a whole line if not a literary genre of travel romances that trace the pre-history of American culture. Adams was perversely fond of digging up problems such nostalgic texts are generally committed to avoiding. Meditating, for instance, on the edifice of Mont-Saint-Michel, Adams recalls several conflicting accounts (some in tapestries, some in poems) of the Battle of Hastings from which England dates its nationhood and about which the record Mont-Saint-Michel tells another version. Not only does he underscore the tangled heritage of England, and thus his Anglo-American (or is it Franco-American?) inheritance, but he also shows that the different interpretations of historical, architectural, and literary texts can make cultural and artistic hierarchies tremble. He is at once "annoyed" and motivated by an anarchical scepticism, one that in a particularly American fashion, refuses to be destructive or simple affirmative as it finds metaphors and interested interpretations where fundamental truths were supposed to have existed:

> The feeling of scepticism before so serious a monument as Mont-Saint-Michel is annoying. The "Chanson de Roland" ought not to be trifled with, at least by tourists in search of art. One is shocked at the possibility of being deceived about the starting point of American genealogy. Taillefer and the song rest on the same evidence that Duke William and Harold and the battle itself rest upon, and to doubt the "Chanson" is to call the very roll of Battle Abbey in question. The whole fabric of society totters; the British peerage turns pale.

Yet doubt he would, and annoy his fellow Harvard historians with sceptical analyses of facts and the empirical historicism by which culture and the curriculum established their heritage and legitimacy. Rather than defer to "science"—or to the "interpretative metaphors" Pound claims to have borrowed from science—Adams brings his criticism to bear on the modern sciences and philosophy as simulated unities or systems to which the arts have mistakenly turned. Adams uncovers the progressive complexity—indeed the original heterogeneity—that preceded the building of the first stratum of such venerable textual and architectural palimpsests as Chartres and Mont-Saint-Michel.

Since the full implications of the critical and parodic thrust of Adams's writing has been glossed over by those readers who appreciate his genteel prose and cultured sensibility more than his destructions of ideal genealogies, it is worth noting his manner of reconstituting a texture of tissue of fragments. He does not lament the ruined state of the churches and other "sacred places" of medieval history. Quite the contrary, he takes advantage of the opportunity: using the flexible medium of his prose, he takes a striking piece from the facade of, say, a Romanesque church and transposes it onto an incomplete, not to say stylistically incompatible, Gothic facade. By this method, which is anathema to history and impossible for architecture, his various fragments become figures in an ever-growing construct that is grounded in complex synechdoches, in which details of various styles represent whole ages that are stitched into Adams's unique prose patchwork that never resolves into a whole book or even an exemplary beginning for a serious art historical study. The ideal edifice he erects is more modern than medieval, more a phantasmagoric exchange of images than a nostalgic recuperation of primitive or organic art:

> Here at Mont-Saint-Michel we have only a mutilated trunk of an eleventh-century church to judge by. We have not even a facade, and we shall have to stop at some Norman village—at Thaon or Ouistreham—to find a west front which might suit the abbey here, but wherever we find it we shall find something more serious, more military, more practical. . . . So, too, the central tower or lantern—the most striking feature of Norman churches—has fallen here at Mont-Saint-Michel, and we shall have to replace it from Cerisy-la-Foret, and Lessay, and Falaise.

Whether or not the modern poet had the proto-modern tourist in mind, the "mutilated trunk," to say nothing of its repair by further fragmentation and the mixing of genres into a sort of collage, anticipates Pound's poetic method. It is worth noting that, while medievalism and Provençal culture in particular were all the rage in Pound's college years, he was especially fond of "The Song of Roland" and granted to its writer and to such troubadours as Bertran de Born a privileged place in his canon of innovators and other heretics. From *Personae* to *The Cantos*, he employed a method of construction that he claimed to have borrowed from Bertran de Born. We have already noted Pound's habit of carving out family trees and preferring "washes" of interpretation over rooted traditions; in this project of fragmentation, he goes a step further than Henry Adams (whom he fashioned the last of a long line of American politicians and active men whose lives were "whole"). He finds that the very poetics of the troubadours involved the piecing together of fragments into anything but an organic whole or an unmediated song. In early long poems, "Na Audiart" and "Near Periogod," for instance, Pound constructs a "composite poem" on the model of the "composite lady of the troubadours," who sent tributes to "real ladies" by anthologizing the ideal features of renowned beauties immortalized by other poets. Thus, in American poems consisting of sometimes partially translated borrowings and stylistic parodies, Pound discloses that in poems written and performed at the same time that the great cathedrals and abbies were slowly being erected, there was no simple relationship between art and life. No one planner, architect, or observer saw the completion of a cathedral, or even the final version of a poem in his lifetime.

Furthermore, the most perfect songs were no more simple reflections of living women than Pound's new American poem, which was to be stitched together out of fragments already doubly textual because they were rooted in poems and not in Nature or Idea.

Pound's closest approach to Adams's architectural reconstructions is his admiration of Sigismundo Malatesta's Tempio (Cantos 13–21, *passim*), that textual layering of pagan/Christian/classical fragments which Pound called "both an apex and in a verbal sense a monumental failure" [*Guide to Kulchur*]. While Pound could accept the heterogeneity of Malatesta's late-Medieval (re)construction, he considered similar American attempts, including William Randolph Hearst's San Simeon, dangerous and inauthentic. When it came to an American Renaissance, he could brook no variety, no individuality. For his version of American culture, Pound chose the rigid, if no less ersatz, center of Fascism. See, for example, his discovery of an Italian version of Jeffersonian agrarianism in *Jefferson and/or Mussolini*. The tangled roots of Pound's Fascism can be read in—or back into—American history. But this is a subterranean line we cannot follow out here.

If Pound was more troubled by his American heritage, his mixed inheritance, Adams was bemused by the prospect of the *new* overtaking the old world. He too brought America with him, carrying his Adams and Quincy grandfathers from New England to his earlier continental ancestors—making, that is, a characteristically American version or reversal of the founding of Rome. In another passage that might be thought to adumbrate Pound's figure of the washes or waves of one culture over another, of modernism obscuring the clear demarcations of the European tradition, Adams confounds genealogy as well as history and geography. He discovers his native New England, as the trace of his own youth, even as he looks down under the foundation of Mont-Saint-Michel:

> From the edge of the platform, the eye plunges down, two hundred and thirty five feet to the wide sands or the wider ocean, as the tides recede or advance, under an infinite sky, over a restless sea, which even we tourists can understand and feel without books or guides. . . . One needs only be old enough in order to be as young as one will. From the top of this Abbey Church one looks across the bay to Avranches, and toward Contances and the Cotentin—the Constantius pagus—whose shore facing us, recalls the coast of New England.

In both *Mont-Saint-Michel* and *The Education* Adams catalogues historical adumbrations and repetitions in the self-reflexive manner usually associated with the most disruptive and de-familiarizing sorts of modernism. The organic intersects with the architectural, as the critic ironically re-stages the fall into complexity that made possible his project of recasting culture into something more exciting because less homogeneous and more clearly marked by interpretation. Adams opens art to science, but to a science that has always been fragmented and in a state of flux. According to Adams, science became baroque or rhetorical after Aquinas, and the baroque is still becoming. And it is American.

Centuries before Adams wrote his idiosyncratic architectural digest—that is, his autobiography of the growth of his own scepticism—there was no ultimate reference point for culture or the arts. Quite apart from his attraction to ruins and monuments, and the apparent nostalgia for the centering figure of the Virgin, Adams celebrates this multiplicity and dynamism. As he digs through layers of supplements to the ancient walls, he remarks the beginnings of the suspicion that organic unity was a mere dream. He suggest that modern science is only the natural—and we would have to say "rhizomatic"—outgrowth of a complexity as fundamental as the dream of organic art, which he criticizes as the "dogma" of orthodoxy and the central Idea. Of the birth of scientific skepticism out of Medieval theology, he says:

> Modern science, like modern art, tends in practice to drop the dogma of organic unity. Some of the medieval habit of mind survives, but even that is said to be yielding before the daily evidence of increasing and extending complexity. The fault, then, was not in man, if he no longer looked at science or art as an organic whole or as the expression of unity. Unity turned itself into complexity, multiplicity, variety and even contradiction. All experience, human and divine, assured man in the thirteenth century that the lines of the universe converged. How was he to know that these lines ran in every conceivable and inconceivable direction, and that at least half of them seemed to diverge from any imaginable centre of unity?

American writers from Emerson to Whitman to Adams to Pound and beyond have naturally—or unnaturally—recognized this complexity and have nonetheless given life to a de-centered tradition, if not a culture, called *America* or American literature or, more simply, modernism. Neither centering nor de-centering has been without its poetic and political dangers.

Robinson Jeffers:
The Women at Point Sur

Brother Antoninus

Beginning with the prologue as a sort of weathering process, we can expect it to furnish the conditioning interval we need for our acclimatization [to *The Women at Point Sur*], orient us into the prospective violence, and at the same time protect us from psychic inundation by too direct an exposure to the blast of action itself. If it is to do this it must be forceful, evocative and intense, and must seize us with the Giant Hand that is the true signature of genius. . . . It is in his magnificent Prelude that Jeffers first possesses us, prepares us to "accept the risk," forces us into the mythological dimension where all the violations may be endured without flinching, and where we may grope forward toward whatever solutions we can find to the ritual of deliverance and ordeal which constitutes the opportunity or the destruction of modern man.

It is one of the masterpieces of Jeffers's art, exhibiting to maximum degree his complex technical skills. And it reveals much about the questions the poem proposes, and some intimation of their answers. I was long of the opinion that it was created well after the inception of the narrative itself. A poet will enter into a theme tentatively, not fully engaged, expecting to deepen his involvement as he goes. Then, finally committed, he turns back and strokes in his opening, able at last to operate somewhere near the level of his subsistent aesthetic commitment. Indeed, the shift in psychic tension between the Prelude and the first section seemed evidence enough that this was the case. But when I examined the Jeffers papers in the Yale Collection of American Literature I saw it was not so. The poet wrote the Prelude as we have it and proceeded immediately to the narrative. Thus we see that it is indeed the psychological matrix out of which the whole

---

From *Robinson Jeffers: Fragments of an Older Fury.* © 1968 by Brother Antoninus. Oyez Longman, 1968.

work develops. More important, it is the "door," the threshold over which we must pass in order to effect a shift in attitude from our normative consciousness, in order to leave the world of "actuality" and enter the world of "myth."

This, the world of myth, is the dimension into which the prologue takes us, and it does so masterfully. Beautiful, intense, vibrant with urgency, flecked with lightning flashes of scorn and repudiation, it hovers over our world like the entry of one of the great storms which it invokes above the Carmel coast and introduces us not only to the climate of mind and the figures we are going to encounter, but also the basic religious symbols that lie in all their primitiveness beneath our culture. It creates the psychic atmosphere which evokes the presence of the "deliverer," the man Barclay himself.

The Prelude opens powerfully:

> I drew solitude over me, on the lone shore,
> By the hawk-perch stones; the hawks and the gulls are never
>   breakers of solitude.

And savagely:

> When the animals Christ was rumored to have died for drew
>   in,
> The land thickening, drew in about me, I planted trees
>   eastward, and the ocean
> Secured the west with the quietness of thunder. I was quiet.

And contemptuously:

> Imagination, the traitor of the mind, has taken my solitude
>   and slain it.
> No peace but many companions; the hateful-eyed
> And human-bodied are all about me: you that love
>   multitude may have them.

It would seem Jeffers is saying that though he prefers solitude and has taken steps to ensure it, the invasion of Carmel in the twenties shifted the psychic balance the region had provided him and overbalanced the soul with the fervid restlessness of the normative American mentality: gregarious, talkative, slap-happy, trivial, mundane, unreflective—all polar opposites to the quietude of the elements. More likely at a far deeper level he is saying that Fame, which has in fact come to him, has touched some somnolent nerve of response, and he must either accept its stimulus and succumb to it, or utterly reject its appeal.

At any rate he has scoffed at our values, and in scoffing intrigued us with the power of the negative. Yet the negative must be uttered, and utterance is positive. He proclaims himself vulnerable.

But why should I make fables again? There are many
Tellers of tales to delight women and the people.
I have no vocation.

The power of the depth throws him back upon the underlying awareness of permanence and stability:

The old rock under the house, the hills
with their
hard roots and the ocean hearted
With sacred quietness from here to Asia.

But he cannot rest there, despite himself he is driven to engage in what he despises:

Make me ashamed to speak of the active little bodies, the
coupling bodies, the misty brainfuls
Of perplexed passion.

Against the immense impersonal gravity and masculine permanence of things, it is this itch, the female sexual itch, that confronts him. Why?
Why not? Carmel, the summer cottages and love-nests of the Jazz Age, week-ending business men with their hot mammas, drunk on green liquor smuggled in by boat from Canada. Carmel, where Aimee Semple McPherson, the torrid evangelist from Southern California, would hole up with her paramour while the nation scoured the byways enthusiastically searching for her kidnapped person.

Humanity is needless.
I said, "Humanity is the start of the race, the gate to break
away from, the coal to kindle,
The blind mask crying to be slit with eye-holes."

That was in "The Tower beyond Tragedy," a flashback into Aeschylus's world, when civilization as we know it was just beginning.

Well, now it is done, the mask slit, the rag burnt, the
starting-post left behind: but not in a fable.

What was then projected as a prophecy has become in actuality a hard fact:

Culture's outlived, art's root-cut, discovery's
The way to walk in.

The poet's duty is no longer to seek ways to prefigure what will be, but to scrawl it out crudely and be done:

Only remains to invent the language to
tell it.
Match-ends of burnt experience
Human enough to be understood,
Scraps and metaphors will serve.

For if the race has burnt itself out, then only burnt out images are necessary to show it to itself. The time when Christ must speak in parables because the people were incapable of apprehending is over. Jeffers reaches for the heart of the parable to show actuality to a post-Christian people:

> The wine was a little too strong for the new wine-skins.

It is important here not to be stung into feeling insulted, into contemptuous dismissal. We are overhearing a man in dialogue with himself. We share, in some measure, his difficulties. Profoundly religious, he loves solitude and permanence, and he seeks out the symbols and images that confirm these truths to himself. But he is shaken, too, with excesses, the fretful and itching acerbations of imagination and dissolution. He has seen those realities increase as the culture proliferated, until by the mid-twenties of this century they were at boiling point. He longs for silence but he is impelled to speak. He despises speaking but speak he must. "The active little bodies, the coupling bodies, the misty brainfuls of perplexed passion." He projects them outside himself, but they are his own projections, and he cannot escape them. For him, a poet, there is only one solution, and that is the creative act. Drawing down within himself, against the stagnation of his conscious mind where the tension has been equalized because the forces countercheck each other, he calls up the great image of creative release, the great archetypal centrality that dominates the Prelude.

> Come storm, kind storm.
> Summer and the days of tired gold
> And bitter blue are more ruinous.
> The leprous grass, the sick forest.
> The sea like a whore's eyes,
> And the noise of the sun,
> The yellow dog barking in the blue pasture,
> Snapping sidewise.

What then is needed? To restore the roots of viability beneath the sterility of corrupt culture. Heinrich Zimmer says:

> Ages and attitudes of man that are long gone by still survive in the deeper unconscious layers of our soul. The spiritual heritage of archaic man (the ritual and mythology that once visibly guided his conscious life) has vanished to a large extent from the surface of the tangible and conscious realm, yet survives and remains ever present in the subterranean layers of the unconscious. It is the part of our being that links us to a remote ancestry and constitutes our involunatry kinship with archaic man and with ancient civilizations and traditions.

It is the sovereign role of the poet to perform this function for modern man. . . .

Now the summer stagnation, image of our rationally dominated culture, in the extremity of its drought, invokes its redeemer, the "kind storm." It is the image of renewal in the creative act, the Dionysian syndrome, and it holds its terrific potential of deliverance: one of those great storms that form on the upper Pacific and start southward bringing winds, rains, and the violence of lightning. This violence is seen as non-human and divine, and it has its correspondence in the human soul:

> When I remembered old rains,
> Running clouds and the iron wind, then the trees trembled.
> I was calling one of the great dancers
> Who wander down from the Aleutian rocks and the open
>   Pacific,
> Pivoting counter-sunwise, celebrating power with the whirl
>   of a dance, sloping to the mainland.
> I watched his feet waken the water
> And the ocean break in foam beyond Lobos;
> The iron wind struck from the hills.

This noble and sublime titanic center of energy serves us as prototype to the figure of Barclay himself—not as a "personification of natural force," for clearly here the storm itself is characterized as an archetypal figure. But the conventionalized rational structure of materialistic civilization is heavily established and refuses to yield.

> You are tired and corrupt,
> You kept the beast under till the fountain's poisoned,
> He drips with mange and stinks through the oubliette
>   window.

Here we are introduced to the underlying psychological apparatus of the poem. The oubliette, a dungeon with an opening only at the top, is a crude symbol of the Freudian version of the unconscious. If the instincts, the "beast," are repressed too long, they will corrupt the conscious powers themselves. Even the recent bloodbath of World War I did not slake or heal these tendencies, for the slaughter was so great that those who might have come back appeased, and hence given balance to society, were themselves killed off, leaving the survivors no better than before:

> The promise-breaker war killed whom it freed,
> And none living's the cleaner.

But the creative potential remains:

> Yet storm comes, the lions hunt
> In the nights striped with lightning. It will come: feed on
>   peace
> While the crust holds.

He warns the complacent, in a fatherly tone:

> to each of you at length a little
> Desolation; a pinch of lust or a drop of terror.

And we make our exit from the areas of rational disquisition as the images fade and blend together in the cadences of appeasement and release, a falling asleep or a drift into Dionysian deliverance:

> Then the lions hunt in the brain of the dying: storm is good,
>   storm is good, good creature,
> Kind violence, throbbing throat aches with pity.

Now we are introduced to one of the principal figures of the drama, Onorio Vasquez, who stands between two worlds, the practical and the visionary. Of all the characters in the drama, only he survives to appear in other Jeffers narratives. He is watching his brothers crucify a hawk, the principal symbol for Jeffers of divinity in act, and by virtue of this crucifixion, is identified with Christ, an identification made earlier by Hopkins in his "Windhover," though it is problematical whether at that time Jeffers had seen that poem—more likely it is an instance of an underlying archetype precipitating an identical insight in two widely separated poets.

> They crucified the creature,
> A nail in the broken wing on the barn wall
> Between the pink splinters of bone and a nail in the other.
> They prod his breast with a wand, no sponge of vinegar,
> "Fly down, Jew-beak."

The hawk, the Christ-like male symbol, introduces Onorio's prophetic mind to its feminine counterpart, a figure corresponding in archetypal dimension to the storm, the great dancer that had preceded her on the water. In the galley proofs of the poem at Yale certain details of her sketch were excised due, according to a note affixed to the portfolio, to the censorship situation at that time. I give the passage, with the kind permission of the curators at Yale, as it exists in the galley proofs.

> What he sees:
> The ocean like sleek gray stone perfectly jointed
> To the heads and bays, a woman walking upon it,
> The curling scud of the storm around her ankles,
> Naked and strong, her thighs the height of the mountain,
>   walking and weeping,
> The shadow of hair under the belly, the jutting breasts
>   like hills, the face in the hands and the hair
> Streaming north.

Now the Christ-hawk identity is deepened. In the mind of Onorio the archetypal woman on the sea is associated with the mother of Jesus:

> "Why are you sad, our lady?" "I had only
>
> one son.
>
> The strange lover never breaks the window-latches again
> When Joseph's at synagogue."

Here the poet accommodates to the modernist interpretation of the miracle of Mary's overshadowing by the Holy Spirit but retains the necessary ambiguity, as the figure "strange lover" fittingly retains the orthodox meaning as well. These ambiguities deepen the Christ-hawk visage into an almost Blakean image of austere divinity:

> Orange eyes, tired and fierce,
> They're casting knives at you now, but clumsily, the knives
> Quiver in the wood, stern eyes the storm deepens.
> Don't wince, topaz eyes.

Old Vasquez and his boys burn the mountain: fire, the symbol of consuming fulfillment, of punishment and purgation. This symbol takes us from the archetypal woman to the young wife who yearns for erotic fulfillment but is frustrate, unable to transmute her need into charismatic encounter, latching the windows but forgetting the door:

> Myrtle Cartwright
> Could sleep if her heart would quit moving the bed-clothes.

This heart-movement introduces Faith Heriot, seen here as a pubescent girl, one of the main figures in the drama to come. She lies to her father, who keeps, not Point Sur but Point Pinos light, to get out in the dark. At last alone she lies under the swinging light of the beacon, another phallic symbol of the restless energizing Spirit, rich with fertility images:

> This girl never goes near the cowshed but wanders
> Into the dunes, the long beam of the light
> Swims over and over her head in the high darkness,
> The spray of the storm strains through the beam but Faith
> Crouches out of the wind in a hollow of the sand
> And hears the sea, she rolls on her back in the clear sand
> Shuddering, and feels the light lie thwart her hot body
> And the sand trickle into the burning places.

We have before this been given the suggestion of the dominant motif, that of strain, but now it rises to an incantatory chant, a function it will maintain throughout the poem:

> Oh crucified
> Wings, orange eyes, open?
> Always the strain, the straining flesh, who feels what God
>   feels
> Knows the straining flesh, the aching desires,

The enormous water straining its bounds, the electric
Strain in the cloud, the strain of the oil in the oil tanks
At Monterey, aching to burn, the strain of the spinning
Demons that make an atom, straining to fly asunder,
Straining to rest at the center,
The strain in the skull, blind strains, force and
    counterforce,
Nothing prevails.

Now we are at the heart of the psychic drama that centers the poem. We have entered the mythological dimension in which the poet is establishing himself: the opposed polarities of an aching mankind and aching Nature, an aching cosmos. Nothing can resolve this tension but release, and such are the opposed forces that release means violence—release means the consummation of the lesser element in the greater, a burnt out filament in a light bulb, Barclay burnt out at the mouth of the Womb-Tomb to end the drama: "Match-ends of burnt experience [just] Human enough to be understood." The end of the affair.

    Now wind rises, introducing another aspect of Spirit (hawk, lover, lightning, wind):

                      At Vasquez' place in the yellow
Pallor of dawn the roof of the barn's lifting, his sons cast
    ropes over the timbers. The crucified
Snaps his beak at them. He flies on two nails.
Great eyes, lived all night?
Onorio should have held the rope but it slid through his
    fingers.
    Onorio Vasquez
Never sees anything to the point. What he sees:
The planted eucalyptuses bent double
All in a row, praying north, "Why everything's praying
And running northward, old hawk anchored with nails
You see that everything goes north like a river.
On a cliff in the north
Stands the strange lover, shines and calls."

The great phallic lighthouse joins the litany of energy-forces assimilated to Spirit.

    Myrtle Cartwright in the seep of dawn can abide no longer.

Her husband is away. She starts through the storm to find her lover. When she flees to her profane lover the lightning as symbol of Spirit overtakes her and covers her like a beast. But it is not a beast:

> The lightnings like white doves hovering her head harmless
>   as pigeons, through great bars of black music.
> She lifts her wet arms. "Come, doves."

The dove was employed as an erotic symbol centuries before Christian iconography applied it to the Holy Spirit. This over-shadowing, this conception, was occasioned by the igniting of the oil tanks by lightning in Monterey. As the atoms split and explode the release from the strain is granted in marriage, the symbols of sexual consummation:

>   The oil tank boils with joy in the north . . .
> roars with fulfilled desire,
> The ring-bound molecules splitting, the atoms dancing apart,
>   marrying the air.

It all builds up to humanity's immolation in the forces behind itself. Human ache of desire will find its consummation, whether as did Myrtle Cartwright, who latched her window against the Spirit but left her door open to the world, or Onorio Vasquez, who longs to immolate his consciousness in a consummation greater than mankind's:

> Don't you see any vision, Onorio Vasquez? "No, for the
>   topazes
> Have dulled out of his head, he soars on two nails,
> Dead hawk over the coast. Oh little brother
> Julio, if you could drive nails through my hands
> I'd stand against the door; through the middle of the palms:
> And take the hawk's place, you could throw knives at me.
> I'd give you my saddle and the big bridle, Julio,
> With the bit that rings and rings when the horse twirls it."
> He smiles. "You'd see the lights flicker in my hair."
> He smiles craftily. "You'd live long and be rich,
> And nobody could beat you in running or riding."
> He chatters his teeth. "It is necessary for someone to be
>   fastened with nails.
> And Jew-beak died in the night. Jew-beak is dead."

Thus ends the prologue. The turning of the storm, the anguish of human desire, the promise of release in physical consummation, all have combined to take us out of our normative consciousness. The archetypal symbols unfold within us in their pristine originality and primitive vigor. We are given to understand that we are not to conceive of this narrative as a sequential account of human events, the drama of the heroic consciousness confronted with nature, or God, or itself. We are instead in the domain of collective myth, and "the myth disregards—does not even know—the individual." Projections of subsistent human consciousness are called up from the deeps and extended into the cruciality of engagement with the cosmos and the spirit. They are given names but they are not to be seen as personalities. . . . They are personifications of the elements of man's inner being which have lost contact with one another and have started forward each on its own path of deliverance.

Thus the solution posited in the possibility of humanity's having passed beyond the need for a redeemer is, as the saying goes, "up for grabs." Everything about these personifications indicates that they are ripe for a deliverer, a true hero, a true superman, who is of the essence of mythical awareness, and who must needs arise if the separating consciousnesses are to be held together. "It is necessary for someone to be fastened with nails." In the debased religiosity and cultural vitiation of the Jazz Age, its triviality, its itching and squirming libido, its profane ignorance and its corrosive cynicism, the anthropocentric version of the God of Christianity will not avail. "Jew-beak is dead." Instead emerges a new hero, a new messiah, a new superman. He will seek to weld all together in a terrible act of unbelievable affirmation—an affirmation beyond the limits of common human desire, beyond common hope. He will free himself through the ancient acts of violation—fornication, incest, rape—and he will carry his followers to the mouth of the tomb. His name is fated to eat like acid, to become a stumbling block to the perplexed literate intelligence of his time. His name is The Rev. Dr. Arthur Barclay, and he is headed for Point Sur. It remains to be seen whether his creator will realize or deny the hunger that gave him birth.

And so, having touched some of the strands of motif and implication that might help us on our way, having immersed ourselves in the compulsive atmosphere of storm, dissolution and renewal that so powerfully pervades the Prelude, we stand at last on the lip of the initiating action, and face forward into the consequential dimension of the myth itself. In treating of the Prelude we have seen the present condition of human collectiveness delineated, its alienation from God and nature, its need of a redeemer to take it back into contact with the making forces of reality, sources of renewal long repressed under metallic surfaces. We have seen, too, something of the individual dimension, the personal adventure posited as initiation rite. A society without religious orientation in depth cries out for a messiah to take it back to its origins. But it cannot produce such a messiah for it has lost the spiritual attitude that makes it possible for him to emerge, and it has jettisoned the techniques that might enable him to perfect himself, be sufficient to the task that would confront him.

Thus it is possible to see in *Point Sur* the two tendencies, the collective and the individual, on a "collision course," and we might read the unfolding of its scenario with that in mind. As the various personifications typified by the cast of characters emerge—Natalia Morhead, Faith Heriot, Maruca,

Randal—their essential rootlessness and inversion signify that they are cut off from centrality, and hence must react like loose flotsam, or metallic particles. Barclay, on the other hand, possessed by the collectivity's need for a messiah, is unable to withstand its compelling demand. It is a demand so overpowering that only the most perfectly formed consciousness could fulfill it, a consciousness which, paradoxically, the collectivity has renounced the capacity to produce. Thus, as it reacts to his presence and becomes more and more intense around him, Barclay himself burns with a more single intensity toward destruction. We are justified, then, in seeing the dénouement at Point Sur as the crisis of a culture, a culture cut off at the roots and delivered to the consequence of its spiritual ignorance.

But, it must be insisted, this is not the position of Jeffers himself. He is registering not the crisis of a culture but the crisis of mankind. For him the more "whole" traditional sacral cultures of the past were no better, essentially, than the painfully rootless ones of today. Why? Because science has shown their beliefs to be as illusionary as ours. The cosmos of Jeffers is essentially a Newtonian one. The religious transposition made available through the shift from Newtonian to Einsteinian physics came too late for him. Nineteenth-century science had demolished the Christian God as an anthropomorphism, and explained religion, no matter what its substance, as mere compensation. The process by which sacral man had staved off disintegration, forms of ritual and meditation sufficient to balance the collective consciousness and produce messiahs in times of crisis—these were, one and all, provisional solutions, efficacious only within the pathetic limits of human consciousness, while those who rose to the bait—Christ, Gautama, Lao Tze—did so out of private impurity. In *Point Sur* Jeffers is putting that solution through its final test-run. He is doing it in order to demonstrate that it will no longer do, has in fact, never done. In "Theory of Truth" he asks over, as we saw, the questions Barclay has asked. Sketching the private impurity of the three great prophets he asks again:

> Then search for truth
> is foredoomed and frustrate?
> Only stained fragments?

And answers:

> Until the mind has turned its love
> from itself and man, from parts to the whole.

And yet, even as he utters it, he gives the game away. Even for himself this solution never sufficed. I am not speaking in terms of the inadequacy of his philosophy; I am speaking in terms of the problem posited by his creative drive. *Point Sur* moves out of the conditions of fragmented and isolated tension we saw in the Prelude and takes its course through a series of inter-reacting exchanges to final crystallization and utter annihilation at the point of conclusion. And whatever the philosophy is saying, the poetry is saying that this is good. All Jeffers's explanations, all his "intentions," do not ring true because they are all belied by the exultation of his verse.

How can this be? The essential attraction-revulsion syndrome upon which the ambivalence is poised is endemic to human nature. But it is so strong in Jeffers that he is willing to intensify contingency in order to clinch it. This is the fact. It could never, for him, suffice to "turn from man," turn "from the parts to the whole." Because to turn, to see, is itself to manifest contingency, and contingency is excruciating. What is the One and what are the Many? To crystallize consciousness in participation in the whole is Jeffers's consuming need, the existence of his verse attests to it. He declares the opposite. He proclaims the necessity, and his willingness, to achieve a life of ego-annulling contemplation. His poetics deny it. Intense, passionate, onrushing, needful and aching, his volcanic rhythms intensify contingency rather than annul it. Yet, somehow, through that crystallized contingency he touches finality, the living glimpse of annihilation. Annihilation. "The most beautiful word." And how are we to conceive of annihilation? It is, essentially, unspeakable; but in a thousand contingent images he evokes it metaphorically. The night. The peace. The quietude. The timelessness. Over and over he creates the images of contingency in order to indicate the substance of his need, which is to pass beyond what he has created, what he has seen, what he has desired.

And in fact the whole effort and achievement of his poem is to establish the ordeal, transmute its agonies into transcendence, and pass beyond transcendence into—what? Well, actually, beatitude. But beatitude as seen from the point of the utter negative. From the positive point of view, beatitude would be the Beatific Vision of the Christian, or the Nirvana of the Buddhist, but Jeffers fights shy of either. They are too conceptual for him. He is aware of the over-mastering presence of God, but the liability of his basic contingency makes him contemptuous of accepting any kind of beatitude based on any kind of deduction from the Reality he has sought.

I suppose his essential role as poet prevents him, actually, from settling for the eventualities of either the philosopher, the seer, or the mystic. Jeffers as poet can only *create* the condition of his beatitude, and when he calls it Annihilation he is thinking of the cancelling *in itself* of that appetitive need within him which is the aesthetic impulse and whose mode is the creative act. So he creates his death, severally, and over and over, in his various narratives and descriptive poems.

In *Tamar* he cast the first spear. He took the *anima*, the feminine principle in himself, and drove it to the point of annihilation, consumed in the fires of the House of Incest. She would not stay dead. In "Apology for Bad Dreams" she haunts him into telling how he encountered her, and years later in a poem called "Come Little Birds" that story is spelled out in detail. "I am Tamar Cauldwell. Tell them I had my desire." Next he took the *animus*, the masculine principle, and drove it to the point of annihilation.

This is Barclay. But neither would the *animus* stay dead. In subsequent narratives he contented himself with exploring the ratios of inter-dependent contingencies and these are more contained, more formally resolved aesthetic structures, and are better liked. But he did not pitch the spear at the absolute again until "At the Birth of an Age" when, in the figure of Gudrun, he cast the *anima* once more. Gudrun does not burn with the same intenseness of naked potentiality that Tamar did; it was as if by that time Jeffers *knew* beforehand, whereas Tamar for him had been pure discovery, as Barclay was pure discovery. But nevertheless in the poem's closing pages the voice of the Nordic Gudrun merges with that of the Oriental Jesus to make a *heiros gamos*, a *conjunctio*, which together are subsumed into that of the Promethean Hanged God, the pure archetype of self-sustaining immolation, which is actually the voice of Barclay purged of its insanity and burning with unspeakable purity, the principle of subsistent consciousness upon which the whole of reality turns and sustains, the principle that Christians themselves perceive as the keynote of all being, and call the Christ:

> If I were quiet and emptied myself of pain,
> > breaking these bonds,
> Healing these wounds: without strain there is nothing.
> > Without pressure, without conditions, without pain,
> Is peace; that's nothing, not-being; the pure night, the
> > perfect freedom, the black crystal. I have chosen
> Being; therefore wounds, bonds, limits and pain; the
> > crowded mind and the anguished nerves, experience
> > and ecstasy.
> Whatever electron or atom or flesh or star or universe cries
> > to me,
> Or endures in shut silence: it is my cry, my silence; I am the
> > nerve, I am the agony,
> I am the endurance. I torture myself
> To discover myself; trying with a little or extreme experiment
> > each nerve and fibril, all forms
> Of being, of life, of cold substance; all motions and netted
> > complications of event,
> All poisons of desire, love, hatred, joy, partial peace, partial
> > vision.
> Discovery is deep and endless,
> Each moment of being is new: therefore I still refrain my
> > burning thirst from the crystal-black
> Water of an end.

So we are not to see *Point Sur* as anything conclusive. We are to see it as a try, a far-cast spear, thrown out of painful ambivalence in an attempt at transcendence. Before the cast was begun the understanding of what transcendence really consisted of was deeply forming in the underlying consciousness, but not articulated. *Tamar* had only glimpsed it. True, "Tower beyond Tragedy" had posited the alternative of contemplation, but the archetypes of imbalance in Jeffers's nature were too acute to accept that. In *Point Sur* he tossed again, the longest, hardest, most intense cast of the spear he was ever to make, and he "touched his answer"—annihilation—the only answer that would ever appease *his* spirit. But he could not keep with it. The secondary calls of contemplation kept positing their claims, and he wrote out his remaining narratives (save one, "The Birth of an Age") to accommodate his needs, rather than discover them.

Now he possesses his answers. His spirit lives on in the annihilative center of the body of poems which constitute his work, the still center of the aesthetic intuition, whose term is beyond mediation, beyond subject and object, beyond contingency, beyond the subsidiary distinctions to the supreme Isness, where all things are annihilated within the abyss of Being, which he, and I, and all men, in our own way and by our own terms, have always called God. "But think on the nothing / Outside the stars," cried Barclay at the last, "the other shore of me, there's peace."

> He ran northward, his followers
> Tired and fell off. He alone, like a burnt pillar
> Smeared with the blood of sacrifice passed across the black
>   hills,
> And then the gray ones, the fire had stopped at a valley.
> He came to a road and followed it, the waste vitality
> Would not be spent. When the sun stood westward he
>   turned
> Away from the light and entered Mal Paso Canyon.
> At the head of the steep cleft men had mined coal
> Half a century before; acres of dry thistles
> Covered the place where men had labored, and Barclay
> Lay down in the mouth of the black pit. After three days,
> Having not tasted water, he was dying and he said:
> "I want creation . . ."

And so the tossed spear has turned in midair and is winging back to life. The ritual of initiation into death has been successful. It is an initiation into renewal. The mythological teleology is preserved, contained in the impenetrable diastole and systole that make up reality. Annihilation is only the entry into the abyss of renewal. Barclay's heroic ordeal, crippled by unpreparedness, propelled by a collective need greater than he could withstand, was not in vain. In the deep psyche of the reader, violation after violation have been passed through, hell-hole after hell-hole penetrated and passed beyond. In death the old life is liberated into the new, and God speaks out of the throat of his mouthpiece:

> "I want creation. The wind over the desert
> Has turned and I will build again all that's gone down.
> I am inexhaustible."

The "Feminine" Language
of Marianne Moore

Bonnie Costello

Several critics of Marianne Moore's poetry have remarked, directly or in-directly, on its "feminine" quality, although it is sometimes difficult to decide just what they mean by this. T. S. Eliot, for instance, concludes his 1923 essay on Moore with a statement he either seems to feel is self-ex-planatory or hasn't really examined: "And there is one final, and 'magnif-icent' compliment: Miss Moore's poetry is as 'feminine' as Christina Rossetti's, one never forgets that it is written by a woman; but with both one never thinks of this as anything but a positive virtue." What can he have in mind? Is it the "restraint" and "humility" that Randall Jarrell talks about in his essay on Moore, entitled "Her Shield"? Is it the ladylike quality, the "chastity" of taste (a term rarely applied to men) that R. P. Blackmur saw as both the virtue and defect of her work? Or perhaps Eliot was thinking of Moore's preoccupation with surfaces and objects of sense experience (especially trivial experience) which he and others have praised as her "genuineness" while they have distinguished genuineness from "great-ness". Men write out of primitive or heroic occasions, women write out of everyday occasions. In his essay about Edna Saint Vincent Millay, "The Poet as Woman," John Crowe Ransom distinguishes Moore for having less "deficiency of masculinity," that is, (and he is explicit about this) "intel-lectual interest" than other women writers. Yet we feel a reserve of pre-judice influencing his view of her, even when his purpose is to applaud, as in "On Being Modern with Distinction." Woman's love, he says in the Millay essay, is a fixation to natural sense objects (woman can't transcend mundane experience). Woman's love is devoted (she has no self). Man has lapsed, since childhood, from natural feelings, and his mind thus grows

From *Women and Language in Literature and Society*, edited by Sally McConnell-Ginet, Ruth Borker, and Nelly Furman. © 1980 by Praeger Publishers.

apart from woman's (woman remains childish). Woman does not go to the office (she has the leisure to be idle and cultivate her tenderness). Woman is set in her "famous attitudes" (woman's mind is full of clichés and household truisms). These assumptions appear, under a gauze of affection, throughout criticism of Moore's poetry. Roy Harvey Pearce begins by praising Moore's modesty and ease, but his parenthetical criticisms make him sound a little insincere in wishing William Carlos Williams, Conrad Aiken, and E. E. Cummings had Moore's female virtue.

Surprisingly, in her staunchly feminist argument, Suzanne Juhasz agrees with the men, both in the way they read the poems and in how they evaluate them. Rather than reexamining the male standards she assumes them a priori. Rather than consider the possible complexity of Moore's predilections and the original strength of her verse, Juhasz accepts past interpretations and simply seeks to explain how Moore's social and historical situation might cause her to "retreat" into the "lesser" qualities of "spinsterly" writing for self-protection. Because she is looking for something else (confessional poetry), Juhasz completely misses the distinctiveness of Moore's inventions. To Juhasz, insofar as Moore's stylistic devices are "feminine" they are defenses.

Moore's art does display much of the taste and manners, the "vanity" as well as the "nobler virtue" our society ascribes to women. She is a lover of ornamental surfaces; she is fascinated with fashion and wrote several articles on the subject; she is "gossipy" and chatty, passing on bits of hearsay and borrowed phrases; she is a collector of knickknacks, her poems are like over-stuffed cupboards, full of irrelevancies and distractions. Moore's life reflected the same tendencies and tastes. Her scrapbooks and library are full of literature on women's dress, interior design, jewelry, ornamental art. Her letters go on for paragraphs describing someone's living room, a new coat, a cat she is caring for. But somehow, when she is describing a friend's hat or a clay bird someone gave her, these particulars seem more important as *occasions* for imaginative response than for their conventional value.

Moore's critics have tended to identify her "feminine" qualities superficially, taking up her lexicon of virtues but applying their own definitions and prejudices to it. In context, I want to suggest, these qualities take on a special, powerful meaning, quite inverted in value. Moore purposely assumes the traditional "household" virtues and attributes in order to redefine them in the action of her poems. Moore's "feminine" virtues and manners do not glass-in or soften reality, do not trivialize experience or diminish the claims of the self, but on the contrary become in various ways the chief sources of energy in her work. Continually in her poetry and in her prose Moore shows a close relationship between moral and technical virtue. As Geoffrey Hartman has observed in a brief note on the poet, "her style does not embody a morality, it is one." The central morality of her style (and the chief source of its vitality) is a resistance to the complacencies of thought and language, to a tendency to accept given forms as descriptive of the world as it is. This is not a passive resistance, for it works in alliance with her mental voracity, continually readjusting the line and pushing against the limits of language. Moore's access to this central concern with the limits of language is through a conventional but redefined femininity. Or, conversely, the breaking up of our assumptions about certain types of virtue and manner is a natural instance of a larger concern for resisting complacencies of thought and language.

This is not, for Moore, an explicitly feminist issue. She nowhere indicates that she thinks of her poems or the values they advocate as particularly "feminine." In fact most of the animal figures that demonstrate these qualities are given male pronouns. But it seems only natural that Moore should select the attributes most readily applied to her as the focus of her efforts to rediscover language. Whether these qualities are a natural or inherited part of her femininity, however, one feels in reading her poems that a man could not have seen the potential in such qualities that Moore has seen and exploited.

One of Moore's favorite categories of virtue, observed throughout her poetry and criticism, is humility, with its analogues, restraint, and modesty. What a nineteenth-century reviewer said of the woman poet Felicia Hemans has been said in other ways (in the quotations above) of Moore: "she never forgets what is due feminine reserve." Indeed, Moore learned well the lesson of Bryn Mawr president Carey Thomas which she quotes in her essay on the "impassioned emancipator": she "behaved not with decorum but with marked decorum." This does not mean that Moore practiced humility without sincerity. Rather, she discovers in it a special value: "humility is a kind of armor." Critics usually take this to mean that by playing down the self, by making few overt claims to authority and power, we avoid subjecting ourselves to envy or attack. Moore's descriptiveness, her extensive use of quotation, her choice of peripheral subject matter, her circumlocution, are all pointed to as technical counterparts of her moral predilections. But what Moore, with Carey Thomas, understood is that strength and power are not necessarily stifled or even contained, but are on the contrary nurtured through acts of self-protection. Aggressive, indecorous, intolerant behavior wastes energy and creativity which can be better sustained and wielded with a certain guardedness. She quotes Thomas's remark: "Bryn Mawr must not be less guarded because it is good." Juhasz and others tend to see nothing but the armor, neglecting what is achieved by its use. Moore compromises nothing in her "self-protective" humility; she gains. Though the idea of "feminine reserve" may conventionally imply an attitude appropriate to inferiority, Moore does not even pretend to weakness. She shows humility to be a reserve, in the sense of a reservoir of power. At the end of "In This Age of Hard Trying," for instance, Moore shows how an apparent "inconsequence of manner" is more effective and durable than aggressive certitude.

IN THIS AGE OF HARD TRYING,
NONCHALANCE IS GOOD AND

"really, it is not the
  business of the gods to bake clay pots." They did not
    do it in this instance. A few
      revolved upon the axes of their worth
  as if excessive popularity might be a pot;

they did not venture the
  profession of humility. The polished wedge
    that might have split the firmament
      was dumb. At last it threw itself away
  and falling down, conferred on some poor fool, a
      privilege.

"Taller by the length of
  a conversation of five hundred years than all
    the others," there was one whose tales
      of what could never have been actual—
  were better than the haggish, uncompanionable drawl

of certitude; his by-
  play was more terrible in its effectiveness
    than the fiercest frontal attack.
      The staff, the bag, the feigned inconsequence
  of manner, best bespeak that weapon, self-protectiveness.
      [All lines quoted from Marianne Moore's poetry are
        taken from *The Complete Poems of Marianne Moore*
        (New York: Viking, 1967).]

Humility, a guarded manner, has the advantage of taking the listener off-guard. And Moore practices her point in a number of ways here. The prosaic, conversational tone, the long, meandering, run-on lines and shifts of figurative level, give the impression of nonchalance. She is not, she seems to suggest, writing anything so grand as a poem. But the design is present, though unobtrusive, acting on our imaginations almost without alerting us. We hardly notice, though we subliminally hear, the careful rhymes, the subtly extended metaphor, the logic of the tale, so that the final lines have a special bold effect in their paradoxical clarity.

Moore's feminine humility, then, is designing: she wants to create and sustain an interest which overt self-assertion or pronounced form would snuff out. Moore's humility and restraint are not passive defenses but ways of gathering force, as a bow is pulled back in order to carry the arrow farther when it is finally released. Such motives and strategies are at work in many of her best poems, especially "The Plumet Basilisk," "The Frigate Pelican," "To a Snail," and "The Pangolin," poems about animals she admires for elusive strengths similar to those she displays in her writing. The end of humility is not self-protection for its own sake so much as "gusto," the spark released in the discovery of and enthusiasm for what is out of our control. In language, "humility is an indispensable teacher, enabling concentration to heighten gusto." Whereas humility associated with women usually implies something negative, a withdrawal, a deference, Moore shows its positive outcome. She is one woman for whom humility is not an end but a means of inspiration and expression.

Humility is not armor against the aggressions of the world on the self so much as against those of the self on the world, against the "disease, My Self," as she calls it. To impose the self and its accumulated structures on the world is to narrow the world and trap the self, a self-defeating gesture. "In Distrust of Merits" takes this theme up directly, but it is always present obliquely in Moore's verse. For her, humility "keeps the world large," preserves a place for something beyond the self that keeps us from complacency and satiation, consequently keeping us alive.

"His Shield" is the poem quoted most often in connection with Moore's idea of the armor of humility. She says it directly: "his shield was his humility." The poem warns against "greed and flattery," insisting that "freedom" is "the power of relinquishing what one would keep." Bravado does not please or improve anything, it simply attracts contenders, and wastes energy fighting them off. "Be dull, don't be envied or armed with a measuring rod." Don't attract envy by flaunting your achievement. This is a traditional code of femininity, but it usually implies that feminine achievement is incommensurate with envy or pride. Let us see how Moore understands her message.

The poem contrasts two kinds of armor, as several critics have pointed out. Moore finds that the spiny covering of the "edgehog miscalled hedgehog with all his edges out . . . won't do." Instead, "I'll wrap myself in salamander skin." The armor of "pig-fur" aggressing on the outside would scare things off. Its force is its inadequacy. But "asbestos" armor endures rather than extinguishes fire. It allows the outside world to enclose without annihilating the subject. Furthermore, it keeps the edges inside, keeps a fire alive internally rather than exhausting it in consuming ego. The ideal is "a lizard in the midst of flames, a firebrand that is life," who is, to use a phrase from Moore's critical essays, "galvanized against inertia." Where possession, and its verbal equivalent, singleminded assertion, imply stasis and complacency, survival and freedom require the constant readjustment of thought. At the level of the sentence, "humility" does not mean that one should be silent, but rather that language should continually be revised in the presence of what it cannot accommodate.

The utopia represented in the poem is an "unconquerable country of unpompous gusto." Power is not compromised, it is simply redistributed. Presbyter John, the hero of the poem, "styled himself but presbyter." Gusto is generated less out of self-aggrandizing conquest or consumption than out of awareness, out of a perpetually perceived difference between himself and the world, and the preservation of that difference and of desire. Resources are never used up in such a country.

Self-denial sounds like an odd basis for utopian experience, however. How can untapped wealth and power be considered as such? Moore manages to develop a sense of wealth without conquest through symbols of the potential effects of power. "Rubies large as tennis / balls conjoined in streams so / that the mountain seemed to bleed." The mountain only *seems* to bleed, but in doing so it marks a potential encounter. Emblematized strength is perpetual, exerted strength expires. Indeed, the emblem of external battle is only realized internally in the struggle for self-possession. The stream of blood, as the internalized warfare of humility, is only the blood stream, the "firebrand that is life."

If we think of the poet as presbyter, the vitality of Moore's lines comes from investing her thought in a presentation of the external world, hence so many poems in a descriptive mode which obliquely suggest a personal attitude. The oddity and apparent awkwardness of her lines comes from that sense of the inadequacy of the "measuring rod" to deal honestly with particulars. In language, "to relinquish what one would keep" is to continually resist available form. One way she does this is by having different forms displace each other to create a variegated surface. Images cut across each other to deny any rigid hierarchy. The "I" of the poem is swallowed up in description. Moral and discursive languages do not preside over the poem, but take their place in a range of languages: commercial, conversational, descriptive, metaphoric. While her lines expand and digress in pursuit of what is always posited as indefinable, they also create images of the self's internal activity, thereby steadying the flux of exploration. Thus, as Geoffrey Hartman has pointed out, "she achieves a dialogue of one, an ironic crossfire of statement that continually denies and reasserts the possibility of a selfless assertion of self . . . the armor she describes is the modesty whereby the self is made strong to resist itself, but also strong to assert its being against voracious dogmatism." The abnegation of self ultimately satisfies the self, for it widens the sphere of response, the self being continually discovered through response to the external world. It declares knowledge a matter of process rather than possession, and it ensures the continuance of that process. The aggressive self is identified in the conquest of one form over another, an impulse to narrow and exclude, which finally entraps the self in the form it has imposed. But the humble self flourishes in the multiplicity of form, identifying with none. It neither narrows its domain nor can be narrowed by the force of others, for it exists in resisting closure. Humility, restraint, paradoxically conduce to freedom.

The armor of humility appears as a recurrent theme and technique in the critical essays as well. "Humility, Concentration and Gusto" opens in the more than metaphorical context of war.

In times like these we are tempted to disregard anything that has not a direct bearing on freedom; or should I say, an obvious bearing, for what is more persuasive than poetry, though as Robert Frost says, it works obliquely and delicately. Commander King-Hall, in his book *Total Victory*, is really saying that the pen is the sword when he says the object of war is to persuade the enemy to change his mind.

Such talk of persuasion would seem on the side of the porcupine's edgy, aggressive "battle dress." But what is persuasive, it turns out, what has bearing on freedom, is humility.

We don't want war, but it does conduce to humility, as someone said in the foreward to an exhibition catalogue of his work, "With what shall the artist arm himself save with his humility?" Humility, indeed, is armor, for it realizes that it is impossible to be original in the sense of doing something that has never been thought of before. Originality is in any case a byproduct of sincerity; that is to say, of feeling that is honest and accordingly rejects anything that might cloud the impression, such as unnecessary commas, modifying clauses, or delayed predicates.

One should not speak from ambition, then, but from honest feeling. The work, as one early critic of "female poetry" said, should "come from the heart, to be natural and true." Humility begins in this essay as a principle of simplicity and "quiet objectiveness," the reduction of self-assertion and the elevation of the external "impression." This is what Ransom "admired" in Millay, "a vein of poetry which is spontaneous, straightforward in diction, and excitingly womanlike; a distinguished objective record of a woman's mind." But humility becomes, as the essay goes on, a principle of difficulty standing for "the refusal to be false." When associated with "sincerity," the principle of humility and restraint becomes an agent of "gusto" by continually turning up a difference between the ways things are described and the way things are. "Gusto thrives on freedom," Moore explains, and freedom is preserved by failures of formal closure, by linguistic deviation. Daniel Berkeley Updike, Moore tells us, "has always seemed to me a phenomenon of eloquence because of the quiet objectiveness of his writing."

And what he says of printing applies equally to poetry. It is true, is it not, that "style does not depend on decoration but on simplicity and proportion"? Nor can we dignify confusion by calling it baroque. Here, I may say, I am preaching to myself, since, when I am as complete as I like to be, I seems unable to get an effect plain enough.

But this is sophisticated humility on Moore's part. What is persuasive is her preaching to herself. Certainly we would not expect her to be less complete than she would like to be, so what might seem like ornament or excess in her verse is justified as honesty. Humility, which upholds an ideal of quiet objectiveness, of simplicity and proportion, also upholds sincerity, which will not force a perception into a dishonestly neat structure. What results from this ironic conflict is a lively play of impulses through a highly variegated, rebellious surface. Though she will not make public claims to "originality," her poems are certainly idiosyncratic and individual, and invite the interest of a public into the special world of a private enchantment.

Moore often speaks of her "natural reticence" in explaining the disobliging difficulty of some of her work. Conventionally, natural reticence belongs to woman's lesser capacity for logical assertion. As a supposedly intuitive rather than analytical creature, woman naturally has trouble being articulate: language is a system of codification and dissection. Moore herself says "feeling at its deepest tends to be inarticulate." But in her verse, once natural reticence gives way to speech it paradoxically causes an overflow of words.

The extreme digressiveness of surface in Moore's poetry has perplexed many critics. Juhasz sees it as deliberate evasiveness, her way "of not talking about what she is talking about and talking about what she is not talking about." Roy Harvey Pearce criticizes her "gossipy" quality and her "uncertainty as to direction." Though Pearce doesn't label these qualities "feminine" he implies as much, and Ransom is explicit. Woman's mind "has no direction or modulation except by its natural health." In other words, women live without purpose or focus beyond their immediate daily cares, to which they respond with inarticulate emotions. Their minds cannot sustain a logical argument or coherent structure because they have no powers of memory or projection, because they live in a continuous present.

Moore takes this digressive mode of thought and examines its special advantages. The mind that follows "its natural health" has a capacity for nuance which evades us where there is "too stern an intellectual emphasis." The "steam roller" mind crushes "all the particles down into close conformity." "As for butterflies, I can hardly conceive of one's attending upon you." The "aimless" mind, like "the magic flute" illogically weaves "what logic can't unweave." It is closer to the center of experience, alive to changes of an unconscious voice. It has a greater capacity for discovery, not blinded by its own hypotheses. It is more inclusive; it has more variety. Through her unwieldy, non-hierarchical structures, her elongated, loquacious sentences, Moore achieves a sense of "continuous present," a sense of the poem in process, the mind experiencing and discovering itself. Moore's prosody works to this same end, through inconspicuous syllabic measure, through dispersed rhyme and run-on lines. Ransom thinks women are always weak on form "because they are not strict enough and expert enough to manage forms, in their default of the discipline under which men are trained." Moore's form is indeed not uniform or abstractly applied; it depends upon movement and changes inflection, unleashing new impulses as they are called up.

Geoffrey Hartman has been unusually sensitive to the force of Moore's "gossipy" meanderings.

> One reads her poems less for their message (always suffused) than for the pleasure of seeing how style may become an act of the living—the infinitely inclusive and discriminating—mind.
>
> This mind, or rather Miss Moore's, is "an enchanting thing"; it takes us by its very irrelevancies. Here too everything is surface; she talks, so to say, from the top of her mind and represents herself as a gossip on the baroque scale. But secretly she is a magician, and distracts on purpose. While her message eludes us through understatement, the poem itself remains teasingly alive through the overstatement of its many tactics, till we accept the conventional rabbit, glorified by prestidigitation. Yet the magic of language becomes intensely moral on further acquaintance and her crazyquilt of thoughts, quotations and sounds resolves into subtler units of meaning and rhythm. The free (but not formless) verse helps break up the automatic emphases of traditional syntax, and respects the more dynamic shifts of the inner, and not merely spoken voice.

Moore's elusive surfaces involve a moral prudence as well as an aesthetic one. She wants to dodge self-consciousness. What male critics have called a certain "fussiness" in Moore, she calls "unconscious fastidiousness" in which she finds "a great amount of poetry." What she seems to describe with the phrase is a kind of impulsive persistence in attempting to manage unmanageable material. Moore sees "unconscious fastidiousness" as an important part of the nurturing process, and imitates the process in her poems. Maternity is the subject of "The Paper Nautilus," and in comparing it to poetry she alters the conventional view of both. We conventionally think of maternal affection as a soft, graceful attitude, and similarly Moore's poetry has been prized, condescendingly, for its "relaxed ease." But the poem describes the process of nurture as a struggle beneath a surface of gentleness, a highly precarious restraint of power. Here unconscious fastidiousness means a high level of attentiveness without the imposition of rigid design which might impede natural development. The health of the eggs somehow depends upon maximum power and maximum restraint. The juxtaposition of "the ram's-horn cradled freight" and "a devilfish" and her eggs reinforces this tension. Later we are told of the shell's relative delicacy (like a wasp nest) and of its strength (like Ionic columns and the force of Parthenon sculpture). The tension described in holding back Hercules is clarified through a notion of a "fortress of love" but not relieved. We have metaphors of maximum impulse without the expiration of energy in action. The paper nautilus must "hide" her "freight" but not "crush" it. The same goes for poets. They too are "hindered to succeed."

> For authorities whose hopes
> are shaped by mercenaries?
> Writers entrapped by
> teatime fame and by
> commuters' comforts? Not for these
> the paper nautilus
> constructs her thin glass shell.

The poem starts by distinguishing two kinds of form, one which is complacent and commercial, generated by petty ambition, (and the association of mercenaries and commuters suggests a male domain) and another kind which will not "entrap" the writer or the audience. Appropriately, Moore will not "entrap" herself and her subject by restricting the tenor of this other kind. Rather, after an initial reference to writers, she shifts into a metaphor for metaphor itself: the shell in which our impression of the world can take shape without calcifying. But the shell is importantly the source and product of a maternal affection, a desire to nurture, in order finally to release the growing object. Her shell does not contain the eggs, or in terms of poetry, is not "the thing itself."

The feminine code of sacrifice says one must "relinquish what one would keep," and this is often applied to maternal relationships. But Moore changes this idea, in an artistic context, to a mode of freedom, not just a duty. Thus "the intensively watched eggs coming from / the shell free it when they are freed." And the mother is free from her state of tension. Freedom, that is, requires differentiation.

We are curious when we sense something like ourselves yet different. Moore knows that observation is always in a way self-interested. Indeed, language is fundamentally of the self and not of the other, so self-expression is inevitable. Her mind follows likeness and finds difference, and again likeness, in the form of statements that are qualified, images which clash, rhymes that are interrupted, deviating detail, almost any form of verbal differentiation. In the process she does not accomplish "objectification" (curiosity is not satisfied) but something more interesting: a composition which metes out likeness and difference, visual and aural as well as semantic. The composition has the rhetorical power both to make associations and to suggest its own limits, since these verbal differences are made to seem like the difference between the world and what we say about it. Moore's compositions are trails of associations which conduct the reader to their source. This identification occurs not only as our vicarious experience of her mental flux, but through her final, subtle self-portraiture. Moore begins by presenting an object apparently for its own sake, but in the process of describing it she borrows the object as a figure of her own activity. This self-portraiture is not the point of arrival of the poet's search for unity or for the thing itself, but a kind of parting embrace of words and things, a form of possession or appropriation that leaves the thing untouched while its ghost performs the function of analogy. Moore pursues the contours of objects for what she can discover of herself, but precisely because she learns about herself through observation of the external world, she can never declare her motive or speak of herself directly. "Imaginary possession" allows her to make associations without assumptions. She never gets to the point at which the idea subverts the observation.

The narcissists and sophisticates in the art world are the constant butt of Moore's satire, though they are "deaf to satire." In "Novices," for instance, she criticizes the "supertadpoles of expression" so attentive to their own egos

> so that they do not know "whether it is the buyer or the
>   seller who gives the money"—
> an abstruse idea plain to none but the artist,
> the only seller who buys and holds on to the money.
> . . . .
> they write the sort of thing that would in their judgment
>   interest a lady;
> curious to know if we do not adore each letter of the alphabet
>   that goes to make a word of it.

These "Will Honeycombs" who "anatomize their work," whose art is highly rational and symmetrical, are "bored by the detailless perspective of the sea," too absorbed in flattering themselves with their intellectual conquests to recognize the irrational power of nature. Moore contrasts their style with "the spontaneous unforced passion of the Hebrew language," which derives its "tempestuous energy" from a complete surrender to the sublimity of nature. In their example Moore shows that the self grows larger by imaginatively embracing something beyond its rational control.

But Moore is not simply advocating unconscious spontaneity or self-annihilation. Moore's is a highly conscious art, its objects derived primarily from books, not wild nature. It is the activity of tracing an "other," of knowing it in relation to oneself, as similar and different, that interests her, and she has called this "imaginary possession." With imaginary possession the mind is free to make associations, but at the same time knows them as such and does not identify them as exclusive truths. The task of "When I Buy Pictures," for instance, is to give both the illusion of a figure in the world who does not affect it, and to make a gesture of possession, to bring what is seen under the control of language.

WHEN I BUY PICTURES

> or what is closer to the truth
> when I look at that of which I may regard myself as the
>   imaginary possessor,

I fix upon what would give me pleasure in my average
        moments:
the satire upon curiosity in which no more is discernible
than the intensity of the mood;
or quite the opposite—the old thing, the medieval decorated
        hat-box,
in which there are hounds with waists diminishing like the
        waist of the hourglass,
and deer and birds and seated people;

The game of imaginary possession involves discretion and humility, not
prohibition:

Too stern an intellectual emphasis upon this quality or that
        detracts from one's enjoyment.
It must not wish to disarm anything; nor may the approved
        triumph easily be honored—
that which is great because something else is small.

Of course these are not "average moments"; they are moments of lumi-
nosity, selected for their suggestiveness. The difference is that between
selection which reveals a will and transformation which emblematizes a
will. Moore does not simply direct her imagery toward a final or overarching
intention. Her mind is attentive to the properties of each object and each
word as it occurs. Age suggests images of age: hatboxes which bear images
of old-fashioned hounds that are shaped like hourglasses whose waists
remind her of time's waste and as these waists diminish the imagery narrows its reference to the matter of fact: deer, birds, and seated people. The
coherence of a part takes her to the next, without rejecting the influence
of the immediate details. But while avoiding "too stern an intellectual emphasis" a surprisingly complex range of associations, built upon the problems of time, distance and complexity, emerges in the movement from one
image to the next, at no cost to the surface randomness of local association:

It may be no more than a square of parquetry; the literal
        biography perhaps,
in letters standing well apart upon a parchment-like expanse;
an artichoke in six varieties of blue; the snipe-legged
        hieroglyphic in three parts;
the silver fence protecting Adam's grave, or Michael taking
        Adam by the wrist.

Parquetry, artichoke, biography, hieroglyphic are all patterns of one kind
or another. The range is inclusive and humorous. These orders are mocked,
but shown to be natural. "Literal biography" is a contradiction reduced to
its formal elements, letters standing well apart. We are directed through
meaningless "orders" to consider our desire for possession, and the poem

moves to emblems of our fall. These unite the previously separate and random problems of time, distance, and complexity raised in the imagery. Poems suppose a hierarchy of elements, but the rhetoric of the list resists our locating ourselves anywhere in particular in the poem. Moore quite consciously tempts our desire for architectonic, mythic structures, our need to privilege the "heroic" moment. She wants these associations while she restrains them from blocking their natural contexts. One does not forfeit the self, then, one does not resign all "views"; one simply explores them discreetly.

Of course the poem itself is a picture for sale. The satire on curiosity is a picture of ourselves since it is, finally, the intensity of the mood which is at issue. Its "opposite," the picture of receding things, draws the curious figure on until it becomes a mirror ("when I look at that of which I may regard myself"). The self does get expressed, through its own enchantment with something else, and this, I think, is what Virginia Woolf means in *A Room of One's Own* when she speaks of a woman's ability to get close to the fountain of creative energy.

While Moore's poetry is in a way "impersonal," in that the self is not the focus or dominant presence, we feel the movement of a distinct personality throughout. Indeed, Moore's very resistance to formal closure becomes for her a means of self-revelation. The "minor defects" of form, as she called unassimilated elements, are marks of style. And it is in style that we know this poet, not in subject or assertion. Though she never advocates "originality," the ambition to supersede the forms others have created, she is a great defender of "idiosyncrasy," an inevitable expression of "honest vision." Idiosyncrasy is connected with sincerity, a kind of non-competitive, oblique presentation of self; it does not require a personal subject or a show of power; it challenges no one.

Emily Watts, in *The Poetry of American Women*, identifies Moore's verse with a tradition of "feminine realism." What she and other critics are pointing to in the use of this term is the combination of "mundane realities," "simple human and natural situations," and "natural sense objects," with ethical generalizations or "household morality." The feminine mind neatly integrates nature and morality. Randall Jarrell, for one, strongly objects to Moore's poetry on the basis of this integration. In clear sexual categories he challenges what he sees as Moore's domestic falsifications, upholding instead the male vision of amoral nature and its corresponding cosmic ambition.

But Moore has transformed the structure of feminine realism (which links observation to ethical generalization) in a number of ways. While she does detail nature, she celebrates her subjects for their recalcitrance. And the morality that accompanies these pictures is one of resisting the mind's impulse to circumscribe experience. In "Sea Unicorns and Land Unicorns," (about the Unicorn Tapestries) Moore points out that the unicorn remains "a puzzle to the hunters." Only the virgin knows him:

Thus this strange animal with its miraculous elusiveness,
has come to be unique,
"impossible to take alive,"
tamed only by a lady inoffensive like itself—
as curiously wild and gentle.

All the poems follow a dictum of resistance even while they move through an apparent structure of observation-moral, for they continually propose definitions only to unravel them. "Integration, too tough for infraction," integration of the mind and the external world, of ethos and nature, is the goal of Moore's poetry, not its claim. And it is based on "efforts of affection" and not on aggression. It is achieved through process, through an open-ended dialectic of observing and making observations, in a continuous present.

While Moore follows the tendency in "feminine realism" to keep an eye on the external object, she is distinctly modern in her awareness of the limits of language to present that object. Moore's "descriptions" break up the conventions of composition, not to protect the self but to bring language into a more adequate relationship to experience, to discover a new realism which resists the habits of mind and eye. But what such resistance to referential conventions does, finally, is bring us into a closer awareness of the surface of language. By blocking the easy transfer from word to picture of meaning, by continually shifting the flow of counters and intruding on conventions which we too readily naturalize, Moore reminds us that we are not actually seeing, but only reading. This technique is especially effective in her poem "An Octopus," a long description of a glacier that concludes with a moral of "relentless accuracy." The extreme difficulty of accurately perceiving the object creates a corresponding difficulty in the words. Often the lengthy and cumbersome sentences lose their syntactic hold on us. We forget the subject or antecedent in the tow of subordinate clauses. Colons and semicolons are suspended between groups without an easy sense of their relation. Appositions become subjects with their own appositions in turn. Participial phrases go on for several lines until we cease even to anticipate their subjects. Where conventional "realism" trusts the parts of speech to represent reality, Moore's language continually demonstrates their failure. In its attempt to circumscribe the viscous presence, the language of "An Octopus," for instance, doubles back on itself with lines that refer outwardly to the objective experience, and inwardly to the experience of reading. "Completing the circle, you have been deceived into thinking that you have progressed." "Neatness of finish! Neatness of finish! Relentless accuracy is the nature of this octopus / with its capacity for fact." Such self-reflective imagery admits that ultimately the "morals" we derive are not natural but represent our efforts to come to terms with nature. In that sense all of Moore's ethical generalizations have to do with her poetic activity.

"Neatness of finish" and "relentless accuracy" sound, in isolation, like mundane lessons. But in the context of this poem they present an enormous challenge to the eye and mind. And Moore proves the point she is making, for instead of rounding off the description with this abstract conclusion, she returns to the particular. She adopts, in the end, a policy of accuracy more relentless than before:

> Is "tree" the word for these things
> "flat on the ground like vines"?
> some "bent in a half circle with branches on one side
> suggesting dust-brushes, not trees;
> some finding strength in union, forming little stunted groves
> their flattened mats of branches shrunk in trying to escape"
> from the hard mountain "planed by ice and polished by the
>   wind"—
> the white volcano with no weather side;
> the lightning flashing at its base,
> rain falling in the valleys, and snow falling on the peak—
> the glassy octopus symmetrically pointed,
> its claw cut by the avalanche
> "with a sound like the crack of a rifle
> in a curtain of powdered snow launched like a waterfall."

The breathlessness of the passage pulls us away from the organizing frame of grammar and syntax and hurls us into the midst of detail. Ethical generalization is returned to the level of perception. And yet even in the midst of detail, the mind makes associations. In this case the associations simply remind us of the controlling presence of language. At the end of the mountain is a curtain of snow; at the end of the poem—is a curtain of snow, the page. Her humility denies both the claims of an achieved realist and those of an achieved moralist; but her struggle for integration is vital and rewarding.

Moore transforms and toughens our understanding of familiar virtues when she uses them as stylistic devices. Humility, affection, reserve, are not passive but dynamic and vital modes of response. They do not protect but rather sustain the self in experience. In her redefinition and revaluation of what have been seen as "feminine" modes of identity, Moore displays a larger, encompassing concern to avoid all complacencies of mind. No container will hold her gusto.

> You have been compelled by hags to spin
>   gold thread from straw and have heard men say:
> "There is a feminine temperament in direct contrast to ours
>
> which makes her do these things. Circumscribed by a
>   heritage of blindness and native

incompetence, she will become wise and will be forced to
give in.
Compelled by experience, she will turn back;

water seeks its own level":
and you have smiled. "Water in motion is far
from level." You have seen it, when obstacles happen to bar
the path, rises automatically.

In describing Ireland, Moore has obliquely celebrated the resilient
power of the "feminine temperament." Ireland survives and deepens its
identity by a combination of persistence and responsiveness. By rising to
meet the shapes experience presents rather than either retreating or im-
posing artificial forms, Moore sustains a vital, creative contact between her
self and her surroundings.

"Advancing Backward in a Circle": Moore as (Natural) Historian

John M. Slatin

Moore writes in "A Grave" (1921) that "repression is not the most obvious characteristic of the sea," and we may say with equal assurance that imitation "is not the most obvious characteristic" of her work. This is hardly surprising, given the original strength of her "reluctance to be unoriginal"; but just as "repression" is a hidden characteristic of the sea, so a concern with imitation is a latent feature of Moore's work from the beginning of her career, and, as the following brief survey will indicate, it comes closer and closer to the surface as time goes on.

In her first published essay, "The Accented Syllable" (October 1916), Moore offers implicit justification for her own increasingly sophisticated use of syllabic verse, arguing that it is virtually impossible to establish or maintain "a distinctive tone of voice" in any other medium. Prose is unacceptable because it has no defense against accidental resemblances: "written tones of voice may resemble one another and . . . a distinctive tone of voice employed by one author may resemble that same tone of voice as employed by another author." Rhymed verse, as Moore calls conventional accentual-syllabic verse, is equally unpromising, because in this "case . . . a distinctive tone of voice is dependent on naturalistic effects, and naturalistic effects are so rare in rhyme as almost not to exist." Worst of all, though, is "free verse," which not only tends naturally toward mimesis but actually encourages deliberate imitation: "So far as free verse is concerned," Moore writes, "it is the easiest thing in the world to create one intonation in the image of another until finally one has assembled a bouquet of vocal exclamation points." Nowhere does she say explicitly that syllabic verse is for her the only satisfactory solution to the problem of distinctive-

From *Twentieth Century Literature* 30, nos. 2/3 (Summer/Fall 1984). © 1984 by Hofstra University Press.

ness; but a careful look at her earlier poems indicates quite clearly that her syllabic patterns give formal expression to what she calls in "Critics and Connoisseurs" (July 1916) "an attitude of self-defense," enabling her to resist the temptation to do "the easiest thing" by preventing her from "creat[ing] one intonation in the image of another."

The real problem is to prevent *herself* from becoming the mere reflected image of another poet, as we see in the early poem "Blake," which I give in its entirety:

> I wonder if you feel as you look at us,
> As if you were seeing yourself in a mirror at the end
>   of a long corridor—walking frail-ly.
> I am sure that we feel as we look at you,
> As if we were ambiguous and all but improbable
>   Reflections of the sun—shining pale-ly.
>   [In quoting Moore I have followed the first
>   published text of each poem.]

Blake, as Moore acknowledges in a letter to Pound four years later, is among "the direct influences bearing on [her]work"; here, though, she sees herself as a pale, attenuated image of him, a distant "mirror" or satellite whose poems shine as "ambiguous and all but improbable / Reflections" of his "sun."

Moore often uses words associated with *light* or *the sun* to designate writers to whom she ascribes both literary mastery and the possession of a visionary power; but her response to that light is deeply ambivalent. In a poem called "You Are Like the Realistic Product of an Idealistic Search for Gold at the Foot of the Rainbow" (later re-titled "To a Chameleon"), published in May 1916, she praises the chameleon for its ability to conceal itself by absorbing light. But it is not always desirable to "snap the spectrum up for food" as the chameleon does; a poem originally drafted in 1915 and published in 1924 presents the sun as a piercing force to be resisted by "An Egyptian Pulled Glass Bottle in the Shape of a Fish," and here she celebrates "that / spectacular and nimble animal the fish, / whose scales turn aside the sun's sword with their polish."

Before 1921, it is far more common to find her trying actively to resist penetration by the light than to find her seeking, chameleon-like, to absorb it. In "Black Earth" (April 1918), the poet "inhabit[s]" an "elephant skin . . . fibred over like the shell of / The coco-nut, [a] piece of black glass through which no light // Can filter." Her pride in her imperviousness is matched by a somewhat envious scorn for the human "Tree trunk without / Roots," whom she images as the "Spiritual / Brother to the coral / Plant, absorbed into which, the equable sapphire light, / Becomes a nebulous green." A few months later, in "The Fish" (August 1918), resistance continues, but "the submerged shafts of the // Sun, split like spun / Glass," have managed to penetrate the "black Jade" of the ocean's surface, with devastating results: the light reveals a "turquoise sea / Of bodies."

By the time "Picking and Choosing" appears in April 1920, Moore has concluded that "the opaque allusion—the simulated flight // upward—accomplishes nothing," that continued resistance to the "sun's sword" is both futile and wrong. Thus in "When I Buy Pictures" (July 1921), she proposes a new set of criteria for the successful work of art:

> It comes to this: of whatever sort it is,
> it must acknowledge the forces which have made it;
> it must be "lit with piercing glances into the life of things;"
> then I "take it in hand as a savage would take a looking-glass."

Rather than resist penetration by the light, the poem must now "be 'lit with piercing glances into the lift of things,' " and this requirement has a twofold bearing on Moore's poetic practice. It means incorporating a larger number of quotations into the poems (as rays of light which also serve to "acknowledge the forces" to which the poem is indebted); and it means *abandoning the syllabic patterns* on which Moore has previously relied as barriers against the light. This is why the new poems which appear in various periodicals between July 1921 and January 1925 are in free verse— the very form Moore had rejected in 1916 on the grounds that were she to use it, "it would be the easiest thing in the world to create one intonation in the image of another."

And this is precisely what she does in the closing lines of "Novices" (February 1923), where a group of young writers, suavely ignorant of the true nature of their craft, are

> "split like a glass against a wall"
> in this "precipitate of dazzling impressions,
> the spontaneous unforced passion of the Hebrew language—
> an abyss of verbs full of reverberation and tempestuous
>   energy,"
> in which action perpetuates action and angle is at variance
>   with angle
> till submerged by the general action;
> obscured by fathomless suggestions of colour,
> by incessantly panting lines of green, white with concussion,
> in this drama of water against rocks—this "ocean of
>   hurrying consonants"
> with its "great livid stains like long slabs of green marble,"
> its "flashing lances of perpendicular lighting" and "molten
>   fires swallowed up,"
> "with foam on its barriers,"
> "crashing itself out in one long hiss of spray."

What we see here is not only a series of quotations joined together to form a composite image of the sea in motion; it is also an effort to "create one intonation in the image of another." The quotations have been carefully arranged so as to replicate, as nearly as possible, the rhythmic effects described in George Adam Smith's analysis of Isaiah 17:12-13. Smith writes in *The Expositor's Bible:*

> The phonetics of the passage are wonderful. The general impression is that of a stormy ocean booming in to the shore and then crashing itself out into one long hiss of spray and foam upon its barriers. The details are noteworthy. In ver. 12 we have thirteen heavy M-sounds, besides two heavy B's, to five N's, five H's, and four sibilants. But in ver. 13 the sibilants predominate; and before the sharp rebuke of the Lord the great, booming sound of ver. 12 scatters out into a long *yish-sha 'oon.* The occasional use of a prolonged vowel amid so many hurrying consonants produces exactly the effect now of the lift of a storm swell out at sea and now the pause of a great wave before it crashes on the shore.

Returning to this passage two or three years after copying it into her reading notebook, Moore discovers in it the prescription for a rhythmic structure which may be filled out by words other than the original ones and adapted to the resources of a language other than the original Hebrew. And as we shall see, in "Bird-Witted" she adapts the principles discovered here to the resources of the syllabic patterns to which she had returned with the composition of "The Steeple-Jack" in 1932; and she will do so again later on, in translating *The Fables of La Fontaine* (1954)—the culminating product of her interest in literary mimesis.

After 1932, Moore's syllabic patterns serve a significantly different function than formerly. They no longer work to secure the distinctiveness of Moore's voice by inhibiting imitation. Instead, they work to celebrate and preserve, where possible, the innocence of the poems' *subjects*—an innocence closely allied with the distinctiveness of the subjects themselves. Because the mode of these celebrations is mimetic, however, it has been too readily assumed by Moore's critics that the poems take their own innocence—and Moore's—for granted; but this is not the case.

It is no accident that "Bird-Witted" takes its title from the writings of Sir Francis Bacon, whom Moore admired both as a literary stylist and as a scientist credited with a major role in the development of modern scientific methods based on careful, empirical observation of natural phenomenon— a development which coincides with the settling of Virginia in the late sixteenth and seventeenth centuries. The poem invites us once more to "Observe the terse Virginian," the mocking-bird to which we are introduced in the fourth stanza of "Virginia Britannia," and to do so with an exact and scrupulous eye; we are no longer to "Behold" it as a static image, as we do in "Virginia Britannia" and in the case of Wordsworth's "child," that "six months darling of a pigmy size!" The invitation here is implicit: instead of being commanded to "Observe," we are shown a triad of young mocking-birds awaiting their mother at feeding-time. The careful observation of this family of birds in action gives an ironic twist, however, to Bacon's concern over what might happen "If a boy be bird-witted," for Moore is interested not only in the empty-headedness of the young (whose sex is of no concern to the poem) but also in the mother-wit of the adult female who has to feed and protect them.

> With innocent wide penguin eyes, three
>   grown fledgling mocking-birds below
> the pussy-willow tree,
>   stand in a row,
> wings touching, feebly solemn,
> till they see
>   their no longer larger
>   mother bringing
> something which will partially
> feed one of them.

The youth of these three birds is crucial: the first thing we learn about them is that their "eyes" are "innocent"—innocent, it will turn out, of that power of observation which would enable them to identify their enemies, and of the capacity for imitation which their mother possesses (though she does not exercise it here), and which depends in turn upon accurate observation.

The young birds are evidently capable of recognizing their mother, but the poet's powers of observation are considerably sharper. As Hugh Kenner has noted, the cries of the "fledgling mocking-birds" are caught in the reiterated double-*ee*'s of the stanza, though for a moment "their cry is muted to the final syllable of 'partially'" when "they see" their mother coming with food. As the feeding begins, their voices are "raised with a new urgency" in the rhyming "squeak" and "meek" and "beak" of the second stanza—decidedly unmusical sounds attesting to their inability to "imitate the call" of anything but broken machinery:

> Towards the high keyed intermittent squeak
>   of broken carriage-springs, made by
> the three similar, meek-
>   coated bird's eye
> freckled forms she comes; and when
> from the beak
>   of one, the still living
>   beetle has dropped
> out, she picks it up and puts
> it in again.

This goes beyond careful attention to detail: as Kenner says, "there is affectionate mimesis in the awkward 'dropped / out' and the businesslike 'she picks it up and puts / it in again.' " The poem is similarly mimetic when, at a crucial stage later on, it stumbles slightly, with one of the birds, then regains its footing and proceeds:

> A dangling foot that missed
> its grasp, is raised
> and finds the twig on which it
> planned to perch.

On a casual reading, it may seem that these birds are the objects of a scrupulously neutral (if sympathetic) attention, of the sort empiricism is supposed to demand. But the eye which initially perceives the young birds' eyes as "innocent" is informed by a moral sense, a knowledge which is by definition not available to innocence itself; and such judgments are specifically disallowed by empirical procedures. The poet's status as observer is in fact the central issue in "Bird-Witted"—though we have no way of knowing this until the fourth stanza, where Moore turns her whole attention to the mother:

> What a delightful note
> with rapid unexpected flute-
> sounds leaping from the throat
> of the astute
> grown bird comes back to one from
> the remote
> unenergetic sun-
> lit air before
> the brood was here? Why has the
> bird's voice become
> harsh?

As Kenner notes, the mother's song "echoes without effort" in the stanza's alternating rhymes, and then "drops into harshness" as the poem moves into the new stanza and enters a critical new phase. But there is a considerable difference between the mimetic effort we have observed so far and the imitative work being performed here.

Uniquely, the stanza just quoted provides no visual data at all; it is wholly devoted to sound. Furthermore, in other stanzas the poem keeps time with the movements of the birds themselves; but the "delightful note . . . leaping from the throat / of the astute / grown bird" is not being sounded now: it only

> comes back to one from
> the remote
> unenergetic sun-
> lit air before
> the brood was here.

It is, then, a "note" sounding not in the ear but in what Wallace Stevens later called "the delicatest ear of the mind," reminding us of a moment of apparently innocent ecstasy (but see "Virginia Britannia") now past, and deliberately recalled—not by the bird, of course, but by the poet. And Moore's act of recall here is no more innocent than the one which, in the closing lines of "Virginia Britannia," balances the full burden of the poem on a single, carefully poised word out of memory.

Again Kenner alerts us to a crucial aspect of what is going on here when he suggests that "Bird-Witted" may have taken its technical inspiration from Pound's *The ABC of Reading*, which had been published just over a year before "Bird-Witted" appeared in January 1936. Pound writes that for the troubadour poets the " 'whole art' of poetry consisted in putting together about six strophes of poetry so that the words and tune should be welded together without joint and without wem"; the poet whose work best exemplified that art, he says, was "the best smith, as Dante called *Arnaut Daniel*, [who] made the birds sing IN HIS WORDS . . . for six strophes WITH the words making sense." This is exactly what Moore has sought to do in "Bird-Witted," and she has done it in a way which both confirms and extends Kenner's hypothesis. For she has used Pound's discussion of Daniel very much as she had earlier used Smith's discussion of Isaiah—as a technical prescription which enables her to give formal, mimetic expression to the interest in Provençal poetry which her reading of Pound's *Cantos* had engendered five years earlier. (She even follows Pound's description of the "perfect strophe" in Daniel "where the bird call interrupts the verse.") Reviewing *A Draft of XXX Cantos* for *Poetry* in October 1931, Moore had written:

> If poetics allure, the Cantos will . . . show that in Provençal minstrelsy we encounter a fascinating precision; the delicacy and exactness of Arnaut Daniel, whose invention, the sestina form, is "like a thin sheet of flame folding and infolding upon itself." *In this tongue . . . is to be found pattern* [my italics]. And the Cantos show the troubadours not only sang poems but *were* poems. . . .
>
> Mr. Pound brings to his reading, master-appreciation; and his gratitude takes two forms; he thanks the book and tells where you may see it. "Any man who would read Arnaut and the troubadours owes great thanks to Emil Levy of Freiburg," he says in *Instigations*. . . . He sings of this in Canto XX. . . .
>
> And as those who love books know, the place in which one read a book or talked of it partakes of its virtue in recollection; so for Mr. Pound the cedars and new-mown hay and far-off nightingale at Freiburg have the glamour of Provence.

Moore's syllabic reinvention of the sestina in "Bird-Witted" is a "very great feat," as Kenner says; but it is much more than a technical tour de force. It is a kind of homage to Pound; and as we shall see, it serves a specific function with respect to Moore's own complex "recollection" in

"Bird-Witted" (and in "Smooth Gnarled Crape Myrtle" as well) of another "far-off nightingale." We must prepare the ground, however, by first taking up the question of memory in a more general way.

For the art of memory seems to function, in Moore's poems of the thirties, as a prelude to, a warning of, and a shield against danger. In "The Steeple-Jack," for instance, Moore relies on the devastatingly accurate memory of the "college student / named Ambrose" to aim her own perception of dangerous untruth at the heart of a community so firmly convinced of its own innocence that its "simple people" are unable to read even the most blatant "sign" of "Danger." Ambrose, we are told, "knows" the scene "by heart," as the poet knows the mockingbird's "delightful note"; the vision revealed by his memory serves as a standard against which to measure "the pitch / of the church // spire" and by which to prove that it is "not true." In the end, it allows us to supply the properly ironic coloring for the opening words of the final stanza: "It could not be dangerous to be living / in a town like this," but it is.

As Moore calls on Ambrose's memory in "The Steeple-Jack," so in "Virginia Britannia" she calls upon her own poetic memory for "intimation" as the poem reaches its crisis—when the forces which are to carry out the moral renovation of America have met with resistance. Memory fuels resistance to danger in "Bird-Witted," too, for here the adult bird's voice has "become // harsh" because, as the present overtakes the lilting rhymes of memory, "A piebald cat" has been "observing" her young, and it is now climbing toward them. She must act *now:*

> The
> parent darting down, nerved by what chills
>   the blood, and by hope rewarded—
> of toil—since nothing fills
>   squeaking unfed
> mouths, wages deadly combat,
> and half kills
>   with bayonet beak and
>   cruel wings, the
> intellectual, cautious-
> ly c r e e p ing cat.

The urgency of the situation is underscored by the fact that the creatures in Moore's poems are rarely so violent, even in self-defense. The jerboa, for example, conceals itself from predators by "assuming [the] colour" of the sand; the plumet basilisk is also hidden by its coloration, that "octave of faulty / decorum"—at least until "nightfall, which is for man the basilisk whose look will kill; but is // for lizards men can / kill, the welcome dark." The frigate-pelican "hides / in the height and in the majestic / display of his art," while the pangolin, an "armoured animal," either "draws away from / danger unpugnaciously / with no sound but a harmless hiss," or "rolls himself into a ball that has / power to defy all effort to unroll it." But the mocking-bird cannot do as the frigate-pelican does: "the majestic / display" of her mimetic "art" will not hide her now, nor will it protect her young; so she must change her tune and go on the attack in order to defend her home ground—as in "Virginia Britannia"—against an invader more coldly calculating, more "intellectual," than herself.

For the mother bird, then, to be "Bird-Witted" is to mobilize instinct against a natural antagonist, to hazard her own life in defense of her young. For the poet, however, it is deliberately to mobilize an "intellectual . . . c r e e p ing" figure which preys upon "innocent wide penguin eye[d]" children: it is to imitate innocence in order to defend it, and to do so in full awareness that the deliberateness of the poem cannot literally protect these or any other birds against attack by a marauding cat; it can, however, mobilize its resources in a parodic defense of the mocking-bird against the kind of treatment Keats accords the nightingale in his famous "Ode."

Moore writes in "Smooth Gnarled Crape Myrtle"—the fourth and final poem in "The Old Dominion" group—that

> "The legendary white-
> eared black bulbul that sings
>   only in pure Sanskrit" should
> be here—"tame clever
> true nightingale."

The " 'tame clever / true nightingale' " is not "here," of course, but to a considerable extent Moore behaves as if it were. Keats asks in the second strophe of the "Ode to a Nightingale" for "a draught of Vintage! . . . Tasting of Flora and the country-green / Dance, and Provencal song," and Moore obliges him, in "Bird-Witted," with a poem about a mocking-bird (syllabically equivalent to the nightingale) which imitates the Provençal "pattern" of Arnaut Daniel. And she goes further: her situation as listener, in the crucial fourth stanza where the bird is invisible, closely parallels the situation in which Keats finds himself in the fifth strophe of his "Ode." He "cannot see" either his surroundings or the bird; lying in "embalmed darkness," he can do nothing in the following strophe but listen:

> Darkling I listen; and, for many a time
>   I have been half in love with easeful Death,
> Called him soft names in many a mused rhyme,
>   To take into the air my quiet breath;
> Now more than ever seems it rich to die,
>   To cease upon the midnight with no pain,
>   While thou art pouring forth thy soul abroad
>   In such an ecstasy!
> Still wouldst thou sing, and I have ears in vain—
>   To thy high requiem become a sod.

Moore is not listening to "such an ecstasy" as Keats hears, but rather remembering a moment from the past; and her own death is not in question. Unlike Keats's "immortal Bird," however, Moore's mocking-bird and her young have indeed been "born for death," and though it is not yet their time to die, the "hungry generations" have appeared—in the form of "A piebald cat"—to "tread [them] down" as they never will Keats's bird. Just as Keats is wrenched back to his "sole self" by the sound of his own voice repeating the word "Forlorn!" as if it were "a bell," so Moore is called back to the present by the suddenly "harsh" voice of the mother bird, inter-rupting her memory of "ecstasy" and forcing her to attend to the emer-gencies of the present. "Bird-Witted" thus justifies its symbolic treatment of the mocking-bird by calling attention to the particular exigencies of its situation in a way that does not concern Keats at all; what we hear in the mocking-bird's song is the "note" of its own insistent perception of danger, rather than the personal note Keats strikes in the "Ode." The implication seems to be that Keats, for all his display of emotion, has transformed the nightingale into a merely "intellectual" symbol of his own desires, and that in doing so he has indulged in a process very similar to that which works upon the mocking-bird itself in "Virginia Britannia."

The mocking-bird enters "Virginia Britannia" in a blur of motion so fast that for a moment we are unable even to identify the "terse Virginian" as a mocking-bird. But the bird, like the reader, is soon arrested by the command to "Observe," and it comes to a stand "on the round stone / topped table with lead cupids grouped to / form the pedestal." The mock-ing-bird has begun to slow, to freeze, long before the end of the stanza, however: it is likened to a statue even as it first comes clearly into focus "with head / held half away, and meditative eye as dead / as sculptured marble / eyes." Now, perched on what is explicitly termed a "pedestal" formed by "lead cupids" in a leaden mockery of loving support, it resembles a statue so closely that it is as if it had been turned to "lead" by the sheer force of the "Care" which "has formed" the scene as if for the express purpose of accommodating and subduing the bird—and by the difficult consonants that slow the rhythm of our reading. It is in this posture that the mocking-bird enters our memory, so that we are implicated with the poet in the alchemical, "intellectual" transmutation of a living creature into a base material.

"Bird-Witted" brings this faintly ominous leaden figure to life again, transforming it into a momentarily animated figure of sound. But Moore's effort to undo the effects of her own "intellectual," Keatsian treatment of the mocking-bird by parodic means is doomed to fail—for parody is a mimetic mode, and must employ Keatsian tactics. As in "Virginia Britan-nia," therefore, the tempo of "Bird-Witted" slows dramatically when the sentence arrives in what seems to be the present, when it comes to the "grown bird" and the predicate that places her "delightful note" in the "remote" past: what we are hearing is a "ditt[y] of no tune" like those which play throughout the "Ode on a Grecian Urn"—a "note" played "Not to the sensual ear" but to "the spirit." We see the mother bird "darting down" to meet the cat, but the engagement is delayed while we are told what impels her to action ("hope . . . of toil"), and when finally she "wages deadly combat / and half kills" her antagonist, the object of the verb is deferred until the last possible moment—deferred not only by syntax, but by typography as well. For in the first three printings of the poem the letters of the final line are more widely spaced than the rest: the mother bird

> wages deadly combat,
> and half kills
> with bayonet beak and
> cruel wings, the
> intellectual cautious-
> ly c r e e p ing cat.

The effect is to freeze the scene: the cat is transfixed as it moves toward its prey, and the mother bird is caught as it were in mid-air, just on the point of attack, by the "intellectual," "unheard" music of the "Ode on a Grecian Urn." Like Keats's "marble men and maidens," Moore's cat and bird will remain so, in the memory of art. When we see them again in "Half Deity," the third poem in the sequence, they have been slightly transformed, but they are still fixed in the same attitudes.

The almost total critical neglect of "Half Deity" may be explained by Moore's decision to omit it from both *The Collected Poems* of 1951 and *The Complete Poems* of 1967—explained, but not justified. The poem is far too important to be ignored. Only one critic, Laurence Stapleton, considers that it "has a rightful place beside the other Virginia poems," but her own treatment is too cursory to specify that "place" or to suggest the poem's crucial bearing on the sequence as a whole.

Like "Virginia Britannia" and "Bird-Witted," "Half Deity" is concerned with the relationship between childhood innocence and adult knowledge, but it explores that relationship more intensively than the others do. "Virginia Britannia" and "Bird-Witted" take the difference between innocence and experience more or less for granted; they can do so, however, only because "Half Deity" offers a rather full account of the passage from one state to the other—an account which is complicated and intensified by Moore's insistence in "Smooth Gnarled Crape Myrtle" that the distance between innocence and guilty knowledge is almost imperceptible: there "is but a / step" between them.

The passage from innocence to experience occurs when the relationship of observer to observed becomes instead a relation between a pursuer and her prey—when, that is, observation becomes an effort not just to secure visual knowledge of a given object but also to possess that object. Or rather, the passage occurs when the observer becomes consciously aware that she is a pursuer already, and that her pursuit must fail of its object: "Half Deity" implies that observation is never innocent of the desire for possession. The difference between child and adult, therefore, is that the latter has "learned to spare" the object of her desire in a way the child has not—for observation, like imitation, has to be "learned," though it has its origin in an instinctive "curiosity." But the adult "spare[s]" the object only from the physical consequences of the possessive urge. Opting for intellectual rather than merely physical possession, the observer makes the object an object of memory instead of immediate sensory experience; she may therefore seem more innocent than the child who attempts to secure the object physically. We have seen that memory may serve as a warning of imminent danger; but it also poses a threat to the integrity of the object, for it transforms and deadens its objects by subordinating them to patterns already formed.

"A subject and an object," says Emerson in "Experience," "—it takes so much to make the galvanic circuit complete, but magnitude adds nothing. What imports it whether it is Kepler and the sphere, Columbus and America, a reader and his book, or puss with her tail?" Pursuit inevitably becomes self-pursuit, and then "the galvanic circuit" can be made "complete" only in a provisional, a metaphorical way, and then only with considerable pain. As Emerson writes earlier in the same essay, "souls never touch their objects." But when the soul *is* the object of the soul's pursuit, as it is in "Half Deity"—when the pursuer deliberately puts on the "aspect" of the innocent observer in an effort to repossess and reanimate her own childhood innocence, which is either a memory or a fiction or both—then the closing of the circle inflicts a sharper pain than the one "puss" must feel when she catches up with "her tail" and bites down. For to capture the memory of one's former innocence is to discover, simultaneously, that what one has in memory is what one has lost in fact, and so to discover the full burden of one's guilt. This, I think, is why Moore elected not to include "Half Deity" in late collections of her work: like "Black Earth" (later renamed "Melancthon"), it is too explicitly self-revealing, and too deeply disturbing, to suit the public image she had come by then to project so successfully.

"Half Deity" begins by carefully establishing the poet in the posture of innocent observer:

> HALF DEITY
> half worm. We all, infant and adult, have
>   stopped to watch the butterfly—last of the
>   elves—and learned to spare the wingless worm
>   that hopefully ascends the tree.

This opening leads us to believe that when the poet stops, a few lines later, "to watch" a "peninsula-tailed" butterfly which "has been / sleeping upright on an elm," she intends only to look at it in order to confirm for herself what others have reported—for "its yellowness / that of the autumn poplar-leaf, by day / has been observed." We assume that she will otherwise "spare" it her attentions, for unlike the sea in "A Grave," she is evidently not "a collector." We have not yet been given reason to consider that our having "learned to spare" the caterpillar, "the wingless worm / that hopefully ascends the tree," says nothing of our eventual response to the butterfly that caterpillar will become; and so we are not distressed when the poet's apparently matter-of-fact observation gives rise to pursuit, because the poet herself takes no visible part in the chase. So far as we can tell, she is the observer and reporter, not the pursuer.

That role is played by another figure, an "infant" "half deity" who appears without warning a third of the way into the poem. "Disguised in butterfly / bush Wedgewood blue, Psyche follows" the butterfly from tree to tree—much as the mocking-bird "drives the / owl" in "Virginia Britannia"—and the action develops so quickly from this point on that we have no time for surprise at the presence in Moore's work of a figure so obviously and so conveniently poetic, no time to consider that the landscape of "The Old Dominion" has suddenly become so thoroughly Romantic that Moore, like Keats, can all "thoughtlessly" happen upon Psyche in a wood. Perhaps, though, we may explain Psyche's sudden appearance by recalling the strange, offhand comment made earlier on, that the butterfly's "yellowness . . . *by day* / has been observed" [my italics]. The phrase implies that the action of the poem takes place at night, and may in fact be a dream—a typically Romantic mode. This might help, too, to account for the specific trees to which Psyche pursues the butterfly. She goes first to a tree whose Latin name, "Micromalus," means "little apple" but suggests as well "little evil," and whose English name, "the midget / crab," calls to mind not only miniature, inedible versions of forbidden fruit but small, painfully grasping creatures as well; then she goes to "the mimosa," the central symbol of Shelley's "The Sensitive Plant," where the tree inhabits a beautiful garden, and lives in a mysterious affinity with a beautiful lady—at least for a time. For "When Winter had gone and Spring came back / The Sensitive Plant was a leafless wreck." And so Psyche leaves the wrecked mimosa and goes straight "from that, to the flowering pomegranate," the tree whose fruit was forbidden to Persephone, who ate it nonetheless and brought winter into the world.

Keats's "Ode to Psyche" begins with the poet's unexpected discovery, as he wanders "in a forest thoughtlessly," of a sleeping couple whom he recognizes as Cupid and Psyche. But Keats—who feared that "there was nothing original to be written in poetry; that its riches were already exhausted—and all its beauties forestalled"—dismisses the "winged boy" without even troubling to name him, for he has no interest in retelling the ancient legend of Cupid and Psyche's love. All his attention is on Psyche, and he revels in his discovery of a subject whose "riches" have not been "exhausted," whose "beauties" have not been "forestalled": Psyche, "latest born" of the goddesses as Moore's butterfly is "last of the elves," was born "too late for antique vows, / Too, too late for the fond believing lyre." No poet has sung her praises, nor made his name inseparable from hers; she has had

> No voice, no lute, no pipe, no incense sweet
>   From chain-swung censer teeming;
> No shrine, no grove, no oracle, no heat
>   Of pale-mouth'd prophet dreaming.
>   (ll. 32–35)

The poet begs her to "let" him fill those offices; declaring, "I will be thy priest," he promises in the final strophe to build in Psyche's honor

>   a fane
> In some untrodden region of my mind,
> Where branched thoughts, new grown with pleasant pain,
>   Instead of pines shall murmur in the wind:
> Far, far around shall those dark-cluster'd trees
>   Fledge the wild-ridged mountains steep by steep;
> And there by zephrys, streams, and birds, and bees,
>   The moss-lain Dryads shall be lull'd to sleep;
> And in the midst of this wide quietness
> A rosy sanctuary will I dress
> With the wreath'd trellis of a working brain,
>   With buds, and bells, and stars without a name,
>   With all the gardener Fancy e'er could feign,
>   Who breeding flowers, will never breed the same:
> And there shall be for thee all soft delight
>   That shadowy thought can win,
> A bright torch, and a casement ope at night,
>   To let the warm Love in!
>   (ll. 50–67)

Keats's "Ode," ostensibly a celebratory gesture occasioned by the poet's discovery of the goddess sleeping in the wood, is transformed by his ambitious desire for originality into an attempt to displace Cupid and possess Psyche for himself. (Compare the similar but far more overt displacement in Whitman's "Song of Myself": "I turn the bridegroom out of bed and stay with the bride myself / I tighter her all night to my thighs and lips.") What Keats ends by building, therefore, is less "a fane" than what Moore calls in "Half Deity" a "flowering, shrewd-scented tropical / device" whose function is to secure the poet's dominion over Psyche by imprisoning her "In some untrodden region of [his] mind."

Similarly, although Psyche's pursuit of the butterfly in "Half Deity" seems to spring from a relatively uncomplicated desire "to watch" it, she

soon finds herself wholly committed to trapping the elusive creature. She
follows it until,

> Baffled not by the quick-clouding serene gray
> moon, but forced by the hot hot sun to pant,
>   she stands on rug-soft grass; though "it is not
>   permitted to gaze informally
>   on majesty, in such a manner as might
>   well happen here." The blind
>   all-seeing butterfly, fearing the slight
> finger, wanders—as though it were ignorant—
> a step further and lights on Zephyr's palm.

Psyche, Zephyr, and the butterfly now form a tableau in which all our
attention is directed to the confrontation of observer and observed, pursuer
and pursued.

> Small unglazed china eyes of butterflies—
>   pale tobacco crown—with the large eyes of
>   the Nymph on them; gray eyes that now are
>   black, for she, with controlled agitated glance
>   observes the insect's face
>   and all's a-quiver with significance
> as in the scene with cats' eyes on the magpie's eyes
> by Goya.

Psyche only "observes the insect's face" here—but the butterfly, rightly
"vexed because curiosity has / been pursuing it," is unable to remain
"calm." For if in "Bird-Witted" the "delightful note" of a "remote" and
untroubled past is recalled as a prelude to danger, "Half Deity" recalls the
"deadly combat" of "Bird-Witted" in the midst of an apparently innocent
confrontation. Psyche's "curiosity" begins to look less innocent, moreover,
when we recall that her marriage to Cupid was annulled when she dis-
obeyed the divine injunction against looking upon his face. And "though
'it is not / permitted to gaze informally / on majesty, in such a manner as
might / well happen' " again " 'here,' " Psyche " 'might / well' " find a
certain sanction for her curiosity in the reflection that—as Alice says elsewhere—" 'A cat may look at a king.' " For that is precisely what does
" 'happen here.' " The analogy to Goya's "scene with cats' eyes on the
magpie's eyes" likens Psyche not to the bird (which would be dubious
enough, since the magpie is a thievish bird) but rather to the "intellectual
cautious / ly c r e e p ing cat" of "Bird-Witted." And the cat is most itself
in preying upon innocence, as readers of earlier poems like "Silence" (where
the cat " 'takes its prey to privacy— / the mouse's limp tail dangling like
a shoelace from its mouth' ") and "Peter" (where the cat is naturally inclined
"to purloin, to pursue" the "hen") will recall.
    All this may seem to set "Half Deity" at odds with the celebration, in

"Bird-Witted," of the effort to repel the predator. But we know by now what "Smooth Gnarled Crape Myrtle" will confirm that "An aspect may deceive." We must consider, too, the poet's lament in the same poem that "Art is unfortunate // One may be a blameless / bachelor and it is but a // step to Congreve"; for there is "but a step" between "Bird-Witted" and "Half Deity." We have seen that "Bird-Witted" inherits from "Virginia Britannia" the memory, in statuary form, of a living creature—a memory which it reanimates by imitating the intricate aural patterns of Arnaut Daniel's verse. But at the very moment when those aural patterns are most conspiciously displayed, the fourth stanza where the poet must carry the tune alone, the imitation of Daniel coincides with the silent memory of the "Ode on a Grecian Urn"; and from then on convergent imitations sustain the formal movement of the verse while gradually returning the bird (and the cat with her) to the initial state of immobility. This is not an innocent stratagem (if there is such a thing) but a desperately conscious one. "Bird-Witted" concentrates upon presenting to the reader the more innocent "aspect" of Moore's poetic enterprise, but it is the peculiar misfortune of an art so wholly mimetic that it must imitate whatever comes into its ken. It is, therefore, only by resorting in desperation to Keats, only by forcing both the mocking-bird and the cat into conformity with the frozen statuary of the Grecian Urn, that Moore prevents herself from taking a mimetic "step further" with the "intellectual cautious- / ly c r e e p ing cat" whose movements the typography has already begun to imitate—prevents herself, that is, from giving the poem an "aspect" as predatory as Psyche's has now become. For, like the poet and the reader in "Virginia Britannia," and like Psyche here, the cat begins by "observing" the "fledgling mocking-birds."

Like the cat, moreover, Psyche is immobilized just when her barely "controlled agitated glance" reveals the true character of her interest in the butterfly. As her "large . . . gray eyes" darken to "black" with excitement, they become so opaque as to recall the "meditative eye" of the "lead- / gray . . . mocking-bird" of "Virginia Britannia"—an eye seemingly "as dead / as sculptured marble / eyes"; but there is a crucial difference between Psyche's eyes and the bird's. The "eyes of the Nymph," apparently so intensely alive, are in fact "sculptured marble," and so are Zephyr's "mirror eyes" and the "Small unglazed china eyes" of the butterfly itself. The action has been brought to a halt by the sudden assertion—apparently against the Keatsian movement of Psyche's pursuit but actually, as the conclusion of "Bird-Witted" attests, in logical confirmation of the end to which that pursuit must lead—of the poet's memory of a "Carved Marble Group by Jean Baptiste Boyer," representing "Psyche trying to capture the butterfly held out on Zephyr's palm."

That memory cannot contain the action for long, however. Reanimated as suddenly as it had been frozen, the butterfly now "springs away, [a] zebra half-deified," and in the next instant the poet takes the irrevocable "step" she had denied herself in "Bird-Witted." She thereby reveals the extent to which her own imitation of Keats, parodic though it may be, has entangled her with Psyche. Until now, the poet has preserved her status as observer of the entire episode; but now she suddenly insults the butterfly, calling after it: "Twig-veined, irascible, / fastidious, stubborn undisciplined zebra! Sometimes one is grateful to / a stranger for looking very nice." So intolerable is it that the butterfly should escape that the poet's voice turns markedly childlike, as though by acting the petulant child for a moment (and she is very like Alice now) she could disguise a deeper, more adult sense of loss and lure the butterfly back.

But "An aspect may deceive," and "looking very nice" is not enough to satisfy the "blind / all-seeing butterfly," which has only wandered on to Zephyr's hand in the first place *"as though* it were ignorant" [my italics]. It sees, therefore, that it is "free / to leave the breeze's hand" as it would not be "free / to leave" the "half-shut" hand Psyche has extended toward it. And so, like Emily Dickinson's "Little Tippler" (Dickinson had "For Poets . . . Keats—and Mr. and Mrs. Browning"),

> it flies, drunken with triviality
> or guided by visions of strength, away till
> diminished like wreckage on the sea,
>> rising and falling easily; mounting
>> the swell and keeping its true course with
>>> what swift majesty, indifferent to
> us, it's gone.

"It's gone," and the poet can only wonder: "Deaf to my / voice, or magnetnice? as it flutters through / airs now slack, now fresh. It has strict ears," she adds ruefully, "when the / West Wind speaks." The lineation here emphasizes the possessive pronoun ("*my* / voice"), and the question brings the poet fully into the open. Psyche has served only as a mask—and not a very effective one at that. The poet's interest in the butterfly is as "intellectual," and therefore as predatory, as Psyche's has become—and she too is immobilized by the weight of her own desire.

But if the butterfly is finally "indifferent / to" anyone who might take an active interest in it, it has yet been drawn as if by a "magnet" to Zephyr, the Shelleyan "West Wind," for whose words it has such "strict ears," and whose "hand spread out was enough / to tempt the fiery tiger-horse to stand." Moore's memory of the "Ode to the West Wind" has served to rescue the poem (and the butterfly) from the impasse to which her imitation of Keats has brought it. As we have seen, what Keats attempts in the "Ode to Psyche" is the attainment of mastery, an ambition which his professed desire to serve the goddess and worship as "priest" at her "fane" cannot conceal; by contrast, in the "Ode to the West Wind" Shelley acknowledges the wind as *his* master. He seeks not to possess its power for himself but rather to be possessed by it as a prophet is possessed by the divine afflatus.

His concern, unlike Keats's, is less for himself than for the "unawakened earth": he wants to borrow the wind's "power" and make it speak his "words," but he wants it not to glorify himself but rather to "quicken a new birth," to arouse the world from its "Winter" sleep to a revolutionary "Spring."

Moore is not, I think, especially concerned with the particular features of the revolution Shelley had in mind, and in fact must have found his doctrines thoroughly incompatible with her own conservative views; but his doctrines are not the issue here. The nature of Moore's interest in Shelley is most clearly indicated by the words of her friend Scofield Thayer, former editor of *The Dial* and a great admirer of Moore and her work, who wrote of Shelley in 1913 that while "many of the poet's ideals now appear scarcely comprehensible, the integrity of his purpose is not the less patent." Thayer's remarks (which Moore transcribed into her reading notebook in November 1928) have a clear bearing on Zephyr's success in attracting the butterfly though he makes no apparent effort to do so. His "hand" is "spread out," giving assurance of "the integrity of his purpose"—an assurance which the "blind / all-seeing butterfly" recognizes, and by which it distinguishes between the Shelleyan Zephyr and the Keatsian Psyche: Zephyr has "no net," and makes no such attempt as Psyche's to "capture the butterfly" in a "half-shut / hand." Nor is Zephyr more "comprehensible" than Shelley: "many of the poet's ideals now appear scarcely comprehensible," says Thayer—and so, Moore writes, Zephyr's "talk was as strange as my grandmother's muff."

Moore's "talk" is "strange," too; but her struggle to "overcome [her] reluctance to be unoriginal"—which has led her actively to pursue "possible comparisons and coincidences" with other writers—has betrayed her into what she perceives as a loss of "integrity." Significantly, Moore does not imitate Shelley in "Half Dcity"; rather, she captures the erratic, fluttering movement of the butterfly by parodying the loosely Pindaric form of Keats's "Ode to Psyche." But parody is only another form of imitation, and even in parody Moore is possessed by the Keatsian obsession with originality which she is struggling to "overcome." Inevitably, then, she becomes Psyche, straining after the butterfly which is the emblem of her own soul, and seeing in her inability to capture it the extent to which, unlike the butterfly, she has departed from her own "true course"—seeing, that is, a loss of self, a loss of innocence and "integrity of purpose." "They that have wings must not have weights," she says early in the poem—but she has no wings. On the contrary, she is so weighted down by memory and desire that, like Psyche, she is immobilized, turned to stone. Even the self whose emblem she strains after is only a memory. The closing line, delivered as an artlessly inconsequent throwaway, lodges the entire poem in the past, reminding us that the poet, for all that she "look[s] very nice" "Disguised in butterfly / bush Wedgewood blue," is not a child but an adult remembering a dream of a childhood long since past: "His talk was as strange as my grandmother's muff."

"Such a life as [Shelley's,]" writes Scofield Thayer, "resembles the sepulchral slab in the pavement of an ancient church; the impertinences of name and insignia are worn away by the feet of time, but the crossed arms remain." The grave thus becomes the image of an inscrutable and anonymous integrity, for Thayer immediately goes on to insist that the incomprehensibility of Shelley's ideals leaves "the integrity of his purpose . . . not the less patent." And so we circle back to "Virginia Britannia," where in the "typical ivied-bower-and-ruined-tower churchyard" of the opening stanza we find that

> A deer-
> track in a church-floor
> brick and Sir George Yeardley's
> coffin tacks and
> tomb remain.

This image is so specific that it bears no obvious relation to Thayer's discusson of Shelley; in the final version, however, the resemblance is much closer. For the identity of the "great sinner" who "lyeth here under the sycamore" is no longer "known": the "impertinences" of Yeardley's "name and insignia" have been "worn away" by revision, leaving only the "deer- / track" and "a fine pavement tomb with engraved top."

But the original image is more fully informed by Thayer's odd analogy than it seems. Yeardley was the only knighted member of the Jamestown colony, and he received his title in recognition of his work in aiding the community to establish itself. Apparently, then, his "tomb" functions in an ironic capacity as an image of justly rewarded integrity, and thus strikes the keynote not only for "Virginia Britannia" but for "The Old Dominion" as a whole. It is "integrity of purpose" that concerns Moore most deeply as she explores what Thayer calls, in the subtitle of his essay on Shelley, "The Poetic Value of Revolutionary Principles." Like Emerson's nature, the landscape of colonial Virginia "offers all her creatures to [the poet] as a picture-language" which, under Moore's scrutiny, reveals the principles inherent in the original "colonizing" of the New World and the subsequent history of America as a nation which owes its existence to the practical application of revolutionary ideals.

We must bear in mind, however, that "An aspect may deceive." For we shall find as the poem proceeds that the "picture-language" of "Virginia Britannia" spells out not a linear history of simple integrity but rather a history of principles perverted in the application and from the start. The history of America as this poem tells us is (to borrow a phrase from "Marriage," but which is originally from Sir Francis Bacon) a history " 'of circular traditions and impostures / committing many spoils' " "Virginia Britannia" is an attempt to rectify that history, to set America back on the "true course" of integrity; as we shall see, however, it works by the apparently paradoxical method of "advancing back- / ward in a circle"—a revolutionary method in the strictest etymological sense of the word "revolution," a method which requires that Moore accept the very perversions she is trying to correct and that she accept them not only in principle but in practice as well. Like Whitman, then—a poet for whom she felt a profound distaste—Moore identifies the form of the poem with the form of America itself, which is the form of its history. For those perversions, those " 'circular traditions and impostures' " and their " 'many spoils,' " are inseparable from the principles to which they give visible expression: they are the history of America. Nowhere is the paradoxical intertwining of principle and perversion, the backward-circling movement of advance, more powerfully evident than in the deliberate use of the word "intimation" to mark the boundary separating the mature poet from the figure of the innocent child and to confess the poet's participation in the circular logic of American history.

The "picture-language" of the Virginia landscape is all the more revealing because it is not entirely the language of nature. As we have seen, [elsewhere], the landscape which the poem purports to describe has been "formed" by the "Care" of an anonymous gardener or gardeners, in painstaking and nostalgic imitation of the landscape the colonists had left behind. What remains for us, however, is a monumental and wholly inadvertent parody, "an almost English" landscape dominated not by the " 'tame clever / true nightingale' " which "should be here" to suit the tastes of " 'one who dresses // in New York but dreams of / London' " (as "Smooth Gnarled Crape Myrtle" puts it), but rather by the hostile, mimetic, statuesque mocking-bird.

The gardeners' efforts to turn Virginia into an earthly Paradise have gone awry, have ended by producing a "Rare unscent- / ed, provident- / ly hot, too sweet, inconsistent flower- / bed" in which "serpentine shadows star- / tle the strangers" while the inhabitants remain curiously oblivious. The grotesquely thickened "stem" of "the white wall-rose," however, is itself a sign of danger: for the "wide-spaced great blunt alternating os- / trich-skin warts that were thorns" signify the " 'many spoils' " which have been committed by "the predatory hand" against which, in "Roses Only" (1917), the rose's thorns provide the only measure of "proof." Nothing is safe here: the "poor unpoison- / ous terrapin likes to / idle near the sea-top" where it makes easy prey; soon "Terrapin / meat and crested spoon / feed the mistress" of that "everywhere open / shaded house on Indian / named Virginian / streams, in counties named for English lords!"

The history of "Virginia Britannia," then, is the history not of integrity stoutly maintained but of "tobacco-crop / gains" memorialized on "church tablets," of mixed motives and cross purposes working "on The Chicka-hominy"—one of those "Indian / named Virginian / streams"—to establish "the Negro (opportunely brought) to / strengthen protest against tyranny." It is a history founded on appropriation:

> Strangler fig, pale fiercely
> unpretentious North American, and Dutch

> trader, and noble
>   Roman, in taking what they
>   pleased—colonizing as we say—
> were not all intel-
>   lect and delicacy.

The Virginian landscape is more than a natural historical record: it is
a work of art predicated upon the colonists' (and their descendants') having
combined the strength to "tak[e] what they / pleased" with an intense
longing "to be unoriginal," to use what they took as the material from
which to construct a simulacrum of the English landscape as a permanent
monument to England and the past—an enormous mortuary sculpture, as
it were. So powerful is that combination of strength and longing that it can
assimilate to its grand design even those native elements which, in breaking
the silence of the grave, threaten to overwhelm the memory of home with
their mockery. Thus the mocking-bird, though as it enters the scene it
"drives the / owl from tree to tree and imitates the call / of whippoorwill
or / lark or katydid," fall silent and turns to "lead" under the spell of the
gardeners' "Care": it is left frozen in its place, "still standing there alone
/ on the round stone- / topped table with lead cupids grouped to / form
the pedestal."
    Nor may we omit Moore's name from the roster of those who have
made "Virginia Britannia" what it is by "taking what they / pleased—
colonizing as we say." For the poem which discovers in the landscape the
long history of appropriation is itself not only the most recent product of
that history, but a "colonizing" power in its own right.

> The slowmoving glossy
> saddle-cavalcade
>
> of buckeye brown surprising
> jumpers; the contrasting work-mule and
>   show-mule and witch-cross door and "strong sweet prison"
> are a part of what
>   has come about, in the black
>   idiom, from advancing back-
> ward in a circle;
>   from taking the Potomac
>   cowbirdlike; and on
> the Chickahominy
> establishing
> the Negro (opportunely brought) to
> strengthen protest against
>   tyranny.

Here Moore registers her own "protest against" the "tyranny" to which
Blacks in America have been and are subject; but in "strengthen[ing]" that
"protest" with a phrase "opportunely brought" into the poem from "the

Black / idiom" she knowingly implicates herself in the very "tyranny" she condemns. The availability of that "idiom" depends, of course, on the institution of slavery, under which "the Negro" was brought to America to sustain the outmoded economy of the South and its "tyrant taste." But Moore uses "the Negro" in a similar way, deliberately appropriating his language to define and sustain the economy of "Virginia Britannia" itself— to enact and "strengthen" the circular logic of its opportunistic history.

Thus Moore is not simply describing a landscape, as she seems to be. Rather, she is extending the method we have seen her use in "Novices" and "Bird-Witted," finding in the construction of the landscape itself the technical principles of composition by which she now composes her own imitative reconstruction of a landscape which is already, in her words, "one of America's most undeniable poems." She is not so much writing "Virginia Britannia," then, as rewriting it, and correcting as she goes (much as she does in revising her own poems, including this one); and she is working along the lines laid down almost a century earlier by Emerson, who writes in "The Poet" (1844) that

> poetry was all written before time was, and whenever we are so finely organized that we can penetrate into that region where the air is music, we hear those primal warblings and attempt to write them down, but we lose ever and anon a word or a verse and substitute something of our own, and thus miswrite the poem.

The original settlers of Virginia, forced to "substitute something of [their] own" for the missing "words" of the English original, have "miswrit[ten] the poem" of Jamestown—and as Emerson tells us a few pages later, "herein is the legitimation of criticism, in the mind's faith that the [poem is] a corrupt version of some text in nature with which [it] ought to be made to tally." Moore's initial response to the colonists' inadvertently parodic miswriting is to counter with a deliberately parodic reconstruction of that parody which both reveals and corrects it. From the outset she intertwines various elements—natural and aritifical, domestic and foreign—so thoroughly that all seem equally out of place in the end, and equally at home as well. In the first stanza, for instance, the alternating pattern formed by "the redbird / the red-coated musketeer / the trumpet-flower, the cavalier," seems to accommodate "the parson, and the / wild parishioner" without strain; but here Moore has already extended the poem well beyond the temporal and chronological limits of what we call Colonial Virginia. In the early seventeenth century "New England was called Northern Virginia," as she points out; and the presence in this closely patterned landscape of "the parson, and the / wild parishioner" points not only to the "deer / track in a church-floor / brick" but also, and more problematically, to a permanent reminder of just how "unEnglish" this "almost English" scene really is. The pairing is a reminder, too, of just how far America has strayed from its "true course," for it recalls the most celebrated adulterous union in nineteenth-century American fiction—the forest meeting between "The Pastor and His Parishioner" in which Hester Prynne persuades Arthur Dimmesdale to join her in fleeing the oppressive strictures of Puritan Boston.

Following Hawthorne's ironic design (for of course Hester and Dimmesdale are foiled by her devilish, cuckolded husband), Moore binds these figures permanently into the American landscape. And she does so with the same "Care" with which she "has formed, a- / mong" the "unEnglish insect sounds" of stanzas which "should sound like a kind of inexhaustible bumble-bee" (as she put it later), "the white wall-rose" with the grotesquely thickened American "stem" whose missing "thorns" are no longer "proof" against "the predatory hand" that governs the landscape. In "Virginia Britannia," however, the "observing" eye does the work of the hand—and "observing" is a very "predatory" activity, as we have had ample occasion to discover.

We cannot gauge the full extent of the eye's rapacity until we consider that it is the poet's simultaneous observance of the forms of the past and of the present which impels her to cast "Virginia Britannia" as a syllabic imitation of the Immortality Ode and, at crucial moments, so complicate that willingness "to be unoriginal" by combining with it the strength to take what she pleases. In doing so—in "colonizing as we say"—Moore reveals the full extent of her unoriginality, of her willingness to let herself be influenced by other writers. For her definition of "colonizing" ("taking what they / pleased") is very nearly identical in phrasing to the definition of influence which Eliot had advanced in his essay "In Memory" of Henry James (1918)—an essay on which Moore relies in "Picking and Choosing," which redefines the complementary relationship between criticism and poetry along the lines of Eliot's discussion: "To be influenced by a writer," says Eliot, "is to have a chance inspiration from him; or to take what one wants." It is Eliot himself who, at a crucial moment in "Virginia Britannia," provides Moore with "a chance inspiration," and it is from his most recent work that she takes "what [she] wants." The mocking-bird to which we have already devoted so much time may be indigenous to Virginia, but like virtually everything in "Virginia Britannia" it has been imported, "opportunely brought" in from elsewhere. It comes from Eliot's short poem "Virginia," one of several small landscapes published under the heading "Words for Music" in the *Virginia Quarterly Review* in April 1934:

> Red river, red river,
> Slow flow heat is silence
> No will is still as a river
> Still. Will heat move
> Only through the mocking-bird
> Heard once?

The mocking-bird belongs to the immediate present; but though it "drives the / owl from tree to tree," it cannot overcome the full burden of the English past. Having been forcefully appropriated by a poet ever-observant of her contemporaries' work, it is introduced into a scene so rigidly determined by the past that the bird is struck dumb and cast in lead. For the scene owes its form to Moore's parodic effort to "Observe" the form of the Immortality Ode—an effort which perpetuates, in turn, the awkward attempts of the original colonists to "Observe" the cherished forms of their own history.

As Moore's corrective measures take effect, as the present begins apparently to free itself from the bonds of the past, there is a corresponding change in the character of Moore's parody. By the penultimate stanza, parody has become anticipatory as well as reminiscent:

> The song-
> bird wakes too soon, to enjoy
> excellent idleness, destroy-
> ing legitimate
> laziness, the unbought toy
> even in the dark
> risking loud whee whee whee
> of joy, the car-
> away-seed-spotted sparrow perched on
> the dew-drenched juniper
> beside the window-ledge;
> the little hedge-
> sparrow that wakes up seven minutes
> sooner than the lark
>
> they say.

But there is no escape from the past. In the final stanza, the delighted, gently mocking anticipation of Shelley's Skylark shades into a much more straightforwardly honorific imitation of the Immortality Ode, and though the anticipatory note remains it has been muted. For "The clouds that gather round the setting sun / Do take a sober colouring from an eye / That hath kept watch o'er man's mortality," and when the poem encounters a group of stationary figures whom even the flaming sunset "can / not move," Moore resorts directly to Wordsworth. This time, in a final, desperate acknowledgment of her own complicity in and responsibility for the American historical process, she takes liberties not only with Wordsworth's formal patterns, but with his language and, most importantly, with his central symbol as well.

Like the "solid- / pointed star" which "stands for hope" at the end of "The Steeple-Jack," like Zephyr in "Half Deity," the child, receiving "an intimation" which she does not seek, seems to hold out the "hope" of escape from the long history of "colonizing" which the poem has developed. But as Moore writes in "The Hero"—one of two companion pieces to "The Steeple-Jack"—hope is not hope "until all ground for hope has / vanished." The child is mother to the woman, an *"historic* metamorphoser" [my italics] like the butterfly in "Half Deity"—and so she is doomed to undergo a process of growth which will invert precisely the transformation of "the wingless worm / that hopefully ascends the tree" into a "weightless" butterfly. The child is already "historic," as Psyche is—a figure caught by poetic memory in the attitude from which, like the butterfly from its cocoon, the predatory, "intellectual" adult emerges into history to stand rooted and grasping in "endless imitation" of an innocence which has already receded into the "remote" past and which she knows from the outset to be permanently lost. "Art is unfortunate."

The Echoing Spell of H. D.'s *Trilogy*

Susan Gubar

In a wonderful children's story called *The Hedgehog,* H. D. focuses on a little girl called "Madge" or "Madgelet" whose name "isn't a name at all" and whose nationality is both English and American, although "You would think she was French too, or Swiss, when you heard her speak." Understandably, she is termed "Madd" by the natives of Leytaux who find it difficult to pronounce her name or understand her language. She, too, has problems understanding them; indeed, her quest in the story is an attempt to discover the meaning of the word *hérisson.* A wild little girl in flight from the rules and regulations of the adult world, such as the demand that she wear horrid thick boots outdoors in the garden, Madge is at the point in her life when she begins to experience self-consciousness. She is fleetingly but frighteningly aware of her separateness from the rest of creation, and it seems fitting that she is searching for an animal whose body provides a kind of natural fortress—armored protection against the slings and arrows of misfortune. This little girl's confusion at the meaning of cultural signs and her identification with the natural world recall a number of wild romantic children who are first lost and then found, but her story—which was, appropriately, written by H. D. for her daughter, Perdita—is a paradigm of a uniquely female quest for maturation that would also concern H. D. in her most ambitious poetic narratives.

Madge learns the secret meaning of the word *hérisson* only after she finds an educated man who owns and interprets for her a book on classical lore that explains how *hérissons* were used by the warriors of Mycenae to make caps and by the Athenians for combing wool. Madge's dependency on Dr. Blum recalls not only H. D.'s subsequent reliance on Dr. Freud, but

From *Contemporary Literature* 19, no. 2 (Spring 1978). © 1978 by the Board of Regents of the University of Wisconsin System.

also her mystification as a child when she "could . . . scarcely distinguish the shape of a number from a letter, or know which was which" on the pages of writing she saw on her father's desk. Sure, then, that her father possessed "sacred symbols," H. D. was conscious ever after that mythic, scientific, and linguistic symbols are controlled and defined by men. She repeatedly describes her alienation from a puzzling system of inherited symbols which do, nevertheless, finally reveal a special meaning to the female initiate. For Madge, the classical references and the successful completion of her quest lead to a joyously personal experience of her own powers which she articulates in her subsequent hymn to the moon, Artemis, who "loved girls, little girls and big girls, and all girls who were wild and free in the mountains, and girls who ran races just like boys along the seashore."

What undercuts the traditional Freudian interpretation of this tale as a little girl's search for the phallus she presumably lacks is precisely this vision of Artemis, embodying Madge's distinctively female joy and her sense that she contains multitudes, that she exists in both the mythic past and the secular present. Far from seeking so-called masculine forms of power, Madge manages to create out of the enigmatic, recalcitrant signs of her culture a new and sustaining story of female freedom. In her fascination with ambiguous signs and stories with "double sorts of meaning," Madge resembles her creator, whose initials stand not only for Hilda Doolittle but also for the *Hermetic Definitions* that would intrigue her with secret meanings made accessible only to those who experience either themselves or their culture as alien. One of H. D.'s most coherent and ambitious poetic narratives, her war *Trilogy*, explores the reasons for her lifelong fascination with the palimpsest. Like Madge, H. D. presents herself as an outsider who must express her views from a consciously female perspective, telling the truth, as Dickinson would say, "slant." Inheriting uncomfortable male-defined images of women and of history, H. D. responds with palimpsestic or encoded revisions of male myths. Thus, like Madge, she discovers behind the recalcitrant and threatening signs of her times a hidden meaning that sustains her quest by furnishing stories of female strength and survival. In the *Trilogy*, through recurrent references to secret languages, codes, dialects, hieroglyphs, foreign idioms, fossilized traces, mysterious signs, and indecipherable signets, H. D. illustrates how patriarchal culture can be subverted by the woman who dares to "re-invoke, recreate" what has been "scattered in the shards / men tread upon [H. D., *Tribute to the Angels*, in *Trilogy* (New York: New Directions, 1973), no. 1, p. 63; parenthetical page references in the text, preceded by the capitalized initials of the volume and the number of the poem, will be to this edition].

While there is never any question for H. D. that she can avoid reinvoking or re-creating, such a posture implies that she never expects to find or make a language of her own. It is significant, I think, that H. D. sees in her famous vision at Corfu a tripod, symbol of "prophetic utterance or occult or hidden knowledge; the Priestess or Pythoness of Delphi sat on the tripod while she pronounced her verse couplets, the famous Delphic utterances which it was said *could be read two ways*" [italics mine]. Throughout her career, H. D. wrote couplets which have been read only one way. Placed in exclusively male contexts, the poetry of Freud's analysand, Pound's girlfriend, and D. H. Lawrence's Isis has been viewed from the monolithic perspective of the twentieth-century trinity of psychoanalysis, imagism, and modernism. While none of these contexts can be discounted, each is profoundly affected by H. D.'s sense of herself as a woman writing about female confinement, specifically the woman writer's struggle against entrapment within male literary conventions. Furthermore, the fact that H. D. wrote her verse so it could be read two ways demonstrates her ambivalence over self-expression: she hides her private meaning behind public words in a juggling act that tells us a great deal about the anxieties of many women poets. Reticence and resistance characterize H. D.'s revisions in the *Trilogy*, where we can trace her contradictory attitudes toward communication: in *The Walls Do Not Fall*, H. D. demonstrates the need for imagistic and lexical redefinition, an activity closely associated with the recovery of female myths, specifically the story of Isis; in *Tribute to the Angels*, she actually begins transforming certain words, even as she revises apocalyptic myth; finally, H. D. translates the story of the New Testament in *The Flowering of the Rod*, feminizing a male mythology as she celebrates the female or "feminine" Word made flesh.

Written in three parts of forty-three poems each, primarily in unrhymed couplets, H. D.'s *Trilogy* was completed between 1944 and 1946, and it deals initially with the meaning of World War II. The title of the first volume, *The Walls Do Not Fall*, reveals the primacy of spatial imagery in H. D.'s analysis of a splintered world where "there are no doors" and "the fallen roof / leaves the sealed room / open to the air" (*WDNF* 1). All of civilized history has failed to create forms that can protect or nurture the inhabitants of this wasteland, and the "Apocryphal fire" threatens even the skeleton which has incomprehensibly survived. The poet is especially vulnerable in a world that worships coercion, for the sword takes precedence over the word. Such so-called non-utilitarian efforts as poetry are deemed irrelevant as books are burned, and the poet who identifies herself as a member of a fellowship of "nameless initiates, / born of one mother" (*WDNF* 13) realizes that only a shift in perspective can redeem this landscape of pain: then the fallen roofs, absent doors, and crumbling walls will be, paradoxically, transformed from houses into shrines. Furthermore, because "gods always face two-ways" (*WDNF* 2), H. D. considers the possibility of scratching out "indelible ink of the palimpsest" to get back to an earlier script on the still-standing walls. However, she knows that her search for "the true-rune, the right-spell" will be castigated as "retrogressive" (*WDNF* 2). In a world dominated by a God who demands *"Thou shall have none other gods but me"* (*WDNF* 37), the entire culture castigates the beauty of "Isis, Aset or Astarte" as the snare of "a harlot" (*WDNF* 2). But from the beginning, H. D. senses that the jealousy of this monotheistic God actually affirms the reality of those "old fleshpots" (*WDNF* 2). Therefore she seeks "to recover old values," although her attempt will be labeled heretical and her rhythm will be identified with "the devil's hymn" (*WDNF* 2).

It is only in the context of her psychological and physical dispossession that H. D.'s famous poem about the spell of the seashell can be fully understood. In her first attempt to "recover the Sceptre, / the rod of power" associated with the healing powers of Caduceus (*WDNF* 3), H. D. portrays herself in the image of the "master-mason" or "craftsman" mollusk within the seashell (*WDNF* 4). No less an emblem of defensive survival in a hostile world than the hedgehog, the mollusk opens its house/shell to the infinite sea "at stated intervals: // prompted by hunger." But, sensing its limits, it "snap[s] shut // at invasion of the limitless" in order to preserve its own existence. Managing to eat without being eaten, the mollusk serves as an object lesson when the poet advises herself and her readers to "be firm in your own small, static, limited // orbit" so that "living within, / you beget, self-out-of-self, // selfless, / that pearl-of-great-price." Self-sufficient, brave, efficient, productive, equipped to endure in a dangerous world, H. D.'s mollusk recalls Marianne Moore's snail whose "Contractility is a virtue / as modesty is a virtue," and Denise Levertov's "Snail" whose shell is both a burden and a grace. Hidden and therefore safe, the mollusk is protected in precisely the way the poet craves asylum: neither fully alive nor fully dead, half in and half out, the mollusk in its shell becomes for H. D. a tantalizing image of the self or soul safely ensconced within the person or body, always and anywhere at home.

But the fascination goes much further because the "flabby, amorphous" mollusk not only protects itself with such impenetrable material as "bone, stone, marble" but also transforms living substance into formal object, and thereby mysteriously creates the beautiful circular patterns of its house and also the perfectly spherical pearl. Shells are associated traditionally with art because the shell is a musical instrument expressing the rhythm of the waves, and H. D. would know that it was Hermes who scooped out the shell of a tortoise, converting it into a lyre which he gave, under duress, to his brother Apollo. Hermes, who later in the *Trilogy* becomes associated with alchemy, reminds us of the transformative power that creates art out of natural objects and that caused the shell to become an important dream symbol for Wordsworth, who hears through it

A loud prophetic blast of harmony;
An Ode, in passion uttered, which foretold
Destruction to the children of the earth
By deluge, now at hand.
(*The Prelude*, 5, 95–98)

Created within the watery world that threatens to overwhelm all of civilization, Wordsworth's shell warns of a return to the beginning in a flood that will cleanse and baptize the earth. H. D.'s shell also forecasts apocalypse; however, she characteristically emphasizes not the onrushing deluge but the paradoxical powerlessness of the infinite waves which cannot break the closed-in "egg in egg-shell."

The self-enclosed, nonreferential completeness of pearl and shell recalls H. D.'s own earlier imagistic poems, but the limits of imagism are what emerge most emphatically since the mollusk can only combat the hostile powers of the sea by snapping shut "shell-jaws." As Gaston Bachelard so brilliantly puts it, while "the animal in its box is sure of its secrets, it has become a monster of impenetrable physiognomy." H. D. has spoken of the power of her verse to "snap-shut neatly," and the analogy implies that these tidy, enclosed poems may be unable to communicate or unwilling even to admit a content. Imprisoned within what amounts to a beautiful but inescapable tomb of form, the mollusk will not be cracked open or digested, but instead remains "small, static, limited," just as H. D.'s early poems refuse any interaction with the external world when they reproduce images that seem shaped by a poet rigidly and self-consciously in control of herself and her material. Far from representing the ultimate statement of her poetics, the seashell poem is a very limited statement, altered and superseded by transformations of this image as the *Trilogy* progresses.

While H. D. discusses her craft in terms of the crafts*man* mollusk, clearly she was drawn to the shell and pearl because of their feminine evocations. Associated iconographically with Venus and the Virgin, the shell is also said to represent the female genitals. It may represent pregnancy, since the pearl is a kind of seed in the womb of the shellfish, or a hope of rebirth, as in the traditionally termed "resurrection shells." This association is supported by the mythic story that Hermes created the lyre from the shell on the very day of his birth, as well as the occasional identification of the seashell with the eggshell. H. D. was careful to elaborate on these aspects of her initial self-portrait in succeeding images of female artistry. But as the poet progresses in her identificaton with overtly feminine forms of creation, shells become associated with "beautiful yet static, empty // old thought, old convention" (*WDNF* 17) as she draws her old self around after her like a "dead shell" (*WDNF* 14). She wants not a shell into which she can withdraw but, on the contrary, an escape from entrapment: "my heart-shell // breaks open" (*WDNF* 25), she proclaims ecstatically when a grain, instead of a pearl, falls into the "urn" of her heart so that "the heart's alabaster / is broken" (*WDNF* 29). The locked-in image of female sexuality and creativity provided by male culture, complete with its emphasis on purity and impenetrability, is finally a "jar too circumscribed" (*WDNF* 31), and the poet renounces "fixed indigestible matter / such as shell, pearl, imagery // done to death" (*WDNF* 32) in her attempt to forge more liberating and nourishing images of survival.

In her next attempt to recover the scepter of power that is Caduceus, H. D. wittily decides not to become the rod itself, which is transformed into an innocent blade of grass, but the snake/worm which travels up the rod in a circuitous spiral toward heaven. Small, parasitic, and persistent, the worm can literally eat its way out of every calamity and sustain life even in the overwhelmingly large world that is its home. Although people cry out in disgust at the worm, it is "unrepentant" as it spins its "shroud," sure in its knowledge of "how the Lord God / is about to manifest" (*WDNF* 6). The enclosing shroud of the worm is a shell that testifies to its divinity since it adumbrates regeneration: the winged headdress, we are told, is a sign in both the snake and the emerging butterfly of magical powers of transformation, specifically of the mystery of death and rebirth experienced by all those who have endured the worm cycle to be raised into a new, higher form. Wrapped in the "shroud" of her own self (*WDNF* 13), the poet feels that she is a part of a poetic race who "know each other / by secret symbols" (*WDNF* 13) of their twice-born experience. Crawling up an "individual grass-blade / toward our individual star" (*WDNF* 14), these survivors are "the keepers of the secret / the carriers, the spinners // of the rare intangible thread / that binds all humanity // to ancient wisdom, / to antiquity" (*WDNF* 15).

It is significant that Denise Levertov centers her discussion of H. D.'s poetry on this sequence of worm poems, voicing her appreciation for poetry which provides "doors, ways in, tunnels through." When Levertov explains that H. D. "showed us a way to penetrate mystery . . . *to enter into* darkness, mystery, so that it is experienced," by darkness she means "not evil but the other side, the Hiddenness before which *man must shed his arrogance*" [italics mine]. In Levertov's poetry, woman is described as "a shadow / . . . drawn out / on a thread of wonder," and this "thread of wonder" links woman to "the worm artist," who tills the soil and thereby pays homage to "earth, aerates / the ground of his living." Levertov makes explicit the relationship between woman and worm artist when she describes one of the "signs" under which she has been living and writing— a "Minoan Snake Goddess" who muses as she stands between two worlds, a symbol of female wisdom and regeneration.

Of course, women from the Fates to Madame Defarge have traditionally been associated with the spinning of fate, the weaving of webs, the ensnaring of men with serpentine allies or embodiments. But H. D. and Levertov reinvent the Lamia-Eve, testimony to modern defilement of Isis, in the innocuous form of the lowly worm who recalls the speaker of Psalm 22: after crying out, "I am a worm and no man; a reproach of men, and despised of the people," the petitioner in the Psalm asks that the God "who took me out of the womb" provide a loving substitute for that loss. Both H. D. and Levertov emphasize the ways in which the worm, like the woman, has been despised by a culture that cannot stop to appreciate an artistry based not on elucidation or appropriation but on homage and wonder at the hidden darkness, the mystery. Both emphasize the worm's ability to provide another womb for its own death and resurrection. With visionary realism, both insist that the only paradise worth seeing exists not behind or beyond but within the dust. While "the keepers of the secret, / the carriers, the spinners" of such "Earth Psalms" are surely men as well as women, they are all associated with traditionally female arts of weaving, with uniquely female powers of reproducing life, and with a pre-Christian tradition that embraces gods (like Ra, Osiris, Amen) who are "not at all like Jehovah" (*WDNF* 16).

The "other side, the Hiddenness" which H. D. and Levertov seek to penetrate consists precisely of those experiences unique to women which have been denied a place in our publicly acknowledged culture, specifically the experiences of female sexuality and motherhood. Told that they embody mystery to men, even if they are indifferent to their bodies' miraculous ability to hide, foster, and emit another life, women may very well experience their own concealed sex organs as curiously mysterious, separate from their consciousness. Furthermore, the abrupt and total biological shifts that distinguish female growth from the more continuous development of men is surely one reason why the worm cycle has always fascinated women. In describing the fears of growing girls, Simone de Beauvoir says, "I have known little girls whom the sight of a chrysalis plunged into a frightened reverie."

Confronting approving images of women that are equally degrading because they trivialize, Emily Dickinson redefines the ornamental butterfly by describing its potential for flight. She experiences confinement as her "Cocoon tightens," realizing that "A dim capacity for Wings / Demeans the Dress" she wears. We see the same conflict portrayed in Judy Chicago's recent portraits of creative women in which what she calls the "butterfly-vagina" struggles in its desire for "easy sweeps of Sky" against the enclosing geometrical boxes and scripts that attempt to contain it in the center of the canvas. Dickinson articulates this sense of contradiction:

> So I must baffle at the Hint
> And cipher at the Sign
> And make much blunder, if at last
> I take the clue divine.

The need for self-transformation creates a dilemma for Dickinson not dissimilar to H. D.'s confusion when she feels ready "to begin a new spiral" (*WDNF* 21) but finds herself thrown back on outworn vocabularies and the terrible feeling that she has failed to achieve metamorphosis. Like Dickinson, who "must baffle at the Hint," H. D. blunders over an "indecipherable palimpsest" (*WDNF* 31) which she cannot read. Floundering, "lost in sea-depth / . . . where Fish / move two-ways" (*WDNF* 30), overwhelmed by confusion at her own "pitiful reticence, // boasting, intrusion of strained

/ inappropriate allusion" (*WDNF* 31), H. D. admits the failure of her own invocations.

Perhaps she has failed because she has tried to evoke Ra, Osiris, Amen, Christ, God, All-father and the Holy Ghost, all the while knowing that she is an "initiate of the secret wisdom, / bride of the kingdom" (*WDNF* 31). The "illusion of lost-gods, daemons" has brought, instead of revelation, the "reversion of old values" (*WDNF* 31) which inhibits, denying as it does the validity of her female perspective. Specifically, she recalls now that the spinners who keep the secret that links humanity to the ancient wisdom are aspects of the female goddess, Isis. She must remain true to her own perspective—"the angle of incidence / equals the angle of reflection" (*WDNF* 32)—and to her own needs and hungers, so she now entreats a new energy: "Hest, // Aset, Isis, the great enchantress, / in her attribute to Serqet, // the original great-mother, / who drove // harnessed scorpions / before her" (*WDNF* 34).

Seeking the "one-truth," to become as wise as "scorpions, *as serpents*" (*WDNF* 35), H. D. can now read her own personal psychic map to find the external realities. Specifically, she can now reevaluate "our secret hoard" (*WDNF* 36). The stars toward which the worm moves in its slow spiral toward the sky are also "little jars . . . boxes, very precious to hold further // unguent, myrrh, incense" (*WDNF* 24). They contain a promise of revelation not very different from shells and cocoons, which can also disclose secret treasures. Modern words, too, may reveal hidden meanings, thereby relinquishing their alien impenetrability, if the poet can somehow perceive their coded, palimpsestic statis. Fairly early in the *Trilogy*, H. D. manages to take some small comfort in the bitter joke wrapped in the pun *"cartouche"*: for her contemporaries, it might mean a gun cartridge with a paper case, but she knows that it once signified the oblong figure in an Egyptian monument enclosing a sovereign's name (*WDNF* 9). This kind of irony offers potential consolation when the poet realizes that it might still be possible to disentangle ancient meanings from corrupt forms, for instance the "Christos-image . . . from its art-craft junk-shop / paint-and-plaster medieval jumble // of pain-worship and death-symbol" (*WDNF* 18). Finally the poet knows and feels

> the meaning that words hide;
>
> they are anagrams, cryptograms,
> little boxes, conditioned
>
> *to hatch butterflies . . .*
> (*WDNF* 39; italics mine).

H. D. learns how to decipher what that other H. D.—Humpty Dumpty—called "portmanteaus," words which open up like a bag or a book into compartments. By means of lexical reconstruction, she begins to see the possibility of purging language of its destructive associations and arbitrariness. Viewing each word as a puzzle ready to be solved and thereby freed not only of modernity but also of contingency, H. D. begins to hope that she can discover secret, coded messages. Surely these must be subversive to warrant their being so cunningly concealed by her culture.

Now *The Walls Do Not Fall* can end in a hymn to Osiris because the poet has managed to "recover the secret of Isis" (*WDNF* 40). Just as H. D. is sure that the destructive signs surrounding her can be redefined for her own renewal, in the ancient myth Isis gathers together the scattered fragments of her lost brother/husband's body and reconstructs him in a happier ending than that to be enacted by the King's men for Humpty Dumpty. The resurrection of Osiris and the reconstruction of the magical power of the Word testify to the healing, even vivifying powers of the poet-Isis who can now see the unity between Osiris and Sirius. Since Sirius is the star representing Isis come to wake her brother from death, such an equation means that the poet glimpses the shared identity of the sibling lovers Osiris and Isis. Approaching this "serious" mystery, H. D. asks, "O, Sire, is" this union between the god and the goddess finally possible (*WDNF* 42)? She can even connect "Osiris" with the "zrr-hiss" of war-lightning. The poet who uses words with reverence can release the coded messages contained or enfolded within them. She has found the "alchemist's key" which "unlocks secret doors" (*WDNF* 30). Although the walls still do not fall, continuing to testify to the divisions and barriers between people, between historical periods, within consciousness itself, they also preserve remnants of written messages—anagrams and cryptograms—which, by providing the link from the present back to the past, allow H. D. to evade the destructive definitions of reality provided by those who utilize the word for modern mastery.

The poet's response in the subsequent volumes of the *Trilogy* to the shattered fragmentation of her world is stated in the first poem of *Tribute to the Angels:* dedicating herself to Hermes Trismegistus, patron of alchemists, H. D. undertakes not merely the archeological reconstruction of a lost past, but also a magical transfiguration not unlike Christ's creation of the sustaining loaves and fishes or the transubstantiation of bread and water into body and blood. Since alchemical art has traditionally been associated with fiery purificaton that resurrects what is decomposing in the grave into a divine and golden form, even the destructive lightning and bombs can now be associated with melting that fuses a new unity, heat that transforms the contents of the dross in the alchemist's bowl into the philosopher's stone. The seashell of *The Walls Do Not Fall* becomes a testimony to such displacement, reappearing as a bowl which is cauldron, grave, and oven, yet another womb in which a new jewel can be created. Now the poet sees the function of the poem/bowl as the transformative redefinition of language itself. Thus she gives us the recipe by which she endows "a word most bitter, *marah*" and a word denigrated, "*Venus*," with more affirmative nurturing meanings: "marah" becomes "Mother" and "Venus" is translated from "venery" to "venerate" (*TA* 8, 12). Similarly, she seeks a way of evading names that definitely label the word-jewel in the bowl: "I do not want to name it," she explains, because "I want to minimize thought, // concentrate on it / till I shrink, // dematerialize / and am drawn into it" (*TA* 14). Seeking a noncoercive vocabulary, a new language that will consecrate what has been desecrated by her culture, H. D. tries to re-establish the primacy of what masculine culture has relegated to a secondary place as "feminine."

Implicitly heretical, Hermes' alchemy is associated with "candle and script and bell," with "what the new-church spat upon" (*TA* 1), and H. D. does not evade the challenge her own alchemical art constitutes to the prevailing Christian conception of the Word. On the contrary, in *Tribute to the Angels* she self-consciously sets her narrative in the context of the Book of Revelation, quoting directly from it in numerous poems in order to question John's version of redemption while offering her own revision. In many poems she seems to be arguing with John directly because his vision appears warped: H. D. quotes John's assertion of the finality of his own account, his admonition that *"if any man shall add // God shall add unto him the plagues,"* even as she determines to alter his story, dedicating herself to making all things new (*TA* 3). She realizes that "he of the seventy-times-seven / passionate, bitter wrongs" is also "he of the seventy-times-seven / bitter, unending wars" (*TA* 3), and she questions the severity and punishing cruelty of John's apocalypse, with its vengeful version of the hidden future. While John sings the praises of seven angels whose seven golden bowls pour out the wrath of God upon the earth, H. D. claims that "my eyes saw" a sign of resurrection: "a half-burnt-out apple-tree / blossoming" (*TA* 23) is the fulfillment of her hopes at the beginning of the *Trilogy* to recover the scepter, the lily-bud rod of Caduceus, which is now associated with the Tree of Life that links heaven and earth, the Cosmic Tree which represents the mysterious but perpetual regeneration of the natural world, the tree that miraculously lodges the coffin of the dead Osiris or the tree on which Christ was hung to be reborn. Aaron's rod which made the bitter (marah) waters sweet when it blossomed in the desert for the wandering children of Israel is converted from a sign of Moses' control to an emblem of a Lady's presence.

Most significantly, H. D. contrasts the final vision of the holy Jerusalem—a city with no need of the sun or the moon because lit by the glory of God, a city which John imagines as the bride of the Lamb—with her own final revelation of redemption. H. D. first describes a Lady in a bedroom lit by the "luminous disc" of the clock by her bedhead, ironically commenting that this room has "no need / of the moon to shine in it" (*TA* 25). But this appearance is only a dream adumbration of the vision of this same Lady who appears when H. D. is "thinking of Gabriel / of the moon-cycle, of the moon-shell, // of the moon-crescent / and the moon at full" (*TA* 28). Far from seeking a place with no need of moonshine, H. D. celebrates a Lady who is actually the representative of lunar time and consciousness. Furthermore, the poet is careful to remind us through a whole series of negatives that this Lady, whom we recognize from the various portraits of the female as she has been worshipped by various cultures, is like none of these previous representatives or incarnations. "None of these / suggest her" as the poet sees her (*TA* 31). H. D.'s vision of the Lady is not hieratic or frozen: "she is no symbolic figure." While she has "the dove's symbolic purity," and "veils / like the Lamb's Bride," H. D. is insistent that "the Lamb was not with her / either as Bridegroom or Child"; not He, but *"we* are her bridegroom and lamb" (*TA* 39; italics mine).

The miraculous transformation in the alchemical bowl and the equally mysterious flowering of the rod find their culmination in this revelation of the muse who is not only the veiled goddess, Persephone, the *Sanctus Spiritus, Santa Sophia,* Venus, Isis, and Mary, but most importantly the female spirit liberated from precisely these mystifications:

> but she is not shut up in a cave
> like a Sibyl; she is not
>
> imprisoned in leaden bars
> in a coloured window;
>
> she is Psyche, *the butterfly,*
> *out of the cocoon.*
>   (*TA* 38; italics mine)

Unnamed and elusive, the Lady recalls in her flight the hatched and winged words of H. D. herself, if only because this visionary Lady carries a book which "is our book" (*TA* 39). Whether this "tome of the ancient wisdom" whose pages "are the blank pages / of the unwritten volume of the new" (*TA* 38) is "a tribute to the Angels" (*TA* 41) or a "tale of a jar or jars" (*TA* 39) that will constitute the next volume of the *Trilogy*, H. D. closely identifies this new Eve who has come to retrieve what was lost at the apple tree with her own liberating revisions of the past. Whatever volume of the poem she may carry or inspire, the Lady reflects H. D.'s hope that her narrative is a "Book of life" (*TA* 36).

As she evokes and thereby reinterprets the inherited signs of her culture which are said to contain the secret wisdom necessary for the attainment of paradise, H. D. implies that "the letter killeth but the spirit giveth life" (2 Corinthians 3:6). It is life that she sees finally created in the crucible "when the jewel / melts" and what we find is "a cluster of garden-pinks / or a face like a Christmas-rose" (*TA* 43). In the final book of the *Trilogy*, the escaping fragrance of such flowering within the pristine glass of a jar represents the poet's success in finding a form that can contain without confining. No longer surrounded by splintered shards, H. D. makes of her jars symbols of aesthetic shape not unlike those of Wallace Stevens or Hart Crane, beautiful and complete objects but also transparencies through which a healing content is made manifest. Purified of their opacity, shell, bowl, and box are now ready to reveal their previously secret and therefore inaccessible hoard. This promise of release is realized fully in *The Flowering of the Rod:* dedicated to the Lady who has escaped conventionally defined categories, the poet readies herself for flight as she asks us to "leave the smouldering cities below" (*FR* 1), the place of deathly skulls, to follow the quest of Christ, who was "the first to wing / from that sad Tree" (*FR* 11) and whose journey is similar to that of the snow-geese circling the Arctic or the mythical migratory flocks seeking paradise.

Not only does H. D. move further back in time in this third volume of the *Trilogy,* but her initial focus on seemingly insignificant animals and her subsequent naming of angelic powers seem to have made it possible for her to finally create human characters as she retells the story of the birth and death of Christ from the unexpected perspective of two participants in the gospel—Kaspar the Magian and Mary Magdala. Furthermore, after two sequences of poems progressing by allusive associations, complex networks of imagery, and repetitive, almost liturgical invocations, the final book of the *Trilogy* embodies the emergence of the poet's sustained voice in a story—if not of her own making—of her own perspective. She takes an unusual stance toward the ancient story to distinguish her vision: claiming to see "what men say is-not," to remember what men have forgot (*FR* 6), she sets out to testify to an event known by everyone but as yet unrecorded (*FR* 12).

Like Christ, who was himself "an outcast and a vagabond" (*FR* 11), and like the poet who is identified with the thief crucified by His side, both Kaspar and Mary are aliens in their society. The inheritor of ancient alchemical tradition, Kaspar owns the jars which hold "priceless, unobtainable-elsewhere / myrrh" (*FR* 13), a "distillation" which some said "lasted literally forever," the product of "sacred processes" which were "never written, not even in symbols" (*FR* 14). As a heathen, he represents prebiblical lore that acknowledges the power of "daemons" termed "devils" by the modern Christian world. His education, however, is a patrimony in an exclusively male tradition that assumes "no secret was safe with a woman" (*FR* 14). Kaspar is shown to be a bit of a prig and something of a misogynist, so it is highly incongruous that Mary Magdala comes to this Arab stranger in his "little booth of a house" (*FR* 13) behind the market. Unmaidenly and unpredictable, Mary is as much of an outcast as Kaspar, if only because of her ability "to detach herself," a strength responsible for her persistence in spite of Kaspar's statement that the myrrh is not for sale: "planted" before him (*FR* 15), Mary identifies herself first as "Mary, a great tower," and then explains that, though she is "Mara, bitter," through her own power she will be "Mary-myrrh" (*FR* 16). Clearly, the coming together of Kaspar and Mary implies the healing of the poet's own sense of fragmentation. Before the jar actually changes hands, however, H. D. dramatizes the discomfort of Simon, who views Mary at the Last Supper as a destructive siren. This "woman from the city" who seems "devil-ridden" to the Christian is recognized by Kaspar as a living embodiment of the indwelling daemons of "Isis, Astarte, Cyprus / and the other four; // he might re-name them, / Ge-meter, De-meter, earth-mother // or Venus / in a star" (*FR* 25).

Only after we have recognized the seemingly antithetical wise man and the whore as common representatives of reverence for the ancient principles of female fertility and creativity does H. D. return to the scene in the booth behind the market to fully describe the vision granted to Kaspar through the intervention of Mary. Here, at the climax of the *Trilogy*, Kaspar recalls the poet's experience with the Lady, for he is graced with a remembrance of "when he saw the light on her hair / like moonlight on a lost river" (*FR* 27). In a fleck or a flaw of a jewel on the head of one of three crowned ladies, Kaspar discovers "the whole secret of the mystery" (*FR* 30). He sees the circles of islands and the lost center island, Atlantis; he sees earth before Adam, Paradise before Eve. Finally, he hears a spell in an unknown langauge which seems to come down from prehistorical times as it translates itself to him:

> *Lilith born before Eve*
> *and one born before Lilith,*
> *and Eve; we three are forgiven,*
> *we are three of the seven*
> *daemons cast out of her.*
>   (*FR* 33)

This is an extremely enigmatic message, but it does seem to imply that a matriarchal genealogy had been erased from recorded history when this ancient female trinity was exorcized as evil, cast out of human consciousness by those who would begin in the Garden with Eve. Since Lilith is a woman who dared pronounce the Ineffable Name and who was unabashed at articulating her sexual preferences, her presence among the crowned or crucified queens seems to promise a prelapsarian vision quite different from that of Genesis: Lilith, Eve, and the unnamed daemon are three of the seven who establish a link back to Kaspar's pagan daemons; together they promise a submerged but now recoverable time of female strength, female speech, and female sexuality, all of which have mysteriously managed to survive, although in radically subdued ways, incarnate in the body of Mary Magdala. As a healer, a shaman of sorts, Kaspar has in a sense recaptured Mary's stolen soul, her lost ancestors; he has established the matriarchal genealogy that confers divinity upon her.

Reading Mary like a palimpsest, Kaspar has fully penetrated the secret of the mystery. H. D. then reverses the chronology of his life, moving backward from his confrontation with this Mary over the jars of myrrh to his delivery of the gift of myrrh to the Virgin Mary. When Kaspar thinks in the ox stall that "there were always two jars" (*FR* 41) and that *"someday*

[he] *will bring the other"* (FR 42), we know that his prophecy has been or will be fulfilled: as he gives the myrrh to the Virgin, we know that he is destined to give the other jar to Mary Magdala, thereby authenticating his vision of the female trinity—his knowledge that the whore is the mother and that Isis, who has been labeled a retrogressive harlot, is actually the regenerative goddess of life. Through the two Marys, Kaspar recovers the aspects of Isis retained by Christianity—the lady of sorrows weeping for the dead Osiris and the divine mother nursing her son, Horus. When marah is shown to be mother the translation is complete, and the poem can end with a new word, as the gift is miraculously appreciated by a Mary who might know that the blossoming, flowering fragrance is the commingling of the magical contents of the jar, the myrrh in her arms, and even perhaps the baby in her lap.

Dramatically ending at the beginning, moving from Apocalypse to Genesis, from death to birth, from history to mystery, H. D. illustrates the cyclical renewal she personally seeks of dying into life. Calling our attention to her own narrative principles, H. D. proclaims: "I have gone forward. / I have gone backward" (FR 8). And as we have seen, her point is precisely the need of going backward in time to recover what has been lost in the past, for this justifies her own progress backward in chronological time throughout the *Trilogy:* proceeding from the modern times of London in *The Walls Do Not Fall* to the medieval cities of *Tribute to the Angels* and back to the ancient deserts of Israel in *The Flowering of the Rod*, she dedicates herself to finding the half-erased traces of a time "When in the company of the gods / I loved and was loved" (WDNF 5). Such a discovery, as we have seen, involves not a learning but a remembering. However, instead of moving backward in a linear, sequential manner, she chooses three time bands that seem to be relatively self-contained, like ever-narrowing circles enclosing some still point of origin. Furthermore, she calls our attention to the disconnectedness of her three time spheres by isolating each within a book of the *Trilogy*. These three distinct periods in time, when taken in themselves, are senseless and directionless, each repeating the other:

> you think, even before it is half-over,
> that your cycle is at an end,
>
> but you repeat your foolish circling—again, again, again;
> again, the steel sharpened on the stone;
>
> again, the pyramid of skulls.
>
> (FR 6)

The senseless wheeling within each of these foolish cycles, caused by the lack of vision that cannot see "then" as an aspect of "now," is fittingly experienced as a tornado (WDNF 32). It can produce only war.

On the other hand, each moment of time in each of these historical cycles is, at least potentially, related to a prehistoric origin, just as all points on the circumference of a circle are related to its center. The poet who understands the palimpsestic symbols of the past in today's imagery can interrupt the "mysterious enigma" that merges "the distant future / with most distant antiquity" (*WDNF* 20). Similarly, seeing down the "deep, deep-well // of th so-far unknown / depth of pre-history," Kaspar realizes "*a point* in time— // he called it a fleck or a flaw in a gem" on a circlet of gems on a lady's head (*FR* 40). Since historical time is envisioned as a series of circles enclosing a prehistoric center, H. D. can describe how Kaspar heard "an echo of an echo in a shell" (*FR* 28), a language he had never heard spoken and which seems translated "as it transmuted its message // through spiral upon spiral of the shell / of memory that yet connects us // with the drowned cities of pre-history" (*FR* 33).

That Kaspar hears "an echo of an echo in a shell" recalls not only the importance of the seashell earlier in the *Trilogy*, but also the fascination of Madge in *The Hedgehog* with Echo, who always answers her caller "Echo":

> Or sometimes just O, O, O, just the same O, getting thin and far
> and far and thin like the sound of water. Echo melts into the hill,
> into the water. Now she is a real person. . . . Echo is the answer
> of our own hearts, like the singing in a sea-shell.

What tantalizes Madge about Echo's response, just as it informed her curiosity about *hérisson*, is the recalcitrance of the word, its refusal to yield up meaning, its emptiness of signification, as well as its ambiguous status as silent sound, the voice of nature, a living remnant of ancient Greece, an aspect of her own voice returned from a far distance, a female utterance of completion and circularity. In *Tribute to Freud*, H. D. returns to the image of the echoing shell when she describes how her unspoken expressions of gratitude go on singing

> like an echo of an echo in a shell—very far away yet very near—
> the very shell substance of my outer ear and the curled involuted
> or convoluted shell skull, and inside the skull, the curled, intricate,
> hermit-like mollusk, the brainmatter itself.

Clearly the spiraling echoes of the shell are a way of recogizing the intimate yet convoluted relationship between a central origin and its distant reaches. Hearing "the echoed syllables of this spell" (*FR* 33), Kaspar remains unsure about the status of his revelation: is it "a sort of spiritual optical-illusion" (*FR* 40)—the answer of his own heart? Or could the echoing shell also contain the secret revealed in *Hermetic Definition*—a sound like that of water, "*Grande Mer*" or "*Mère*"?

Echo, we should remember, was punished for her only "failing," her fondness for talk, by being deprived of the power of speaking first. In this respect, she serves as a paradigm of the secondary status of women who have traditionally been reduced to supporting, assuaging, serving, and thereby echoing the work, wishes, and words of men. Specifically, she serves as a model for H. D.'s sense of her own belatedness as she repeats the warped words she experiences as prior authorities on her own spiritual and psychic experiences. Echo does manage, however, to express her desires, even as she mocks the speech of those she mimics. Like Echo, H. D. felt cursed because she was denied control over her own speech, destined to repeat the language of another's making, and therefore hidden, if not obliterated, from her own creations. However, just as Echo manages to express her desires, even making sexual advances by dropping certain words and altering her inflection, H. D. manages to get her secrets sung, making of her echoes a personal response to the literary and linguistic conventions she inherits. Moreover, as a symbol of retreat from the danger of meaning into protective obscurity, the echoing shell is an understandably attractive image for H. D., who can define her art as "merely" derivative. Using the langauge of another's creation is, after all, a foolproof defense against being defined by one's verse and thereby confined within the prisonhouse of language. H. D.'s story is always "different yet the same as before" (*TA* 39), and therefore "only" a repetition. Herein lies both the strength and the weakness of her art, as well as the reason why the echo is yet another infinity decipherable (and therefore indecipherable) palimpsest.

Whether derivative or transmuted sound, however, the spiraling echo of the shell makes all of the enclosures of the first two poems comprehensible as metamorphoses of the circle. The shell with its spherical pearl, the bowl containing the gold, the boxes hatching butterflies, even the jars are circles surrounding a magical potent center. In an evocation of the spiraling turns of the worm approaching its star, the migratory geese of *The Flowering of the Rod* seek paradise by circling "till they drop from the highest point of the spiral / or fall from the innermost center of the ever- / narrowing circle" (*FR* 5). Their drowning would be a welcome end for the poet, who feels now that "only love is holy and love's ecstasy // that turns and turns and turns about one centre, / reckless, regardless, blind to reality" (*FR* 6). The islands encircled by water, especially the lost center of Atlantis, become a fitting symbol of the time of prehistoric eternity. The poet seeks this center because it can serve as an escape from the repetitions of history and because it is an entrance to creative stasis. Such a center is neither temporally nor spatially bound: its potential for unfolding gains it extension in space as it detemporalizes the present into an emblem of both the past and the future.

Finally we see the circumference as a flower which, contained in the grain or seed,

> opened petal by petal, a circle,
> and each petal was separate
>
> yet still held, as it were,
> by some force of attraction

to its dynamic centre;
and the circle went on widening

and would go on opening
. . . to infinity.

(*FR* 31)

Participating in a mystical literary tradition that extends from Dante to Roethke, H. D. evokes the unbroken, unfolding circle to satisfy her longing to "equilibrate" (*FR* 5) the antagonisms between desert and arctic, spring and winter, silence and sound, to heal the struggle between father and mother, thereby establishing a harmony dramatized by the recognition of commonality between Kaspar and Mary Magdala and by the image of the androgynous center of the flower. Seeking to be drawn into the center, H. D. finds in resurrection "a sense of direction" taking her "straight to the horde and plunder, / the treasure, the store-room, // the honeycomb" to "food, shelter, fragrance" (*FR* 7). While H. D. never denies the place of men in such an origin, she does end the *Trilogy* with an emphasis on the feminine that extends Kaspar's consciousness of prelapsarian time as a time of woman worship: she celebrates the baby or myrrh cradled in the arms of a woman whose sex is represented as a circle on a stem ♀—the sacred *ankh* which is the symbol of life in Egypt. The medieval definition of God as the sphere whose center is everywhere and whose circumference is nowhere has been radically feminized by a writer who sees the outstretched wings of the butterfly or the beauty of the "lunar rainbow" (*WDNF* 32) as alternative examples of the "arc of perfection" (*TA* 43). Here again H. D. serves as a paradigm for other women writers, such as Marge Piercy, whose sequences of poems entitled "The Spring Offensive of the Snail" celebrates encircling, blossoming lovers; Monique Wittig, who makes the circle an emblem of her Amazon utopia; Margaret Atwood, who focuses on circularity in her revision of the myth of Circe's island; and Adrienne Rich, who circles around the wreck with a book of outworn myths.

H. D. would not and does not deprive the center of its inaccessible mystery or the circumference of its distance from origin. On the contrary, as one of Jung's precursors, she testifies to the continued need for approaching the center, for retelling and rewriting and adding to a palimpsest even as she realizes that such an approach is a regression, and that—as the word "re-cover" implies—she hides what she seeks to reveal. Denise Levertov celebrates just this reverence for the unknowable in H. D.'s poetry when she explains that H. D. went "further, further out of the circle of known light, further in toward an unknown center." This center is the secret; for example, the final transaction between Kaspar and Mary Magdala which is never represented in the *Trilogy* or even adequately explained. If in some ways Kaspar the Magian was right that "no secret was safe with a woman" (*FR* 14), he nevertheless failed to realize that the woman who models her speech on that of Echo or Sibyl, or (less hopefully) Cassandra or Philomel, would be telling a secret that retains the power of its hidden mystery. Singing a spell which conforms to none of the words she had ever heard spoken, H. D. reveals the ways in which one woman mythologizes herself and her gender, asserting herself as the center of the universe in a radical reversal and revision of the inherited images she so brilliantly echoes.

John Ransom's Poetry

Randall Jarrell

The subject matter of Ransom's poetry is beautifully varied: the poems are about everything from Armageddon to a dead hen. All their subjects are linked, on the surface, by Ransom's persistent attitude, tone, and rhetoric; at bottom they are joined, passively, by being parts of one world—joined, actively, by fighting on one side or the other in the war that is going on in that world. On one side are Church and State, Authority, the Business World, the Practical World, men of action, men of affairs, generals and moralists and applied mathematicians and philosophers you set your watch by—efficient followers of abstraction and ideals, men who have learned that when you know how to use something you know it. There is a good deal of rather mocking but quite ungrudging credit—if little fondness— given to this side of things, the motor or effector system which, after all, does run the world along its "metalled ways" of appetency (our version of Tennyson's "ringing grooves of change"). But Ransom's affection goes out to that other army, defeated every day and victorious every night, of so-lightly-armed, so-easily-vanquished skirmishers, in their rags and tags and trailing clouds, who run around and around the iron hoplites pelting them with gravel and rosemary, getting killed miserably, and—half the time, in the pure pleasure or pain of being—forgetting even that they are fighting, and wandering off into the flowers at the edge of the terrible field. Here are the "vessels fit for storm and sport," not yet converted into "miserly merchant hulls"—the grandfather dancing with his fierce grandsons, in warpaint and feathers, round a bonfire in the back yard, having "performed ignominies unreckoned / Between the first brief childhood and the second," but now "more honorable . . . in danger and in joy." In these ranks are children and the old, women—innocent girls or terrible beauties

From *Poetry and the Age.* © 1953 by Randall Jarrell. Knopf, 1953.

or protecting housewives, all above or below or at the side of the Real World—lovers, dreams, nature, animals, tradition, nursery rhymes, fairy tales, everything that is at first or at last "content to feel / What others understand." Sometimes the poems are—as Empson might say—a queer mixture of pastoral and childcult. Although the shepherds are aging and the children dead, half of them, and the fox-hunters not making much headway against the overweening Platonism of the International Business Machine Company, it is all magical: disenchantment and enchantment are so prettily and inextricably mingled that we accept everything with sad pleasure, and smile at the poems' foreknowing, foredefeated, mocking, half-acceptant pain. For in the country of the poems wisdom is a poor butterfly dreaming that it is Chuang-tze, and not an optimistic bird of prey; and the greatest single subject of the romantics, pure potentiality, is treated with a classical grace and composure.

The most important thing to notice about this treatment, the rhetorical machinery of the poems, is that it is not a method of forcing intensity, of creating a factitious or at least arbitrary excitement, as most modern rhetoric is. Instead of listening through the hands, with closed eyes, as one is sucked deeper and deeper into the maelstrom, one listens with one's eyes open and one's head working about as well as it usually works. Most writers become over-rhetorical when they are insisting on more emotion than they actually feel or need to feel; Ransom is just the opposite. He is perpetually insisting, by his detached, mock-pedantic, wittily complicated tone, that he is not feeling much at all, not half so much as he really should be feeling—and this rhetoric becomes over-mannered, too-protective, when there is not much emotion for him to pretend not to be feeling, and he keeps on out of habit. Ransom developed this rhetorical machinery—tone, phrasing, properties, and all the rest—primarily as a way of handling sentiment or emotion without ever seeming sentimental or over-emotional; as a way of keeping the poem at the proper aesthetic distance from its subject; and as a way for the poem to extract from its subject, no matter how unpleasant or embarrassing, an unembarrassed pleasure. He was writing in an age in which the most natural feeling of tenderness, happiness, or sorrow was likely to be called sentimental; consequently he needed a self-protective rhetoric as the most brutal or violent of poets did not—such a poet, on being told that some poem of his was a delirium of pointless violence, had only to reply, with a satisfied smile, "Yes, isn't it?" One can say, *very* crudely, that Ransom's poems are produced by the classical, or at worst semi-classical, treatment of romantic subjects. Both the subjects and the treatment of the poems are Impractical, so far as Ransom's war of the worlds (of Feeling and of Power) is concerned; but the Latinity, mixed generality and peculiarity, and mocking precision of the vocabulary, the sharp intelligence of the tone, are always acknowledging or insisting that we can live only by trading with the enemy—that the heart has its reasons, a mighty poor grade of them, too—that the poet himself is an existence away from the Innocent Doves he mourns for.

I suppose that the quality of Ransom's rhetoric—so different from Laforgue's and Corbière's in form, though fairly similar in some of its functions—was suggested by his profession, by Oxford, by the lingering rhetoric of the South, by the tradition of rhetoric in the ministry, and by his own quite classical education and interests. And I imagine that he had before his eyes, as haunting, more-than-embarrassing examples of the direct treatment of sentimental subjects, some of his own early poems. But by the thirties—as you can see from "Prelude to an Evening," in which most of his rhetoric has disappeared—he could afford an exact, grave directness.

Ransom seems in his poems, as most modern poets do not, sympathetic and charming, full of tenderness and affection, wanting the light and sorry for the dark—moral and condemning only when he has to be, not because he wants to be; loving neither the sterner vices nor the sterner virtues. He has the personal seriousness that treats the world as it seems to him, not the solemnity that treats the really important things, the world as everybody knows it is. His poems are full of an affection that cannot help itself, for an innocence that cannot help itself—for the stupid travelers lost in the maze of the world, for the clever travelers lost in the maze of the world. The poems are not a public argument but personal knowledge, personal feeling; and their virtues are the "merely" private virtues—their characters rarely vote, rarely even kill one another, but often fall in love.

The poems have none of that traumatic passion for Authority, any Authority at all, that is one of the most unpleasant things in our particular time and our particular culture. To tell the truth, the poems are out of place in this most Pharisaical of ages: a time that wanted its artists ruins among its ruins, or else signposts pointing from them to some Heavenly or Earthly City as different as possible from everything, everything; a time that damned Gentile and Jew alike for lacking—of all possible things!—the proper relationship to, or appreciation of, Evil; a time that told each random smile that a smile is nothing but repressed hostility, or sexual sublimation, or ignorance, or evasion, or an escape, or Original Sin, or bourgeois complacency, or a hundred other things each worse than the last; a time that had learned, as no other ever had, that it was a time different from all other times, a last age different from all the ages. It tried, with little success, to forgive the poems for having made a small garden, and not a large crater—for having saved no one by joining a Party or attacking a Party, by exposing the shallowness and corruption of our middle-class culture, by maintaining a paradoxical and ecstatic relationship with God, or by doing anything else that one would expect a poem to do. Instead the poems told stories. Stories!

The attitude of the poems is quiet and complicated; it neither satisfied the expectations nor spoke for the causes of any large body of readers. Any of the poems could have been called, "With Mixed Feelings"; and the feelings of most of their readers may have been mixed-up, but they certainly weren't mixed. The poems were so transparently dialetical that no one called them that: they set out both struggling sides of things, saw both as cater-cornered, corrugated, kaleidoscopic mixtures—all their steady states, even, were hardened and habitual struggles of opposites. (Look at "Painted Head," "The Equilibrists," "Spectral Lovers," "Here Lies a Lady," and many other poems, where all this is plain.) Once I took a little girl to a Tarzan movie; and as each new actor, each new cannibal, each new leopard and monkey and crocodile came on the scene, she would whisper to me desperately: "Is that a *good* one? Is that a *bad* one?" This great root-notion, this imperative at the bottom of our beings, is ill satisfied by Ransom's poems, anomalous things that keep whispering to us, "Both"—that keep whispering to us, "Neither." Perhaps it is best to call them, as Winters does, an "ambiguous and unhappy connective" between the "Experimental Generation" and the "Reactionary Generation"; and certainly, to one so precariously assured of certain certainties as Winters, poems that speak of uncertainties with such ambiguous sureness must seem unhappy.

In Ransom's best poems every part is subordinated to the whole, and the whole is realized with astonishing exactness and thoroughness. Their economy, precision, and restraint give the poems, sometimes, an individual but impersonal perfection; and Ransom's feel for the exact convention of a particular poem, the exact demands of a particular situation, has resulted in poems different from each other and everything else, as unified, individualized, and unchangeable as nursery rhymes. Who could want or imagine anything different in "Here Lies a Lady," in "Captain Carpenter"? They have the composed and inexhaustible ambiguity of things. Some of Ransom's queer fabulous allegories are close, in form, to Kafka's. If you read "Captain Carpenter" (or *Metamorphosis*, for that matter) to a quite uncultivated audience, it will be delighted with what happens but puzzled about what it means—even "Here Lies a Lady," which seems to an ordinarily cultivated reader almost too immediate to be called allegory, is a puzzling joy to such hearers, since the identification between one's own life or lives in general and the "six little spaces of chill and six of burning," the automatic application of the conceit, occurs to them with difficulty. But Ransom's poetry is not "modernist" poetry at all, normally (notice the difference when it becomes so, in "Painted Head"); and it is remarkable how much narrative, dramatic, not-lyric, not-highbrow interest the best poems have.

Sometimes Ransom uses a version of that ironic-familiar treatment of the past that was so common in the twenties, but he uses it for freshness, sensation by shock, and not for "debunking." More often he does the exact opposite, and treats the present—or future or what has no time at all—in terms of a specific past:

> Till knowing his need extreme, and his heart pure,
> Christ let them dress him his thick chevelure,
> And soon his beard was glozed and sweetly scented.

And very often he is mocking, and pretends to discredit, by the extravagance or incongruity of his terms, precisely what he wishes us to realize that we do believe and cannot help believing.

It is interesting to compare one of Ransom's mock-medieval, carefully mannered poems inside a chosen convention, with one of those pieces of music, composed at the same time, which also were set inside some arbitrarily chosen convention out of the past. And this reminds one of Stravinsky's remark that Wagner "made an organ" of his orchestra—which could also mean, interpreted past reason, that in Wagner all the contradictions are synthesized in a sort of transcendental unity of intensity. In Ransom the contradictions are clear, exactly contradictory, not fused in arbitrary overall emotion; one admires the clear, sharp, Mozartian lightness of texture of the best poems. And occasionally their phrasing is magical— light as air, soft as dew, the real old-fashioned enchantment:

> Go and ask Robin to bring the girls over
> To Sweetwater, said my Aunt; and that was why
> It was like a dream of ladies sweeping by
> The willows, clouds, deep meadowgrass, and the river.
>
> Robin's sisters and my Aunt's lily daughter
> Laughed and talked, and tinkled light as wrens
> If there were a little colony all hens
> To go walking by the steep turn of Sweetwater.
>
> Let them alone, dear Aunt, just for one minute
> Till I go fishing in the dark of my mind:
> Where have I seen before, against the wind,
> These bright virgins, robed and bare of bonnet,
>
> Flowing with music of their strange quick tongue
> And adventuring with delicate paces by the stream,—
> Myself a child, old suddenly at the scream
> From one of the white throats which it hid among?

Not Nausicaa, not Pharaoh's daughter bending among the rushes, gazed with a purer astonishment.

It seems to me that Ransom's best poems are "Captain Carpenter," "Antique Harvesters," "Painted Head," "Here Lies a Lady," "Judith of Bethulia," "Janet Waking," "Prelude to an Evening," "Bells for John Whiteside's Daughter," "Dead Boy," "Tom Tom the Piper's Son," "Vision by Sweetwater," and "Old Mansion." Besides these, "The Equilibrists," "Necrological," and "Armageddon" are elaborately mannered but fairly successful poems of an odd kind; the new version of "Vaunting Oak" has kept all the charm of the old, and has got rid of most of its embarrassing pieces of mannerism and rhetoric; and "Piazza Piece" and "Lady Lost" are good examples of Ransom's microscopic success. (What beautiful *lieder* five or six of Ransom's poems would make!) And the last stanzas of "Puncture" and "Conrad in Twilight" are plainly Ransom at his best.

Only one of the poems I have mentioned—"Vision by Sweetwater"— is omitted from the *Selected Poems*. One can imagine Ransom's "Mighty slight, mighty slight" as he left it out, but this was a real mistake, the only important mistake in the book. Few poets have ever picked their best poems so surely, or disliked their weak or impossibly mannered poems so effectively: the whole *Selected Poems* is a little triumph of omission and revision, a piece of criticism that makes a great deal of the criticism one might otherwise write entirely unnecessary. (Why condemn a poem, or turn up one's nose at a phrase, that the poet has already omitted or replaced? This implicit criticism of his own poetry is superior to any of Ransom's overt criticism of other people's.) Perhaps "Her Eyes," "Survey of Literature," and "Dog" might have been replaced. "Survey of Literature" is a fairly popular poem, but it seems to me no more than a recipe, a few half-fleshed-out rhymes, and a moral. "Then there was poor Willie Blake / He foundered on sweet cake" is so queer a judgment, about a poet whose favorite word was *howl*, that one decides it is not a judgment but a rhyme. And "Dog" reminds one of what Goldsmith said about the way Johnson's little fishes would have talked—though here, of couse, they are parodying themselves on purpose.

A good many people, wondering what Ransom's poems grew out of, must have gone back to the book he published in 1918. At first reading *Poems about God* is shockingly, almost impossibly different from Ransom's later poetry. (Though in the opening poem one comes upon *escheat*, the word that, along with its backward brother *estopped*, was later to become the "little phrase of Vinteuil's" or national anthem of the Fugitives.) Most of the time one is bumping over the furrows of a crude, broad, direct, Southern pastoral, full of reapers and sermons and blackberry pie, quite as country as anything in the early Frost. Many people might recognize, in "Hurrying home on a windy night / And hearing tree-tops rubbed and tossed," the familiar accents of a marginal Arcadia; but who would suppose them Ransom's? Most of the earlier *Poems about God* are old-fashioned, amateurishly direct jobs that remind you of the Longfellow-Whittier-Lowell section in your sixth grade reader, and there are a few surprisingly close to popular doggerel: "There's a patch of trees at the edge of the field / And a brown little house that is kept so warm." A poem about a practical farmer who, by cutting away the roses at the edge of his field, always got a bigger yield than his neighbors has a name like a steam-roller: "One Who Rejected Christ." But along with the raw innocence of some of the poems there is the raw knowledge that replaces innocence: the "hulk of heaving meat" that "in his vomit laid him down" to die. Some of these earlier poems are nothing but the revulsion and condemnation that are the direct response of innocence and goodness to the evil of the world: at first one is separated from the other absolutely, but afterwards, occasionally, they begin to be joined in the sweet-sour, good-and-evil, steady struggle of opposites that is usual in Ransom's mature poems. The practical and impractical are already at their war: the swimmer floating far down in the cool green depths, with no more need of senses, work, wife, life itself, hears the scolding watch of the world tick grimmer and grimmer, "O *wicked* swimmer!" The preacher being resolutely Christian at Christmas to the little daughter who impatiently says, "I know, I know," begs her father to talk about Santa Claus, and at last weeps, defeated—this is the first of many such poems about children, the first of many such defeats by the world of morals, business, and science. And in "Prayer," when God groans despairingly over the prayers of a poor old woman, several seraphim forget their harping to scold: "O what a wicked woman, / To shrew his splendid features out of shape!"

"The Power of God" is the first poem to have some of Ransom's elaborate biblical-pedantic rhetoric; but in many of the poems one can already see his characteristic use of the situation or tone or *gestalt* of the ballad or fairy tale. One smiles at the plain broad beginning of his many-branched myth of Woman: "I have seen women by these bad roads, / Thank God for that"; but in the poems at the back of the book one finds very different things; and, remembering "Antique Harvesters," one smiles delightedly at Ransom's sympathetic and mocking account of that young Hellenist in Tennessee who

> Cursed the paternity that planted me
> One green leaf in a wilderness of autumn;
> And wept, as fitting such a fruitful spirit
> Sealed in a yellow tomb.

One realizes, "Why, it wasn't a mutation—this is Ransom after all"; one has not only seen some of the cruder attitudes, afterwards refined or contradicted, that underlie the later poems, one has wound up in the later poems.

Ransom's poetry shows no individual influences of any real importance. (The Bible, fairy tales, and such are important general influences.) Once, in the early "Geometry," Ransom rewrote Hardy in Hardy's own language: "Unprofited by the centuries / He still plants on as crazily / As in his drivelling infancy." And the beginning of "Night Voices," from Ransom's second book, is Hardy being biblical. Occasionally in *Poems about God* there is a slight flavor of Robinson; and "Tom Tom the Piper's Son" is a working out of a Robinson theme with more grace, concentration, and purity than Robinson could have brought to it himself. Ransom must be almost the only person in the world who has been influenced (though too slightly to talk about, except for fun) by both early and late Yeats: so that as one reads, in *Poems about God,*

> Must I confess before the pack
> Of babblers, idiots, and such?

one remembers a couple of late-Yeats phrases in Ransom's "Address to the Scholars of New England." But when one reads, in "Old Mansion," the phrases "we beautifully trusted" and "with my happier angel's own temerity," one decides that this is a natural similarity, not simply James.

Ransom has noticeably influenced at least three good poets: Robert Graves, Allen Tate, and Robert Penn Warren. But all three were influenced more by his accident than by his essence, and their best poems show no trace of him. To expect Tate's and Warren's poems to be much influenced by Ransom's is like expecting two nightmares to be influenced by a daydream; and Graves, who might have been more affected, ended with a style all his own only after undergoing considerably more mesmeric American influences.

As Blake said, there is no competition between true poets. Ransom is plainly a member of that strange wonderful family, with about as much individual difference and as much family likeness as is common; and his poems profess their limitations so candidly, almost as a principle of style, that it is hardly necessary to say they are not poems of the largest scope or of the greatest intensity. But it is only fair to say that Ransom is one of the best, most original, and most sympathetic poets alive; and it is easy to see that his poetry will always be cared for, since he has written poems that are perfectly realized and occasionally almost perfect—poems that the hypothetical generations of the future will be reading page by page with Wyatt, Campion, Marvell, and Mother Goose.

But one hates to end on such a grave yew-like note, and had rather cover the last page with a picture, a recollected Breughelish landscape of the country of Ransom's poems. In the center of everything—but unseen, like the blind spot in the middle of one's eye—is the practical world of business and science and morality, a vortex that is laboring to suck everything into its transforming revolutions. In the foreground there is a girl weeping for a dead pet; or simply a girl, dead; and her parents are mourning—in their dry, wistful, pedantic way, full of sentiment and knowledge—this pure potentiality which they have tried helplessly to shelter, but which existence itself has brought to nothing. Nearby the girl, grown up now, stands under the great hollow oak that whispers gently to its daughter—stands torn with pure love, pure pain, as she watches the "serpent's track" of the bicyclist pumping his winding way uphill, carrying the last of all letters to her lover: who walks with blank bitter dryness through the bare wet woods, slashing with a cane at weeds, full of abstraction, morality, and baffled oblivious non-attachedness, a man who has seen through everything except the process of seeing through everything. Children are playing in the vacant lots, animals are playing in the forest. Everything that the machine at the center could not attract or transform it has forced out into the suburbs, the country, the wilderness, the past; out there are the fairy tables and nursery rhymes, chances and choices, dreams and sentiments and intrinsic aesthetic goods—everything that doesn't pay and doesn't care. Out there are the old men, like children now—the defeated Way of an old world—and the gods of that way: Christ and Anti-Christ arming themselves for their tourney; Lamb and Paraclete and Exegete; the friar poring doubtfully over the bloody leaves of the battlefield; Grimes, the old scapegoat, old campaigner, hardened and professional in the habit of atonement, careless of those he dies for:

> Blue blazed the eyes of Grimes in the old manner,—
> The flames of eyes which jewel the head of youth
> Were strange in the leathery phiz of the old campaigner,—
> Smoke and a dry word crackled from his mouth
> And the wind ferried them South.

And there are beauties dangerous as Judith of Bethulia, tenderhearted plant-loving spinsters, lovers embracing like acrobats on a tight-rope, lovers quarreling and wandering through the dewy night like ghosts. Out there are things queer and unchangeable as anything in Grimm: a Quixote who loses on his quests arms, legs, eyes, everything but his tongue and the "old heart in his bust"—and at last those; Tom Tom the Piper's Son, the changeling pulling his little black coat tight about him, glaring around with little grey eyes; the Maiden accosted among the roses of the trellis of the piazza by Death, who has come for her in a dustcoat; the "fine woman" turned into a timid lady bird; the lady whose life was "six little spaces of chill and six of burning." Was she not lucky? Here is old Robert Crocodile: who went to Oxford, carried an umbrella, turned into a society psychoanalyst—an echoingly metaphysical one—and at last sank back into the ooze of the Ohio Everglades, where to this day "floating he lies extended many a rood" among all his kinsfolk.

Eliot's *Ash-Wednesday*

Hugh Kenner

*What then, shall I continually "fall" and never "rise"? "turn away" and
not once "turn again"? Shall my rebellions be "perpetual"?*
                                        —LANCELOT ANDREWES

*A beautiful and ineffectual angel, beating in the void his luminous wings
in vain.*
                                        —MATTHEW ARNOLD

A thin, firm minor music, of ceremonious intricacy, dissolving the world
of Tiresias, Hamlet, and Mrs. Equitone, creating in the zone vacated by
that world "a place of solitude where three dreams cross"; a visionary
precision in which a symbolic stair has (incidentally) a banister, and three
symbolic leopards sit quietly because their stomachs are full; a wholly transparent network of allusions, tacitly nourished, like a nervous system, from
secret sources among which research will discover nothing irrelevant; a
religious poem which contains no slovenly phrase, no borrowed zeal, no
formulated piety: this improbable achievement subsumes for good the secular Eliot whose traces of Original Richard Savage precipitated in his poems
an arresting residue of gritty substantiality. We are to hear no more of how

> Apeneck Sweeney spreads his knees
> Letting his arms hang down to laugh,

nor will such a detail as "rats' feet over broken glass" momentarily usurp
the world.

> And a time for the wind to break the loosened pane
> And to shake the wainscot where the field-mouse trots,
> And to shake the tattered arras woven with a silent motto.

In these lines from *East Coker* we see images from one of Eliot's familiar
constellations functioning in a new way. The trotting field-mouse is a figure
in a poemscape, not like the rat in *The Hollow Men* the synedoche of some
omnipresent world. The most arresting images now *recede;* intensity inheres
in the design of the whole passage, not in the immutable phrase. His former

---

From *The Invisible Poet: T. S. Eliot.* © 1959 by Hugh Kenner. Methuen, 1965.

idiom had tended toward opacity. Its savour lay in the gestures of real speech exactly caught. The vice that menaced it was a certain succinct impenetrability ("this broken jaw of our lost kingdoms"). The language after *Ash-Wednesday* is characteristically open, even tranquil, its aim a ritual translucency, its lapses into facility and small talk. Some withdrawal from individual speech has occurred, which resembles a loss of vigour, though the vigour is rather dispersed than evaporated. This poetry is related less intimately now to the speaking voice than to renovated decorums of the impersonal English language. Its substance even becomes to some extent its own decorousness

> —every phrase
> And sentence that is right (where every word is at home,
> Taking its place to support the others, . . .
> The common word exact without vulgarity,
> The formal word precise but not pedantic,
> The complete consort dancing together),
> Every phrase and every sentence is an end and a beginning,
> Every poem an epitaph.

This points to the animating principle of *Ash-Wednesday*, its own autonomous virtuosity in a universe implying adjacent spiritual states, but wholly compounded of verbal suggestions. From node to node of its own structure, from zone to zone, the poem moves swiftly like a swallow, and without flutter. Arrived in each zone, it circles and searches before passing on, making its way in this fashion from the zone of feeling dominated by "Because . . ." to the domain of "although . . . ," from a ratiocinative submission ("Because I know . . ." "Consequently I rejoice . . .") in the place where "there is nothing again," to a tension among substantial presences ("And the weak spirit quickens to rebel / For the bent golden-rod and the lost sea smell") that has no use for "because" and "consequently."

What is achieved—we are driven to impersonal summary—is a tension: more than the Magus achieved. He arrived at a disenchantment which "another death" might make right. Sweeney too lost the taste for created things. The centre of perception that moves through *Ash-Wednesday* (a focal point as specific as an "I" can be, but too wholly absorbed in its own spiritual states to be called a protagonist), the "I," the Voice, the "finite centre," begins where the Magus left off, and moves on: not at the last merely "no longer at ease here, in the old dispensation," but installed in a realm of superior wakefulness where

> the lost heart stiffens and rejoices
> In the lost lilac and the lost sea voices
> And the weak spirit quickens to rebel
> For the bent golden-rod and the lost sea smell
> Quickens to recover
> The cry of quail and the whirling plover

> And the blind eye creates
> The empty forms between the ivory gates
> And smell renews the salt savour of the sandy earth.

Here every noun, verb and adjective pulls two ways. The heart is lost to the world and lost in the world. It stiffens with life and with rebellion. The lilac is lost in belonging to the world that has been renounced, and the heart "rejoices" either to applaud its departure or to bring it back transfigured: this last a thin possibility inhering only in the overtone emphatic placement confers upon "rejoices," a possibility so nearly illusory that the phrase "weak spirit" remains appropriate in its presence. The senses, by the same implication of transfiguration and recovery, renew "the salt savour of the sandy earth"; but the parallel with the delusions created by the "blind eye" and the doubtful force of "sandy" (Is it really fruitful earth? What are its relations with "the desert in the garden" of part 5 and with the desert of "the blessing of sand" in part 2?) increase the tension of implicit delusion. From which follows—

> Suffer us not to mock ourselves with falsehood
> Teach us to care and not to care
> Teach us to sit still
> And even among these rocks,
> Our peace in His will
> And even among these rocks
> Sister, mother
> And spirit of the river, spirit of the sea,
> Suffer me not to be separated
> And let my cry come unto Thee.

"Teach us to care and not to care." The tension itself is a good. This line and its companion have not the context of resignation that sponsored their first appearance in part 1; or rather, the resignation is of greater purity. The ambivalent "separated" rejects internal separation as well as separation from God. Without specifying what evades specification, it is permissible for commentary to suggest that the opposite pull of the senses and the devotional spirit—of God's creation and God—is to be maintained as a fruitful and essential equivocalness, not "solved" by relegating one half of the being to the earth and the other half to heaven, nor yet, as in the Buddhist Fire Sermon, by becoming "weary of the knowledge of the visible" and so "empty of desire." A temptation to deny the senses must be resisted, rather as Becket in *Murder in the Cathedral* contends with the temptation to appoint himself martyr.

That is where the poem goes. It arrives there by a climbing of stairs, a vision, and a vertigo of assonances where

> the unstilled world still whirled
> About the centre of the silent Word.

Before the stairs, it undergoes a dismemberment of all corporeality, by three white leopards; over this scene of macabre tranquillity presides the goodness of a Lady who subsequently withdraws herself

> In a white gown, to contemplation, in a white gown.

The composition of this strange scene includes a juniper tree, bones, and a desert, dreamily static like an invention of the Douanier Rousseau's. It is evidently the first phase of that which is constructed "upon which to rejoice," according to the proposal in the first section of all:

> Because I cannot hope to turn again
> Consequently I rejoice, having to construct something
> Upon which to rejoice
>
> And pray to God to have mercy upon us
> And I pray that I may forget
> These matters that with myself I too much discuss
> Too much explain

The middle sections of the poem, consequently, neither discuss nor explain, but pursue that "logic of the imagination" for which in his introduction to Perse's *Anabase* Eliot in 1930 claimed a status coequal with that of the familiar logic of concepts. The first part, however, allies itself to that zone of consciousness where discussion is carried on, and with the aid of a form which suggests a strict form in echoing the melodic freedom of the Cavalcanti *ballate*, it adapts the ceremonious wraith of a syllogism to the uses of an ideal self-examination.

> Because I do not hope to turn again
> Because I do not hope
> Because I do not hope to turn
> Desiring this man's gift and that man's scope
> I no longer strive to strive towards such things
> (Why should the agèd eagle stretch its wings?)
> Why should I mourn
> The vanished power of the usual reign?

"Perch'io non spero di tornar gia mai . . ." so Guido Cavalcanti expecting to die in exile commences the dialogue with the Ballata he is sending to his distant lady: the dialogue with the Ballata is the Ballata itself, much as Eliot's resolve to construct something upon which to rejoice is itself an element in the construction.

> Because no hope is left me, Ballatetta,
> Of return to Tuscany,
> Light-foot go thou some fleet way
> Unto my Lady straightway,
> And out of her courtesy
> Great honour will she do thee.
>
> > [Ezra Pound's translation]

With Cavalcanti's plight is associated the mood of Shakespeare, one of his hundred moods:

> When in disgrace with fortune and men's eyes,
> I all alone beweep my outcast state
> And trouble deaf heaven with my bootless cries,
> And look upon myself and curse my fate:
> Wishing me like to one more rich in hope,
> Featured like him, like him with friends possessed,
> Desiring this man's art and that man's scope.

This English Renaissance fit of the sulks, readily cured by thinking of something else ("haply I think on thee"), is transcended by Cavalcanti's irremediable plight just as Cavalcanti's is transcended by the metaphysical despair of Ash-Wednesday, when the Christian universe examines its own unworthiness. The *Ash-Wednesday* language bears a similar relation to Shakespeare's: it is emptied of irrelevant specificity: the speaker does not quaintly "trouble deaf heaven" but moves as if through the phases of some liturgy, in an unpunctuated *stil nuovo*, cadenced rather than counted, pre-Elizabethan, not mediaeval, a language never spoken anywhere, though never remote in its deliberate bare elegance from the constructions (if not the energies) of actual speech. Though the cadences swing with the untrammelled gravity of a Foucault pendulum, the idiom is devoid of copiousness: when we come upon "the infirm glory of the positive hour" we are aware of "infirm" and "positive," two deliberate words, neither one resonant, each salient in the grave nerveless ambience. So with "the one veritable transitory power": these rare polysyllables bring with them an air of exactness without momentum. The energy of the line has precisely expended itself in establishing two precise words, and there is none left over to propel the next line to some rhetorical pitch. The next line is simply, "Because I cannot drink."

The other dimension of the opening is an insistent mellifluousness, nearly Tennysonian, located in the long vowels and associating itself with the recurrent pairings of identical words ("I no longer strive to strive towards such things"; "Because I know I shall not know") and with the liturgical repetition of constructions, phrases, and whole lines. It is this quality that sets the language of *Ash-Wednesday* at a remove from speech, so much so that we are driven for analogy as far as the Laureate's *Holy Grail*:

> Then every evil word I had spoken once,
> And every evil thought I had thought of old,
> And every evil deed I ever did,
> Awoke and cried, "This Quest is not for thee."
> And lifting up mine eyes, I found myself
> Alone, and in a land of sand and thorns,
> And I was thirsty, even unto death;
> And I too cried, "This Quest is not for thee."

This Victorian ceremony of iterations is crude beside Eliot's austere gestures of withdrawal and submission; neverthelesss, it appears to have been under his eye. A few lines later Sir Percivale is telling of the delusions that beset him on his quest; he came to a brook with apple trees,

> But even while I drank the brook, and ate
> The goodly apples, all these things at once
> Fell into dust and I was left alone
> And thirsting in a land of sand and thorns.

which may be the source of

> Because I cannot drink
> There, where trees flower, and springs flow, for there is
>   nothing again

Percivale proceeds to encounter what Eliot calls "the infirm glory of the positive hour," in the shape of a knight

> In golden armour with a crown of gold
> About a casque all jewels; and his horse
> In golden armour jewell'd everywhere;

he likewise fell into dust. Later in *The Holy Grail* Sir Lancelot climbs stairs towards a vision—

> up I climb'd a thousand steps
> With pain: as in a dream I seem'd to climb
> For ever;

the vision when he encounters it is veiled.

By way of Tennyson, *Ash-Wednesday* is united with certain *Waste Land* themes: the quester, the Chapel Perilous, the elusive vision associated with a lady. By way of Dante, the lady, appearing on three planes, gathers divinity. In the desert she is withdrawn to contemplation, like the earthly Beatrice. In the vision that follows the scene on the stairs, she appears veiled in white and blue, capable of making strong the fountains and fresh the springs, functioning in the economy of the poem somewhat as Beatrice does in Canto 30 of the *Purgatorio*. Though she goes "in Mary's colour" she is not Mary; yet she is perhaps also "the veiled sister" of part 5, who may pray "for those who wait in darkness," and who in the finale of the poem is so closely associated with the "holy mother" as to be virtually identified with her.

When we first become aware of her, she is not, however, a wholly settling presence; there is even something a little sinister in the indifference of her withdrawal ("in a white gown, to contemplation, in a white gown") after the leopards have completed their feast. She is in more than one way a "Lady of silences," and if she is "Calm and distressed / Torn and most whole," those are qualities not only of supernatural compassion, but of natural derangement, proper to the sphere of the Hyacinth girl's unnerving simplicity, and to the fact that the positive hour's glory ("looking into the heart of Light, the silence") is "infirm." Not that these vaguely troubling implications are of any salience; the remote, cool ritual verse obliterates all but our most determined attention to the normal range of certain words. In part 2, with its "I who am here dissembled" and its willed forgetting, we inhabit a *protective* peace, dreamlike, just below the threshold of a less soothing wakefulness. Parts 3 and 4 are not so fragile; the "devil of the stairs" and the "cloud of tears" do not menace a dream, they are components of a vision.

Plainly the speaker is in some unspecifiable way thrusting past experiences into the destructive element of symbol, though it is pointless to fuss about the poem's sequence of events, or to determine which of its scenes may be recollections, which presences. It is true that the verbs in parts 2, 3 and 4 are chiefly in the past tense, but Eliot's tenses are frequently opportunisms, as in "Triumphal March," for dimming or vivifying. Grammatically, five minutes ago is as much in the past as twenty years ago. In part 4, however, we hear of "the years that walk between," and are at liberty to suppose that the lady who once enlivened the Waste Land, "made cool the dry rock and made firm the sand," did so on the far side of those years, in "the positive hour," perhaps, and that the injunction "Sovegna vos," if we are to press the parallel with Arnaut's speech in *Purgatorio*, Canto 26, is addressed to her out of a present metaphorical fire. For the years restore her:

> Here are the years that walk between, bearing
> Away the fiddles and the flutes, restoring
> One who moves in the time between sleep and waking,
> 　　　wearing
> White light folded, sheathed about her, folded,
> The new years walk, restoring
> Through a bright cloud of tears, the years, restoring
> With a new verse the ancient rhyme.

The parallel with the iterated participles that introduce *The Waste Land* seems deliberate: on that occasion, a "covering" and an umbilical "feeding" that resist the Spring's breeding, mixing, and stirring; on this occasion, a welcoming of what the new years bring even as they seem to be taking gratifying things away. They restore "with a new verse, the ancient rhyme," not only enhancing the present but bestowing meaning on the neutral past. As we are to be told in *The Dry Salvages*,

> 　　approach to the meaning restores the experience
> In a different form, beyond any meaning
> We can assign to happiness.

The "white gown" of her faintly unsettling withdrawal in part 2 is now "white light," as she moves in the time between sleep and waking. The function of her departure and restoration is somewhat explicated in *Marina*, an Ariel Poem published a few months after *Ash-Wednesday*. Here an epigraph from Seneca's *Hercules Furens* tugs against the explicit parallels with Shakespeare's *Pericles* sufficiently hard to arouse a slight but stubborn possibility that the speaker may be mocking himself with falsehood. The epigraph, spoken by a man who has slaughtered his children and is now recovering sanity, tends to align certain motifs of *Pericles* with the Eliotic sequence of perhaps-drowned women, though it is true that when Shakespeare's hero threw his queen into the sea he supposed her already dead. In the shipboard scene (5:1) in which the king's lost daughter is restored to him as prelude to the recovery of his wife, Pericles supposes for a time that he is enjoying only "the rarest dream that e'er dull sleep did mock sad fools withal." He asks the apparition,

> But are you flesh and blood?
> Have you a working pulse? And are no fairy?

Eliot's speaker asks,

> What is this face, less clear and clearer
> The pulse in the arm, less strong and stronger—
> Given or lent? more distant than stars and nearer than
>   the eye.

The pulse may be his own, the face a vision; he next evokes

> Whispers and small laughter between leaves and hurrying
>   feet
> Under sleep, where all the waters meet.

The sleeping and waking worlds are equivocally mingled throughout the poem, and we are not required to suppose someone passing, as Pericles did, from one to the other. A curious passage intermingling the decrepitude of his ship ("the rigging weak and the canvas rotten") with his realization that the dream-child was of his making leads into the evocation of

> This form, this face, this life
> Living to live in a world of time beyond me; let me
> Resign my life for this life, my speech for that unspoken,
> The awakened, lips parted, the hope, the new ships.

New life, new ships, and the daughter belong to the same perhaps illusory dispensation. "I made this," in the same way, points both to the ship and to the child: "between one June and another September" may or may not be a nine-month interval. The "bowsprit cracked with ice and paint cracked with heat" suggests some such lurid journey as the Ancient Mariner's, now "become unsubstantial." The daughter, or the possibility of her presence, at least for the duration of Eliot's most elusive poem, suspends nervewracking actualities:

> What seas what shores what granite islands towards my
> timbers
> And woodthrush calling through the fog
> My daughter.

In *Ash-Wednesday* the woman who "moves in the time between sleep and waking" comes like the daughter in *Marina* out of the past to bestow a transitory happiness which can transfigure the world, and which after its pleasure has faded like music, leaves the world, past and present, better understood. This is the reverse of Eliot's Lazarus plot, in which someone's passing through leaves the ambience troubled. It is an event he never represents as happening at the behest of present actuality: always at the bidding of an awakened memory. Present actuality is the actuality of "Triumphal March," or if it is subtler than that it is Bradley's "immediate experience," a circle closed on the outside.

> This is the use of memory:
> For liberation—not less of love but expanding
> Of love beyond desire, and so liberation
> From the future as well as the past . . .
> . . . See, now they vanish,
> The faces and places, with the self which, as it could, loved
> them,
> To become renewed, transfigured, in another pattern.
> (*Little Gidding*)

What we are entitled to prize in the natural present is "tension." A new verse may perhaps restore the ancient rhyme, and a verse is not only something added to a poem but etymologically a turning again; nevertheless the last section of *Ash-Wednesday* begins "Although I do not hope to turn again." The emphasis of the final prayer,

> Suffer us not to mock ourselves with falsehood
> Teach us to care and not to care
> Teach us to sit still,

is explicated by Eliot in specific terms five years later, in the play about the Canterbury Bishop who was tempted not to resist his enemies, and finally succeeded in not resisting them, but not as he had been tempted. There are ways of not caring and of sitting still that constitute mocking ourselves with falsehood. The function of the journey detailed in *Ash-Wednesday* is to arrive at a knowledge of the modes and possibilities of temporal redemption sufficient to prevent our being deluded by a counterfeit of the negative way. The 1920s were full of elegant sceptics, and T. S. Eliot was one of their heroes, but he does not return the compliment.

Ghosts and Roses: T. S. Eliot

Gregory S. Jay

> *Follow the feet*
> *Of the walker, the water-thrush. Follow the flight*
> *Of the dancing arrow, the purple martin. Greet*
> *In silence the bullbat. All are delectable. Sweet sweet sweet*
> *But resign this land at the end, resign it*
> *To its true owner, the tough one, the sea-gull.*
> *The palaver is finished.*
> —"Cape Ann"

In part 5 of *The Dry Salvages* the seas and sailors drop away. The poet begins his turn toward exploration of another approach to ecstasy, one that will culminate in the "double part" he assumes when he meets the ghost in *Little Gidding*. As *The Dry Salvages* closes, the chaos of interpretative methods ("these are usual / Pastimes and drugs") motivates the recurrent hope of order: "But to apprehend / The point of intersection of the timeless / With time, is an occupation for the saint." Thus, "For most of us, there is only the unattended / Moment, the moment in and out of time," the again repeated moment "lost in a shaft of sunlight, / The wild thyme unseen, or the winter lightning." These new repetitions are now "hints and guesses" pointing to the Christian philosophy of a divine repetition: "The hint half-guessed, the gift half understood, is Incarnation." The Incarnation is God's strange repetition in time, as Christ figures the archetype of the revisionist. He is the ideal *figura* of which personal repetitions are prefigurations, as they seek the Spirit of the moment in representative reembodiments.

One poetic "saint" who glimpsed this mystery is Dante, whose *Paradiso* concludes with puzzlement at "our image" in the divine Light and with a reconciliation among the stars: "I wished to see how the image conformed to the circle and how it has its place therein; but my own wings were not sufficient for that, save that my mind was smitten by a flash wherein its wish came to it. Here power failed the lofty phantasy; but already my desire and my will were revolved, like a wheel that is evenly moved, by the Love which moves the sun and the other stars" (*Paradiso*, canto 33). By a fiery flash of the divine, Dante receives the mystery, but cannot record it, for his receptive faculty for images ("fantasia") remains human. He experiences an Annunciation of the Word made flesh; yet, its representation is reserved

From *T. S. Eliot and the Poetics of Literary History*. © 1983 by Louisiana State University Press.

for the Word itself, while the poet's words record the feeling of this illumination. Love is the emotion of divinity, the unrepresentable height and
depth inspiring poet and universe. Dante carries away a souvenir of this
passionate moment in his poetic remembrance; his vision is not of the
mystery's solution, but of the revolving love of its repetition in time. Eliot
alludes to this moment in Dante ("to my thinking the highest point that
poetry has ever reached or ever can reach") to prepare the way for his own
version of the *Paradiso* in *Little Gidding*. His love for Dante's poem moves
him to attempt its reincarnation. He will end his own climactic work by
repeating the end of Dante's, and the approach to its meaning will in this
other time alter Dante in yet another fulfillment of the mystery's promise.

Fire is the element of *Little Gidding*. The refining purgatorial fire now
burns with enlightenment, as the pentecostal flame and the flash of Dante.
As "un fulgore" had shown the Incarnation to Dante, so Dante will be
reincarnated and show himself in Eliot's poem. This meeting of the living
and the dead crosses the normal categories of time and bestows meaning
upon them through other patterns. *Little Gidding* transfigures the occupation of the saint, finds in its intertextuality the "intersection of the timeless
/ With time." This violation of temporal rules recalls the simultaneous order
of literature in "Tradition and the Individual Talent" and gives a dramatic
account of such an encounter between the disciple and "some dead master." Thus, when the scene is set, it is "Midwinter spring," a confusion of
the regulated order imposed on phenomena and called "natural." Designations of identity are exposed as reductions of the mystery. This undoing
of classifications parallels the earlier sense that "Words strain, / Crack and
sometimes break, under the burden" of stamping a single identity on disparate objects by obscuring the difference that makes possible the abstraction producing the signifier. Those trained in the ways of comparative
philology, such as Nietzsche and Eliot, were quick to probe the philological
relativity of language. Eliot assimilated this questioning of the signifier to
his own systematic interrogation of language and emotion, locating the
problem in the process of representation, or what he called remembrance:
"In perception we intend the object; in recollection we intend a complex
which is composed of image and feeling. We do not intend to remember
simply the object, but the object as we remember it. And this new object
is much more *the experience* than the *past object*, for we try to remember how
we felt toward the past object." A word repeats conventionally, limiting
meaning. Poetic repetition "unknows" words and moments in another
discourse. They pass through exile into humiliation, their repetition sig-
naling love and their remembrance incarnating the spirit that knows, or
unknows, itself through them.

This interpretative process is "Suspended in time, between pole and
tropic," antinomies undone by the "pentecostal fire" that "Stirs the dumb
spirit" to transfigured speech of "the spring time . . . not in time's convenant . . . Not in the scheme of generation." The exploration leads not

to the eternal, for that would be only the timeless, but to the "uncertain hour before the morning" in section 2, when the "unimaginable" trods the pavement. We have come ashore, as at the end of *The Waste Land,* but these lands are in a very strange order. Their principle of conjunction is not unlike that binding the fragments and quotes at the end of the earlier poem. What is different is the absence of hysteria, the calm passion of this entrance into that that passeth understanding. The "broken king" comes again, de-throned, repeating the Fisher King and King Charles, now humbled, with-out hope or fear of restoration to authority. Here "at the end of the journey" knight and poet discover the errancy that disrupts the "scheme of gener-ation," turning each word and each accomplishment into prelude and benediction.

> And what you thought you came for
> Is only a shell, a husk of meaning
> From which the purpose breaks only when it is fulfilled
> If at all. Either you had no purpose
> Or the purpose is beyond the end you figured
> And is altered in fulfilment.

Undoing the temporal and historical structure of figural interpretation, Eliot's fulfillments break their *figurae,* reach back and alter the purposes of signs.

The fulfillment here is not the original figure in a different, exalted form that had been prefigured: rather these fulfillments choose their past figures, empty them, and make them "only a shell, a husk of meaning." Figural interpretation had resolved the ambiguity of original and copy in-herent in the etymology of *figura* by the construction of a teleological model of figural purposes. The times were reconciled by the links to the logos figural interpretation assumed; the new testaments emptied the authority of the old and inverted their priority, turning them into hints and guesses of themselves, the new texts. Although the doctrine described a movement forward from figure to fulfillment, the actual motion ran backward as the modern moment secured itself by revising the purposeful significance of the ancient. The poet, then, working at this actual level, accepts the in-evitable transfiguraton of his authority and words by others in their inter-pretations, accepts the new worlds of meaning that break, "If at all," beyond the end the poet figured, constantly altering his text in new ful-fillments. It would be hard to believe that Eliot was unaware of the theory of the figural and of the history of the term, especially in light of his modest education in Romance philology and his assimilation of the Christian his-toriographical model. In any case, the essence of the practice is contained in Augustine's *Confessions* and in Dante's *Commedia,* two of Eliot's principal inspirations. Eliot's transfigurational poetics emerge as a revision of Chris-tian historiography and theology, English political history, the literature of remembrance and autobiography, the philosophy of belated perception, the literacy criticism of historical formalism, and his own personal quest for a reconciliation with America and mutability.

Figural breaks are the eternal recurrence of "the world's end" repeating "in place and time, / Now and in England." A simple notion of the end of history would still involve "mere sequence— / Or even development." *Little Gidding* puts an end to the end of history and begins history as altered repetitions, a constant intersection.

> And what the dead had no speech for, when living,
> They can tell you, being dead: the communication
> Of the dead is tongued with fire beyond the language of
> > the living.

Thus, the theoretical model is propounded and ready for application in the conjunction of a dead master speaking in fiery tongues.

> In the uncertain hour before the morning
> > Near the ending of interminable night
> > At the recurrent end of the unending
> After the dark dove with the flickering tongue
> > Had passed below the horizon of his homing
> > While the dead leaves still rattled on like tin
> Over the asphalt where no other sound was
> > Between three districts whence the smoke arose
> > I met one walking, loitering and hurried
> As if blown towards me like the metal leaves
> > Before the urban dawn wind unresisting.
> > And as I fixed upon the down-turned face
> That pointed scrutiny with which we challenge
> > The first-met stranger in the waning dusk
> > I caught the sudden look of some dead master
> Whom I had known, forgotten, half recalled
> > Both one and many; in the brown baked features
> > The eyes of a familiar compound ghost
> Both intimate and unidentifiable.
> > So I assumed a double part, and cried
> > And heard another's voice cry: "What! are *you* here?"

Forgotten and half-recalled, intimate and unidentifiable, the familiar compound ghost characterizes the eerie temporality and mixed identities of the literary text. This meeting and conversation may be read as Eliot's condensed summary of his poetic philosophy, the last act and statement of the individual's struggle with inheritance and futurity. In "What Dante Means to Me" (1950), Eliot says "This section of a poem—not the length of one canto of the Divine Comedy—cost me far more time and trouble than any passage of the same length that I have ever written." The recently published manuscripts of the poem prove the point.

The conception was clear at the start: an "imitation" of Dante's terza rima, a reenactment of the master-disciple scenes Eliot so often cited, the compounding of Yeats with Dante, Shelley, and others, and the echo of Hamlet's ghost. But in the first draft the concluding advice given by this ghost, some twenty-four lines, treats other themes than the published text. The distance between the warden and the ghost appears greater, the alienation more severe. "I was always dead," the speaker says in one version of their meeting, "Always revived, and always something other, / And he a face changing." Recalling King Hamlet's "Remember me," the manuscript ghost's answering injunction is of a different sort.

> Remember rather the essential moments
>   That were the times of birth and death and change
>   The agony and the solitary vigil.
> Remember also fear, loathing and hate,
>   The wild strawberries eaten in the garden,
>   The walls of Poitiers, and the Anjou wine,
> The fresh new season's rope, the smell of varnish
>   On the clean oar, the drying of the sails,
> Such things as seem of least and most importance.
> So, as you circumscribe this dreary round,
>   Shall your life pass from you, with all you hated
>   And all you loved, the future and the past.
> United to another past, another future,
>   (After many seas and after many lands)
>   The dead and the unborn, who shall be nearer
> Than the voices and the faces that were most near.

The *Quartets* sometimes fall to flatness of cadence and sense in the pursuit of a common style. The recourse to Eliot's cherished nautical imagery suggests the importance of this section, but it comes out a pale reflection of *The Dry Salvages*. This version lapses into vagueness compared to the final copy, its reconciliation seemingly unearned and complacent. Its defect, as Eliot wrote in a letter to John Hayward, was "the lack of some acute personal reminiscence."

He supplies the personal touch through Yeats's influence, inspired by the late lyrics of tragic gay wisdom. Not surprisingly, the 1940 essay on Yeats focuses on influence and maturity. While writing the *Quartets*, Eliot sets down in his appreciation of Yeats the poetic principle guiding his own work, finally admitting the primacy of a "second impersonality" wherein the poet makes a general symbol of his personal experience. Redefining himself through Yeats, Eliot offers in this essay his mature position on language and social change. It is important for an understanding of the *Quartets'* approach to the meaning of current, catastrophic historical experiences. Embodied in the *Quartets,* and in numerous essays of the period after 1939, this attitude culminated a debate that had begun in *The Sacred*

Wood's attack on Arnold: "Born into a world in which the doctrine of 'Art for Art's sake' was generally accepted, and living on into one in which art has been asked to be instrumental to social purposes, he held firmly to the right view which is between these, though not in any way a compromise between them, and showed that an artist, by serving his art with entire integrity, is at the same time rendering the greatest service he can to his own nation and to the whole world."

For all Yeats's importance, however, Dante still dominates the compound. Of him, Eliot says "that of the very few poets of similar stature there is none, not even Virgil, who has been a more attentive student of the *art* of poetry, or a more scrupulous, painstaking and *conscious* practitioner of the *craft*." Having already written extensively on Dante, Eliot in 1950 means "to talk informally about his influence upon myself," in particular about the philosophy behind the composition of *Little Gidding*." He does so in a technical manner, like Poe's account of how he wrote "The Raven," an account the veracity of which Eliot himself doubted. So we may also suspect Eliot's retrospect. The concentration on craft turns the passage's "rending pain of re-enactment" into only a craftsman"s training. This half-truth eludes admisson of the pain of comparing one's own soul to those of the Yeatses and the Dantes.

Eliot spends the first pages of his last Dante essay on the theory of poetic debts, citing his own enrichment by Laforgue and Baudelaire. He reiterates his belief that the young poet should apprentice himself to minor poets, but with his usual genealogical metaphors he cautions that the older poet can learn little unless he faces "exalted . . . distant ancestors" and "great masters," as Dante faced Virgil and as Eliot tried to face Yeats and Dante and Shakespeare. Confessing his earlier anxiety of influence, Eliot now sees how the mature poet can only rise by competition with the great, who will not leave him alone anyway. Praising Shelley's "translation" of Dante in "The Triumph of Life" as better than his own, he states that "the influence of Dante, where it is really powerful, is a *cumulative* influence: that is, the older you grow, the stronger the domination becomes." *Little Gidding* submits to this domination while inscribing it in the same structure of revisionary control over the precursors pioneered by Dante. This repetition lessens the threat, paying back old debts and stamping new coinages as palimpsests on the old.

Eliot has "range over some varieties of 'influence' in order to approach an indication, by contrast, of what Dante has meant to me." In *The Waste Land*, he recounts, he intended to "establish a relationship between the medieval inferno and modern life," insinuating that to forget Dante, or any past's potential, is a sin of the modern inferno, a symptom if not a cause of its pernicious ennui. The parallel works in *Little Gidding*, too, written in reaction to the repetition that was World War II: "But the method is different: here I was debarred from quoting or adapting at length—I borrowed and adapted freely only a few phrases—because I was imitating." Imitation here acts like translation and transfiguraion, differentiated from the shoring of archaeologized ruins. The recollection of pieces joins a larger metamorphic repetition of style, stance, and theme as Eliot identifies with the dead master. If the transumption prevails and the dead join in chorus with the living, then the poetic father does become "like an admired elder brother." In the scheme of generations the anxiety of domination forms a hierarchy of fathers and sons, disparate rival temporalities. In the scheme of poetry, "not in time's covenant," matured poets are as brothers, contemporaneous and adjacent colleagues. Imitation disciplines the poem with a high linguistic standard. The poem undergoes askesis, metering the transfusion from other authors. As Eliot said of Yeats, "The course of improvement is towards a greater and greater starkness." The same is said of Dante.

The common stylistic effort, tied to a theme of the "gifts reserved for age," replaces the quest for individual authority, except as it can be made to symbolize the general. Through imitation or repetition, originality exists as the compound of what Dantesque standards can produce through the contemporary poet. In this case, repetition is not death, not the sign of exhausted sensibility or the horror of meaningless recurrence. It is the shared project of poets. Repetition and imitation order history. They interpret discontinuity by an abstraction of the Same, yet remain open to the altered fulfillments wrought by desire, accident, and fate. Thus, Eliot brings Dante to bear upon the morning after an air raid, a modern moment of breakage brought to comprehension by imitation, and the resulting poem supplements what was once the meaning of the *Commedia*. Eliot's emphasis on technique implies that one sustenance he seeks in that morning is the renewed assurance that the tongues of poetic fire can match those of material destruction. The submission of the poem to an impersonal linguistic goal coincides with the effort to place an eruptive event in a consoling frame.

Seven of the first eight lines of the imitation begin with prepositional or adverbial phrases. The syntax dramatizes the key act of placement, difficult when time and seasons are suspended. As Hugh Kenner has noted, "no other *Quartet* is so explicitly located in time as this one in which time is conquered." Still, the reiteration of "In . . . Near . . . At . . . After . . . While . . . Over . . . Between" speaks of a profound difficulty of location. The reader and the text meet, as do the warden and the ghost, at an uncertain intersection of poetic crossroads, turning the streets of London into a literary labyrinth. Eliot's lines are in the first person, but deceptively so, for the singular identity of this "I" is immediately denied by the reader's knowledge that his is the Dantesque "I" as well. This "I" is neither Eliot nor Dante nor any other poet, but an intertextual compound ("I was always dead, / Always revived, and always something other"), "the recognition of a temperament akin to one's own, and in another aspect the discovery of one's own form. These are not two things, but two aspects of the same thing." And the encounter cannot be wholly located in the text, for it is with "That pointed scrutiny with which we challenge / The first-met stranger in the waning dusk" that "I caught the sudden look of some dead

master." The insertion of the universalizing "we" depersonalizes the encounter, reminding us as readers that the scene is also an allegory of our
own meeting with this text, that we are also the "I" and Eliot is also "some
dead master." This prefiguration recalls the mix of "I" and "you" in "Song
of Myself," which enables a metamorphosis of author into text, text into
the fulfilled meaning of the text, meaning into the identity of the reader.
Whitman's final lines are also outside time's covenant, in literature's simultaneity. Self-consciously, Whitman's poem addresses the reader across
the decades, marking the text as crossroads.

> You will hardly know who I am or what I mean
> But I shall be good health to you nevertheless
> And filter and fibre your blood.
>
> Failing to fetch me at first keep encouraged,
> Missing me one place search another,
> I stop somewhere waiting for you.

We should also recall the time-traveling of "Crossing Brooklyn Ferry." The
uncanny Whitman enters the compound, master of temporal shuttlings
and shuffler of pronominal identities.

    The "double part" Eliot plays does the poets in different voices. Ec-
static, he is beside himself and compounded, "still the same, / Knowing
myself yet being someone other." He is "being" in the "other" as the
"other" lives through him, "In concord at this intersection time / Of meeting
nowhere." He speaks to himself. The dialogue that follows is the self-
reflection of the present conducted through the past, reflected across time
and meant to prepare the future. So compounded beyond time, this ghost,
unlike Hamlet's father, does not command the son to a stultifying
obedience.

> Last season's fruit is eaten
> And the fullfed beast shall kick the empty pail.
> For last year's words belong to last year's language
> And next year's words await another voice.

The ghost tacitly approves Eliot's method, rehearsing its thought and theory
while forgiving them. As he is soon to acknowledge, this theory makes his
own existence possible in the untimely dawn of this text. The ghost con-
secrates the poem's askesis, its clear-sighted submission to the ravages of
time. The "fullfed beast" aptly images the cycle of poetic usurpation that
Bloom has schematized and that Eliot accepts as fate. The distance between
time-bound languages, here seemingly so irrevocable, closes even as it is
pronounced: this is an imitation of Dante and Yeats, and it does manage
to bring "last year's words" to life again in "another voice." Kenner says
that "no other Voice in Eliot's repertoire articulates with such authority."

    But what is the nature of this authority, and by whom has it been
authored? Eliot constructs his authority by a mingled borrowing of tomes
and tones. We feel the ghost's authority because a poet has craftily shaped

him that way: the ghost is an allegory of authority, built consciously out of the rhetoric of wisdom. This authority is a ghost, the nonpresence and nonabsence of sunlit truth, a compound whose persuasive voice depends on convention, history, and humility. Eliot had once found Yeats "perhaps a little too much the weather-worn Triton among the streams," quoting "Vacillation," a poem consciously appropriated by *Little Gidding*. Eliot works to save his poem from the charge by taming Yeats with Dante. Eliot steals their authority and then makes it speak in his own measure, in the passage where Yeats's dancer moves in Dante's "refining fire."

The fate of ghostly authority sung, "the passage now presents no hindrance / To the spirit unappeased and peregrine / Between two worlds become much like each other." Translated from the distant shore of Hades, the ghost depends on the present and the poet for life and authority, and vice versa. Ritually murdered by beasts, his resurrection can be of use to "next year's words." Feeling the need to mute the voice of Yeats, Eliot inserts a translation of Mallarmé: "Since our concern was speech, and speech impelled us to purify the dialect of the tribe." The allusion, from "The Tomb of Edgar Poe," compounds Mallarmé, Eliot, and Poe together in the craftsman's task. Mallarmé's poem, however, bitterly protests the hostility and incomprehension that met Poe's work.

> Just as eternity transforms him at last unto Himself,
> The Poet rouses with a naked sword
> His age terrified at not having discerned
> That death was triumphant in that strange voice.

It required French translation and imitation to resurrect Poe or at least to mark his grave (a story of transatlantic influence Eliot tells in "From Poe to Valéry"). The dismal ignominy suffered by Poe and revenged by Mallarmé inspires Eliot's own funereal colloquy, his tomb of Dante, Yeats, Poe, Shelley, Mallarmé, Shakespeare, Whitman, Swift, and others. Eliot cannot assume Mallarmé's resentful tone, because he is himself a part of the compound. Yeats's voice returns to deliver the final advice on the ironic, sad "gifts reserved for age / To set a crown upon your lifetime's effort," as Mallarmé's crown for Poe becomes Eliot's Yeatsian crown of thorns.

The embarrassment Eliot feels at the Triton's weathered reflections on his aged self prompts him to divide his echo, severing the counsel of wisdom from introspection by dramatically representing it as speech to a disciple. Though the words pertain to the ghost's experience, the pronouns and tone are carefully restricted to avoid self-pity and direct attention toward the aspirant. We sense that these sufferings have been the ghost's, but his particular experience is no more than the general symbol. "First, the cold friction of expiring sense" robs the sensual and sexual of power "As body and soul begin to fall asunder." To this loss of physical powers is added "the conscious impotence of rage / At human folly, and the laceration / Of laughter at what ceases to amuse." These might be the Sweeney poems or the vitriol of *After Strange Gods*.

Such attitudes, self-centered and superior, must yield to the wisdom of humility and repetition.

> And last, the rending pain of re-enactment
>   Of all that you have done, and been; the shame
>   Of motives late revealed, and the awareness
> Of things ill done and done to others' harm
>   Which you took for exercise of virtue.
>   Then fools' approval stings, and honour stains.
> From wrong to wrong the exasperated spirit
>   Proceeds, unless restored by that refining fire
>   Where you must move in measure, like a dancer.

The rending pain of reenactment cuts through the *Four Quartets* and is their subject and technique, as the dancer from Yeats embodies the concord of form and content, of actor and action. Many motives are late revealed: the nostalgia for childhood bliss; adolescent rebellion against home's constraints; the longing for transcendent knowledge; the hope of poetic success; the trials of love; the calamities of history; the desire to restore ancestral orders; the dream of new ships, of a language that could carry exploring old men past Byzantium's glitter to a justified paradise. The "exercise of virtue," in retrospect, had also been an evasion of self-knowledge in a waste of ill-conceived opinions "done to others' harm." Eliot carries Dante's method to its logical conclusion, consigns himself to hell, purgatory, and judgment. The "refining fire" now burning with the announcements of pentecostal flames is a text and a state of the soul: it is a processing of identity through other corrective voices, an intertextual conflagration wherein "you must move in measure, like a dancer." If one reads the scene as, among other things, an interior agon between recurrent self-images, then it epotimizes what Lawrence Lipking isolates as a major purpose of *Four Quartets:* to self-consciously reread the entirety of Eliot's career in poetry, selecting and shaping its fragments into some version of that epic unity or coherent view of life that he believed distinguished great poets from mere versifiers.

The poet and the man measure steps among the living and the dead, choreograph a pattern of connections, displacements, and repositionings. There are no intermissions for the dancer of endless humility, no resting on the ground or in the heavens. This dancer's pained ecstasy is performed in the theater of repetition. Knowledge of self and other comes through representation, as a reading of the dance of estrangements and homecomings, their motives, virtues, and ends. The poet begins and ends on that estranging stage: "I cannot find any alternative for either 'enchantment' or 're-enactment' which does not either lose or alter meaning. 'Re-enacting' is weak as a substantive; and I want to preserve the association of 'enact'—to take the part of oneself on a stage for oneself as the audience." So goes the drama of "impersonality."

With the end of the ghost's speech, the curtain falls on this scene of instruction, while it rises on that of the encompassing poem itself. The theater that is the poem starts up; the reader in the audience watches as the section closes at dawn and reenacts in its ending the beginning of Hamlet.

> The day was breaking. In the disfigured street
>   He left me, with a kind of valediction,
>   And faded on the blowing of the horn.

Eliot rejected an editorial suggestion by Hayward concerning these lines on the grounds that it would "mean my losing the allusion to Hamlet's ghost," the specter he had not even mentioned in his early essay on the play. The allusion does more than just effect a neat symmetry between the all-clear siren and the crowing of the cock that dismissed Hamlet's father "like a guilty thing / Upon a fearful summons." That moment comes at the beginning of the tragedy, this at the end. The conflation and inversion help to situate this part of the poem as a kind of prologue to what is possible. It holds open the possibility of reversing the tragic course of Shakespeare's play, in which the son is doomed by the return of the dead and the callousness of the living. The horn comes after the destructive night, leaving us in a yet "uncertain hour" to face the days this colloquy has prepared for. The play, the reenactment of these words, is left in the audience-reader's hands. The street has been "disfigured" as well as transfigured. The puns on the former term include ruination, depopulation, and the confusion of destruction. But on this literary street, disfiguration also means the compounding of various poetic "figures" into this "dead master." Language has disfigured experience and made a strange place accessible. Figures are "breaking," sounding a farewell to past identities.

There is "a kind of valediction" at the end of certain speech, a diction of breakings and dawnings that also bids a reverent good-bye to what it disfigures. This valediction forbids mourning, for this morning sees the patterned reconciliation of double parts. The allusion to Donne's poem fits the implication of distance reserved in measurement. Donne and his lady assume their double parts: "If they be two, they are two so / As stiff twin compasses are two." The precision of Donne's conceit and the faith he has in his centering love bring him expertly home.

> And though it in the center sit,
>   Yet when the other far doth roam,
> It leans and hearkens after it,
>   And grows erect, as that comes home.
> Such wilt thou be to me, who must
>   Like th'other foot, obliquely run;
> Thy firmness makes my circle just,
>   And makes me end where I begun.

The circle, so often invoked in discussions of the *Quartets*, appears at first to manage this section of *Little Gidding*. It moves from the "uncertain hour before morning" through the "intersection time" and back to the breaking of day. The firmness of the style and the ghost's poetically constructed authority make Eliot's circle "just," as it does justice to each of the many parts played by tradition and the individual talent. Where he ends, with the lessons of the past, is where he sat down to write this "imitation" of Dante. Yet, the foot of Eliot's compass is a ghost, a shadowy figure obliquely running. His ending beginning is a breaking of the circle. The blowing of the horn trumpets the fading of even a ghostly center, leaving poet and reader at the recurrent dawning of the ending. Donne's poem recollects reunion in a metaphor of circumscriptions; Eliot's poem repeats Donne's and breaks it into reinscriptions that can never be exactly measured.

Breaking occurs in repetition, as repetition disfigures what it represents. Thus, in the light of the eclipse, dawn breaks on the "present," and memory find its vocation.

> This is the use of memory:
> For liberation—not less of love but expanding
> Of love beyond desire, and so liberation
> From the future as well as the past.

Eliot goes on to reject the notion of memory as nostalgic recollection and to repudiate thinking of the future as if it were simply perpetuation or recovery.

> History may be servitude,
> History may be freedom. See, now they vanish,
> The faces and places, with the self which, as it could, loved
>   them,
> To become renewed, transfigured, in another pattern.

The same interplay of recollection and repetition pertains to "history." The weight of historical inheritance lightens when "servitude" to the past becomes the "freedom" of transfiguration/disfiguration. The end of Western history, here in England and always, ceases to be a privileged, unique catastrophe. It, too, dismally repeats and must be made the occasion of a renewal sprung from disillusion. Because "history is a pattern / Of timeless moments," Eliot believes that "A people without history / Is not redeemed from time" by forgetfulness or resignation to the Same. The timelessness of ghostly moments and their passions depends on the purpose of the historical memory. Condemned to repeat history in interpretation, humanity at least has the option of refusing to repeat it in action. Wars are revenge tragedies, directed at another whose conquest offers the delusion of purgation. Against this, Eliot counsels relinquishment, though not appeasement.

Eliot supports the war against fascism. What he questions, most pointedly in "The Idea of a Christian Society," is the "validity of a civilisation" centered on the economic imperative; a civilization deluded by the promise of recuperated investments, living as if fresh profits could erase the traces of human loss and degradation without accounting for their wastes. Eliot wondered if the combatants were dissimilar only in the degree to which they would brutalize and exploit life for political power and economic gain. Through an odd lens compounded of Marx and Christ, which often yielded strange visions, Eliot interrogated that "organization of society on the principle of private profit, as well as public destruction" reigning throughout the West, connecting the Allies and Axis in a single pattern. On this, that the root causes of the war were economic and spiritual, Pound and Eliot largely agreed. The fires of the war present an opportunity for reexamining the servitude to ruling ideologies perpetuated by corrupt desires and bad memories. Time will reduce all to vanity; freedom may be facilitated by bidding farewell to them, allowing them to vanish in the revision of humility. The war provides the "objective correlative" of the meditation that is *Little Gidding*. How we are to recover from it, how its irreparable losses are to be fit into a progressive, profitable philosophical economy, poetry cannot say without disfiguring and disillusioning the partisans on every side.

Incarnating breakage, the war repeats the pattern Eliot finds in memory and literature. In fact, the poems of the *Quartets* link their subjects and levels of discourse in a general philosophical argument about the economy of waste and enrichments, in which the war is but another, if terrifying, example. In section 5 of *Little Gidding* the argument moves from the particular manifestation of the war to the general reflection on loss, value, and the aberrant economy they figure when covenants of measurement are suspended. Adjusted to the surprises at play in remembrance, the poem economically transfigures its own recollections of itself: "What we call the beginning is often the end / And to make an end is to make a beginning / The end is where we start from." Previously we had started from "home." Home ends now; our being at home in the poem is ending. We shall soon start up from the text, go home, begin again, and find home transfigured as this text produces a different text from the one we had initially figured. The "home" we come to is a process of understanding characterized by its identification with the structure of language.

> And every phrase
> And every sentence that is right (where every word is at home,
> Taking its place to support the others,
> The word neither diffident nor ostentatious,
> An easy commerce of the old and the new,
> The common word exact without vulgarity,
> The formal word precise but not pedantic,
> The complete consort dancing together)
> Every phrase and every sentence is an end and a beginning,
> Every poem an epitaph.

The ideal "commerce" set off in parentheses might be assimilated to a

theology of poetic formalism or unanxious influence were it not equally
asserted that every poem is "an epitaph." The poem, or any utterance,
elegizes. It commemorates loss, marking the grave of that passionate moment language can only approach belatedly in a representation. And it
marks its own grave, too, dies onto the page: "And any action / Is a step
to the block, to the fire, down the sea's throat / Or to an illegible stone:
and that is where we start." We are at home with illegible stones, in the
graveyard/library of tumbled expressions, "dancing together" with the
dead.

The act of writing violates the calm of supposed securities, marks the
whiteness of the page and moment with a darkness into which we read.
Reading starts with the illegible, and the illegible is its end. Reading repeats
the act of disfiguring/transfiguring as it produces yet another pattern of
language: every interpretation an epitaph. That pattern in turn appears
illegible to the future that castrates, murders, loves, and resurrects it. Inscriptions, like the entombed Madeline Usher, break from their crypts with
meanings beyond the figured purpose, called from their graves by their
living literary lovers. Writing and reading supplement each other's destructive acts, die into each other's embrace, are each other's ghostly double,
and reproduce life in their narrative. The process is memory's, too, and
also conditions the formation of knowledge about identity, time, and being:
"We are born with the dead." The poem will itself die and in its final stanza
be born with the dying lines gathered up and returned from their previous
incarnations. These last lines of the *Quartets* create an Eliotic palimpsest,
its form of repetition perfectly tuned to the theme of a renewal in illegibility,
an ecstatic unknowing of past versions. Unceasing exploration arrives
"where we started" and knows "the place for the first time" as an epitaph,
thus a liberation. To know "Through the unknown, remembered gate" is
to write/remember the place out of place, to be in a present place and know
it as the displacement of where we have been. What was remembered was
unknown, and it is known now by a repetition that occurs "When the last
of earth left to discover / Is that which was the beginning." By repeating
his American beginnings ("the source of the longest river / The voice of
the hidden waterfall / And the children in the apple-tree") the poet unknows
them. They are severed from enchainment to past meaning or future deliverance and are made sights of rediscovery. They were

> Not known, because not looked for
> But heard, half-heard, in the stillness
> Between two waves of the sea.

These moments, "Quick now, here, now, always—" signify the evanescent
and ungraspable sensations of the moment, always flickering just before
language arrives to take them home and make them known. Known, like
woman to this imagination, they fall. The imagination may figure for us,
remembering, the idea of a virgin present "Between two waves of the sea,"

like Aphrodite sprung from the breakers of past and future. In the wake of this breaking is not an absence, but the fully resounding language of ghostly compounds, voicing real beauties.

Understanding this loss and gain, readying conservation for metamorphosis into projection, the imagination, compounded of emotion and intellect, suffers a sea change to "A condition of complete simplicity / (Costing not less than everything)." Possessed by way of dispossession, the poet treasures remembered beauties as potential repetitions, recurrences exceeding the taxonomy of living and dead, same and different—and in that excess known for the first time. These categories break, in literature as in life, when the convenant of identity and abstration is distracted, revolved as in Dante's final canto of the *Paradiso* by the loving will that explores the illegible details of passionate moments. The writing of exploration recovers by awakening/dying into the eternity of transfiguring, disillusioning dawns. An altered sense is given to Emerson's prophetic assertion at the beginning of *Nature* that "the sun shines to-day also." Night and day forever interpenetrating, the divine sun always a ghost on the horizon, losses are tossed up, and memories supplied that they may burn to light the presence of day.

> And all shall be well and
> All manner of thing shall be well
> When the tongues of flame are in-folded
> Into the crowned knot of fire
> And the fire and the rose are one.

Eliot ends reenvisioning Dante's paradisial end, recalling the ingathering of "substances and accidents and their relations" that are "bound by love in one single volume." Disfigured by Eliot, the vision incorporates an image of passionate and destructive change in the connotations now carried by flame and fire. This fire combines the actions of disintegration and revision in producing its transfigurations of the past. The flames of poetic tongues gather, laced rather than fused, in a knot that reserves their individual strands as they are tied together in a singular incendiary device. The "crowned knot of fire" stands for the torchlight that is tradition, the intersection world, the suspended timing of texts and repetitions burning to illuminate the darkness they discover at beginning and end. A dazzling metaphor, the fiery knot lights the paths of literature and consciousness, consuming the fuels of desire. So conceived and put to the torch, "the fire and the rose are one." The rose of perfection, recollection, and order is also "in-folded" in the erotic and literary fire, thus uniting the hue of natural passion with the color of the tongues of flame to form a final figure for personal and poetic history.

The rose garden is on fire. The desire for unity, consummation, bliss, the eternal recurrence of the Same, undergoes its last askesis. Polysemous, the emblem of the rose unites nature's Eros with poetry's theology in order to refine the longings and delusions of both. As a knot of fire, the rose becomes an eternal flame of enlightened disillusionment, a process of love that gains energy from its losses of identity and grows strong in the repetition of other times it heatedly ingathers. Love, as the overcoming of self-consciousness and the repetition of an ancient pattern in modern figures, renews itself just as the poem is renewed by entwining itself with its precursors. Purged of its illusions, the rose dances in the "tongues of flame" that repeat and inspire it, re-marking the measures of poetry and love.

Conrad Aiken: The Self
against the Sky

Delmore Schwartz

Most poets publish too many poems. Consequently their collected volumes
are disorderly, overgrown parks in which the reader is lost and masterpieces
are obscured by volubility and prolixity. This is certainly true of Wordsworth, as it is true of Browning, and to a lesser extent true of Keats, Shelley,
Tennyson, Swinburne, and Robinson, among others. The real difficulty is
that it is necessary, often, to write a great deal in order to write a few good
poems, and the poet has no certain way of knowing whether he is about
to write a good or bad poem.

But then, at the other extreme, there are some poets—and this volume
shows that Aiken is one of them—who reach their full meaning and being
only when they write a great deal and are read in bulk. Hardy is perhaps
the best example. In a literal sense his work would not exist if he had not
written more than a thousand pages of lyric poems; if, indeed, he had not
written a great many poems which are in themselves weak, poor, or defective, but give his work a rich completeness which no single poem contains. And the complication is increased by the deception of the anthology:
the jewels of anthologies invariably misrepresent poets like Hardy and
Aiken, just as they sustain the vulgar, natural tendency to regard poetry
as consisting of purple passages, isolated eloquence, and excited language.

Hence this volume of collected poems, which contains the work of
forty years, is valuable in that it helps to remove such obstructions as
anthological habitation, the false lights of literary fashion, and the complex,
contradictory impressions which accumulate during a long and complex
poetic career. But far more important than that, the inclusive character of
the volume makes possible a new experience of all of Aiken's work. Poems
which at first seemed unimportant in themselves gain a new and profound

From *The New Republic* 129, no. 14 (November 2, 1953). © 1953 by *The New Republic*.

meaning as phases and stages of a long progress and pilgrimage. And other poems, which seemed when they appeared separately to be only charming and delightful lyrics, exist now in a new light, possessing an underlying seriousness which was not at first apparent.

The progress and pilgrimage begins and ends with the situation of modern man, the situation of the modern ego naked and alone in the midst of a cosmos which may be as meaningless as it is enormous, or which may have a hidden meaning, but which certainly makes every hope and belief subject to the torment of doubt. This sense of existence arose with the overwhelming triumph of physical science; it haunted and obsessed the poetry of the nineteenth century (which is the reason that Arnold's "Dover Beach" is the most representative poem of the century); and it presents itself less directly in most modern poetry only because it has been taken for granted: there is no longer a conflict between the world pictures of religion and of science because the religious image of the world has long since ceased to be a literal and *visual* part of consciousness.

Where other modern poets take the modern image of the cosmos as, at most, a point of departure, or a background irrelevant to human concerns and values, in Aiken's work it is always present as an inevitable awareness, as a kind of cold night which surrounds all things, like the sky itself. Whatever the subject, object, or emotion of the poem, it *is* framed within this awareness: everything may be a dream, hallucination, illusion, or delusion, as everything is subject to time, nature, and death. The self is hidden from the self by the very nature of the self, as it is removed from true certainty about love, knowledge, nature, and society. The mind and every object of the mind exist within an inexhaustible mystery and abyss:

> Then came I to the shoreless shore of silence
> Where never summer was, nor shade of tree,
> Nor sound of water, nor sweet light of the sun,
> But only nothing and the shore of nothing,
> Above, below, around, and in my heart.

But no matter how great the darkness, one cannot live by darkness. One must confront the darkness of existence—the silence of the stars, the depths of the atom, the gulf between each conscious being—with all the attitudes which the imagination makes possible. This is the essential center of Aiken's poetry. It has often been admired for the wrong reasons or misunderstood because it is a veritable fountain of attitudes toward existence as a whole. He is a metaphysical poet in the old sense of metaphysical which has virtually nothing to do with the metaphors of John Donne. The wind does not merely blow; "the wind blows from Arcturus"; a human being cannot be seen within a narrative or dramatic framework, but " . . . it was there, at eight o'clock, I saw / Vivien and the infinite together."

The universe of the Milky Way and of the atom is the context within which any particular thing must be perceived. Within this cosmic perspective, all particulars are subordinated, and reduced to scale, a necessary virtue which makes the surface of the poetry seem to the careless reader at once too rhetorical and too bare. This superficial reading is encouraged by the wonderful musical quality which Aiken's poetry has always possessed, and it persists only because the symbolic and emotional function of every statement is not perceived, and the underlying attitudes are not grasped.

These attitudes can hardly be formulated exactly into intellectual abstractions. They resist prose formulation, and naturally, since they achieve actuality only through the concreteness of rhythm and tone. Their variety and their uniqueness also evade the platitude of the formula, which is a way of saying again that only a reading of this collected volume will show how important a poet Aiken is. What is possible is an approximation of the scope and span of attitude. At one extreme there is the child and the angel, "the simple voice that says . . . Here is a letter from the other world, / Here is news from the land of the everlasting." At the other extreme there is the celebration and praise of Lazarus, of one who has walked in the valley of the shadow, and returned, joyous and triumphant, to say: "Give us this day our daily death that we / May learn to live." Moving through the phases between these two extremes, there is always a sense of "the causeless melancholy of the rain," "the cold treble" of the piano, the sound of "a surf of leaves when the wind blows." And the hard-earned affirmation with which the poet most often concludes is a declaration of the godhead of the self, agonized and miraculous.

The Poetry of a Supreme Technician: Conrad Aiken

Dudley Fitts

Whatever stature the work of Conrad Aiken may ultimately assume in the long run of criticism, we can affirm now, without risking prematurity of judgment, that he is one of the supreme technicians of modern English poetry. There are few writers, either in prose or in verse, who can challenge his mastery of language, who give us anything comparable to his assurance in controlling the most powerful and varied and nervous resources of expression. His writing has the inevitability of the highest art; it is, rhetorically, definitive. The very first lines of this new book are an example:

> Fanfare of northwest wind, a bluejay wind
> announces autumn, and the Equinox
> rolls back blue bays to a far afternoon.

Such verses reward the closest investigation; the placing of the caesura, with the resultant contrapuntal interplay of the subordinate cadences and the great arc of rhythm; the delicate modulation, by inversion and assonance, of the melody—all true, all demonstrable; together with what is less demonstrable but no less true: an inventive power, beyond language itself, that makes the sweep and the space and the color happen on the page before our eyes. And happen not merely here, or in other scattered instances, but constantly in these poems; and constantly in the earlier poems, as far back as we can go. The unalterable concord of image, of diction, of musical phrase; this is the signature of Conrad Aiken.

Unfortunately the public, or that part of the public that is conscious of poetry at all, finds it a too special signature. It must; otherwise Aiken would have had more than the considerable but still perfunctory recognition that he has been given. It is not too much to say that he is our least

From *The New Republic* 133, no. 26 (December 26, 1955). © 1955 by *The New Republic*.

considered major poet: the artist whom everyone acknowledges, whom everyone thereupon forgets to recall. The canons of contemporary poetry itself are partly to blame. The art is so private, so much a matter of poet A writing for himself, or, at most, with a reluctant ear cocked in the direction of poets B and C, that the man who is composing openly and in the great tradition is regarded with some dismay, as though he were either a throwback or an uncomfortable kind of ghost. Moreover, we are not used to the courtesy of grace.

A poet may puzzle us, tickle us, shock us, and we accept him as a good man accepts his fate; let a poet try to delight us, and we think of what happened to the poor dear Victorians. So art can defeat itself, it seems: no surface so lovely can be quite respectable. Such a state of mind will assent to the static little symbolists and formalists on all sides of us and deny a true poet his praise chiefly because he is true. So it may be, partly, with Conrad Aiken.

Partly, but not wholly. There can be such a thing as too much art, too great a preoccupation with the instrument; and then rhetoric, in the uneasy sense of the word, is a danger. It is here, I think, rather than in the withdrawn self-searching temper of the poet's mind, that the harmful qualifications lie. It is perilous to speak with the tongues of angels and not of men if the substance of what is spoken is not also memorable. And although I find much in these poems that is just, and much more that is privately or nostalgically poignant, I do not generally find a significance to match the style. I am oddly most moved, though certainly not most impressed, by passages that the poet clearly intends to be subordinate:

> the divine touch that in the radiant fingertips
> could at once create, with a magician's eloquence,
> nothing from something, or something from nothing:
> as, out of the untouched piano,
> a shabby chord, a threadbare tune, the banal air
> squealing from the midnight juke-box, where,
> at the corner saloon, over the tepid beer,
> you sit and stare—

It is all there, it is inevitable; yet the mind is fascinated by it, not compelled, not possessed. It has the quality of supreme improvisation, a grace and truth that beguile us without quite touching the heart. A falling short, maybe; if so, it is happening at a level that few of our poets have even dreamed of.

Notes on E. E. Cummings's Language

R. P. Blackmur

In his four books of verse, his play, and the autobiographical *Enormous Room*, Mr. Cummings has amassed a special vocabulary and has developed from it a special use of language which these notes are intended to analyze and make explicit. Critics have commonly said, when they understood Mr. Cummings's vocabulary at all, that he has enriched the language with a new idiom; had they been further interested in the uses of language, they would no doubt have said that he had added to the general sensibility of his time. Certainly his work has had many imitators. Young poets have found it easy to adopt the attitudes from which Mr. Cummings has written, just as they often adopt the superficial attitudes of Swinburne and Keats. The curious thing about Mr. Cummings's influence is that his imitators have been able to emulate as well as ape him; which is not so frequently the case with the influence of Swinburne and Keats. Mr. Cummings is a school of writing in himself; so that it is necessary to state the underlying assumptions of his mind, and of the school which he teaches, before dealing with the specific results in poetry of those assumptions.

It is possible to say that Mr. Cummings belongs to the anti-culture group; what has been called at various times vorticism, futurism, dadaism, surrealism, and so on. Part of the general dogma of this group is a sentimental denial of the intelligence and the deliberate assertion that the unintelligible is the only object of significant experience. These dogmas have been defended with considerable dialectical skill, on the very practical premise that only by presenting the unintelligible as viable and actual *per se* can the culture of the *dead intelligence* (Brattle Street, the Colleges, and the Reviews) be shocked into sentience. It is argued that only by denying to

From *R. P. Blackmur's Language as Gesture: Essays in Poetry.* © 1952 by R. P. Blackmur, renewed 1980 by Elizabeth Blackmur. Harcourt, Brace, 1952.

the intelligence its function of discerning quality and order can the failures of the intelligence be overcome; that if we take things as they come without remembering what has gone before or guessing what may come next, and if we accept these things at their face value, we shall know life, at least in the arts, as it really is. Nothing could be more arrogant, and more deceptively persuasive to the childish spirit, than such an attitude when held as fundamental. It appeals to the intellect which wishes to work swiftly and is in love with immediate certainty. A mind based on it accepts every fragment of experience as final and every notion as definite, yet never suffers from the delusion that it has learned anything. By an astonishing accident, enough unanimity exists among these people to permit them to agree among themselves; to permit them, even, to seem spiritually indistinguishable as they appear in public.

The central attitude of this group has developed, in its sectaries, a logical and thoroughgoing set of principles and habits. In America, for example, the cause of the lively arts has been advanced against the ancient seven; because the lively arts are necessarily immediate in appeal and utterly transitory. Thus we find in Mr. Cummings's recent verse and in his play *Him* the side show and the cabaret set up as "inevitable" frames for experience. Jazz effects, tough dialects, tough guys, slim hot queens, barkers, fairies, and so on, are made into the media and symbols of poetry. Which is proper enough in Shakespeare where such effects are used ornamentally or for pure play. But in Cummings such effects are employed as substance, as the very mainstay of the poetry. There is a continuous effort to escape the realism of the intelligence in favor of the realism of the obvious. What might be stodgy or dull because not properly worked up into poetry is replaced by the tawdry and by the fiction of the immediate.

It is no great advantage to get rid of one set of flabby generalities if the result is merely the immersion of the sensibility in another set only superficially less flabby. The hardness of the tough guy is mostly in the novelty of the language. There is no hardness in the emotion. The poet is as far from the concrete as before. By denying the dead intelligence and putting on the heresy of unintelligence, the poet only succeeds in substituting one set of unnourished conventions for another. What survives, with a deceptive air of reality, is a surface. That the deception is often intentional hardly excuses it. The surface is meant to clothe and illuminate a real substance, but in fact it is impenetrable. We are left, after experiencing this sort of art, with the certainty that there was nothing to penetrate. The surface was perfect; the deceit was childish; and the conception was incorrigibly sentimental: all because of the dogma which made them possible.

If Mr. Cummings's tough-guy poems are excellent examples of this sentimentality, it is only natural that his other poems—those clothed in the more familiar language of the lyric—should betray even more obviously, even more perfectly, the same fault. There, in the lyric, there is no pretense at hardness of surface. We are admitted at once to the bare emotion. What is most striking, in every instance, about this emotion is the fact that, insofar as it exists at all, it is Mr. Cummings's emotion, so that our best knowledge of it must be, finally, our best guess. It is not an emotion resulting from the poem; it existed before the poem began and is a result of the poet's private life. Besides its inspiration, every element in the poem, and its final meaning as well, must be taken at face value or not at all. This is the extreme form, in poetry, of romantic egoism: whatever I experience is real and final, and whatever I say represents what I experience. Such a dogma is the natural counterpart of the denial of the intelligence.

Our interest is not in the abstract principle, but in the results of its application in poetry. Assuming that a poem should in some sense be understood, should have a meaning apart from the poet's private life, either one of two things will be true about any poem written from such an attitude as we have ascribed to Mr. Cummings. Either the poem will appear in terms so conventional that everybody will understand it—when it will be flat and no poem at all; or it will appear in language so far distorted from convention as to be inapprehensible except by lucky guess. In neither instance will the poem be genuinely complete. It will be the notes for a poem, from which might flow an infinite number of possible poems, but from which no particular poem can be certainly deduced. It is the purpose of this paper to examine a few of the more obvious types of distortion which Mr. Cummings has practiced upon language.

The question central to such a discussion will be what kind of meaning does Mr. Cummings's poetry have; what is the kind of equivalence between the language and its object. The pursuit of such a question involves us immediately in the relations between words and feelings, and the relations between the intelligence and its field in experience—all relations which are precise only in terms themselves essentially poetic—in the feeling for an image, the sense of an idiom. Such relations may only be asserted, may be judged only tentatively, only instinctively, by what seems to be the disciplined experience, but what amounts, perhaps, only to the formed taste. Here criticism is appreciation. But appreciation, even, can take measures to be certain of its grounds, and to be full should betray the constant apprehension of an end which is the necessary consequence, the proper rounding off, of just those grounds. In the examination of Mr. Cummings's writing the grounds will be the facts about the words he uses, and the end will be apprehended in the quality of the meaning his use of these words permits.

There is one attitude toward Mr. Cummings's language which has deceived those who hold it. The typographical peculiarities of his verse have caught and irritated public attention. Excessive hyphenation of single words, the use of lower case "i," the breaking of lines, the insertion of punctuation between the letters of a word, and so on, will have a possible critical importance to the textual scholarship of the future; but extensive consideration of these peculiarities today has very little importance, carries almost no reference to the *meaning* of the poems. Mr. Cummings's experiments in typography merely extend the theory of notation by adding to the number, *not* to the *kind*, of conventions the reader must bear in mind, and are dangerous only because since their uses cannot readily be defined, they often obscure rather than clarify the exact meaning. No doubt the continued practice of such notation would produce a set of well-ordered conventions susceptible of general use. At present the practice can only be "allowed for," recognized in the particular instance, felt, and forgotten: as the diacritical marks in the dictionary are forgotten once the sound of the word has been learned. The poem, after all, only takes wing on the page, it persists in the ear.

Considering typographical peculiarities for our present purposes as either irrelevant or unaccountable, there remain the much more important peculiarities of Mr. Cummings's vocabulary itself; of the poem *after* it has been read, as it is in the mind's ear, as it is on the page only for reassurance and correction.

If a reader, sufficiently familiar with these poems not to be caught on the snag of novelty, inspects carefully any score of them, no matter how widely scattered, he will especially be struck by a sameness among them. This sameness will be in two sorts—a vagueness of image and a constant recurrence of words. Since the one depends considerably upon the other, a short list of some of Mr. Cummings's favorite words will be a good preliminary to the examination of his images. In *Tulips and Chimneys* words such as these occur frequently—thrilling, flowers, serious, absolute, sweet, unspeaking, utter, gradual, ultimate, final, serene, frail, grave, tremendous, slender, fragile, skillful, carefully, intent, young, gay, untimid, incorrigible, groping, dim, slow, certain, deliberate, strong, chiseled, subtle, tremulous, perpetual, crisp, perfect, sudden, faint, strenuous, minute, superlative, keen, ecstatic, actual, fleet, delicious, stars, enthusiastic, capable, dull, bright. In listing these as favorite words, it is meant that these words do the greater part of the work in the poems where they occur; these are the words which qualify the subject matter of the poems, and are sometimes even the subjects themselves. Observe that none of them, taken alone, are very *concrete* words; and observe that many of them are the rather *abstract*, which is to say typical, *names* for precise qualities, but are not, and cannot be, as *originally important* words in a poem, very precise or very concrete or very abstract: they are middling words, not in themselves very much one thing or the other, and should be useful only with respect to something concrete in itself.

If we take Mr. Cummings's most favored word "flower" and inspect the uses to which he puts it, we should have some sort of key to the kind of poetry he writes. In *Tulips and Chimneys* the word "flower" turns up, to a casual count, forty-eight times, and in *&*, a much smaller volume, twenty-one times. We have among others the following: smile like a flower, riverly is a flower; steeped in burning flowers; last flower; lipping flowers; more silently than a flower; snow flower; world flower; softer than flowers; forehead a flight of flowers; feet are flowers in vases; air is deep with flowers; slow supple flower of beauty; flower-terrible; flower of thy mouth; stars and flowers; mouth the new flower; flowers of silence; god's flowers; flowers of reminding; dissonant flowers; flower-stricken air; Sunday flower; tremendous flower; speaking flower; flowers of kiss; futile flowers, etc., etc. Besides the general term there is a quantity of lilies and roses, and a good assortment of daisies, pansies, buttercups, violets, and chrysanthemums. There are also many examples of such associated words as "petals" and "blooms" and "blossoms," which, since they are similarly used, may be taken as alternative to flowers.

Now it is evident that this word must attract Mr. Cummings's mind very much; it must contain for him an almost unlimited variety and extent of meaning; as the mystic says god, or at least as the incomplete mystic repeats the name of god to every occasion of his soul, Mr. Cummings in some of his poems says flower. The question is, whether or not the reader can possibly have shared the experience which Mr. Cummings has had of the word; whether or not it is possible to discern, after any amount of effort, the precise impact which Mr. Cummings undoubtedly feels upon his whole experience when he uses the word. "Flower," like every other word not specifically the expression of a logical relation, began life as a metaphor, as a leap from feeling to feeling, as a bridge in the imagination to give meaning to both those feelings. Presumably, the amount of meaning possible to the word is increased with each use, but only the meaning *possible*. Actually, in practice, a very different process goes on. Since people are occupied mostly with communication and argument and conversation, with the erection of discursive relationships, words are commonly spoken and written with the *least* possible meaning preserved, instead of the most. History is taken for granted, ignored, or denied. Only the outsides of words, so to speak, are used; and doubtless the outsides of words are all that the discursive intellect needs. But when a word is used in a poem it should be the sum of all its appropriate history made concrete and particular in the individual context; and in poetry all words act *as if* they were so used, because the only kind of meaning poetry can have requires that all its words resume their full life: the full life being modified and made unique by the *qualifications* the words perform one upon the other in the poem. Thus even a very bad poem may seem good to its author, when the author is not an acute critic and believes that there is life in his words merely because there was life (and a very different sort of life, truly) in the feelings which they represent. An author should remember, with the Indians, that the reality of a word is anterior to, and greater than, his use of it can ever be; that there is a perfection to the feelings in words to which his mind cannot hope to attain, but that his chief labor will be toward the approximation of that perfection.

We sometimes speak of a poet as a master of his words, and we sometimes say that a man's poetry has been run away with by words—meaning that he has not mastered his words but has been overpowered by his peculiar experience of certain among them. Both these notions are commonly improper, because they represent misconceptions of the nature of poetry in so far as they lay any stress upon originality, or the lack of it, in the poet's use of words. The only mastery possible to the poet consists in that entire submission to his words which is perfect knowledge. The only originality of which the poet is properly capable will be in the choice of order, and even this choice is largely a process of discovery rather than of origination. As for words running away with a poet or a poem, it would be more accurate to say that the poet's *ideas* had run away with him than his words.

This is precisely what has occurred to Mr. Cummings in his use of the word "flower" as a maid of all work. The word has become an idea, and in the process has been deprived of its history, its qualities, and its meaning. An idea, the intellectual pin upon which a thought is hung, is not transmissible in poetry as an important element in the poem and ought only to be employed to pass over, with the greatest possible velocity, the area of the uninteresting (what the poet was not interested in). That is, in a poem whose chief intent was the notation of character and yet required a descriptive setting, the poet might well use for the description such vague words as space and time, but could not use such words as goodness or nobleness without the risk of flatness. In Mr. Cummings's poetry we find the contrary; the word "flower," because of the originality with which he conceives it, becomes an idea and is used to represent the most interesting and most important aspect of his poem. Hence the center of the poem is permanently abstract and unknowable for the reader, and remains altogether without qualifications and concreteness. It is not the mere frequency of use that deadens the word flower into an idea; it is the kind of thought which each use illustrates in common. By seldom saying *what* flower, by seldom relating immitigably the abstract word to a specific experience, the content of the word vanishes; it has no inner mystery, only an impenetrable surface.

This is the defect, the essential deceit, we were trying to define. Without questioning Mr. Cummings, or any poet, as to sincerity (which is a personal attitude, irrelevant to the poetry considered) it is possible to say that when in any poem the important words are forced by their use to remain impenetrable, when they can be made to surrender nothing actually to the senses—then the poem is defective and the poet's words have so far deceived him as to become ideas merely. Mr. Cummings is not so much writing poetry, as he is dreaming, idly ringing the changes of his reveries.

Perhaps a small divagation may make clearer the relation of these remarks to Mr. Cummings's poems. Any poetry which does not consider itself as much of an art and having the same responsibilities to the consumer as the arts of silversmithing or cobbling shoes—any such poetry is likely to do little more than rehearse a waking dream. Dreams are everywhere ominous and full of meaning; and why should they not be? They hold the images of the secret self, and to the initiate dreamer betray the nerve of life at every turn, not through any effort to do so, or because of any inherited regimen, but simply because they cannot help it. Dreams are like that—to the dreamer the maximal limit of experience. As it happens, dreams employ words and pictorial images to fill out their flux with a veil of substance. Pictures are natural to everyone, and words, because they are prevalent, seem common and inherently sensible. Hence, both picture and word, and then with a little stretching of the fancy the substance of the dream itself, seem expressible just as they occur—as things created, as the very flux of life. Mr. Cummings's poems are often nothing more than the report of just such dreams. He believes he knows what he knows, and no doubt he does. But he also believes, apparently, that the words which he encourages most vividly to mind are those most precisely fitted to put his poem on paper. He transfers the indubitable magic of his private musings from the cell of his mind, where it is honest incantation, to the realm of poetry. Here he forgets that poetry, so far as it takes a permanent form, is written and is meant to be read, and that it cannot be a mere private musing. Merely because his private fancy furnishes his liveliest images, is the worst reason for assuming that this private fancy will be approximately experienced by the reader or even indicated on the printed page.

But it is unfair to limit this description to Mr. Cummings; indeed, so limited, it is not even a description of Mr. Cummings. Take the *Oxford Book of English Verse*, or any anthology of poems equally well known, and turn from the poems printed therein of such widely separated poets as Surrey, Crashaw, Marvell, Burns, Wordsworth, Shelley, and Swinburne, to the collected works of these poets respectively. Does not the description of Mr. Cummings's mind at work given above apply nearly as well to the bulk of this poetry as to that of Mr. Cummings, at least on the senses' first immersion? The anthology poems being well known are conceived to be understood, to be definitely intelligible, and to have, without inspection, a precise meaning. The descent upon the collected poems of all or of any one of these authors is by and large a descent into tenuity. Most of their work, most of any poet's work, with half a dozen exceptions, is tenuous and vague, private exercises or public playthings of a soul in verse. So far as he is able, the reader struggles to reach the concrete, the solid, the definite; he must have these qualities, or their counterparts among the realm of the spirit, before he can understand what he reads. To translate such qualities from the realm of his private experience to the conventional forms of poetry is the problem of the poet; and the problem of the reader, likewise, is to come well equipped with the talent and the taste for discerning the meaning of those conventions as they particularly occur. Neither the poet's casual language nor the reader's casual interlocution is likely to be much help. There must be a ground common but exterior to each: that is the poem. The best poems take the best but not always the hardest reading; and no doubt it is so with the writing. Certainly, in neither case are dreams or simple reveries enough. Dreams are natural and are minatory or portentous; but except when by accident they fall into forms that fit the intelligence, they never negotiate the miracle of meaning between the poet and the poem, the poem and the reader.

Most poetry fails of this negotiation, and it is sometimes assumed that the negotiation was never meant, by the poet, to be made. For the poet, private expression is said to be enough; for the reader, the agitation of the senses, the perception of verbal beauty, the mere sense of stirring life in the words, are supposed sufficient. If this defense had a true premise—if the poet did express himself to his private satisfaction—it would be un-answerable; and to many it is so. But I think the case is different, and this is the real charge against Mr. Cummings: the poet does not ever express himself privately. The mind cannot understand, cannot properly know its own musings until those musings take some sort of conventional form. Properly speaking a poet, or any man, cannot be adequate to himself in terms of himself. True consciousness and true expression of consciousness must be external to the blind seat of consciousness—man as a sensorium. Even a simple image must be fitted among other images, and conned with them, before it is understood. That is, it must take a form in langauge which is highly traditional and conventional. The genius of the poet is to make the convention apparently disappear into the use to which he puts it.

Mr. Cummings and the group with which he is here roughly associ-ated, the anti-culture or anti-intelligence group, persist to the contrary. Because experience is fragmentary as it strikes the consciousness it is thought to be essentially discontinuous and therefore essentially unintel-ligible except in the fragmentary form in which it occurred. They credit the words they use with immaculate conception and there hold them unques-tionable. A poem, because it happens, must mean something and mean it without relation to anything but the private experience which inspired it. Certainly it means something, but not a poem; it means that something exciting happened to the writer and that a mystery is happening to the reader. The fallacy is double: they believe in the inexorable significance of the unique experience; and they have discarded the only method of making the unique experience into a poem—the conventions of the intelligence. As a matter of fact they do not write without conventions, but being ig-norant of what they use, they resort most commonly to their own inefficient or superficial conventions—such as Mr. Cummings's flower and doll. The effect is convention without substance; the unique experience becomes a rhetorical assurance.

If we examine next, for the sake of the greatest possible contrast, one of the "tough" poems in *is 5*, we will find a similar breach with the concrete.

The use of vague words like "flower" in the lyrical poems as unexpanded similes, is no more an example of sentimental egoism than the use of vague conventions about villains. The distortion differs in terms but is essentially identical.

Sometimes the surface of the poem is so well constructed that the distortion is hard to discover. Intensity of process occassionally triumphs over the subject. Less frequently the subject itself is conceived directly and takes naturally the terms which the language supplies. The poem numbered One-XII in *is 5* is an example in so far as the sentimental frame does not obscure the process.

> now dis "daughter" uv eve (who aint precisely slim) sim

> ply don't know duh meanin uv duh woid sin in
> not disagreeable contras tuh dat not exactly fat

> "father" (adjustin his robe) who now puts on his flat hat

It is to be noted in this epigram, that there is no inexorable reason for either the dialect or the lapses from it into straight English. No one in particular is speaking, unless it be Mr. Cummings slumming in morals along with he-men and lady social workers, and taking it for granted that the dialect and the really refined language which the dialect exercises together give a setting. There are many other poems in *is 5*, more sentimental and less successful, where the realism is of a more obvious sort; not having reference to an ideal so much as to a kind of scientific reality. That is, there is an effort to ground an emotion, or the facts which make the emotion, in the style of the character to whom the emotion happens. It is the reporter, the man with the good ear for spoken rhythms, who writes out of memory. The war poems and the poem about Bill and his chip (One-XVI) are examples. Style in this sense (something laid on) is only an attribute; is not the man; is not the character. And when it is substituted for character, it is likely to be sentimental and melodramatic. That is, the emotion which is named in the poem (by one of its attributes) is in excess of its established source (that same attribute). There is a certain immediate protection afforded to this insufficiency by the surface toughness, by the convention of burlesque; as if by mocking oneself one made sure there was something to mock. It is a kind of trickery resulting from eager but lazy senses; where the sensation itself is an excess, and appears to have done all the work of intuition and intelligence; where sensation seems expert without incorporation into experience. As if sensation could be anything more than the idea of sensation, so far as poetry goes, without being attached to some central body of experience, genuinely understood and *formed* in the mind.

The intrusion of science into art always results in a sentimental realism and always obfuscates form when that science is not kept subordinate to the qualitative experience of the senses—as witness the run of sociological novels. The analogues of science, where conventions are made to do the work of feeling instead of crowning it, are even more dangerous. Mr. Cummings's tough guy and his hard-boiled dialects are such analogues.

Mr. Cummings has a fine talent for using familiar, even almost dead words, in such a context as to make them suddenly impervious to every ordinary sense; they become unable to speak, but with a great air of being bursting with something very important and precise to say. "The bigness of cannon is *skillful* . . . enormous rhythm of *absurdity* . . . *slimness* of *evenslicing* eyes are chisels . . . electric Distinct face haughtily vital *clinched* in a swoon of *synopsis* . . . my friend's being continually whittles *keen* careful futile *flowers*," etc. With the possible exception of the compound *evenslicing* the italicized words are all ordinary words; all in normal contexts have a variety of meanings both connotative and denotative; the particular context being such as to indicate a particular meaning, to establish precisely a feeling, a sensation or a relation.

Mr. Cummings's contexts are employed to an opposite purpose in so far as they wipe out altogether the history of the word, its past associations and general character. To seize Mr. Cummings's meaning there is only the free and *uninstructed* intuition. Something precise is no doubt intended; the warrant for the belief is in the almost violent isolation into which the words are thrown; but that precision can seldom, by this method, become any more than just that "something precise." The reality, the event, the feeling, which we will allow Mr. Cummings has in mind, is not sensibly in the word. It is one thing for meaning to be difficult, or abstruse—hidden in its heart, that is. "Absent thee from *felicity* a while," Blake's "Time is the *mercy* of eternity" are reasonable examples; there the mystery is inside the words. In Mr. Cummings's words the mystery flies in the face, is on the surface; because there is no inside, no realm of possibility, of essence.

The general movement of Mr. Cummings's language is away from communicable precision. If it be argued that the particular use of one of the italicized words above merely makes that word unique, the retort is that such uniqueness is too perfect, is sterile. If by removing the general sense of a word the special sense is apotheosized, it is only so at the expense of the general sense itself. The destruction of the general sense of a word results in the loss of that word's individuality; for in practice the character of a word (which is its sense) is manifest only in good society, and meaning is distinguished only by conventional association. Mr. Cummings's use of words results in a large number of conventions, but these conventions do not permeate the words themselves, do not modify their souls or change their fates; they cannot be adopted by the reader because they cannot be essentially understood. They should rather be called inventions.

If we take a paragraph from the poem beginning on page thirty in *is 5,* we will discover another terminus of the emotional habit of mind which produced the emphasis on the word "flower" in *Tulips and Chimneys.*

the Bar.tinking luscious jigs dint of ripe silver with warmlyish
wetflat splurging smells waltz the glush of squirting taps plus slush

of foam knocked off and a faint piddle-of-drops she says I ploc
spittle what the lands thaz me kid in no sir hopping sawdust you
kiddo he's a palping wreaths of badly Yep cigars who jim him
why gluey grins topple together eyes pout gestures stickily point
made glints squinting who's a wink bum-nothing and money fuz-
zily mouths take big wobbly foot-steps every goggle cent of it get
out ears dribbles soft right old feller belch the chap hic summore
eh chuckles skulch.

Now the point is that the effect of this whole paragraph has much in
common with the effect of the word "flower." It is a flower disintegrated,
and the parts are not component; so that by presenting an analysis of his
image Mr. Cummings has not let us into its secret: the analysis is not a
true analysis, because it exhibits, finally, what are still only the results, not
the grounds, of his private conventions, his personal emotions. It is indubitable that the words are alive; they jostle, even overturn, the reader
in the assurance of their vitality; but the notion of what their true vitality
is remains Mr. Cummings's very own. The words remain emotive. They
have a gutsy air of being something, but they defeat themselves in the
effort to say what, and come at last to a bad end, all fallen in a heap.

The easiest *explanation* of the passage would be to say that each separate
little collection of words in it is a note for an image; an abstraction, very
keen and lively in Mr. Cummings's mind, of something very precise and
concrete. Some of the words seem like a painter's note, some a philologist's.
But they are all, as they are presented, notes, abstractions, ideas—with
their concrete objects unknown—except to the most arbitrary guess. The
guess must be arbitrary because of the quantity, not the quality, of the
words employed. Mr. Cummings is not here overworking the individual
words, but by heaping so many of them together he destroys their individuality. Meaning really residual in the word is not exhausted, is not even
touched; it must remain abstract and only an emotional substitute for it
can be caught. The interesting fact about emotional substitutes in poetry,
as elsewhere, is their thinness, and the inadequacy resulting from the thinness. The thinness is compulsory because they can, so far as the poem is
concerned, exist only as a surface; they cannot possess tentacular roots
reaching into, and feeding on, feelings, because the feelings do not exist,
are only present by legerdemain. Genuine emotion in poetry perhaps does
not *exist* at all; though it is none the less real for that, because a genuine
emotion does not need the warrant of existence: it is the necessary result,
in the mind, of a convention of feelings: like the notion of divine grace.

In *Tulips and Chimneys* there is a poem whose first and last lines supply
an excellent opposition of proper and improper distortion of language.

the Cambridge ladies who live in furnished souls

. . . .

the
moon rattles like a fragment of angry candy

In the context the word "soul" has the element of surprise which is surprise at *justness*, at *aptness;* it fits in and finishes off the notion of the line. "Furnished souls" is a good, if slight, conceit; and there is no trouble for the reader who wishes to know what the line means: he has merely to *extend* his knowledge slightly, just as Mr. Cummings merely extended the sense of his language slightly by releasing his particular words in this particular order. The whole work that the poet here demands of his reader is pretty well defined. The reader does not have to *guess;* he is enabled to *know.* The reader is not collecting data, he is aware of a meaning.

It would be unfair not to quote the context of the second line.

> the Cambridge ladies do not care, above
> Cambridge if sometimes in its box of
> sky lavender and cornerless, the
> moon rattles like a fragment of angry candy

We can say that Mr. Cummings is putting beauty next to the tawdry; juxtaposing the dead with the live; or that he is being sentimentally philosophical in verse—that is, releasing from inadequate sources something intended to be an emotion.

We can go on illustrating Mr. Cummings's probable intentions almost infinitely. What Mr. Cummings likes or admires, what he holds dear in life, he very commonly calls flowers, or dolls, or candy—terms with which he is astonishingly generous; as if he thought by making his terms general enough their vagueness could not matter, and never noticed that the words so used enervate themselves in a kind of hardened instinct. We can understand what Mr. Cummings intended by "moon" and "candy" but in the process of understanding, the meaning of the words themselves disappears. The thrill of the association of "rattles" with "moon" and "angry" with "candy" becomes useless as a guide. "Rattles" and "angry" can only be continued in the meaning of the line if the reader supplies them with a force, a definiteness of suggestion, with which Mr. Cummings has not endowed them.

The distortion is here not a release of observation so keen that commonplace language would not hold it; it is not the presentation of a vision so complete that words must lose their normal meanings in order to suggest it. It is, on the contrary, the distortion of the commonplace itself; and the difficulty about a commonplace is that it cannot be known, it has no character, no fate, and no essence. It is a substitute for these.

True meaning (which is here to say knowledge) can only exist where some contact, however remote, is preserved between the language, forms, or symbols in which it is given and something concrete, individual, or sensual which inspired it; and the degree in which the meaning is seized will depend on the degree in which the particular concreteness is realized. Thus the technique of "meaning" will employ distortion only in so far as the sense of this concreteness is promoted by it. When contrast and con-

tradiction disturb the ultimate precision of the senses the distortion involved is inappropriate and destructive. Mr. Cummings's line about the
moon and candy does not weld a contradiction, does not identify a substance by a thrill of novel association. It leaves the reader at a loss; where
it is impossible to *know*, after any amount of effort and good will, what the
words mean. If it be argued that Mr. Cummings was not interested in
meaning then Mr. Cummings is not a serious poet, is a mere collector of
sensations, and can be of very little value to us. And to defend Mr. Cummings on the ground that he is in the pretty good company of Swinburne,
Crashaw, and Victor Hugo, is partly to ignore the fact that by the same
argument all four also enjoy the companionship of Mr. Guest. Such defense
would show a very poor knowledge of the verses of Mr. Cummings, who
is nothing if not serious in the attempt to exhibit precise knowledge. His
interest in words and in their real meaning is probably greater than that
of most poets of similar dimensions. He has consciously stretched syntax,
word order, and meaning in just the effort to expand knowledge in poetry;
and his failure is because he has gone too far, has lost sight of meaning
altogether—and because, perhaps, the experience which he attempts to
translate into poetry remained always personal to him and was never
known objectively as itself. By his eagerness Mr. Cummings's relation to
language has become confused; he has put down what has meant much
to him and can mean little to us, because for us it is not put down—is only
indicated, only possibly there. The freshness and depth of his private experience is not denied; but it is certain that, so far as its meaning goes, in
the poetry into which he translated it, sentimentality, empty convention,
and commonplace rule. In short, Mr. Cummings's poetry ends in ideas
about things.

When Mr. Cummings resorts to language for the *thrill* that words may
be made to give, when he allows his thrill to appear as an equivalent for
concrete meaning, he is often more successful than when he is engaged
more ambitiously. This is true of poets like Swinburne and Poe, Shelley
and the early Marlowe: where the first pair depended almost as much upon
thrill as Mr. Cummings in those poems where they made use of it at all,
and where the second pair, particularly Marlowe, used their thrills more
appropriately as ornament: where all four were most successful in their
less ambitious works, though perhaps not as interesting. Likewise, today,
there is the example of Archibald MacLeish, whose best lines are those that
thrill and do nothing more. So that at least in general opinion Mr. Cummings is in this respect not in bad company. But if an examination of thrill
be made, whether in Mr. Cummings's verse or in that of others, it will be
shown that the use of thrill has at heart the same sentimental impenetrability that defeats the possibility of meaning elsewhere. Only here, in the
realm of thrill, the practice is comparatively less illegitimate. Thrill, by itself,
or in its proper place, is an exceedingly important element in any poem: it
is the circulation of its blood, the *quickness* of life, by which we know it,

when there is anything in it to know, most intimately. To use a word for its thrill, is to resurrect it from the dead; it is the incarnation of life in consciousness; it is movement.

But what Mr. Cummings does, when he is using language as thrill, is not to resurrect a word from the dead: he more often produces an apparition, in itself startling and even ominous, but still only a ghost: it is all a thrill, and what it is that thrilled us cannot be determined. For example in *XLI Poems,* the following phrases depend considerably for their effect upon the thrill that is in them: "Prisms of sharp *mind;* where strange birds *purr;* into the *smiting* sky *tense* with *blending;* ways cloaked with *renewal;* sinuous riot; *steeped* in burning flowers; little kittens who are called *spring;* electric Distinct face haughtily vital clinched in a *swoon* of synopsis; unreal *precise* intrinsic fragment of actuality; an orchid whose *velocity* is *sculptural;* scythe takes *crisply* the *whim* of thy *smoothness;* perpendicular *taste;* wet stars, etc., etc." (The italics are mine.)

Take especially the phrase, "scythe takes *crisply* the *whim* of thy *smoothness.*" We know in the poem that it is the scythe of death and that it is youth and beauty (in connection with love) that is to be cut off. So much is familiar, is very conventional; and so the conventional or dead emotion is placed before us; the educated reader receives it and reacts to it without a whimper. But Mr. Cummings must not have been content with presenting the conventional emotion in its conventional form; he felt bound to enliven it with metaphor, with overtones of the senses and the spirit: so that he substituted for the direct statement a rather indirect image combining three unusually sensed words for the sake of the *thrill* the special combination might afford. As the phrase stands there is no precision in it. There is a great suggestion of precision about it—like men going off to war; but precisely *what* is left for the reader to guess, to supply from his own heart. By themselves *whim* and *smoothness* are abstract quality words; and in order for them to escape the tensity, the dislocated strain, of abstractness and gain the intensity, the firm disposition, of concrete meaning, they should demand a particular reference.

Smoothness is probably the smoothness of the body and is used here as a kind of metonymy; but it may be pure metaphor and represent what is really to die—the spirit—taken in its physical terms; or it may be that all that is to be understood is a pure tautology. And so on. Even with this possible variety of reference, *smoothness* would not be objectionable, were it the only word in the phrase used in this way, or were the other words used to clarify the *smoothness.* But we have also the noun *whim* bearing directly on *smoothness* and the adverb *crisply* which while it directly modifies *takes,* really controls the entire phrase. Taken seriously *whim,* with reference to the smoothness of either the body or the spirit or the love it inspires, is to say the least a light word; one might almost say a "metrical" word, introduced to stretch the measure, or because the author liked the sound of it, or enjoyed whimsy. It diminishes without limiting the possibilities of *smoothness.* Because it is here, in the phrase, it is inseparable from the phrase's notion of smoothness; yet instead of assisting, tends to prevent what that notion of smoothness is from being divulged.

Crisply is even more difficult to account for; associated with a scythe it perhaps brings to mind the sound of a scythe in a hayfield, which is surely not the reference here intended; it would be very difficult for such a crispness to associate itself with death, which the scythe represents, or *whim*, or *smoothness* in either the spiritual or fleshly sense. If it implies merely a cleanness, a swiftness of motion in the apparition of death, some other word would have seemed better chosen. If this analysis be correct, the three words are unalterably combined by the force of *crisply* in such a way as to defeat the only possible sense their *thrilling* use would have had. They are, so to speak, only the notions of themselves and those selves must remain forever unknown. All we are left with in such a phrase as this is the strangeness which struck us on our first encounter; and the only difference is that the strangeness is the more intensified the more we prolong the examination. This is another test of poetry: whether we understand the *strangeness* of a poem or not.

As it happens there is an exquisite example of the proper use of this strangeness, this thrill, in another poem of Mr. Cummings: where he speaks of a cathedral before whose face "the streets turn *young* with rain." While there might be some question as to whether the use of *young* presents the only adequate image, there is certainly no question at all that the phrase is entirely successful: that is, the suggestive feeling in *young* makes the juncture, the emotional conjugation, of streets and rain transparent and perfect. This may be so because there is no element of essential contradiction, in the terms of feeling, between the emotional word *young* and the factual words *streets* and *rain*; or because, positively, what happens to the context by the insertion of *young* is, by a necessary leap of the imagination, someting qualified. *Young* may be as abstract a word by itself, as purely relative and notional a word, as any other; but here it is brought into the concrete, is fixed there in a proper habitation. Just because reference is not commonly made either to young streets or young rain, the combination here effected is the more appropriate. The surprise, the contrast, which lend force to the phrase, do not exist in the poem; but exist, if at all, rather in the mind of the reader who did not foresee the slight stretch of his sensibility that the phrase requires—which the phrase not only requires, but necessitates. This, then, is a *strangeness* understood by its own viableness. No preliminary agreement of taste, or contract of symbols, was necessary.

The point is that Mr. Cummings did not here attempt the impossible, he merely stretched the probable. The business of the poet who deals largely with tactual and visual images, as Mr. Cummings does, for the meat of his work, is to escape the prison of his private mind; to use in his poem as little as possible of the experience that happened to him personally, and on the other hand to employ as much as possible of that experience as it is data.

It is idle for a critic to make the familiar statement that the mind of the writer is his work or that "the style is the man," when by mind and man is meant the private experience of the author. So far as, in this sense, the mind *is* the work or the style *is* the man, we can understand the work or the style only through an accidental unanimity; and what we understand is likely to be very thin—perhaps only the terms of understanding. For the author himself, in such circumstances, can have understood very little more. He has been pursuing the impossible, when the probable was right at hand; he has been transcending his experience instead of submitting to it. And this is just what Mr. Cummings does in the phrases quoted above.

It would be ungracious to suppose that as a poet "a swoon of synopsis" did not represent to Mr. Cummings a very definite and very suggestive image. But to assent to that image would be a kind of *tour de force*; the application of such assent would imply that because the words appear, and being words contain notions, they must in this particular instance exhibit the undeniable sign of interior feeling. The proper process of poetry designs exactly what the reader will perceive; that is what is meant when a word is said to be inevitable or *juste*. But this exactness of perception can only come about when there is an extreme fidelity on the part of the poet to his words as living things; which he can discover and control—which he must learn, and nourish, and stretch; but which he cannot invent. This unanimity in our possible experience of words implies that the only unanimity which the reader can feel in what the poet represents must be likewise exterior to the poet; must be somehow both anterior and posterior to the poet's own experience. The poet's mind, perhaps, is what he is outside himself with; is what he has learned; is what he knows; it is also what the reader knows. So long as he is content to remain in his private mind, he is unknowable, impenetrable, and sentimental. All his words perhaps must thrill us, because we cannot know them in the very degree that we sympathize with them. But the best thrills are those we have without knowing it.

This essay has proceeded so far on the explicit assumption that the poems of Mr. Cummings are unintelligible, and that no amount of effort on the part of the reader can make them less so. We began by connecting Mr. Cummings to two schools, or groups, which are much the same essentially—the anti-culture group which denies the intelligence and the group, not limited to writers, of which the essential attitude is most easily defined as sentimental egoism or romantic idealism. Where these schools are most obviously identical is in the poetry they nourish: the avowed interest is the relentless pursuit of the actual in terms of the immediate as the immediate is given, without overt criticism, to the ego. Unintelligibility is a necessary consequence of such a pursuit, if by the intelligible we mean something concrete, qualified, permanent, and public. Poetry, if we understand it, is not in immediacy at all. It is not given to the senses or to the free intuition. Thus, when poetry is written as if its substance were immediate and given, we have as a result a distorted sensibility and a violent inner confusion. We have, if the poet follows his principles, something abstract, vague, impermanent, and essentially private. When every sensation and every word is taken as final and perfect, the substance which sensations report and for which words must stand remains inexplicable. We can understand only by accident.

Of course there is another side to the matter. In a sense anyone can understand Mr. Cummings and his kind by the mere assertion that he does understand. Nothing else is needed but a little natural sympathy and a certain aptness for the resumption of a childish sensibility. In much the same way we understand a stranger's grief—by setting up a private and less painful simulacrum. If we take the most sentimental and romantic writers as they come, there will be always about their work an excited freshness, the rush of sensation and intuition, all the ominous glow of immediacy. They will be eagerly at home in the mystery of life. Adroitness, expertness, readiness for any experience, will enlighten their activities even where they most miserably fail. They are all actors, ready to take any part, for they put themselves, and nothing else, into every part they play. Commonly their real success will depend on the familiarity of the moments into which they sink themselves; they will depend on convention more than others, because they have nothing else to depend on.

So with the poetry of Mr. Cummings we might be altogether contented and pleased, were he himself content with the measure of his actual performance. But no poetry is so pretentious. No poetry ever claimed to mean more; and in making this claim it cannot avoid submitting itself, disastrously, to the criticism of the intelligence. So soon as we take it seriously, trying to discover what it really says about human destiny and the terms of love and death, we see how little material there is in this poetry except the assurance, made with continuous gusto, that the material exists. We look at the poetry. Sometimes one word, in itself vague and cloudy, is made to take on the work of an entire philosophy—like flower. Sometimes words pile themselves up blindly, each defeating the purport of the others. No feeling is ever defined. No emotion betrays a structure. Experience is its own phantoms, and flows willy-nilly. With the reality of experience the reality of language is lost. No metaphor crosses the bridge of tautology, and every simile is unexpanded. All the "thought" is metonymy, yet the substance is never assigned; so in the end we have only the thrill of substance.

Such an art when it pretends to measure life is essentially vicarious; it is a substitute for something that never was—like a tin soldier, or Peter Pan. It has all the flourish of life and every sentimental sincerity. Taken for what it is, it is charming and even instructive. Taken solemnly, as it is meant to be, the distortion by which it exists is too much for it, and it seems a kind of baby-talk.

John Brooks Wheelwright:
In the American Grain

John Ashbery

The pure products of America don't always go crazy: Dr. Williams himself
is a demonstration of this. But the effort of remaining both pure and American can make them look odd and harassed—a lopsided appearance characteristic of much major American poetry, whose fructifying mainstream
sometimes seems to be peopled mostly by cranks (Emerson, Whitman,
Pound, Stevens), while certified major poets (Frost, Eliot) somehow end
up on the sidelines. This is suggested again by the unexpected appearance
of [a] voluminous *Collected Poems* by [a poet] who now seems destined to
pass abruptly from the status of minor to major crank.

John Wheelwright [is] full of tics and quirks; [he] frequently writes as
though poetry could not be a vehicle of major utterance, as though it were
itself a refutation of any such mythic nonsense; in [his hands] the poem is
not so much a chronicle of its own making as of its unmaking. Often, as
in "North Atlantic Passage," the final product looks like a mess of disjointed
notes for a poem. Yet [Wheelwright] finishes by stretching our recognition
of what a poem can be and in so doing carries the notion of poetry a little
higher and further. [He] seems destined to end up, albeit kicking and
struggling, as classic American.

Unexpected is perhaps not the word for the publication of Wheelwright's *Collected Poems;* it was first announced on the jacket of a small
pamphlet of his *Selected Poems* published by New Directions in 1941, a few
months after Wheelwright was killed by a drunken driver in Boston at the
age of forty-three. Why the present volume has been in the works for so
long is not explained, and is all the more inexplicable in view of Wheelwright's close ties with so many well-known writers of his time, to whom

From *The New York Review of Books* 20, no. 2 (February 22, 1973). © 1973 by The New York
Review, Inc.

many of the poems are dedicated: Robert Fitzgerald, Malcolm Cowley, Matthew Josephson, James Agee, Archibald MacLeish, Allen Tate, Howard Nemerov, Horace Gregory, and Wheelwright's brother-in-law S. Foster Damon, to name a few. If at least some of these were his close friends it seems strange that no one, including James Laughlin (another dedicatee), has managed until now to rescue this brilliant poet's work from obscurity.

Perhaps there was some kind of opposition from the family, and one suspects also that many of the writers with whom "Jack" was on close terms appreciated his engaging personality and odd political views (Boston Brahmin-Anglo-Catholic-Trotskyite) but drew the line at his "recalcitrant" (the apt word is that of his editor, Alvin Rosenfeld) verse. Three volumes— *Rock and Shell, Mirrors of Venus, Political Self-Portrait*—were published in his lifetime by the Boston publisher Bruce Humphries in tiny editions and have long been unobtainable, as has the New Directions pamphlet; a fourth collection, *Dusk to Dusk,* was ready for publication at the time of Wheelwright's death and now appears for the first time in the *Collected Poems,* along with some hitherto uncollected poems.

Besides the mystery of the book's long-delayed arrival, Mr. Rosenfeld's thoughtful preface leaves several other questions unanswered. Where are the original texts of the previously unpublished poems, and how were the present readings established? The fact that a poem published in the 1941 *Selected Poems* as "Staircase Thoughts" appears here in somewhat different form as *"Esprit d'Escalier,"* while another now called "In the Bathtub, to Mnemosyne" was printed in the earlier volume as "Bathtub Thoughts" with a final stanza which has here been omitted, suggests that significantly different versions of other poems might well exist.

One wonders too about the sketches for a long poem on St. Thomas (the skeptic-believer Wheelwright's favorite saint) which Mr. Rosenfeld says were "deemed too fragmentary for publication," and whether there are other such fragments. What happened to the book on American architecture which Wheelwright, whose father was for a time city architect of Boston and built among other things the Stadium Bridge in Cambridge and the troubadour-style Lampoon Building, was working on at the end of his life? These are, of course, secondary questions which will have to await a later stage of Wheelwright scholarship; meanwhile one hopes that the present volume will initiate that stage.

Wheelwright is a difficult poet, not merely for the erudition he presupposes, though this in itself is intimidating. His own footnotes usually compound the difficulties. One poem, he says, "is a literal contradiction to Oliver Wendell Holmes's *The Voiceless*"; another "quotes the Hymnal, the Psalter, the Bhagavad Gita, Oliver Wendell Holmes, Stonewall Jackson, and an anonymous ejaculation made at the Jamestown [*sic*] Flood." Elsewhere it is a question of Baring-Gould's *Lost and Hostile Gospels,* "Walker's translation of a Nestorian novel on the Acts of Thomas," "Maurice Samuel's translation of Edmond Flegg's *Jewish Anthology*," Böhme, Engels, Dietzgen, "the *Journal* of Pastor Higgenson," and, even more to the point, episodes from the poet's private life: " 'Lobster Cove,' an essay in pastoral, represents what occupied the end of a day at the Madame Goss House in Annisquam, on Cape Ann, while the Author was brushing up some chores for the Damons." (The reader will look in vain for a poem with this title in the *Collected Poems*; it was one of the titles, here omitted, of the nine groups of poems that comprise *Political Self-Portrait*.)

I say even more to the point because Wheelwright's literary references, if they could be tracked down, would finally be of as little help in explicating the poetry as are the unstated facts of his biography, which are given the same telescoped, allusive treatment. This is not to say that the references don't matter; they, or their abstruseness, matter crucially in the long theological epics, where there are stretches unrelieved by the chiaroscuro glitter of the equally obdurate but less programmatic lyrics. But the difficulty proceeds less from arcane allusions than from Wheelwright's peculiarly elliptical turn of mind which convolutes and compresses clarities to the point of opacity. There is no more point in doing one's homework first than there is with the *Cantos:* one has to wade in, grasping at what is graspable and letting the extraordinarily charged lyrical climate accustom one little by little to the at first blinding brightness or darkness.

Ellipsis is not a principle of construction, as with Pound, nor is there a willful, romantic obscuring impulse like Crane's. Wheelwright demands that we follow a logic perceptible to him but only intermittently so to us, and that we be prepared to abandon it without warning for another kind of poetic logic. If Crane's poetry presents a baroque façade, Wheelwright's is the architectural underpinnings and calculations that would support such a façade, which we glimpse only rarely in his calmer, lyrical moments. Meanwhile the feats of engineering that we can take in are almost enough in themselves.

It is best perhaps to start with the shorter, seemingly easier poems, not because they are actually easier but because they contain some of his most radically original poetry unburdened by a narrative or dialectical function. This one, "Familiar," is from *Dusk to Dusk:*

> O, gilded Boston State House; O, gleaming Irish hair!
> I saw Lady Bountiful taking a walk in clean sunlight.
> A goodlooking girl, if only she hadn't lips for eyelids.
> I thought I saw two persons, and I got all mixed up.
> You see, it was this way . . . Lady Bountiful was modestly,
>   even stylishly
> dressed in two dimensions. But Lady Bountiful's shadow
> had three dimensions, and crept behind like
> pickpocket stenches of belches of Welch wenches.

Even while beginning to wonder what this is all about, one is overtaken by its conviction. I think it succeeds, just as I think the very next one, "Stranger," doesn't:

> (While Boston blossoms into one brown rose)
> how is it, Girlie, on your way
> from Saroyan's whimsy play
> *Over the hills and Far Away*
> to suffocate black incubator babies
> that you carry a tall walking stick
> embossed with the many-breasted Artemis;
> but rubbed on its prepuce nether tip?
> Did you lift it from my steady's mother?

In both cases I am unsure of what is being said, but also fairly sure that it doesn't matter, that we are in the presence of something as dumbfounding as Cubism must have seemed to its first spectators and as valid as it now looks in retrospect.

Even at his most direct Wheelwright is up to something other than what appears, as in "Dinner Call," a poem about a posthumous visit from Amy Lowell. The setting owes something to the Eliot of "Aunt Helen" and "The *Boston Evening Transcript.*" The specter of the poetess arrives "while my Aunt and I were sitting round the house / waiting for the time to come for us to be sitting / and waiting for the time to drink our tea, / what brought her to Nantucket seven months after decent burial? / Digging up color for *Scrimshaw and Jade Fish?*" Miss Lowell gossips about her recent post-mortem activities as this seemingly prosaic but incredible domestic scene unfolds:

> When Anna carried in the urn; the lamp, slop-bowl, the pot,
>   etcetera for tea, the Sacrament of tact; Aunt Dolly lit
>   the alcohol.
> Whereat, from that oracular orifice and steaming snout of
>   repartee, the kettle's grape tendril of vapor gushed:
> "Amy's got next the tripod of cookies,—great girl; she helps
>   herself while helping others . . . (It's hot spit shut my
>   eye.)
> Let's let her let us help ourselves,—look how she takes up
>   the entire settle." (The lamp went out.)

She departs and the narrator accompanies her for a while until their paths separate:

> But I turned for "Good-bye" to Amy Lowell, Biggest
>   Traveling One-Man Show since Buffalo Bill caught the
>   Midnight Flyer to contact Mark Twain;
> "One would be inclined, at moments, to doubt the entire
>   death!" I shouted.
> Grinning from ear to ear, she shouted back: "Mr. Brooks,
>   you are perfectly right;—one would be."

We know, because Matthew Josephson mentions it in a recent memoir of Wheelwright in *Southern Review*, that Wheelwright met Amy Lowell at the home of one of his aunts; that he once nettled her at a lecture she gave at Harvard by asking, "Miss Lowell, how do you write when you have nothing to say?" and that he later explained he had merely meant, "How does *one* write when *one* has nothing to say?" Yet the poem, which Josephson calls "a rather jocular elegy for Miss Lowell," seems to work on a number of levels: first as anecdote, though even here much remains to be explained. Why is the ghost returning? Why the sarcastic parting at the end? Wheelwright alludes to their exchange at Harvard, but a reader unfamiliar with the incident might well take it as another fictive bauble and miss the point.

Obviously the poem is satirical, but who or what is being satirized? If it is Miss Lowell, we are not told why. Wheelwright's attitude toward her and her poetry is tongue-in-cheek but uncommitted. And what is the function of the ghastly evocation of her corpse, straight out of *El Topo:* "As the lime rose, her neck turned grey, like stale ashes / of cigars; but gushes of dead blood mounted her neck. / They flowed through her head; the cheeks turned red; the lips / glowed like scars. But her eyes? Her eyes were frightened." Yet finally these questions scarcely matter. What matters is that the poem is alive and crackling with satire loosened from its object; it stands free of its narrative armature, though it could scarcely have come into being without it.

This is true of much of the poetry, including the long poems, and it points to a central problem: that lacking the precise reference, which is often not literary but autobiographical, we are forced back on the tributary beauties of the language, which are however frequently so substantial as to carry the poem alone. In this Wheelwright resembles another rediscovered Yankee crackpot genius, Charles Ives, whose gifts didn't rule out occasional lapses into tedium which cannot and should not be isolated from the rest, because they too stem from an ambitious plan which was completely apparent only to its author but whose energy enlivens even the barren passages. Nevertheless there will have to be a study of Wheelwright's sources before major poems such as the arcane closet drama "Morning," published here for the first time, can be appraised for more than their coldly felicitous Landor-like purple passages.

Still, almost any random page from Wheelwright makes one want to persevere. A suggestion of the difficulties and delights ahead can be found in the remarkable *ars poetica* (of a sort) called "Verse + Radio = Poetry," published by Rosenfeld and S. Foster Damon in *Southern Review* (Spring 1972):

> The music of poetry is more than sound—its music consists in the presentation of ideas as themes repeated, contradicted, and developed like musical ideas. . . . Ideological music is closely related to disassociation of associated ideas and the association of the

disassociated. This philosophical process must constantly go on, in answer to constantly changing society, for ages and generations and for individuals from childhood to old age and from mood to mood. This makes spirits athletic, not only to guard against the change but to welcome change. The poetry keeps you awake. If it makes you dream, it warns you that you are half asleep.

I can't leave Wheelwright without quoting in full one of his most beautiful poems, "Why Must You Know?" from *Rock and Shell*, to which one can return again and again, savoring it without penetrating its secret:

—"What was that sound we heard
fall on the snow?"
—"It was a frozen bird.
Why must you know?
All the dull earth knows the good
that the air, with claws and wings
tears to the scattered questionings
which burn in fires of our blood."
"Let the air's beak and claws carry my deeds
far, where no springtime thaws the frost for their seeds."
—"One could fathom every sound
that the circling blood can tell
who heard the diurnal syllable,
while lying close against the ground."
"My flesh, bone and sinew now would discern
hidden waters in you Earth, waters that burn."
—"One who turns to earth again
finds solace in its weight; and deep
hears the blood forever keep
the silence between drops of rain."

The clear mystery, the cold passion, and the warm intelligence are there in equal proportion.

Allen Tate's Poetry

Cleanth Brooks

Allen Tate's poetry illustrates a structure of violent synthesis. He constantly throws his words and images into active contrast. Almost every adjective in his poetry challenges the reader's imagination to follow it off at a tangent. For instance, in the "Ode to the Confederate Dead," November becomes not "drear" November, "sober" November, but *"Ambitious* November with the humors of the year" [italics mine]. The "curiosity of an angel's stare" is not "idle" or "quiet" or "probing" or any other predictable adjective, but "brute" curiosity. This is the primary difficulty that Tate's poetry presents to the reader who is unacquainted with his dominant themes: the surface of the poem, in its apparently violent disorder, may carry him off at tangents.

There is some justification, therefore, for approaching Tate's poetry through an account of his basic themes—all the more since these themes are closely related to the poetic method itself. We may conveniently begin by examining a very important passage in his essay "Humanism and Naturalism." In discussing attitudes toward history, he describes two ways of viewing the past. The first is that which gives what may be called the scientist's past, in which events form a logical series; the second is that which gives what Tate himself calls the "temporal past."

> The logical series is quantitative, the abstraction of space. The temporal series is, on the other hand, space concrete. Concrete, temporal experience implies the existence of a temporal past, and it is the foundation of the religious imagination; that is to say, the only way to think of the past independently of . . . naturalism is

to think religiously; and conversely, the only way to think religiously is to think in time. Naturalistic science is timeless. A doctrine
based upon it, whether explicitly or not, can have no past, no idea
of tradition, no fixed center of life. The "typically human" is a
term that cannot exist apart from some other term; it is not an
absolute; it is fluid and unfixed.

To de-temporize the past is to reduce it to an abstract lump. To
take from the present its concrete fullness is to refuse to let standards work from the inside. It follows that "decorum" must be
"imposed" from above. Thus there are never specific moral problems (the subject matter of the arts) but only fixed general doctrines
without subject matter—that is to say, without "nature."

In other words, the artist today finds that his specific subject matter
tends to be dissolved in abstractions of various sorts. His proper subjects—
specific moral problems—are not to be found in an abstract, logical series,
for in such a series there are no standards of any sort—and nothing specific,
nothing concrete.

Tate's preoccupation with history and time in his poetry is thus closely
related to John Crowe Ransom's characteristic problem: that of man living
under the dispensation of science—modern man suffering from a disso-
ciation of sensibility.

Tate goes on to say in the same essay: "The 'historical method' has
always been the anti-historical method. Its aim is to contemporize the past.
Its real effect is to detemporize it. The past becomes a causal series, and
timeless." Tate's concern here is with the neohumanists, but the generalization may be applied to the arts without distorting it too violently. Carl
Sandburg, for example, will supply an example pat to our purpose. Consider his "Four Preludes on Playthings of the Wind."

After the first Prelude with its "What of it? Let the dead be dead,"
and after the second Prelude which describes an ancient city (Babylon?)
with its cedar doors and golden dancing girls and with its ultimate destruction, Prelude Three begins:

> It has happened before.
> Strong men put up a city and got
>   a nation together,
> And paid singers to sing and women
>   to warble: We are the greatest city,
>   the greatest nation,
>   nothing like us ever was.

But as the poem goes on to point out, the ultimate dancers are the rats,
and the ultimate singers, the crows. The poet's intention, presumably, is
to contemporize the past. The real effect is to detemporize it. Babylon or
Nineveh becomes interchangeable with Chicago. Chicago receives a certain

access of dignity from the association; Babylon, a certain humanity and
reality; and the poet is allowed to imply, with a plausible finality, that
human nature fundamentally doesn't change.

Sandburg's primary impulse seems to be a revulsion from the "literary"
past—the people of the past, too, hired singers, ran night-clubs, and joined
booster societies. But Sandburg's contemporizing of the past springs also—
probably unconsciously—from the fact that he is immersed in a scientific
civilization.

Tate not only cannot accept Sandburg's detemporized past; he must
strive actively to ascertain what meaning the past can have for modern
man who has so many inducements to consider it merely as a logical series.
This, I take it, is the primary theme of "The Mediterreanean," "Aeneas at
Washington," and even—in a varied form—of the "Ode to the Confederate
Dead." Aeneas possessed a concrete past—moved from a particular Troy
to found a particular Rome. We, on the other hand, who have "cracked
the hemispheres with careless hand," in abolishing space have also abolished time. The poem is not a lament, nor is it a "sighing for vanished
glories." It is a recognition and an exploration of our dilemma. Modern
man, like the Aeneas of Tate's poem, is obsessed with the naturalistic view
of history—history as an abstract series. He sees

> all things apart, the towers that men
> Contrive I too contrived long, long ago.

But Aeneas has been acquainted with another conception of history.

> Now I demand little. The singular passion
> Abides its object and consumes desire
> In the circling shadow of its appetite.

(We may gloss the last quoted lines as follows: In his "Religion and the
Old South," Tate argues that the naturalistic view of history is intent on
utility; but in the case of concrete history, the "images are only to be
contemplated, and perhaps the act of contemplation after long exercise
initiates a habit of restraint, and the setting up of absolute standards which
are less formulas for action than an interior discipline of the mind.")

Modern man with his tremendous historical consciousness is thus confronted with a dilemma when asked for the meaning of his actions:

> Stuck in the wet mire
> Four thousand leagues from the ninth buried city
> I thought of Troy, what we had built her for.

The problem of history receives a somewhat similar treatment in the
fine "Message from Abroad." The form into which the problem is cast is
peculiarly that of the American confronted with the lack of "history" of his
own land and thrown up against the immense "history" of Europe. Stated
in somewhat altered form, it is the problem of man, who requires a history

in which he can participate personally, lost in the vast museum galleries
of Western civilization.

> Provençe,
> The Renascence, the age of Pericles, each
> A broad, rich-carpeted stair to pride
> . . . they're easy to follow
> For the ways taken are all notorious,
> Lettered, sculptured and rhymed.

But "those others," the ways taken by his ancestors, are

> incuriously complete, lost,
> Not by poetry and statues timed,
> Shattered by sunlight and the impartial sleet.

He can find, to make those ways,

> Now only
> The bent eaves and the windows cracked,
> The thin grass picked by the wind,
> Heaved by the mole.

The tall "red-faced" man cannot survive the voyage back to Europe:

> With dawn came the gull to the crest,
> Stared at the spray, fell asleep
> Over the picked bones, the white face
> Of the leaning man drowned deep.

And the poet is finally forced to admit that he cannot see the ancestors,
and can merely conjecture

> What did you say mornings?
> Evenings, what?
> The bent eaves
> On the cracked house,
> That ghost of a hound. . . .
> The man red-faced and tall
> Will cast no shadow
> From the province of the drowned.

Obviously Tate's poetry is not occupied exclusively with the meaning
of history. But his criticism of merely statistical accounts of reality serves
as an introduction to the special problems of his poetry in much the same
way that Ransom's comments on the relation of science to the myth serve
as an approach to his.

Attention to his criticism will illuminate, for example, the positive position from which he comments on our present disintegration:

> The essential wreckage of your age is different,
> The accident the same; the Annabella
> Of proper incest, no longer incestuous:
> In an age of abstract experience, fornication
> Is self-expression, adjunct to Christian euphoria.
>   ("Causerie")

Or, to make the application to the subject of poetry itself, one may quote from the same poem:

> We have learned to require
> In the infirm concessions of memory
> The privilege never to hear too much.
> What is this conversation, now secular,
> A speech not mine yet speaking for me in
> The heaving jelly of my tribal air?
> It rises in the throat, it climbs the tongue,
> It perches there for secret tutelage
> And gets it, of inscrutable instruction.

The situation described is peculiarly that of the modern poet. His speech is a mass of clichés—of terms which with their past associations seem too grandiloquent and gaudy, or, with their past content emptied, now seem meaningless. "Vocabulary / Becomes confusion," and without vocabulary man is lost.

> Heredity
> Proposes love, love exacts language, and we lack
> Language. When shall we speak again? When shall
> The sparrow dusting the gutter sing? When shall
> This drift with silence meet the sun? When shall
>   I wake?

We may state the situation in still other terms: Man's religion, his myths, are now merely private fictions. And as Tate has remarked in one of his essays, "a myth should be in conviction immediate, direct, overwhelming, and I take it that the appreciation of this kind of imagery is an art lost to the modern mind." The lover in Tate's "Retroduction to American History," has lost his appreciation of such imagery. He "cannot hear. . . . His very eyeballs fixed in disarticulation. . . . his metaphors are dead."

Tate's metaphors are very much alive; it is through the production of energetic metaphor, of live "myths" that the poet attempts to break through the pattern of "abstract experience" and give man a picture of himself as man. Hence his preoccupation with time and mortality and "specific moral problems." But as a matter of integrity, he cannot take the short cut which Tennyson tends to take to these subjects. One cannot find a living relation between the present and the past without being honest to the present—

and that involves taking into account the anti-historical character of our present.

In his "Retroduction to American History," the poet asks why "in such serenity of equal fates"—that is, why, if life is merely a causal sequence, merely abstract experience—has Narcissus "urged the brook with questions?" In a naturalistic world, the brook, like Mr. Ransom's cataract, is only so much water; and we have the absurdity which the poet proceeds to point out:

> Merged with the element
> Speculation suffuses the meadow with drops to tickle
> The cow's gullet; grasshoppers drink the rain.

Self-scrutiny, introspection, in a purely mechanistic universe, is merely a romantic gesture—"Narcissism." In the "Ode to the Confederate Dead," Narcissism figures again, though without a specific symbol.

As Tate has written: "The poem is 'about' solipsism or Narcissism, or any other *ism* that denotes the failure of the human personality to function properly in nature and society. Society (and 'nature' as modern society constructs it) appears to offer limited fields for the exercise of the whole man, who wastes his energy piecemeal over separate functions that ought to come under a unity of being. . . . Without unity we get *the remarkable self-consciousness* of our age [italics mine]."

In the "Ode," the Narcissism of the present forms one term of the contrast; the "total" world in which the dead soldiers fulfilled themselves, the other. But the poet refuses to take the easy romantic attitude toward the contrast. The world which the dead soldiers possessed is not available to the speaker of the poem, for that kind of world is the function of a society, not something which can be wrought out by the private will. Moreover, the poet is honest: the leaves, for him *are* merely leaves.

The irony expressed in the poem, then, is not the romantic irony of the passage quoted from Tate's criticism in chapter 3. It is a more complex irony, and almost inevitably, a self-inclusive irony. Such an irony is found also in "Last Days of Alice," "The Sonnets at Christmas," "The Meaning of Life," and "The Meaning of Death."

Before considering these poems, however, it is well to note a further criticism of naturalism in Tate's prose. The naturalistic view of experience (history as an abstract series) suggests an "omnipotent human rationality." It can only predict success. The poet (who, by virtue of being a poet, is committed to the concrete and particular) is thus continually thrown into the role of Tiresias.

A number of Tate's poems are ironical treatments of rationality, "The Eagle," for example. It is not the heart which fears death, but the mind, "the white eagle." And in the "Epistle to Edmund Wilson," "The mind's a sick eagle taking flight." The theme is most powerfully stated in the last of the "Sonnets of the Blood." The brother is cautioned to

> Be zealous that your numbers are all prime,
> Lest false division with sly mathematic
> Plunder the inner mansion of the blood,
> . . . .
> . . . the prime secret whose simplicity
> Your towering engine hammers to reduce,
> Though driven, holds that bulwark of the sea
> Which breached will turn unspeaking fury loose
> To drown out him who swears to rectify
> Infinity.

If the blood is a symbol of the nonrational, concrete stuff of man which resists abstract classification, by the same token it symbolizes man's capacity to be more than an abstract integer, and therefore signifies man's capacity for sin. In an age of abstract experience sin is meaningless.

In "Last Days of Alice," the logical, self-consistent but inhuman world of *Through the Looking-Glass* becomes an ironical symbol of the modern world. The poet maintains most precisely the analogy between Alice gazing "learnedly down her airy nose" into the abstract world of the mirror, and modern man who has also turned his world into abstraction. The subsidiary metaphors—"Alice grown . . . mammoth but not fat," symbolizing the megalomania of the modern; Alice "turned absent-minded by infinity" who "cannot move unless her double move," symbolizing the hypostasis of the modern—grow naturally out of the major symbolism. The poem is witty in the seventeenth-century sense; the reference to the Cheshire cat with his abstract grin, a witty comparison. But the wit, the sense of precision and complexity, is functional. It contributes the special quality of irony necessary to allow the poet to end his poem with the positive outcry:

> O God of our flesh, return us to Your Wrath,
> Let us be evil could we enter in
> Your grace, and falter on the stony path!

Man's capacity for error, his essential unpredictability, is referred to in a number of Tate's poems. It is the basis of the beautiful "Ode to Fear."

> My eldest companion present in solitude,
> Watch-dog of Thebes when the blind hero strove:
> 'Twas your omniscience at the cross-road stood
> When Laius, the slain dotard, drenched the grove.
>
> Now to the fading, harried eyes immune
> Of prophecy, you stalk us in the street
> From the recesses of the August noon,
> Alert world over, crouched on the air's feet.
>
> You are the surety to immortal life,
> God's hatred of the universal stain.

There is an especially rich development of this theme in the twin poems, "The Meaning of Life" and "The Meaning of Death." The first opens with a dry statement of the point as if in a sort of apologetic monotone:

> Think about it at will; there is that
> Which is the commentary; there's that other,
> Which may be called the immaculate
> Conception of its essence in itself.

But the essence must not be turned into mere abstraction by the commentary, even though the commentary is so necessary that the essence is speechless without it. The poet goes on to apologize for the tone of tedious explication:

> I was saying this more briefly the other day
> But one must be explicit as well as brief.
> When I was a small boy I lived at home
> For nine years in that part of old Kentucky
> Where the mountains fringe the Blue Grass,
> The old men shot at one another for luck;
> It made me think I was like none of them.
> At twelve I was determined to shoot only
> For honor; at twenty not to shoot at all;
> I know at thirty-three that one must shoot
> As often as one gets the rare chance—
> In killing there is more than commentary.

Our predicament is that the opportunity for any meaningful action rarely offers itself at all.

With the last lines the poet shifts the tone again, modulating from the half-whimsical, personal illustration into a brilliant summarizing figure:

> But there's a kind of lust feeds on itself
> Unspoken to, unspeaking; subterranean
> As a black river full of eyeless fish
> Heavy with spawn; with a passion for time
> Longer than the arteries of a cave.

The symbol of the concrete, irrational essence of life, the blood, receives an amazing amplification by its association with the cave. The two symbols are united on the basis of their possession of "arteries." The blood is associated with "lust," is "subterranean" (buried within the body), is the source of "passion." But the added metaphor of the cave extends the association from those appropriate to an individual body to something general and eternal. The reference to the fish may be also a fertility symbol. But the fish are "eyeless" though "Heavy with spawn." The basic stuff of life lacks eyes—cannot see even itself; and filled with infinite potentialities, runs its dark, involved, subterranean course. The metaphor is powerful and rich, but it gives no sense of having been spatchcocked on to the poem. The blood symbol is worked out only in terms of the cave symbol; the two cannot be broken apart. Moreover, it has been prepared for in the casual personal allusion which precedes it. It too is a part of "old Kentucky / Where the mountains fringe the Blue Grass."

"The Meaning of Death" also begins quietly, as "An After-Dinner Speech." The speech is addressed to us, the moderns, who have committed ourselves to commentary—complete, lucid, and full. We have no passion for time—have abolished time.

> Time, fall no more.
> Let that be life—time falls no more. The threat
> Of time we in our own courage have foresworn.
> Let light fall, there shall be eternal light
> And all the light shall on our heads be worn
>
> Although at evening clouds infest the sky
> Broken at base from which the lemon sun
> Pours acid of winter on a useful view.

The concession announced by "although" is important in developing the tone. Incorrigible optimists that we are, we say hopefully that there shall be eternal light although one must admit that the evening light does not suggest the warmth of life but freezes the landscape with cold, pours acid upon it, turns it into something which is a vanity and meaningless. (The psychological basis for the symbolism here is interesting. The "lemon sun" indicates primarily the color of the evening sun, but "lemon" carries on over into a suggestion of something acid and astringent.)

But, the poet observes, our uneasiness is really groundless. Tomorrow surely will bring "jocund day" and the colors of spring. If one in boyhood connected fear with the coming on of the dark at evening, that was merely because one was a small boy. We, at least, have given up that past with its irrationalities and superstitions:

> Gentlemen! let's
> Forget the past, its related errors, coarseness
> Of parents, laxities, unrealities of principle.
>
> Think of tomorrow. Make a firm postulate
> Of simplicity in desire and act
> Founded on the best hypotheses;
> Desire to eat secretly, alone, lest
> Ritual corrupt our charity.

Ritual implies a respect for the thing as thing; it implies more than an abstract series—implies a breach in our strict naturalism. That naturalism must be maintained

> Lest darkness fall and time fall
> In a long night

and thus spoil our plans for the conquest of time—spoil our plans for the reduction of everything to abstraction where, we hope,

> learned arteries
> Mounting the ice and sum of barbarous time
> Shall yield, without essence, perfect accident.

The past phrase suggests the final metaphor of "The Meaning of Life," and with the final line of this poem, the speaker drops his ironical pretense of agreement with the "gentlemen" and shifts into another quality of irony, a deeper irony, returning to the cave metaphor: "We are the eyelids of defeated caves." We are the generation that has broken with history, the generation that has closed the mouth of the cave. The word "eyelids" indicates the manner of the closing: the suggestion is that the motion is one of languor and weariness as one might close his eyelids in sleep. The vitality is gone.

A similar theme is to be found in "The Oath" though the setting and the treatment of the theme in this poem are very different. The two friends are sitting by the fire in the gathering twilight.

> It was near evening, the room was cold,
> Half-dark; Uncle Ben's brass bullet-mould
> And powder-horn and Major Bogan's face
> Above the fire in the half-light plainly said:
> There's naught to kill but the animated dead.
> Horn nor mould nor major follows the chase.

Then one of the friends proposes the question, "Who are the dead?"

> And nothing more was said.
> So I, leaving Lytle to that dream,
> Decided what it is in time that gnaws
> The aging fury of a mountain stream
> When suddenly as an ignorant mind will do
> I thought I heard the dark pounding its head
> On a rock, crying: *Who are the dead?*
> Then Lytle turned with an oath—By God it's true!

The thing that is true is obvious that *we* are the dead. The dead are those who have given in to abstraction, even though they may move about and carry on their business and be—to use the earlier phrase in the poem—the "animated dead." A mountain stream ceases to be a mountain stream when its bed has become worn level. It might even be termed a "defeated" mountain stream when it has lost the activity which gave its career meaning.

Hart Crane: The Long Way Home

Sherman Paul

Crane's "task" is what Rilke would have called *The Bridge*, the large work that had become his destiny, that took up all his growth and, by expressing all that he had been given to express, completed his development. And Crane recognized this when, in the act of desperation that brought him a benefactor, he wrote Otto Kahn that "besides the poems collected into my forthcoming volume I have partially written a long poem, the conception of which has been in my mind for some years." In saying this he allowed himself a poet's license—or merely that of applying for grants—for only "Atlantis" was "partially written," and the conception, which had been in his mind since the spring of 1923, had simply been there, advanced not at all, to judge from the way he put it—"a new cultural synthesis of values in terms of our America." This vague description derives from Waldo Frank, or from what Munson had written about him, and it is important, less for what it tells us about the completed poem than for the way it locates its beginning in Frank's thought and invokes the tutelary friend upon whom Crane relied most in the long travail of getting it written. He wrote Kahn, too, for the same reason he talked so much about *The Bridge:* to bind himself to it. He asked Kahn's help not only because his condition was unusually desperate—he was "foot-loose in the world," the Cleveland home having been sold, he was without a job and living off friends, and he was distressed by his mother's silence—but because he needed in a decisive way, at this critical creative moment, to precipitate his fate. By accepting Kahn's stake, he staked his life on this poem. (And Kahn's stake was insured by his life!) That he had, as he wrote his mother in a pompously defensive letter telling of his good fortune, "the first real opportunity to use my talents unhampered by fear and worry for the morrow" was itself, he soon learned, a severe condition.

Crane began and ended the year 1926, during which the conception of *The Bridge* was finally worked out and much of the poem was written, at Patterson, New York—at Addie Turner's farmhouse, his new home, which he shared, not necessarily unfortunately, with the Tates. Conditions of work were especially important to him. (How often he expended time and money in making a room his own and placed himself within the shelter of a beneficent maternal presence! The Isle of Pines, he told his mother, was "the most ideal place and 'situation' I've ever had for work," chiefly, he went on to say, because of Mrs. Simpson's interest in his work and generous attention to his needs.) But just as important for creativity as this security, this enclosing of the self, was an attendant risk—the challenge of the task, those "tests" of materials and imagination he speaks of, which were set him by the age but which, it seems, he sometimes put in his own way by reading (Spengler's *The Decline of the West* is the immediate example), by correspondence (at this time he resumed with Munson their discussion of the nature of poetry and of his limitations as a poet), and by the presence of friends (in this instance Allen Tate, whose conviction of the wrongness of *The Bridge*, based as it was on Tate's allegiance to Eliot's views, was undoubtedly made known to Crane before the foreword to *White Buildings*).

Though Crane began to work enthusiastically on *The Bridge*, he worked in fear of failure—in fear of failing to countervail Eliot's "poetic determinism of our age," that the world ends "Not with a bang but a whimper." Mostly he read, in a fruitful eclectic way, in order to prepare a rich poetic soil—"to incorporate [the materials] in the subconscious," as he said of his reading of Marco Polo. And mostly he worked on the Columbus section (later called "Ave Maria"), which was not the adventitious beginning it seems but the necessary beginning of the return to the self upon which the composition of *The Bridge*—"this structure of my dreams" he called it—depended. In the letter to Otto Kahn in which he outlined his early progress on the poem and thereby put an end to the first period of concentrated work, he said that "mid-ocean is where the poem begins." And that, in fact, is where his own creative activity began, and where creative necessity, not hindered but served by the quarrel with the Tates, brought him. An early letter to his grandmother foretells this outcome: "I have been reading the *Journal of Christopher Columbus* lately—of his first voyage to America, which is concerned mostly with his cruising around the West Indies. It has reminded me many times of the few weeks I spent on the Island [the Isle of Pines]."

By April Crane had reached an impasse. Intense pressure of commitment had prompted the premature account of the poem to Otto Kahn, and this, in turn, had blocked him. "I'm afraid," he told Munson, "that I've so systematically objectivized my theme and its details that the necessary 'subjective lymph and sinew' is frozen." Though he never acknowledged it in words, he needed, after the initial creative sally, to descend more deeply into himself; the creative source of the poem was there and he had not yet reached it. And so, all unconsciously, he may be said to have brought on the crisis—an unduly severe but not uncommon one of bitter feeling, urgent creative necessity, and financial extremity—from which, in this instance, only his mother could satisfactorily deliver him. The letter in which he told her of the "hideous" situation in the Turner farmhouse implicated her in the fate of his poem; it put her affection to the test and made all but impossible the refusal of the island property ("this refuge," as he now called it) she had always refused him before: "If you feel at all sympathetic to this situation of mine I wish you *this time* be generous enough to let me go to the Island and finish my poem there." This time she did (reason enough for naming the Columbus section "Ave Maria"). Her generous act—even her wedding to Charles Curtis, which she arranged to take place in New York City prior to Hart's departure—contributed to his self-possession and to the repossession of his past. For the island was both family ground (he speaks variously of "the house my grandfather built," "my grandmother's place," and the "sure . . . ground" of "my parents' property") and "Eden." In reaching it he had journeyed back, had actually discovered the verdant isle: "To me," he told the Browns, "the mountains, strange greens, native thatched huts, perfume, etc. brought me straight to Melville." A profound compulsion of his being moved him to this journey, but he saw with new eyes—was "surprised," he said, "that I didn't carry away more definite impressions from my first visit 11 years ago."

Was it necessary for Crane to discover the Caribbean world in order to write about Columbus? Probably not: no more than it was necessary for him to carry out archaeological studies in preparation for "The Dance." It is true that he spent much of his time assimilating that world ("Mine own true self has been chewing its cud, mostly, i.e., trying to imagine itself on the waters with Cristobal Colon"), and that he was pleased that the voyage by schooner he made to Grand Cayman had enabled him to give the verses of "Ave Maria" a veritable sea rhythm. But his essential activity was at a deeper level, figuratively expressed by the remainder of the earlier sentence—"and trying to mend the sails so beautifully slit by the Patterson typhoon."

He wasted little time in reaching the Isle of Pines and toward the restoration of his spirit wisely chose Waldo Frank to accompany him there. In his recently published *Virgin Spain* (the title "Ave Maria" may also allude to this), Frank had used Columbus, the "mystic mariner," as his spokesman and had placed him, at the end of the book, in debate with Cervantes over the spiritual future of America. Frank, moreover, was the foremost exponent of the "mystic tradition" that for him began with Whitman, and positive faith for him was exemplified in art by what he called the "apocalyptic method"—the acceptance of the chaos of contemporary life and its transfiguration in new forms. It is to this faith that Crane referred when he told Munson, in the letter on Eliot's "stern conviction of death," that *Virgin Spain* was a "document of the spirit . . . " and when, later, at the height of creative excitement, he addressed Frank as "Dear repository of my faith." On completing the book, he wrote Frank that " 'The Port of Columbus' [the concluding chapter] is truly something of a prelude to my intentions for *The Bridge*"; and the book, described by Frank as "Symphonic History," was very much in his mind when he wrote Otto Kahn that his poem would be an "eloquent document" with an "unusually symphonic form." More than anyone, Frank, it seems, was necessary to Crane's task—and its re-sumption. That Frank, usually preoccupied with his own writing, con-sented to come with him was an act incalculably generous, capping his always sympathetic attention to Crane's work. Without his encouragement, Crane probably would not have completed *The Bridge*.

Crane later named the immediate work he had to do—"get into myself again"—and this was accomplished in several ways. By mid-June he had written two of his finest poems, "O Carib Isle!" and "Repose of Rivers." The former commemorates the experience of elemental exposure at Grand Cayman, which provided him a landscape of vastation. Like the best of the island poems—"Island Quarry" and "The Idiot," which were written later—it is death-haunted, haunted specifically by spiritlessness, power-lessness. It shows the depth of negation he had to reach and how writing itself—the creative force he wished to liberate—helped him to reach and overcome it. "O Carib Isle!" is not so much a poem of despair as of gathering strength. "Repose of Rivers" is similarly therapeutic, for in it Crane was able to work through and free himself (for the time) from the restrictive hold of the past. "Here," as he says in "Key West," an inferior poem devoted to the same end—"Here has my salient faith annealed me." The illness following the voyage to Grand Cayman was also salutary, and so was the skepticism concerning *The Bridge* to which the reading of Spengler had given full play. Referring to Spengler's book, he later told Frank that it was "a very good experience for ripening some of *The Bridge*," and so, he realized, had been the "many 'things' and circumstances that seem to have uniformly conspired in a strangely symbolical way toward the present speed of my work." The "ripening" he speaks of here was a consequence of the "rotted seed of personal will" (the phrase is from *Virgin Spain*). Crane's spiritual dying had released the creative self, the "positive center of action, control, and beauty" to which, he found, everything suddenly, wonderfully rushed.

"A hurricane in the spirit"—Rilke's description of creative possession admirably conveys the overwhelming fury of the month during which Crane brought to some stage of expression all but three of the fifteen poems comprising *The Bridge*. Rilke was describing the "nameless storm" that overtook him and granted him in a few days the power to complete the *Duino Elegies*: "All that was fiber, fabric in me, framework," he says, "cracked and bent." Except for the fact that Rilke finished his task, Crane's situation is comparable, marked by the joy and gratitude of the artist who has been given so much. "I feel an absolute music in the air again," he wrote Frank on July 24, less than a week after he had begun, as he said later, to "spill" over. Here he announced the writing of "To Brooklyn Bridge," and the receipt of the contract for *White Buildings*, which must have been as heartening as the "news of Allen Tate's generosity [in promising to do the foreword]," a "truly beautiful" act, he said, that "refreshed me a great deal." On July 26 he wrote Frank that "my plans are soaring again, the conception swells" and enclosed "Ave Maria"; on July 29 he sent the Cowleys "Cutty Sark"; on August 3 he sent Frank a new version of "Atlantis" and the gloss notes that "a reaction to Eliot's *Waste Land* notes put . . . in [his] head," commented favorably on Tate's foreword to *White Buildings*, which Munson had sent him ("clever, valiant, concise and beautiful"), and told of how he was trying to steady himself in readiness for the several poems of "Powhatan's Daughter." Toward that pivotal section of the poem, on August 12 he reported his reading of Sandburg's *The Prairie Years* and noted that two of the "Three Songs" had "just popped out" and the third, "Virginia," was about to follow; that "The Tunnel" was nearly done, along with "Calgary Express" (a section omitted from *The Bridge* but partly used in "The River"); and that the poem he was constructing—he likened himself to a "sky-gack or girder-jack"—though only half finished, was "already longer than *The Waste Land*." In this letter he wrote Frank that he was "happy, quite well, and living as never before"; and in a letter of August 19 he informed him that he was living completely in his poem and "having the time of my life." That phrase ended with "just now, anyway," and signaled cessation. "Work continues. 'The Tunnel', now," he told Frank on August 23; but by the time he wrote again, from Havana, on September 3, the storm was over.

He had gone to Havana to recover himself after "doing more writing than all the last three years together (a glorious triumph!)," but his mother, to whom he had written this, was undergoing the dissolution of her second marriage, and her emotional distress destroyed the benefit of his holiday and interrupted the course of his work. The hurricane that shattered the Hart plantation in October also forced him home to Patterson, but it was the lesser power, unmentioned in the list of things headed by his mother's "unrestrained letters," that, he confessed to Charlotte Rychtarik, "nearly killed me." He may have "managed to come through, at least with my skin," as he told her, and he may have been secure enough in his accomplishment to wait out, without worry, the subsequent doldrum, as he told Frank toward the end of November, but bitterness filled him and old guilts burdened him. "Nothing but illness and mental disorder in my family," he wrote Wilbur Underwood in December, "—and I am expected by all the middle-class ethics and dogmas to rush myself to Cleveland and devote myself interminably to nursing, sympathizing with woes which I have no sympathy for because they are all unnecessary, and bolstering up the faith in others toward concepts which I long ago discarded as crass and cheap." Even the appearance of *White Buildings* at the end of the year did not lift his depression. In the letter telling his mother of its publication, he described the insomnia he was suffering in terms vaguely reminiscent of "Southern Cross" and "The Tunnel": "when I do 'sleep' my mind is plagued by an endless reel of pictures, startling and unhappy—like some endless cinematograph." And then, recalling what he had staked on his poem, he charged her with the fact that "I'm trying my best—both to feel the proper sentiments to your situation and keep on with my task." "*The Bridge*," he reminded her, "is an important task—and nobody else can ever do it."

Crane never again attained the creative situation—the explosive poise—he had known on the Isle of Pines. He remained at Patterson during much of 1927, working intermittently at both old and new portions of the poem, but he did not complete it. Family and financial worries distracted him. By August he was, as so often in the past, looking for a job, only now in dismay of delaying further the completion of his nearly finished poem. In September he sent Kahn the manuscript of all he had done, along with an account of his intentions (this prompted perhaps by the criticism of Tate and Winters), in the hope, it seems, of duplicating all that his earlier good fortune had brought him. And in October, when Kahn supplemented with travel money an allowance from his father, he looked forward to a winter in Martinique ("a much pleasanter island than the Isles of Pines"), where he expected to finish the poem. But his mother, always reluctant to have him beyond easy reach, urged him to remain in New York City— which he did. And later, when Eleanor Fitzgerald found employment for him as the companion of Herbert A. Wise, a wealthy young man who was going to California for his health, he was able to join his mother, who, having secured her divorce, had, in her impetuous way, gone there to live.

The terrible quarrel with his mother in which Hart disclosed his homosexuality and following which fled California like a "thief in the night" is the most dramatic episode with which to mark the disequilibrium that had already become evident in the months following his return from the Isle of Pines. Crane seemed unable to rally the creative force needed to complete his poem and, consequently, seemed unable, where decision was required, to decide in its favor. Perhaps Martinique would have helped him. But he chose instead to honor his "responsibilities" and go to California, where he yielded to an environment whose decadence mirrored his own disgust and abetted his self-destructiveness. The letters from California, though sometimes heady with drink, are among his best: observant, serious, full of energy. They witness a great and greatly troubled spirit, whose reading in the prophets of the time (Wyndham Lewis, Ramon Fernandez, and Waldo Frank) and the essential critics (I. A. Richards and Jessie Weston) and the classic modern literature (Proust and Gide) indicates the disorientation he was trying to stem, and whose most demoralized and unguarded letters, like that to Slater Brown on February 22, 1928, expose the pristine sensibility only death would overcome.

In the letters of this time Crane attributed to the "spiritual disintegration of our period"—a theme addressed by his friends Frank and Munson—his own inability to complete *The Bridge*. "When I get some of the points [of contemporary speculation] a little more definitely arranged," he told Isidor Schneider, "then maybe I'll have more nerve to continue my efforts on *The Bridge*." Like the earlier skepticism over Spengler, this uncertainty over ideas was genuine but only symptomatic of deeper sources of difficulty. Where poetry was concerned—his discovery of Hopkins, for example—he showed no hesitancy, and even at his most defenseless ("As for Hart Crane," he wrote in reply to Munson, whose *Destinations* he had just read, "I know him too well to disagree on as many points as I once did") he held fast to his essential view ("I still stake some claims on the pertinence of the intuitions."). Put simply, his disorientation followed from the frustration of the profoundest claims of his being and was immediately due to the demands and disorientation of his mother, as the violence of their break-up indicates.

But break-up did not relieve it nor enable him, as he wrote Waldo Frank from Patterson in June, to complete *The Bridge* "this summer." The shame of precipitate departure, the guilt of irresponsibility (he left his mother to care for his dying grandmother), the fear that his father, with whom he was on good terms, would now learn of his homosexuality, the terrible emotional wound whose consequences he saw in the projected indifference of his friends—all this compounded it. So did the final contest with his mother over the legacy left him by Grandmother Hart, who died in September, and his further flight to Europe, where he was now free to go.

Writing to Frank from Paris, in February 1929, Crane said that the previous year, lost as far as *The Bridge* was concerned, was "the most decisive of my life," but that he now needed "more strength than ever." A long letter to the Rychtariks, relating in detail all that had contributed to the break-up, accounts for this—and for the willingness with which he gave himself to the "carnival" life of Paris. The noteworthy news of this letter tells of Harry and Caresse Crosby's promise to publish *The Bridge* in a fine edition. But perhaps of greater significance for Crane and the subsequent course of his life is the plan he said he had had but in hatred of his mother had given up of "buying a little country place in Connecticut, for her ultimate home as much as mine."

Crane accomplished nothing in Europe but his humiliation. He was jailed for disorderly conduct in La Santé and beaten, the necessary conclusion, perhaps, of the logic of return that moved him almost from the time of his arrival. At the end of July he embarked for home. And there—at Patterson and Columbia Heights—under pressure of deadline and at heavy expense of will and drink (and with the good offices of friends), he completed *The Bridge* during the months of the declining year that brought the Wall Street crash and the suicide of Harry Crosby.

From August through December Crane revised, in what he described as "fevers of work," the proofsheets of the poem and added to it "Cape Hatteras," "Indiana," and "Quaker Hill." In May he had written Isidor Schneider that the poem would be published in the fall "regardless"—that is, as it was then, without those sections which he said might be incorporated, should he ever write them, in a later edition. But with publication impending he was more respectful of his poem and its conception. "Don't rush along too fast, though—please!" is the reiterated plea of his correspondence with Caresse Crosby: "Please be patient. The book must have these sections." For they were not negligible, mere "accent marks" as he said of "Quaker Hill," and their significance, not insignificance, explains his not having written them earlier. In them he had, finally, to resolve problems of faith and feeling whose centrality is suggested by the briefest labels: Whitman, mother, friends-community-home. By December 26 this difficult work was done and he was relieved at last of what he had come to consider "the 5-year load of The Bridge."

In the spring of 1930 *The Bridge* appeared in two excellent editions, one published by the Crosbys' Black Sun Press and the other by Liveright. Except for his replies to its critics—among them friends who had shared in the work—Crane's task was done.

II

At almost every stage, *The Bridge* was a controversial poem. Criticism—opposition—seems to have mounted in ratio to the degree of its completion, and on publication it was for the most part greeted with openly hostile reviews, the most damaging, Crane felt, by his friends Yvor Winters and Allen Tate. Tate had already expressed his basic strictures in the foreword to *White Buildings,* which he wrote during the year in which he had lived and quarreled with Crane; and Winters, who had reviewed *White Buildings,* had accepted Tate's "evaluation and definition of Hart Crane's genius" and made it his point of departure. Their criticism—and that of Munson in *Destinations* (his essay on Crane is subtitled "Young Titan in the Sacred Wood")—is similar, having for its grounds an appreciation of Eliot's account of the modern sensibility and the ethical-religious demands made on poetry by the New Humanists, who, in the years Crane devoted to *The Bridge,* had again become prominent and powerful. With the later criticism of Crane by R. P. Blackmur, these vigorously held and expressed views—position papers in the contemporary debate on the modern spirit—created the perspective in which *The Bridge* and the imagination that fashioned it have almost always been treated. With this encumbrance of criticism it has been difficult to see the poem freshly, or, as Bachelard would say, in an open "admirative" way, but this is what we must now try to do.

How splendidly the dedicatory poem opens and fills its imaginative space with the reverberations of its images—images whose invitation to poetic reverie can hardly be surpassed.

> How many dawns, chill from his rippling rest
> The seagull's wing shall dip and pivot him,
> Shedding white rings of tumult, building high
> Over the chained bay waters Liberty—

The poem begins with the renewal of creation and with its own birth. And in its beginning is its end. The point of departure is the place of return. *The Bridge*, constituted by all that occurs between "Proem" and "Atlantis," describes a circle, the most pervasive figure of the poet's world.

The opening lines evoke a familiar prospect—New York harbor as it might be seen at dawn when looking seaward from Brooklyn Bridge—and express the sense of liberation, the dilation of spirit, afforded by it. In pitch and rising rhythm suspending on "Liberty," they strike up for a new world, for the freedom and creation—the freedom of creation—depicted in the movement (flight, soaring, and dance) of the seagull, Crane's tutelary bird. ("Constantly your seagull ["the white bird"] has floated in my mind," he told Gaston Lachaise, "and it will mean much to me to have it.") This is not the scavenging gull of *Paterson* 4, but the gull of "The Wanderer," a poem opening also in New York harbor and treating a poet's dedication to America and to the renewal of creation, a poem whose importance to Crane may have been hinted at in the epigraph from Job with which he introduced *The Bridge*. Its kin are many, among them the bird with whose free spirit Wordsworth identifies in *The Prelude* and the hawk in Thoreau's *Walden*: symbols of "all that's consummate and free," of the self, fulfilled in and liberated by the powers of imagination and spirit.

The scene, like that of "Crossing Brooklyn Ferry," is eternally recurring and warrants faith in the future. ("How many" suggests this, and "shall" invokes the future, bends the poem toward it.) The coming of dawn—the radiant hope of beginnings insisted on by the writers of *The Seven Arts* group—is the expectation of the poem. But the dawn does not come of itself so much as through the agency of the seagull, as the effulgence of its motion. The bird is harbinger, creator. It rises from the waters "Shedding white rings of tumult"—shedding light, white circles of perfect harmony— and the dance of its being, its "building high," enacted in the poem's movement, is an upward vortex, while the "tumult" is its cry of birth and creative play as well as a reminder of the downward vortex, the chill and darkness, the "rest," from which it has ascended. This light-giving flight brings to view—may be said to create—the Statue of Liberty and is, in itself, an act of liberty, the free action of the spirit over the "chained bay waters." Accordingly, as the imagery of the last stanza indicates, it is a paradigm of the bridge.

Seagull and statue intertwined: the importance of this bright wonderful image is stressed by the brevity of its appearance. "Liberty" also "forsake[s] our eyes" with the departure of the gull; it, too, becomes "apparitional." And what was actual thereby becomes visionary, a presence to be pursued, like the woman of "The Harbor Dawn." We are permitted only a glimpse of the goddess, the first in the poet's pantheon to be presented, although historically she may be the last, assuming all that Crane invests in the more prominent Mary and Pocahontas. "Liberty" stands in the harbor welcoming the voyager, a supreme image of homecoming for Crane, who spoke his double need—for response and imaginative freedom, security and risk—in "To Liberty":

> Out of the seagull cries and wind
> On this strange shore I build
> The virgin.

And just as the image of the ascending gull recalls the moth of his earliest poem, so these lines of explicit comment on the initial stanza of "Proem" recall "C 33" and the fledgling poet's justification and devotion; "O Materna! to enrich thy gold head / And wavering shoulders with a new light shed." At the beginning of *The Bridge*, the poet, looking to sea, counts on poetry, an energy of the self, to liberate him and to bring him home.

Turning on "Liberty," the poem itself describes a curve like the "inviolate curve" of the gull and quickly enacts a momentous transition from space to confinement, imaginative liberty to routine, reality present (beheld) to reality lost (remembered, imagined in interior space, longed for)—from dawn, that is, to "day," the working day, which fails the expectations of the dawn by being dark. With remarkable compression, the second stanza places us in the business world of "Faustus and Helen" and "Recitative." And the gull, who in its flight "forsake[s] our eyes" (and all the affirmative possibilities of the self), is now assimilated to "sails," an image as white and fleeting ("apparitional") that evokes the spacious past of discovery and sea adventure (the world of "Ave Maria" and "Cutty Sark") and, in the context of an office worker's reverie, represents the deepest longing of the soul. What the "inviolate curve" of the gull intends and the sail summons us to is deferred ("filed away" covers it too) until we are freed, as in "Faustus and Helen," from the routine that characterizes modern civilization (suggested also by paper work, finance, skyscrapers, and machinery). Then we may seek the "world dimensional," that "somewhere / Virginal perhaps, less fragmentary, cool."

Only with this pursuit in mind does the poet distinguish himself from the "multitudes" for whom he speaks, and then in order to propose an object worthy of their desire. Though the first three stanzas represent a diminution in intensity of seeing—from beholding to dreaming to fantasizing passively—there is no diminishment of its necessity. The poet sub-scribes to the belief, from Proverbs, that where there is no vision the people perish. When he thinks of "cinemas" it is not only because he associates "panoramic sleights" with the gull's vanishing flight, but because, even though they ultimately cheat the multitudes, they show their inextinguish-able desire for the true magic of revelation. Though in their removes from the source (object) of vision—the light of some "flashing scene / Never disclosed"—the multitudes are in Plato's cave, they are also in church—the church that the movies, especially remarked in the twenties, had be-come. Their attitude ("bent toward," where "bent" is read as "kneel" and "toward" is read as a transcendental preposition) is religious, albeit secular and parodic, and prepares us for the revelation of the bridge, a true object of devotion, which the poet, moving from darkness to light and from disappointment to fulfillment, discloses in all of its radiant splendor:

> And Thee, across the harbor, silver-paced
> As though the sun took step of thee, yet left
> Some motion ever unspent in thy stride,—
> Implicitly thy freedom staying thee!

The image is vital, not mechanical: the bridge, an organic structure, has what Louis Sullivan called "mobile equilibrium"; and as a roadway for the sun it is an arc of the cosmic circle. And it recalls the dawn-bringing gull of stanza one. "Thee" rhymes with "Liberty." The poet, in showing us the path of the soul to reality, restores the epiphanic glory of the beginning. Again the poem is at peak, and now the bridge becomes its focus, to be variously characterized in the next five stanzas and invoked in the con-cluding two.

Before turning to these stanzas something more should perhaps be said about the third stanza. It works to distinguish the poet from the "mul-titudes" but, as "Van Winkle" shows, its imagery carries his private burden. The most notable thing about it is the violated curve of desire, the terrible want always frustrated (refused: "Never disclosed"), a pattern of expec-tation and disappointment first traced in the poet's case in his boyhood. In "Van Winkle," where memory flashes it out of his own dark depths, he remembers

> the Sabbatical, unconscious smile
> My mother almost brought me once from church
> And once only. . . .

> It flickered through the snow screen, blindly
> It forsook her at the doorway, it was gone
> Before I had left the window. It
> Did not return with the kiss in the hall.

In this episode, the poem—and the poet's quest—has its origin. "Forsake":

"forsook." And in considering the bridge to which he directs our attention, it may help us understand the deification and celebration of this answerer.

Stanzas five to nine are a litany—a catalog somewhat in Whitman's fashion—of the attributes and occasions of the bridge. In the first, the bridge provides a platform for spiritual release, in this instance the death leap of the "bedlamite" who has fled the subway (the "Tunnel," or inferno of industrial civilization and of isolation), ascended the parapets of the bridge, and there, "shrill shirt ballooning," like a gull, taken flight. The concluding line—"A jest falls from the speechless caravan"—is Whitman-like in its matter-of-fact tone and cadence, and perhaps in its ambiguity. For "jest" may refer to the bedlamite as well as to the kind of remark called forth in moments of extremity. That it "falls," in contrast to the "ballooning" shirt— both arrested in the instant of the poet's own "flashing scene"—conveys a positive value even though the negative is present. "To die," as Whitman said, "is different from what any one supposed, and luckier."

The next stanza maintains the values established in stanzas one and four. Significantly, the bridge is set against the artifacts with which the poet defines modern civilization: Wall Street, a dark confining metallic space associated with the mechanical by the image of the acetylene torch—that is, by the busy construction of skyscrapers, these conveyed in the images of "rip-tooth" and of towering (yet "cloud-flown": gull-abandoned) derricks. The bridge, again, is not presented in its mechanical but in its vital aspect. Though it is a part of the scene (seen), the very center of it, it belongs to another world: to the eternal, spiritual, pristine, spacious, natural world of the "*North* Atlantic," the cool new world of the harbor dawn, as the further contrast of "noon" and "afternoon" suggests. And even now, in the frenzy of modern life, the bridge responds to the spirit ("breathe") and is "still," at peace.

Crane wrote Waldo Frank that, in "Atlantis," which he was again working on in January 1926, the bridge was becoming "a ship, a world, a woman, a tremendous harp." It is world and ship here, and both are related to each other. "Cables breathe" is descriptively accurate in respect to the actual bridge, just as "flashing scene," in an earlier stanza, is in respect to the movies of that time. Crane is invariably true to the actual, and his metaphors, accordingly, are never far-fetched. In the context of ocean setting ("North Atlantic"), "cables" acquire nautical significance, and animated by "breathe" (breath), they evoke the image of sails. And so the bridge is a ship—sailing ship, and gull—and the world it belongs to is both natural (spiritual) and past. The bridge is a curve of time, simultaneously past-present-future. It exists in the present as a vital presence of the past, and the future it portends will possess values—new only because rediscovered—that are associated with the past.

The progression of this litany is most clearly one of increasing religious identification; of mounting fervor, too, culminating in stanza eight and subsiding in the wonderful peace of stanza nine. In stanza seven, the weakest, the bridge is asserted to be a redemptive agency—again because vital ("Vibrant"). The referents are vague ("that heaven of the Jews," "guerdon," "accolade"), but evoke religious and archaic associations, chiefly those of chivalric times, and do the work of transition. What the poet asserts, however, is what he hopes to receive ("reprieve and pardon"). Syntactical parallelism and rhyme indicate what is important to him: "Accolade thou dost bestow"; "Vibrant reprieve and pardon thou dost show." The bridge neither withholds nor hides, and its accolade is conferred by embrace.

Such is the logic by which the bridge becomes the answerer of stanza eight and the holy mother of stanza nine. In stanza eight the wonder of

> O harp and altar, of the fury fused,
> (How could mere toil align thy choiring strings!)

is heightened by the immediate recollection of Blake's great poem to creation, "The Tyger," no image of which is employed by Crane, the association being achieved instead at a deeper level by "fury fused" and the interrogatory character of the parenthetical exclamation. Blake's poem speaks in these lines for Crane's awareness of the terrible but joyous energies and awful grandeur of art, of the difficulty of synthesizing (to use his theoretical word for "fuse") the contraries of experience. It speaks for Roebling's achievement and that of his own "song." By joining the mechanical (the forge of creation) and the natural (the tyger), Blake's poem also confirms the mysterious double nature of the bridge, Crane's tyger, burning brightly in the darkness of the next stanza, but in a way moderated perhaps by the moderating stanza of Blake's poem:

> And when the stars threw down their spears,
> And water'd heaven with their tears,
> Did he smile his work to see?
> Did he who made the Lamb make thee?

The evocation of divinity is powerful in Crane's lines—"Terrific," used in the sense of awe-inspiring, is fitting. For the bridge, framed by divinity, is also the instrument with which we entreat divinity: an instrument of religious celebration ("harp and altar") and the "threshold" from which the prophet, pariah, and lover launch their petitions—the "pledge," "prayer," and "cry" whose answers, imputed here, are assured in the next stanza, which concludes the sentence begun by the poet's outcry.

Now with the coming of night the masculine divinity of creation becomes the feminine divinity of love, or rather we see this aspect of divinity's nature, a nature similarly presented in "Ave Maria." Night overtakes the poem without our knowing it, but, as in "Faustus and Helen," it is a time consecrated by woman. Not Helen, however, but Mary is associated with the "traffic lights," which move across the bridge, delineating it—"immaculate sigh of stars, / Beading thy path"—even as the continuous movement "condense[s] eternity," reveals the radiant bridge fully, in its supreme office: "And we have seen night lifted in thine arms." This image of the mother, recalling the pietà, is among the greatest in Crane's work. It is the culminating image of his litany and is presented as the revelation hitherto undisclosed ("we have seen"). In the curve of lights from pier to pier, the bridge, which is more commonly recognized as spanning the abyss, is represented as sustaining the darkness of the world. Its most powerful meaning for Crane—he ascribes eternity to it—is in its upholding arms.

And so he invokes it in his dark time. The concluding stanzas may be considered separately, even though they fulfill the development of the litany, because in them the poet speaks *in propria persona*, thereby focusing the poem, hitherto focused on the bridge, on himself—on his own position in respect to the bridge and his need for its spiritual agency. At the end of the poem we find him awaiting the dawn of its beginning. He is not waiting passively, but, as "I waited" suggests, humbly.) We have moved through an entire day—the temporal span of *The Bridge* (as also of "Song of Myself")—and now move out of the darkness into the rest of *The Bridge*. We stand beneath the bridge, in its shadow, not, as at the end, in "Atlantis," on it; for "the darkness," as Crane maintained, is part of the poet's business: the condition and point of departure for a journey, a trial, a passage into light. The time is probably late December, past Christmas (the "fiery parcels" of the brightly lit Manhattan skyline are "all undone"), and past midnight. Yet the winter solstice, the darkest time, portends the light, just as Christmas portends redemption and the gentle, purifying snow (submerging "an iron year") the blessing of love.

Of these hopeful changes—of the vital process that brings them to pass—the bridge is guarantor, an eternal wakefulness ("O Sleepless") overseeing the restless movement of history ("the river"). Always in motion, it has life, a cosmic energy like that of the sun, which earlier "took step of thee" and whose diurnal course over the continent is now represented by its "inviolate curve": "Vaulting the sea, the prairies' dreaming sod." Again the bridge figures as part of the circle of life; and it is an awakener, not merely vaulting the prairie but bringing forth . . . its hidden life. Its magnitude and height above us comport with divinity, but so does the dovelike nature of its spirit ("sometime sweep, descend" recalling the seagull), which the poet, finally, petitions: "Unto us lowliest sometime sweep, descend / And of the curveship lend a myth to God."

With this personal request, psychological-spiritual meanings are added to the geographical points (east and west) of the poem. The poet asks for intervention of spirit, for his own quickening by the divinity he recognizes and celebrates in the world. For the act of descent empowers the poem, "a myth to God" ("descend" rhymes with and controls the meaning of "lend"); it complements the upward flight of the seagull, a "curveship" too. And these visible motions of spirit, like the poem the poet wishes to create, are the "concrete *evidence* of the *experience* of a recognition"; they are instances of "the real connective experience, the very 'sign manifest' on which rests the assumption of a godhead." We should not invest "myth" too heavily, certainly not with the religious and philosophical expectations of Crane's friends. The poem is concerned with myth but is itself not necessarily mythic. Nor is it religious, though Crane said that "the very idea of a bridge . . . is a form peculiarly dependent on . . . spiritual convictions." It does not aspire to anything so grand (and doctrinal), but merely to poetry, an "affirmation of experience," and an affirmative experience of the kind Williams rendered in "The Wanderer":

> And with that a great sea-gull
> Went to the left, vanishing with a wild cry—
> But in my mind all the persons of godhead
> Followed after.

"Proem: To Brooklyn Bridge" is an invocatory prayer—an equivalent perhaps of the traditional invocation to the muse—that also does the work of Whitman's "Inscriptions." It introduces us to the poet's themes and to the "thematic anticipations" noted in part by Frederick Hoffman. More formally integrated with the poem than "Inscriptions," it does more. In many significant ways it is a single version of the entire poem: an instance of its situation, duration, landscapes, mediating consciousness, poetic (symbolic) action, and "logic of metaphor." In naming the bridge, it centers and localizes the poem, establishes a point in history and geography, in time and space; and in invoking the bridge, it begins the symbolization upon which the success of the poem depends. No more ludicrous than the Eiffel Tower, the bridge is a symbol, of the order of Whitman's "grass," that acquires meaning by participating in concrete situations. In speaking of the frequently expressed wish of overcoming the "meaningless life of our industrial society . . . [by] introducing value through creating new symbols," Dorothy Lee addresses the problem Crane recognized in writing "Proem": "symbols in themselves have no value, and they cannot convey value to a situation. Only after they have participated in a situation can they have value, and then only in so far as the situation itself holds value." Since individual experience initiates this acquisition of meaning, the poet, for whom the bridge already possesses meaning at the beginning of the poem, speaks for himself and enables us, by means of the poem (to invoke, in this instance, is to evoke), to enter his experience and come into his meanings. And since a symbol "grows in meaning, and even changes in meaning," he will present the bridge in various situations, as he does so exemplarily in "Proem" by using the cubist technique of shifting perspectives, a technique that brings much together in the name of the bridge and represents one of the ways in which the entire poem, the poet's journey of consciousness, becomes a totality of meaning, the "Word" of a simultaneously apprehended "logic of metaphor" as well as the warrant of his identification with life.

Langston Hughes:
Evolution of the Poetic Persona

Raymond Smith

Langston Hughes's career as a poet began with the publication of "The Negro Speaks of Rivers" in the June 1921 issue of *The Crisis*, the journal of Negro life and opinion edited by W. E. B. Du Bois. By 1926, before the poet reached the age of twenty-five, he had published his first volume of poems, *The Weary Blues*. Of this volume Alain Locke, the leading exponent of "The New Negro," announced that the black masses had found their voice: "A true people's poet has their balladry in his veins; and to me many of these poems seem based on rhythms as seasoned as folksongs and on moods as deep-seated as folk-ballads. Dunbar is supposed to have expressed the peasant heart of the people. But Dunbar was the showman of the Negro masses; here is their spokesman." With the publication of his second volume of poems, *Fine Clothes to the Jew* (1927), Hughes was being referred to as the "Poet Laureate of the American Negro." During a visit to Haiti in 1932, he was introduced to the noted Haitian poet Jacques Roumain, who referred to Hughes as "the greatest Negro poet who had ever come to honor Haitian soil." When the noted Senegalese poet and exponent of African Negritude, Léopold Senghor, was asked in a 1967 interview "In which poems of our, American, literature [do] you find evidence of Negritude?" his reply was "Ah, in Langston Hughes; Langston Hughes is the most spontaneous as a poet and the blackest in expression!" Before his death in 1967, Hughes had published more than a dozen volumes of poetry, in addition to a great number of anthologies, translations, short stories, essays, novels, plays, and histories dealing with the spectrum of Afro-American life.

Of the major black writers who first made their appearance during the

From *Studies in the Literary Imagination* 7, no. 2 (Fall 1974). © 1974 by the Department of English, Georgia State University.

exciting period of the 1920s commonly referred to as "the Harlem Renaissance," Langston Hughes was the most prolific and the most successful. As the Harlem Renaissance gave way to the Depression, Hughes determined to sustain his career as a poet by bringing his poetry to the people. At the suggestion of Mary McLeod Bethune, he launched his career as a public speaker by embarking on an extensive lecture tour of the South. As he wrote in his autobiography: "Propelled by the backwash of the 'Harlem Renaissance' of the early 'twenties, I had been drifting along pleasantly on the delightful rewards of my poems which seemed to please the fancy of kindhearted New York ladies with money to help young writers. . . . There was one other dilemma—how to make a living from *the kind of writing I wanted to do.* . . . I wanted to write seriously and as well as I knew how about the Negro people, and make *that* kind of writing earn me a *living.*" The Depression forced Hughes to reconsider the relation between his poetry and his people: "I wanted to continue to be a poet. Yet sometimes I wondered if I was barking up the wrong tree. I determined to find out by taking poetry, *my* poetry, to *my* people. After all, I wrote about Negroes, and primarily *for* Negroes. Would they have me? Did they want me?"

Though much of the poetry Hughes was to write in the thirties and afterward was to differ markedly in terms of social content from the poetry he was producing in the twenties, a careful examination of his early work will reveal, in germinal form, the basic themes which were to preoccupy him throughout his career. These themes, pertaining to certain attitudes towards America and vis-a-vis his own blackness, had in fact been in the process of formulation since childhood. Hughes's evolution as a poet cannot be seen apart from the circumstances of his life which thrust him into the role of poet. Indeed, it was Hughes's awareness of what he personally regarded as a rather unique childhood which determined him in his drive to express, through poetry, the feelings of the black masses. Hughes's decision to embark on the lecture tour of Southern colleges in the 1930s is not to be taken as a rejection of his earlier work; it was merely a redirection of energies towards the purpose of reaching his audience. Hughes regarded his poetry written during the height of the Harlem Renaissance as a valid statement on Negro life in America. The heavily marked volumes of *The Weary Blues, Fine Clothes to the Jew,* and *The Dream Keeper* (published in 1932 but consisting largely of selections from the two earlier volumes), used by Hughes for poetry readings during the thirties and forties and now in the James Weldon Johnson Collection at Yale University, indicate that Hughes relied heavily on this early work and in no way rejected it as socially irrelevant.

Hughes's efforts to create a poetry that truly evoked the spirit of Black America involved a resolution of conflicts centering around the problem of identity. For Hughes, like W. E. B. Du Bois, saw the black man's situation in America as a question of dual-consciousness. As Du Bois wrote in his *The Souls of Black Folk* (1903): "It is a peculiar sensation, this double-consciousness, this sense of always looking at oneself through the eyes of others, of measuring one's soul by the tape of a world that looks on in amused contempt and pity. One ever feels his twoness,—an American, a Negro; two souls, two thoughts, two unreconciled strivings; two warring ideals in one body, whose dogged strength alone keeps it from being torn asunder." Hughes was to speak of this same dilemma in his famous essay, published in 1927, concerning the problems of the black writer in America, "The Negro Artist and the Racial Mountain": "But this is the mountain standing in the way of any true Negro art in America—this urge within the race toward whiteness, the desire to pour racial individuality into the mold of American standardization, and to be as little Negro and as much American as possible." In *The Weary Blues* (New York: Knopf, 1926), Hughes presented the problem of dual-consciousness quite cleverly by placing two parenthetical statements of identity as the opening and closing poems, and titling them "Proem" and "Epilogue." Their opening lines suggest the polarities of consciousness between which the poet located his own persona: "I am a Negro" and "I, Too, Sing America." Within each of these poems, Hughes suggests the interrelatedness of the two identities: the line "I am a Negro" is echoed as "I am the darker brother" in the closing poem. Between the American and the Negro, a third identity is suggested: that of the poet or "singer." It is this latter persona which Hughes had assumed for himself in his attempt to resolve the dilemma of divided consciousness. Thus, within the confines of these two poems revolving around identity, Hughes is presenting his poetry as a kind of salvation. If one looks more closely at Hughes's organization of poems in the book, one finds that his true opening and closing poems are concerned not with identity but with patterns of cyclical time. "The Weary Blues" (the first poem) is about a black piano man who plays deep into the night until at last he falls into sleep "like a rock or a man that's dead." The last poem, on the other hand, suggests a rebirth, an awakening, after the long night of weary blues: "We have tomorrow / Bright before us / Like a flame." This pattern of cyclical time was adopted in the opening and closing poems of *Fine Clothes to the Jew*, which begins in sunset and ends in sunrise. Again, it is the blues singer (or poet) who recites the song: "Sun's a risin', / This is gonna be ma song." The poet's song, then, is Hughes's resolution to the problem of double-consciousness, of being an American and being black.

Hughes viewed the poet's role as one of responsibility: the poet must strive to maintain his objectivity and artistic distance, while at the same time speaking with passion through the medium he has selected for himself. In a speech given before the American Society of African Culture in 1960, Hughes urged his fellow black writers to cultivate objectivity in dealing with blackness: "Advice to Negro writers: Step *outside yourself*, then look back—and you will see how human, yet how beautiful and black you are. How very black—even when you're integrated." In another part of the speech, Hughes stressed art over race: "In the great sense of the word, anytime, any place, good art transcends land, race, or nationality, and color drops away. If you are a good writer, in the end neither blackness nor whiteness makes a difference to readers." This philosophy of artistic distance was integral to Hughes's argument in the much earlier essay "The Negro Artist and the Racial Mountain," which became a rallying call to young black writers of the twenties concerned with reconciling artistic freedom with racial expression: "It is the duty of the younger Negro artist if he accepts any duties at all from outsiders, to change through the force of his art that old whispering 'I want to be white' hidden in the aspirations of his people, to 'Why should I want to be white? I am a Negro—and beautiful!' " Hughes urged other black writers to express freely, without regard to the displeasure of whites *or* blacks, their "individual dark-skinned selves." "If white people are glad, we are glad. If they are not, it doesn't matter. We know we are beautiful, and ugly too. If colored people are pleased we are glad. If they are not, their displeasure doesn't matter either. We build our temples for tomorrow, strong as we know how, and we stand on top of the mountain, free within ourselves." In this carefully thought-out manifesto, Hughes attempted to integrate the two facets of double-consciousness (the American and the Negro) into a single vision—that of the poet. His poetry had reflected this idea from the beginning, when he published "The Negro Speaks of Rivers" at the age of nineteen. Arna Bontemps, in a retrospective glance at the Harlem Renaissance from the distance of almost fifty years, was referring to "The Negro Speaks of Rivers" when he commented: "And almost the first utterance of the revival struck a note that *disturbed* poetic tradition" (italics mine).

In Hughes's poetry, the central element of importance is the affirmation of blackness. Everything that distinguished Hughes's poetry from the white avant-garde poets of the twenties revolved around this important affirmation. Musical idioms, jazz rhythms, Hughes's special brand of "black-white" irony, and dialect were all dependent on the priority of black selfhood:

> I am a Negro:
>   Black as the night is black
>   Black like the depths of my Africa.

Like Walt Whitman, Hughes began his career as a poet confident of his power. Unlike Whitman, however, who celebrated particular self ("Walt Whitman, the cosmos"), Hughes celebrated racial, rather than individual, self. Hughes tended to suppress the personal element in his poetry, appropriating the first person singular as the fitting epitome of universal human tendencies embodied in race. "The Negro Speaks of Rivers" seems almost mystical in comparison to Whitman's physicality:

> I've known rivers:
> Ancient, dusky rivers.
> My soul has grown deep like the rivers.

One could venture too far in this comparison; of course, Whitman declared himself the poet of the soul as well as the body. Few would deny he had mystical tendencies.

In Hughes, however, there is little hint of the egotism in which Whitman so frequently indulged. Indeed, Hughes was hesitant to introduce the element of the personal into his poetry. In an essay published in the journal *Phylon* in 1947 on his "adventures" as a social poet, Hughes remarked that his "earliest poems were social poems in that they were about people's problems—whole groups of people's problems—rather than my own personal difficulties." Hughes's autobiographical account of the writing of "The Negro Speaks of Rivers" confirms this point, and sheds light on the process by which Hughes transformed personal experiences into archetypal racial memories. The poem had evolved out of personal difficulties with his father, who had emigrated to Mexico when Langston was a child, and had not seen his son in over a decade. Hughes had been summoned unexpectedly by his father to join him in the summer of 1919, hoping to persuade the son to enter into the business world. The elder Hughes felt nothing but contempt for the country and the race he had left behind. The following conversation, recorded in Hughes's autobiography *The Big Sea*, suggests the irreconcilable differences between the two:

> "What do you want to be?"
> "I don't know. But I think a writer."
> "A writer?" my father said. "A writer?
> Do you think they make money? . . . Learn something you can make a living from anywhere in the world, in Europe or South America, and don't stay in the States, where you have to live like a nigger with niggers."
> "But I like Negroes," I said.

The following summer, on a train trip to Mexico, Hughes's dread of the eventual confrontation with his father over his future vocation led to the writing of the poem: "All day on the train I had been thinking about my father, and his strange dislike of his own people. I didn't understand it, because I was Negro, and I liked Negroes very much." Despite Hughes's severe emotional state, the poem itself displays little hint of the personal anxiety that led to its creation.

Perhaps the closest Hughes ever came to incorporating his personal anxiety into a poem was his "As I Grew Older," published initially in 1925, and later included in *The Weary Blues*. The poem is almost reduced to abstractions; it is a landscape of nightmare, a bleak and existential examination of blackness. The poet begins by recalling his "dream," once "bright like a sun," but now only a memory. A wall which separates the poet from his dream suddenly appears, causing him severe anxiety. It is at this point that the poet is thrust back upon himself and forced to seek an explanation for his dilemma:

> Shadow.
> I am black.

These two lines appearing at the center of the poem provide the key to his despair and to his salvation. As he begins to realize that his blackness is the cause of his being separated from his dream, he simultaneously realizes that blackness is central to his ontology. It is as much a physical reality as it is a metaphysical state of mind. In order for the dream to be restored, the spiritual and the physical blackness must be reintegrated. As the poet examines his hands, which are black, he discovers the source of his regeneration as a full person:

> My hands!
> My dark hands!
> Break through the wall!
>
> Find my dream!
> Help me to shatter this darkness,
> To smash this night,
> To break this shadow
> Into a thousand lights of sun,
> Into a thousand whirling dreams
> Of sun!

In order for the poet to transcend his temporal despair, he must accept the condition of his blackness completely and unequivocally. The poem thus ends, not in despair, but rather in a quest for self-liberation, dependent on the affirmation "I am black!"

The words have been used much earlier by another poet, W. E. B. Du Bois, far better known as the founder of the NAACP, editor of *The Crisis*, and lifelong champion of black pride. His poem "The Song of the Smoke," published in the magazine *Horizon* in 1899, opened with the words:

> I am the smoke king,
> I am black.

Later in the poem, Du Bois wrote these ringing lines:

> I will be black as blackness can,
> The blacker the mantle the mightier the man,
> My purpl'ing midnights no day may ban.
>
> I am carving God in night,
> I am painting hell in white.
> I am the smoke king.
> I am black.

The poem, published when Hughes was five years old, prefigures the point time, fifteen years later, when the careers of the two—Du Bois and

Hughes—would converge, with the publication of Hughes's poem "The Negro Speaks of Rivers," in Du Bois's journal *The Crisis*, with the poem's dedication also going to Du Bois.

This early connection between Hughes and Du Bois is important, for it was Du Bois who was calling for a renaissance of black culture as early as 1913, in an essay on "The Negro in Literature and Art": "Never in the world has a richer mass of material been accumulated by a people than that which the Negroes possess today and are becoming conscious of. Slowly but surely they are developing artists of technic who will be able to use this material." By 1920, Du Bois was actually using the word "renaissance" in referring to the new awakening of black creativity in the arts: "A renaissance of Negro literature is due; the material about us in the strange, heartrending race tangle is rich beyond dream and only we can tell the tale and sing the song from the heart." This editorial in *The Crisis*, almost certainly read by Hughes, must have encouraged him to submit the poem for publication. In his autobiography, Hughes credited Du Bois and *The Crisis* for publishing his first poems and thus giving his literary career its first official boost: "For the next few years my poems appeared often (and solely) in *The Crisis*. And to that magazine, certainly, I owe my literary beginnings, insofar as publication is concerned."

While Hughes certainly owed Du Bois a debt of gratitude for his official entrance upon the literary scene, it seems that Hughes's very special sensitivity as a budding young poet developed organically from his experiences as a child. Though he did credit Dunbar and Sandburg among his influences, these literary mentors pale in light of what Hughes had to say about his method of poem-writing: "Generally, the first two or three lines come to me from something I'm thinking about, or looking at, or doing, and the rest of the poem (if there is to be a poem) flows from those first few lines, usually right away." This spontaneity of approach worked both for and against Hughes. Many of his poems, written in hasty response to some event reported in yesterday's newspaper, for example, have badly dated. The spontaneity that resulted in his best poetry came from the depths of his own experiences as a black man in America, though these personal experiences often were disguised as archetypal ones.

The tension between his awareness of growing up black and his acceptance of the "dream" of America, however tenuously defined, provided the dynamic for his poetry. From an early age, Hughes developed the distinction between the social versus the physical implication of black identity in America: "You see, unfortunately, I am not black. There are lots of different kinds of blood in our family. But here in the United States, the word 'Negro' is used to mean anyone who has *any* Negro blood at all in his veins. In Africa, the word is more pure. It means *all* Negro, therefore *black*." During a trip to Africa as a merchant seaman in 1922, he discovered that the Africans who "looked at me . . . would not believe I was a Negro." The semantic confusion was of American origin. Whatever the semantic distinctions, Hughes desired to be accepted as Negro by the Africans, and was disappointed with their reaction to him.

Hughes's middle American background (he grew up in Lawrence, Kansas) sheltered him from some of the more blatant forms of racial prejudice toward Negroes in other regions of the country. When he lived in Topeka, he attended a white school, his mother having successfully challenged the school board to have him admitted. Most of his teachers were pleasant, but there was one "who sometimes used to make remarks about my being colored. And after such remarks, occasionally the kids would grab stones and tin cans out of the alley and chase me home." For a while he lived with his maternal grandmother, from whom he heard "beautiful stories about people who wanted to make the Negroes free, and how her father had had apprenticed to him many slaves . . . so that they could work out their freedom. . . . Through my grandmother's stories always life moved, moved heroically toward an end. . . . Something about my grandmother's stories . . . taught me the uselessness of crying about anything." Hughes's poem "Aunt Sue's Stories," published in *The Crisis* in July of 1921, furnishes an example of how Hughes transformed such memories into poetry. His childhood was not a happy one in Lawrence, as he related in his autobiography, and he turned to books for solace. Parallels between his childhood experiences and later poems abound. Many of his poems focused on unhappy or wrongly treated children, for whom the American dream had no relevance. This empathy with wronged children had its origins with Hughes's own unhappiness as a child.

Many of his poems about black laborers originated out of his difficulties in finding work while in school. A job he had in a hotel, cleaning toilets and spitoons, while only in the seventh grade, was to result in one of his more well-known poems, "Brass Spitoons," included in his second volume of poetry *Fine Clothes to the Jew* (1927). Four decades after a local theatre owner put up a sign "NO COLORED ADMITTED" in Lawrence, Kansas, Hughes would recall the event in *Ask Your Mama:*

> IN THE QUARTER OF THE NEGROES
> WHERE THE RAILROAD AND THE RIVER
> HAVE DOORS THAT FACE EACH WAY
> AND THE ENTRANCE TO THE MOVIE'S
> UP AN ALLEY UP THE SIDE

A beating administered by a group of white toughs in Chicago the summer before the Chicago riots would be transformed into "The White Ones" seven years later:

> I do not hate you,
> For your faces are beautiful, too.
> I do not hate you,
> Your faces are whirling lights of loveliness

and splendor, too.
Yet why do you torture me,
O, white strong ones,
Why do you torture me?

These parallels between Hughes's early life and his later poetry indicate that he had formulated certain attitudes towards his race and towards white America before he had even considered the idea of becoming a poet.

It was only by accident that he became a poet. He was elected to the position of class poet at Cleveland's Central High because, as he humorously recalled, he was a Negro, and Negroes were supposed to have "rhythm." "In America most white people think, of course, that *all* Negroes can sing and dance, and have a sense of rhythm. So my classmates, knowing that a poem had to have rhythm, elected me unanimously—thinking, no doubt, that I had some, being a Negro. . . . It had never occurred to me to be a poet before, or indeed a writer of any kind." Thus the role of poet was thrust upon Hughes by accident, or perhaps, by design, because he was Negro in a white society. It was the social implications of his blackness, however, that fitted him for the role. The incidents of his childhood and youth had marked Langston Hughes as a black man, and his poetry would affirm his acceptance of the mission, to be a spokesman for the black masses.

At the same time, Hughes could not deny the double nature, the dual-consciousness of being an American as well as a black. The very fact that he had been chosen by his classmates as class poet *because* he was Negro only accentuated his separateness from them. By the same token, he had never completely been exposed to the full brunt of prejudice, American-style, during his youth. Up until the time of his Southern lecture tour of 1931, his acquaintance with Southern mores had been merely peripheral. Indeed, he often began these programs by explaining how truly "American" his upbringing had been: "I began my program by telling where I was born in Missouri, that I grew up in Kansas in the geographical heart of the country, and was, therefore very American." His audiences, which consisted largely of Southern Negroes, must have found his initial declaration of Americanism rather disorienting. As Hughes himself explained in his autobiography, this first-hand encounter with racial prejudice in the South provided an introduction to an important aspect of racial heritage to which he had never been fully exposed: "I found a great social and cultural gulf between the races in the South, astonishing to one who, like myself, from the North, had never known such uncompromising prejudices."

In a poem published in *The Crisis* in 1922, Hughes outlined his ambivalence towards the region in rather chilling imagery:

The child-minded South
Scratching in the dead fire's ashes
For a Negro's bones.

He indicated in the poem's conclusion that the South had a strong attraction, but that he was more comfortable in resisting its allure:

> And I, who am black, would love her
> But she spits in my face.
> And I, who am black,
> Would give her many rare gifts
> But she turns her back upon me.

In the same year that Hughes published "The South," Jean Toomer published *Cane*. One of the poems in *Cane*, "Georgia Dusk," evoked similar imagery:

> A feast of moon and men and barking hounds,
>   An orgy for some genius of the South
>   With blood-hot eyes and cane-lipped scented mouth,
> Surprised in making folk-songs from soul sounds.

Where Toomer's *Cane* was the product of direct experience (a six-month sojourn in Georgia as a rural schoolteacher), Hughes's South was an imaginatively evoked nightmare. The last lines of Hughes's poem suggest that he was not yet ready to embrace the Southern experience as Toomer had done. Hughes's Gothic South was a far cry from Toomer's seductive lines in "Carma":

> Wind is in the cane. Come along.
> Cane leaves swaying, rusty with talk,
> Scratching choruses above the guinea's squawk,
> Wind is in the cane. Come along.

If Hughes feared the direct Southern confrontation during the twenties, he found much to admire in those Southern blacks who came to settle in the teeming cities of the North, and from them he derived material for his poetry. In seeking communal identity through them, Hughes overemphasized the exotic, as this passage from *The Big Sea* indicates: "I never tired of hearing them talk, listening to the thunderclaps of their laughter, to their troubles, to their discussions of the war and the men who had gone to Europe from the Jim Crow South. . . . They seemed to me like the gayest and the bravest people possible—these Negroes from the Southern ghettoes—facing tremendous odds, working and laughing and trying to get somewhere in the world." The passage suggests the attitude of a sympathetic observer rather than that of an engaged participant. In some ways, Hughes's attitude towards Southern Negroes was directly counter to that of his father's. According to Langston, the elder Hughes "hated Negroes. I think he hated himself, too, for being a Negro. He disliked all of his family because they were Negroes and remained in the United States." Hughes, on the other hand, proudly affirmed his racial heritage. Where his father rejected both race and country, Hughes could reject neither.

At the end of his lecture programs in the South, Hughes would recite his poem "I, Too, Sing America." As often as he invoked this poem, he would be reaffirming his faith in the American dream. Some of Hughes's earliest poems reveal an almost childlike faith in the American ideal, as in the opening lines of the following, first published in 1925:

> America is seeking the stars,
> America is seeking tomorrow,
> You are America,
> I am America
> America—the dream,
> America—the vision.
> America—the star-seeking I.

The same poem affirmed the unity of black and white America:

> You of the blue eyes
> And the blond hair,
> I of the dark eyes
> And the crinkly hair,
> You and I
> Offering hands.

This affirmation of racial unity had a direct relation to Hughes's experience with racial integration at Cleveland's Central High, where he was often elected to important class positions because of his acceptability to various white ethnic factions: "Since it was during the war, and Americanism was being stressed, many of our students, including myself, were then called down to the principal's office and questioned about our belief in Americanism. . . . After that, the principal organized an Americanism Club in our school, and . . . I was elected President" (*The Big Sea*). While this experience might serve to strengthen his faith in an ideal America, it also, paradoxically, reinforced his sense of separateness as a Negro. His race was clearly an advantage in terms of popularity among his peers; still, it was his color which marked him as different.

At the same time, Hughes's experience in racial integration set him apart from the experience of those Negroes from the South whose life-style he so admired. Hughes must have realized that his experience vis-a-vis that of most black Americans was rather unique. Though he claimed at times to have had a typical Negro upbringing, it was nevertheless different, as he pointed out in this passage from *The Big Sea*: "Mine was not a typical Negro family. My grandmother never took in washing or worked in service or went to church. She had lived in Oberlin and spoke perfect English, without a trace of dialect. She looked like an Indian. My mother was a newspaper woman and a stenographer then. My father lived in Mexico City. My grandfather had been a congressman." In addition, Hughes harbored no grudges against white society: "I learned early in life not to hate *all* white people. And ever since, it has seemed to me that *most* people are generally good, in every race and in every country where I have been."

Hughes often sought to dispel the distinction between American and Negro by affirming his nationality in no uncertain terms. The following incident from his autobiography illustrates this point. He had been teaching English to Mexicans during his final summer in Mexico with his father. The teacher who was to replace him was a white American woman who found it incredible that a Negro could be capable of teaching anything:

> When she was introduced to me, her mouth fell open and she said: "Why, Ah-Ah thought you was an American."
> I said: "I am American!"
> She said: "Oh, Ah mean a white American."
> Her voice had a Southern drawl.
> I grinned.

Another incident from his autobiography concerns his refusal to deny his race. On the return trip to the United States from Mexico after his first summer there, Hughes attempted to purchase an ice cream soda in St. Louis. The following exchange took place:

> The clerk said: "Are you a Mexican or a Negro?"
> I said: "Why?"
> "Because if you're a Mexican, I'll serve you," he said. "If you're colored, I won't."
> "I'm colored," I replied. The clerk turned away to wait on someone else. I knew I was home in the U. S. A.

These incidents were to have their counterparts in his poetry, where he could affirm with equal assurance his two credos of identity: "I am a Negro" and "I, Too, Sing America." But while affirming these polar commitments, Hughes was alienated from both of them. As a black man, he was aware that his race had never been granted full participation in the American dream. His exposure to the possibilities of that dream, however, through his experience with racial integration, and his relative innocence (this was to disappear, of course) in matters of Southern mores, would distinguish his circumstances from the lot of the black masses, with whom he sought to identify to the extent of becoming their spokesman. This peculiar set of conditions allowed Hughes to assume a degree of sophistication in racial matters quite unusual among his contemporaries, white or black. This sophistication, coupled with his insistence on maintaining the necessary aesthetic distance of the artist, provided the stimulus for his poetry and endowed the poet with a sense of mission. He was absolutely confident of his self-imposed mission as a poet of the black masses. His familiarity with white Bohemian intellectual circles in New York during the twenties provided him with the additional stimulus of communicating his message across racial lines. Thus two kinds of poetry emerged in the twenties: the black vernacular poetry, utilizing dialect, jazz talk, and everyday subject matter; and "message" poetry, which concentrated on the position of the black man in white America. *The Weary Blues*, Hughes's first book, contained much of this message poetry, besides some experiments in jazz poetry ("The Cat and the Saxophone," "Blues Fantasy," "Negro Dancers"), and additional nonracial lyrics. The second book, *Fine Clothes to the Jew*, concentrated almost entirely on the vernacular subject matter, and contained many poems written in blues dialect. These two tendencies in Hughes's early work were to predominate throughout his career.

Shakespeare in Harlem (1942), for example, may be considered a sequel to *Fine Clothes*, while *Montage of a Dream Deferred* (1951) integrated the vernacular subject matter with the thematic concerns introduced in *The Weary Blues*. *Montage*, along with *Ask Your Mama* (1961), will probably remain Hughes's most important achievements in poetry since his work of the twenties. *Ask Your Mama*, permeated with humor, irony, and exciting imagery, contains echoes of "The Negro Speaks of Rivers," "As I Grew Older," and "The Cat and the Saxophone." As in these earlier poems, Hughes transforms personal experiences and observations into distillations of the Black American condition.

Hughes wrote in his autobiography: "My best poems were all written when I felt the worst. When I was happy, I didn't write anything." When he first began writing poetry, he felt his lyrics were too personal to reveal to others: "Poems came to me now spontaneously, from somewhere inside. . . . I put the poems down quickly on anything I had at hand when they came into my head, and later I copied them into a notebook. But I began to be afraid to show my poems to anybody, because they had become very serious and very much a part of me. And I was afraid other people might not like them or understand them." These two statements regarding his poetry suggest deep underlying emotional tensions as being the source of his creativity. And yet the personal element in Hughes's poetry is almost entirely submerged beneath the persona of the "Negro Poet Laureate." If, as Hughes suggested, personal unhappiness was the groundstone for his best work, it then follows that, in order to maintain the singleness of purpose and devotion to his art, he would be required to sacrifice some degree of emotional stability. Thus poetry became a kind of therapy, masking deeper emotional tensions. We know from his autobiography that Hughes experienced two severe emotional breakdowns. The first one had to do with a break with his father over the course of his vocation; the second followed upon a break with his wealthy white patroness in the late twenties over the kind of poetry he was writing. Both of these emotional traumas were directly related to his decision to become a poet of his people.

The persona of the poet was the role Hughes adopted in his very first published poem, as *the Negro* in "The Negro Speaks of Rivers." It was a persona to which he would remain faithful throughout his lengthy career. The link between his personal experiences and his poetry has been suggested in this paper. It cannot be defined because it seems clear that Hughes suppressed the more frightening excursions into his own personal void. Poetry was an outlet as well as a salvation. Only occasionally, as in the poem "As I Grew Older," does Hughes provide a window upon his inner anxieties, and even in this poem the real root of these anxieties is hidden, and the poem becomes an allegory of the black man's alienation in white America.

Hughes's early attempts in the twenties to fill the role of Poet Laureate of the Negro led him to create a body of work that was organic in nature. The traditional literary sources of inspiration were for the most part bypassed. The source of his poetry was to be found in the anonymous, unheard black masses: their rhythms, their dialect, their life styles. Hughes sought to incorporate this untapped resource of black folk language into a new kind of poetry. His personal experiences, as related in his autobiography, combined with this folk material to provide thematic dimension to his work. The basic themes regarding the American dream and its possibilities for the black man were always in his poetry. The tension between the unrealized dream and the realities of the black experience in America provided the dynamic. This tension between material and theme laid the groundwork for the irony which characterized Hughes's work at its best.

Countee Cullen and Keats's "Vale of Soul-Making"

Ronald Primeau

In *The Anxiety of Influence* Harold Bloom suggests that "poetic history" is "indistinguishable from poetic influence, since strong poets make that history by misreading one another, so as to clear imaginative space for themselves." By "misreading," Bloom means not "mis-taking" but rather what he calls "clinamen," something more akin to what Lucretius meant by a "*swerve* of the atoms so as to make changes possible in the universe. A poet swerves away from his precursor, by so reading his precursor's poem as to execute a *clinamen* in relation to it." I am of course oversimplifying Bloom's detailed discussion, in order to emphasize his theory of poetry as the product of the anxiety of influence; for it provides a way to reexamine the much-discussed yet little-understood anxieties in Countee Cullen's reading of Keats. Almost without exception, commentators on Cullen cite Keats as his chief "poetic model." While the similarities in structure, imagery, and theme are unmistakable, critics have stressed overt links evidenced in direct allusions and have, at the same time, neglected even more crucial (though more subtle) thematic connections. Cullen's attempts at once to grow through identification with Keats and to free himself from such influences in the very process of assimilating them exemplify many of the tensions in his career.

Cullen was attracted to (indeed, almost obsessed by) Keats's repeated and even ritualized insistence that pleasure and pain are always bound up in each other in the sensuous complexity of felt existence. While the suffering of the artist has become almost a cliché in literary history, the creative dimensions of pain and uncertainty—what Keats called the "Vale of Soul-Making"—above all else drew Cullen to the distant poet with whom he

From *Papers on Language and Literature* 12, no. 1 (Winter 1976). © 1976 by the Board of Trustees, Southern Illinois University.

had little else in common. The well-known remarks in Keats's letters suggest a significant parallel:

> Do you not see how necessary a World of Pains and troubles is to school an Intelligence and make it a soul? A place where the heart must feel and suffer in a thousand diverse ways! Not merely is the Heart a Hornbook, It is the Mind's Bible, it is the Mind's experience, it is the teat from which the Mind or intelligence sucks its identity—As various as the Lives of Men are—so various become their soul.

The emphasis that Cullen gives to the creativity inherent in bittersweet experiences is paralleled throughout the Afro-American literary tradition. Among the key values "that seem frequently to be reflected by Negro folk literature and by outstanding Negro writers," George E. Kent includes "an acceptance of the role of suffering in retaining one's humanity and in retaining some perspective on the humanity of the oppressor." What Cullen found in Keats's poems is consistent with, and reinforces, this basic pattern. In a perceptive review and analysis of Cullen's major themes, Bertram L. Woodruff has suggested that he uses the five "anodynes" of "Love, Beauty, Faith in Man, Belief in Christ, and Poetry" in order to "assuage the anguish of living." Woodruff notes the fact that Cullen, like Keats, seems to feel that "his joys are not at the full until they are sharpened into pains." This sharpening of sensitivity until the full range of human experience is forged into a grid of pleasure-pain is at the center of Cullen's own experience as well as the chief stimulus attracting him to Keats. From his own experiences, Cullen fuses joys and difficulties to create what Keats called "the sweetness of the pain."

Ironically, poems in which Cullen refers directly to Keats display far less of the intensity he achieves in his other more subtle treatments of the same material. In "For John Keats" he accomplishes little more than an echo of the epitaph on Keats's grave in Rome's Protestant Cemetery: "Not writ in water, nor in mist, / Sweet lyric throat, thy name; / Thy singing lips that cold death kissed / Have seared his own with flame." Although the imagery reflects elemental human quests, the patterns he achieves are neither original nor particularly striking. Similarly, "To Endymion" expresses "the bright immortal lie / Time gives to those detractors of your name" in a series of Keatsian allusions that are for the most part too explicit. "Your star is steadfast now" suggests "Bright star . . . ," and "Long shall she stammer forth a broken note" echoes Keats's wish in his *Endymion* that he might "stammer where old Chaucer us'd to sing." Other examples, though this one suffices, reinforce the critical opinion that Cullen was more hurt than helped by this encounter with Keats.

One other famous and directly allusive lyric—"To John Keats, Poet at Spring Time"—is more lyrical and somewhat more intense. In his version of the Adonais myth, Cullen attempts to merge life and death, pain and

joy through the transforming and liberating energies of beauty, specifically
of music. As the imagery focuses on the unavoidable difficulties of passing
time

> Spring beats
> Her tocsin call to those who love her,
> And lo! the dogwood petals cover
> Her breast with drifts of snow

the speaker identifies with nature, beauty, and the poet:

> And while my head is earthward bowed
> To read new life sprung from your shroud,
> Folks seeing me must think it strange
> That merely spring should so derange
> My mind. They do not know that you,
> John Keats, keep revel with me, too.

The scene Cullen creates is again built on qualified assertions typical in
Keats's odes. The season is a spring that "never was," a time that "the
lyric ghost" of Keats heightens beyond its own capacities. In fact "Spring
never was so fair and dear / As Beauty makes her *seem* this year" (italics
mine). Poetic "Beauty" thus awakens in the speaker a "pulsing" power
that blends the music of the leaves, the harp, and his poetic song. The
intensity is strikingly Keatsian as through the dust fingers push "The Vision
Splendid to a birth." The dead poet's cry (his poem) continues in "bud and
blossom," and "John Keats still writes poetry." Bewilderment in "Folks
seeing me" (readers) and references to the "merely spring" is therefore
both ironic and quite literal.

One could go on citing countless such examples of Cullen's attraction
to Keats as a significant poetic precursor. Their common ground is always
their persistent and almost obsessive drive to render poetically the realities
of bittersweet human experience. Most often in direct allusions, invocations
bordering on idolatry, and blatant parallels, Cullen fails to overcome an
influence that truly became a burden. But Cullen also read Keats creatively,
and in poems where he is able to establish a distance between his precursor
and his own experiences, the influence is stronger even where it is least
perceptible. Through a process of closure, Cullen read more into Keats than
is generally assumed to be there. Drawing upon his own needs and am-
bitions, Cullen made his best use of Keats and at the same time freed himself
from his precursor by placing his own experiences in a position of
prominence.

Beyond such observable parallels, what has been overlooked in discussions of Cullen's indebtedness to Keats is his own distinctive reworking
of themes and techniques. In his more subtle modifications of Keats, Cullen
selected, rearranged, and reshaped poetic materials by impressing his own
experiences on his responses to what he read. The poems most successfully

forged from his reading communicate a sense of authentic existence. Ironically, then, his reading of Keats is most influential not in what is sometimes called his "non-racial" verse but rather in poetry he created out of his most intensely personal experiences as a black man and black poet.

Parallels in the works of the two distant poets speak also to many of the controversies surrounding the influence of white poets on the black art of the Harlem Renaissance. Cullen's ability to render his own experience in poems was to some extent limited by his choice of culturally white aesthetic forms. The oft-repeated argument that Cullen and others in the Harlem Renaissance often wrote for white audiences and with white standards in mind is well known. But the truths in this basic assumption should not be used to dismiss Cullen's achievements in his own time. Nor should we overlook the subtle influences on poems in which he does convey his experiences authentically. Everything that attracted Cullen to Keats (or to anyone else) depended in large part on his ability to come to grips with his own experience. In short, Cullen's personal experiences as a black man and poet within a given historical reference helped to shape his responses to Keats in distinctive ways and prompted him at the same time to transform what he found in his reading into the creation of his own poems. In what is usually considered his "racial" poetry, Cullen's absorption of Keats is more pervasive and liberating than in the obviously allusive and formal elegies.

In "The Shroud of Color" the speaker describes "being dark" in terms similar to the intensity of contraries central to Keats's odes:

> There is a hurt
> In all the simple joys which to a child
> Are sweet; they are contaminate, defiled
> By truths of wrongs the childish vision fails
> To see; too great a cost this birth entails.

Grappling with tensions and contradictions, the speaker embodies both the intensity of Keats's "burst joy's grape" in "Ode on Melancholy" and the hopelessness characteristic of Keats's poems and letters to Fanny Brawne:

> I strangle in this yoke drawn tighter than
> The worth of bearing it, just to be man.
> I am not brave enough to pay the price
> In full; I lack the strength to sacrifice.

Cullen's poem may be likened to a long Keatsian dream-vision in which the speaker explores elemental feelings and attempts to place all the world's sufferings and joys together in epic panorama:

> All was struggle, gasping breath, and fight.
> A blind worm here dug tunnels to the light,
> And there a seed, racked with heroic pain,
> Thrust eager tentacles to sun and rain.

The speaker languishes with "groans / From tangled flesh and interlocked bones," lamenting especially the pain of being black in a world serving those "whose flesh is fair." Yet as a "strange wild music smote / A chord long impotent" in his being, the pattern of sorrow reverses itself in what James Baldwin terms "celebration of what is constant." The speaker fights his way through, and in the process affirms difficulty itself by expressing the hope such endurance brings for creative growth:

> And somehow it was borne upon my brain
> How being dark, and living through the pain
> Of it, is courage more than angels have. . . .
>
> . . . .
>
> The cries of all dark people near or far
> Were billowed over me, a mighty surge
> Of suffering in which my puny grief must merge
> And lose itself.

Structurally and thematically Cullen creates striking parallels with what he found regularly in Keats. But his subject is clearly the experience which is both personal and collective as it is embodied in the Afro-American oral tradition which Cullen knew well. His conclusion is therefore experientially authentic and shaped into poetic conflicts very like what he found in Keats's odes:

> Right glad I was to stoop to what I once had spurned,
> Glad even unto tears; I laughed aloud; I turned
> Upon my back, and though the tears for joy would run,
> My sight was clear; I looked and saw the rising sun.
> ("The Shroud of Color")

Cullen often repeats this basic pattern of Keats's odes: a speaker in pursuit of a seemingly unrealizable goal modifies his quest to accept, and in the process to reaffirm and to remake what is difficult but realizable in day to day human experience. His affirmation brings pleasure and pain as the speaker trades escape for a difficult, inevitable, yet imaginative involvement in human existence in time.

In his extended series of "Epitaphs" Cullen pursues in shorter, almost clipped form his preoccupation with dreams ("I have wrapped my dreams in a silken cloth"), his theme of affirmation of process as an answer to time's destructive powers ("This lovely flower fell to seed;" but "She held it as her dying creed / That she would grow again"), and his compulsion toward the inter-relatedness of joy and sorrow: "Mirth was a crown upon his head; / Pride kept his twisted lips apart / In jest, to hide a heart that bled." Although these short lyrics are among Cullen's best-known works, they are seldom read alongside others in which he alludes directly to Keats. When seen together, Keats's influence and Cullen's working within the Afro-American poetic tradition become more complex than either alone is usually considered. In "If You Should Go" the speaker expresses the view that night is needed to define the day; he then extends this theme to the fading of a dream:

> A dream,
> When done, should leave no trace
> That it has lived, except a gleam
> Across the dreamer's face.

In "She of the Dancing Feet Sings," the speaker, much like the dreamers in Keats's odes, rejects perfection as an unrealizable and ultimately inhuman state:

> And how would I thrive in a perfect place
> Where dancing would be sin,
> With not a man to love my face,
> Nor an arm to hold me in?

thus recalling the "Ode to a Nightingale": "But here there is no light." "The Wise" also repeats the Keatsian pattern of withdrawal from and then reentry into painful complexity: "Dead men alone bear frost and rain / On throbless heart and heatless brain, / And feel no stir of joy or pain." The poem is a death-wish that is undercut nonetheless by Cullen's ironic juxtaposition of contrary states of love and hate, heat and cold, growth and death. The speaker's conclusion is thus appropriately ambiguous in its partially ironic longing to freeze the flux of time and to stop painful initiation into the painful world of process: "Strange, men should flee their company, / Or think me strange who long to be / Wrapped in their cool immunity." Curiously, Cullen places "To John Keats" between "The Wise" and "Requiescam" in arranging the selections in *On These I Stand*. The three poems complement each other by working and reworking the theme of death as a bittersweet end to both joy and pain; taken together, the three poems describe death as a complex of relief and loss. Whereas "To John Keats" is a hopeful "Adonais" and "The Wise" an expression of unresolved conflict, "Requiescam" is a bitter wish that "my life's cold sun were setting / To rise for me no more."

In many conventional sonnets Cullen rewrote Keats by transforming the themes and techniques he found in the older poet into the terms of his own experience. Typically in the sonnets "a crucifix" displaces Keats's imagery of autumn as "the noblest way . . . fraught with too much pain." Cullen also links "what was said before" with what will be said "countless centuries from now again" when a poet "warped with bitterness and pain" will "brew" his poems "hoping to salve his sore." Again in this one in a series of untitled sonnets, a Keatsian "throbbing" unifies his obsession with the intermingling of pain and pleasure in the eternizing creativity of poetry. In emphasizing anguish and disdain in several poems Cullen echoes the despair that dominates in Keats's "Isabella." In "Sonnet Dialogue" the speaker's realization that "the worm shall tread the lion down" suggests the "wormy circumstance" in "Isabella."

Many of Cullen's most conventional lyrics also take on added dimensions when read as further orchestrations of his persistent blending of joy and suffering. His lays of the unrequited lover again often resemble the desperateness of Keats's poems to Fanny Brawne. "The Love Tree" relates a tale of "pale lovers chancing here" who

> pluck and eat, and through their veins a sweet
> And languid ardor play, their pulses beat
> An unimagined tune, their shy lips meet
> And part, and bliss repeat again.

Yet this growth in love reveals another variation on a basic Keatsian theme: "'Twas break of heart that made the Love Tree grow." Further examples of Cullen's attraction to Keats's themes multiply. In "Love's Way," the cup is "shared down to the last sweet dregs." And in "Protest," the speaker once more affirms process in his acceptance of human existence as a "time to live, to love, bear pain and smile."

In "More Than a Fool's Song" Cullen unobtrusively builds a catalog of opposites:

> Court pleasure in the halls of grief;
>
> . . . .
> . . . The World's a curious riddle thrown
> Water-wise from heaven's cup;
> The souls we think are hurtling down
> Perhaps are climbing up.

Just as "The Foolish Heart" "needs a grave / To prove to it that it is dead," the speaker of "Bright Bindings" seeks "flesh gifted to ache and bleed." In "After a Visit," Cullen describes man's fall from grace as a recoiling from pain and a destructive withdrawal from involvement in the experiential that can be remedied only by reentry into a complex and painful regenerative process:

> I had known joy and sorrow I had surely known,
> But out of neither any piercing note was blown.
> Friends had been kind and surely friends had fruitless been,
> But long ago my heart was closed, panelled within.

Again the Keatsian pattern of resolution closes the poem:

> And shame of my apostasy was like a coal
> That reached my tongue and heart and far off frigid soul,
> Melting myself into myself, making me weep
> Regeneration's burning tears, precluding sleep.

Cullen's best-known works, such as "Heritage," "From the Dark

Tower," and "The Black Christ," are also glossed significantly by an understanding of his attraction to, and reshaping of, Keatsian themes and techniques. The ironies that Cullen is able to sustain regularly in his major works are analogous to what Kenneth Burke has now classically referred to as "symbolic action" in Keats's odes. Reading "Ode on a Grecian Urn" as "a viaticum that leads, by a series of transformations, into the oracle 'Beauty is truth, truth beauty,' " Burke established inseparable links between stylistic pattern and a thematic "abolishing of romanticism through romanticism." This fusion of structure and theme results in what Walter Jackson Bate has called "that process of symbolic debate in which a dominant symbol or concept, after being postulated at the start, becomes the motif in a counterpoint of withdrawal, qualifications, and partial return." Cullen found this poetic structure best able to reflect his own experiences, and he drew upon this fusion of experiential and poetic structure in order to express the tensions in his own life. Keats's often quoted discussion of the "Vale of Soul-Making" summarizes his most important influences on Cullen's style and thought:

> Suppose a rose to have sensation, it blooms on a beautiful morning it enjoys itself—but there comes a cold wind, a hot sun—it cannot escape it, it cannot destroy its annoyances—they are as native to the world as itself: no more can man be happy in spite, the worldly elements will prey upon his nature— . . . I say "*Soul-Making*" Soul as distinguished from an Intelligence—There may be Intelligences or sparks of the divinity in millions—but they are not Souls till they acquire identities, till each one is personally itself.

Cullen repeatedly worked such themes and structures directly into his shorter poems and then reworked them carefully into his major works so as to adjust them to his developing needs. Direct parallels can be seen once again in "Two Thoughts of Death":

> While I hang poised between the dead
> And quick, into omniscience fanned,
> My mind shall glow with one rich spark
> Before it ends in endless dark. . . .
>
> . . . .
> And as my day throbs into dusk,
> This heart the world has made to bleed,
> While all its red stream deathward flows,
> Shall comprehend just why the seed
> Must agonize to be the rose.

In his reading of Keats, Cullen was at his best able to transform the stylistic patterns he found by merging them with the oral and folk traditions that were a part of his own experience. The resultant merging of theme and structure accounts for both the productive tensions and the puzzling

ambiguities and controversies created by his major works. In writing on
"the symbolic texture" of Cullen's "self-critical enquiry into the nature and
function of the African idyll in the Black American's consciousness," Lloyd
W. Brown traces the "mythic nature" of his "sentimental fantasies about
cultural roots." Just as the speakers of Keats's odes dream unreal dreams
that reflect real tensions inherent in everyday human problems, so also—
following Brown's reading—"Heritage" embodies images that are "unreal"
and yet "reflect a very real psychological need." For the speaker in "Heritage," careful rendering of fantasy mirrors tensions in his thinking and
expresses what Brown calls his "desire to establish a Black frame of reference." Keats's poems are, of course, not the only place Cullen would
find such preoccupations. But in this context, his response to Keatsian
imagery and poetic form brought him closer to, rather than farther from,
an understanding of his own experience and a developing poetic form in
which to express the paradoxes of that experience. Again in Brown's view,
"What is paramount are the psycho-existential needs which these myths
protect, and which the writers themselves analyze in serious and self-
conscious terms."

"Heritage," Cullen's most famous poem, needs no commentary here.
In the long soliloquy the speaker captures the contraries and poised energy
typical of the concentrated expression and expansive paradox in Keats's
odes:

> So I lie, whose fount of pride,
> Dear distress, and joy allied,
> In my somber flesh and skin,
> With the dark blood dammed within
> Like great pulsing tides of wine
> That, I fear, must burst the fine
> Channels of the chafing net
> Where they surge and foam and fret.

Here the parallels to Keats's themes (distress and joy allied), imagery
("dammed within"), and fusion of theme and structure ("burst the fine
channels") are both overt and sufficiently blended into Cullen's own experience as he transforms his influences into his own statements. The result
is a more subtle and effective influence that often is ignored.

Cullen's own experience merges with the Keatsian influence again in
his subtle attack on Christianity in "Heritage." Although he knew little
about either African or Eastern cultures, he was certain that a white Christ
offered the black man at best a fragmented symbol of his own experience:

> Ever at Thy glowing altar
> Must my heart grow sick and falter,
> Wishing He I served were black,
> Thinking then it would not lack
> Precedent of pain to guide it.

Again Cullen's emphasis on the creative dimensions of pain and the ability to identify with suffering is obvious. And once more his magnetic pull toward the conceptual influenced his choice of the poetic vehicle in which to express the guidance of precedent.

The full range and complexity of influences on Cullen's career await fuller exploration. His indebtedness to the spirituals, to shouts and work songs, to Dunbar (surely underestimated during the Renaissance), and to minor poets of Cullen's own time such as Georgia Douglas Johnson, Frank Horne, and Helene Johnson needs extensive examination and evaluation. Recognition of the complexity of Cullen's response to Keats indicates some of the directions further study might take. Although he often speaks from behind Du Bois's "veil" and reflects the tension of experiences within the double life, Cullen tends more toward the conceptual and the philosophical rather than the concrete dramatic rhythms dominant in the oral tradition. Enmeshed in controversy most of his career, Cullen's own goals and accomplishments within the limitations imposed by his own times are underestimated. In 1927 he told an interviewer for the Chicago *Bee* that in his works he tried to capture the distinctive experiences of the Negro, "his joys and sorrows, mostly the latter." His obsessive drive to create at least a workable balance between the intellectual and the sensuous, the mythological and the deeply personal further attracted him to Keats. Cullen's subject was always—in a variety of forms and in repeated reworkings— again in his own words, "the heights and depths of emotions which I feel as a Negro."

Biographical Notes

Edwin Arlington Robinson (1869–1935), raised in Gardiner, Maine, attended Harvard for two years then returned home to stay until the death of his parents when he was twenty-two. Thereafter he lived in furnished rooms around New York City. From middle age he summered regularly at the MacDowell Colony in Peterborough, New Hampshire. He dedicated his quiet life entirely to serious writing. His first volume, *The Torrent and the Night Before* (1896), privately printed, favorably impressed the literary figures his friends mailed it to, but Robinson's way was made by Kermit Roosevelt, the President's son, who found a copy of *The Children of the Night* (1897) in the Groton School library and recommended it to his father. Theodore Roosevelt wrote an essay celebrating the second edition of the book. With the publication of *Captain Craig* (1902), the President secured Robinson a sinecure at the New York Customs House, a position he held throughout Roosevelt's tenure. The poet, rescued from his earlier job as a subway inspector, spent these five years of grace establishing himself in literature and never took another job. His work breaks neatly into sonnets and dramatic narratives, or monologues. The characters most often are remarkable failures, the setting frequently "Tilburn," a town very like Gardiner, Maine. His volumes include: *The Town down the River* (1910), *The Man against the Sky* (1916), *Merlin* (1917), *Lancelot* (1920), *The Three Taverns* (1920), *Avon's Harvest* (1921), three *Collected Poems* (1921, 1927, 1937), *Roman Bartholow* (1923), *The Man Who Died Twice* (1924), *Dionysus in Doubt* (1925), *Tristram* (1927), *Sonnets 1889–1927* (1928), *Cavender's House* (1929), *The Glory of the Nightingales* (1930), *Selected Poems* (1931), *Nicodemus* (1932), *Tamaranth* (1934), and *King Jasper* (1935).

Paul Laurence Dunbar (1872–1906) was born in Dayton, Ohio, to parents who had been slaves in Kentucky. He became a celebrated literary figure with the publication of his second book, *Majors and Minors* (1895), which was passionately reviewed by William Dean Howells. He lectured widely, and wrote a musical, four novels, and many stories. His early death after a prolonged illness caused national mourning. His books of poems include: *Oak and Ivy* (1893), *Lyrics of Lowly Life* (1896), *Lyrics of the Hearthside* (1899), *Lyrics of Love and Laughter* (1903), and *Lyrics of Sunshine and Shadow* (1905).

Robert Lee Frost (1874–1963), born to a New England family in San Francisco, moved as a boy to the farm and mill country north of Boston, the backdrop of his poems. Independent by nature and necessity, Frost attended both Dartmouth and Harvard briefly, and passed through jobs as a mill hand, school teacher, and newspaper editor. He married Elinor White, his fellow high-school valedictorian. He farmed for several years. His poems were not well received until he moved to England, where Ezra Pound and others promoted his first book, *A Boy's Will* (1913). His book *North of Boston* (1914) established his reputation, and he returned to the United States to settle on a New Hampshire farm. His subsequent books include *Mountain Interval* (1916), *New Hampshire* (1923), *West-Running Brook* (1928), two *Collected Poems* (1930, 1939), *A Further Range* (1936), *Steeple Bush* (1947), and *In the Clearing* (1962). He also published two blank-verse plays in biblical settings, *A Masque of Reason* (1945) and *A Masque of Mercy* (1947). Frost lectured widely and taught occasionally at Amherst, Harvard, and the University of Michigan. His wife preceded him in death by many years, as did three of their five children.

Wallace Stevens (1879–1955) was born in Reading, Pennsylvania, and educated at Harvard and New York University Law School. He made his career as an executive. As a special student at Harvard, he studied French and German, became friendly with George Santayana, and was president of the *Harvard Advocate*. Before law school he was unhappily employed at the New York *Herald Tribune*. He worked briefly in a law partnership that failed, then for a series of firms in New York; he joined the legal staff of one insurance company, then took a job with another. He was finally transferred to Hartford, where he remained with the Hartford Accident and Indemnity Company, ending as Vice President. In his later life he studied the history of his family.

Stevens never left America. He lived quietly at home, keeping both business and literary associates from the door. He did have a wide acquaintance in each of his worlds. He made rambunctious outings in bohemian Greenwich Village and took trips with "the boys" to Key West. He married Elsie Moll, a young woman from home, just as he started his insurance career. His daughter, Holly, has played a role in editing his literary legacy.

Stevens published in student magazines at Harvard. His work appeared in the best literary periodicals throughout his life, with substantial hiatuses after college and following the publication of his first book, *Harmonium* (1923, rev. 1931). He also wrote essays, collected in *The Necessary Angel* (1951). The other books of poems include: *Ideas of Order* (1936), *Owl's Clover* (1936), *The Man with the Blue Guitar* (1937), *Parts of a World* (1942), *Transport to Summer* (1947), *The Auroras of Autumn* (1950), *Selected Poems* (1953), *Collected Poems* (1954), *Opus Posthumous* (1957), and *The Palm at the End of the Mind* (1971).

(Nicholas) Vachel Lindsay (1879–1931), born to evangelical Christian parents in Springfield, Illinois, attended Hiram College and studied art in Chicago and New York. He became a celebrated tramp, preaching on temperance, reciting verse, and trading broadsides of his poetry for food and lodging. He developed his own theology and preached his "Gospel of Beauty." His first two volumes of poems, *General William Booth Enters into Heaven and Other Poems* (1913) and *The Congo and Other Poems* (1914), brought him a literary reputation as an innovator as well as popular acclaim. He married a woman he met while performing. They had two children. Lindsay became a fixture on the lecture circuit, unable to escape an endless tour reciting the title poems of his first two books. He committed suicide with poison.

Besides poetry, Lindsay wrote memoirs and political essays and one of the first books on movies, *The Art of the Moving Picture* (1916). His friend Edgar Lee Masters wrote his biography. His later collections include *The Daniel Jazz* (1920), *Collected Poems* (1923, rev. 1925), and *Johnny Appleseed* (1928).

Edgar Lee Masters (1868–1950), born in Kansas and raised near Springfield, Ohio, practiced law for thirty years in Chicago. He was for some time a partner of Clarence Darrow. He published *Book of Verse* (1898) as a young man and a play in blank verse, *Maximilian* (1902), but only became known with *Spoon River Anthology* (1915). Such promoters as Harriet Monroe grouped him with Carl Sandburg and Vachel Lindsay as a poet using new verse techniques to bring unfamiliar material into poetry. Masters wrote novels, autobiography, biographies of Lindsay, Whitman, and Twain, and a history of Chicago. His study of Lincoln was intended to deflate Sandburg's hagiography. His subsequent volumes of poetry include: *Starved Rock* (1919), *Domesday Book* (1920), *The New Spoon River* (1924), *Invisible Landscapes* (1935), *Poems of People* (1936), *Illinois Poems* (1941), and *The Sangamon* (1942).

Carl August Sandburg (1878–1967) was born in Galesburg, Illinois, to Swedish immigrants, and spent his youth as an itinerant laborer. He gained an interest in education while a soldier in the Spanish-American War and returned to Galesburg to attend Lombard College. After college, Sandburg worked first as an advertising writer, then joined in socialist politics as a polemicist and reporter as well as organizer. He was secretary to Milwaukee's Social Democratic mayor. With the waning of midwestern socialism, Sandburg became a foreign correspondent in Scandinavia and finally an editorial writer for the Chicago *Daily News*. He held that position for fifteen years until retirement.

Sandburg's poems became known when Harriet Monroe's *Poetry* published a selection including "Chicago." *Chicago Poems* (1916) set the colloquial, impressionistic, politically liberal tone followed in *Cornhuskers* (1918), *Smoke and Steel* (1920), *Slabs of the Sunburnt West* (1922), *Good Morning, America* (1928), and *The People, Yes* (1936). He compiled an important collection of American folksong, *The American Songbag* (1927). He wrote three popular books of nonsense for children, an immense novel tracing three centuries of an American family, memoirs, and a six-volume work chronicling the life of Abraham Lincoln. Other books of poems include two *Complete Poems* (1950, 1970), *Harvest Poems 1910–1960* (1960), *Wind Song* (1960), and *Honey and Salt* (1963).

Sara Teasdale (1884–1933), born in St. Louis, was educated at home and in private academies. She traveled in the American Southwest, Europe, and the Near East. She settled with her husband, an exporter, in New York, where she died after many years of poor health. She edited collections of poetry and worked with composers to set her verse to music. The books of poems include: *Sonnets to Duse and Other Poems* (1907), *Helen of Troy* (1911), *Rivers to the Sea* (1915), *Love Song* (1917), *Flame and Shadow* (1920), *Dark of the Moon* (1926), *Strange Victory* (1933), and the posthumous *Collected Poems* (1937).

Elinor Hoyt Wylie (1885–1925), born in New Jersey to a family distinguished in politics, was educated at schools for young ladies as well as at Bryn Mawr. Shortly after the birth of her son, she left her first husband to elope with a married man to England. After several years in Europe the couple returned and married, and Wylie began publishing her poems. She left her second husband to marry the poet William Rose Benet. She died of a stroke five years later.

As a young woman, Wylie was torn between painting and poetry. She had success as a novelist and spent a good deal of her money accumulating a distinguished Shelley library. She moved widely in New York literary society. Many novels of the time include a character based on her. Wylie's books of poems include: *Incidental Numbers* (1912), *Nets to Catch the Wind* (1921), *Black Armour* (1923), *One Person* (1928), *Trivial Breath* (1928), *Collected Poems* (1932), and *Last Poems* (1943).

Edna St. Vincent Millay (1892–1950), born in Rockland, Maine, published poems in the children's magazine *St. Nicholas* as a teenager. They attracted the attention of a patron who sent her to Vassar after preparation at Barnard. At school she appeared in many plays, and achieved national celebrity with the poem "Renascence" in the annual *The Lyric Year*. In 1917 *Renascence and Other Poems* appeared. Millay moved to New York City to live as a Greenwich Village bohemian. She acted with the Provincetown Players and struck up friendships with Floyd Dell, Arthur Fiske Davis, and Edmund Wilson. Millay was devoted to her mother and her sisters. She also developed a close relationship with the Dutchman Eugen Boissevain, who largely curtailed his world-wide business dealings to marry Millay and live with her on a Berkshire farm. Less well known than her sonnets are her volumes of poems addressing social problems. She also wrote several plays in verse, translated Baudelaire, and published prose sketches under the pseudonym Nancy Boyd. The books of poetry include: *A Few Figs from Thistles* (1920), *Second April* (1921), *The Ballad of the Harp-Weaver* (1923), *The Buck in the Snow* (1928), *Fatal Interview* (1931), *Wine from the Grapes* (1934), *Conversation at Midnight* (1937), *Huntsman, What Quarry?* (1939), *Make Bright the Arrows* (1940), *The Murder of Lidice* (1942), *Collected Sonnets* (1941), *Collected Lyrics* (1943), *Collected Poems* (1956), and the posthumous *Mine the Harvest* (1954).

William Carlos Williams (1883–1963), born in Rutherford, New Jersey, and educated at the University of Pennsylvania Medical School, returned to his home to practice general medicine for the rest of his life. He studied at Paris and Geneva as a teenager, in Leipzig after medical school, and interned in New York. His father came from Birmingham, England, and his mother from Puerto Rico. As a student in Philadelphia, Williams became friends with Ezra Pound and H. D. He associated himself with the international literary society of his youth, and his home in New Jersey was an object of pilgrimage to young authors in his mature years. He wrote essays, manifestos, novels, stories, plays, and memoirs. His books of poetry include: *Poems* (1909), *The Tempers* (1913), *Al Que Quiere!* (1917), *Kora in Hell* (1920), *Spring and All* (1923), *Collected Poems 1921–1931* (1934), *An Early Martyr* (1935), *Adam and Eve in the City* (1936), *The Complete Collected Poems, 1906–1938* (1938), *Paterson, Book I* (1946), *Paterson, Book II* (1948), *The Clouds* (1948), *Selected Poems* (1949, rev. 1963), *Paterson, Book III* (1949), *The Collected Later Poems* (1950, rev. 1963), *The Collected Earlier Poems* (1951), *Paterson, Book IV* (1951), *The Desert Music* (1954), *Journey to Love* (1955), *Paterson, Book V* (1958), *Pictures from Brueghel* (1962), *Paterson* (1963), and *Imaginations* (1970).

Ezra Weston Loomis Pound (1885–1972), born in Hailey, Idaho, and raised in Pennsylvania, was educated at Hamilton College and the University of Pennsylvania. He was fired with full pay from an instructorship at Wabash College for having a woman in his room, and traveled on that money to Europe, where he began a career as poet, critic, and a promoter of artists. He lived thereafter in England, then Paris, then Italy. He only visited the United States twice, once to Washington, D.C., to lobby for an isolationist policy toward the Axis powers. He returned to that city the second time in chains, to spend eventually twelve years in a hospital for the insane, judged unfit to stand trial as a war criminal. To list Pound's important friendships would be to write a history of Modernism in all arts. His cultural researches led to a passion for the reform of economic society, and it was as a Fascist collaborator that he entered the machine of American justice. After his release was secured by a network of prominent associates, Pound returned to Italy, where he died. His books of literary criticism include: *The Spirit of Romance* (1910, rev. 1952), *Instigations* (1920), *ABC of Reading* (1934), *Make It New* (1934), *Polite Essays* (1937), and *Literary Essays* (1954). His books of poetry include: *A Lume Spento* (1908), *A Quinzaine for This Yule* (1908), *Personae* (1909), *Exultations* (1909), *Canzoni* (1911), *Ripostes* (1912), *Lustra* (1916), *Quia Pauper Amavi* (1919), *Umbra: The Early Poems* (1920), *Hugh Selwyn Mauberley* (1920), *Poems, 1918–1921* (1921), *Personae: Collected Poems* (1926; rev. 1949), *Selected Poems* (1928), *Homage to Sextus Propertius* (1934), *The Cantos* (1948, 1965, 1970), *Selected Poems* (1949; rev. 1957).

(John) Robinson Jeffers (1887–1962), born in Pittsburgh to an academic family, traveled widely in Europe before arriving in California as a teenager. He graduated from Occidental College. He inherited a small income on which he depended for the rest of his life. Studying medicine at the University of Southern California, he fell in love with a fellow student, Mrs. Una Call Kuster. Frustrated, Jeffers wandered, sampling graduate studies at universities in the United States and abroad. Una divorced her husband and Jeffers stopped wandering. They

settled for a lifetime in Carmel, California, sojourning at times in New Mexico. Over the years Jeffers built a tower next to his house, by hand, with boulders he stole from the beach at night.

Jeffers wrote short lyrics and long narrative poems. His first volumes, *Flagons and Apples* (1912) and *Californians* (1916), contained both. It was the narratives of his third book, *Tamar and Other Poems* (1924), that first won distinction for their author. The title poem resets the Old Testament story in modern California, and is accompanied by a version of the Orestes legend. For the rest of his career, Jeffers made poems of the harsher ancient stories and fashioned new epics of incest and murder in the California hills. He wrote plays, achieving national success with Judith Anderson's production of his adaptation of Euripides' *Medea* (1946). Throughout his life he wrote lyrics describing the beauty of Carmel. His many works include: *Roan Stallion* (1925), *The Women at Point Sur* (1927), *Poems* (1928), *Cawdor and Other Poems* (1928), *Thurso's Landing* (1932), *Solstice and Other Poems* (1935), *Selected Poetry* (1938), *The Double Axe and Other Poems* (1948, rev. 1971), *Hungerfield and Other Poems* (1954), and *Selected Poems* (1965).

Marianne Craig Moore (1887–1972), born in St. Louis and educated at Bryn Mawr, taught in commercial schools and worked as a librarian. She edited *The Dial* from 1925 to 1929. After living for eleven years in Greenwich Village, Moore moved in 1929, to Brooklyn, close to the Dodgers, where she lived until 1966, when she returned to Manhattan. Her friends H. D. and Bryher published her first book, *Poems* (1921), without Moore's knowledge at the Egoist Press in London. Thereafter Moore published *Observations* (1924), *Selected Poems* (1935), *The Pangolin, and Other Verse* (1936), *What Are Years?* (1941), *Nevertheless* (1944), *Collected Poems* (1951), *Like a Bulwark* (1956), *O to Be a Dragon* (1959), *The Arctic Ox* (1964), *Tell Me, Tell Me* (1966), *Complete Poems* (1967), and *The Fables of Jean de la Fontaine* (1954), a verse translation. She published two collections of essays, *Predilections* (1955) and *Idiosyncracy and Technique* (1958).

Hilda Doolittle (H. D.) (1888–1961) was born in Bethlehem, Pennsylvania, was educated at Bryn Mawr, and lived her adult life in England, Switzerland, Italy, and Greece. She began a friendship with Ezra Pound and William Carlos Williams as a student in Philadelphia. Her marriage with the British author Richard Aldington ended just after the First World War. H. D.'s established reputation as the textbook Imagist ignores her long poems and trilogies, plays and novels, and work in mixed prose and verse. She wrote memoirs and romans à clef, including an account of her analysis under Sigmund Freud. Her volumes of poetry include: *Sea Garden* (1916), *Hymen* (1921), *Heliodora and Other Poems* (1924), *Collected Poems* (1925), *Red Roses for Bronze* (1931), *The Walls Do Not Fall* (1944), *Tribute to the Angels* (1945), *The Flowering of the Rod* (1946), *By Avon River* (1949), *Selected Poems* (1957), and *Hermetic Definition* (1972).

John Crowe Ransom (1888–1974) was born in Pulaski, Mississippi, to a family with southern traditions. His father was a minister, and a great-uncle helped found the Ku Klux Klan. Ransom graduated from Vanderbilt, then served in France as a first lieutenant in the field artillery. After work in classics and mathematics at Christ Church College, Oxford, as a Rhodes scholar, Ransom returned to Vanderbilt to join the English department. A traditionalist, he was a leader of the Agrarians and an editor of *The Fugitive*. Two of his early works of criticism, *God without Thunder: An Unorthodox Defense of Orthodoxy* (1930) and *The World's Body* (1938), attack the materialism of the modern age. Ransom left Vanderbilt for Kenyon College, where he founded the *Kenyon Review*. This most influential journal abandoned regional tradition to promote new writing congenial to the teachings of Ransom's *The New Criticism* (1941). His books of poems include: *Poems about God* (1919), *Chills and Fever* (1924), *Grace after Meat* (1924), *Two Gentlemen in Bonds* (1927), *Selected Poems* (1945; rev. 1963, 1969).

Thomas Stearns Eliot (1888–1965), born in St. Louis and educated at Harvard, established himself in London. His father was a successful industrialist, and his mother the author of a verse drama and biographer of her father-in-law, the man who brought Unitarianism to St. Louis. After Harvard, Eliot studied philosophy at the Sorbonne and Merton College, Oxford, then taught school and clerked in a bank before achieving success in literature. For the balance of his life he was editor, and later director, of a publishing house. He also edited the review *Criterion*. He won the Nobel Prize in literature in 1948. Eliot became a British subject and an Anglo-Catholic in middle life. He married twice. His first marriage, plagued by the mental illness of his wife, ended at her death after several years' separation.

Eliot wrote both criticism and poetry all his adult life. The criticism examines culture at large and society as well as literature. These interests flow together in the religious verse dramas and pageants Eliot began writing in middle age. The books of criticism include: *Ezra Pound: His Metric and Poetry* (1917), *The Sacred Wood* (1920), *Homage to John Dryden* (1924), *For Lancelot Andrewes: Essays on Style and Order* (1928), *Dante* (1929), *The Use of Poetry and the Use of Criticism* (1933), *Notes toward the Definition of Culture* (1948), and *On Poetry and Poets* (1957). The books of poems include: *Prufrock and Other Observations* (1917), *Poems* (1919), *Ara Vos Prec* (1920), *The Waste Land* (1922), *Poems 1909–1935* (1936), *Old Possum's Book of Practical Cats* (1939), *The Waste Land and Other Poems* (1940), *East Coker* (1940), *Burnt Norton* (1941), *The Dry Salvages* (1941), *Little Gidding* (1942), *Four Quartets* (1943), *Poems Written in Early Youth* (1950), and *Collected Poems 1909–1962*. The dramatic works include: *The Rock: A Pageant Play* (1934), *Murder in the Cathedral* (1935), *The Family Reunion* (1939), *The Cocktail Party* (1950), *The Confidential Clerk* (1954), and *The Elder Statesman* (1958).

Conrad Potter Aiken (1889–1973), at the age of eleven, discovered his parents' bodies after a murder-suicide in their Savannah, Georgia, home. Both his father, a surgeon, and his mother, the daughter of a Congregational minister, had moved to the South from New England. Young Aiken returned there to the care of a great-aunt in New Bedford, Massachusetts. He entered Harvard with the class of 1911 and graduated in 1912 after the first of many visits to Europe. A life-long friendship with T. S. Eliot started in college. Aiken moved to Boston, where he always returned after travels abroad and sojourns in England. Later he lived on Cape Cod.

Aiken made a career as a man of letters. He reviewed contemporary poets for the magazines, wrote a London column for the *New Yorker*, edited the Modern Library's *Twentieth-Century American Poetry* (1941), filled the Chair of Poetry at the Library of Congress, and worked in the Federal Writers Project. He was an early critic of Emily Dickinson. He wrote novels, plays, short stories, and a remarkable psychological memoir, *Ushant: An Essay* (1952, rev. 1971).

Aiken wrote book-length philosophic verse and sonnet sequences as well as briefer lyrics. His volumes include: *Earth Triumphant* (1914), *Nocturne of Remembered Spring* (1917), *The House of Dust: A Symphony* (1920), *Priapus and the Pool* (1922), *John Deth* (1930), *Preludes for Memnon* (1931), *Time in the Rock* (1936), *And in the Human Heart* (1940), *Brownstone Eclogues* (1942), *The Soldier* (1944), *The Kid* (1947), *A Letter from Li Po* (1955), *Sheepfold Hill* (1958), *The Morning Song of Lord Zero* (1963), two *Selected Poems* (1929, 1961), and *Collected Poems* (1953).

Edward Estlin Cummings (1894–1962), born in Cambridge, Massachusetts, took degrees at Harvard and joined a volunteer ambulance corps in France one year before the United States entered the war. Once there, Cummings was interrogated by French police investigating irreverent remarks discovered in the letters of another volunteer. When officials demanded that Cummings swear he hated the Germans, the poet insisted that he loved the French. The account of his subsequent imprisonment, *The Enormous Room* (1922), a prose work, attracted much attention, and his books of poetry began to appear shortly thereafter. They include: *Tulips and Chimneys* (1923), *&* (1925), *is 5* (1926), *ViVa* (1931), *No Thanks* (1935), *1/ 20* (1936), *Collected Poems* (1938), *50 Poems* (1940), *1 x 1* (1944), *Poems 1923–1954* (1954), and

Poems (1958). They consistently expand on the winning integrity and the petty willful idiosyncracy that landed him in jail. His other works include the plays *Him* (1927) and *Santa Claus* (1946), a diary of travel in the USSR, *Eimi* (1933), and *i* (1953), six "nonlectures" given at Harvard. Though he resided for many years at Patchin Place in New York's Greenwich Village, he was the son of a minister at Boston's Old South Church and considered himself a part of the grand northern New England tradition.

John Brooks Wheelwright (1896–1940) was born and lived his entire life in Boston. The descendant of Boston clerics and merchants, he added color to a rich family tradition with a life of eccentricity, moral commitment, and high sensibility. He lectured on socialism from a soapbox in South Boston, in a raccoon coat worn over a fine waistcoat. No hypocrite, he simply was committed to quality as much as to justice. He died while walking, struck by a speeding truck. His books include: *Rock and Shell* (1933), *Mirrors of Venus* (1938), *Political Self-Portrait* (1940), and the posthumous *Dusk to Dusk*, included in *Collected Poems* (1971).

(John Orley) Allen Tate (1899–1979) was born in Winchester, Kentucky, to a strongly southern family. He studied at Georgetown and the University of Virginia before taking his bachelor's degree magna cum laude from Vanderbilt. He and his roommate, Robert Penn Warren, fell in with the literary group at that college, and Tate became an editor of *The Fugitive*. A poem published there brought a letter from Hart Crane, starting a strong friendship. An influential literary critic, Tate reviewed widely, helped edit *Hound and Horn*, and edited *The Sewanee Review*. He published collections including *Reactionary Essays on Poetry and Ideas* (1936), *Reason in Madness* (1941), and *The Man of Letters in the Modern World* (1957). He taught at the University of Minnesota for seventeen years. A strong regionalist, he contributed to Agrarian symposia and wrote biographies of Stonewall Jackson and Jefferson Davis, as well as a novel set in the South. Tate was married three times: first to the novelist Caroline Gordon, second to the writer Isabella Gardner, and third to Helen Heinz. His books of poetry include: *Mr. Pope and Other Poems* (1928), *Poems 1928–1931* (1932), *The Mediterranean and Other Poems* (1936), *Selected Poems* (1937), *The Winter Sea* (1944), *Poems 1920–1945* (1947), *Poems 1922–1947* (1948), *Two Conceits for the Eye to Sing, if Possible* (1950), *Poems* (1960), *Poems* (1961), and *The Swimmers and Other Selected Poems* (1970).

(Harold) Hart Crane (1899–1932) was born in Garretsville, Ohio, the child of a stormy marriage. When his parents finally divorced, Crane moved to New York, his home. He never finished high school nor started college. He sometimes returned to visit his parents in Ohio. He had several affairs with men, and pursued a friendship with Allen Tate that began with a shared love and hate of T. S. Eliot's poetry and ended with an argument over household chores while rooming with the southern poet and his wife. Crane never settled down, but worked most frequently in advertising. He committed suicide from a passenger ship returning to New York from Mexico, after saying goodbye to his woman companion in their stateroom.

His books of poems are: *White Buildings* (1926), *The Bridge* (1930), and, posthumously, *Collected Poems* (1933), *Seven Lyrics* (1966), *The Complete Poems and Selected Letters and Prose* (1966), and *Ten Unpublished Poems* (1972).

(James) Langston Hughes (1902–1967) was born in Joplin, Missouri. His parents separated early but remained fully involved in his life. He studied for a year at Columbia University, then left to live the drifter's life aboard ship and in Paris. He adopted a serious attitude at Vachel Lindsay's urging. Hughes, a busboy, slipped Lindsay some verses while serving him dinner, and the performing poet read them at his evening recital. The younger poet returned to college, Lincoln University in Pennsylvania, where he won a national prize for undergraduate poetry, and published a novel the year of his graduation. Thereafter Hughes wrote for a living, and his total body of work is enormous, including poetry, plays, novels,

newspaper columns, musicals, and autobiography. He never married; in later years he dropped in on the man of letters Arna Bontemps and his wife when he wanted family warmth.

Hughes's artful newspaper columns about the character Jesse B. Semple (a.k.a. Simple) are selected in *The Best of Simple* (1961). His novels are *Not without Laughter* (1930) and *Tambourines to Glory* (1958). His collections of stories include *The Ways of White Folks* (1934) and *Something in Common* (1963). His autobiographies are *The Big Sea* (1940) and *I Wonder as I Wander* (1956). Hughes's books of poems include: *The Weary Blues* (1926), *Fine Clothes to the Jew* (1931), *The Negro Mother* (1931), *The Dream Keeper and Other Poems* (1932), *Scottsboro Limited* (1932), *A New Song* (1938), *Shakespeare in Harlem* (1942), *Jim Crow's Last Stand* (1943), *Fields of Wonder* (1947), *One Way Ticket* (1949), *Montage of a Dream Deferred* (1951), *Selected Poems* (1959), *Ask Your Mama* (1961), and *The Panther and the Lash* (1967).

Countee Cullen (1903–1946), born in New York, took his bachelor's degree at New York University and a master's degree at Harvard. His father was a Methodist Episcopal minister. He was married for one year to Yolande Du Bois, daughter of W. E. B. Du Bois. Cullen worked as assistant editor of *Opportunity: Journal of Negro Life*, spent a Guggenheim fellowship in Paris, and taught in New York's public schools for the rest of his career. He vacationed in France whenever possible. In addition to his poetry, he did some stage adaptation, wrote a novel entitled *One Way to Heaven*, and edited an anthology of black verse, *Caroling Dusk* (1927). His books of poems include: *Color* (1925), *Copper Sun* (1927), *The Ballad of the Brown Girl* (1927), *The Black Christ* (1929), *The Medea* (1935), and *On These I Stand* (1947).

Contributors

Harold Bloom, Sterling Professor of the Humanities at Yale University, is the author of *The Anxiety of Influence, Poetry and Repression,* and many other volumes of literary criticism. His forthcoming study, *Freud: Transference and Authority,* attempts a full-scale reading of all of Freud's major writings. A MacArthur Prize Fellow, he is general editor of five series of literary criticism published by Chelsea House.

Conrad Aiken, poet and novelist, edited the Modern Library anthology *Twentieth-Century American Poetry,* and wrote the introduction to an edition of Emily Dickinson which did much to create her reputation. His many reviews are collected in *A Reviewer's ABC* (1958).

Myron Simon is Professor of English and Comparative Literature at the University of California at Riverside. He has edited *Teacher and Critic: Essays by and about Austin Warren,* with Harvey Gross, and *Transcendentalism and Its Legacy,* with Thornton W. Parsons.

Richard Poirier is Distinguished Professor of English at Rutgers University and Editor of Raritan. His books of criticism include *The Performing Self* and *Robert Frost: The Work of Knowing.*

Charles Berger is Associate Professor of English at Yale University. He is the author of *Forms of Farewell: The Late Poetry of Wallace Stevens.*

Marie Borroff is William Lampson Professor of English at Yale University. She is the author of *Language and the Poet: Verbal Artistry in Frost, Stevens, and Moore,* and *Sir Gawain and the Green Knight: A Stylistic and Metrical Study.*

Hyatt Waggoner is Professor of English at Brown University. His books include *American Poets from the Puritans to the Present* and *American Visionary Poetry.*

Paul Mariani, a poet and critic, is Professor of English at the University of Massachusetts at Amherst. He is the author of *Crossing Cocytus and Other Poems, William Carlos Williams: A New World Naked*, and *A Usable Past: Essays on Modern and Contemporary Poetry*.

Kathryne V. Lindberg is Assistant Professor of English at Harvard University. Her article is excerpted from her forthcoming book, *Reading Pound Reading: The Nietzschean Indirections of Modernism*.

Brother Antoninus (William Everson), a sometime Dominican monk, writes frequently on the poetry of Robinson Jeffers. His other publications are poetry, including *The Hazards of Holiness* (1962) and *River-Root* (1976).

Bonnie Costello is Associate Professor of English at Boston University and the author of *Marianne Moore: Imaginary Possessions*.

John M. Slatin is Assistant Professor of English at the University of Texas at Austin. He has recently completed *The Savage's Romance*, a book-length study of Moore's place in the Anglo-American poetic tradition.

Susan Gubar is Professor of English at Indiana University. She is editor, with Sandra Gilbert, of *The Madwoman in the Attic, Shakespeare's Sisters: Feminist Essays on Women Poets*, and *The Norton Anthology of Literature by Women: The Tradition in English*.

Randall Jarrell, the poet, is remembered as a critic for such books as *Poetry and the Age* and the recent collection *Kipling, Auden, and Co.: Essays and Reviews, 1935–1964*.

Hugh Kenner teaches at Johns Hopkins University. He is the canonical critic of Anglo-American literary "modernism," widely admired for his studies of Joyce, Eliot, Pound, and Wyndham Lewis.

Gregory S. Jay teaches English at the University of Alabama. He has written extensively upon contemporary criticism.

Delmore Schwartz, the poet, was an editor of *Partisan Review* and reviewed widely in many publications. His criticism is collected in *Selected Essays* (1970). He translated Rimbaud's *A Season in Hell* (1939), and wrote plays and stories. His book of poems, *Summer Knowledge* (1959), won the Bollingen Prize.

Dudley Fitts, instructor of English at Phillips Academy, Andover, translated the plays of Aristophanes. He collaborated with Robert Fitzgerald on other translations, wrote poems, and edited the Yale Series of Younger Poets.

R. P. Blackmur was Resident Fellow, then Professor of English at Princeton University. He is remembered for his poems as well as his criticism. His collections of essays include *Language as Gesture* (1952) and *Form and Value in Modern Poetry* (1957).

John Ashbery, the poet, is a critic of the visual arts. His books of poetry include *Self-Portrait in a Convex Mirror, The Tennis-Court Oath and Other Poems*, and *The Wave*.

Cleanth Brooks is Professor Emeritus of English at Yale University. He is the author of *Modern Poetry and the Tradition*, and editor, with R. W. B. Lewis and Robert Penn Warren, of *American Literature: The Makers and the Making*.

Sherman Paul is Professor of English at the University of Iowa. He is the author of studies of Emerson, Thoreau, Charles Olson, and Edmund Wilson.

Raymond Smith earned a degree in American Studies at Yale University. He has written and organized exhibits on vernacular American photography.

Ronald Primeau is the author of a study of Edgar Lee Masters, *Beyond Spoon River*, and numerous articles relating poets of this period to Keats and Shelley.

Bibliography

EDWIN ARLINGTON ROBINSON

Barnard, Ellsworth. *Edwin Arlington Robinson: Centenary Essays*. Athens: University of Georgia Press, 1969.
————. *Edwin Arlington Robinson: A Critical Study*. New York: Macmillan, 1952.
Cary, Richard, ed. *Appreciation of Edwin Arlington Robinson*. Waterville, Maine: Colby College Press, 1969.
Fussell, Edwin S. *Edwin Arlington Robinson: The Literary Background of a Traditional Poet*. Berkeley: University of California Press, 1954.
Howe, Irving. "A Grave and Solitary Voice: An Appreciation of Edwin Arlington Robinson." In *The Critical Point: On Literature and Culture*, 96–108. New York: Horizon Press, 1973.
Murphy, Francis, ed. *Edwin Arlington Robinson: A Collection of Critical Essays*. Englewood Cliffs, N.J.: Prentice-Hall, 1970.
Simon, Myron. *The Georgian Poetic*, 84–85. Berkeley: University of California Press, 1975.
Winters, Yvor. *Edwin Arlington Robinson*. Norfolk, Conn.: New Directions, 1946.
Wolf, H. R. "E. A. Robinson and the Integration of Self." In *Modern American Poetry: Essays in Criticism*, edited by Jerome Mazzaro, 40–59. New York: David McKay, 1970.

PAUL LAURENCE DUNBAR

Flusche, Michael. "Paul Laurence Dunbar and the Burden of Race." *Southern Humanities Review* 11 (Winter 1977): 49–61.

Martin, Jay. " 'Jump Back Honey': Paul Laurence Dunbar and the Rediscovery of American Poetical Traditions." *Bulletin of the Midwestern Modern Language Association* 7, no. 2 (1974): 40–53.

————, ed. *Singer in the Dawn: Reinterpretations of Paul Laurence Dunbar.* New
York: Dodd, Mead, 1975.

Revell, Peter. *Paul Laurence Dunbar.* Boston: Twayne, 1979.

ROBERT FROST

Baker, Carlos. "Frost on the Pumpkin." In *The Echoing Green,* 186–212.
Princeton: Princeton University Press, 1984.

Bloom, Harold, ed. *Modern Critical Views: Robert Frost.* New York: Chelsea
House, 1986.

Bogan, Louise. "Robert Frost." In *A Poet's Alphabet,* 160–63. New York:
McGraw-Hill, 1970.

Cook, Reginald L. *The Dimensions of Robert Frost.* New York: Rinehart, 1958.

————. *Robert Frost: A Living Voice.* Amherst: University of Massachusetts
Press, 1974.

Cowley, Malcolm. "Robert Frost: A Dissenting Opinion." In *A Many-Win-
dowed House,* 201–12. Carbondale: Southern Illinois University Press,
1970.

Dickey, James. "Robert Frost." In *Babel to Byzantium: Poets and Poetry Now,*
200–209. New York: Farrar, Straus & Giroux, 1968.

Donoghue, Denis. "Robert Frost." In *Connoisseurs of Chaos: Ideas of Order
in Modern American Poetry.* New York: Macmillan, 1965.

Eberhart, Richard. "Robert Frost in the Clearing." *Southern Review* 11
(Spring 1975): 260–68.

Harris, Kathryn Gibbs, ed. *Robert Frost: Studies of the Poetry.* Boston: G. K.
Hall, 1979.

Kemp, John C. *Robert Frost and New England: The Poet as Regionalist.* Princeton: Princeton University Press, 1979.

Lentricchia, Frank. *Robert Frost: Modern Poetics and the Landscapes of Self.*
Durham, N.C.: Duke University Press, 1975.

————. "The Poet's Meaning and the Poem's World." In *Modern Poetry,*
edited by John Hollander, 485–500. New York: Oxford University
Press, 1968.

Poirier, Richard. *Robert Frost: The Work of Knowing.* New York: Oxford University Press, 1977.

Pritchard, William. *Frost: A Literary Life Reconsidered.* New York: Oxford
University Press, 1984.

Ryan, Alvan S. "Frost and Emerson: Voice and Vision." *Massachusetts Review* 1 (1959): 5–23.

Sears, John F. "The Subversive Performer in Frost's 'Snow' and 'Out,
Out—.' " In *The Motive for Metaphor,* edited by Francis Blessington.
Boston: Northeastern University Press, 1983.

Tharpe, Jac L., ed. *Frost: Centennial Essays.* Jackson: University Press of Mississippi, 1974.

———. *Frost: Centennial Essays II.* Jackson: University Press of Mississippi, 1976.

———. *Frost: Centennial Essays III.* Jackson: University Press of Mississippi, 1978.

Vitelli, James R. "Robert Frost: The Contrarieties of Talent and Tradition." *New England Quarterly* 47 (1974): 351–67.

Warren, Robert Penn. "The Themes of Robert Frost." In *Selected Essays,* 118–36. New York: Random House, 1958.

Winters, Yvor. "Robert Frost: Or, The Spiritual Drifter as Poet." In *The Function of Criticism,* 157–88. Denver: Alan Swallow, 1957.

WALLACE STEVENS

Baird, James. *The Dome and the Rock: Studies in the Poetry of Wallace Stevens.* Baltimore: Johns Hopkins University Press, 1968.

Benamon, Michel. *Wallace Stevens and the Symbolist Imagination.* Princeton: Princeton University Press, 1972.

Bloom, Harold. *Wallace Stevens: The Poems of Our Climate.* Ithaca: Cornell University Press, 1977.

———, ed. *Modern Critical Views: Wallace Stevens.* New York: Chelsea House, 1985.

Borroff, Marie. *Language and the Poet: Verbal Artistry in Frost, Stevens and Moore.* Chicago: University of Chicago Press, 1979.

———, ed. *Wallace Stevens: A Collection of Critical Essays.* Englewood Cliffs, N.J.: Prentice-Hall, 1963.

Brazeau, Peter. *Parts of a World: Wallace Stevens Remembered.* New York: Random House, 1983.

Brown, Ashley, and Robert S. Haller, eds. *The Achievement of Wallace Stevens.* Philadelphia: Lippincott, 1962.

Buttel, Robert. *Wallace Stevens: The Making of Harmonium.* Princeton: Princeton University Press, 1967.

Buttel, Robert, and Frank Doggett, eds. *Wallace Stevens: A Celebration.* Princeton: Princeton University Press, 1980.

Doggett, Frank. *Stevens' Poetry of Thought.* Baltimore: Johns Hopkins University Press, 1966.

Fuchs, Daniel. *The Comic Spirit of Wallace Stevens.* Durham, N.C.: Duke University Press, 1963.

Kermode, Frank. *Wallace Stevens.* New York: Grove, 1960.

Litz, A. Walton. *Introspective Voyager: The Poetic Development of Wallace Stevens.* New York: Oxford University Press, 1972.

MacCaffrey, Isabel G. "The Other Side of Silence: 'Credences of Summer' as an Example." *Modern Language Quarterly* 30 (1969): 417–38.

Martz, Louis L. *The Poem of the Mind*. New York: Oxford University Press, 1966.

Middlebrook, Diane Wood. *Walt Whitman and Wallace Stevens*. Ithaca: Cornell University Press, 1974.

Miller, J. Hillis. *Poets of Reality*. Cambridge: Harvard University Press, 1965.

Morse, Samuel French. *Wallace Stevens: Poetry as Life*. New York: Pegasus, 1970.

Pack, Robert. *Wallace Stevens: An Approach to His Poetry and Thought*. New Brunswick, N.J.: Rutgers University Press, 1958.

Pearce, Roy Harvey, and J. Hillis Miller, eds. *The Act of the Mind: Essays on the Poetry of Wallace Stevens*. Baltimore: Johns Hopkins University Press, 1965.

Riddel, Joseph. *The Clairvoyant Eye: The Poetry and Poetics of Wallace Stevens*. Baton Rouge: Louisiana State University Press, 1965.

Sukenick, Ronald. *Musing the Obscure*. New York: New York University Press, 1967.

Vendler, Helen H. *On Extended Wings: Wallace Stevens' Longer Poems*. Cambridge: Harvard University Press, 1969.

VACHEL LINDSAY

Chenetier, Marc. " 'Free-Lance in the Soul-World': Toward a Reappraisal of Vachel Lindsay's Works." *Prospects: Annual of American Cultural Studies* 2 (1976): 497–512.

———. "Sign and Symbol in Vachel Lindsay's Poetic and Graphic Work." In *Poetic Knowledge: Circumference and Centre*, edited by Joseph T. Swann and Roland Hagenbuchle, 122–27. Bonn: Bouvier, 1980.

Engler, Balz. "Vachel Lindsay and the Town of American Vision." *Literature in Performance* 3, no. 1 (1982): 27–32.

Flanagan, John T., ed. *Profile of Vachel Lindsay*. Columbus: Merrill, 1970.

Wesling, Donald. "What the Canon Excludes: Lindsay and American Bardic." *Michigan Quarterly Review* 21 (1982): 479–85.

EDGAR LEE MASTERS

Barnstone, Willis. "Introduction." In *The New Spoon River*, by Edgar Lee Masters. New York: Macmillan, 1968.

Burgess, Charles E. "Edgar Lee Masters: The Lawyer as Writer." In *The Vision of this Land*, edited by John E. Hallwas and Dennis J. Reader, 55–73. Macomb: An Essays in Literature Book, Western Illinois University, 1976.

Derleth, August. "Masters and the Revolt from the Village." *Colorado Quarterly* 8 (1959): 164–67.

Flanagan, John T. *Edgar Lee Masters: The Spoon River Poet and His Critics*. Metuchen, N.J.: Scarecrow Press, 1974.

Hahn, Henry. "Evolution in the Graveyard." *Midwest Quarterly* 10 (1969): 275–90.

Primeau, Ronald. *Beyond Spoon River—The Legacy of Edgar Lee Masters*. Austin: University of Texas Press, 1981.

———. "Shelley and Edgar Lee Masters' 'Amphimixis.' " *Old Northwest* 1 (1975): 141–57.

CARL SANDBURG

Alexander, William. "The Limited American, the Great Loneliness, and the Singing Fire: Carl Sandburg's 'Chicago Poems.' " *American Literature* 45 (March 1973): 67–83.

Allen, Gay Wilson. *Carl Sandburg*. Minneapolis: University of Minnesota Press, 1972.

Crowder, Richard. *Carl Sandburg*. New York: Twayne, 1964.

Duffy, Bernard. "The Struggle for Affirmation—Anderson, Sandburg, Lindsay." In *The Chicago Renaissance in American Letters: A Critical History*, 194–238. East Lansing: Michigan State University Press, 1954.

Hoffman, Daniel G. "Sandburg and 'The People': His Literary Populism Appraised." *Antioch Review* 10 (1950): 265–78.

Mayer, Charles W. "*The People, Yes:* Sandburg's Dreambook for Today." In *The Vision of This Land*, edited by John E. Hallwas and Dennis J. Reader, 82–91. Macomb: An Essays in Literature Book, Western Illinois University, 1976.

Rexroth, Kenneth. "Search for Sandburg." *The Nation* 186 (February 22, 1958): 171–72.

Williams, William Carlos. "Carl Sandburg's Complete Poems." *Poetry* 78 (1951): 345–51.

SARA TEASDALE

Carpenter, Margaret Haley. *Sara Teasdale: A Biography*. Norfolk: Pentelic, 1977.

Drake, William. *Sara Teasdale, Woman and Poet*. San Francisco: Harper & Row, 1979.

Perry, Ruth, and Maurice Sagoff. "Sara Teasdale's Friendships." *New Letters* 46, no. 2 (1979): 101–7.

Sprague, Rosemary. *Imaginary Gardens: A Study of Five American Poets*. Philadelphia: Chilton, 1969.

Swafford, Russell Anne, and Paul Ramsay. "The Influence of Sara Teasdale on Louise Bogan." *CEA Critic: An Official Journal of the College English Association* 41, no. 4 (1979): 7–12.

ELINOR WYLIE

Benet, William Rose. *The Prose and Poetry of Elinor Wylie*. Norton, Mass.: Wheaton College Press, 1934.

ıth. "Poets and Laureates." *The Southern Review* 2 (1936):

'm. "The Owl and the Nightingale." *The Dial* 74 (June 1923):

_ *Life and Art of Elinor Wylie.* Baton Rouge: Louisiana State
___ıversity Press, 1983.

Gray, Thomas A. *Elinor Wylie.* New York: Twayne, 1969.

Kelly, Edward H. " 'The Eagle and the Mole': The Affective Fallacy Revis-
ited." *English Record* 21, no. 2 (1970): 57–59.

Tate, Allen. "Elinor Wylie's Poetry." *The New Republic* (September 7, 1932):
107.

Wright, Celeste Turner. "Elinor Wylie: The Glass Chimaera and the Mino-
taur." *Women's Studies* 7 (1980): 159–70.

EDNA ST. VINCENT MILLAY

Dobbs, Jeanine. "Edna St. Vincent Millay and the Tradition of Domestic
Poetry." *Journal of Women's Studies in Literature* 1 (1979): 89–106.

Fairley, Irene R. "Millay in Feminist Perspective: Critical Trends of the 70's."
Tamarack 1, no. 1 (1981): 28–31.

Farr, Judith. "Elinor Wylie, Edna St. Vincent Millay, and the Elizabethan
Sonnet Tradition." In *Poetic Traditions of the English Renaissance*, edited
by Maynard Mack and George deForest Lord, 287–305. New Haven:
Yale University Press, 1982.

Jones, Phyllis M. "Amatory Sonnet Sequences and the Female Perspective
of Elinor Wylie and Edna Saint Vincent Millay." *Women's Studies* 10
(1983): 41–61.

Klemans, Patricia A. " 'Being Born a Woman': A New Look at Edna St.
Vincent Millay." *Colby Library Quarterly* 15 (1979): 7–18.

Stanbrough, Jane. "Edna St. Vincent Millay and the Language of Vulner-
ability." In *Shakespeare's Sisters: Feminist Essays on Women Poets*, edited
by Susan Gubar and Sandra M. Gilbert, 183–99. Bloomington: Indiana
University Press, 1979.

WILLIAM CARLOS WILLIAMS

Angoff, Charles, ed. *William Carlos Williams: Papers by Kenneth Burke, Emily
Mitchell Wallace, Norman Holmes Pearson, A.M. Sullivan.* Rutherford,
N.J.: Fairleigh Dickinson University, 1974.

Bloom, Harold, ed. *Modern Critical Views: William Carlos Williams.* New York:
Chelsea House, 1986.

Coles, Robert. *William Carlos Williams: The Knack of Survival in America.* New
Brunswick, N.J.: Rutgers University Press, 1975.

Cushman, Stephen. *William Carlos Williams and the Meanings of Measure.*
New Haven: Yale University Press, 1985.

Doyle, Charles. *William Carlos Williams: The Cr.*
ledge & Kegan Paul, 1980.

Field 29 (Fall 1983). Special William Carlos Williams

Joswick, Thomas P. "Beginning With Loss: The Poetı.
Williams' *Kora in Hell: Improvisation.*" *Texas Studies in* out-
guage 19 (1977): 98–118.

Juhasz, Suzanne. *Metaphor and the Poetry of Williams, Pound* s
Lewisburg, Pa.: Bucknell University Press, 1974.

Kenner, Hugh. *A Homemade World: The American Modernist Writers*
York: Knopf, 1975.

Kronick, Joseph G. "William Carlos Williams' Search for an 'America.
Place." In *American Poetics of History: From Emerson to the Moderns*. Baton
Rouge: Louisiana State University Press, 1984.

Levertov, Denise. "William Carlos Williams 1883–1963" and "William Carlos Williams and the Duende." In *The Poet and the World*. New York:
New Directions, 1973.

Levin, Harry. "William Carlos Williams and the Old World." In *Memories
of the Moderns*. New York: New Directions, 1980.

Mariani, Paul L. "William Carlos Williams." In *A Usable Past*. Amherst:
University of Massachusetts Press, 1984.

————. *William Carlos Williams: A New World Naked*. New York: McGraw-
Hill, 1981.

Marling, William. *William Carlos Williams and the Painters 1909–1923*. Athens:
Ohio University Press, 1982.

Mazzaro, Jerome, ed. *William Carlos Williams: The Later Poems*. Ithaca: Cornell
University Press, 1973.

Miller, J. Hillis. *Poets of Reality*. Cambridge, Mass.: Belknap, 1966.

————. "Williams." In *The Linguistic Moment*. Princeton: Princeton University Press, 1985.

————, ed. *William Carlos Williams: A Collection of Critical Essays*. Englewood
Cliffs, N.J.: Prentice-Hall, 1966.

Rapp, Carl. *William Carlos Williams and Romantic Idealism*. Hanover, N.H.:
University Press of New England, 1984.

Riddel, Joseph. *The Inverted Bell: Modernism and the Counterpoetics of William
Carlos Williams*. Baton Rouge: Louisiana State University Press, 1974.

Sayre, Henry M. "Ready-Mades and Other Measures: The Poetics of Marcel
Duchamp and William Carlos Williams." *Journal of Modern Literature* 8
(1980): 3–22.

Tomlinson, Charles, ed. *William Carlos Williams: A Critical Anthology*. Har-
mondsworth: Penguin, 1972.

Waggoner, Hyatt H. "William Carlos Williams: Naturalizing the Unearthly." In *American Visionary Poetry*. Baton Rouge: Louisiana State
University Press, 1982.

Wagner, Linda Welshimer. *William Carlos Williams: A Reference Guide*. Boston: G. K. Hall, 1978.

e American Background. London:

.iams. New York: Twayne, 1968.
.rmerly Newsletter), 1975–.

Weaver, Mike
Cambri~
Whitaker, ~
The Willi~Andre. *The Tale of the Tribe: Ezra Pound and the Modern*
.rinceton: Princeton University Press, 1980.

.dld, ed. *Modern Critical Views: Ezra Pound*. New York: Chelsea
~se, 1986.

.ds, John Steven. "Larvatus Prodeo: Semiotic Aspects of the Ideograms
in Pound's *Cantos*." *Paideuma* 9 (1980): 289–307.

Davenport, Guy. *Cities on Hills: A Study of I–XXX of Ezra Pound's* Cantos.
Ann Arbor, Mich.: UMI Research Press, 1983.

Davie, Donald. *Ezra Pound*. New York: Viking, 1975.

———. *Ezra Pound: Poet as Sculptor*. New York: Oxford University Press,
1964.

Eastham, Scott. *Paradise and Ezra Pound: The Poet as Shaman*. Lanham, Md.:
University Press of America, 1983.

Froula, Christine. *To Write Paradise: Style and Error in Pound's* Cantos. New
Haven: Yale University Press, 1984.

Hesse, Eva, ed. *New Approaches to Ezra Pound: A Co-Ordinated Investigation
of Pound's Poetry*. Berkeley: University of California Press, 1969.

Kenner, Hugh. *The Poetry of Ezra Pound*. Norfolk, Conn.: New Directions,
n.d. [1951]; Kraus, Millwood, N.Y., 1974.

———. *The Pound Era*. Berkeley: University of California Press, 1971.

Levy, Alan. *Ezra Pound: The Voice of Silence*. Sag Harbor, N.Y.: Permanent
Press, 1983.

Link, Franz H. "Pound's Imagist Alba: Myth as Cognitive Method." In
*Poetic Knowledge: Circumference and Centre: Papers from the Wuppertal Sym-
posium 1978*, edited by Roland Hagenbuechle and Joseph T. Swann,
128–40. Bonn: Bouvier Verlag Herbert Grundmann, 1980.

McDougal, Stuart Y. *Ezra Pound and the Troubador Tradition*. Princeton:
Princeton University Press, 1972.

Nicholls, Peter. *Ezra Pound: Politics, Economics, and Writing: A Study of the
Cantos*. London: Macmillan, 1984.

Nolde, John H. *Blossoms from the East: The China Cantos of Ezra Pound*. Orono:
National Poetry Foundation, University of Maine, 1983.

Pearlman, Daniel D. "The Anti-Semitism of Ezra Pound." *Contemporary
Literature* 22 (1981): 104–15.

———. *The Barb of Time: On the Unity of Ezra Pound's* Cantos. New York:
Oxford University Press, 1969.

Perloff, Marjorie. "Pound/Stevens: Whose Era?" *New Literary History* 13
(1982): 485–510.

———. "The Portrait of the Artist as Collage-Text: Pound's *Gaudier-Brzeska* and the 'Italic' Texts of John Cage." *American Poetry Review* 11 (1982): 19–29.

———. *The Poetics of Indeterminacy: Rimbaud to Cage*. Princeton: Princeton University Press, 1981.

Wilhelm, J. J. *The American Roots of Ezra Pound*. New York: Garland, 1985.

ROBINSON JEFFERS

Alexander, John R. "Conflict in the Narrative Poetry of Robinson Jeffers." *The Sewanee Review* 80 (Winter 1972): 85–99.

Antoninus, Brother [William Everson]. *Robinson Jeffers: Fragments of an Older Fury*. Berkeley, Calif.: Oyez Press, 1968.

Boyers, Robert. "A Sovereign Voice: The Poetry of Robinson Jeffers." *The Sewanee Review* 77 (Summer 1969): 487–507.

Brophy, Robert J. *Robinson Jeffers: Myth, Ritual, and Symbol in His Narrative Poems*. Cleveland: Case Western Reserve University Press, 1973.

Carpenter, Frederic I. *Robinson Jeffers*. New York: Twayne, 1962.

Coffin, Arthur B. *Robinson Jeffers: Poet of Inhumanism*. Madison: University of Wisconsin Press, 1971.

Commager, Henry Steele. "The Cult of the Irrational." In *The American Mind*, 120–40. New Haven: Yale University Press, 1950.

Fitts, Dudley. "The Hellenism of Robinson Jeffers." In *The Kenyon Critics*, edited by John Crowe Ransom, 307–12. Cleveland: World Publishing, 1951.

Hotchkiss, Bill. *Jeffers: The Sivaistic Vision*. Auburn, Calif.: Blue Oak Press, 1975.

Nolte, William. "Robinson Jeffers: A Defense." *Virginia Quarterly Review* 42 (Spring 1966): 257–72.

Squires, Radcliffe. *The Loyalties of Robinson Jeffers*. Ann Arbor: University of Michigan Press, 1956.

Zaller, Robert. *The Cliffs of Solitude: A Reading of Robinson Jeffers*. New York: Cambridge University Press, 1983.

MARIANNE MOORE

Abbott, Craig S. *Marianne Moore: A Descriptive Bibliography*. Pittsburgh: University of Pittsburgh Press, 1977.

Bloom, Harold, ed. *Modern Critical Views: Marianne Moore*. New York: Chelsea House, 1986.

Borroff, Marie. *Language and the Poet: Verbal Artistry in Frost, Stevens and Moore*. Chicago: University of Chicago Press, 1979.

Costello, Bonnie. *Marianne Moore: Imaginary Possessions*. Cambridge: Harvard University Press, 1981.

Davenport, Guy. "Marianne Moore." In *The Geography of the Imagination*, 114–23. San Francisco: North Point Press, 1981.

Glatstein, Jacob. "Marianne Moore." Translated by Doris Vidaver. *Yiddish* 6, no. 1 (1985): 67–73.

Newlin, Margaret. " 'Unhelpful Hymen!': Marianne Moore and Hilda Doolittle." *Essays in Criticism* 27, no. 3 (1977): 216–30.

Phillips, Elizabeth. *Marianne Moore*. New York: Frederick Ungar, 1982.

Poesis: A Journal of Criticism 6, no. 3/4 (1985). *A Celebration of H. D. and Marianne Moore.*

Stapleton, Lawrence. *Marianne Moore: The Poet's Advance*. Princeton: Princeton University Press, 1978.

Tomlinson, Charles, ed. *Marianne Moore: A Collection of Critical Essays*. Englewood Cliffs, N.J.: Prentice-Hall, 1969.

Twentieth Century Literature 30, no. 2/3 (1984). Special Marianne Moore issue.

H. D. (HILDA DOOLITTLE)

DuPlessis, Rachel Blau. "Romantic Thralldom in H. D." *Contemporary Literature* 20 (1979): 178–203.

DuPlessis, Rachel Blau, and Susan Stanford. "Woman Is Perfect: H. D.'s Debate with Freud." *Feminist Studies* 7 (1981): 417–30.

Friedman, Susan. "Creating a Woman's Mythology: H. D.'s *Helen in Egypt*." *Women's Studies* 5 (1977): 163–97.

Gelpi, Albert. "Hilda in Egypt." *The Southern Review* 18 (1982): 233–50.

Gilbert, Sandra M. "H. D.? Who Was She?" *Contemporary Literature* 24 (1983): 496–511.

Gubar, Susan. "The Echoing Spell of H. D.'s *Trilogy*." *Contemporary Literature* 19 (1978): 196–218.

———. "Sapphistries." *Signs* 10 (1984): 43–62.

Morris, Adelaide. "Reading H. D.'s 'Helios and Athene.' " *The Iowa Review* 12, no. 2/3 (1981): 155–63.

Poesis: A Journal of Criticism 6, no. 3/4 (1985). *A Celebration of H. D. and Marianne Moore.*

JOHN CROWE RANSOM

Brooks, Cleanth. "The Doric Delicacy." *The Sewanee Review* 56 (1948): 402–15.

Buffington, Robert. *The Equilibrist: A Study of John Crowe Ransom's Poems, 1916–1963*. Nashville: Vanderbilt University Press, 1970.

———. "The Poetry of the Master's Old Age. *Georgia Review* 25 (1972): 5–16.

———. "Ransom's Poetics: 'Only God, My Dear.' " *Michigan Quarterly Review* 12 (1973): 353–60.

Jarrell, Randall. "John Ransom's Poetry." *The Sewanee Review* 56 (1948): 378–90.

Marston, Jane. "Persona and Perspective in John Crowe Ransom's Poetry." *Mississippi Quarterly* 30 (1977): 59–70.

Schwartz, Delmore. "Instructed of Much Morality." *The Sewanee Review* 54 (1946): 439–48.

Warren, Robert Penn. "John Crowe Ransom: A Study in Irony." *Virginia Quarterly Review* 11 (1935): 93–112.

Wellek, Rene. "John Crowe Ransom's Theory of Poetry." In *Literary Theory and Structure: Essays in Honor of William K. Wimsatt*. New Haven: Yale University Press, 1973.

Williams, Miller. *The Poetry of John Crowe Ransom*. New Brunswick, N.J.: Rutgers University Press, 1972.

Young, Thomas D., ed. *John Crowe Ransom: Critical Essays and a Bibliography*. Baton Rouge: Louisiana State University Press, 1968.

T. S. ELIOT

Bloom, Harold, ed. *Modern Critical Views: T. S. Eliot*. New York: Chelsea House, 1985.

Drew, Elizabeth. *T. S. Eliot: The Design of His Poetry*. New York: Scribner's, 1949.

Frye, Northrop. *T. S. Eliot*. New York: Grove, 1963.

Gallup, Donald. *T. S. Eliot: A Bibliography*. Rev. ed. New York: Harcourt Brace Jovanovich, 1969.

Gardner, Helen. *The Art of T. S. Eliot*. New York: Dutton, 1959.

Gordon, Lyndall. *Eliot's Early Years*. Oxford: Oxford University Press, 1977.

Grant, Michael, ed. *T. S. Eliot: The Critical Heritage*. 2 vols. London: Routledge & Kegan Paul, 1982.

Jay, Gregory S. *T. S. Eliot and the Poetics of Literary History*. Baton Rouge: Louisiana State University Press, 1983.

Kenner, Hugh. *The Invisible Poet: T. S. Eliot*. New York: Harcourt Brace Jovanovich, 1969.

————, ed. *T. S. Eliot: A Collection of Critical Essays*. Englewood Cliffs, N.J.: Prentice-Hall, 1962.

Kermode, Frank, ed. *Selected Prose of T. S. Eliot*. New York: Harcourt Brace Jovanovich, 1975.

Kojecký, Roger. *T. S. Eliot's Social Criticism*. New York: Farrar, Straus & Giroux, 1972.

Lucy, Sean. *T. S. Eliot and the Idea of Tradition*. London: Cohen & West, 1960.

Margolis, John D. *T. S. Eliot's Intellectual Development*. Chicago: University of Chicago Press, 1972.

Martin, Graham, ed. *Eliot in Perspective: A Symposium*. New York: Humanities Press, 1970.

Matthiessen, F. O. *The Achievement of T. S. Eliot*. 3rd ed. New York: Oxford University Press, 1958.

Moody, A. L. *Thomas Stearns Eliot, Poet.* Cambridge: Harvard University Press, 1981.

Schneider, Elizabeth. *T. S. Eliot: The Pattern in the Carpet.* Berkeley: University of California Press, 1975.

Scofield, Martin. "T. S. Eliot's Images of Love." *Critical Quarterly* 18 (Autumn 1976): 5–26.

Serio, John N. "Landscape and Voice in T. S. Eliot's Poetry." *Centennial Review* 26 (Winter 1982): 33–50.

Smith, Grover. *T. S. Eliot's Poetry and Plays.* Chicago: University of Chicago Press, 1974.

Spender, Stephen. *T. S. Eliot.* New York: Penguin, 1975.

Tate, Allen, ed. *T. S. Eliot: The Man and His Work.* London: Chatto & Windus, 1967.

Unger, Leonard. *T. S. Eliot: Moments and Patterns.* Minneapolis: University of Minnesota Press, 1967.

CONRAD AIKEN

Blanshard, Rufus A. "Pilgrim's Progress: Conrad Aiken's Poetry." *Texas Quarterly* 1 (Winter 1958): 135–48.

Denney, Reuel. *Conrad Aiken.* Minneapolis: University of Minnesota Press, 1964.

Hagenbuchle, Helen. "Antennae of the Race: Conrad Aiken's Poetry and the Evolution of Consciousness." *Huntington Library Quarterly* 45, no. 3 (Summer 1982): 215–26.

Hoffman, Frederick J. *Conrad Aiken.* New York: Twayne, 1962.

Lawrence, Seymour, ed. *Conrad Aiken Number: Wake II.* New York: Wake Editions, 1952.

Lerner, Arthur. *Psychoanalytically Oriented Criticism of Three American Poets: Edgar Allan Poe, Walt Whitman, and Conrad Aiken.* Rutherford, N.J.: Farleigh Dickinson University Press, 1970.

Martin, Jay. *Conrad Aiken, A Life of His Art.* Princeton: Princeton University Press, 1962.

Peterson, Houston. *The Melody of Chaos.* New York: Longmans, Green, 1931.

E. E. CUMMINGS

Baum, Stanley Vergil, ed. *Esti: eec; E. E. Cummings and the Critics.* East Lansing: Michigan State University Press, 1962.

Davenport, Guy. "Satyr and Transcendentalist." *Parnassus* 8, no. 2 (1980): 42–50.

Dumas, Bethany K. *E. E. Cummings: A Remembrance of Miracles.* London: Vision, 1974.

Friedman, Norman. *E. E. Cummings: A Collection of Critical Essays.* Englewood Cliffs. N.J.: Prentice-Hall, 1972.

————. *E. E. Cummings: The Art of His Poetry*. Baltimore: Johns Hopkins University Press, 1960.

Kennedy, Richard S. *Dreams in the Mirror: A Biography of E. E. Cummings*. New York: Liveright, 1979.

Marks, Barry Alan. *E. E. Cummings*. New York: Twayne, 1964.

Norman, Charles. *E. E. Cummings, The Magic Maker*. Indianapolis: Bobbs-Merrill, 1972.

Rotella, Guy, ed. *Critical Essays on E. E. Cummings*. Boston: G. K. Hall, 1984.

Triem, Eve. *E. E. Cummings*. Minneapolis: University of Minnesota Press, 1969.

Wagner, Linda W. "E. E. Cummings: A Review of the Research and the Criticism." *Resources for American Literary Study* 11, no. 2 (1981): 184–214.

JOHN BROOKS WHEELWRIGHT

Howard, Richard. "Four Originals." *Poetry* 72 (1973): 351–53.

Rosenfeld, Alvin H., and S. Foster Damon. "John Wheelwright: New England's Colloquy with the World." *The Southern Review* 8 (1972): 310–28.

Wald, Alan M. *The Revolutionary Imagination: The Poetry and Politics of John Wheelwright and Sherry Mangan*. Chapel Hill: University of North Carolina Press, 1983.

Warren, Austin. "Introduction: John Brooks Wheelwright." In *Collected Poems of John Wheelwright*, edited by Alvin H. Rosenfeld, xiii–xxii. New York: New Directions, 1982.

ALLEN TATE

Bradford, M. E. *Rumors of Mortality: An Introduction to Allen Tate*. Dallas: Argus Academic Press, 1969.

Brooks, Cleanth. "Allen Tate and the Nature of Modernism." *The Southern Review* 12 (1976): 685–97.

Davie, Donald. "Theme and Action." *Parnassus* 6, no. 2 (1978): 64–73.

Donoghue, Denis. "Nuances of a Theme by Allen Tate." *The Southern Review* 12 (1976): 698–713.

Fuller, Roy. "Tate Full Length." *The Southern Review* 14 (1978): 233–44.

Squires, Radcliffe. *Allen Tate: A Literary Biography*. New York: Pegasus, 1971.

————. "Allen Tate and the Pastoral Vision." *The Southern Review* 12 (1976): 733–43.

————, ed. *Allen Tate and His Work: Critical Evaluations*. Minneapolis: University of Minnesota Press, 1972.

Warren, Austin. "Homage to Allen Tate." *The Southern Review* 9 (1973): 753–77.

Williamson, Alan. "Allen Tate and the Personal Epic." *The Southern Review* 12 (1976): 714–32.

Young, Thomas Daniel. "Allen Tate's Double Focus: The Past in the Present." *Mississippi Quarterly* 30 (1977): 517–25.

HART CRANE

Andreach, Robert J. *Studies in Structure, The Stages of the Spiritual Life in Four Modern Authors.* New York: Fordham University Press, 1964.

Antoninus, Brother [William Everson]. "Our Modern Sensibility." *Commonweal* 77 (October 26, 1962): 111–12.

Butterfield, R. W. *The Broken Arc: A Study of Hart Crane.* Edinburgh: Oliver & Boyd, 1969.

Combs, Robert Long. *Vision of the Voyage: Hart Crane and the Psychology of Romanticism.* Memphis: Memphis State University Press, 1978.

Hanley, Alfred. *Hart Crane's Holy Vision: "White Buildings."* Pittsburgh, Pa.: Duquesne University Press, 1981.

Hazo, Samuel John. *Hart Crane, An Introduction and Interpretation.* New York: Barnes & Noble, 1963.

———. *Smithereened Apart: A Critique of Hart Crane.* Athens: Ohio University Press, 1977.

Hinton, Norman D., and Lise Rodgers. "Hart Crane's 'The Moth that God Made Blind.' " *Papers on Language and Literature* 16 (Summer 1980): 87–95.

Horton, Philip. *Hart Crane, The Life of an American Poet.* New York: Viking, 1957.

Irwin, John T. "Naming Names: Hart Crane's 'Logic of Metaphor.' " *The Southern Review* 11 (1975): 284–99.

Lewis, R. W. B. *The Poetry of Hart Crane: A Critical Study.* Westport, Conn.: Greenwood, 1978.

Strier, Richard. "The Poetics of Surrender: An Exposition and Critique of New Critical Poets." *Critical Inquiry* 2 (1975): 171–89.

Trachtenberg, Alan, ed. *Hart Crane: A Collection of Critical Essays.* Englewood Cliffs, N.J.: Prentice-Hall, 1982.

Vogler, Thomas A. *Preludes to Vision, The Epic Venture of Blake, Wordsworth, Keats and Hart Crane.* Berkeley: University of California Press, 1971.

LANGSTON HUGHES

Barksdale, Richard K. *Langston Hughes: The Poet and His Critics.* Chicago: American Library Association, 1977.

Brown, Lloyd W. "The Portrait of the Artist as a Black American in the Poetry of Langston Hughes." *Studies in Black Literature* 5, no. 1 (1974): 24–27.

Davis, Arthur P. "Langston Hughes." In *From the Dark Tower*, 61–72. Washington, D.C.: Howard University Press, 1974.

Dixon, Melvin. "Rivers Remembering Their Source: Comparative Studies in Black Literary History—Langston Hughes, Jacques Romain, and Negritude." In *Afro-American Literature: The Reconstruction of Instruction*, edited by Dexter Fisher and Robert B. Stepto, 25–43. New York: Modern Language Association, 1979.

Miller, R. Baxter. " 'A Mere Poem': 'Daybreak in Alabama,' A Resolution to Langston Hughes' Theme of Music and Art." *Obsidian* 2, no. 2 (1976): 30–37.

———. "Langston Hughes and the 1980s: Rehumanization of Theory." *Black American Literature Forum* 15, no. 3 (1981): 83–84.

———. "Langston Hughes, His Times and Humanistic Techniques." In *Black American Literature and Humanism*, edited by R. Baxter Miller, 11–26. Lexington: University Press of Kentucky, 1981.

———. " 'No Crystal Stair': Unity, Architecture, and Symbol in Langston Hughes' Poems on Women." *Negro American Literature Forum* 9 (1975): 109–14.

O'Daniel, Therman B., ed. *Langston Hughes, Black Genius: A Critical Evaluation*. New York: William Morrow, 1971.

Onwuchekwa, Jemie. *Langston Hughes: An Introduction to the Poetry*. New York: Columbia University Press, 1976.

Randall, Dudley. "The Black Aesthetic in the Thirties, Forties, and Fifties." In *The Black Aesthetic*, edited by Addison Gayle, Jr., 212–21. New York: Anchor, 1972.

Smith, Raymond. "Langston Hughes: Evolution of the Poetic Persona." *Studies in the Literary Imagination* 7, no. 2 (1974): 49–64.

Waldron, Edward E. "The Blues Poetry of Langston Hughes." *Negro American Literature Forum* 5 (1971): 140–49.

COUNTEE CULLEN

Baker, Houston A., Jr. *A Many-Colored Coat of Dreams: The Poetry of Countee Cullen*. Detroit: Broadside, 1974.

Christian, Barbara. *Spirit Bloom in Harlem: The Search for a Black Aesthetic during the Harlem Renaissance: The Poetry of Claude McKay, Countee Cullen, and Jean Toomer*. Ph.D. diss., Dept. of Modern Language and Literature, Columbia University, 1970.

Ferguson, Blanche E. *Countee Cullen and the Negro Renaissance*. New York: Dodd, Mead, 1966.

Lomax, Michael L. "Countee Cullen: A Key to the Puzzle." *Studies in the Literary Imagination* 7, no. 2 (1974): 39–48.

Perry, Margaret. *A Bio-Bibliography of Countee Cullen, 1903–1946*. Greenwich, Conn.: Greenwich Publishing, 1971.

Shucard, Alan R. *Countee Cullen*. Boston: Twayne, 1984.

Acknowledgments

The Edwin Arlington Robinson section of the Introduction (originally entitled "Bacchus and Merlin: The Dialectic of Romantic Poetry in America") by Harold Bloom is from *The Ringers in the Tower* by Harold Bloom, © 1971 by the University of Chicago. Reprinted by permission of the University of Chicago Press.

"Edwin Arlington Robinson" by Conrad Aiken from *A Reviewer's ABC*, edited by Rufus A. Blanshard, © 1958 by Conrad Aiken. Reprinted by permission of Meridian Books.

"Paul Laurence Dunbar and Dialect Poetry" (originally entitled "Dunbar and Dialect Poetry") by Myron Simon from *A Singer in the Dawn: Reinterpretations of Paul Laurence Dunbar*, edited by Jay Martin, © 1975 by Jay Martin. Reprinted by permission of the author, the editor, and Dodd, Mead & Company, Inc.

"Robert Frost: Choices" (originally entitled "Choices") by Richard Poirier from *Robert Frost: The Work of Knowing* by Richard Poirier, © 1977 by Oxford University Press. Reprinted by permission.

"Echoing Eden: Frost and Origins" by Charles Berger, © 1986 by Charles Berger. Reprinted by permission of the author.

"Stevens's *An Ordinary Evening in New Haven*" (originally entitled "*An Ordinary Evening in New Haven*") by Harold Bloom from *Wallace Stevens: The Poems of Our Climate* by Harold Bloom, © 1976 by Cornell University. Reprinted by permission of Cornell University Press.

"Wallace Stevens's World of Words: An Always Incipient Cosmos" by Marie Borroff from *Language and the Poet: Verbal Artistry in Frost, Stevens and Moore* by Marie Borroff, © 1979 by the University of Chicago.

Reprinted by permission of the author and the University of Chicago Press.

"Sic Transit Gloria: Six Famous Poets: Vachel Lindsay, Edgar Lee Masters, Carl Sandburg, Sara Teasdale, Elinor Wylie, Edna St. Vincent Millay" (originally entitled *"Sic Transit Gloria:* Six Famous Poets") by Hyatt Waggoner from *American Poets: From the Puritans to the Present* by Hyatt Waggoner, © 1968 by Hyatt Waggoner. Reprinted by permission of the author and Houghton Mifflin Co., Inc.

"The Eighth Day of Creation: Rethinking Williams's *Paterson*" (originally entitled "The Eighth Day of Creation: Rethinking *Paterson*") by Paul Mariani from *Twentieth Century Literature* 21, no. 3 (1975), © 1975 by Hofstra University Press. Reprinted by permission. This essay later appeared in *A Usable Past: Essays on Modern and Contemporary Poetry* (University of Massachusetts Press, 1984).

"Rhizomatic America: Ezra Pound" (originally entitled "Rhizomatic America") by Kathryne V. Lindberg from *Reading Pound Reading: The Nietzschean Indirections of Modernism* by Kathryne V. Lindberg, © 1986 by Oxford University Press. Reprinted by permission.

"Robinson Jeffers: *The Women at Point Sur*" by Brother Antoninus from *Robinson Jeffers: Fragments of an Older Fury* by Brother Antoninus, © 1968 by Brother Antoninus. Reprinted by permission of Oyez Longman Publishing Co. and the William Morris Agency.

"The 'Feminine Language' of Marianne Moore" by Bonnie Costello from *Women and Language in Literature and Society,* edited by Sally McConnell-Ginet, Ruth Borker, and Nelly Furman, © 1980 by Praeger Publishers. Reprinted by permission of the publisher. The poems in the essay are reprinted by permission of Faber & Faber.

" 'Advancing Backward in a Circle': Moore as (Natural) Historian" (originally entitled " 'Advancing Backward in a Circle': Marianne Moore as (Natural) Historian") by John M. Slatin from *Twentieth Century Literature* 30, nos. 2-3 (Summer/Fall 1984), © 1984 by Hofstra University Press. Reprinted by permission.

"The Echoing Spell of H. D.'s *Trilogy*" by Susan Gubar from *Contemporary Literature* 19, no. 2 (Spring 1978), © 1978 by the Board of Regents of the University of Wisconsin System. Reprinted by permission.

"John Ransom's Poetry" by Randall Jarrell from *Poetry and the Age* by Randall Jarrell, © 1953 by Randall Jarrell. Reprinted by permission of Random House and Mary Jarrell.

"Eliot's *Ash-Wednesday*" (originally entitled *"Ash-Wednesday"*) by Hugh Kenner from *The Invisible Poet: T. S. Eliot* by Hugh Kenner, © 1959 by Hugh

Kenner. Reprinted by permission of the author and Methuen & Co., Ltd.

"Ghosts and Roses: T. S. Eliot" (originally entitled "Ghosts and Roses") by Gregory S. Jay from *T. S. Eliot and the Poetics of Literary History* by Gregory S. Jay, © 1983 by Louisiana State University Press. Reprinted by permission.

"Conrad Aiken: The Self against the Sky" (originally entitled "The Self against the Sky") by Delmore Schwartz from *The New Republic* 129, no. 14 (November 2, 1953), © 1953 by *The New Republic*.

"The Poetry of a Supreme Technician: Conrad Aiken" (originally entitled "The Poetry of a Supreme Technician") by Dudley Fitts from *The New Republic* 133, no. 26 (December 26, 1955), © 1955 by *The New Republic*.

"Notes on E. E. Cummings's Language" by R. P. Blackmur from *R. P. Blackmur's Language as Gesture: Essays in Poetry* by R. P. Blackmur, © 1952 by R. P. Blackmur, renewed 1980 by Elizabeth Blackmur. Reprinted by permission of Harcourt Brace Jovanovich.

"John Brooks Wheelwright: In the American Grain" (originally entitled "In the American Grain") by John Ashbery from *The New York Review of Books* 20, no. 2 (February 22, 1973), © 1973 by The New York Review, Inc. Reprinted by permission.

"Allen Tate's Poetry" by Cleanth Brooks from *Modern Poetry and the Tradition* by Cleanth Brooks, © 1939 by the University of North Carolina Press. Reprinted by permission of the author and publisher.

"Hart Crane: The Long Way Home" (originally entitled "The Long Way Home") by Sherman Paul from *Hart's Bridge* by Sherman Paul, © 1972 by the Board of Trustees of the University of Illinois. Reprinted by permission of the author and the University of Illinois Press.

"Langston Hughes: Evolution of the Poetic Persona" by Raymond Smith from *Studies in the Literary Imagination* 7, no. 2 (Fall 1974), © 1974 by the Department of English, Georgia State University. Reprinted by permission. The notes have been omitted.

"Countee Cullen and Keats's 'Vale of Soul-Making' " by Ronald Primeau from *Papers on Language and Literature* 12, no. 1 (Winter 1976), © 1976 by the Board of Trustees, Southern Illinois University. Reprinted by permission.

Index

413